SPRING

The Spring 1.x Primer

April 22, 2007

SourceBeat

The Spring 1.x Primer
by Matt Raible

Published by SourceBeat, LLC, Highlands Ranch, Colorado.

Managing Editor: Sarah Hogan
Technical Editors: Scott Nicholls, Cos DiFazio, and Dion Almaer
Copy Editor: Mary Beth Curran
Cover Designer: Max Hays

ISBN: 0974884375

CONTENTS

Chapter 5: Advanced Spring MVC 117

Chapter 6: View Options... 155

Chapter 11: Web Framework Integration 387

DEDICATION

To Abbie and Jack — the coolest kids in town.

ABOUT THE AUTHOR

Matt Raible currently resides in Denver, Colorado, where he runs Raible Designs, a consultancy that specializes in open source Java frameworks and Ajax development. Matt has been surrounded by computers for most of his life, even though he grew up in the backwoods of Montana without electricity.

Matt is an author (*Spring Live*, *Pro JSP*), an active Java open-source contributor, and a blogger at raibledesigns.com. He is the founder of AppFuse, a project that allows you to get started quickly with Java frameworks, and he is a committer on the Apache Roller project.

Matt is an avid mountain biker, skier, and golfer. When he's not developing and promoting open source, he's making life wonderful for his two children, Abbie and Jack.

PREFACE

Thank you for buying *Spring Live*. This book is the result of my thoughts and experiences while learning the Spring Framework from 2004 to 2006. During that time, I made more than 10 updates of this book. You're currently reading the final update, which I last made in the fall of 2006.

While I was writing this book, a lot of things happened to me. I traveled to Norway, became a father for the second time (Hi, Jack!), and traveled to many conferences to talk about Spring. The whole experience was quite a ride — thanks to SourceBeat for the opportunity to write this book and to the creators and maintainers of the Spring Framework for making it all possible.

This book is an introduction to the Spring Framework. It's written for developers who have no experience with Spring but do have web development experience.

Unlike traditional books, this book has changed, grown, and become better over the past two years. Although the 1.0 version was fun to write, the updates to this book were more exciting. Together, we acted as a team to produce an in-depth, pragmatic, and interesting book about the Spring Framework. As you provided feedback, I improved existing content in the book and added new content that you said interested you. This book is yours as much as it is mine.

What I discovered, though, is that Spring is such a popular subject, one book can't handle it alone. I talked to Matt Filios, the president of SourceBeat, and we are breaking out various Spring topics for other books. A book about Spring Acegi Security is under way, and other books are in the works. Another book that covers the open source project I founded, AppFuse, is also in progress.

As the Spring Framework continues to grow and improve, you will need more books like Spring Live to help you keep up and do your job. If you know of upcoming projects that are using a certain technology in Spring, let me know; the information might be good fodder for another Spring book.

If you are interested in writing for SourceBeat, visit the web site at www.sourcebeat.com. I won't kid you: Writing a book isn't easy, but it is rewarding.

This book is managed similar to an open source project. Each update of the book has been announced on my Spring Live blog. All of the source code I developed in each chapter is available at sourcebeat.com/downloads. This page has links to download before and after snapshots of each chapter's code.

If you find issues or would like to request features for future books, please enter them in JIRA. For general discussion questions, you can use the Spring Live Forums or Equinox User Mailing List. I've also set up a Confluence wiki for tracking FAQs and updates. You can also send email to me directly a mattr@sourcebeat.com.

Thanks to Atlassian for the JIRA and Confluence software and to Javalobby for hosting the weblog and forums.

To my ex-wife, Julie — thanks for your support and love while flying down this crazy highway call Life.

Sincerely,

Matt Raible

http://raibledesigns.com

INTRODUCTION

This book is written for Java developers who are familiar with web frameworks. Its main purpose is to help Java developers learn Spring and evaluate it against other frameworks. One of my hopes is to compare Spring with other web frameworks — or at least show how it can be integrated with other frameworks, such as Struts, WebWork, and maybe even Tapestry down the road. This book contains a usable sample application that includes Spring code to wire DAOs and services together.

This book does have a bit of a Struts perspective to it because I have been a Struts developer for almost three years, and Struts is the most popular web framework today. It is only natural that I use my experience in my writing.

Chapter Summaries
....

CHAPTER 1: INTRODUCING SPRING

This chapter covers the basics of Spring, including how it came to be and why it's getting so much press and rave reviews. This chapter compares the traditional way of resolving dependencies (binding interfaces to implementations using a Factory Pattern) and illustrates how Spring does it all in XML. It also briefly covers how Spring simplifies the Hibernate API.

This chapter includes the following sections:

- The history of Spring
- About Spring
- Why everyone loves it
- How Spring makes J2EE easier

CHAPTER 2: SPRING QUICK-START TUTORIAL

This chapter is a tutorial that steps you through writing a simple Spring web application using the Struts Model-View-Controller (MVC) framework for the front end, Spring for the middle-tier glue, and Hibernate for the back end. In *Chapter 4: Spring's MVC Framework*, this application will be refactored to use the Spring MVC framework.

This chapter covers writing tests to verify functionality, configuring Hibernate and transactions, loading Spring's *applicationContext.xml* file, setting up dependencies between business services and DAOs, and wiring Spring into the Struts application.

This chapter includes the following sections:

- Overview
- Download Struts and Spring
- Create project directories and an Ant build file
- Create unit test for persistence layer
- Configure Hibernate and Spring
- Implement **UserDAO** with Hibernate
- Run unit test and verify CRUD with DAO
- Create manager and declare transactions
- Create unit test for Struts action
- Create action and model (**DynaActionForm**) for web layer

- Run unit test and verify CRUD with action
- Complete JSPs to allow CRUD through a web browser
- Verify JSP's functionality through your browser
- Add validation using Commons Validator

CHAPTER 3: THE BEANFACTORY AND HOW IT WORKS

The **BeanFactory** represents the heart of Spring, so it's important to know how it works. This chapter covers how bean definitions are written and covers their properties, dependencies, and autowiring. You will also read about the logic behind making singleton beans (versus prototypes) and then delve into Inversion of Control (IoC), how it works, and the simplicity it brings. This chapter dissects the lifecyle of a bean in the **BeanFactory** so that you better understand how it works. In addition, you will inspect the applicationContext.xml file for the MyUsers application you created in *Chapter 2: Spring Quick-Start Tutorial*.

This chapter includes the following sections:

- About the **BeanFactory**
- A bean's lifecycle in the **BeanFactory**
- The **ApplicationContext**: Talking to your beans

CHAPTER 4: SPRING'S MVC FRAMEWORK

This chapter describes the many features of Spring's MVC framework. It shows you how to replace the Struts layer in MyUsers with Spring and covers the **DispatcherServlet**, various controllers, handler mappings, view resolvers, validation, and internationalization. It also briefly covers Spring's JSP tags.

This chapter includes the following sections:

- Overview
- Testing Spring controllers
- Configure **DispatcherServlet** and **ContextLoaderListener**
- **SimpleFormController**: Method lifecycle review
- Spring's JSP tags

CHAPTER 5: ADVANCED SPRING MVC

This chapter covers advanced topics in web frameworks, particularly validation and page decoration. In it, you will read about using Tiles or SiteMesh to decorate a web application. It also demonstrates how the Spring Framework handles validation and shows examples of using it in the web business layers. Finally, it outlines a strategy for handling exceptions in the controllers and describes how to upload files and send email messages.

This chapter includes the following sections:

- Overview
- Templating with SiteMesh
- Templating with Tiles
- Validating the Spring way
- Using Commons Validator
- Exception handling in controllers
- Uploading files
- Intercepting the request
- Sending email

CHAPTER 6: VIEW OPTIONS

This chapter covers the view options in Spring's MVC architecture. At the time of this writing, the options are JSP, Velocity, FreeMarker, XSLT, PDF, and Excel. This chapter is a reference for configuring all Spring-supported views. It also contains a brief overview of how each view works and compares constructing a page in MyUsers with each option. Additionally, it focuses on internationalization for each view option.

This chapter includes the following sections:

- Overview
- Views and **ViewResolvers**
- Testing the view with **jWebUnit**
- JSP
- Velocity
- FreeMarker
- XSLT
- Excel
- PDF

CHAPTER 6.5: JASPERREPORTS

JasperReports is a powerful open source Java reporting tool that delivers many content types for printing. It currently supports PDF, HTML, XLS, CSV, and XML files. Unlike the view types in *Chapter 6: View Options*, JasperReports is designed for reporting and is an excellent tool for rendering printable pages.

This chapter includes the following sections:

- Environment setup
- Configuration
- Creating the report
- Integrating JasperReports into MyUsers
- iReport issues

CHAPTER 7: PERSISTENCE STRATEGIES: HIBERNATE, iBATIS, JDBC, JDO, AND OJB

Hibernate is quickly becoming a popular choice for persistence in Java applications, but sometimes it doesn't fit. If you have an existing database schema — or even pre-written SQL — sometimes it's better to use JDBC or iBATIS (which supports externalized SQL in XML files). This chapter refactors the MyUsers application to support both JDBC and iBATIS as persistence framework options. It also implements the UserDAO using JDO and OJB to showcase Spring's excellent support for these frameworks.

This chapter includes the following sections:

- Overview
- Hibernate
- iBATIS

CHAPTER 8: TESTING SPRING APPLICATIONS

This chapter covers how to use test-driven development to create high-quality, well-tested, Spring-based applications. You will learn how to test your components using tools such as EasyMock, jMock, and DbUnit. For the controllers, you will learn how to use Cactus for in-container testing and Spring Mocks for out-of-container testing. Last, you will learn how to use jWebUnit and Canoo's WebTest for testing the web interface.

This chapter includes the following sections:

- Overview
- JUnit
- Testing the database layer
- DbUnit
- Testing the service layer

 • Testing the web layer

CHAPTER 9: AOP

Aspect-Oriented Programming (AOP) has received a lot of attention in the Java community in the last couple of years. What is AOP and how can it help you in your applications? This chapter will cover the basics of AOP and provide some useful examples of how AOP might help you.

This chapter includes the following sections:

 • Overview
 • Logging example
 • Definitions and concepts
 • Practical AOP examples

CHAPTER 10: TRANSACTIONS

Transactions are an important part of J2EE, allowing you to view several database calls as one and roll them back if they don't all succeed. One of the most highlighted features of EJBs is declarative transactions. This chapter demonstrates how Spring simplifies using declarative and programmatic transactions.

This chapter includes the following sections:

 • Overview
 • J2EE transaction management
 • Managing transactions with Spring
 • Spring transaction managers

CHAPTER 11: WEB FRAMEWORK INTEGRATION

Spring has its own web framework, but it also integrates well with other frameworks. This capability allows you to leverage your existing knowledge and still use Spring to manage your business objects and data layer. This chapter explores Spring integration with four popular web frameworks: JSF (JavaServer Faces), Struts, Tapestry, and WebWork.

This chapter includes the following sections:

 • Overview
 • JavaServer Faces (JSF)
 • Struts
 • Tapestry

- WebWork
- Framework comparison
- Tips and tricks
- Recommended reading

CHAPTER 12: SECURITY

This chapter covers how you can configure authentication and authorization using traditional J2EE (container-managed) security and the Acegi Security framework for Spring. It also shows how you can use Acegi Security to protect and prevent method invocations on Spring-managed beans and configure Access Control Lists (ACLs).

This chapter includes the following sections:

- Overview
- J2EE authentication
- Acegi Security system for Spring
- Acegi Security versus J2EE security
- Authorization

CHAPTER 13: ADVANCED FORM PROCESSING

Spring MVC is a full-fledged web application framework. It can easily handle complex data types, nested forms, indexed properties, and wizards. It even has a "page flow" component that allows you to configure navigation rules external to your controllers.

This chapter includes the following sections:

- Non-string fields
- Drop-down lists and check boxes
- Nested objects and indexed properties
- **AbstractWizardFormController**
- Spring Web Flow

APPENDIX A: EXAMPLES AND REFERENCES

This appendix includes explicit examples of JSF, Tapestry, and WebWork integration.

This appendix includes the following sections:

- JSF and Spring CRUD Example

- Tapestry and Spring CRUD example
- WebWork and Spring CRUD example

ACKNOWLEDGMENTS

I'd like to thank my ex-wife, Julie, for being such a great mother and terrific wife. Your ability to entertain Abbie and comfort Jack at the same time is amazing. Thank you for building our home and giving birth to Jack while I wrote this book. Abbie and Jack, thanks for reminding me that work is not as important as playing with you. Your smiles and giggles always make my day.

I'd like to thank my parents, Joe and Barb, for instilling in me the passion to learn. I learned a lot about computers from my Dad's passion for them. Dad, thanks for being such a good role model and great friend. To my sister, Kalin, I appreciate your listening to all my stories when we walked home from the bus stop. I can't help but think that my storytelling as a child helped me become an author.

Thanks to Rod Johnson for providing J2EE developers with such a great framework for developing J2EE applications more easily. Juergen, Colin, Keith, and the rest of the Spring Framework team — keep up the coding! Your time, commitment and user support are greatly appreciated. Open source is a great way to develop software, and your team is one of the best.

To the SourceBeat founders, Matt Filios and James Goodwill, thanks for the opportunity to write and to do it such an innovative way. SourceBeat is a great model from which readers will truly benefit. Scott, Cos, and Dion, I appreciate all the time you spent plowing through the code in *Spring Live* and ensuring all the examples worked. You've been great technical editors.

INTRODUCING SPRING

The basics of Spring and its history

This chapter covers the basics of Spring, including how it came to be and why it's getting so much press and rave reviews. This chapter compares the traditional way of resolving dependencies (binding interfaces to implementations using a factory pattern) and illustrates how Spring does it all in XML. It also briefly covers how Spring simplifies the Hibernate API.

THE HISTORY OF SPRING

Rod Johnson is the ingenious inventor of Spring. It started from infrastructure code in his book, *Expert One-on-One J2EE Design and Development*, in late 2002. In it, Rod explains his experiences with J2EE and how Enterprise JavaBeans (EJBs) are often overkill for projects. He believes a lightweight, JavaBeans-based framework can suit most developers' needs. If you're a developer and haven't read this book, I highly recommend that you do.

The framework he described eventually became known as the Spring Framework when it was open sourced on SourceForge in February 2003. At this point, Rod was joined by Juergen Hoeller as lead developer and right-hand man of Spring. Rod and Juergen have added many other developers over the last several months. At the time of this writing, 38 developers are on Spring's committer list. Rod and Juergen wrote a book titled *Expert One-on-One J2EE Development without EJB* that describes how Spring solves many of the problems with J2EE.

The architectural foundations of Spring have been developed by Rod since early 2000 (before Struts or any other frameworks I know of). These foundations were built from Rod's experiences building infrastructure on a number of successful commercial projects. Spring's foundation is constantly being enhanced and reinforced by hundreds (possibly thousands) of developers. All are bringing their experience to the table, and you can literally watch Spring become stronger day-by-day. Its community is thriving, its developers are enthusiastic and dedicated, and it's quite possibly the best thing that has ever happened to J2EE.

ABOUT SPRING

According to the Spring web site: "Spring is a layered J2EE application framework based on code published in *Expert One-on-One J2EE Design and Development* by Rod Johnson." At its core, Spring provides a means to manage your business objects and their dependencies. For example, using Inversion of Control (IoC), Spring allows you to specify that a Data Access Object (DAO) depends on a **DataSource**. It also allows a developer to code to interfaces and simply define the implementation using an XML file. Spring contains many classes that support other frameworks (such as Hibernate and Struts) to make integration easier.

Following J2EE design patterns can be cumbersome and unnecessary at times (and in fact often become anti-patterns). Spring is like following design patterns, but everything is simplified. For example, rather than writing a **ServiceLocator** to look up Hibernate Sessions, you can configure a **SessionFactory** in Spring. This configuration allows you to follow the best practices of J2EE field experts rather than trying to figure out the latest pattern.

WHY EVERYONE LOVES IT

If you follow online forums such as TheServerSide.com or JavaLobby.org, you've probably seen Spring mentioned. It has even more traction in the Java blogging community (such as JavaBlogs.com and JRoller.com). Many developers are describing their experiences with Spring and praising its ease of use.

Not only does Spring solve developers' problems, it also enforces good programming practices such as coding to interfaces, reducing coupling, and allowing for easy testability. In the modern era of programming, particularly in Java, good developers are practicing test-driven development (TDD). TDD is a way of letting your tests, or clients of your classes, drive the design of those classes. Rather than building a class and then trying to retrofit the client, you're building the client first. This way, you know exactly what you want from the class you're developing. Spring has a rich test suite of its own that allows for easy testing of your classes.

Compare this practice to "best practices" from J2EE, where the blueprints recommend that you use EJBs to handle business logic. EJBs require an EJB container to run, so you need to start up your container to test them. When's the last time you started up an EJB server like WebLogic, WebSphere, or JBoss? It can test your patience if you need to do it over and over to test your classes.

COMMON CRITICISMS OF SPRING

With success, there's always some criticism. The most compelling argument I've seen against Spring is that it's not a "standard," meaning it's not part of the J2EE specification and it hasn't been developed through the Java community process. The same folks who argue against Spring advocate EJBs, which are a standard. In my opinion, the main reason for standards is to ensure portability across appservers. The code you develop for one server should run on another, but porting EJBs from one EJB container to another is not as simple as it should be. Different vendors require different deployment descriptors, and there's no common way of configuring data sources or other container dependencies. In contrast, coding business logic with Spring is highly portable across containers — with no changes to your code or deployment descriptors.

Although Spring "makes things easier," some developers complain that it's "too heavyweight." However, Spring is really an *á la carte* framework from which you can pick and choose what you want to use. The development team has segmented the distribution so you can use only the Java ARchives (JARs) you need.

How Spring works

The *J2EE Design and Development* book illustrates Spring and how it works. Spring is a way to configure applications using JavaBeans. When I say "JavaBeans," I mean Java classes with *getters* and *setters* (also called *accessors* and *mutators*) for its class variables. Specifically, if a class exposes setters, Spring configures that class. Using Spring, you can expose any of your class dependencies (that is, a database connection) with a setter and then configure Spring to set that dependency. Even better, you don't have to write a class to establish the database connection; you can configure that in Spring, too. This dependency resolution has a name: *Inversion of Control (IoC)* or *dependency injection*. Basically, it's a technical term for wiring dependent objects together through some sort of container.

Spring has seven individual modules, and each has its own JAR file. Figure 1.1 is a diagram[1] of the seven modules:

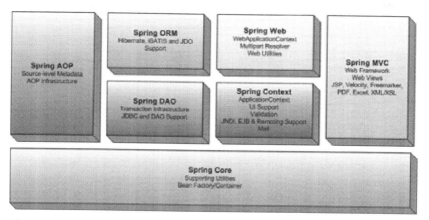

Figure 1.1: Overview of the Spring Framework

---

1. This diagram is based on one from Spring's reference documentation.

In the MyUsers application that you will develop in *Chapter 2: Spring Quick-Start Tutorial,* you will use several of the modules above, but not all of them. Furthermore, you'll only be using a fraction of the functionality in each module.

The diagram in Figure 1.2 shows the Spring modules that MyUsers will be using.

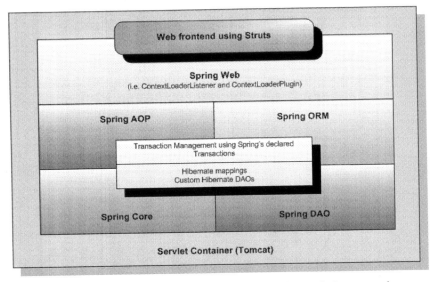

Figure 1.2: Spring middle tier using Struts for the web framework

HOW SPRING MAKES J2EE EASIER

In Figure 1.2, you can see that Spring provides a lot of pieces for the application you'll be building. At first glance, it looks intrusive, and you might think that you'll to need to know a lot about Spring. Not true, my friend. In most cases, you won't even see Spring's API being used. For instance, in the middle tier, you will set up declarative transactions and set DAOs on the business delegates. Your code will not see a single import from Spring or any factory patterns to figure out which DAO implementation to use. You simply configure it all in an XML file — and *voilá!* — clean design is yours.

The following sections cover some of the processes that Spring simplifies.

CODING TO INTERFACES

Coding to interfaces allows developers to advertise the methods by which their objects will be used. It's helpful to design your application using interfaces because you gain a lot of flexibility in your implementation. Furthermore, communicating among the different tiers using interfaces promotes loose coupling of your code.

EASY TESTABILITY

Using TDD is the best way to rapidly produce high-quality code. It allows you to drive your design by coding your clients (the tests) before you code interfaces or implementations. In fact, modern IDEs such as Eclipse and IDEA will allow you to create your classes and methods on-the-fly as you're writing your tests. Spring-enabled projects are easy to test for two reasons:

- You can easily load and use all your Spring-managed beans in a JUnit test. This capability allows you to interact with them as you normally would from any client.

- Your classes won't bind their own dependencies. This feature allows you to ignore Spring in your tests and set mock objects as dependencies.

REDUCING COUPLING: FACTORY PATTERN VERSUS SPRING

In order to have an easily maintainable and extendable application, it's not desirable to tightly couple your code to a specific resource (for example, you may have code that uses SQL that is specific to a database type). Of course, it's often easier to code to a specific database if the proprietary functionality helps you get your job done quicker. When you do end up coding proprietary functionality into a class, the J2EE patterns recommend that you use a factory pattern to decouple your application from the implementing class.

In general, it's a good idea to create interfaces for the different layers of your application. Creating these interfaces allows the individual layers to be ignorant of the implementations that exist. A typical J2EE application has three layers:

- Data layer: Contains classes that talk to a database or other data storage system.

- Business logic: Contains classes that hold business logic and provide a bridge between the GUI layer and the data layer.

- User interface: Contains classes and view files used to compose a web or desktop interface to a user.

Figure 1.3 is a graphical representation of a typical J2EE application.

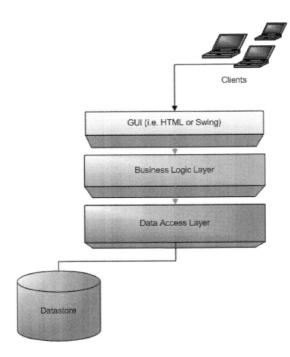

Figure 1.3: A typical J2EE application

A factory pattern (also known as the abstract factory and factory method from the Gang-of-Four patterns) allows you to easily switch from one implementation to another by using a couple of factory classes. Typically, you'll create an abstract **DAOFactory** class and a factory class for the specific implementation (such as **DAOFactoryMySQL**). For more information, see Core J2EE Patterns — Data Access Object from the J2EE patterns catalog.

CONFIGURING AND BINDING CLASS DEPENDENCIES

The factory pattern is a complicated J2EE pattern. Not only does it require two classes to set up, but it also introduces issues with managing dependencies of those "factoried" objects. For instance, if you're getting a DAO from the factory, how do you pass in a connection (rather than opening one for each method)? You can pass it in as part of the constructor, but what if you're using a DAO implementation that requires a Hibernate Session? You could make the constructor parameter a **java.lang.Object** and then cast it to the required type, but it just seems ugly.

The better way is to use Spring to bind interfaces to implementations. Everything is configured in an XML file, and you can easily switch out your implementation by modifying that file. Even better, you can write your unit tests so no one knows which implementation you're using — and you can run them for numerous implementations. It works great with iBATIS and Hibernate DAO implementations. Because the test is in fact a client, it's a great way to ensure the business logic layer will work with an alternative DAO implementation. Listing 1.1 is an example of getting a **UserDAO** implementation using Spring:

Listing 1.1

```
ApplicationContext ctx =
    new ClassPathXmlApplicationContext
        ("/WEB-INF/applicationContext.xml");
UserDAO dao = (UserDAO) ctx.getBean("userDAO");
```

You'll have to configure the **userDAO** bean in the */WEB-INF/applicationContext.xml* file. Listing 1.2 is a code snippet from *Chapter 2: Spring Quick-Start Tutorial.*

Listing 1.2

```
<bean id="userDAO"
    class="org.appfuse.dao.hibernate.UserDAOHibernate">
    <property name="sessionFactory">
        <ref local="sessionFactory"/>
    </property>
</bean>
```

If you want to change the implementation of **UserDAO**, all you need to change is the "class" attribute in Listing 1.2. It's a cleaner pattern that you can use throughout your application. All you need to do is add a few lines to your beans definition file. Furthermore, Spring manages the Hibernate Session for this DAO for you via the **sessionFactory** property. You don't even need to worry about opening and closing it anymore.

NOTE: Spring is often referred to as a "lightweight container" because you talk to its **ApplicationContext** in order to get instantiated objects. The objects are defined in a *context file* (also called *beans definition file*). This file is simply an XML file with a number of **<bean>** elements. In a sense, it's a "bean container" or an "object library," where everything has been set up and is ready to be used. It's not really a container in the traditional sense (such as Tomcat or WebLogic), but more of a "configured beans provider."

OBJECT-RELATIONAL MAPPING TOOLS

Another example of Spring's usability is its first-class support for object-relational mapping (ORM) tools. The first advantage of using the ORM support classes is you don't need to try/catch many of the checked exceptions that these APIs throw. Spring wraps the checked exceptions with runtime exceptions, allowing developers to decide whether they want to catch exceptions. Listing 1.3 is an example of a **getUsers()** method from a **UserDAOHibernate** class without Spring:

Listing 1.3

```
public List getUsers() throws DAOException {
    List list = null;

    try {
        list = ses.find("from User u order by upper(u.username)");
    } catch (HibernateException he) {
        he.printStackTrace();
        throw new DAOException(he);
    }

    return list;
}
```

Listing 1.4 is an example using Spring's Hibernate support (by extending **Hiber-nateDaoSupport**), which is much shorter and simpler:

Listing 1.4

```
public List getUsers() {
    return getHibernateTemplate()
            .find("from User u order by upper(u.username)");
}
```

From these examples, you can see how Spring makes it easier to decouple your application layers and your dependencies — *and* it handles configuring and binding a class's dependencies. It also greatly simplifies the API to use ORM tools, such as Hibernate.

SUMMARY
. . . .

This chapter covered the history of Spring, why everyone loves it, and how it makes J2EE development easier. Examples compared the traditional factory pattern with Spring's **ApplicationContext** and provided a before and after view of developing with Hibernate.

Spring's **ApplicationContext** can be thought of as a "bean provider" that handles instantiating objects, binding their dependencies and providing them to you preconfigured.

Chapter 2: Spring Quick-Start Tutorial is a tutorial for developing a web application that uses Spring, Hibernate and Struts to manage users in a database. This application will demonstrate how Spring simplifies J2EE and TDD. *Chapter 3: The BeanFactory and How It Works* examines the Spring Core module, as well as the lifecycle of the beans it manages. The BeanFactory is the heart and brain of Spring — controlling how objects work together and providing them with the support they need to survive.

SPRING QUICK-START TUTORIAL

Developing your first Spring web application

This chapter is a tutorial that steps you through writing a simple Spring web application using the Struts Model-View-Controller (MVC) framework for the front end, Spring for the middle-tier glue, and Hibernate for the back end. In Chapter 4: Spring's MVC Framework, this application will be refactored to use the Spring MVC framework.

This chapter covers writing tests to verify functionality, configuring Hibernate and transactions, loading Spring's applicationContext.xml file, setting up dependencies between business services and DAOs, and wiring Spring into the Struts application.

OVERVIEW

You will create a simple application for user management that does basic CRUD (Create, Retrieve, Update and Delete). This application is called MyUsers, and it will be the sample application throughout the book. It's a three-tiered web app with an action that calls a business service, which in turn calls a DAO. The diagram in Figure 2.1 shows a brief overview of how the MyUsers application will work when you finish this tutorial. The numbers below indicate the order of flow — from the web (**UserAction**) to the middle tier (**UserManager**) to the data layer (**UserDAO**) — and back again.

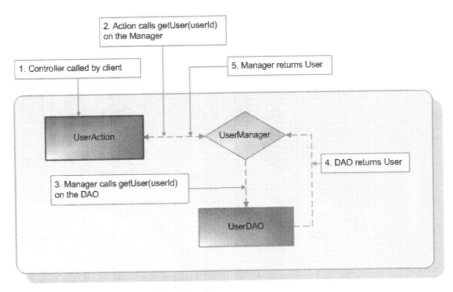

Figure 2.1: MyUsers application flow

This application uses Struts as the MVC framework because most readers are familiar with Struts. The real power of Spring lies in its declarative transactions, dependency binding and persistence support (for example Hibernate and iBATIS). *Chapter 4: Spring's MVC Framework* refactors this application to use Spring's MVC framework.

Below are the ordered steps you will perform:

1   Download Struts and Spring.

2   Create project directories and an Ant build file.

3   Create a unit test for the persistence layer.

4   Configure Hibernate and Spring.

5   Create Hibernate DAO implementation.

6   Run the unit test and verify CRUD with DAO.

7   Create manager and declare transactions.

8   Create a unit test for the Struts action.

9   Create an action and model **(DynaActionForm)** for the web layer.

10 Run the unit test and verify CRUD with action.

11 Create JavaServer Pages (JSPs) to allow CRUD through a web browser.

12 Verify the JSPs' functionality through your browser.

13 Add validation using Commons Validator.

DOWNLOAD STRUTS AND SPRING[1]

1   Download and install the following components:

- Java Development Kit (JDK) 1.4.2 (or above)
- Tomcat 5.0+
- Ant 1.6.1+

2   Set up the following environment variables:

- JAVA_HOME
- ANT_HOME
- CATALINA_HOME

3   Add the following to your PATH environment variable:

- JAVA_HOME/bin
- ANT_HOME/bin
- CATALINA_HOME/bin

To develop a Java-based web application, developers usually download JARs, create a directory structure, and create an Ant build file. For a Struts-only application, this can be simplified by using the *struts-blank.war*, which is part of the standard Struts distribution. For a web app using Spring's MVC framework, you can use the *webapp-minimal* application that ships with Spring. Both of these are nice starting points, but neither simplifies the Struts-Spring integration nor takes into account unit testing. Therefore, I created Equinox, both for this book and to help developers get started quickly with Spring.

Equinox is a bare-bones starter application for creating a Spring-based web application. It has a pre-defined directory structure, an Ant build file (for compiling, deploying and testing), and all the JARs you will need for a Struts, Spring and Hibernate-based web app. Much of the directory structure and build file in Equinox is taken from my open source AppFuse application. Therefore, Equinox is really just an "AppFuse Light" that allows rapid web app development with minimal setup. Because it is derived from AppFuse, you will see many references to it in package names, database names and other areas. This is done purposefully so you can migrate from an Equinox-based application to a more robust AppFuse-based application.

In order to start MyUsers, download Equinox 1.0 from sourcebeat.com/downloads and extract it to an appropriate location.

---

1. You can learn more about how I set up my development environment on Windows at raibledesigns.com/wiki/Wiki.jsp?page=DevelopmentEnvironment.

CREATE PROJECT DIRECTORIES AND AN ANT BUILD FILE

To set up your initial directory structure and Ant build file, extract the Equinox download onto your hard drive. I recommend putting projects in *C:\Source* on Windows and *~/dev* on Unix or Linux. For Windows users, now is a good time set your HOME environment variable to *C:\Source*. The easiest way to get started with Equinox is to extract it to your preferred source location, cd into the *equinox* directory and run **ant new -Dapp.name=myusers** from the command line.

WARNING: You must have the *CATALINA_HOME* environment variable set, or building MyUsers will not work. This is because its *build.xml* depends on a *catalina-ant.jar* file for running Tomcat's Ant tasks (covered shortly). As an alternative, you can specify a *tomcat.home* property in *build.properties* that points to your Tomcat installation.

At this point, you should have the directory structure shown in Figure 2.2 for the MyUsers web app:

Figure 2.2: MyUsers application directory structure

TIP: I use Cygwin (www.cygwin.com) on Windows, which allows me to type forward-slashes, just like Unix/Linux. Because of this, all the paths I present in this book will have forward slashes. Please adjust for your environment accordingly (that is, use backslashes (\) for Windows' command prompt).

Equinox contains a simple but powerful *build.xml* file to deploy, compile and test using Ant. For all the Ant targets available, type **ant** in the *MyUsers* directory. The return should look like the code in Listing 2.1:

Listing 2.1

```
[echo] Available targets are:

[echo] compile   --> Compile all Java files
[echo] war       --> Package as WAR file
[echo] deploy    --> Deploy application as directory
[echo] deploywar --> Deploy application as a WAR file

[echo] install   --> Install application in Tomcat
[echo] remove    --> Remove application from Tomcat
[echo] reload    --> Reload application in Tomcat
[echo] start     --> Start Tomcat application
[echo] stop      --> Stop Tomcat application
[echo] list      --> List Tomcat applications

[echo] clean --> Deletes compiled classes and WAR
[echo] new --> Creates a new project
```

Equinox supports Tomcat's Ant tasks. These tasks are already integrated into Equinox, but showing you *how* they were integrated will help you understand how they work.

TOMCAT AND ANT

Tomcat ships with a number of Ant tasks that allow you to install, remove and reload web apps using its manager application. The easiest way to declare and use these tasks is to create a properties file that contains all the definitions. In Equinox, a *tomcatTasks.properties* file is in the base directory with the contents in Listing 2.2:

Listing 2.2

```
deploy=org.apache.catalina.ant.DeployTask
undeploy=org.apache.catalina.ant.UndeployTask
remove=org.apache.catalina.ant.RemoveTask
reload=org.apache.catalina.ant.ReloadTask
start=org.apache.catalina.ant.StartTask
stop=org.apache.catalina.ant.StopTask
list=org.apache.catalina.ant.ListTask
```

A number of targets are in *build.xml* for installing, removing and reloading the application. See Listing 2.3:

Listing 2.3

```xml
<!-- Tomcat Ant Tasks -->
<taskdef file="tomcatTasks.properties">
    <classpath>
        <pathelement
            path="${tomcat.home}/server/lib/catalina-ant.jar"/>
    </classpath>
</taskdef>

<target name="install" description="Install application in Tomcat"
    depends="war">
    <deploy url="${tomcat.manager.url}"
        username="${tomcat.manager.username}"
        password="${tomcat.manager.password}"
        path="/${webapp.name}"
        war="file:${dist.dir}/${webapp.name}.war"/>
</target>

<target name="remove" description="Remove application from Tomcat">
    <undeploy url="${tomcat.manager.url}"
        username="${tomcat.manager.username}"
        password="${tomcat.manager.password}"
        path="/${webapp.name}"/>
</target>

<target name="reload" description="Reload application in Tomcat">
    <reload url="${tomcat.manager.url}"
        username="${tomcat.manager.username}"
        password="${tomcat.manager.password}"
        path="/${webapp.name}"/>
</target>

<target name="start" description="Start Tomcat application">
    <start url="${tomcat.manager.url}"
        username="${tomcat.manager.username}"
        password="${tomcat.manager.password}"
        path="/${webapp.name}"/>
</target>

<target name="stop" description="Stop Tomcat application">
    <stop url="${tomcat.manager.url}"
        username="${tomcat.manager.username}"
        password="${tomcat.manager.password}"
        path="/${webapp.name}"/>
</target>

<target name="list" description="List Tomcat applications">
```

```
      <list url="${tomcat.manager.url}"
          username="${tomcat.manager.username}"
          password="${tomcat.manager.password}"/>
  </target>
```

In the targets listed in Listing 2.3, several `${tomcat.*}` variables need to be defined. These are in the *build.properties* file in the base directory. By default, they are defined as follows (see Listing 2.4):

Listing 2.4

```
# Properties for Tomcat Server
tomcat.manager.url=http://localhost:8080/manager
tomcat.manager.username=admin
tomcat.manager.password=admin
```

To make sure the **admin** user is able to access the manager application, open the *$CATALINA_HOME/conf/tomcat-users.xml* file and verify that the following line exists. If it does not exist, you must create it. Note that the **roles** attribute may contain a comma-delimited list of roles. (See Listing 2.5.)

Listing 2.5

```
<user username="admin" password="admin" roles="manager"/>
```

To test this change, save *tomcat-users.xml* and start Tomcat. Then navigate to the *MyUsers* directory from the command line and try running **ant list**. You should see a list of currently running applications on your Tomcat server., similar to the example in Figure 2.3.

Figure 2.3: Results of the `ant list` command

Now you can install MyUsers by running **ant deploy**. Open your browser and go to localhost:8080/myusers. The "Welcome to Equinox" window displays, as in Figure 2.4:

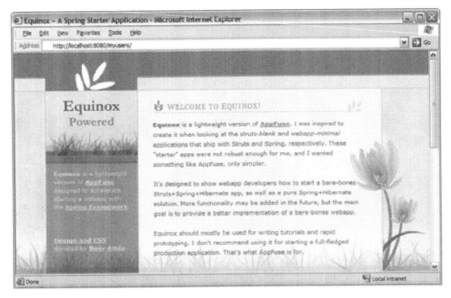

Figure 2.4: Equinox Welcome page

WARNING: In order for the in-memory HSQLDB to work correctly with MyUsers, start Tomcat from the same directory from which you run Ant. Type **$CATALINA_HOME/bin/startup.sh** on Unix/Linux and **%CATALINA_HOME%\ bin\startup.bat** on Windows. You can also change the database settings to use an absolute path.

In the next few sections, you will develop a **User** object and a Hibernate DAO to persist that object. You will use Spring to manage the DAO and its dependencies. Last, you will write a business service that uses transparent aspect-oriented programming (AOP) and declarative transactions.

CREATE UNIT TEST FOR PERSISTENCE LAYER

In the MyUsers app, you will use Hibernate for your persistence layer. Hibernate is an object-relational (O/R) framework that relates Java objects to database tables. It allows you to very easily perform CRUD (Create, Retrieve, Update, Delete) on these objects. Spring makes working with Hibernate even easier. In my experience, switching from a Hibernate-only solution to Spring+Hibernate reduced lines of code by about 75%. This code reduction was sponsored by the removal of a ServiceLocator class, a couple of **DAOFactory** classes, and using Spring's runtime exceptions instead of Hibernate's checked exceptions.

Writing a unit test will help you formulate your **UserDAO** interface. To create a JUnit test for your **UserDAO**, complete the steps below:

1   Create a **UserDAOTest.java** class in the *test/org/appfuse/dao* directory. This class should extend **BaseDAOTestCase**, which already exists in this package. This parent class initializes Spring's **ApplicationContext** from the *web/WEB-INF/applicationContext.xml* file. Listing 2.6 is the code you will need to begin writing your *UserDAOTest.java*:

Listing 2.6

```
package org.appfuse.dao;

// use your IDE to handle imports

public class UserDAOTest extends BaseDAOTestCase {
    private User user = null;
    private UserDAO dao = null;

    protected void setUp() throws Exception {
        super.setUp();
        dao = (UserDAO) ctx.getBean("userDAO");
    }

    protected void tearDown() throws Exception {
        super.tearDown();
        dao = null;
    }
}
```

NOTE: Automatically importing necessary classes is a nice feature of modern IDEs such as Eclipse and IDEA. Equinox contains the project necessary for both of these IDEs.

This class won't compile yet because you haven't created your **UserDAO** interface. Before you do that, write a couple of tests to verify that CRUD works on the **User** object.

2   Add the **testSave** and **testAddAndRemove** methods to the **UserDAOTest** class, as shown in Listing 2.7:

Listing 2.7

```
public void testSaveUser() throws Exception {
    user = new User();
    user.setFirstName("Rod");
    user.setLastName("Johnson");

    dao.saveUser(user);
    assertNotNull("primary key assigned", user.getId());
    log.info(user);
    assertNotNull(user.getFirstName());
}

public void testAddAndRemoveUser() throws Exception {
    user = new User();
    user.setFirstName("Bill");
    user.setLastName("Joy");

    dao.saveUser(user);

    assertNotNull(user.getId());
    assertEquals(user.getFirstName(), "Bill");

    if (log.isDebugEnabled()) {
        log.debug("removing user...");
    }

    dao.removeUser(user.getId());

    assertNull(dao.getUser(user.getId()));
}
```

From these test methods, you can see that you need to create a **UserDAO** with the following methods:

- **saveUser(User)**
- **removeUser(Long)**
- **getUser(Long)**
- **getUsers()** (to return all the users in the database)

3   Create a *UserDAO.java* file in the *src/org/appfuse/dao directory* and populate it with the code in Listing 2.8:

NOTE: If you are using an integrated development environment (IDE) such as Eclipse or IDEA, a "lightbulb" icon will appear to the left of a non-existent class and allow you to create it on-the-fly.

Listing 2.8

```
package org.appfuse.dao;

// use your IDE to handle imports

public interface UserDAO extends DAO {
    public List getUsers();
    public User getUser(Long userId);
    public void saveUser(User user);
    public void removeUser(Long userId);
}
```

Finally, in order for the **UserDAOTest** and **UserDAO** to compile, create a **User** object to persist.

4   Create a **User.java** class in the *src/org/appfuse/model* directory and add **id**, **firstName** and **lastName** as member variables, as shown in Listing 2.9:

Listing 2.9

```
package org.appfuse.model;
public class User extends BaseObject {
    private Long id;
    private String firstName;
    private String lastName;

  /*
    Generate your getters and setters using your favorite IDE:
    In Eclipse:
     Right-click -> Source -> Generate Getters and Setters
   */
}
```

Notice that you're extending a **BaseObject** class. It has the following useful methods: **toString()**, **equals()** and **hashCode()**. The latter two are required by Hibernate.

> **NOTE:** In a real-world application, these methods should not be in a parent class, but rather in each subclass. Making them abstract in the **BaseObject** class can help to enforce this rule. **Commonclipse** is an Eclipse plugin that can generate these methods for you.

After creating the **User** object, open the **UserDAO** and **UserDAOTest** classes and resolve missing imports with your IDE.

CONFIGURE HIBERNATE AND SPRING

Now that you have the Plain Old Java Object (POJO), create a mapping file so Hibernate can persist it.

1   In the *src/org/appfuse/model* directory, create a file named *User.hbm.xml* with the contents in Listing 2.10:

Listing 2.10

```xml
<?xml version="1.0" encoding="UTF-8"?>
<!DOCTYPE hibernate-mapping PUBLIC
    "-//Hibernate/Hibernate Mapping DTD 2.0//EN"
    "http://hibernate.sourceforge.net/hibernate-mapping-2.0.dtd">

<hibernate-mapping>
    <class name="org.appfuse.model.User" table="app_user">

        <id name="id" column="id" unsaved-value="0">
            <generator class="increment" />
        </id>
        <property name="firstName" column="first_name"
            not-null="true"/>
        <property name="lastName"
            column="last_name" not-null="true"/>

    </class>
</hibernate-mapping>
```

2   Add this mapping to Spring's *applicationContext.xml* file in the *web/WEB-INF* directory. Open this file and look for **<property name="mappingResources">** and change it to the code in Listing 2.11:

Listing 2.11

```xml
<property name="mappingResources">
    <list>
        <value>org/appfuse/model/User.hbm.xml</value>
    </list>
</property>
```

In the *applicationContext.xml* file, you can see how the database is set up and Hibernate is configured to work with Spring. Equinox is designed to work with an HSQL database named db/appfuse. It will be created in your project's *db* directory. Details of this configuration will be covered in the *How Spring is configured in Equinox* section.

3   Run **ant deploy reload** (with Tomcat running) and see the database tables being created as part of Tomcat's console log (see Listing 2.12):

Listing 2.12

```
INFO - SchemaExport.execute(98) | Running hbm2ddl schema export
INFO - SchemaExport.execute(117) | exporting generated schema to
database
INFO - ConnectionProviderFactory.newConnectionProvider(53)
    | Initializing connection provider:
        org.springframework.orm.hibernate
            .LocalDataSourceConnectionProvider
INFO - DriverManagerDataSource.getConnectionFromDriverManager(140) |
    Creating new JDBC connection to [jdbc:hsqldb:db/appfuse]
INFO - SchemaExport.execute(160) | schema export complete
```

TIP: If you'd like to see more (or less) logging, change the log4j settings in the *web /WEB-INF/classes/log4j.xml* file

4   To verify that the **app_user** table was actually created in the database, run
    ant browse to bring up a HSQL console. You should see the HSQL
    Database Manager, as shown in Figure 2.5:

NOTE: If you don't see the **app_user** table when running **ant browse**, it's
because you didn't start Tomcat from the same directory in which you're running
Ant.

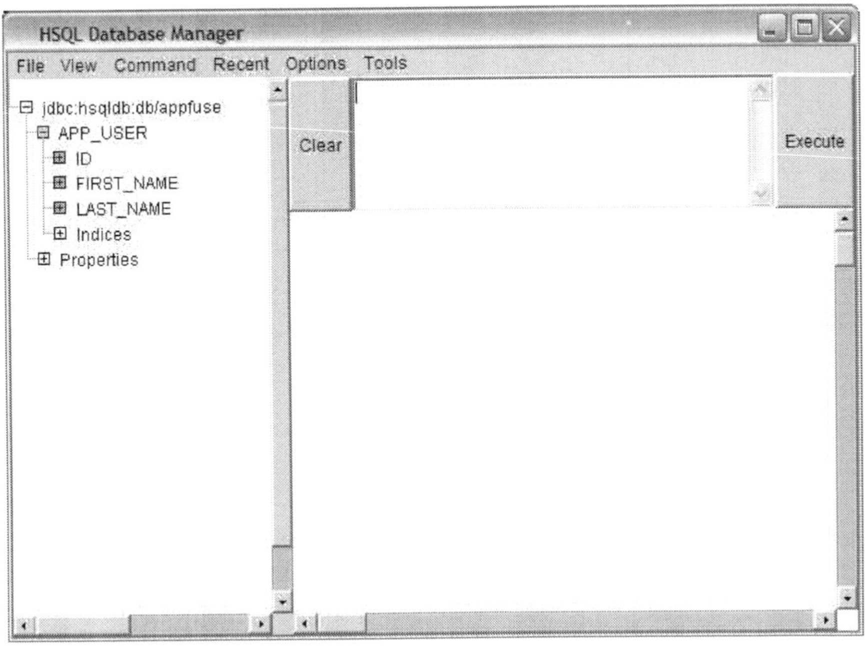

Figure 2.5: HSQL database manager

How Spring is configured in Equinox

It is very easy to configure any J2EE-based web application to use Spring. At the very least, you can simply add Spring's `ContextLoaderListener` to your *web.xml* file (see Listing 2.13):

Listing 2.13

```
<listener>
    <listener-class>
        org.springframework.web.context.ContextLoaderListener
    </listener-class>
</listener>
```

This is a `ServletContextListener` that initializes when your web app starts up. By default, it looks for Spring's configuration file at *WEB-INF/applicationContext.xml*. You can change this default value by specifying a `<context-param>` element named `contextConfigLocation`. An example is provided in Listing 2.14:

Listing 2.14

```
<context-param>
    <param-name>contextConfigLocation</param-name>
    <param-value>/WEB-INF/sampleContext.xml</param-value>
</context-param>
```

The **<param-value>** element can contain a space or comma-delimited set of paths. In Equinox, Spring is configured using this Listener and its default **contextConfigLocation**.

So, how does Spring know about Hibernate? This is the beauty of Spring: it makes it very simple to bind dependencies together. Look at the full contents of your *applicationContext.xml* file (see Listing 2.15):

Listing 2.15

```
<?xml version="1.0" encoding="UTF-8"?>
<!DOCTYPE beans PUBLIC "-//SPRING//DTD BEAN//EN"
    "http://www.springframework.org/dtd/spring-beans.dtd">

<beans>
    <bean id="dataSource"
        class="org.springframework.jdbc.datasource
            .DriverManagerDataSource">
        <property name="driverClassName">
            <value>org.hsqldb.jdbcDriver</value>
        </property>
        <property name="url">
            <value>jdbc:hsqldb:db/appfuse</value>
        </property>
        <property name="username"><value>sa</value></property>
        <!-- Make sure <value> tags are on same line - if they're not,
            authentication will fail -->
        <property name="password"><value></value></property>
    </bean>

    <!-- Hibernate SessionFactory -->
    <bean id="sessionFactory"
        class="org.springframework.orm.hibernate
            .LocalSessionFactoryBean">
        <property name="dataSource">
            <ref local="dataSource"/>
        </property>
        <property name="mappingResources">
            <list>
                <value>org/appfuse/model/User.hbm.xml</value>
            </list>
        </property>
```

```
            <property name="hibernateProperties">
            <props>
                <prop key="hibernate.dialect">
                    net.sf.hibernate.dialect.HSQLDialect
                </prop>
                <prop key="hibernate.hbm2ddl.auto">create</prop>
            </props>
            </property>
        </bean>

        <!-- Transaction manager for a single Hibernate SessionFactory -->
        <bean id="transactionManager"
            class="org.springframework.orm.hibernate
                .HibernateTransactionManager">
            <property name="sessionFactory">
                <ref local="sessionFactory"/>
            </property>
        </bean>
    </beans>
```

The first bean (**dataSource**) represents an HSQL database, and the second bean (**sessionFactory**) has a dependency on that bean. Spring just calls **setData-Source** (**DataSource**) on the **LocalSessionFactoryBean** to make this work. If you wanted to use a Java Naming and Directory Interface (JNDI) **DataSource** instead, you could easily change this bean's definition to something similar to Listing 2.16:

Listing 2.16

```
<bean id="dataSource"
    class="org.springframework.jndi.JndiObjectFactoryBean">
    <property name="jndiName">
        <value>java:comp/env/jdbc/appfuse</value>
    </property>
</bean>
```

Also note the **hibernate.hbm2ddl.auto** property in the **sessionFactory** definition. This property creates the database tables automatically when the application starts. Other possible values are *update* and *create-drop*.

The last bean configured is the **transactionManager** (and nothing is stopping you from using a Java Transaction API — JTA — transaction manager), which is necessary to perform distributed transactions across two databases. If you want to use a JTA transaction manager, simply change this bean's class attribute to **org.springframework.transaction.jta.JtaTransactionManager**.

Now you can implement the **UserDAO** with Hibernate.

IMPLEMENT USERDAO WITH HIBERNATE

To create a Hibernate implementation of the UserDAO, complete the following steps:

1   Create a *UserDAOHibernate.java* class in *src/org/appfuse/dao/hibernate* (you will need to create this directory/package). This file extends Spring's **HibernateDaoSupport** and implements **UserDAO**. See Listing 2.17.

Listing 2.17

```
package org.appfuse.dao.hibernate;

// organize imports using your IDE

public class UserDAOHibernate extends HibernateDaoSupport implements
    UserDAO {
    private Log log = LogFactory.getLog(UserDAOHibernate.class);

    public List getUsers() {
        return getHibernateTemplate().find("from User");
    }

    public User getUser(Long id) {
        return (User) getHibernateTemplate().get(User.class, id);
    }

    public void saveUser(User user) {
        getHibernateTemplate().saveOrUpdate(user);

        if (log.isDebugEnabled()) {
            log.debug("userId set to: " + user.getId());
        }
    }

    public void removeUser(Long id) {
        Object user = getHibernateTemplate().load(User.class, id);
        getHibernateTemplate().delete(user);
    }
}
```

Spring's **HibernateDaoSupport** class is a convenient super class for Hibernate DAOs. It has handy methods you can call to get a Hibernate **Session**, or a **SessionFactory**. The most convenient method is **getHibernateTemplate()**, which returns a **HibernateTemplate**. This template wraps Hibernate checked exceptions with runtime exceptions, allowing your DAO interfaces to be Hibernate exception-free.

Nothing is in your application to bind **UserDAO** to **UserDAOHibernate**, so you must create that relationship.

2   For Spring to recognize the relationship, add the lines in Listing 2.18 to the *web/WEB-INF/applicationContext.xml* file.

Listing 2.18

```
<bean id="userDAO"
class="org.appfuse.dao.hibernate.UserDAOHibernate">
    <property name="sessionFactory">
        <ref local="sessionFactory"/>
    </property>
</bean>
```

This sets a Hibernate **SessionFactory** on your **UserDAOHibernate** (which inherits **setSessionFactory()** from **HibernateDaoSupport**). Spring detects if a **Session** already exists (that is, it was opened in the web tier), and it uses that one instead of creating a new one. This allows you to use Hibernate's popular "Open Session in View" pattern for lazy loading collections.

RUN UNIT TEST AND VERIFY CRUD WITH DAO

Before you run this first test, tune down your default logging from informational messages to warnings.

1   Uncomment the **<logger>** settings for *net.sf.hibernate* and *org.springframework* in the *log4j.xml* file (in *web/WEB-INF/classes*).

2   Run **UserDAOTest** using **ant test**. If this wasn't your only test, you could use **ant test -Dtestcase=UserDAO** to isolate which tests are run. After running this, your console should have a couple of log messages from your tests, as shown in Figure 2.6:

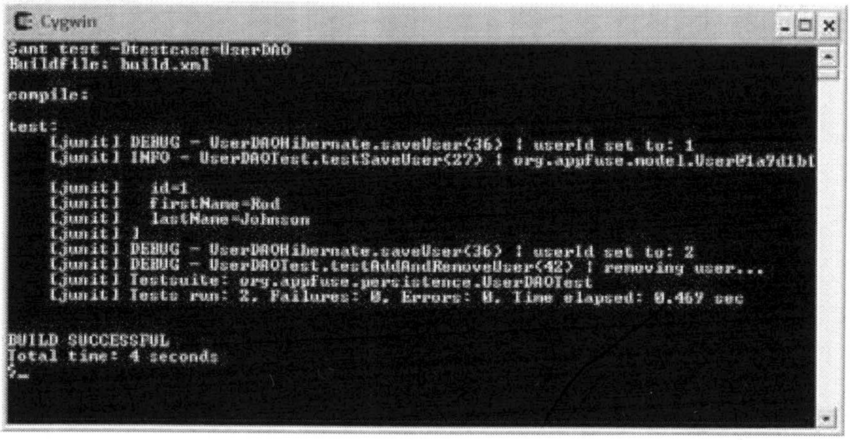

Figure 2.6: Results of the `ant test -Dtestcase=UserDAO` command

CREATE MANAGER AND DECLARE TRANSACTIONS

A recommended practice in J2EE development is to keep your layers separated. That is to say, the data layer (DAOs) shouldn't be bound to the web layer (servlets). Using Spring, it's easy to separate them, but it's useful to further separate these tiers with a business service class.

The main reasons for using a business service class are:

- Most presentation tier components execute a unit of business logic. It's best to put this logic in a non-web class so a web service or rich platform client can use the same API as a servlet.

- Most business logic can take place in one method, possibly using more than one DAO. Using a business service class allows you to use Spring's declarative transactions feature at a higher business logic level.

The **UserManager** interface in the MyUsers application has the same methods as the **UserDAO**. The main difference is the manager is more web friendly; it accepts strings where the **UserDAO** accepts longs, and it returns a **User** object in the **saveUser()** method. This is convenient after inserting a new user (for example, to get its primary key). The manager (or business service) is also a good place to put any business logic that your application requires.

1   Start the services layer by first creating a **UserManagerTest** class in *test /org/appfuse/service* (you have to create this directory). This class extends JUnit's TestCase and contains the code in Listing 2.19:

Listing 2.19

```
package org.appfuse.service;

// use your IDE to organize imports

public class UserManagerTest extends TestCase {
    private static Log
        log = LogFactory.getLog(UserManagerTest.class);
    private ApplicationContext ctx;
    private User user;
    private UserManager mgr;

    protected void setUp() throws Exception {
        String[] paths = { "/WEB-INF/applicationContext.xml" };
        ctx = new ClassPathXmlApplicationContext(paths);
        mgr = (UserManager) ctx.getBean("userManager");
    }

    protected void tearDown() throws Exception {
        user = null;
        mgr = null;
    }

    // add testXXX methods here
}
```

In the **setUp()** method in Listing 2.19, you are loading your *applicationContext.xml*
file into the **ApplicationContext** variable using **ClassPathXmlApplication-
Context**. Several methods are available for loading the **ApplicationContext**:
from the classpath, the file system or within a web application. These methods will
be covered in the *Chapter 3: The BeanFactory and How It Works.*

    2   Code the first test method to verify that adding and removing a **User**
object with the **UserManager** completes successfully (see Listing 2.20):

Listing 2.20

```
public void testAddAndRemoveUser() throws Exception {
    user = new User();
    user.setFirstName("Easter");
    user.setLastName("Bunny");

    user = mgr.saveUser(user);

    assertNotNull(user.getId());

    if (log.isDebugEnabled()) {
        log.debug("removing user...");
```

```
        }
        String userId = user.getId().toString();
        mgr.removeUser(userId);

        user = mgr.getUser(userId);
        assertNull("User object found in database", user);
    }
```

This test is really an *integration test* rather than a *unit test* because it uses all the real components it depends on. To be more like a *unit test*, you would use EasyMock or a similar tool to *fake* the DAO. Using this, you could even get away from loading Spring's **ApplicationContext** and depending on any of Spring's APIs. I recommend the test we created because it tests all the internals that our project depends on (Spring, Hibernate, our classes), including the database. *Chapter 9: Testing Spring Applications* covers refactoring the **UserManagerTest** to use mocks for its DAO dependency.

3   To compile the **UserManagerTest**, create the **UserManager** interface in the *src/org/appfuse/service* directory. Use the code in Listing 2.21 to create this class in the **org.appfuse.service** package:

Listing 2.21

```
package org.appfuse.service;

// use your IDE to handle imports

public interface UserManager {
    public List getUsers();
    public User getUser(String userId);
    public User saveUser(User user);
    public void removeUser(String userId);
}
```

4   Now create a new subpackage called **org.appfuse.service.impl** and create an implementation class of the **UserManager** interface (see Listing 2.22)

Listing 2.22

```
package org.appfuse.service.impl;

// use your IDE to handle imports

public class UserManagerImpl implements UserManager {
    private static Log
        log = LogFactory.getLog(UserManagerImpl.class);
```

```
                   private UserDAO dao;

                   public void setUserDAO(UserDAO dao) {
                       this.dao = dao;
                   }

                   public List getUsers() {
                       return dao.getUsers();
                   }

                   public User getUser(String userId) {
                       User user = dao.getUser(Long.valueOf(userId));

                       if (user == null) {
                           log.warn("UserId '" + userId + "'
                               not found in database.");
                       }

                       return user;
                   }

                   public User saveUser(User user) {
                       dao.saveUser(user);

                       return user;
                   }

                   public void removeUser(String userId) {
                       dao.removeUser(Long.valueOf(userId));
                   }
               }
```

This class has no indication that you're using Hibernate. This is important if you ever want to switch your persistence layer to use a different technology.

This class has a private dao member variable, as well as a **setUserDAO()** method. This allows Spring to perform its dependency binding magic and wire the objects together. Later, when you refactor this class to use a mock for its DAO, you'll need to add the **setUserDAO()** method to the **UserManager** interface.

5   Before running this test, configure Spring so **getBean("userManager")** returns the **UserManagerImpl** class. In *web/WEB-INF/application-Context.xml*, add the lines in Listing 2.23:

Listing 2.23

```
<bean id="userManager"
    class="org.appfuse.service.impl.UserManagerImpl">
    <property name="userDAO"><ref local="userDAO"/></property>
</bean>
```

The only problem with this is you're not leveraging Spring's AOP and, specifically, declarative transactions.

6 To do this, change the `userManager` bean to use a `ProxyFactoryBean`. A `ProxyFactoryBean` creates different implementations of a class, so that AOP can intercept and override method calls. For transactions, use `TransactionProxyFactoryBean` in place of the `UserManagerImpl` class. Add the bean definition in Listing 2.24 to the context file:

Listing 2.24

```
<bean id="userManager"
    class="org.springframework.transaction.interceptor
        .TransactionProxyFactoryBean">
    <property name="transactionManager">
        <ref local="transactionManager"/>
    </property>
    <property name="target">
        <ref local="userManagerTarget"/>
    </property>
    <property name="transactionAttributes">
        <props>
            <prop key="save*">PROPAGATION_REQUIRED</prop>
            <prop key="remove*">PROPAGATION_REQUIRED</prop>
            <prop key="*">PROPAGATION_REQUIRED,readOnly</prop>
        </props>
    </property>
</bean>
```

You can see from this XML fragment that the `TransactionProxyFactoryBean` must have a `transactionManager` property set, and `transactionAttributes` defined.

7 Tell this transaction proxy the object you're mimicking: `userManagerTarget`. As part of this new bean, change the old `userManager` bean to have an `id` of `userManagerTarget`. See Listing 2.25.

Listing 2.25

```
<bean id="userManagerTarget"
    class="org.appfuse.service.impl.UserManagerImpl">
    <property name="userDAO"><ref local="userDAO"/></property>
</bean>
```

After editing *applicationContext.xml* to add definitions for **userManager** and **user-ManagerTarget**, run **ant test -Dtestcase=UserManagerTest** to see the console output displayed in Figure 2.7:

Figure 2.7: Results of the **ant test -Dtestcase=UserManagerTest** command

If you'd like to see the transactions execute and commit, add the XML in Listing 2.26 to the *log4j.xml* file:

Listing 2.26

```
<logger name="org.springframework.transaction">
    <level value="DEBUG"/> <!-- INFO does nothing -->
</logger>
```

Running the test again will give you a plethora of Spring log messages as it binds objects, creates transactions, and then commits them. You'll probably want to remove the above logger after running the test.

Congratulations! You've just implemented a Spring/Hibernate solution for the back end of a web application. You've also configured a business service class to use AOP and declarative transactions. This is no small feat; give yourself a pat on the back!

CREATE UNIT TEST FOR STRUTS ACTION

The business service and DAO are now functional, so let's slap an MVC framework on top of this sucker! Whoa, there — not just yet. You can do the C (Controller), but not the V (View). Continue your TDD path by creating a Struts action for managing users.

The Equinox application is configured for Struts. Configuring Struts requires putting some settings in *web.xml* and defining a *struts-config.xml* file in the *web/WEB-INF* directory. Since there is a large audience of Struts developers, this chapter deals with the Struts way first. *Chapter 4: Spring's MVC Framework* deals with the Spring way. If you'd prefer to skip this section and learn the Spring MVC way, see that chapter.

To develop your first Struts action unit test, create a **UserActionTest.java** class in *test/org/appfuse/web*. This class extends **MockStrutsTestCase** and contains the code in Listing 2.27:

Listing 2.27

```
package org.appfuse.web;

// use your IDE to handle imports

public class UserActionTest extends MockStrutsTestCase {

    public UserActionTest(String testName) {
        super(testName);
    }

    public void testExecute() {
        setRequestPathInfo("/user");
        addRequestParameter("id", "1");
        actionPerform();
        verifyForward("success");
        verifyNoActionErrors();
    }
}
```

CREATE ACTION AND MODEL (DYNAACTIONFORM) FOR WEB LAYER

1   Create a **UserAction.java** class in *src/org/appfuse/web*. This class extends **DispatchAction**, which you will use in a few minutes to dispatch to the different CRUD methods of this class. See Listing 2.28.

Listing 2.28

```
package org.appfuse.web;

// use your IDE to handle imports

public class UserAction extends DispatchAction {
    private static Log log = LogFactory.getLog(UserAction.class);
```

```
public ActionForward execute(ActionMapping mapping,
    ActionForm form,
                            HttpServletRequest request,
                            HttpServletResponse response)
throws Exception {
    request.getSession().setAttribute("test", "succeeded!");

    log.debug("looking up userId: " + request.getParameter("id"));

    return mapping.findForward("success");
}
}
```

2   To configure Struts so that the */user* request path means something, add an *action-mapping* to *web/WEB-INF/struts-config.xml*. Open this file and add the code in Listing 2.29 as an action-mapping:

Listing 2.29

```
<action path="/user" type="org.appfuse.web.UserAction">
    <forward name="success" path="/index.jsp"/>
</action>
```

3   Execute **ant test -Dtestcase=UserAction** and you should get the lovely "BUILD SUCCESSFUL" message.

4   Add a *form-bean* definition to the *struts-config.xml* file (in the **<form-beans>** section). For the Struts **ActionForm**, use a **DynaActionForm**, which is a JavaBean that gets created dynamically from an XML definition. See Listing 2.30.

Listing 2.30

```
<form-bean name="userForm"
    type="org.apache.struts.action.DynaActionForm">
    <form-property name="user" type="org.appfuse.model.User"/>
</form-bean>
```

You're using this instead of a concrete **ActionForm** because you only need a thin wrapper around the **User** object. Ideally, you could use the **User** object, but you'd lose the ability to validate properties and reset checkboxes in a Struts environment. Later, I'll show you how Spring makes this easier and allows you to use the **User** object in your web tier.

5   Modify your **<action>** definition to use this form and put it in the request (see Listing 2.31):

Listing 2.31

```
<action path="/user" type="org.appfuse.web.UserAction"
    name="userForm" scope="request">
    <forward name="success" path="/index.jsp"/>
</action>
```

6   Modify your **UserActionTest** to test the different CRUD methods in your action, as shown in Listing 2.32:

Listing 2.32

```
public class UserActionTest extends MockStrutsTestCase {

    public UserActionTest(String testName) {
        super(testName);
    }

    // Adding a new user is required between tests because HSQL creates
    // an in-memory database that goes away during tests.
    public void addUser() {
        setRequestPathInfo("/user");
        addRequestParameter("method", "save");
        addRequestParameter("user.firstName", "Juergen");
        addRequestParameter("user.lastName", "Hoeller");
        actionPerform();
        verifyForward("list");
        verifyNoActionErrors();
    }

    public void testAddAndEdit() {
        addUser();

        // edit newly added user
        addRequestParameter("method", "edit");
        addRequestParameter("id", "1");
        actionPerform();
        verifyForward("edit");
        verifyNoActionErrors();
    }

    public void testAddAndDelete() {
        addUser();

        // delete new user
        setRequestPathInfo("/user");
        addRequestParameter("method", "delete");
        addRequestParameter("user.id", "1");
        actionPerform();
```

```
                verifyForward("list");
                verifyNoActionErrors();
        }

        public void testList() {
                addUser();
                setRequestPathInfo("/user");
                addRequestParameter("method", "list");
                actionPerform();
                verifyForward("list");
                verifyNoActionErrors();

                List users = (List) getRequest().getAttribute("users");
                assertNotNull(users);
                assertTrue(users.size() == 1);
        }
}
```

7   Modify the **UserAction** so your tests will pass and it can handle CRUD
requests. The easiest way to do this is to write edit, save and delete
methods. Be sure to remove the existing **execute** method first.
Listing 2.33 is the modified **UserAction.java**:

Listing 2.33

```
public class UserAction extends DispatchAction {
        private static Log log = LogFactory.getLog(UserAction.class);
        private UserManager mgr = null;

        public void setUserManager(UserManager userManager) {
                this.mgr = userManager;
        }

        public ActionForward delete(ActionMapping mapping,
                ActionForm form,
                                    HttpServletRequest request,
                                    HttpServletResponse response)
        throws Exception {
                if (log.isDebugEnabled()) {
                        log.debug("entering 'delete' method...");
                }

                mgr.removeUser(request.getParameter("user.id"));

                ActionMessages messages = new ActionMessages();
                messages.add(ActionMessages.GLOBAL_MESSAGE,
                                new ActionMessage("user.deleted"));

                saveMessages(request, messages);
```

```
        return list(mapping, form, request, response);
    }

    public ActionForward edit(ActionMapping mapping, ActionForm form,
                              HttpServletRequest request,
                              HttpServletResponse response)
    throws Exception {
        if (log.isDebugEnabled()) {
            log.debug("entering 'edit' method...");
        }

        DynaActionForm userForm = (DynaActionForm) form;
        String userId = request.getParameter("id");

        // null userId indicates an add
        if (userId != null) {
            User user = mgr.getUser(userId);

            if (user == null) {
                ActionMessages errors = new ActionMessages();
                errors.add(ActionMessages.GLOBAL_MESSAGE,
                        new ActionMessage("user.missing"));
                saveErrors(request, errors);

                return mapping.findForward("list");
            }

            userForm.set("user", user);
        }

        return mapping.findForward("edit");
    }

    public ActionForward list(ActionMapping mapping, ActionForm form,
                              HttpServletRequest request,
                              HttpServletResponse response)
    throws Exception {
        if (log.isDebugEnabled()) {
            log.debug("entering 'list' method...");
        }

        request.setAttribute("users", mgr.getUsers());

        return mapping.findForward("list");
    }

    public ActionForward save(ActionMapping mapping, ActionForm form,
                              HttpServletRequest request,
                              HttpServletResponse response)
```

```
throws Exception {
    if (log.isDebugEnabled()) {
        log.debug("entering 'save' method...");
    }

    DynaActionForm userForm = (DynaActionForm) form;
    mgr.saveUser((User)userForm.get("user"));

    ActionMessages messages = new ActionMessages();
    messages.add(ActionMessages.GLOBAL_MESSAGE,
                new ActionMessage("user.saved"));
    saveMessages(request, messages);

    return list(mapping, form, request, response);
    }
}
```

Now that you've modified this class for CRUD, perform the following steps:

8 Modify *struts-config.xml* to use the `ContextLoaderPlugin` and configure Spring to set the `UserManager`. To configure the `ContextLoaderPlugin`, simply add the code in Listing 2.34 to your *struts-config.xml* file:

Listing 2.34

```
<plug-in
    className="org.springframework.web.struts.ContextLoaderPlugin">
    <set-property property="contextConfigLocation"
        value="/WEB-INF/applicationContext.xml,
                /WEB-INF/action-servlet.xml"/>
</plug-in>
```

This plug-in will load the *action-servlet.xml* file by default. Since you want your test actions to know about your managers, you must configure the plug-in to load *applicationContext.xml* as well.

NOTE: Using the `ContextLoaderPlugin` is one of many ways to integrate a Struts web tier with a Spring middle tier. Other options are covered in *Chapter 12: Web Framework Integration*.

9 For each action that uses Spring, define the action mapping to `type="org.springframework.web.struts.DelegatingActionProxy"` and declare a matching Spring bean for the actual Struts action. Therefore, modify your action mapping to use this new class.

10 Modify your action mapping to work with `DispatchAction`.

In order for the **DispatchAction** to work, add **parameter="method"** to the mapping. This indicates (in a URL or hidden field) which method should be called. At the same time, add forwards for the **edit** and **list** forwards that are referenced in your CRUD-enabled **UserAction** class. See Listing 2.35.

Listing 2.35

```
<action path="/user"
    type="org.springframework.web.struts.DelegatingActionProxy"
    name="userForm" scope="request" parameter="method">
    <forward name="list" path="/userList.jsp"/>
    <forward name="edit" path="/userForm.jsp"/>
</action>
```

Be sure to create the *userList.jsp* and *userForm.jsp* files in the *web* directory of MyUsers. You don't need to put anything in them at this time.

> **11** As part of this plug-in, configure Spring to recognize the **/user** bean and to set the **UserManager** on it. Add the bean definition in Listing 2.36 to *web/WEB-INF/action-servlet.xml*.

Listing 2.36

```
<bean name="/user" class="org.appfuse.web.UserAction"
    singleton="false">
    <property name="userManager">
        <ref bean="userManager"/>
    </property>
</bean>
```

In this definition you're using **singleton="false"**. This creates new actions for every request, alleviating the need for thread-safe actions. Since neither your manager nor your DAO contains member variables, this should work without this attribute (defaults to **singleton="true"**).

> **12** Configure messages in the *messages.properties* **ResourceBundle**.

In the **UserAction** class are a few references to success and error messages that will appear after operations are performed. These references are keys to messages that should exist in the **ResourceBundle** (or *messages.properties* file) for this application. Specifically, they are:

- **user.saved**
- **user.missing**
- **user.deleted**

Add these keys to the *messages.properties* file in *web/WEB-INF/classes*, as in Listing 2.37:

Listing 2.37

```
user.saved=User has been saved successfully.
user.missing=No user found with this id.
user.deleted=User successfully deleted.
```

This file is loaded and made available to Struts via the **<message-resources>** element in *struts-config.xml* (see Listing 2.38):

Listing 2.38

```
<message-resources parameter="messages"/>
```

RUN UNIT TEST AND VERIFY CRUD WITH ACTION

Run the **ant test -Dtestcase=UserAction**. It should result in the output displayed in Figure 2.8:

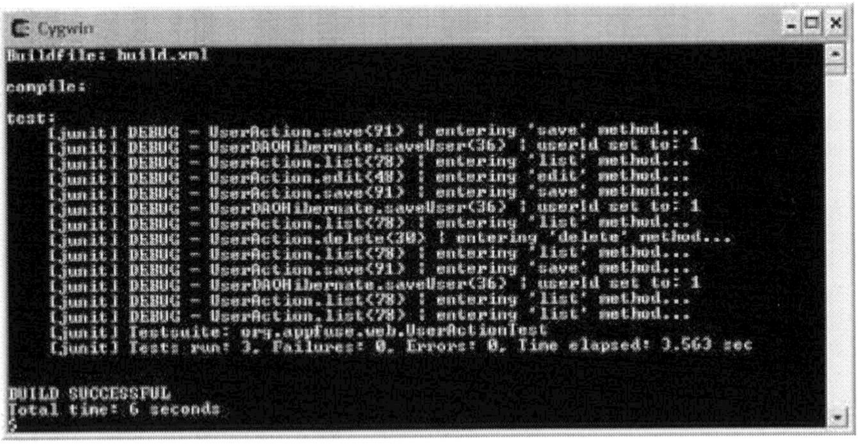

Figure 2.8: Results of the `ant test -Dtestcase=UserAction` command

COMPLETE JSPS TO ALLOW CRUD THROUGH A WEB BROWSER

Perform the following steps to complete JSPs and allow CRUD through a web browser.

1   Add code to your JSPs (*userForm.jsp* and *userList.jsp*) so that they can render
the results of your actions. If you haven't already done so, create a
userList.jsp file in the *web* directory. Now add some code so you can see the
all the users in the database. In the code in Listing 2.39, the first line
includes a *taglibs.jsp* file. This file contains all the JSP tag library declarations
for this application, mostly for Struts tags, JavaServer Pages Standard Tag
Library (JSTL), and SiteMesh (which is used to "pretty up" the JSPs).

Listing 2.39

```
<%@ include file="/taglibs.jsp"%>

<title>MyUsers ~ User List</title>

<button onclick="location.href='user.do?method=edit'">
    Add User</button>

<table class="list">
<thead>
<tr>
    <th>User Id</th>
    <th>First Name</th>
    <th>Last Name</th>
</tr>
</thead>
<tbody>
<c:forEach var="user" items="${users}" varStatus="status">
<c:choose>
    <c:when test="${status.count % 2 == 0}"><tr class="even">
        </c:when>
    <c:otherwise><tr class="odd"></c:otherwise>
</c:choose>
    <td><a href="user.do?method=edit&amp;id=${user.id}">${user.id}
        </a></td>
    <td>${user.firstName}</td>
    <td>${user.lastName}</td>
</tr>
</c:forEach>
</tbody>
</table>
```

You can see a row of headings (in the **<thead>**). JSTL's **<c:forEach>** tag iterates
through the results and displays the users.

2   Populate the database so you can see some actual users. You have a choice:
you can do it by hand, using **ant browse**, or you can add the target in
Listing 2.40 to your *build.xml* file:

Listing 2.40

```
<target name="populate">
    <echo message="Loading sample data..."/>
    <sql driver="org.hsqldb.jdbcDriver"
        url="jdbc:hsqldb:db/appfuse"
        userid="sa" password="">
        <classpath refid="classpath"/>

        INSERT INTO app_user (id, first_name, last_name)
            values (5, 'Julie', 'Raible');
        INSERT INTO app_user (id, first_name, last_name)
            values (6, 'Abbie', 'Raible');

    </sql>
</target>
```

VERIFY JSP'S FUNCTIONALITY THROUGH YOUR BROWSER

To verify JSP's functionality through your web browser, perform the following steps:

1   With this JSP and sample data in place, view this JSP in your browser. Run **ant deploy reload**, then go to localhost:8080/myusers/user.do? method=list. The window in Figure 2.9 displays:

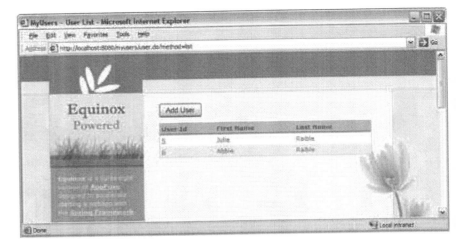

Figure 2.9: Results of `ant deploy reload` command

2   This example doesn't have an internationalized page title or column headings. Do this by adding some keys to the *messages.properties* file in *web /WEB-INF/classes*. See Listing 2.41.

Listing 2.41

```
user.id=User Id
user.firstName=First Name
user.lastName=Last Name
```

The modified, i18n-ized header should now resemble the code in Listing 2.42:

Listing 2.42

```
<thead>
<tr>
    <th><bean:message key="user.id"/></th>
    <th><bean:message key="user.firstName"/></th>
    <th><bean:message key="user.lastName"/></th>
</tr>
</thead>
```

Note that JSTL's `<fmt:message key="..."> ` tag could also be used. If you wanted to add sorting and paging to this table, use the display tag (`displaytag.sf.net`). Listing 2.43 is an example of using this JSP tag:

Listing 2.43

```
<display:table name="users" pagesize="10" styleClass="list"
    requestURI="user.do?method=list">
    <display:column property="id" paramId="id" paramProperty="id"
        href="user.do?method=edit" sort="true"/>
    <display:column property="firstName" sort="true"/>
    <display:column property="lastName" sort="true"/>
</display:table>
```

Please refer to the display tag's documentation for internationalization of column headings.

3   Now that you've created your list, create the form where you can add/edit data. If you haven't already done so, create a *userForm.jsp* file in the *web* directory of MyUsers. Listing 2.44 is the code to add to this JSP to allow data entry:

Listing 2.44

```
<%@ include file="/taglibs.jsp"%>

<title>MyUsers ~ User Details</title>

<p>Please fill in user's information below:</p>

<html:form action="/user" focus="user.firstName">
<input type="hidden" name="method" value="save"/>
<html:hidden property="user.id"/>
<table>
<tr>
    <th><bean:message key="user.firstName"/>:</th>
    <td><html:text property="user.firstName"/></td>
</tr>
<tr>
    <th><bean:message key="user.lastName"/>:</th>
    <td><html:text property="user.lastName"/></td>
</tr>
<tr>
    <td></td>
    <td>
        <html:submit styleClass="button">Save</html:submit>
    <c:if test="${not empty param.id}">
        <html:submit styleClass="button"
            onclick="this.form.method.value='delete'">
            Delete</html:submit>
    </c:if>
    </td>
</tr>
</table>
</html:form>
```

NOTE: If you're developing an application with internationalization (i18n), replace the informational message (at the top) and the button labels with `<bean:message>` or `<fmt:message>` tags. This is a good exercise for you. For informational messages, I recommend key names like *pageName.message* (such as `userForm.message`) and button names like *button.name* (such as `button.save`).

---

4   Run **ant deploy** and perform CRUD on a user from your browser.

ADD VALIDATION USING COMMONS VALIDATOR
. . . .

To enable validation in Struts, perform the following steps:

1   Add the **ValidatorPlugIn** to *struts-config.xml*.

2   Create a *validation.xml* file that specifies that **lastName** is a required field.

3   Change the **DynaActionForm** to a **DynaValidatorForm**.

4   Configure validation for the **save()** method, but not for others.

5   Add validation errors to *messages.properties*.

ADD THE VALIDATOR PLUG-IN TO STRUTS-CONFIG.XML

Configure the validator plug-in by adding the XML fragment in Listing 2.45 to your *struts-config.xml* file (right after the Spring plug-in):

Listing 2.45

```
<plug-in className="org.apache.struts.validator.ValidatorPlugIn">
    <set-property
        property="pathnames" value="/WEB-INF/validator-rules.xml,
                                    /WEB-INF/validation.xml"/>
</plug-in>
```

From this you can see that the validator is going to look for two files in the *WEB-INF* directory: *validator-rules.xml* and *validation.xml*. The first file, *validator-rules.xml*, is a standard file that's distributed as part of Struts. It defines all the available validators, as well as their client-side JavaScript functions. The second file, *validation.xml*, contains the validation rules for each form.

EDIT VALIDATION.XML TO REQUIRE LASTNAME

The *validation.xml* file has a number of standard elements to match its Document Type Definition (DTD), but you only need the **<form>** and **<field>** elements you see below. Please refer to the validator's documentation for more information. Add the **<formset>** (see Listing 2.46) between the **<form-validation>** tags in *web /WEB-INF/validation.xml*:

Listing 2.46

```
<formset>
    <form name="userForm">
        <field property="user.lastName" depends="required">
            <arg0 key="user.lastName"/>
        </field>
    </form>
</formset>
```

CHANGE DYNAACTIONFORM TO DYNAVALIDATORFORM

Now change the **DynaActionForm** to a **DynaValidatorForm** in *struts-config.xml*.
See Listing 2.47.

Listing 2.47

```
<form-bean name="userForm"
    type="org.apache.struts.validator.DynaValidatorForm">
...
```

CONFIGURE VALIDATION FOR THE SAVE() METHOD, BUT NOT FOR OTHERS

One unfortunate side effect of using Struts' **DispatchAction** is that validation is
turned on at the mapping level. In order to turn validation off for the list and edit
screen, you could create a separate mapping with **validate="false"**. For
example, AppFuse's **UserAction** has two mappings: */editUser* and */saveUser*.
However, there's an easier way that requires less XML and only slightly more Java.

1. In the mapping for **/user**, add **validate="false"**.

2. In **UserAction.java**, modify the **save()** method to call
    form.**validate()** and return to the edit screen if any errors are found.
    See Listing 2.48.

Listing 2.48

```
if (log.isDebugEnabled()) {
    log.debug("entering 'save' method...");
}

// run validation rules on this form
ActionMessages errors = form.validate(mapping, request);
if (!errors.isEmpty()) {
    saveErrors(request, errors);
    return mapping.findForward("edit");
}

DynaActionForm userForm = (DynaActionForm) form;
```

When working with **DispatchAction**, this is cleaner than having two mappings
with one measly attribute changed. However, the *two mappings* approach has some
advantages:

- It allows you to specify an **input** attribute that indicates where to go when
  validation fails.

- You can declare a **roles** attribute on your mapping to specify who can access that mapping. For instance, anyone can see the "edit" screen, but only administrators can save it.

3 Run **ant deploy reload** and try to add a new user without a last name. You will see a validation error indicating that last name is a required field, as in the example in Figure 2.10:

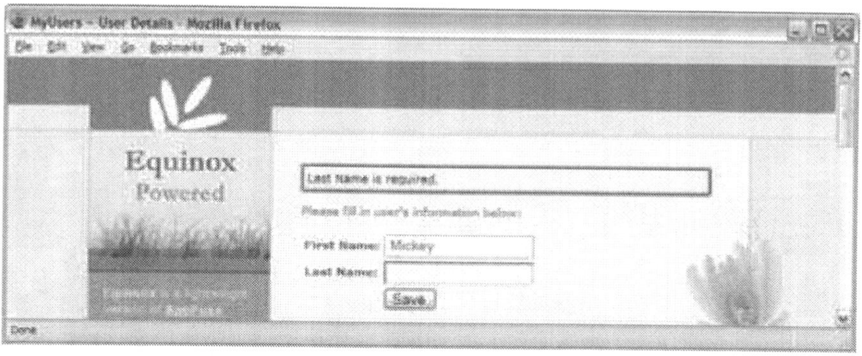

Figure 2.10: Result of the **ant deploy reload** command

Another nice feature of the Struts validator is client-side validation.

4 To enable this quickly, add an **onsubmit** attribute to the **<form>** tag (in *web/ userForm.jsp*), and a **<html:javascript>** tag at the bottom of the form. See Listing 2.49.

Listing 2.49

```
<html:form action="/user" focus="user.firstName"
    onsubmit="return validateUserForm(this)">
. . .
</html:form>

<html:javascript formName="userForm"/>
```

Now if you run **ant deploy** and try to save a user with a blank last name, you will get a Java-Script alert stating that "Last Name is required." The one issue with the short form of the **<html:javascript>** tag is that it puts all of the validator's Java-Script functions into your page. There is a better way: Include the JavaScript from an outside page (which is itself generated). How to do this will be covered in *Chapter 5: Advanced Spring MVC.*

Congratulations! You've just developed a web app that talks to a database, implements validation, and even displays success and error messages. In *Chapter 4: Spring's*

MVC Framework, you will convert this application to use Spring's MVC framework. In *Chapter 5: Advanced Spring MVC*, you will add exception handling, file uploading, and emailing features. *Chapter 6: View Options* will explore alternatives to JSP, and you'll add alternative DAO implementations using iBATIS, JDO and Spring's JDBC in *Chapter 8: Persistence Strategies: Hibernate, iBATIS, JDBC, JDO, and OJB.*

SUMMARY

Spring is a great framework for reducing the amount of code you have to write. If you look at the number of steps in this tutorial, most of them involved setting up or writing code for Struts. Spring made the DAO and manager implementations easy. It also reduced most Hibernate calls to one line and allowed you to remove any Exception handling that can sometimes be tedious. In fact, most of the time I spent writing this chapter (and the MyUsers app) involved configuring Struts.

I have two reasons for writing this chapter with Struts as the MVC framework. The first is because I think that's the framework most folks are familiar with, and it's easier to explain a Struts-to-Spring migration than it is to explain a JSP/servlet-to-Spring migration. Second, I wanted to show you how writing your MVC layer with Struts can be a bit cumbersome. In *Chapter 4: Spring's MVC Framework*, you'll refactor the web layer to use Spring's MVC framework. I think you'll find it a bit refreshing to see how much easier and more intuitive it is.

THE BEANFACTORY AND HOW IT WORKS

An introduction to the bean definitions, the BeanFactory, and ApplicationContext

The **BeanFactory** *represents the heart of Spring, so it's important to know how it works. This chapter covers how bean definitions are written and covers their properties, dependencies, and autowiring. You will also read about the logic behind making singleton beans (versus prototypes) and then delve into Inversion of Control (IoC), how it works, and the simplicity it brings. This chapter dissects the lifecycle of a bean in the* **BeanFactory** *so that you better understand how it works. In addition, you will inspect the applicationContext.xml file for the MyUsers application you created in Chapter 2: Spring Quick-Start Tutorial.*

Spring is an excellent tool for integrating IoC into your application because it uses a **BeanFactory** *to manage and configure beans. In most cases, you won't interact with the* **BeanFactory***; instead, you will use the* **ApplicationContext***, which adds more enterprise-level J2EE functionality, such as internationalization (i18n), custom converters (for converting string types into object types), and event publication/notification.*

This chapter covers how the **BeanFactory** *works, how IoC works as it relates to the* **BeanFactory***, how to configure beans for the* **BeanFactory***, and how to use the* **ApplicationContext***.*

ABOUT THE BEANFACTORY

The **BeanFactory** is an internal interface that configures and manages virtually any Java class. The **XMLBeanFactory** reads *bean definitions* from an XML file, while the **ListableBeanFactory** reads definitions from properties files. When the **BeanFactory** is created, Spring validates each bean's configuration. However, the properties of each bean are not set until the bean is created. Singleton beans are instantiated by the **BeanFactory** at startup time, while other beans are created on demand. According to the **BeanFactory**'s javadocs, "There are no constraints on how the definitions could be stored: LDAP, RDBMS, XML, properties file, etc." At the time of this writing, only XML and properties file implementations exist. Since the **XMLBeanFactory** is the most commonly used method to configure J2EE applications, this chapter uses XML for all examples.

NOTE: For reading bean definitions from properties files, you can use **PropertiesBeanDefinitionReader**.

The **BeanFactory** is a workhorse that initializes beans and calls their lifecycle methods. It should be noted that most lifecycle methods only apply to singleton beans. Spring cannot manage prototype (non-singleton) lifecycles. This is because, after they're created, prototypes are handed off to the client and the container loses track of it. For prototypes, Spring is really just a replacement for the **new** operator.

A BEAN'S LIFECYCLE IN THE BEANFACTORY

Figure 3.1 illustrates a bean's *lifecycle*. An outside force controls the bean, which is the IoC container. The IoC container defines the rules by which the bean operates. The rules are *bean definitions*. The bean is *pre-initialized* through its dependencies. The bean then enters the *ready* state where the beans are ready to go to work for the application. Finally, the IoC container *destroys* the bean.

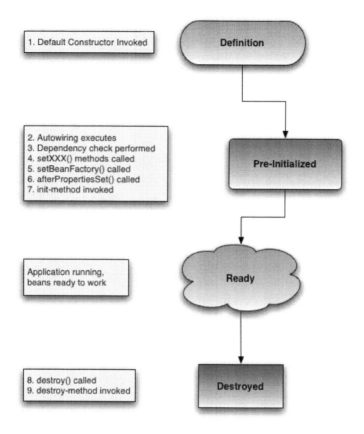

Figure 3.1: A bean's lifecycle

INVERSION OF CONTROL (IOC)

IoC is a powerful concept in application development. One form of IoC is *dependency injection*, as described by Martin Fowler. Dependency injection uses the Hollywood principle: "Don't call me, I'll call you." In other words, your classes don't look up or instantiate the classes they depend on. The *control is inverted* and some form of container sets the dependencies. Using IoC often leads to much cleaner code and provides an excellent way to de-couple dependent classes. Dependency injection exists in three forms:

- Setter-based: Classes are typically JavaBeans, with a no-arg constructor, and with *setters* for the IoC container to use when wiring dependencies. This is the variant recommended by Spring. While Spring supports constructor-based injection, a large number of constructor arguments can be difficult to manage.

- Constructor-based: Classes contain constructors with a number of arguments. The IoC container discovers and invokes the constructor based on the number of arguments and their object types. This approach guarantees that a bean is not created in an invalid state.

- Getter-based (or method injection): This is similar to setter-based, except you add a getter to your class. The IoC container overrides this method when it runs inside, but you can easily use the getter you specify when testing. This approach has only recently been discussed; more information is available on TheServerSide.

Listing 3.1 is an example of a class before it's been made IoC-ready. It is a Struts action called **ListUsers** that depends on a **UserDAO**, which, in turn, requires a connection as part of its constructor.

Listing 3.1

```
public class ListUsers extends Action {

    public ActionForward execute(ActionMapping mapping,
                                 ActionForm form,
                                 HttpServletRequest request,
                                 HttpServletResponse response)
    throws Exception {
        // get a connection from the database
        Connection conn = DatabaseUtils.getConnection();
        UserDAO dao = DAOFactory.createUserDAO("hibernate", conn);

        List users = dao.getUsers();

        DatabaseUtils.closeConnection(conn);
        return mapping.findForward("success");
    }
}
```

This design is ugly because the class's dependency is in the code and can't be substituted with an alternative implementation. Clean it up by implementing an IoC-ready **ListUsers** class, as in Listing 3.2.

Listing 3.2

```
public class ListUsers extends Action {
    private UserDAO dao;
    public void setUserDAO(UserDAO userDAO) {
        this.dao = userDAO;
    }

    public ActionForward execute(ActionMapping mapping,
```

```
                                        ActionForm form,
                                        HttpServletRequest request,
                                        HttpServletResponse response)
        throws Exception {
            List users = dao.getUsers();

            return mapping.findForward("success");
        }
    }
```

The above class doesn't contain any lookup code. This makes it clean and workable for testing. For instance, in your test you can use a **Mock** object for the DAO to eliminate any dependencies on your data tier. A good IoC container allows you to wire a connection (or **DataSource**) to the **UserDAO**. With Spring, you can choose to wire connections in the data layer, or use a filter to open a connection per request.

THE BEAN DEFINITION EXPOSED

A bean definition, or **<bean>**, is really quite simple, as illustrated by the example in Listing 3.3:

Listing 3.3

```
<bean id="example" class="org.appfuse.util.Converter"/>
```

At the very least, a bean has an **id** (or *name*) attribute and a **class** attribute. You don't have to set any properties on the bean if you don't want to, but that's similar to invoking **new** on an object. Most bean definitions contain some kind of property setting, unless they're simply used to bind interfaces to implementations (emulating the factory pattern).

The first required bean attribute is **id**. Like any good XML document, the bean definition's allowed attributes and child elements are dictated by a DTD. The DTD for Spring is appropriately named *spring-beans.dtd*. The **id** attribute of a bean is a real XML ID, which means it must be unique throughout the XML document. You can only define one **id** per bean. To add aliases to a bean, or to use illegal XML characters in a bean's **id**, specify the **name** attribute. This attribute allows one or more bean ids, each separated by a comma or semicolon. Using an **id** attribute is the preferred and recommended way to configure beans.

The second required bean attribute is **class**. While Spring can manage practically any Java class, the most common pattern is a default (empty) constructor with setters for dependent properties. The value specified in this attribute must be a fully-qualified class name (package name + class name). Otherwise, you can use the **parent** attribute. This can be useful if you want to duplicate a class and override its properties.

Table 3.1 lists all the attributes that you can define in a `<bean>` element.

Table 3.1: `<bean>` attributes

Attribute	Description	Frequency of Use
`id`	This XML ID element enables reference checking. To use a name that's illegal as an XML ID (such as 1 or 2), use the optional **name** attribute. If you specify neither an id nor a name, Spring assigns the class name as the `id`.	High
`name`	Use this attribute to create one or more aliases illegal as an `id`. Multiple aliases can be comma- or space-delimited. Use this attribute if you use the `ContextLoaderPlugin` with Struts and Spring manages your actions.	Medium
`class`	The `class` and `parent` attributes are interchangeable. A bean definition must specify the fully qualified name of the class (package name + class name) or the name of the `parent` bean. **Note:** A `child` bean definition that references a `parent` can override property values of the `singleton` attribute. It inherits all of the parent's other attributes, such as `lazy-init` and `autowire`.	High
`parent`		Low
`singleton`	This attribute determines whether the bean is a `singleton` (one shared instance returned by all calls to `getBean(id)`), or a `prototype` (independent instance resulting from each call to `getBean(id)`). The default value is `true`.	Low
`abstract`	If `true`, the `BeanFactory` will not try to instantiate the bean. Use this attribute when defining parent beans for concrete `child` bean definitions. The default value is `false`.	Low
`lazy-init`	If `true`, the bean will be lazily initialized. If `false`, it will be instantiated on startup by bean factories that perform eager initialization of singletons.	Low

Table 3.1: `<bean>` attributes (continued)

Attribute	Description	Frequency of Use
`autowire`	This attribute controls the *autowiring* of bean properties. If used, Spring automatically figures out the dependencies using one of the following modes: **no:** (Default) You must define bean references in the XML file using the `<ref>` element. Recommended to make documentation more explicit. **byName:** Autowires by property name. If a DAO exposes a `dataSource` property, Spring will try to set this to the value of the `"dataSource"` bean in the current factory. **byType:** Autowires if exactly one bean of the property type is in the factory. **constructor:** Same as `byType` for constructor arguments.	Low
	autodetect: Chooses the `constructor` or `byType` through inspection of the bean class. **Note:** While this attribute reduces the size of your XML file, it reduces the readability and self-documentation supplied by declaring properties. For larger applications, autowiring is discouraged because it removes the transparency and structure from collaborating classes.	
`dependency-check`	This attribute checks to see whether all of a bean's dependencies (expressed in its properties) are satisfied. **None:** No dependency checking (the default). Properties with no value specified are not set. **simple:** Checks type dependencies, including primitives and strings. **object:** Checks other beans in the factory. **all:** Includes both of the above types.	Low

Table 3.1: `<bean>` attributes (continued)

Attribute	Description	Frequency of Use
`depends-on`	This attribute names the beans that this bean depends on for initialization. The `BeanFactory` will guarantee that these beans are initialized first.	Low
`init-method`	This is a **no-argument** method to invoke after setting a bean's properties.	Low
`destroy-method`	This is a **no-argument** method to invoke on factory shutdown. **Note:** This method is invoked only on **singleton** beans!	Low

CONFIGURING PROPERTIES AND DEPENDENCIES

The **BeanFactory** could be compared to EJB's lifecycle, except Spring is much simpler; you can wire up pretty much *any* class, and you don't need to extend or implement interfaces. With bare-bones EJBs, you're required to implement many lifecycle classes that you may never even use. With Spring-managed beans, you can manage the lifecycle using **init-method** and **destroy-method** attributes, and you only need to implement interfaces if you want to physically talk to the **BeanFactory** during the initialization process.

A bean *property* is a member variable of a class. For example, your bean might have a **maxSize** property and a method to set it, as in Listing 3.4:

Listing 3.4

```
private int maxSize;

public void setMaxSize(int maxSize) {
     this.maxSize = maxSize;
}
```

You can set the value of **maxSize** by using the XML fragment in Listing 3.5 on your bean's definition:

Listing 3.5

```
<property name="maxSize"><value>1000</value></property>
```

TIP: In Spring 1.2, you can use the shorter **value** attribute in Listing 3.6:

Listing 3.6

```
<property name="maxSize" value="1000"/
```

A bean *dependency* is a property the bean *depends on* in order to operate. Dependencies refer to other classes, rather than simple values. For instance, the **dataSource** property in Listing 3.7 refers to another bean. The **dataSource** is a *dependency* of the **sessionFactory** bean, whereas the **mappingResources** is just a property with values.

Listing 3.7

```
<bean id="sessionFactory" class="...">
    <property name="dataSource">
        <ref local="dataSource"/>
    </property>
    <property name="mappingResources">
        <list>
            <value>org/appfuse/model/User.hbm.xml</value>
        </list>
    </property>
    ...
</bean>
```

In this example, the reference to the **dataSource** bean is set using a **<ref>** tag.

TIP: Using Spring 1.2, you can express a **<ref>** dependency with the **ref** attribute, as in Listing 3.8.

Listing 3.8

```
<property name="dataSource" ref="dataSource"/>
```

SPECIFYING DEPENDENCIES WITH <REF>

The **<ref>** tag that points to the dataSource uses a **local** attribute to point to the **dataSource** bean. In addition to local, other options exist for pointing to dependent beans. The following list shows the available attributes for the **<ref>** element:

- Bean: Finds the dependent bean in either the same XML file or another XML file that has been loaded into the **ApplicationContext**. The **<ref>** attribute defaults to this scope.

- Local: Finds the dependent bean in the current XML file. This attribute is an XML **IDREF**, so it must exist or validation will fail.

- External: Finds the bean in another XML file and does not search the current XML file.

From this list, **<ref bean="..."/>** and **<ref local="..."/>** are most commonly used. **Bean** is the most flexible option, allowing you to move beans between files, but **local** has the convenience of built-in XML validation.

In addition to specifying values from string, you can also read values from a **.properties** file using the **PropertyPlaceHolderConfigurer** class. Listing 3.9 is an example using a **database.properties** file in the classpath.

Listing 3.9

```
<bean id="propertyConfigurer"
    class="org.springframework.beans.factory.config
        .PropertyPlaceholderConfigurer">
    <property name="location">
        <value>classpath:database.properties</value>
    </property>
</bean>

<bean id="dataSource"
    class="org.springframework.jdbc.datasource
        .DriverManagerDataSource">
    <property name="driverClassName">
        <value>${db.driverName}</value>
    </property>
    <property name="url"><value>${db.url}</value></property>
    <property name="username"><value>${db.username}
        </value></property>
    <property name="password"><value>${db.password}
        </value></property>
</bean>
```

You can use a special **<null/>** element to set a property to Java's null value. An empty value, **<value></value>**, will result in setting an empty string (**""**).

PRE-INITIALIZING YOUR BEANS

To pre-initialize your beans is to prepare them to work for your application. You do this by configuring their properties and dependencies. The following sections cover the most critical steps of this process.

AUTOWIRING

Even though autowiring is not recommended for larger applications as noted below, you may choose to use it for your smaller ones. If you choose to autowire a bean, I recommend that you use **autowire="byName"** because it's good practice to keep the names of your setters and bean ids in synch.

For example, you could define the **UserDAO** from *Chapter 2: Spring Quick-Start Tutorial* with autowiring, and then you wouldn't need to specify the **sessionFactory** property. See Listing 3.10.

Listing 3.10

```
<bean id="userDAO" autowire="byName"
    class="org.appfuse.dao.hibernate.UserDAOHibernate"/>
```

If you use **autowire="byType"**, Spring will look for a bean that is a Hibernate **SessionFactory**. The problem with this approach is that you may have multiple session factories talking to two databases. With **byName**, you can give those beans different names and label your setters appropriately. The **constructor** and **auto-detect** options will suffer from the same affliction, since they employ **byType** under the covers.

> **NOTE:** Autowiring causes you to lose the self-documenting features of the XML file, but it allows you to develop faster. Without autowiring, you'll know what a bean's dependencies are because they're specified in XML. With autowiring, you might have to look at a class's Javadocs or source to figure it out. Also, though rare, the **BeanFactory** could autowire some dependencies that you didn't want set.

DEPENDENCY CHECKS

Defining a **dependency-check** attribute in your bean's definition is useful when you want to ensure that all properties are properly set on a bean. A properly structured bean has default values. Some properties may not be needed in certain scenarios, limiting this feature's usefulness. The default is **none**, meaning dependency checking is not activated, but you can enable this on a per bean basis. A **simple** verifies primitive types and set collections. An **object** value checks a bean's dependencies (also called collaborators). The **all** value includes both **simple** and **object**.

SETXXX()

The **setXXX()** methods are simply the setters that inject dependencies into a class. These properties are configured in the context file and can be primitives (that is, int or boolean), object types (Long, Integer), null values or references to other objects.

To demonstrate how each of these types is set, the Smorgasbord class in Listing 3.11 has all the previously mentioned property types:

Listing 3.11

```java
package org.appfuse.model;

// organize imports with your IDE

public class Smorgasbord extends BaseObject {
    private Log log = LogFactory.getLog(Smorgasbord.class);
    private int daysToJavaOne;
    private boolean attendingJavaOne;
    private Integer streetsInDenver;
    private Long peopleInDenver;
    private DataSource dataSource;

    public void setDaysToJavaOne(int daysToJavaOne) {
        this.daysToJavaOne = daysToJavaOne;
    }

    public void setAttendingJavaOne(boolean attendingJavaOne) {
        this.attendingJavaOne = attendingJavaOne;
    }

    public void setStreetsInDenver(Integer streetsInDenver) {
        this.streetsInDenver = streetsInDenver;
    }

    public void setPeopleInDenver(Long peopleInDenver) {
        this.peopleInDenver = peopleInDenver;
    }

    public void setDataSource(DataSource dataSource) {
        this.dataSource = dataSource;
    }

    public String toString() {
        log.debug(super.toString());
        return super.toString();
    }
}
```

Rather than writing a unit test for this class example, use the dependency-check attribute in the bean's definition, as well as the init-method attribute to call its toString() method. See Listing 3.12.

NOTE: For your professional applications, I strongly recommend always writing a unit test.

Listing 3.12

```
<bean id="smorgasbord" class="org.appfuse.model.Smorgasbord"
    dependency-check="all" init-method="toString">
    <property name="daysToJavaOne"><value>14</value></property>
    <property name="attendingJavaOne"><value>true</value></property>
    <property name="streetsInDenver"><value>334</value></property>
    <property name="peopleInDenver"><value>3000000</value></property>
    <property name="dataSource"><ref local="dataSource"/></property>
</bean>
```

You can turn on informational logging for the `org.springframework.beans` package by adding the code in Listing 3.13 to *web/WEB-INF/classes/log4j.xml*:

Listing 3.13

```
<logger name="org.springframework.beans">
    <level value="INFO"/>
</logger>
```

Now if you run any tests or deploy and run MyUsers, you should see the output shown in Figure 3.2 in your console. This example uses **ant test -Dtestcase= UserDAO**.

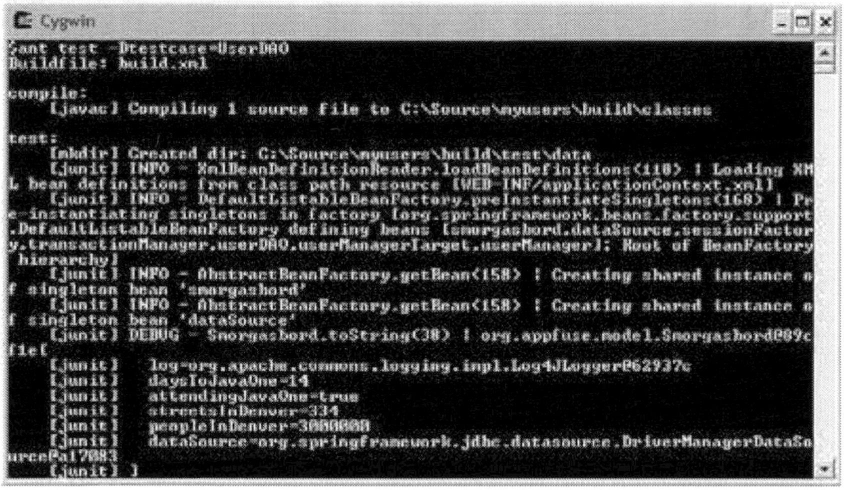

Figure 3.2: Output from `ant test -Dtestcase=UserDAO`

SETBEANFACTORY()

After the initialization methods are called, the **BeanFactory** checks for classes implementing the **BeanFactoryAware** and **BeanNameAware** interfaces. These interfaces provide a means for beans to find out more information about where they came from and who they are. The **BeanFactoryAware** interface defines one method (see Listing 3.14):

Listing 3.14

```
public void setBeanFactory(BeanFactory beanFactory)
throws BeansException;
```

If you implement this interface, it references to the **BeanFactory**, which you can use to look up other beans. It basically documents a bean's origins.

In order for a bean to discover its **id**, use the **BeanNameAware** interface. This interface has a single method (see Listing 3.15):

Listing 3.15

```
public void setBeanName(java.lang.String name);
```

In most cases, you won't need access to the **BeanFactory** because you can talk to other beans by wiring them as dependencies (using **<ref bean="..."/>**). Accessing the bean's name may be helpful if you want to configure the same class as two different beans with different dependency implementations. Using this, you can perform conditional logic based on which **name** is configured.

After calling methods from the **BeanFactoryAware** and **BeanNameAware** interfaces, beans enter into a *ready* state. This is when your application has completed starting up (in Tomcat, for example).

AFTERPROPERTIESSET()

You can configure your beans for post-initialization processing using one of two approaches: 1) use the **init-method** attribute as illustrated in the previous example or 2) implement **InitializingBean** and its **afterPropertiesSet()** method. (The diagram shows both methods, but only one is required.) Clearly, using **init-method** is a much cleaner and simpler way to do this. However, implementing **InitializingBean** can be helpful for testing when you're not using Spring to manage your beans. For instance, you can call this method in your tests and verify that your mock objects have been set correctly. It's also useful for guaranteeing that your bean will be configured correctly; you're not depending on someone to write the bean's definition correctly.

The earlier example injected property values into the **Smorgasbord** class. It set primitive values, object values, and even a reference (**dataSource**) to another bean in the factory. Not only does Spring's DTD support simple **<value>** elements in properties, it also supports setting **Properties**, **Lists** and **Maps**. Listing 3.16 is an example (from Spring's documentation) of using these more complex properties:

Listing 3.16

```xml
<!-- results in a setPeople(java.util.Properties) call -->
<property name="people">
    <props>
        <prop key="HarryPotter">The magic property</prop>
        <prop key="JerrySeinfeld">The funny property</prop>
    </props>
</property>
<!-- results in a setSomeList(java.util.List) call -->
<property name="someList">
    <list>
        <value>a list element followed by a reference</value>
        <ref bean="dataSource"/>
    </list>
</property>
<!-- results in a setSomeMap(java.util.Map) call -->
<property name="someMap">
    <map>
        <entry key="aString">
            <value>just some string</value>
        </entry>
        <entry key="aBean">
            <ref bean="dataSource"/>
        </entry>
    </map>
</property>
```

NOTE: In Spring 1.2, the **<entry>** element can use a **key-ref** attribute to refer to a dependent bean (see Listing 3.17):

Listing 3.17

```xml
<entry key="ds" key-ref="dataSource"/>
```

INIT-METHOD

The **init-method** attribute of a bean definition calls a method after all the properties of a bean have been set. This has the same functionality as implementing the **InitializingBean** interface, except that it doesn't tie your bean to Spring.

READY STATE

After your beans have been pre-initialized and any **setup** methods have been called, they enter into a ready state. The ready state means that your application can get these beans and use them as needed. The entire lifecyle to enter the ready state is very quick. It increases based on the number of beans in your app. However, it only occurs at startup.

DESTROYING BEANS

When you shut down (or reload) your application, beans that are singletons once again get lifecycle methods called on them. First, beans that implement the **DisposableBean** interface will have their **destroy()** methods called. Next, beans with a **destroy-method** specified in their bean definitions will have that method invoked.

THE APPLICATIONCONTEXT: TALKING TO YOUR BEANS

Understanding the **BeanFactory** is important when developing with Spring, but you probably won't need to interface with it in your application. In most cases, you'll use the **ApplicationContext**, which adds more enterprise-level, J2EE functionality, such as internationalization (i18n), custom converters (for converting string types into object types) and event publication/notification. An **ApplicationContext** is instantiated with bean definition files and beans can be easily retrieved using **context.getBean("beanId")**. Instantiating the **ApplicationContext** and loading the bean definition XML files is the hardest part, so let's look at the different ways to do this.

GET THAT CONTEXT!

Spring gives you many options for loading its bean definitions. In the current release (1.0.2), bean definitions must be loaded from files. You could also implement your own **ApplicationContext** and add support for loading from other resources (such as a database). While many *contexts* are available for loading beans, you'll only need the few that are listed below. The others are internal classes that are used by the framework itself.

- **ClassPathXmlApplicationContext**: Loads context files from the classpath (that is, *WEB-INF/classes* or *WEB-INF/lib* for web applications).

It initializes using a **new ClassPathXmlApplicationContext(path)**, where **path** is the path to the file or files. The **path** argument can also be a string array of paths and supports Ant-style pattern matching for grabbing multiple files with similar names (see the **PathMatcher** javadoc for more details). This class is useful for loading the context in unit tests. (See Listing 3.18.)

Listing 3.18

```
String[] paths = {"/WEB-INF/applicationContext*.xml"};
ApplicationContext ctx = new ClassPathXmlApplicationContext(paths);
```

* **FileSystemXmlApplicationContext**: Loads context files from the file system, which is nice for testing. It initializes using a **new FileSystem-XmlApplicationContext (path)** where **path** is a relative or absolute path to the file. The **path** argument can also be a string array of paths and supports Ant-style pattern matching for grabbing multiple files with similar names. This class typically ties you to a single platform. (See Listing 3.19.)

Listing 3.19

```
String[] paths =
    {"c:/source/myusers/web/WEB-INF/applicationContext*.xml"};
ApplicationContext ctx = new FileSystemXmlApplicationContext(paths);
```

* **StaticApplicationContext**: Allows programmatic registration of beans, rather than loading bean definitions from files. Very useful for testing. (See Listing 3.20.)

Listing 3.20

```
StaticApplicationContext ctx = new StaticApplicationContext();
Map properties = new HashMap();
properties.put("basename", "messages");
ctx.registerSingleton("messageSource",
                      ResourceBundleMessageSource.class,
                      new MutablePropertyValues(properties));
ctx.refresh();
```

* **XmlWebApplicationContext**: Loads context files internally by the **ContextLoaderListener**, but can be used outside it. For instance, if you are running a container that doesn't load listeners in the order specified in *web.xml*, you might need to use this class in another listener. (See Listing 3.21.)

Listing 3.21

```
XmlWebApplicationContext ctx = new XmlWebApplicationContext();
context.setServletContext(ctx);
context.refresh();
```

TIP: If your container doesn't load listeners in the specified order, you can write your own listener (see Listing 3.22) that extends **ContextLoaderListener**. This way, you can control the initialization of the **ApplicationContext** and use it after initializing it.

Listing 3.22

```
public class StartupListener extends ContextLoaderListener
    implements ServletContextListener {

    public void contextInitialized(ServletContextEvent event) {

        // call Spring's context ContextLoaderListener to initialize
        // all the context files specified in web.xml
        super.contextInitialized(event);
// get beans from WebApplicationContext in servletContext
    }
}
```

Most Spring applications are configured to have more than one context file. Loading multiple files is easy: specify each by name, or use the wildcard syntax. Another option is to use an **<import>** element in an existing context file. This element must appear between the **<beans>** and first **<bean>** definition. All paths in the **resource** attribute are assumed to be relative to the current file. See Listing 3.23.

Listing 3.23

```
<beans>
    <import resource="applicationContext-hibernate.xml"/>
    <import resource="conf/applicationContext-security.xml"/>

    <bean id="firstBean" class="..."/>
```

Once you've obtained a reference to a context, you can get references to beans using **ctx.getBean("beanId")**. Of the above contexts, **ClassPathXmlApplicationContext** is the most flexible. It doesn't care where the files are, as long as they're in the classpath. This allows you to move files around and simply change the classpath.

TIPS FOR UNIT TESTING AND LOADING CONTEXTS

Writing unit tests with Spring is generally pretty easy. Spring-ready beans can be instantiated and tested sans-container with mocks put into the setters. Testing is also easy because of Spring's interface-based design, which allows you to choose how to test implementing classes. Testing with the least amount of setup can be achieved by using a **ClassPathXmlApplicationContext**, getting a reference to your bean, and calling methods on it. This method allows you to write your tests to interfaces, not to implementation classes. If you decide to swap out implementations (by changing the **class** attribute of your bean), you don't have to change anything in your test.

However, one issue with using this is the **ApplicationContext** can take a few seconds to initialize. As your application grows, the time-to-initialize will increase. Furthermore, if you load the context in a **setUp()** method, the context will be instantiated each time before a **testXXX()** method is called. Luckily, a couple of simple solutions exist to load the context only once per **TestCase**. The first is to use JUnit's **TestSetup** class in a suite, or you can put the context-loading code in a static block of your test. See Listing 3.24.

Listing 3.24

```
protected static ApplicationContext ctx = null;

static {
    ctx = new ClassPathXmlApplicationContext("/appContext.xml");
}
```

The second solution is to directly test the implementation classes, without ever using Spring's **BeanFactory** or **ApplicationContext**. This generally involves creating an instance with the **new** operator, setting its dependencies manually, and invoking methods to test. Using this technique allows you to replace dependent classes with mock objects, which can speed up your tests and isolate them from their environment dependency.

More information on unit testing will be given in *Chapter 9: Testing Spring Applications.*

INTERNATIONALIZATION AND MESSAGESOURCE

Internationalization, or i18n, is an important concept in application development, particularly in web applications. It's likely that your users will originate from other countries and will speak different languages. They'll probably have their browsers set to show sites in their native language first.

The **ApplicationContext** interface extends the **MessageSource** interface, which gives it messaging (i18n) functionality. In conjunction with the **Hierarchichal-MessageSource**, capable of hierarchical message resolving, these are the basic interfaces Spring provides to resolve messages. When loading an **Application-Context**, it searches for a bean with the name **messageSource** defined in its context. If no such bean is found in the current or parent contexts, a **StaticMessageSource** will be created so that **getMessage()** calls don't fail.

Two **MessageSource** implementations exist in the current Spring code base. They are **ResourceBundleMessageSource** (which reads from a *.properties* file) and **StaticMessageSource** (hardly used, but allows for adding messages programmatically). Listing 3.25 is an example **messageSource** bean definition that will load *messages.properties* from the classpath:

Listing 3.25

```
<bean id="messageSource"
    class="org.springframework.context.support
       .ResourceBundleMessageSource">
    <property name="basename"><value>messages</value></property>
</bean>
```

If you want to specify multiple **ResourceBundles**, you can set the **basenames** property instead of the single-value **basename** property, as in Listing 3.26.

Listing 3.26

```
<property name="basenames">
    <list>
        <value>messages</value>
        <value>errors</value>
    </list>
</property>
```

The next chapter defines a **messageSource** bean and interacts with it to get error and success messages.

EVENT PUBLISHING AND SUBSCRIBING

The **ApplicationContext** supports event handling via the **ApplicationEvent** class and **ApplicationListener** interface. If you'd like to use this functionality, you can implement **ApplicationListener** in a bean and when an **Application-Event** is published to the context, your bean will be notified.

The following list describes the three standard Spring events.

- **ContextRefreshedEvent**: Event published when the
  ApplicationContext is initialized or refreshed. Initialized here means
  that all beans are loaded, singletons are pre-instantiated and the
  ApplicationContext is ready for use.

- **ContextClosedEvent**: Event published when the
  ApplicationContext is closed, using the **close()** method on the
  ApplicationContext. "Closed" here means that singletons are
  destroyed.

- **RequestHandledEvent**: A web-specific event telling all beans that a
  HTTP request has been serviced (this will be published after the request
  has been finished). Note that this event is only applicable for web
  applications using Spring's **DispatcherServlet**.

You can also implement custom events by calling the **publishEvent()** method on
the **ApplicationContext**. See Spring's Reference documentation for an example.

A CLOSER LOOK AT MYUSERS' *APPLICATIONCONTEXT.XML*

In the MyUsers application from *Chapter 2: Spring Quick-Start Tutorial*, you loaded
your bean definitions from *web/WEB-INF/applicationContext.xml*. In this file, several
beans are defined. Of the seven beans defined in this file, only three of them
(**userDAO**, **userManagerTarget**, and **/user**) refer to classes that you created. This
really shows the power of Spring: four of the classes you used (**dataSource**,
sessionFactory, **transactionManager**, and **userManager**) are internal Spring
classes upon which you set properties.

Now that you understand how a bean definition XML file is composed, I encourage
you to take a closer look at the *applicationContext.xml* file from MyUsers. I think you
will notice that it's rather simple and easy to comprehend.

SUMMARY

In this chapter, you learned about IoC, which was recently aliased as *dependency injection* by Martin Fowler. Injecting dependencies using a container like Spring is a clean
and powerful way to configure applications and reduce couplinsg.

The **BeanFactory** and bean definitions are the driving force behind Spring's IoC
container, allowing you to specify dependencies and control your class's lifecycles in
XML. Knowing how the **BeanFactory** works and how bean definitions are specified will help you to become an extremely efficient developer with Spring. Knowing
how properties are set — whether they're string types, object types, or references to
other beans — is a tremendous asset. You can also define more complex properties
such as properties, lists and maps. This is where you will be wiring up your entire

application, rather than in code itself. Now, your code is loosely coupled, and can take care of its concerns, and you can think of the **ApplicationContext/BeanFactory** as the container that couples everything together.

In *Chapter 4: Spring's MVC Framework*, you will convert the MyUsers application from *Chapter 2: Spring Quick-Start Tutorial* to use Spring's MVC framework. I think you'll be amazed at how simple web development with Spring is, once you've gotten the internals set up and configured.

SPRING'S MVC FRAMEWORK

Spring MVC: A web framework with a lifecycle

This chapter describes the many features of Spring's MVC framework. It shows you how to replace the Struts layer in MyUsers with Spring and covers the **DispatcherServlet**, *various controllers, handler mappings, view resolvers, validation, and internationalization. It also briefly covers Spring's JSP tags.*

OVERVIEW

Chapter 3: The BeanFactory and How It Works explored Spring's BeanFactory and its lifecycle, which you can use to control how to invoke and use your beans. Spring carries this concept into the web tier and allows you to easily use dependency injection in its MVC framework. In popular frameworks like Struts and WebWork, controllers usually contain a single method: **execute()**. The framework, regardless of whether a **GET** or **POST** request is sent, will call this method. It's up to the developer to code any logic needed in this method; for example, you may populate dropdown lists, handle validation errors, and set up the view to add a new record. You can code multiple methods in a Struts or WebWork Action and then dispatch to them based on request parameters or button names, but it doesn't change the fact that the method call doesn't care which request method (**GET** versus **POST**) you use.

Spring's MVC is a bit friendlier. It offers two controllers: a **Controller** interface and a **SimpleFormController** class. The **Controller** is best suited for displaying read-only data (such as list screens), while the **SimpleFormController** handles forms (such as edit, save, delete). The **Controller** interface in Listing 4.1 is quite simple, containing a single **handleRequest(request, response)** method.

Listing 4.1

```
package org.springframework.web.servlet.mvc;

import javax.servlet.http.HttpServletRequest;
import javax.servlet.http.HttpServletResponse;
```

```
import org.springframework.web.servlet.ModelAndView;

public interface Controller {

    /**
     * Process the request and return a ModelAndView object which the
     * DispatcherServlet will render. A null return is not an error:
     * It indicates that this object completed request processing
     * itself, thus there is no ModelAndView to render.
     */
    ModelAndView handleRequest(HttpServletRequest request,
                               HttpServletResponse response)
        throws Exception;
}
```

The **handleRequest()** method returns a **ModelAndView** class. This class holds both the model and the view, which are both very distinct. The *model* is the information that you intend to display, and the *view* is the logical name where you want to display it. The model can be a single object with a name, or it can be a **java.util.Map** containing several objects. The view can be a **View** object (which is an interface for the different view types), or it can be a string name that is determined by a **ViewResolver**. *Chapter 6: View Options* meticulously covers the rich set of views available in Spring.

The **SimpleFormController** is a concrete class with several methods that are invoked while processing a data-entry form. The reason one is an interface and the other is a super-class is primarily for flexibility. All controllers in Spring use the **Controller** interface, whereas the **SimpleFormController** is an implementation with default settings for many of its methods. If you don't need all the rich functionality of a **FormController**, you can extend the **AbstractCommandController** to populate your command beans from an **HttpServletRequest**. Spring's MVC has a deep **FormController** hierarchy that is out of the scope of this chapter. In most cases, you simply won't need them and **SimpleFormController** will fulfill most requirements. *Chapter 14: Advanced Form Processing* covers using the **Abstract-WizardFormController** and Spring Web Flow for multi-page forms.

The **SimpleFormController** calls two distinct sets of methods: one for **GET** request methods, which prepare the form to be displayed, and one for **POST** request to process the information extracted from the form. This corresponds with how most web applications work; a **GET** signifies an "edit," while a **POST** signifies a "save" or "delete." This allows for easy isolation of the two operations. In Struts, you can achieve similar functionality using a **DispatchAction** (or one of its subclasses). In *Chapter 2: Spring Quick-Start Tutorial*, you used a **DispatchAction** to separate the CRUD operations into different methods. Spring's approach is better; you can re-use methods for all CRUD actions. In the *SimpleFormController: Method life-cyle review* section near the end of this chapter, you will see the purpose of the different methods in the **SimpleFormController** and the order in which they are called.

This chapter covers only what you need to know to develop a simple web application with validation, including the following topics:

*   Unit-testing Spring controllers
*   Configuring **DispatcherServlet** and **ContextLoaderListener**
*   Creating a unit test for **UserController** (to display a list of users)
*   Creating **UserController** and configuring it in *action-servlet.xml*
*   Creating *userList.jsp* to display list of users
*   Creating a unit test for **UserFormController** (edits, saves, and deletes users)
*   Creating **UserFormController** and configuring it in *action-servlet.xml*
*   Creating *userForm.jsp* to allow editing of the user's information
*   Configuring Commons Validator for Spring
*   **SimpleFormController** — Method lifecycle review
*   Spring's JSP tags
*   Handling non-string fields: Integer, double, and date
*   Populating drop-down lists and handling check boxes
*   Displaying and editing nested objects and indexed properties
*   Using **AbstractWizardFormController** and Spring Web Flow

Chapter 14: Advanced Form Processing covers more advanced features and techniques for working with Spring MVC.

As previously mentioned, Spring's MVC framework is a bit different from traditional frameworks like Struts and WebWork. With Spring, you use two controllers for master/detail screens. With Struts, you often use one Action for deleting, editing, saving and listing rows in a database table. "Listing" is the process of getting all the rows to display from a particular table. This satisfies most of what you need to do in web applications. With Spring MVC, rather than having one controller do all the work, it's simpler to create a controller for the listing (master) and another for the delete/edit/save (detail).

TIP: If you don't want to create a new controller for every list screen, you can use a **MultiActionController** that has separate methods for each list screen.

NOTE: *Chapter 12: Web Framework Integration* conducts a detailed analysis of Spring MVC versus the more popular MVC frameworks available: Struts, WebWork,

Tapestry, and JavaServer Faces (JSF). It covers the strengths and weaknesses of each and demonstrates how Spring's middle tier can integrate with each of them.

In this chapter, and throughout this entire book, use a good Java IDE to do the exercises. Eclipse and IntelliJ's IDEA are excellent ones, and each chapter's downloads accommodate both of them. The FAQ for this book contains tutorials on how to set up both IDEs to run your unit tests and use the Spring IDE Eclipse plug-in for editing/validating context files (wiki.sourcebeat.com/display/SPL /FAQ).

TESTING SPRING CONTROLLERS

When I first started working with Spring's MVC framework, I found it somewhat difficult to test. This was surprising, because one of Spring's advertised benefits is "Applications built using Spring are very easy to unit test."[1] While it was easy to test controllers (those classes that drive list screens), it was a bit more difficult to test a `SimpleFormController`. The main problem I had was that none of the recommended solutions (such as Mock Objects) had APIs to handle the tasks you normally do in a web application: setting request parameters/attributes, grabbing information from application scope, etc. With Struts, you can use `StrutsTest-Case`, which does a very nice job of providing mock implementations of most Struts and Servlet API classes.

Because Spring is open source, I was able to dig in and see what the developers were using internally to test the controllers. It turned out they had a number of home-grown mocks, which covered most of the Servlet APIs that I needed. Shortly after discovering that, the Spring team cleaned up these mocks for public consumption and added them to the Spring distribution. You'll be using these classes when you write your unit tests. If you'd like to use similar mocks in your project, be sure to include *spring-mock.jar* in your classpath.

In this chapter, like previous ones, you can follow along and do the examples as you go. The easiest way to do this is to download the **MyUsers Chapter 4** bundle from sourcebeat.com/downloads. This download is similar to the Equinox package you downloaded for *Chapter 2: Spring Quick-Start Tutorial*. However, it has all Struts-related material removed and is designed to be a pure Spring (with Hibernate) application. It contains all the JARs you will need in this chapter in its *web/WEB-INF/lib* directory.

You can also use the application you developed in *Chapter 2: Spring Quick-Start Tutorial*. If you go this route, download the **Chapter 4** JARs from sourcebeat.com /downloads. The next section covers how Spring is configured in the downloaded

---

1. From Rod Johnson's Introducing the Spring Framework on TheServerSide.com.

bundle. It also shows what you need to modify if you're converting the Struts-based application from *Chapter 2: Spring Quick-Start Tutorial.*

CONFIGURE DISPATCHERSERVLET AND CONTEXTLOADERLISTENER

Spring's MVC framework is similar to Struts in that it uses a single instance of a controller by default. You can change your controllers to create new instances for every request as well, by adding **singleton="false"** to your controller's bean definition. This way, if you prefer WebWork's new-action-per-request, you can still get that functionality.

Spring MVC has a single servlet that handles all requests, similar to most Java web frameworks.[2] It's called the **DispatcherServlet** and is responsible for dispatching requests to handlers, which have mappings to tell it where to go next. In the **MyUsers Chapter 4** download, the **DispatcherServlet** is already configured in the *web/WEB-INF/web.xml* file. Its mapping is set to **.html*, which means that this servlet will handle any URLs ending in *.html*.

If you're modifying the application created in *Chapter 2: Spring Quick-Start Tutorial,* you'll need configure the MyUsers application to use the **DispatcherServlet** for its front controller, rather than Struts' **ActionServlet**. See the instructions in the following section. You can skip to the *Create unit test for UserController* section if you downloaded the bundle for this chapter.

MODIFY WEB.XML TO USE SPRING'S DISPATCHERSERVLET

At this point, you should have the MyUsers project set up on your hard drive. To begin, open *web/WEB-INF/web.xml* and modify the **action** servlet's **<servlet-class>** from the code in Listing 4.2:

Listing 4.2

```
<servlet>
    <servlet-name>action</servlet-name>
    <servlet-class>
        org.apache.struts.action.ActionServlet
    </servlet-class>
    <load-on-startup>1</load-on-startup>
</servlet>
```

To the code in Listing 4.3.

---

2. This is a core J2EE pattern called **Front Controller**.

Listing 4.3

```
<servlet>
    <servlet-name>action</servlet-name>
    <servlet-class>
        org.springframework.web.servlet.DispatcherServlet
    </servlet-class>
    <load-on-startup>1</load-on-startup>
</servlet>
```

In addition, change the action's `<servlet-mapping>` from *.do* to *.html*. You're serving up HTML, so it makes sense to use this instead of .do. Also, there's no point in advertising the web framework you're using. See Listing 4.4.

Listing 4.4

```
<servlet-mapping>
    <servlet-name>action</servlet-name>
    <url-pattern>*.html</url-pattern>
</servlet-mapping>
```

By default, the `DispatcherServlet` looks for an XML file named *servletname-servlet.xml* in the *WEB-INF* directory. In this case, it'll find and load the *action-servlet.xml* once you create it. This file contains all of the web controllers and settings used in MyUsers.

In *Chapter 2: Spring Quick-Start Tutorial*, you used the Spring plug-in for Struts (`ContextLoaderPlugin`) to load the bean configuration files. However, the `ContextLoaderListener` was also configured in your *web.xml* file. This caused the *applicationContext.xml* file to be loaded twice. This was so you could unit test your Action classes without loading any context files manually.

NOTE: This listener will only work with Servlet 2.3 containers, so if you're on an older container, use the `ContextLoaderServlet`.

Since the `ContextLoaderListener` is already configured in *web.xml*, no further configuration is needed on your part. If you have more than one file with bean definitions, you need to add a `contextConfigLocation` context parameter to indicate the different files. For example, to do this in MyUsers, you would add the XML fragment in Listing 4.5 to *web.xml*, directly after the `sitemesh` filter and before its `<filter-mapping>`:

Listing 4.5

```
<context-param>
    <param-name>contextConfigLocation</param-name>
    <param-value>
        /WEB-INF/applicationContext1.xml
        /WEB-INF/applicationContext2.xml
    </param-value>
</context-param>
```

> **TIP:** Notice that the paths to the two files are space-delimited. These paths can also be comma-delimited. You can also use an asterisk to for wildcard filename matching (for example, */WEB-INF/applicationContext-*.xml*).

Those are the basic steps to configure a Java web application to use Spring's MVC framework. Here's a review of the steps:

1   In *web.xml*, add a **<servlet>** definition for **DispatcherServlet** and configure its **<servlet-mapping>**.

2   If you have more than one context file, define a **contextConfigLocation** **<context-param>** with the paths to your bean configuration files.

3   Add a **<listener>** definition for **ContextLoaderListener**.

REMOVE STRUTS AND ADD SPRING FILES

Remove the **UserAction** and **UserActionTest** Struts classes, as well as a few Struts JARs in *web/WEB-INF/lib*. Listing 4.6 lists some commands to accomplish this quickly:

Listing 4.6

```
rm src/org/appfuse/web/UserAction.java
rm test/org/appfuse/web/UserActionTest.java
rm web/WEB-INF/lib/struts*
rm web/WEB-INF/struts-config.xml
```

Now remove the definition for the **UserAction** class from *action-servlet.xml*. Delete the lines in Listing 4.7 from the file:

Listing 4.7

```
<bean name="user" class="org.appfuse.web.UserAction"
singleton="false">
```

```
        <property name="userManager">
            <ref bean="userManager"/>
        </property>
    </bean>
```

Download the **Chapter 4** JARs to your hard drive. Put the JAR files in the *web /WEB-INF/lib* directory. The *spring.jar* file contains Spring 1.2 RC1 (Equinox 1.0 ships with Spring 1.0.2), the *spring-mock.jar* file contains mocks for the Servlet API, and the *spring-sandbox.jar* file contains Commons Validator support. Another file, *validator-rules.xml* is also in the download; put this file in the *web/WEB-INF* directory. Configuring validation will be covered later in this chapter.

Now you're ready to begin developing your controllers.

CREATE UNIT TEST FOR USERCONTROLLER

To practice TDD, start by writing a unit test for the **UserController**. This class returns a list of all the users from a business service class (**UserManager**). If you're not familiar with TDD, here's a good definition from Dave Thomas's blog:

"Test-driven development is an important way of thinking about coding. It's about using tests to gain perspective on your design and implementation. You listen to what the tests are telling you, and alter to code accordingly. Finding it hard to test something in isolation? Refactor your code to reduce coupling. Is it impossible to mock out a particular subsystem? Look at adding facades or interfaces to make the separation cleaner. Tests drive the design, and tests verify the implementation."

To create a JUnit Test for the controller, create a *UserControllerTest.java* file in *test /org/appfuse/web* (you might need to create this directory/package). This class should extend **junit.framework.TestCase** and have a **setUp()** method defined to load the context files using an **XmlWebApplicationContext**. The main reason for using this *ContextLoader* over a **ClassPathXmlApplicationContext** is so web-only beans can be instantiated. Web-only beans are those that require a **WebApplicationContext** to be present. See Listing 4.8.

Listing 4.8

```
public void setUp() {
    String[] paths = {"/WEB-INF/applicationContext.xml",
                      "/WEB-INF/action-servlet.xml"};
    ctx = new XmlWebApplicationContext();
    ctx.setConfigLocations(paths);
    ctx.setServletContext(new MockServletContext(""));
    ctx.refresh();
}
```

The preceding code will instantiate any beans defined in their respective XML files. Now write a **testXXX** method in order to test your controller. This is where TDD comes into play. The test will drive the design. Write a test method to retrieve a list of users, verify the success, and confirm the view returned is the one you expect. Listing 4.9 is the entire **UserControllerTest**, so you can easily integrate it into your project. The **testGetUsers()** is the method you're most interested in.

Listing 4.9

```
package org.appfuse.web;

// use your IDE (Eclipse and IDEA rock!) to add imports

public class UserControllerTest extends TestCase {

    private XmlWebApplicationContext ctx;

    public void setUp() {
        String[] paths = {"/WEB-INF/applicationContext.xml",
                          "/WEB-INF/action-servlet.xml"};
        ctx = new XmlWebApplicationContext();
        ctx.setConfigLocations(paths);
        ctx.setServletContext(new MockServletContext(""));
        ctx.refresh();
    }

    public void testGetUsers() throws Exception {
        UserController c = (UserController)
                              ctx.getBean("userController");
        ModelAndView mav =
            c.handleRequest((HttpServletRequest) null,
                            (HttpServletResponse) null);
        Map m = mav.getModel();
        assertNotNull(m.get("users"));
        assertEquals(mav.getViewName(), "userList");
    }
}
```

TIP: When writing tests for your own project, create a **BaseControllerTestCase** that extends **TestCase** and all your *ControllerTest classes extend. In this class's **setUp()** method, you can load the context for all child tests. If you do this, be sure to call **super.setUp()** when overriding **setUp()** in child classes.

In the **testGetUsers()** method, you're grabbing the **UserController** and invoking its **handleRequest()** method, which returns a **ModelAndView** class. This method is common to all Spring controllers, so you'll actually use this same method to test your **FormController** classes. The **ModelAndView** class is a unique concept in web frameworks. It contains information about the next page (the view) and what data to expose to it (the model). With Struts, the model and view are separated. The model is usually put into the request (or session) scope, and **Actions** typically return **ActionForwards**, which are just fancy wrappers around URLs.

CREATE USERCONTROLLER
AND CONFIGURE ACTION-SERVLET.XML

Now that you've written your unit test, it's time to create the **UserController** class so you can get it to compile. First, create a *UserController.java* file in *src/org /appfuse/web* (you may need to create this directory/package). This class should implement the **Controller** interface and its **handleRequest(request, response)** method. You're also going to need to use the **UserManager** to talk to get the list of users, so you'll need to add a private **userManager** variable and a **setUserManager()** method for Spring's IoC container to use. When you configure this controller (bean) in the next section, you'll add the **UserManager** as a dependency. So far, you have the class structure in Listing 4.10:

Listing 4.10

```
package org.appfuse.web;

// Modern IDEs support easy importing

public class UserController implements Controller {
    private static Log
        log = LogFactory.getLog(UserController.class);
    private UserManager mgr = null;

    public void setUserManager(UserManager userManager) {
        this.mgr = userManager;
    }

    // put handleRequest() method here
}
```

Now implement the **handleRequest()** method to get a list of users and route the user to **userList.jsp**. See Listing 4.11.

Listing 4.11

```
public ModelAndView handleRequest(HttpServletRequest request,
                                  HttpServletResponse response)
throws Exception {
    if (log.isDebugEnabled()) {
        log.debug("entering 'handleRequest' method...");
```

```
        }

    return new
        ModelAndView("userList", "users", mgr.getUsers());
    }
```

This method is quite simple; in fact, it would be only one line without the logging statement at the beginning!

Compiling the **UserControllerTest** class should work now, but if you try to run the test (using **ant test -Dtestcase=UserController**), it will fail with the error in Listing 4.12:

Listing 4.12

```
[junit] No bean named 'userController' is defined:
org.springframework.beans.factory.support
    .DefaultListableBeanFactory defining beans
[dataSource,sessionFactory,transactionManager,
    userDAO,userManagerTarget,
    userManager]; root of BeanFactory hierarchy
```

This error is saying that the **userController** bean is not defined in any loaded context files. To make the test pass, edit the *action-servlet.xml* file in the *web/WEB-INF/* directory. The *action-servlet.xml* file starts similar to any other Spring context file with the DTD at the top and the beginning **<beans>** element.

Adding a **userController** bean definition should cause this file to look like the code in Listing 4.13:

Listing 4.13

```
<?xml version="1.0" encoding="UTF-8"?>
<!DOCTYPE beans PUBLIC "-//SPRING//DTD BEAN//EN"
    "http://www.springframework.org/dtd/spring-beans.dtd">

<beans>
    <bean id="userController" class="org.appfuse.web.UserController">
        <property name="userManager" ref="userManager"/>
    </bean>
</beans>
```

Now your **UserControllerTest** should run just fine. You can execute it by running **ant test -Dtestcase=UserController** or run it as a JUnit test in Eclipse or IDEA.

TIP: You can find instructions for setting up MyUsers in Eclipse and IDEA in this book's FAQ at http://wiki.sourcebeat.com/display/SPL/FAQ.

From the command line, the output should look similar to Figure 4.1.

Figure 4.1: Running `UserControllerTest`

CREATE USERLIST.JSP TO DISPLAY LIST OF USERS

Now that the `UserController` is working, you must configure Spring so it knows the `userList` view actually points to the *userList.jsp* file. The simplest way to do this is to use the `InternalResourceViewResolver`, which resolves names to files. It allows you to add a *prefix* and a *suffix*, so you can easily control where your JSPs reside. Add the XML block in Listing 4.14 to *action-servlet.xml*, after the `userController` bean definition

Listing 4.14.

```
<bean id="viewResolver"
    class="org.springframework.web.servlet.view.
        InternalResourceViewResolver">
    <property name="viewClass"
        value="org.springframework.web.servlet.view.JstlView"/>
    <property name="prefix" value="/"/>
    <property name="suffix" value=".jsp"/>
</bean>
```

In the `viewResolver` definition in Listing 4.14, notice that you're specifying a `JstlView` class for the `viewClass` property. This is so you can use JSTL's `<fmt:message>` tag, which requires a bit of preparation to use its i18n features with Spring MVC. The prefix is "/" and the suffix is ".jsp." If you need to move your JSPs to */WEB-INF/pages*, all you'll need to change is the prefix.

By adding the **viewResolver** definition, the **userList** view name in **UserController** will be resolved to **/userList.jsp**. You can use several other **ViewResolvers** depending on your view technology of choice. These will be covered in *Chapter 6: View Options*.

Now you need to configure URLs in the application so that the */users.html* URL will invoke the **UserController** class. To do this, Spring MVC requires you to define a **HandlerMapping** bean and define which URLs go to which controllers. In most cases, the **SimpleUrlHandlerMapping** is all you'll need. It allows you to specify **url-patterns** to bean names. In order to map */users.html* to the **userController** bean, add the code in Listing 4.15 to *web/WEB-INF/action-servlet.xml*.

Listing 4.15

```
<bean id="urlMapping"
    class="org.springframework.web.servlet.handler
        .SimpleUrlHandlerMapping">
    <property name="mappings">
        <props>
            <prop key="/users.html">userController</prop>
        </props>
    </property>
</bean>
```

Listing 4.16

```
<bean name="/users.html" class="org.appfuse.web.UserController">
    <property name="userManager" ref="userManager"/>
</bean>
```

If you're modifying the application you created in *Chapter 2: Spring Quick-Start Tutorial*, you'll need to modify some JSPs. The *web/taglibs.jsp* file should contain the code in Listing 4.17:

Listing 4.17

```
<%@ page language="java" errorPage="/error.jsp" %>
<%@ taglib uri="http://java.sun.com/jstl/core_rt" prefix="c" %>
<%@ taglib uri="http://java.sun.com/jstl/fmt" prefix="fmt" %>
<%@ taglib uri="http://www.springmodules.org/tags/commons-validator"
    prefix="html" %>
<%@ taglib uri="http://www.springframework.org/tags"
    prefix="spring" %>
<%@ taglib uri="http://www.opensymphony.com/sitemesh/decorator"
    prefix="decorator"%>
```

The *web/messages.jsp* file should have the code in Listing 4.18:

Listing 4.18

```
<%-- Success Messages --%>
<c:if test="${not empty message}">
    <div class="message">${message}</div>
    <c:remove var="message" scope="session"/>
</c:if>
```

1 Create a *userList.jsp* file in the *web* directory. This file may already exist.

2 Add code so you can see the all the users in the database. In Listing 4.19, the first line includes the *taglibs.jsp* file. This file contains all the JSP Tag Library declarations for this application, mostly for JSTL and SiteMesh (which is used to "pretty up" the JSPs).

Listing 4.19

```
<%@ include file="/taglibs.jsp"%>

<title>MyUsers ~ User List</title>

<button onclick="location.href='editUser.html'">Add User</button>

<table class="list">
<thead>
<tr>
    <th><fmt:message key="user.id"/></th>
    <th><fmt:message key="user.firstName"/></th>
    <th><fmt:message key="user.lastName"/></th>
</tr>
```

```
</thead>
<tbody>
<c:forEach var="user" items="${users}" varStatus="status">
<c:choose>
  <c:when test="${status.count % 2 == 0}"><tr class="even"></c:when>
  <c:otherwise><tr class="odd"></c:otherwise>
</c:choose>
    <td><a href="editUser.html?id=${user.id}">${user.id}</a></td>
    <td>${user.firstName}</td>
    <td>${user.lastName}</td>
</tr>
</c:forEach>
</tbody>
</table>
```

As an alternative to JSTL's **<fmt:message>** tag, you can use the **<spring:message>** tag. To do so, just replace **<fmt:message key="..."/>** with **<spring:message code="..."/>**. This tag is a more full-featured than the JSTL counterpart and allows default messages, as well as HTML and JavaScript escaping. (The JSTL tags are a standard and portable across any web framework that uses JSPs.)

NOTE: The prefix used for the Spring's JSP tags is configurable in *web/taglibs.jsp*. You can easily use **<s:...>** instead of **<spring:...>**.

---

3   To enable i18n message lookups (for the **<fmt:message>** tag), you must add a **messageSource** bean to *web/action-servlet.xml*. See Listing 4.20.

Listing 4.20

```
<bean id="messageSource"
    class="org.springframework.context.support
        .ResourceBundleMessageSource">
    <property name="basename" value="messages"/>
    <property name="useCodeAsDefaultMessage" value="true"/>
</bean>
```

The **basename** property refers to "messages," which means *look for messages.properties at the root of the classpath*. If you'd like to use more than one *.properties* file, you can use the **basenames** property with a **<list>** of **<values>**. For example, see Listing 4.21:

Listing 4.21

```
<property name="basenames">
    <list>
```

```
        <value>messages</value>
        <value>errors</value>
    </list>
</property>
```

> NOTE: The `ResourceBundleMessageSource` depends on Java's `Resource-
> Bundle`, which caches loaded bundles indefinitely. With this class, reloading a
> bundle during VM executing is not possible. If you need such functionality, you can
> use the `ReloadableResourceBundleMessageSource`.

To use this bean instead, move your *messages.properties* file to the *web/WEB-INF*
directory and add the bean definition in Listing 4.22 to *web/WEB-INF/action-
servlet.xml*.

Listing 4.22

```
<bean id="messageSource"
    class="org.springframework.context.support
    .ReloadableResourceBundleMessageSource">
    <property name="basename" value="/WEB-INF/messages "/>
    <property name="cacheSeconds" value="1"/>
</bean>
```

To test that you've configured Spring's handlers and resolvers correctly, as well as
modified *userList.jsp* successfully, start Tomcat, deploy MyUsers (**ant deploy**) and
view localhost:8080/myusers/users.html in your browser. To add users to the database, run **ant populate**. See Figure 4.2.

> NOTE: If running **ant populate** doesn't cause users to show up in the list, see
> the FAQ at http://wiki.sourcebeat.com/display/SPL/FAQ.

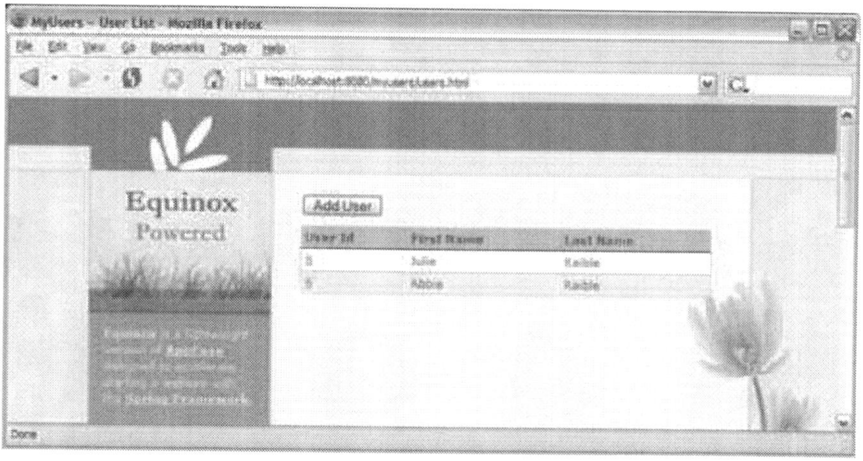

Figure 4.2: User list

If your screen looks like Figure 4.2, congratulations! If not, you can post a message to the Spring Live Forums (www.javalobby.org/forums/forum.jspa?forumID=174) to get help.

CREATE UNIT TEST FOR USERFORMCONTROLLER

The list screen was the easy part since it simply retrieves and displays data. Now you must create a controller and JSP to handle editing database records. Since you are practicing TDD, start by creating a unit test for the **UserFormController** (that you haven't created yet). To do this, create a *UserFormControllerTest.java* file in the *test/org/appfuse/web* directory. This file should extend JUnit's **TestCase** class and have the following **setUp()** and **tearDown()** methods. See Listing 4.23.

Listing 4.23

```
package org.appfuse.web;

// resolve imports using your IDE

public class UserFormControllerTest extends TestCase {
    private static Log log =
        LogFactory.getLog(UserFormControllerTest.class);
    private XmlWebApplicationContext ctx;
    private UserFormController c;
    private MockHttpServletRequest request;
    private ModelAndView mv;
    private User user;

    public void setUp() throws Exception {
        String[] paths =
```

```
                 { "/WEB-INF/applicationContext.xml",
                   "/WEB-INF/action-servlet.xml" };
        ctx = new XmlWebApplicationContext();
        ctx.setConfigLocations(paths);
        ctx.setServletContext(new MockServletContext(""));
        ctx.refresh();
        c = (UserFormController) ctx.getBean("userFormController");

        // add a test user to the database
        UserManager mgr = (UserManager) ctx.getBean("userManager");
        user = new User();
        user.setFirstName("Matt");
        user.setLastName("Raible");
        user = mgr.saveUser(user);
    }

    public void tearDown() {
        ctx = null;
        c = null;
        user = null;
    }

    // put testXXX methods here
}
```

The **setUp()** method in this class is very similar to the **setUp()** method in **User-ManagerTest** from *Chapter 2: Spring Quick-Start Tutorial*, except that it also loads *action-servlet.xml*. Separating your business components and data layer classes between the two files allows you to easily switch out the MVC framework without even touching *applicationContext.xml*. This is very powerful for decoupling your different tiers and allows for easy refactoring.

The **UserFormController** you'll be developing has many functions. It retrieves a **User** object from the **UserManager**, and it has the ability to save and/or delete that user. Looking at and testing each feature individually should make the features (and tests) a bit easier to understand.

The first feature to test is editing a user. Add a **testEdit()** method to your **User-FormControllerTest** class. The **Mock*** classes you'll see in this section are from Spring's Servlet API mocks, which allow for easy testing of controllers. See Listing 4.24.

Listing 4.24

```
    public void testEdit() throws Exception {
        log.debug("testing edit...");
        request = new MockHttpServletRequest
            ("GET", "/editUser.html");
```

```
        request.addParameter("id", user.getId().toString());
        mv = c.handleRequest(request, new MockHttpServletResponse());
        assertEquals("userForm", mv.getViewName());
    }
```

The **MockHttpServletRequest** class you see in this method is from *spring-mock.jar*, which contains test-friendly mocks for most of the Servlet API. This class makes it easy to call **GET** and **POST** methods on a given URI (Uniform Resource Indicator). It has a number of constructors, each listed in Listing 4.25.

Listing 4.25

```
    public MockHttpServletRequest(ServletContext servletContext)
    public MockHttpServletRequest(ServletContext servletContext,
                                  String method, String URI)
    public MockHttpServletRequest()
    public MockHttpServletRequest(String method, String URI)
```

The **UserFormControllerTest** class will not compile until you create the **User-FormController** class. If you're using an IDE such as IDEA or Eclipse, it will actually prompt you with an icon on the left to auto-create the new class.

CREATE USERFORMCONTROLLER AND CONFIGURE IT IN ACTION-SERVLET.XML

Start by creating a *UserFormController.java* file in *src/org/appfuse/web*. This class should extend **SimpleFormController**, which is a concrete **FormController** implementation that provides configurable form and success views. It automatically resubmits to the form view when validation errors occur, and displays the success view when a submission is valid. This class provides many methods to override in the lifecycle of displaying a form, as well as submitting a form.

This is one of the unique things about Spring's MVC framework versus others like Struts or WebWork. The latter frameworks typically only provide one method for you to override, and you don't have as much control over what happens when. Of course, with Spring's MVC you don't *have* to override its lifecycle methods; it's simply an option if you need it. Toward the end of this chapter is a detailed overview of the different lifecycle methods and when they're called.

The **UserFormController** is simple so you can easily grasp how Spring MVC works. In fact, you only need to override two methods: **onSubmit()** and **form-BackingObject()**. The **onSubmit()** method handles form posts and the **form-BackingObject()** method gives the request an object that matches the fields in your HTML form. This method is a convenient location to fetch existing records, as well as good place to instantiate empty objects (for example, to display an empty form). This method's default implementation simply creates a new empty object. In Spring's terminology, this object is called a "**command** class."

By default, command objects in a **SimpleFormController** are request-scoped. If you want to change this behavior, you can add **setSessionForm(true)** to your controller's constructor.

Listing 4.26

```
public MyFormController() {
    super();
    setSessionForm(true);
}
```

If your command object is session-scoped, the same object will be re-used across the entire form edit-and-submit process. If your command object is request-scoped, the **formBackObject()** will be called on both edit and submit. The default implementation of this method calls **BaseCommandController.createCommand()**, which creates a new instance of the command class.

The code in Listing 4.27 only shows how to implement "edit" functionality, since that's all you're testing at this point. When editing an object, no **POST** occurs; therefore, there's no **onSubmit()** method implemented.

Listing 4.27

```
package org.appfuse.web;

// resolve imports using your IDE

public class UserFormController extends SimpleFormController {
    private static Log log =
        LogFactory.getLog(UserFormController.class);
    private UserManager userManager = null;

    public void setUserManager(UserManager userManager) {
        this.userManager = userManager;
}

    public UserFormController() {
        super();
        setCommandClass(User.class);
    }

    protected Object formBackingObject(HttpServletRequest request)
    throws ServletException {
        String id = RequestUtils.getStringParameter(request, "id",
"");

        if (!"".equals(id)) {
            return userManager.getUser(id);
        } else {
```

```
        return new User();
      }
   }
}
```

From this code, you can see how the **formBackingObject()** method simply creates an empty object for adds, and a populated object for edits. The **Request-Utils** class used in this method is convenient for auto-converting types (for example, String→Long, String→Boolean, etc.)

Now it's time to configure this controller in your *web/WEB-INF/action-servlet.xml* file. In this bean's definition, you will set a fair amount of declarative values: the formView, the command class, and its name. This is also where you will inject its dependency on the **UserManager**. Listing 4.28 is the **userFormController** definition you need to add.

Listing 4.28

```
<bean id="userFormController"
    class="org.appfuse.web.UserFormController">
    <property name="commandName" value="user"/>
    <property name="formView" value="userForm"/>
    <property name="successView" value="redirect:users.html"/>
    <property name="userManager" ref="userManager"/>
</bean>
```

In this definition, the **commandName** property is optional. If you choose not to specify this property, it will default to **command**. The main reason for specifying the name is because Commons Validator keys off this name for its validation rules. In the next section, when you create the JSP for this controller, you'll see where the **commandName** property is used. It is not by any code in this controller, nor in its Test class.

TIP: Many of the properties specified in this bean definition can also be set in the **UserFormController** class's constructor. For example, setting the **command-Class** property is required, but it's set in the constructor instead. You could also set it in the bean definition using the code in Listing 4.29:

Listing 4.29

```
<property name="commandClass" value="org.appfuse.model.User"/>
```

You also might notice the **redirect:** prefix used by the **successView**. This indicates you want to send a redirect to the next controller. Another option is to wrap the logical view name with a **RedirectView** class as in Listing 4.30:

Listing 4.30

```
return new ModelAndView(new RedirectView(getSuccessView()));
```

You can also use a **forward:** prefix. An example of using this prefix is given in Listing 4.31. Using redirect is usually the best option to solve the duplicate submit problem that occurs in web applications.

Listing 4.31

```
<property name="successView" value="forward:users.html"/>
```

In *action-servlet.xml*, you'll need to add a URL mapping so that *editUser.html* resolves to use the **userFormController** bean. Do this by adding an additional line to the **mappings** property of the **urlMapping** bean. See Listing 4.32.

Listing 4.32

```
<property name="mappings">
    <props>
        <prop key="/users.html">userController</prop>
        <prop key="/editUser.html">userFormController</prop>
    </props>
</property>
```

TIP: Because you have full control over the URLs for your controllers, you could also use something like Listing 4.33:

Listing 4.33

```
<property name="mappings">
    <props>
        <prop key="/user/index.html">userController</prop>
        <prop key="/user/edit.html">userFormController</prop>
    </props>
</property>
```

Run the **UserFormControllerTest** in your IDE or from the command line. Figure 4.3 shows the output on the command line from running **ant test -Dtestcase=UserFormController**.

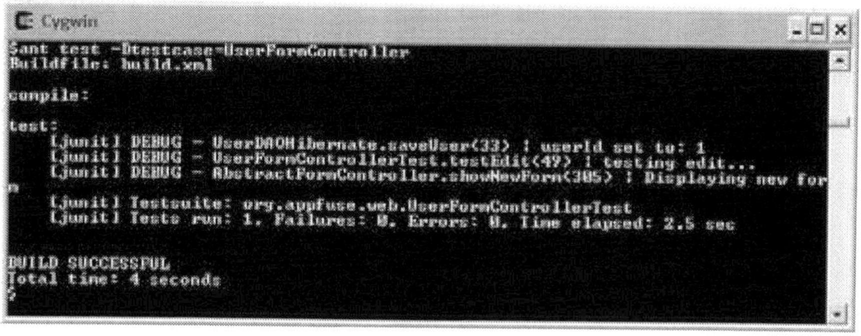

Figure 4.3: Run `UserFormControllerTest`

If you see something similar to Figure 4.3, nice work! Next, you need to create the JSP to display the results of the edit action.

CREATE USERFORM.JSP TO VIEW USER INFORMATION

In the Struts version of this application, the *userForm.jsp* was simple; relying on Struts' `<html:form>` and `<html:text>` JSP tags to make things easy. Unfortunately, Spring doesn't currently have similar simplistic form-specific tags. However, they have good reasons. The main premise behind the lack of rich form tags is to give the user maximum control over the HTML. Because Spring's form-handling tags do not generate any HTML, the user has complete control over it. Since several Struts folks are migrating to Spring, there have been some discussions on the mailing list of producing something similar. At the time of this writing, an enhancement request is in Spring's JIRA to add JSP 2.0 tag files for easier form syntax.

Besides unobtrusive form-handling tags, Spring allows you to configure your form's action URL to whatever you like. This may be annoying because it requires more typing, as though you're hard-coding the URL to the controller.

Struts will prepend the **contextPath**, and append the suffix you defined in *web.xml* (such as **.do*). See Listing 4.34.

Listing 4.34

```
<html:form action="/user">
```

With Spring, an equivalent action declaration looks like Listing 4.35:

Listing 4.35

```
<form action="<c:url value="/user.html"/>">
```

You could also use relative paths, which makes the Spring version require less typing than the Struts version. See Listing 4.36.

Listing 4.36

```
<form action="user.html">
```

The `<c:url>` version prepends your application's **contextPath** (for example, /*myusers*), allowing you to easily move the JSP to a subfolder. Furthermore, it gives you full control over the extension you want to use. This works very nicely if you want to have secure and unsecure sections of your application. You can define servlet-mappings in *web.xml* (such as **.html* and **.secure*) and then protect any **.secure* URLs. You cannot do this with Struts because the form action's URL is always filled in for you.

The next difference between a Struts JSP and a Spring JSP is how Spring binds object values to form input fields. Struts' input tags look up information from the `<html:form>` tag and match properties to getters in the **ActionForm**. Spring's `<spring:bind>` tag allows you to *bind* getters (properties) in your command object with input fields. Compare the differing syntax for the **firstName** input field. If you were using Struts, you'd use an `<html:text>` tag. See Listing 4.37:

Listing 4.37

```
<html:text property="user.firstName"/>
```

Using Spring, the syntax is more verbose. See Listing 4.38.

Listing 4.38

```
<spring:bind path="user.firstName">
    <input type="text" name="${status.expression}"
        value="${status.value}"/>
    <span class="fieldError">${status.errorMessage}</span>
</spring:bind>
```

NOTE: You can use `${status.expression}` or the name of the property itself (for example, **firstName**).

Struts' **ActionForms** are very similar in their functionality. However, Spring allows easier binding to your domain objects, eliminating the need (in many cases) to develop a form just to handle web input. One case where you may still need a "web-only form object" is when you want to combine two domain objects into one form or if you want to put two forms on one page.

In Listing 4.39, you will find the full code for *web/userForm.jsp*.

Listing 4.39

```
<%@ include file="/taglibs.jsp"%>

<title>MyUsers ~ User Details</title>

<p>Please fill in user's information below:</p>

<form method="post" action="<c:url value="/editUser.html"/>">
<spring:bind path="user.id">
<input type="hidden" name="id" value="${status.value}"/>
</spring:bind>
<table>
<tr>
    <th><fmt:message key="user.firstName"/>:</th>
    <td>
        <spring:bind path="user.firstName">
        <input type="text" name="${status.expression}"
               value="${status.value}"/>
        <span class="fieldError">${status.errorMessage}</span>
        </spring:bind>
    </td>
</tr>
<tr>
    <th><fmt:message key="user.lastName"/>:</th>
    <td>
        <spring:bind path="user.lastName">
        <input type="text" name="${status.expression}"
               value="${status.value}"/>
        <span class="fieldError">${status.errorMessage}</span>
        </spring:bind>
    </td>
</tr>
<tr>
    <td></td>
    <td>
        <input type="submit" class="button"
            name="cancel" value="Cancel"/>
    </td>
</tr>
</table>
</form>
```

At this point, you should be able to view a user's record through your browser. Run **ant deploy** and start Tomcat. Then run **ant populate** and go to localhost:8080 /myusers/editUser.html?id=5 in your browser. The retrieved page should resemble the one in Figure 4.4.

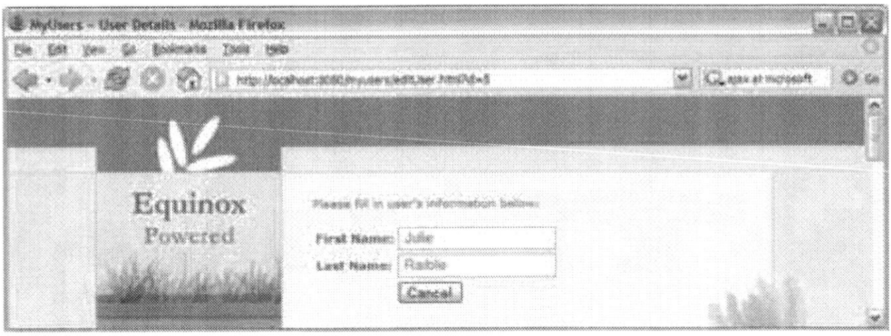

Figure 4.4: View user

If you click on the **Cancel** button on this screen, you'll be sent to the list screen because the default implementation of **SimpleFormController** sends you to view defined by the **successView** property.

MODIFY USERFORMCONTROLLERTEST TO TEST SAVING A USER

After viewing a user's information, the next logical step is updating their information. Add a **testSave()** method to your **UserFormControllerTest** class. See Listing 4.40.

Listing 4.40

```
public void testSave() throws Exception {
    request = new MockHttpServletRequest
        ("POST", "/editUser.html");
    request.addParameter("id", user.getId().toString());
    request.addParameter("firstName", user.getFirstName());
    request.addParameter("lastName", "Updated Last Name");

    mv = c.handleRequest(request, new MockHttpServletResponse());

    String errorsKey = BindException.ERROR_KEY_PREFIX +
                            c.getCommandName();
    Errors errors = (Errors) mv.getModel().get(errorsKey);
    assertNull(errors);
    assertNotNull(request.getSession().getAttribute("message"));
}
```

This method is making a **POST** request to the **UserFormController**, followed by verifying no errors exist and a success message is present. This is the first time you've seen the **Errors** interface in this chapter. This is an interface that is implemented by an object to store and expose information about data binding or validation errors.

MODIFY USERFORMCONTROLLER TO IMPLEMENT SAVING A USER

To implement *save* logic in the **UserFormController**, you need to override the **initBinder()** and **onSubmit()** methods from **SimpleFormController**. The **initBinder()** method is where you'll register property editors to convert strings into non-string types. In the example in Listing 4.41, you must register a data binder to handle the **java.lang.String** → **java.lang.Long** conversion for **user.setId()**.

Listing 4.41

```
protected void initBinder(HttpServletRequest request,
                          ServletRequestDataBinder binder) {
    NumberFormat nf = NumberFormat.getNumberInstance();
    binder.registerCustomEditor(Long.class,
        new CustomNumberEditor(Long.class, nf, true));
}

public ModelAndView onSubmit(HttpServletRequest request,
                             HttpServletResponse response,
                             Object command,
                             BindException errors)
throws Exception {
    if (log.isDebugEnabled()) {
        log.debug("entering 'onSubmit' method...");
    }

    User user = (User) command;

    userManager.saveUser(user);
    // put success message into session so it survives redirects
    request.getSession().setAttribute("message",
            getMessageSourceAccessor().getMessage("user.saved",
            new Object[]
                { user.getFirstName() + ' ' + user.getLastName() }
            ));

    return new ModelAndView(getSuccessView());
}
```

You can also see how simple the **onSubmit()** method is; it calls the **UserManager** to save the **User** object and returns a **ModelAndView**. In this example, a success message is saved into the session, and it's retrieved with the *web/messages.jsp* that's included in the SiteMesh decorator, which *Chapter 5: Advanced Spring MVC* covers in depth. See Listing 4.42.

Listing 4.42

```
<c:if test="${not empty message}">
    <div class="message">${message}</div>
    <c:remove var="message" scope="session"/>
</c:if>
```

NOTE: Another option is to add the success message to the `ModelAndView` —
and it'll be added to the redirected URL as a request parameter. Listing 4.43 is an
example.

Listing 4.43

```
userManager.saveUser(user);
String message = getMessageSourceAccessor()
                    .getMessage("user.saved",
                    new Object[] { user.getFirstName() + ' ' +
                                    user.getLastName() });

return new ModelAndView(getSuccessView(), "message", message);
```

To display success messages using this technique, modify *web/messages.jsp* to
resemble the code in Listing 4.44:

Listing 4.44

```
<c:if test="${not empty param.message}">
    <div class="message">${param.message}</div>
</c:if>
```

There are several other submit methods you can override to handle a form's submit
process. See Listing 4.45.

Listing 4.45

```
ModelAndView onSubmit(Object command) throws Exception
ModelAndView onSubmit(Object command,  BindException errors)
void doSubmitAction(Object command) throws Exception
```

Of these methods, the second is recommended when you want to build your own
`ModelAndView`, and the third is recommended when you simply want to forward to
the success view.

The **initBinder()** method is responsible for doing the string-to-property conversion for the command class. In this example, a **CustomNumberEditor** converts the **user.id** property, which is a **java.lang.Long**. A list of built-in property editors you can use in this method is listed in Table 4.1.

Table 4.1: Built-in Property Editors

Class	Description	Registered by Default?
ByteArrayProperty-Editor	Editor for byte arrays. Strings will simply be converted into their corresponding byte representations. Registered by default by **BeanWrapperImpl**.	Yes
ClassEditor	Parses strings representing classes to actual classes and the other way around. When a class is not found, an **IllegalArgumentException** is thrown.	Yes
CustomBoolean-Editor	Customizable property editor for Boolean properties. Registered by default by **BeanWrapperImpl**, but can be overridden by registering custom instance of it as custom editor.	Yes
CustomCollection-Editor	Property editor for collections; converts any source collection to a given target collection type.	Yes, for **Set**, **SortedSet** and **List**
CustomDateEditor	Customizable property editor for **java.util.Date**; supports a custom **DateFormat**.	No
CustomNumberEditor	Customizable property editor for any **Number** subclass such as **Integer, Long, Float, Double**.	Yes
FileEditor	Capable of resolving strings to file objects.	Yes

Table 4.1: Built-in Property Editors

Class	Description	Registered by Default?
InputStreamEditor	One-way property editor capable of taking a text string and producing (via an intermediate **ResourceEditor** and **Resource**) an **InputStream**, so **Input-Stream** properties may be directly made capable of resolving strings to file objects. Note that the default usage will not close the **InputStream** for you.	Yes
LocaleEditor	Capable of resolving strings to locale objects and vice versa (the string format is **[language]_ [country]_[variant]**, which is the same thing the **toString()** method of locale provides; registered by default by **Bean-WrapperImpl**.	Yes
PropertiesEditor	Editor for **java.util.Proper-ties** objects.	Yes
StringArray-PropertyEditor	Editor for string arrays.	Yes
StringTrimmer-Editor	Property editor that trims strings.	Yes
URLEditor	Editor for java.net.URL to directly feed a URL property instead of using a string property.	Yes

a) Table is based on Spring's reference documentation: www.springframework.org/docs/reference /validation.html#beans-beans-conversion.

In this example, adding a new user and updating an existing one doesn't require any special logic because Hibernate will handle that on the back end. Now if you run **ant test -Dtestcase=UserFormController**, you should see something similar to Figure 4.5.

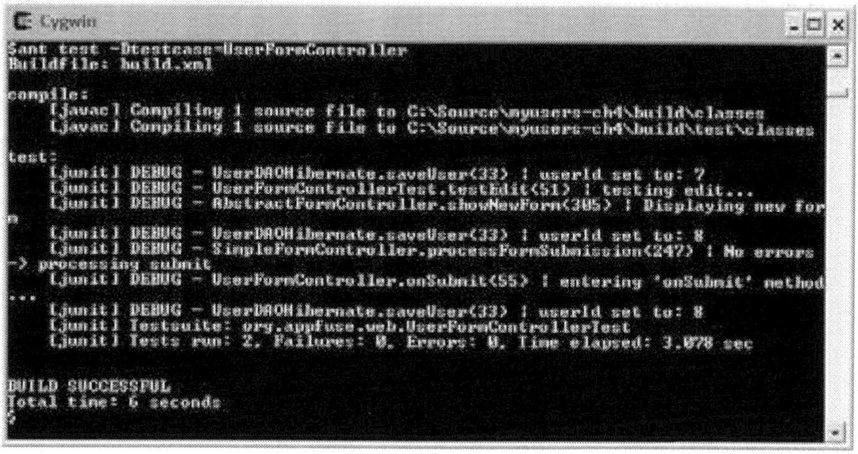

Figure 4.5: Running `UserFormControllerTest`

MODIFY USERFORM.JSP TO ALLOW SAVING A USER

You've proven the `UserFormController` works, now you need to enable "save" functionality in the *web/userForm.jsp*. Add a **Save** button to the form in this JSP. See Listing 4.46

Listing 4.46

```
<td>
    <input type="submit" class="button"
            name="save" value="Save"/>
    <input type="submit" class="button" name="cancel"
            value="Cancel"/>
</td>
```

Since the **Save** and **Cancel** buttons are both submit buttons, you need to add some logic to recognize when the **Cancel** button has been clicked. By overriding the `processFormSubmission()` method in the `UserFormController` class, you can easily get the desired cancel functionality. See Listing 4.47.

Listing 4.47

```
/**
 * Redirect to the successView when cancel button has been pressed.
 */
public ModelAndView processFormSubmission(HttpServletRequest request,
                                        HttpServletResponse response,
                                        Object command,
                                        BindException errors)
```

```
throws Exception {
    if (request.getParameter("cancel") != null) {
        return new ModelAndView(getSuccessView());
    }

    return super.processFormSubmission
        (request, response, command, errors);
}
```

Now you should be able to run **ant deploy reload** and add a new user. Figure 4.6 shows the success message after adding "Jack Raible."

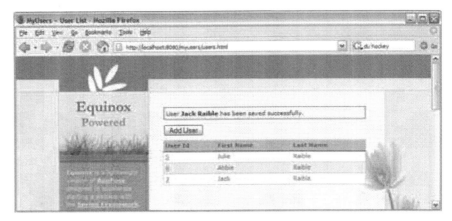

Figure 4.6: Add user success message

MODIFY USERFORMCONTROLLER TO TEST DELETING A USER

The last CRUD feature you need to add is *delete* functionality. First, add the **testDelete()** method to **UserFormControllerTest**. See Listing 4.48.

Listing 4.48

```
public void testDelete() throws Exception {
    request = new MockHttpServletRequest("POST", "/editUser.html");
    request.addParameter("delete", "");
    request.addParameter("id", user.getId().toString());
    mv = c.handleRequest(request, new MockHttpServletResponse());
    assertNotNull(request.getSession().getAttribute("message"));
}
```

In this method, you're sending a delete parameter with no value. This is because you're simply trying to replicate clicking on the **Delete** button, and you don't care what its value is. In HTML-based forms, the name of the button that's clicked is sent as a request parameter, while the other button names are not sent as request parameters.

MODIFY USERFORMCONTROLLER TO IMPLEMENT DELETING A USER

To add delete functionality to the **UserFormController** class, you only need to add some logic to check for delete versus save. See Listing 4.49.

Listing 4.49

```
public ModelAndView onSubmit(HttpServletRequest request,
                             HttpServletResponse response,
                             Object command,
                             BindException errors)
throws Exception {
    if (log.isDebugEnabled()) {
        log.debug("entering 'onSubmit' method...");
    }

    User user = (User) command;

    if (request.getParameter("delete") != null) {
        userManager.removeUser(user.getId().toString());
        request.getSession().setAttribute("message",
                getMessageSourceAccessor().
                    getMessage("user.deleted",
                    new Object[] {
                       user.getFirstName() + ' ' +
                       user.getLastName()}));
    } else {
        userManager.saveUser(user);
        request.getSession().setAttribute("message",
                getMessageSourceAccessor().getMessage("user.saved",
                    new Object[] {user.getFirstName() + ' ' +
                        user.getLastName()}));
    }

    return new ModelAndView(getSuccessView());
}
```

Running the **UserFormControllerTest** with **ant test -Dtestcase=UserForm** should now pass. See Figure 4.7.

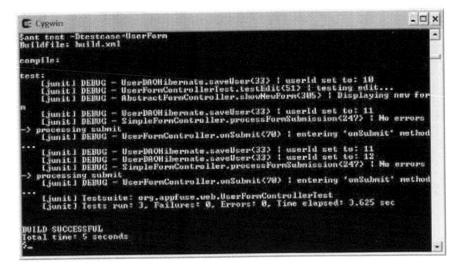

Figure 4.7: Running `UserFormControllerTest`

MODIFY USERFORM.JSP TO ALLOW DELETING A USER

Adding a **Delete** button to the *web/userForm.jsp* is the next step in this process. See Listing 4.50.

Listing 4.50

```
        <input type="submit" class="button" name="save" value="Save"/>
    <c:if test="${not empty param.id}">
        <input type="submit" class="button"
            name="delete" value="Delete"/>
    </c:if>
    <input type="submit" class="button" name="cancel" value="Cancel"/>
```

The `<c:if>` statement hides the **Delete** button when adding a new user. Running `ant deploy reload` should allow you to delete an existing user, like Figure 4.8 and Figure 4.9 show.

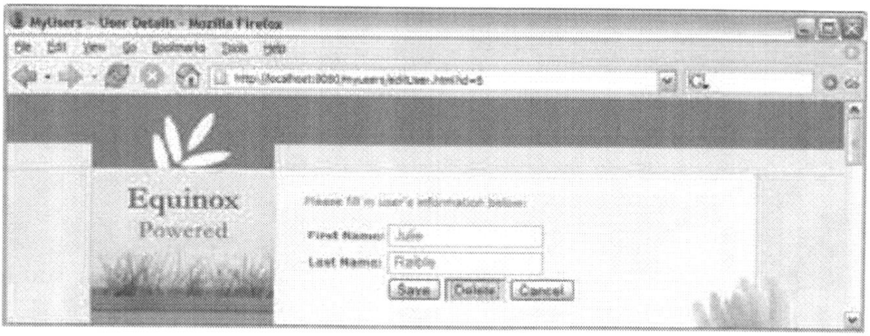

Figure 4.8: Deleting a user

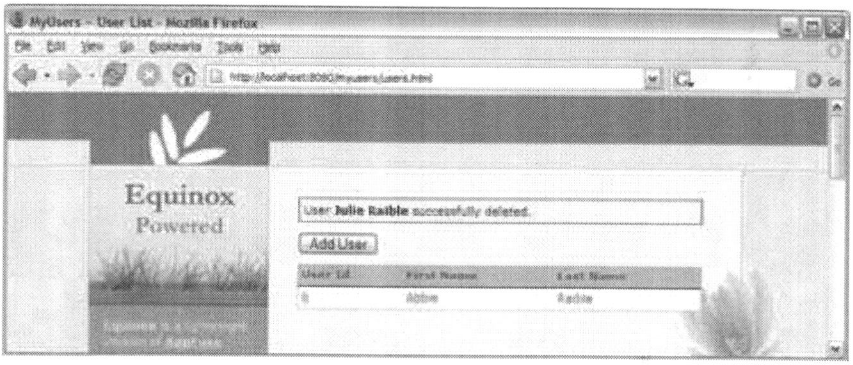

Figure 4.9: Delete user success message

In Spring controllers, there's generally a lack of exception handling. This is primarily to keep things simple. *Chapter 5: Advanced Spring MVC* covers an exception handling strategy.

The last thing you need to do is add validation.

CONFIGURE COMMONS VALIDATOR FOR SPRING

At the time of this writing, Spring 1.2 RC1 has been released, and it does not contain a built-in declarative validation framework. The core validation framework requires that you create classes that implement the `org.springframework.validation` `.Validator` interface. After creating a validator implementation for your command class, you can reference it as the `validator` property of your `FormController`. Using this method is covered in the next chapter.

Daniel Miller added support for using Commons Validator with Spring. The code for using Commons Validator with Spring MVC was recently moved from Spring's

CVS sandbox to the Spring Modules project on java.net. The code in this section uses the 0.1 release from this project.

For Struts users, using the validation framework they're familiar with should make Spring MVC even easier. To migrate the *validation.xml* file from Struts to Spring MVC, you only need to change a few attribute values: the **formName** (**user-Form→user**) and the field names (removing **user** because you're not wrapping it with a **DynaActionForm**). The modified-for-Spring version is as follows in Listing 4.51:

Listing 4.51

```
<form-validation>
    <formset>
        <form name="user">
            <field property="lastName" depends="required">
                <arg0 key="user.lastName"/>
            </field>
        </form>
    </formset>
</form-validation>
```

In the preceding XML, the form **name** should match the value of the **commandName** property in your controller's bean definition. The field's property value should match the name of your input fields, and the key refers to an i18n key in *web/WEB-INF/classes/messages.properties*. More information on writing validation rules is available in the Validator User Guide at struts.apache.org/struts-doc-1.2.x/userGuide/dev_validator.html.

The download for this chapter has a *validator-rules.xml* file (in *web/WEB-INF*) that is different from the one that ships with Struts. This file defines all of the Spring-specific classes and methods to use for validation, as well as defining JavaScript methods for client-side validation.

To add declarative validation to the user form in the MyUsers application, you'll need to complete the following steps.

1   At the bottom of *web/userForm.jsp* add a JSP tag that renders the JavaScript for client-side validation. See Listing 4.52.

Listing 4.52

```
<html:javascript formName="user"/>
```

NOTE: The one-line JavaScript tag in Listing 4.52 is not the recommended way to configure client-side validation with Commons Validator. The above method is used for simplicity and results in all the JavaScript functions being included in the final

HTML. *Chapter 5: Advanced Spring MVC* outlines a cleaner way, where the functions are referenced from an external JavaScript file.

2   Add an **onsubmit** handler to the **<form>** in *web/userForm.jsp*. The **validateUser()** is a JavaScript function that will be generated by the **<html:javascript>** tag. The name of this method will always be **validateXXX**, where *XXX* is the uppercase name of the **formName**. See Listing 4.53.

Listing 4.53

```
<form method="post" action="<c:url value="/editUser.html"/>"
    onsubmit="return validateUser(this)">
```

Also, add an **onclick** attribute to the **Cancel** button so validation doesn't kick in when you click **Cancel**. See Listing 4.54.

Listing 4.54

```
<input type="submit" class="button" name="cancel" value="Cancel"
    onclick="bCancel=true"/>
```

3   To notify Spring that you want to use Commons Validator as your validation engine, add a couple of **<bean>** definitions to *web/WEB-INF /action-servlet.xml*. See Listing 4.55.

Listing 4.55

```
<bean id="validatorFactory"
    class="org.springmodules.commons.validator
        .DefaultValidatorFactory">
    <property name="validationConfigLocations">
        <list>
            <value>/WEB-INF/validator-rules.xml</value>
            <value>/WEB-INF/validation.xml</value>
        </list>
    </property>
</bean>

<bean id="beanValidator"
    class="org.springmodules.commons.validator.DefaultBeanValidator">
    <property name="validatorFactory" ref="validatorFactory"/>
</bean>
```

The **validatorFactory** bean loads the validator's methods and class mappings (*validator-rules.xml*), as well as the application-specific validation rules (*validation.xml*). The second bean (**beanValidator**) applies validation to any POJO.

4   To configure your **UserFormController** to use the **beanValidator** for validation, you simply need to add a **validator** property to the **userFormController** definition. See Listing 4.56.

Listing 4.56

```
<property name="validator" ref="beanValidator"/>
```

NOTE: The developers of Spring plan to add their own declarative validation framework in the future. In the meantime, you can use Commons Validator.

Run **ant deploy reload**, open your browser to localhost:8080/myusers /editUser.html and try to add a new user without specifying a last name; you should see the JavaScript alert in Figure 4.10:

Figure 4.10: Client-side validation message

If you want to make sure things are *really* working as expected, turn off JavaScript and ensure that server-side validation is working. This is easy in Mozilla Firefox; just go to **Tools→ Options→Web Features** and uncheck **Enable JavaScript**. Now if you clear the **lastName** field and save the form, you should see the something like Figure 4.11:

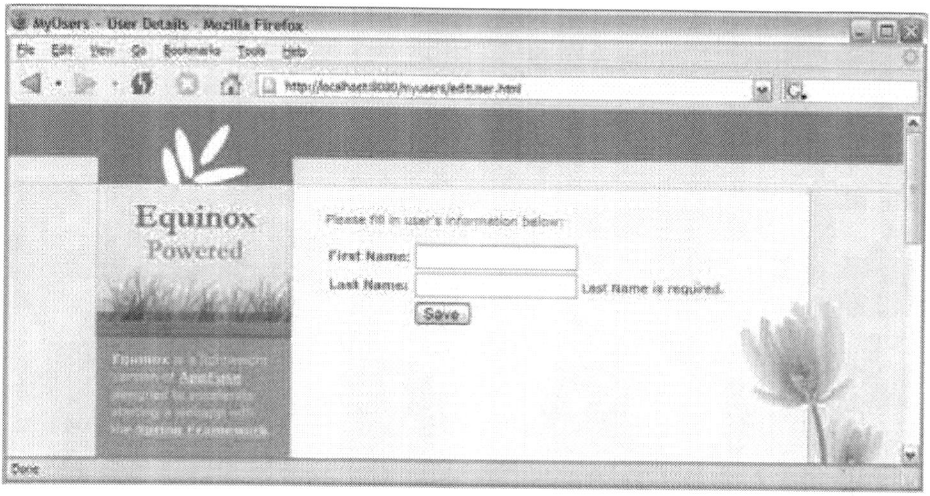

Figure 4.11: Server-side validation message

To capture all the errors at the top of your JSP (like Struts), add the code in Listing 4.57 to the top of the JSP, just after the `<title>` element.

Listing 4.57

```
<spring:bind path="user.*">
    <c:if test="${not empty status.errorMessages}">
    <div class="error">
        <c:forEach var="error" items="${status.errorMessages}">
            <c:out value="${error}" escapeXml="false"/><br/>
        </c:forEach>
    </div>
    </c:if>
</spring:bind>
```

If you add this code, run **ant deploy** and click **Save** without adding a `lastName` (with JavaScript turned off). Your screen should resemble Figure 4.12:

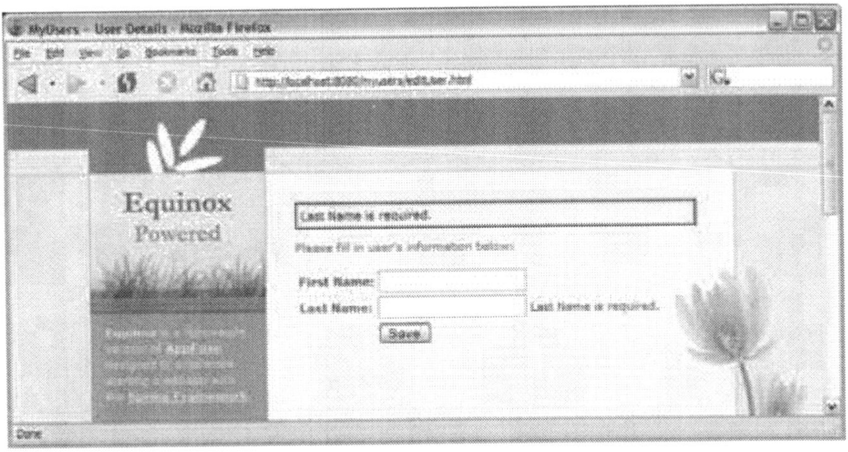

Figure 4.12: User details form with alert

To review, there are four steps to integrating Commons Validator and configuring your validation rules:

1   Add *springmodules-validator-0.1.jar* to your classpath and define **validatorFactory** and **beanValidator** beans. Download *validator-rules.xml* and put it in your *WEB-INF* directory.

2   Use **<property name="validator" ref="beanValidator"/>** as the validator property of your controller.

3   Define your form validation rules in a *WEB-INF/validation.xml* file.

4   Add an **<html:javascript>** tag to your JSP and add an onsubmit handler (for the form) to enable client-side validation.

You've just created a web application that uses Spring for its MVC layer. *Congratulations!*

SIMPLEFORMCONTROLLER: ## METHOD LIFECYLE REVIEW

The **SimpleFormController** is one of many **CommandControllers** in Spring's MVC package. These controllers interact with domain objects and dynamically bind parameters from the request to the objects. In comparison to Struts, Spring is much cleaner because it doesn't require your domain objects to implement an interface or extend a superclass. The only two that you'll likely need are **SimpleFormController** and **AbstractWizardFormController**.

- **SimpleFormController** is a concrete **FormController** that provides configurable form and success views, and an **onSubmit** chain for convenient overriding. It automatically resubmits to the form view in case of validation errors, and renders the success view in case of a valid submission.

- **AbstractWizardFormController** is a **FormController** for typical wizard-style workflows. In contrast to classic forms, wizards have more than one page view. Because of this, various methods allow the user to go next, back, cancel or finish.

Using **SimpleFormController** can be a bit overwhelming at first. Read its Java-Docs, which describe the lifecycle (that is, workflow) of its methods. Figure 4.13 illustrates the lifecycle for a **GET** request, and Figure 4.14 shows a **POST** request's lifecycle. In the exercises so far, you have not overridden the **referenceData()** method, which is useful for fetching ancillary data. Using this method is covered in the *Drop-down lists and check boxes* section in *Chapter 14: Advanced Form Processing*.

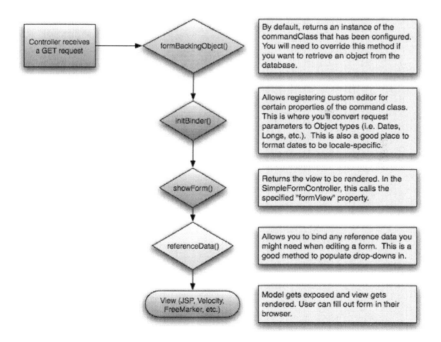

Figure 4.13: SimpleFormController lifecycle - GET request

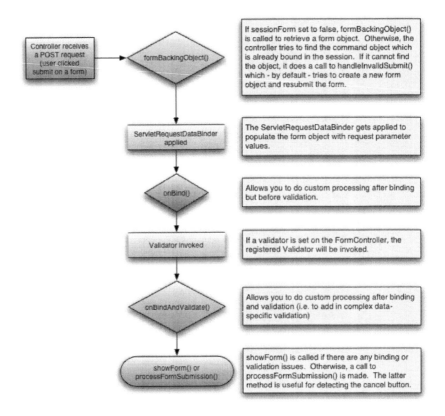

Figure 4.14: SimpleFormController lifecycle - POST request

These diagrams should give you a better understanding of the Spring's **FormCon-troller**'s lifecycle. Knowing these methods and when they're called can be helpful when developing applications with Spring MVC.

SPRING'S JSP TAGS

We briefly touched on the **<spring:bind>** tag when modifying *userForm.jsp*; now look at the other JSP tags available. Below is a list of current tags that ship with Spring by default.

- **spring:bind** binds command object properties to form fields. This tag exposes a **status** variable in the **pageContext**. This variable can be grabbed with JSP's Expression Language (EL); **${status.value}** will give you a properties value, and **${status.errorMessage}** will display any errors associated with a property. This is the most useful tag in Spring's taglib.

- **spring:hasBindErrors** provides support for binding the errors for an object. This tag seems to be most useful for checking a command object if it has bind errors.

- **spring:transform** provides support for transforming properties not contained by a command object using PropertyEditors associated with the command object. This can be useful if you need to transform data from the **referenceData()** method (for example, drop-downs). It must be used *inside* a **spring:bind tag**. It's not currently used in any of Spring's sample apps.

- **spring:message** is similar to JSTL's **<fmt:message>** tag, but it supports Spring's **MessageSource** concept. It also works with Spring's locale support. JSTL's **<fmt:message>** tag has fulfilled all my i18n needs with Spring MVC. It's not currently used in any of Spring's sample apps.

- **spring:htmlEscape** sets the default HTML escape value for the current page. The default is **false**. You can also set a **defaultHtmlEscape** *web.xml* context-param. Using the tag in a JSP overrides any settings in *web.xml*. It's not currently used in any of Spring's sample apps.

- **spring:theme** looks up the theme message in the scope of the current page. This tag will be covered in detail in *Chapter 5: Advanced Spring MVC* when talking about templating.

From the above list, you can see that many of the core tags are not used. Therefore, you've already seen the most important one: **spring:bind**.

SUMMARY

This chapter covered a lot of material. It covered unit testing and using *spring-mock.jar* to test controller classes, then it demonstrated how to convert the MyUsers application to use Spring MVC instead of Struts. Through this process, you learned how to create a controller unit test and how to configure *action-servlet.xml* for controllers, handlers, and resolvers. You saw how to modify a Struts JSP to use Spring tags and how to add declarative validation with Commons Validator. You learned about the **SimpleFormController**'s lifecycle and Spring's JSP tags.

In the later half of this chapter, advanced form processing was covered. This section showed you how to bind to non-string fields, populate drop-down lists, and handle check boxes. In addition, you learned how to display and edit nested objects and lists of objects. The `AbstractWizardFormController` was used to create a wizard, and a brief introduction to Spring Web Flow was provided.

This chapter was designed to show you the basics of developing web applications with Spring MVC. *Chapter 5: Advanced Spring MVC* will cover more advanced validation and web site page decoration (also called templating). You'll also learn how to handle exceptions in controllers and how to do a simple file upload. For more advanced form processing features in Spring MVC, please see *Chapter 14: Advanced Form Processing*.

ADVANCED SPRING MVC

Integrating Tiles and SiteMesh for page decoration, implementing validation, handling exceptions, uploading files, and sending email

This chapter covers advanced topics in web frameworks, particularly validation and page decoration. In it, you will read about using Tiles or SiteMesh to decorate a web application. It also demonstrates how the Spring Framework handles validation and shows examples of using it in the web business layers. Finally, it outlines a strategy for handling exceptions in the controllers and describes how to upload files and send email messages.

OVERVIEW

Several years ago, web developers didn't have frameworks to help them develop Java/JSP-based applications. They were more concerned with getting it done than doing it right. Today, numerous frameworks are available to accelerate a developer's efficiency. They have built-in page decoration, validation engines, exception handling, and file upload. Some even support interceptors, which can interrupt a web request and perform logic on-the-fly.

Spring supports all of these features as well. This chapter explores how to configure page decoration frameworks such as SiteMesh and Tiles in your Spring-based web application. It then shows how you can build from your Struts Validator knowledge and use the Commons Validator with Spring (which nicely supports client-side validation with JavaScript). After validation, this chapter covers exception handling, applying interceptors, and uploading files. Lastly, it briefly covers sending email messages.

This may sounds like a lot to accomplish in one chapter, but it will be simple and easy to understand. Furthermore, all of these technologies and concepts will be viewed in the context of the MyUsers application. At the end of this chapter, you'll have a reference application that employs all of these features.

TEMPLATING WITH SITEMESH

SiteMesh is an open source layout and page decoration framework from the Open-Symphony project. It was originally created over 5 years ago, when Joe Walnes downloaded the first Sun servlet engine and wrote it using servlet chains. Over the years, the basic design has stayed the same; content is intercepted and parsed, and a decorator mapper finds a decorator and merges everything. Figure 5.1 shows a simplistic example of how this works.

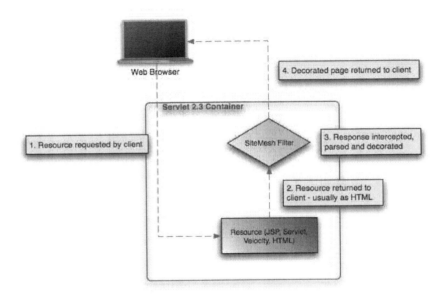

Figure 5.1: How SiteMesh works

Skinning is an essential element to every web application. The ability to edit one or two files to change the *entire* layout of an application is necessary for maintainability. SiteMesh is a simple decoration framework and is very easy to install and configure.

INSTALLATION AND CONFIGURATION

If you're using the application you developed in *Chapter 4: Spring's MVC Framework*, SiteMesh is already configured. To start from scratch (without SiteMesh), you must download the **MyUsers Chapter 5** bundle from sourcebeat.com/downloads. None of the topics for this chapter have been configured in the downloaded application. After downloading it, extract it to *myusers-ch5* and then copy *myusers-ch5* to *myusers-site-mesh*.

> **NOTE:** You will copy *myusers-ch5* to *myusers-tiles* when you install and configure Tiles.

Run **ant remove clean install** while Tomcat is running; your screen should resemble Figure 5.2 when you open localhost:8080/myusers. This is much different and quite bland when compared with previous screens you've seen. Installing and configuring SiteMesh will allow you to pretty it up a bit.

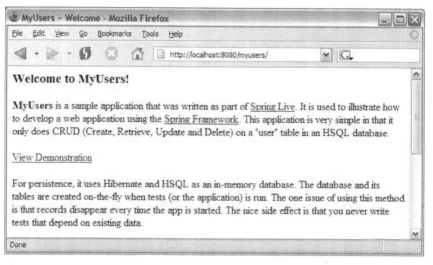

Figure 5.2: the MyUsers application before SiteMesh

STEP 1: CONFIGURE SITEMESH IN WEB.XML

The *sitemesh-2.1.jar* is already in the *web/WEB-INF/lib* directory of *myusers-sitemesh*, so you don't have to install that. However, if you were installing SiteMesh from scratch, you would download it from www.opensymphony.com/sitemesh.

1   Open your *web.xml* file (in *web/WEB-INF*) to edit.

2   At the top of this file, right after the **<display-name>** and before the **<context-param>**, add the **<filter>** definition in Listing 5.1:

Listing 5.1

```
<filter>
    <filter-name>sitemesh</filter-name>
    <filter-class>
        com.opensymphony.module.sitemesh.filter.PageFilter
    </filter-class>
</filter>
```

3   After the `<context-param>` and before the `<listener>` element, add the `<filter-mapping>` in Listing 5.2:

Listing 5.2

```
<filter-mapping>
    <filter-name>sitemesh</filter-name>
    <url-pattern>/*</url-pattern>
    <dispatcher>REQUEST</dispatcher>
    <dispatcher>FORWARD</dispatcher>
</filter-mapping>
```

The `<dispatcher>` elements in the `<filter-mapping>` above are new to Servlet 2.4. These dispatchers (as well as `ERROR`) allow you to map filters to more than just requested URLs.

STEP 2: CREATE CONFIGURATION FILES

Use the following steps to create your configuration files.

1   Create a *sitemesh.xml* file in *web/WEB-INF*, as shown in Listing 5.3:

Listing 5.3

```
<sitemesh>
    <page-parsers>
        <parser default="true"
            class="com.opensymphony.module.sitemesh.parser
                .FastPageParser"/>
        <parser content-type="text/html"
            class="com.opensymphony.module.sitemesh.parser
                .FastPageParser"/>
        <parser content-type="text/html;charset=ISO-8859-1"
            class="com.opensymphony.module.sitemesh.parser
                .FastPageParser"/>
    </page-parsers>

    <decorator-mappers>
        <mapper
          class="com.opensymphony.module.sitemesh.mapper
            .ConfigDecoratorMapper">
            <param name="config" value="/WEB-INF/decorators.xml"/>
        </mapper>
    </decorator-mappers>
</sitemesh>
```

This file configures *page-parsers* and *decorator-mappers*. The page-parsers are configured to parse certain content-types, and it's unlikely you'll ever need to change these values. Both the **FastPageParser** (shown here) and the **HTMLPageParser** build an **HTMLPage** object from an HTML document. The **HTMLPageParser** was written to provide similar functionality as the **FastPageParser** and to make it simpler to add custom features, such as user-defined rules.

The **ConfigDecoratorMapper** is one of several possible *decorator-mappers*. Specifically, it tells SiteMesh to read decorators and mappings from the **config** property, which is */WEB-INF/decorators.xml* by default. Because you're using the default, you could remove the **<param>** element in *sitemesh.xml* and everything would work the same. The *decorators.xml* file specifies which URL patterns will use which decorators.

2   Create a *decorators.xml* file in *web/WEB-INF* and put the XML in Listing 5.4 into it.

Listing 5.4

```
<decorators defaultdir="/decorators">
    <decorator name="default" page="default.jsp">
        <pattern>/*</pattern>
    </decorator>
</decorators>
```

STEP 3: CREATE A DECORATOR

Finally, build a *decorator* that will act as the template to wrap the pages in your application. If you're familiar with Tiles, this is the same thing as creating a *base layout*.

1   Create a *web/decorators/default.jsp* file, as was configured in the *decorators.xml* file.

2   Put the code in Listing 5.5 into the *default.jsp* file:

Listing 5.5

```
<!DOCTYPE html PUBLIC "-//W3C//DTD XHTML 1.0 Transitional//EN"
    "http://www.w3.org/TR/xhtml1/DTD/xhtml1-transitional.dtd">

<%@ include file="/taglibs.jsp"%>

<html xmlns="http://www.w3.org/1999/xhtml" xml:lang="en">
<head>
    <title><decorator:title default="MyUsers"/></title>
    <meta http-equiv="content-type"
        content="text/html; charset=utf-8"/>
    <link href="${ctx}/styles/global.css" type="text/css"
        rel="stylesheet"/>
    <link href="${ctx}/images/favicon.ico" rel="SHORTCUT ICON"/>
    <decorator:head/>
    <!-- HTML & Design contributed by Boer Attila
        (http://www.calcium.ro) -->
```

```
        <!-- Found at
            http://www.csszengarden.com/
                ?cssfile=/083/083.css&page=2 -->
</head>
<body>
<a name="top"></a>
<div id="container">
    <div id="intro">
        <div id="pageHeader">
            <h1><span>Welcome to Equinox</span></h1>
            <div id="logo" onclick="location.href='
                <c:url value="/"/>'"
                onkeypress="location.href='
                    <c:url value="/"/>'"></div>
            <h2><span>Spring Rocks!</span></h2>
        </div>

        <div id="quickSummary">
            <p>
                <strong>Equinox</strong> is a lightweight version
                <a href="http://raibledesigns.com/appfuse">
                    of AppFuse</a> designed
                to accelerate starting a webapp with the
                <a href="http://www.springframework.org">
                    Spring Framework</a>.
            </p>
            <p class="credit">
                <a href=
                    "http://www.csszengarden.com/
                        ?cssfile=/083/083.css">
                Design and CSS</a>
                    donated by <a href="http://www.calcium.ro">
                Bo&eacute;r Attila</a>.
            </p>
        </div>

        <div id="content">
            <%@ include file="/messages.jsp"%>
            <decorator:body/>
        </div>
    </div>

    <div id="supportingText">
        <div id="underground">
            <decorator:getProperty property="page.underground"/>
        </div>
        <div id="footer"></div>
    </div>

</div>
```

```
    <div id="linkList">
        <div id="linkList2">
        </div>
    </div>

  </div>

  </body>
  </html>
```

The important elements to look for are the **<decorator:*>** tags, which are highlighted in yellow. At the top of the document, a **<decorator:title>** grabs the **<title>** tag from JSP pages that are wrapped, and the **<decorator:head/>** tag pulls in anything defined in **<head>**. In the middle, a **<decorator:body/>** tag grabs the "body" of the page. Lastly, the **<decorator:getProperty>** tag pulls in a **<content>** tag that's defined in your decorated JSPs. Listing 5.6 is an example from the *index.jsp* page:

Listing 5.6

```
<content tag="underground">
    <h3>Additional Information</h3>
    <!-- more content here -->
</content>
```

Add the **<decorator>** taglib directive to *web/taglibs.jsp*. Add the line in Listing 5.7 at the bottom of this file:

Listing 5.7

```
<%@ taglib uri="http://www.opensymphony.com/sitemesh/decorator"
    prefix="decorator" %>
```

Run **ant deploy reload** and open your browser to localhost:8080/myusers; you should see a decorated page as in Figure 5.3.

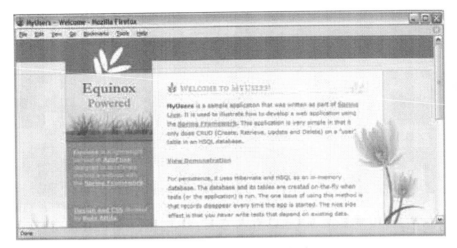

Figure 5.3: The MyUsers application after SiteMesh

This is a clean and simple, yet attractive design. For the most part, your decorated pages can use standard HTML elements. Yet they don't need all the elements (such as `<html>`, `<body>`) that static pages require. Even better, SiteMesh doesn't care what server-side technology you use for your application; it works with CGI, PHP, Servlets, Velocity, and FreeMarker. This makes it very Spring-friendly since Spring supports so many different view technologies (covered thoroughly in *Chapter 6: View Options*).

TEMPLATING WITH TILES

Tiles is a templating and document layout engine much like SiteMesh. Tiles is the default layout engine for Struts, while most SiteMesh users tend to use WebWork (mainly due to the fact that both WebWork and SiteMesh come from OpenSymphony). Cedric Demoulin originally wrote Tiles and released it shortly after Struts 1.0. Initially, it was a separate add-on to Struts, much like the Validator. Much of the work in Struts 1.1 was devoted to extracting useful components from Struts into the Jakarta Commons projects. Because no one had the time to extract it, Tiles did not become a separate project, but became a part of the core Struts (in *struts.jar*).

The next few sections show you how to configure Tiles to work with Spring's MVC framework.

INSTALLATION AND CONFIGURATION

The instructions below are for Struts 1.1, with which Tiles is integrated; hence, it does not have its own version number.

Copy *myusers-ch5* to *myusers-tiles*. If you haven't downloaded *myusers-ch5* yet, you can download it from sourcebeat.com/downloads. At this point, if you run **ant remove clean install**, your screen will look like it did before the *Templating with SiteMesh* section (see Figure 5.1).

STEP 1: CONFIGURE SPRING TO RECOGNIZE TILES

You need to configure Spring to recognize Tiles.

1   For Spring to recognize Tiles and use it for rendering views, create a **tilesConfigurer** bean definition in the *action-servlet.xml* file in *web/ WEB-INF*, as shown in Listing 5.8:

Listing 5.8

```
<bean id="tilesConfigurer"
    class="org.springframework.web.servlet.view.tiles
        .TilesConfigurer">
    <property name="factoryClass"
        value="org.apache.struts.tiles.xmlDefinition
            .I18nFactorySet"/>
    <property name="definitions">
        <list>
            <value>/WEB-INF/tiles-config.xml</value>
        </list>
    </property>
</bean>
```

2   Change the **viewClass** property of the **viewResolver** bean from **JstlView** to **TilesJstlView**. You can also delete the **prefix** and **suffix** values in this bean definition. Listing 5.9 is the replacement viewResolver bean definition:

Listing 5.9

```
<bean id="viewResolver"
class="org.springframework.web.servlet.view
    .InternalResourceViewResolver">
    <property name="requestContextAttribute" value="rc"/>
    <property name="viewClass"
        value="org.springframework.web.servlet.view.tiles
            .TilesJstlView"/>
</bean>
```

The **TilesJstlView** class will now resolve any view names to definition names. For instance, in the **UserController** class, it returns the **userList** view from the

handleRequest() method. This will now render the **userList** definition in Listing 5.10.

Listing 5.10

```
return new ModelAndView("userList", "users", mgr.getUsers());
```

Another example is the **formView** property of the **UserFormController** class. In *action-servlet.xml*, it's set to userForm, which will render the userForm definition.

STEP 2: CREATE A BASE LAYOUT

Now you must create a *base layout* JSP. This is a template (equivalent to SiteMesh's *decorator*) that controls the layout of the page and where certain components are inserted.

   1   Create a *web/layouts/baseLayout.jsp* file. Fill this file with the code in Listing 5.11:

Listing 5.11

```
<!DOCTYPE html PUBLIC "-//W3C//DTD XHTML 1.0 Transitional//EN"
    "http://www.w3.org/TR/xhtml1/DTD/xhtml1-transitional.dtd">

<%@ include file="/taglibs.jsp"%>

<html xmlns="http://www.w3.org/1999/xhtml" xml:lang="en">
<head>
    <title><tiles:getAsString name="title"/></title>
    <meta http-equiv="content-type"
        content="text/html; charset=utf-8"/>
    <link href="${ctx}/styles/global.css" type="text/css"
        rel="stylesheet"/>
    <link href="${ctx}/images/favicon.ico" rel="SHORTCUT ICON"/>
    <!-- HTML & Design contributed by Boer Attila
        (http://www.calcium.ro) -->
    <!-- Found at
        http://www.csszengarden.com/
            ?cssfile=/083/083.css&page=2 -->
</head>
<body>
<a name="top"></a>
<div id="container">
    <div id="intro">
        <div id="pageHeader">
            <h1><span>Welcome to Equinox</span></h1>
            <div id="logo" onclick="location.href='
                <c:url value="/"/>'"
```

```
            onkeypress="location.href='
                <c:url value="/"/>'"></div>
        <h2><span>Spring Rocks!</span></h2>
    </div>

    <div id="quickSummary">
        <p>
            <strong>Equinox</strong> is a lightweight version
            <a href="http://raibledesigns.com/appfuse">
                of AppFuse</a> designed
            to accelerate starting a webapp with the
            <a href="http://www.springframework.org">
                Spring Framework</a>.
        </p>
        <p class="credit">
            <a href="http://www.csszengarden.com/?cssfile=
                /083/083.css">
            Design and CSS</a> donated by
                <a href="http://www.calcium.ro">
            Bo&eacute;r Attila</a>.
        </p>
    </div>

    <div id="content">
        <%@ include file="/messages.jsp"%>
        <tiles:insert attribute="content"/>
    </div>
</div>

<div id="supportingText">
    <div id="underground">
        <c:out value="${underground}" escapeXml="false"/>
    </div>
    <div id="footer"></div>
</div>

<div id="linkList">
    <div id="linkList2">
    </div>
</div>

</div>

</body>
</html>
```

This file is very similar to the *web/decorators/default.jsp* that you created for SiteMesh, except that it uses the **tiles** JSP tag instead of the **decorator** tag. Therefore, you must add the **tiles** tag to the *web/taglibs.jsp* file.

2   Add the `tiles` tag to the *web/taglibs.jsp* file. This file should look like Listing 5.12 after making the change:

Listing 5.12

```
<%@ page language="java" errorPage="/error.jsp" %>
<%@ taglib uri="http://java.sun.com/jstl/core_rt" prefix="c" %>
<%@ taglib uri="http://java.sun.com/jstl/fmt" prefix="fmt" %>
<%@ taglib uri="http://www.springframework.org
    /tags/commons-validator"
    prefix="html" %>
<%@ taglib uri="http://www.springframework.org/tags"
    prefix="spring" %>
<%@ taglib uri="http://jakarta.apache.org/struts/tags-tiles"
    prefix="tiles" %>
```

STEP 3: CREATE PAGE DEFINITIONS

Tiles supports two methods of configuring *page definitions*: configure a page's definition in a JSP, and configure each page definition in an XML file. The second method gives a cleaner separation of concerns and allows your JSPs to be agnostic to the fact that Tiles is using them.

1   To create page definitions for MyUsers, create a *tiles-config.xml* file in *web/ WEB-INF* and populate it with the XML in Listing 5.13:

Listing 5.13

```
<?xml version="1.0" encoding="UTF-8" ?>
<!DOCTYPE tiles-definitions PUBLIC
    "-//Apache Software Foundation
        //DTD Tiles Configuration 1.1//EN"
    "http://jakarta.apache.org/struts/dtds/tiles-config_1_1.dtd">

<tiles-definitions>
    <!-- base layout definition -->
    <definition name="baseLayout" path="/layouts/baseLayout.jsp">
        <put name="title" value="MyUsers"/>
    </definition>

    <!-- index definition -->
    <definition name="index" extends="baseLayout">
        <put name="title" value="MyUsers ~ Welcome"/>
        <put name="content" value="/index.jsp"/>
    </definition>

    <!-- user list definition -->
    <definition name="userList" extends="baseLayout">
        <put name="title" value="MyUsers ~ User List"/>
```

```
      <put name="content" value="/userList.jsp"/>
   </definition>

   <!-- user form definition -->
   <definition name="userForm" extends="baseLayout">
      <put name="title" value="MyUsers ~ User Details"/>
      <put name="content" value="/userForm.jsp"/>
   </definition>
</tiles-definitions>
```

The above file defines the page titles here instead of in the JSPs.

2   To produce clean HTML in your application, delete the **<title>** elements
     from *userList.jsp* and *userForm.jsp* in the *web* directory. There is no easy way
     to control the title in the JSP as with SiteMesh.

3   Configure Spring so it can resolve URLs to Tiles definitions by adding a
     bean definition. The **UrlFilenameViewController** class is declared in
     the *action-servlet.xml* as follows in Listing 5.14:

Listing 5.14

```
<bean id="filenameController"
   class="org.springframework.web.servlet.mvc
       .UrlFilenameViewController"/>
```

4   In order to render the index page (*/index.html*) of the MyUsers application,
     configure the **urlMapping** bean with an additional mapping (see
     Listing 5.15):

Listing 5.15

```
<prop key="/index.html">filenameController</prop>
```

5   Run **ant remove clean install** to see a similar view to the SiteMesh
     result (see Listing 5.2) when you go to localhost:8080/myusers/users.html.

The problem that you'll experience now is that if you go to localhost:8080/myusers,
it shows the *index.jsp* page with no decoration.

6   Solve this by renaming *index.jsp* to *welcome.jsp* and create a new *index.jsp* file
     with the contents in Listing 5.16:

Listing 5.16

```
<%@ include file="/taglibs.jsp"%>

<tiles:insert definition="index"/>
```

7 Change *tiles-config.xml* to use the *welcome.jsp* for the content page (see Listing 5.17):

Listing 5.17

```
<definition name="index" extends="baseLayout">
    <put name="title" value="MyUsers ~ Welcome"/>
    <put name="content" value="/welcome.jsp"/>
</definition>
```

While the previous solution works, it can be a real pain to create two JSPs to solve problems like this one. Therefore, I recommend using a servlet filter to redirect certain URLs to others. Using this solution, you must configure your application so that the root URL invokes the */index.html* URL. You cannot do this using the **<welcome-file-list>** in *web.xml*, so use Paul Tuckey's **URLRewriteFilter** to make it happen.

NOTE: Paul Tuckey's rewrite filter is modeled after **mod_rewrite** for the Apache HTTP server. It redirects or forwards requested URLs in order to create tidy URLs, do browser detection, or gracefully handle moved content.

The *urlrewrite-1.2.jar* is already in *web/WEB-INF/lib*, so you only need to configure it in *web.xml* and add its configuration file.

8 Open *web.xml* and add the **<filter>** definition in Listing 5.18:

Listing 5.18

```
<filter>
    <filter-name>UrlRewriteFilter</filter-name>
    <filter-class>
        org.tuckey.web.filters.urlrewrite.UrlRewriteFilter
    </filter-class>
</filter>
```

9 Add its mapping (in Listing 5.19):

Listing 5.19

```
<filter-mapping>
    <filter-name>UrlRewriteFilter</filter-name>
    <url-pattern>/*</url-pattern>
    <dispatcher>REQUEST</dispatcher>
    <dispatcher>FORWARD</dispatcher>
</filter-mapping>
```

10 Configure this filter's rules by creating an *urlrewrite.xml* file in the *web/ WEB-INF* directory (see Listing 5.20):

Listing 5.20

```xml
<?xml version="1.0" encoding="utf-8"?>
<!DOCTYPE urlrewrite PUBLIC "-//tuckey.org
    //DTD UrlRewrite 1.0//EN"
    "http://tuckey.org/res/dtd/urlrewrite1.dtd">

<urlrewrite>
    <rule>
        <from>/$</from>
        <to type="forward">index.html</to>
    </rule>
    <rule>
        <from>/index.jsp</from>
        <to type="forward">index.html</to>
    </rule>
</urlrewrite>
```

This configuration will route both localhost:8080/myusers and localhost:8080/ myusers/index.jsp to localhost:8080/myusers/index.html, thereby invoking Spring's **DispatcherServlet**. The **/index.html** mapping will call the **file-nameController** bean, which will use the URL to figure out it needs to render the **index** definition.

Finally, you must fix *index.jsp* so it sets the **underground** content as a request variable for the definition to pick up. With SiteMesh, you were able to set content from the JSP using the **<content>** tag and the **<decorator:getProperty>** tag in your decorator. Tiles does not have similar functionality, but you can mimic this pattern by setting a request attribute with JSTL.

11 Open *web/index.jsp* and change the **<content tag="…">…</content>** to the code in Listing 5.21:

Listing 5.21

```jsp
<c:set var="underground" scope="request">
...
</c:set>
```

This text will be picked up and rendered by the line in Listing 5.22 in *layouts/base-Layout.jsp*:

Listing 5.22

```jsp
<c:out value="${underground}" escapeXml="false"/>
```

NOTE: This solution also works with SiteMesh if you'd prefer not to use its
proprietary `<content>` tags.

The last couple of sections have given you the knowledge you need to configure the
two most popular page layout and decoration engines. They both work with
Spring's MVC framework and they're both relatively easy to configure (especially
now that you have this guide). I recommend SiteMesh, because it is easier to work
with, especially with new applications.

VALIDATING THE SPRING WAY

Currently, Spring does not ship with the Commons Validator setup that the
MyUsers application uses. It does, however, have a fairly simple validation system
you can use, if you don't want to use Commons Validator. All you need to do is
create a class that implements `org.springframework.validation.Validator`,
which has the methods in Listing 5.23:

Listing 5.23

```
/**
 * Return whether or not this object can validate objects
 * of the given class.
 */
boolean supports(Class clazz);

/**
 * Validate an object, which must be of a class for which
 * the supports() method returned true.
 * @param obj  Populated object to validate
 * @param errors  Errors object we're building.
 * May contain errors for this field relating to types.
 */
void validate(Object obj, Errors errors);
```

1   Disable Commons Validator in your *userForm.jsp* file. Simply remove the
    `onsubmit` attribute of the `<form>` tag (see Listing 5.24):

Listing 5.24

```
<form method="post" action="<c:url value="/editUser.html"/>">
```

2   Create a class named `UserValidator` in the *src/org/appfuse/web* directory
    (see Listing 5.25):

Listing 5.25

```
package org.appfuse.web;

// use your IDE to organize imports

public class UserValidator implements Validator {
    private Log log = LogFactory.getLog(UserValidator.class);

    public boolean supports(Class clazz) {
        return clazz.equals(User.class);
    }

    public void validate(Object obj, Errors errors) {
        if (log.isDebugEnabled()) {
            log.debug("entering 'validate' method...");
        }
        User user = (User) obj;

        ValidationUtils.rejectIfEmptyOrWhitespace(errors,
            "lastName", "errors.required", "Value required.");
    }
}
```

In the preceding code, this validator only supports the **User** class, and its **validate()** method will return an error if the **lastName** variable is empty.

3 To configure this validator in *action-servlet.xml*, simply add the bean definition in Listing 5.26:

Listing 5.26

```
<bean id="userValidator" class="org.appfuse.web.UserValidator"/>
```

4 Change the **validator** property of the **userFormController** bean to use **userValidator** instead of **beanValidator** (see Listing 5.27):

Listing 5.27

```
<property name="validator" ref="userValidator"/>
```

5 Run **ant deploy reload** and try to add a new user without a last name. To prove the **UserValidator** is being invoked, check your logs for the debug message when entering the validate method. Using this validation mechanism can be very powerful when you want to do more sophisticated validation (such as comparing properties against database values).

The next section reviews setting up Commons Validator for a Spring application and using it to verify the **lastName** field is not empty. Then it will show you how to use both Commons Validator's declarative validation and the **Validator** interface to create a validation chain.

USING COMMONS VALIDATOR

Chapter 4: Spring's MVC Framework covered using Commons Validator's declarative validation framework in detail; however, because this chapter explores validation, here is a step-by-step overview of what you need to do:

1   Create a *validation.xml* file in *web/WEB-INF* and define your validation rules in it.

2   Download the *Spring-specific validation-rules.xml* file and install it in *web/WEB-INF.* This file is included in the bundle for this chapter.

3   Add **validatorFactory** and **beanValidator** bean definitions to *web/WEB-INF/action-servlet.xml.*

4   Configure your **FormController** bean to use **beanValidator** for its **validator** property.

These steps enable server-side validation, but not client-side validation. The method from *Chapter 4: Spring's MVC Framework* works, but it includes all of the JavaScript validation functions in the page. A better way is to refer to a standalone JavaScript file that the user's browser can cache. The following instructions assume you have no client-side validation configured on your form.

1   Add an **onsubmit** attribute to the **<form>** on which you want to enable validation. (See Listing 5.28.)

Listing 5.28

```
<form method="post" action="<c:url value="/editUser.html"/>"
    onsubmit="return validateUser(this)">
```

2   At the bottom of the form, add the lines of code in Listing 5.29 to write JavaScript function calls for the form's rules and to include the standalone JavaScript file. If you try this in MyUsers, be sure to replace the existing **<html:javascript>** tag.

Listing 5.29

```
<html:javascript formName="user"
    staticJavascript="false" xhtml="true" cdata="false"/>
<script type="text/javascript"
    src="<c:url value="/scripts/validator.jsp"/>"></script>
```

> **3** Create a *validator.jsp* file in *web/scripts* (you must create the *scripts* directory) with the code in Listing 5.30:

Listing 5.30

```
<%@ page language="java" contentType="javascript/x-javascript" %>
<%@ taglib uri="http://www.springmodules.org
    /tags/commons-validator" prefix="html" %>

<html:javascript dynamicJavascript="false"
    staticJavascript="true"/>
```

The most difficult part about using Commons Validator is the setup and configuration process. Once you have that in place, creating the rules is simple. You can even use XDoclet to generate the rules from your POJOs.

XDOCLET

XDoclet is an open source code-generation engine. It enables Attribute-Oriented Programming for Java, so you can add more significance to your code by adding metadata (attributes) to your Java sources. To add this metadata, you use special JavaDoc tags. For more information, please refer to the XDoclet web site at xdoclet.sourceforge.net/xdoclet/resources.html. The metadata attributes that XDoclet uses are also called *annotations*. This concept has received such praise and use that annotations have been added as a feature in J2SE 5.

At the time of this writing, this functionality doesn't exist in an XDoclet release, but it is checked into XDoclet's CVS.

> **1** To generate your validation rules from your POJOs, define a **<webdoclet>** task that uses the **<springvalidationxml>** task. An example is given in Listing 5.31:

Listing 5.31

```
<target name="webdoclet"
    description="Generate web deployment descriptors">
    <taskdef name="webdoclet"
        classname="xdoclet.modules.web.WebDocletTask">
        <classpath>
```

```
            <path refid="xdoclet.classpath"/>
        </classpath>
    </taskdef>
    <webdoclet destdir="${webapp.target}/WEB-INF"
        force="${xdoclet.force}"
        mergedir="metadata/web"
        excludedtags="@version,@author"
        verbose="true">
        <fileset dir="src"/>
        <springvalidationxml/>
    </webdoclet>
</target>
```

2   Add **@spring.validator** tags to your POJO's setters, as follows in
     Listing 5.32:

Listing 5.32

```
/**
 * @spring.validator type="required"
 */
public void setLastName(String lastName) {
    this.lastName = lastName;
}
```

The preceding code will generate the same *validation.xml* file that you are using in
MyUsers, which makes **lastName** a required field. This example demonstrates how
simple XDoclet can make declarative validation. If you'd like more information
about XDoclet, please refer to AppFuse or build XDoclet from CVS.

CHAINING VALIDATORS

The previous two examples set a **validator** property on the **userFormController**. The bean referenced in this property referred to the custom **userValidator** or to Commons Validator's **beanValidator**, which reads its rules from an
XML file. With Spring MVC, you can actually add multiple validators by setting a
validators property as follows in Listing 5.33:

Listing 5.33

```
<property name="validators">
    <list>
        <ref bean="beanValidator"/>
        <ref bean="userValidator"/>
    </list>
</property>
```

This creates a sort of *validation chain* that can do simple validation using Commons Validator and more complex validation with a custom **Validator** implementation.

VALIDATING IN BUSINESS DELEGATES

While validation in the web tier seems to be the most common practice, there is a demand for validation in the business layer as well. Below is a simple example of how to use Spring's validation in your middle tier.

1   In *UserManagerImpl.java*, you can change the **saveUser()** method to the code in Listing 5.34:

Listing 5.34

```
public User saveUser(User user) {
    BindException errors = new BindException(user, "user");
    new UserValidator().validate(user, errors);
    if (errors.hasErrors()) {
        throw new RuntimeException
            ("validation failed!", errors);
    }
    dao.saveUser(user);

    return user;
}
```

2   Write a unit test to verify that the exception is thrown in *UserManagerTest.java*. See Listing 5.35.

Listing 5.35

```
public void testWithValidationErrors() {
    user = new User();
    user.setFirstName("Bill");

    try {
        user = mgr.saveUser(user);
        fail("Validation exception not thrown!");
    } catch (Exception e) {
        log.debug(e.getCause().getMessage());
        assertNotNull(e.getCause());
    }
}
```

3   Run the test using **ant test -Dtestcase=UserManager**; you should see output similar to Figure 5.4.

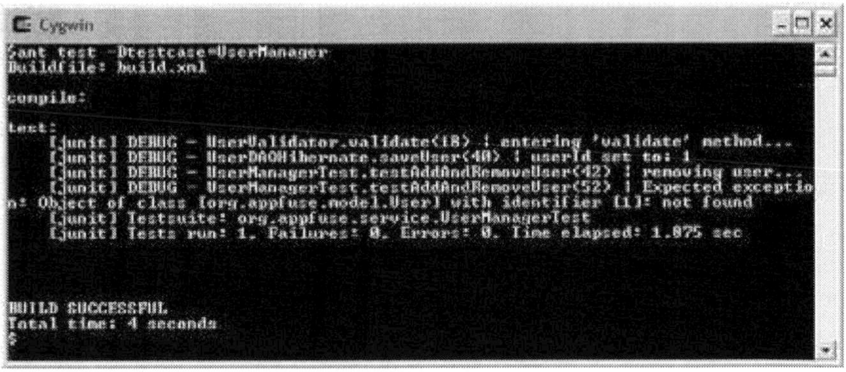

Figure 5.4: Running the `UserManagerTest`

This example has a hard-coded validator, but it is not necessary to hard-code which validator to use. You could add a `setValidator()` method to the `UserManager-Impl` (and its interface), then use dependency injection to set the `validator` property declaratively in your *applicationContext.xml* file. To make this work, you need to declare your validator bean in *applicationContext.xml* or load *action-servlet.xml* in your test. Overall, it's much easier to configure and use validation in the web tier.

SPRING'S FUTURE DECLARATIVE VALIDATION FRAMEWORK

At the time of this writing, Commons Validator is the only declarative validation framework that's been released to support Spring MVC. The `Valang Validator` is part of the Spring Modules project, but it hasn't been released yet. There are plans for declarative validation being part of Spring, but it hasn't been developed yet. Keith Donald, a core developer for Spring, provided a few details about it:

- A simple, consistent interface for defining new validation rules (rule providers simply implement a single `boolean test(argument)` method).

- Support for bean property expressions (for example, `minProperty` must be less than `maxProperty`). The property access strategy will be pluggable and not limited to Java beans (for example, allowing map-backed storage, or buffered `form` objects on the rich client side of the house).

- Support for complex nested expressions (and/or/not), and all relational operators ($>$, $>=$, $<$, $<=$, $!=$, $==$).

- Support for applying different sets of rules based on context or use case.

- A reporting subsystem capable of iterating over rule structures, performing validation, and capturing/generating error message results. This allows you to assemble complex rules on-the-fly without having to hard code a lot of static messages; the reporter is capable of generating rule messages from the underlying structures automatically.

- Report field typing hints (the rules associated with a field to let the user know what they're expected to type).

- Integration with Spring Rich Client Platform (RCP) and Spring MVC environments.

From this list, you can see that validation in Spring has a very bright future.

EXCEPTION HANDLING IN CONTROLLERS

Exception handling is something that every web application should have. The Servlet API provides a simple mechanism for mapping particular exceptions and error codes to specific views. In Equinox, for example, the following clause in its *web.xml* file says that "if a page is not found" go to the *404.jsp* page (see Listing 5.36):

Listing 5.36

```
<error-page>
    <error-code>404</error-code>
    <location>/404.jsp</location>
</error-page>
```

The XML in Listing 5.37 says that any "500: Internal Server Errors" should go to *error.jsp*. If you're seeing a lot of 500 errors when developing your application, you need better exception handling.

Listing 5.37

```
<error-page>
    <error-code>500</error-code>
    <location>/error.jsp</location>
</error-page>
```

In addition to *web.xml* error-pages, you should tell your JSP pages to go to an error page when they encounter an exception. The MyUsers application does this in *web/ taglibs.jsp*, where you specify **errorPage="/error.jsp"**. In *web.xml*, you can additionally declare certain exceptions go to certain pages using the **<exceptiontype>** mapping. See Listing 5.38.

Listing 5.38

```
<error-page>
    <exception-type>
        org.appfuse.service.UserNotFound
    </exception-type>
    <location>/userNotFound.html</location>
</error-page>
```

WARNING: SiteMesh has a bug in Tomcat; it will not decorate `<error-page>` mappings in your *web.xml* file. If you want to map exceptions in *web.xml*, write these pages so they can stand alone without being decorated.

While the Servlet API provides an easy way to handle exceptions, it's difficult to extract information from the exception and perform logic on that information. It's difficult to put try/catch statements in controllers because they take up a fair amount of lines. It's so much cleaner to call a business delegate's method. An easy way to avoid try/catching exceptions in your controllers is by adding **throws Exception** to the **onSubmit()** method in a **FormController**. In frameworks such as Struts, you can do this on your actions and then declaratively map exceptions to views. In other words, you can specify (in XML) that when *X* exception is thrown, the user should be forwarded to an action, a Tiles' definition, or a JSP.

The ability to forward to a particular view for a specific exception is also possible with Spring. The easy way to do this is to define a **SimpleMappingExceptionResolver** in your *action-servlet.xml* file and specify which exceptions go to which view name.

   1   Add the definition in Listing 5.39 in *web/WEB-INF/action-servlet.xml*.

Listing 5.39

```
<bean id="exceptionResolver"
    class="org.springframework.web.servlet.handler
        .SimpleMappingExceptionResolver">
    <property name="exceptionMappings">
        <props>
            <prop key="org.springframework.dao
                .DataAccessException">
                dataAccessFailure
            </prop>
        </props>
    </property>
</bean>
```

In the preceding code, **dataAccessFailure** refers to the name of a view that the **viewResolver** bean can determine. To Tiles users, this might refer to a definition in *tiles-config.xml*.

2   To test that the preceding mapping works, modify the **UserDAOTest** (in *test/org/appfuse/dao*). Near the bottom of the **testAddAndRemoveUser()** method is the line in Listing 5.40:

Listing 5.40

```
assertNull(dao.getUser(user.getId()));
```

3   Replace this line with the code in Listing 5.41 to ensure that an exception is thrown when a user isn't found:

Listing 5.41

```
try {
    user = dao.getUser(user.getId());
    fail("User found in database");
} catch (DataAccessException dae) {
    log.debug("Expected exception: " + dae.getMessage());
    assertNotNull(dae);
}
```

4   Modify the **getUser()** method in **UserDAOHibernate** (in *src/org/ appfuse/dao*) to throw an exception when a user is not found (see Listing 5.42):

Listing 5.42

```
public User getUser(Long id) {
    User user =
        (User) getHibernateTemplate().get(User.class, id);
    if (user == null) {
        throw new ObjectRetrievalFailureException
            (User.class, id);
    }
    return user;
}
```

5   Verify that everything is working as planned by running **ant test -Dtestcase=UserDAO.**

6   Create a *dataAccessFailure.jsp* file in the *web* folder. See Listing 5.43.

Listing 5.43

```jsp
<%@ include file="/taglibs.jsp" %>

<h3>Data Access Failure</h3>
<p>
    <c:out value="${requestScope.exception.message}"/>
</p>

<!--
<%
Exception ex = (Exception) request.getAttribute("exception");
ex.printStackTrace(new java.io.PrintWriter(out));
%>
-->

<a href="<c:url value='/'/>">&#171; Home</a>
```

If you're using the MyUsers project with SiteMesh, this is all you need to do. Tiles users must add a step:

7   Add a **dataAccessFailure** definition in *tiles-config.xml* as in Listing 5.44.

Listing 5.44

```xml
<definition name="dataAccessFailure" extends="baseLayout">
    <put name="title" value="Data Access Failure"/>
    <put name="content" value="/dataAccessFailure.jsp"/>
</definition>
```

TIP: You can mix and match view classes, such as using JSTL for one view and Tiles for the next. You can do this by using a **ResourceBundleViewResolver** for the **viewResolver** and specifying a properties file with the view's names and paths. You can see an example of this in the Petclinic sample application that ships with Spring. However, this won't help you mix SiteMesh and Tiles.

---

8   Run **ant deploy reload** and open localhost:8080/myusers/ editUser.html?id=100; you should see an error page stating that this user doesn't exist.

Figure 5.5: Handling a `DataAccessException`

If you need more robust functionality than the `SimpleMappingExceptionRe-solver` gives you, look at implementing the `HandlerExceptionResolver` for a more customized `ExceptionResolver`.

UPLOADING FILES

Every so often, you might run into a requirement to upload files in your web application. The good news is that Spring MVC provides support for uploading files. Better yet, you get a choice of file upload implementations: *Commons FileUpload* or *COS FileUpload*.

NOTE: If you're using a Servlet 2.2 container, you will not be able to use Spring's built-in file upload support. However, Commons FileUpload has excellent support for doing file uploads with a 2.2 container.

---

1   Define a bean with an ID of `multipartResolver` in *web/WEB-INF/action-servlet.xml*. See Listing 5.45.

Listing 5.45

```
<bean id="multipartResolver"
    class="org.springframework.web.multipart.commons
        .CommonsMultipartResolver"/>
```

This bean provides *multipart* support to the `DispatcherServlet`. A *multipart* request is an `HttpServletRequest` that contains both binary and text data. You indicate that you want a form to submit a multipart request by adding an `enctype="multipart/form-data"` attribute to an HTML `<form>`. When Spring detects a multipart request, it simply wraps the current request with its `Multi-`

partHttpServletRequest, which allows you to access normal **HttpServletRequest** methods, as well as a few new ones (like **getFile(String name)**).

2   To implement a file upload feature in MyUsers, add the preceding bean definition, as well as two classes: a **FileUpload** command class and a **SimpleFormController** to handle the uploading process. Create the command class for this example in *src/org/appfuse/web* with the contents in Listing 5.46:

Listing 5.46

```
package org.appfuse.web;

public class FileUpload {
    private byte[] file;

    public void setFile(byte[] file) {
        this.file = file;
    }

    public byte[] getFile() {
        return file;
    }
}
```

3   In the same directory, create a **FileUploadController** class that extends **SimpleFormController**. In the code in Listing 5.47, the most important part is the **initBinder()** method, which registers a **PropertyEditor** to grab the uploaded file's bytes. Without this, the upload process will fail.

Listing 5.47

```
package org.appfuse.web;

// use your IDE to organize imports

public class FileUploadController extends SimpleFormController {
    private static Log
        log = LogFactory.getLog(FileUploadController.class);

    public FileUploadController() {
        super();
        setCommandClass(FileUpload.class);
    }

    protected void initBinder(HttpServletRequest request,
                              ServletRequestDataBinder binder)
```

```
    throws ServletException {
        binder.registerCustomEditor(byte[].class,
                                new ByteArrayMultipart
                                    FileEditor());
    }

    protected ModelAndView onSubmit(HttpServletRequest request,
                                HttpServletResponse response,
                                Object command,
                                BindException errors)
    throws ServletException, IOException {

        FileUpload bean = (FileUpload) command;
        byte[] bytes = bean.getFile();

        // cast to multipart file so we can get additional
            information
        MultipartHttpServletRequest multipartRequest =
            (MultipartHttpServletRequest) request;
        CommonsMultipartFile file =
            (CommonsMultipartFile)
                multipartRequest.getFile("file");

        String uploadDir =
            getServletContext().getRealPath("/upload/");

        // Create the directory if it doesn't exist
        File dirPath = new File(uploadDir);

        if (!dirPath.exists()) {
            dirPath.mkdirs();
        }

        String sep = System.getProperty("file.separator");

        if (log.isDebugEnabled()) {
            log.debug("uploading to: " + uploadDir + sep +
                    file.getOriginalFilename());
        }

        File uploadedFile = new File(uploadDir + sep +
                                    file.getOriginalFilename());
        FileCopyUtils.copy(bytes, uploadedFile);

        // set success message
        request.getSession().setAttribute("message", "Upload
completed.");

        String url = request.getContextPath() + "/upload/" +
                    file.getOriginalFilename();
```

```
        Map model = new HashMap();
        model.put("filename", file.getOriginalFilename());
        model.put("url", url);

        return new ModelAndView(getSuccessView(), "model", model);
    }
}
```

4   Put the controller's bean definition in *action-servlet.xml* (see Listing 5.48)

Listing 5.48

```xml
<bean id="fileUploadController"
    class="org.appfuse.web.FileUploadController">
    <property name="commandClass">
        <value>org.appfuse.web.FileUpload</value>
    </property>
    <property name="formView"><value>fileUpload</value>
        </property>
    <property name="successView">
        <value>fileUpload</value>
    </property>
</bean>
```

5   Define the URL to access this controller by adding another **<prop>** to the **urlMapping** bean. See Listing 5.49.

Listing 5.49

```xml
<prop key="/fileUpload.html">fileUploadController</prop>
```

6   Create *web/fileUpload.jsp* with an upload form and a link to display an uploaded file. See Listing 5.50.

Listing 5.50

```jsp
<%@ include file="/taglibs.jsp"%>

<h3>File Upload</h3>

<c:if test="${not empty model.filename}">
<p style="font-weight: bold">
    Uploaded file (click to view):
        <a href="${model.url}">${model.filename}</a>
</p>
</c:if>

<p>Select a file to upload:</p>
```

```
<form method="post" action="fileUpload.html"
    enctype="multipart/form-data">
    <input type="file" name="file"/><br/>
    <input type="submit" value="Upload" class="button"
        style="margin-top: 5px"/>
</form>
```

SiteMesh users have added what they need at this point. Tiles users, add the following step.

7   Add a definition for the **fileUpload** view. See Listing 5.51.

Listing 5.51

```
<definition name="fileUpload" extends="baseLayout">
    <put name="title" value="My Users ~ File Upload"/>
    <put name="content" value="/fileUpload.jsp"/>
</definition>
```

8   To verify success, open your browser to localhost:8080/myusers/ fileUpload.html. Your browser window should resemble the view in Figure 5.6.

Figure 5.6: Selecting a file to upload

After uploading a file, you should see a screen similar to Figure 5.7.

WARNING: Some files (such as **.html*) will not allow viewing by clicking on the file name, so I recommend choosing *LICENSE.txt* in the *myusers* directory.

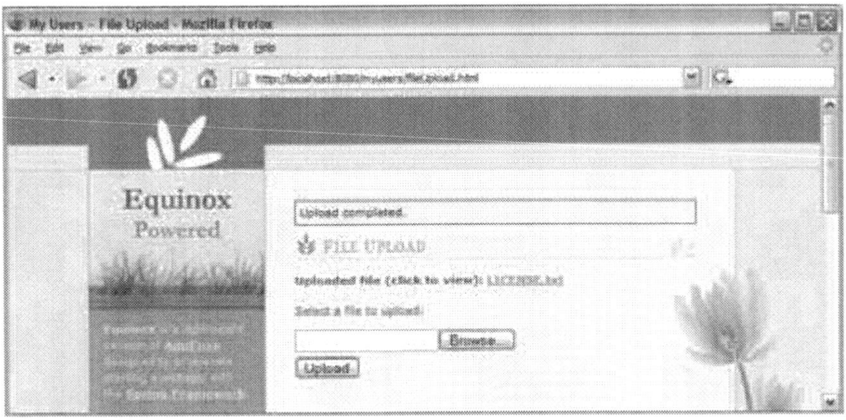

Figure 5.7: Successful file upload

Congratulations! Now you know how to perform a file upload with Spring. *Chapter 9: Testing Spring Applications* covers unit-testing the **FileUploadController**.

INTERCEPTING THE REQUEST

Many MVC frameworks have the ability to specify interceptors for controllers. Interceptors are classes that intercept the request and perform some sort of logic for controlling flow, setting request attributes, and so forth. They are similar to servlet filters, the major difference being that filters are configured in *web.xml* and interceptors are configured in a framework configuration file.

The **HandlerInterceptor** is an interface that contains methods for intercepting the executing of a handler before execution (**preHandle**), after execution (**postHandle**), and after rendering the view (**afterCompletion**). A couple of useful built-in Spring interceptors are the **OpenSessionInViewInterceptor** and the **UserRoleAuthorizationInterceptor**. The first is Hibernate-specific, while the second prevents certain roles from accessing certain URLs.

TIP: The **OpenSessionInViewInterceptor** has a sister filter (**OpenSession-InViewFilter**) with the same functionality. Both are used for lazy-loading Hibernate-managed objects when the view renders. The filter is MVC-framework agnostic.

The following example configures and uses the **UserRoleAuthorizationInterceptor**. Configure the MyUsers application to protect a particular URL pattern. Lock down the entire application so only users with a **tomcat** role can access it and then configure the interceptor to allow only users with a **manager** role to upload files.

1   Add the code in Listing 5.52 to the very bottom of the *web.xml* file in *web/WEB-INF*:

Listing 5.52

```
<security-constraint>
    <web-resource-collection>
        <url-pattern>/*</url-pattern>
    </web-resource-collection>

    <auth-constraint>
        <role-name>tomcat</role-name>
        <role-name>manager</role-name>
    </auth-constraint>
</security-constraint>

<login-config>
    <auth-method>BASIC</auth-method>
    <realm-name>My Users</realm-name>
</login-config>

<security-role>
    <role-name>tomcat</role-name>
</security-role>

<security-role>
    <role-name>manager</role-name>
</security-role>
```

2   Run **ant deploy reload** and go to localhost:8080/myusers. You will be prompted to log in. Use the user name **tomcat** and password **tomcat** to log in with the **tomcat** role, and use **admin/admin** to log in with the **manager** role. These users and roles are configured in Tomcat's *conf/tomcat-users.xml* file (in the *$CATALINA_HOME* directory).

3   To add an interceptor to only allow managers to upload files, define **UserRoleAuthorizationInterceptor** as a bean in *web/WEB-INF/action-servlet.xml* (see Listing 5.53)

Listing 5.53

```
<bean id="managersOnly"
    class="org.springframework.web.servlet.handler
        .UserRoleAuthorizationInterceptor">
    <property name="authorizedRoles" value="manager"/>
</bean>
```

4   Add a new **SimpleUrlHandlerMapping** that uses this interceptor on the
    /fileUpload.html mapping. See Listing 5.54.

Listing 5.54

```
<bean id="managerMappings"
    class="org.springframework.web.servlet.handler
        .SimpleUrlHandlerMapping">
    <property name="interceptors">
        <list>
            <ref bean="managersOnly"/>
        </list>
    </property>
    <property name="mappings">
        <props>
            <prop key="/fileUpload.html">
                fileUploadController
            </prop>
        </props>
    </property>
</bean>
```

5   Close your browser (to log out) and reopen to localhost:8080/myusers/
    fileUpload.html. The login prompt displays. If you log in as **tomcat**/
    tomcat, you will see a 403 error page, which means that access is denied.

TIP: You can easily customize this page by specifying a 403 **<error-page>** in
web.xml.

6   Log in again with **admin**/**admin**, but remember to close your browser to
    erase your previous login credentials.

This is just a simple example of using an interceptor to control access to a URL.
You could easily use this same configuration with a different class and URL
mapping to do other things (for example, to make sure certain attributes are always
in the request).

SENDING EMAIL

Email is an excellent notification system; it also can act as a rudimentary workflow
system. Spring makes sending email messages easy, and it hides the complexity of
the underlying mail system. The main interface of Spring's mail support is called
MailSender. It also has a **SimpleMailMessage** class that encapsulates common
attributes of a message (**from**, **to**, **subject**, **message**). If you want to send email

messages with attachments, you can use the `MimeMessagePreparator` to create and send messages.

Create a simple example in the `FileUploadController` to send an email message when the file upload has completed. In *Chapter 10: AOP*, you will extract this logic out into a `NotificationAdvice` class.

1   Add a `mailSender` bean to *action-servlet.xml*. The `host` property should match an SMTP server that does not require authentication. If your host requires authentication, you can add `username` and `password` properties. See Listing 5.55.

Listing 5.55

```
<bean id="mailSender"
    class="org.springframework.mail.javamail
        .JavaMailSenderImpl">
    <property name="host" value="localhost"/>
</bean>
```

NOTE: Using the `JavaMailSenderImpl` class requires that you include *activation.jar* and *mail.jar* in your classpath. These files are included in the **Chapter 5** download bundle.

2   Add a property and setter for `MailSender` in the `FileUploadController` class. At the same time, add a property/setter combination for a `SimpleMailMessage`. Setting the `SimpleMail-Message` with dependency injection allows you to configure a default `from` and `subject` in *action-servlet.xml*. See Listing 5.56.

Listing 5.56

```
private MailSender mailSender;
private SimpleMailMessage message;

public void setMailSender(MailSender mailSender) {
    this.mailSender = mailSender;
}

public void setMessage(SimpleMailMessage message) {
    this.message = message;
}
```

3   To specify the defaults values for an email message, add the XML in Listing 5.57 to *action-servlet.xml*.

Listing 5.57

```
<bean id="mailMessage"
    class="org.springframework.mail.SimpleMailMessage">
    <property name="from">
        <!-- The <value> and CDATA below
             must be on the same line -->
        <value><![CDATA[Uploader
            <springlive@sourcebeat.com>]]></value>
    </property>
    <property name="subject">
        <value>File finished uploading</value>
    </property>
</bean>
```

4   Modify the **fileUploadController** bean definition to inject the
     mailSender and **message** properties. See Listing 5.58.

Listing 5.58

```
<bean id="fileUploadController"
    class="org.appfuse.web.FileUploadController">
    <property name="formView" value="fileUpload"/>
    <property name="successView" value="fileUpload"/>
    <property name="mailSender" ref="mailSender"/>
    <property name="message" ref="mailMessage"/>
</bean>
```

5   Add the code in Listing 5.59 to the end of the **onSubmit()** method in
     FileUploadController (before returning the **ModelAndView**):

Listing 5.59

```
// Notify user that file has finished uploading
SimpleMailMessage
    msg = new SimpleMailMessage(this.message);
msg.setTo("matt@raibledesigns.com");
msg.setText("File \"" + file.getOriginalFilename() +
            "\" has finished uploading.");
try {
    mailSender.send(msg);
} catch (MailException ex) {
    log.error(ex.getMessage());
}
```

TIP: Be sure to change the email address for **msg.setTo()** or you'll just be sending
the email to me!

This example simply logs exceptions because it's not critical that this message be sent. If notification email messages are critical in your application, handle the exception with a `SimpleMappingExceptionResolver`.

6   To test the previous configuration (you must have access to an SMTP server), run **ant deploy reload**, go to localhost:8080/myusers/ fileUpload.html, and log in as **admin/admin**. Then upload a file and wait for the email message. You should see a result similar to Figure 5.8.

Figure 5.8: File finished uploading an email message

> **TIP:** You can also configure the `mailSession` bean to use a `MailSession` object from JNDI. You can learn more about this on TheServerSide.com, as well as how to use Velocity templates in the article titled *"Sending Velocity-based Email with Spring."*

SUMMARY

This chapter covered several advanced Spring MVC topics. You learned how to configure and use the two most popular page decoration frameworks: SiteMesh and Tiles. Validation is an essential part of web application, and you saw how to configure Commons Validator, as well as how to implement a native Spring validator. Exception handling is important too, and you should now have a grasp of how to throw and handle exceptions. Uploading files is easy once you have an example, which you now have from this chapter. Interceptors are similar to servlet filters, but Spring has some built-in ones that can be quite useful, like the **User-RoleAuthorizationInterceptor**. Finally, you saw how using email as a notification mechanism is much easier by using Spring's JavaMail support. *Chapter 6: View Options* explores the different views that Spring supports, including Velocity, FreeMarker, XML/XSL, Excel, and PDF.

VIEW OPTIONS

Using Spring with JSP, Velocity, FreeMarker, XSLT, PDF, and Excel

This chapter covers the view options in Spring's MVC architecture. At the time of this writing, the options are JSP, Velocity, FreeMarker, XSLT, PDF, and Excel. This chapter is a reference for configuring all Spring-supported views. It also contains a brief overview of how each view works and compares constructing a page in MyUsers with each option. Additionally, it focuses on internationalization for each view option.

OVERVIEW

In J2EE applications, JSPs have become the *de facto* standard for constructing views because they're the only page-templating option provided by the J2EE 1.4 specification. However, other options are quickly gaining recognition. Velocity and FreeMarker are templating technologies that use syntax similar to JSP 2.0. XML and XSL can be helpful when pulling XML data and transform it, or to serve up different views (via XSL) on the fly. XMLC is similar to the templating technologies, except its syntax is plain HTML and it uses the **id** attribute to locate and replace dynamic text. Finally, outputting data as PDF and Excel formats is great for reporting and producing portable documents. In this chapter, you will learn how to use each of these technologies with Spring's MVC framework. Before learning how to configure the different views, it's important to understand how Spring determines views.

VIEWS AND VIEWRESOLVERS

Spring ships with a number of **ViewResolvers**, which allow you to de-couple your controllers from your view. In your controller, you simply specify a logical name for a view and Spring resolves that name to a specific view type. The **View** interface prepares the request and hands it over to the view technology you have configured.

In its loose-coupling spirit, Spring makes it easy to configure your view choice in one of your XML context files.

In *Chapter 4: Spring's MVC Framework*, you saw how controllers return a **ModelAndView**. This object contains the name of a view that the specified **ViewResolver** uses to determine what to show to the user. Throughout this chapter, you will learn how each **ViewResolver** works. Table lists the **ViewResolvers** currently available in Spring.

Table 6.1: Spring **ViewResolvers**

ViewResolver	Description	Useful For
AbstractCaching- ViewResolver	This abstract **ViewResolver** caches views. Lots of views need preparation before you can use them; extending from this view resolver enables caching of views.	Extending a view to implement caching in a custom resolver
ResourceBundle- ViewResolver	This implementation of **ViewResolver** uses bean definitions from a **ResourceBundle**, specified by the bundle basename. The bundle is typically defined in a properties file located in the classpath.	Mixing different views, such as JSP and Velocity
UrlBased- ViewResolver	This simple implementation of **ViewResolver** allows for direct resolution of symbolic view names to URLs without an explicit mapping definition. This is appropriate if your symbolic names match the names of your view resources in a straightforward manner without the need for arbitrary mappings.	Resolving symbolic view names to URLs, without explicit mapping definition
InternalResource- ViewResolver	This convenient subclass of **UrlBasedViewResolver** supports **InternalResourceView** (such as servlets and JSPs), and subclasses like **JstlView** and **TilesView**. You can specify the view class for all views generated by this resolver via **setViewClass**.	Supporting JSPs and Tiles

Table 6.1: Spring `ViewResolvers`

ViewResolver	Description	Useful For
Velocity- ViewResolver	This convenient subclass of `AbstractTemplateViewResolver` supports `VelocityView` (that is, Velocity templates) and custom subclasses.	Supporting Velocity Views
FreeMarker- ViewResolver	This convenient subclass of `AbstractTemplateViewResolver` supports `FreeMarkerView` (that is, FreeMarker templates) and custom subclasses of it.	Supporting FreeMarker Views

In most cases, you won't need to choose which `ViewResolver` to use; you will simply use the one that your view technology requires. The exception is the `ResourceBundleViewResolver`, which allows you to choose different view classes for each view name. You will learn how to configure and use each Spring-supported view technology before using this resolver.

Each view technology section will show you how to configure the view resolver and how to implement pages for that technology. The best way to learn is to follow along with the exercises in this chapter. To do this, download the **MyUsers Chapter 6** bundle from sourcebeat.com/downloads. This project tree contains all the JARs you will use in this chapter. You can also use the application you've been developing in previous chapters. If you go this route, download the **Chapter 6** JARs from sourcebeat.com/downloads.

TIP: If you choose to use your existing work, you might want to remove the security you added to demonstrate *interceptors*. This will allow you to test the view without logging in each time.

Before getting into view options, write a unit test to verify the basic functionality of listing, adding, saving, and deleting a user.

TESTING THE VIEW WITH JWEBUNIT

jWebUnit is an open source project hosted on SourceForge. It offers a simple API on top of **HttpUnit** for testing web applications.

1   If you downloaded the **Chapter 6** bundle or the **Chapter 6** JARs, you don't need to add JARs to your application. Otherwise, download jWebUnit version 1.2 and put the following JARs in *web/WEB-INF/lib*:

- *jwebunit-1.2.jar*
- *httpunit-1.5.4.jar*
- *Tidy.jar*

2   If you're developing with Eclipse or IDEA, modify your project's classpath to include these JARs. For Eclipse 3.0, this is at Project /Properties/Project Build Path/Libraries Tab. In IDEA 4.5, this is at File /Settings/Project Settings:Paths/Libraries Tab.

TIP: Instructions are available for building and testing the MyUsers application in Eclipse and IDEA.

---

3   Create a test by creating a new **UserWebTest.java** class in *test/org /appfuse/web* that extends **WebTestCase** by using the code in Listing 6.1:

Listing 6.1

```
package org.appfuse.web;

// use your IDE to organize imports

public class UserWebTest extends WebTestCase {

    public UserWebTest(String name) {
        super(name);
        getTestContext().setBaseUrl
            ("http://localhost:8080/myusers");
    }

    public void testWelcomePage() {
        beginAt("/");
        assertTitleEquals("MyUsers ~ Welcome");
    }

    public void testAddUser() {
        beginAt("/editUser.html");
        assertTitleEquals("MyUsers ~ User Details");
        setFormElement("id", "");
        setFormElement("firstName", "Spring");
        setFormElement("lastName", "User");
        submit("save");
        assertTextPresent("saved successfully");
    }
}
```

```
public void testListUsers() {
    beginAt("/users.html");

    // check that table is present
    assertTablePresent("userList");

    //check that a set of strings are present
        somewhere in table
    assertTextInTable("userList",
            new String[] {"Spring", "User"});
}

public void testEditUser() {
    beginAt("/editUser.html?id=" + getInsertedUserId());
    assertFormElementEquals("firstName", "Spring");
    submit("save");
    assertTitleEquals("MyUsers ~ User List");
}

public void testDeleteUser() {
    beginAt("/editUser.html?id=" + getInsertedUserId());
    assertTitleEquals("MyUsers ~ User Details");
    submit("delete");
    assertTitleEquals("MyUsers ~ User List");
}

/**
 * Convenience method to get the id of the inserted user
 * Assumes last user in table is "Spring User"
 */
protected String getInsertedUserId() {
    beginAt("/users.html");
    assertTablePresent("userList");
    assertTextInTable("userList", "Spring");
    String[][] sparseTableCellValues =
            getDialog()
                .getSparseTableBySummaryOrId("userList");
    return sparseTableCellValues
        [sparseTableCellValues.length-1][0];
}
}
```

4   In order for jWebUnit to work, modify a bit of the HTML in the existing
    JSPs. The **testListUsers()** method contains the line in Listing 6.2:

Listing 6.2

```
assertTablePresent("userList");
```

This line verifies that a `<table>` is present in the rendered page. In order for this to work, the table must have an `id` attribute with a value of `userList`.

5   Open *web/userList.jsp* and add this attribute so your HTML looks like Listing 6.3:

Listing 6.3

```
<table class="list" id="userList">
```

6   Since jWebUnit performs in-container testing (it expects a server to be running), you must run **ant clean deploy** and start Tomcat (**ant deploy reload** if Tomcat is already running).

7   Run this test from your IDE or from the command line using **ant test -Dtestcase=UserWeb**.

WARNING: You may have to delete the database if this test doesn't pass on your first attempt (stop Tomcat and delete **db** in your working directory).

---

8   To separate the out-of-container and in-container tests in the *build.xml* file, exclude classes with "WebTest" in their name from being executed in the **test** target. Locate this target in the *build.xml* file and add the line in Listing 6.4:

Listing 6.4

```
<batchtest todir="${test.dir}/data" unless="testcase">
    <fileset dir="${test.dir}/classes">
        <include name="**/*Test.class*"/>
        <exclude name="**/*WebTest.class"/>
    </fileset>
</batchtest>
```

9   Add a new **test-web** target right after the existing **test** target, as in Listing 6.5.

Listing 6.5

```
<target name="test-web" depends="compile"
    description="Runs tests that required a running server">
    <property name="testcase" value="WebTest"/>
    <antcall target="test"/>
</target>
```

10   Run all your out-of-container tests using **ant test** and all the in-container tests using **ant test-web**.

JSP

The MyUsers sample application you've been developing has been using JSP 2.0. This version of JSP is much simpler than previous versions in that you can use its EL to retrieve values for display. This is not only useful for eliminating scriptlets, but its syntax is similar to that used in Velocity and FreeMarker. JSF (the J2EE standard web application framework) uses JSPs out of the box. Many folks believe that JSF will quickly become the dominant way of writing Java-based web application, so the information below is applicable for JSF applications as well.

VIEWRESOLVER CONFIGURATION

In order to use JSP and the JSTL in particular, you must define an **InternalResourceViewResolver** in *web/WEB-INF/action-servlet.xml*. See Listing 6.6.

Listing 6.6

```
<bean id="viewResolver"
    class="org.springframework.web.servlet.view
        .InternalResourceViewResolver">
    <property name="requestContextAttribute" value="rc"/>
    <property name="viewClass"
        value="org.springframework.web.servlet.view.JstlView"/>
    <property name="prefix" value="/"/>
    <property name="suffix" value=".jsp"/>
</bean>
```

In the above bean definition, the **requestContextAttribute** exposes Spring's **RequestContext** object as the variable **rc**. If you're using JSPs, it's unlikely that you'll need to use this variable, but you can use it to grab your application's **contextPath** (that is, */myusers*) using **${rc.contextPath}**. This object is necessary for views that do not have access to the servlet request (for example, Velocity and FreeMarker templates). The **prefix** and **suffix** values are convenient ways to make the view name a friendly name rather than a hard-coded path.

As an example, move the JSPs you created from the *web* directory to *web/WEB-INF/jsp* (you'll need to create the *jsp* directory). Figure 6.1 shows what your project tree should look like at this point. Leave the following JSPs in the *web* directory because they're either error pages or used in the SiteMesh decorator: *404.jsp, error.jsp, index.jsp, messages.jsp* and *taglibs.jsp*.

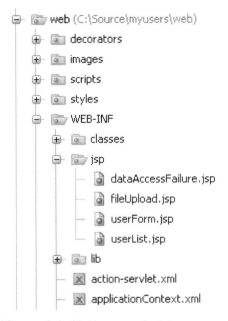

Figure 6.1: MyUsers project tree

To configure Spring to recognize the new location of your JSPs, change the **prefix** of the **viewResolver** bean to */WEB-INF/jsp/*. See Listing 6.7.

Listing 6.7

```
<property name="prefix" value="/WEB-INF/jsp/"/>
```

To test this, make sure Tomcat is running and execute **ant remove**. Executing the **remove** target will delete the application from Tomcat, ensuring that your JSPs aren't left in the root directory of your application. Then type **ant deploy** and wait for Tomcat to reinstall your application. Finally, run **ant test-web**.

JSTL

In the previous **viewResolver** bean definition, a **viewClass** property is set. See Listing 6.8.

Listing 6.8

```
<property name="viewClass"
    value="org.springframework.web.servlet.view.JstlView"/>
```

The value of the property refers to the view class Spring uses to determine the viewable page. In this case, it's using **JstlView**. This class is helpful because it exposes Spring's local and message bundle to JSTL's formatting and message tags. If you're using JSPs, this is the view class you'll want to use.

THE DISPLAY TAG

If you're using JSP and displaying lists of data, use the display tag library. The display tag is a JSP tag that provides paging and sorting tables of data. To show you its functionality, implement it in the MyUsers application. The JAR file for version 1.0 (RC1) is included in the download for this chapter, as well as any CSS and images. You can also download it from SourceForge.

   1   Change the *userList.jsp* file in *web/WEB-INF/jsp* to have the contents in Listing 6.9:

Listing 6.9

```
<%@ include file="/taglibs.jsp"%>
<%@ taglib uri="http://displaytag.sf.net" prefix="display" %>

<head>
    <title>MyUsers ~ User List</title>
    <link href="styles/displaytag.css"
        type="text/css" rel="stylesheet"/>
</head>

<button onclick="location.href='editUser.html'">Add User</button>

<display:table name="${users}"
    class="list" requestURI="" id="userList"
    export="true">
    <display:column property="id"
        sort="true" href="editUser.html"
        paramId="id" paramProperty="id" titleKey="user.id"/>
    <display:column property="firstName" sort="true"
        titleKey="user.firstName"/>
    <display:column property="lastName" sort="true"
        titleKey="user.lastName"/>
    <display:setProperty name="basic.empty.showtable"
        value="true"/>
</display:table>
```

   2   Run **ant deploy reload** and go to localhost:8080/myusers/users.html in your browser. You should see a table like the one in Figure 6.2. The table is sorted by first name.

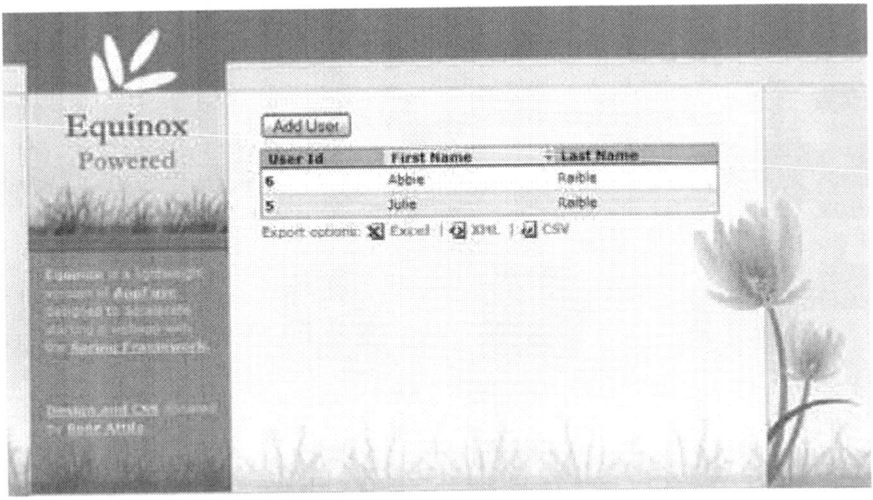

Figure 6.2: The display tag, sorted by first name

Use the **Excel, XML,** and **CSV** links at the bottom of the table to export the table to the indicated format. This tag library also supports exporting to PDF, but it's disabled by default. To enable it, create a *displaytag.properties* file in *web/WEB-INF/classes* and add the text in Listing 6.10.

Listing 6.10

```
export.pdf=true
```

After making this change, run **ant deploy reload** to see a PDF export option. This feature requires an iText JAR in your classpath, which is already in the download for this chapter. For further configuration options available in this file, see displaytag.sourceforge.net/configuration.html.

TIP: Use this tag library in your next demo. Most people will be impressed by the ability to sort columns in a web application.

TILES

Tiles is a mature page decoration framework that *Chapter 5: Advanced Spring MVC* covered. The **viewResolver** bean's configuration for Tiles is similar to JSTL; simply set the **viewClass** property to use **TilesView** or **TilesJstlView**. The JSTL version gives you all the features of **TilesView**, and it gives you access to JSTL's formatting tags in your pages. See Listing 6.11.

Listing 6.11

```
<property name="viewClass"
    value="org.springframework.web.servlet.view.tiles
        .TilesJstlView"/>
```

To use Tiles, you must set up a bean in *web/WEB-INF/action-servlet.xml* to read your Tiles configuration file. The easiest way to do this is to use Spring's `TilesConfigurer` class and specify your definition files. See Listing 6.12.

Listing 6.12

```
<bean id="tilesConfigurer"
    class="org.springframework.web.servlet.view.tiles
        .TilesConfigurer">
    <property name="factoryClass"
        value="org.apache.struts.tiles.xmlDefinition
            .I18nFactorySet"/>
    <property name="definitions">
        <list>
            <value>/WEB-INF/tiles-config.xml</value>
        </list>
    </property>
</bean>
```

Using JSPs to code your view is a common way to develop J2EE applications. However, it's not the only way. You can use other template frameworks like Velocity or FreeMarker, both of which are lightweight and fast. Better yet, Spring makes them *very* easy to use and eliminates the hard part of using them: setup and configuration.

VELOCITY

Velocity is an open source project hosted by Apache at jakarta.apache.org/velocity. Its primary use is generating dynamic web pages for web browsers. However, since it is a templating technology, you can use it wherever you need templates (for example, sending HTML-based email messages). Velocity runs the same in any J2EE container, giving it an advantage over JSPs, which can have quirky behavior and performance issues from one container to the next. Velocity has a templating language called Velocity Template Language (VTL) that uses syntax similar to JSP 2.0's EL. For example, to print out the value of a `lastName` property on a user object, you would use `${user.lastName}` in JSP 2.0. In Velocity, the syntax doesn't have to change at all: `${user.lastName}`. This is known as *formal reference notation*. You can also use the *shorthand* syntax: **$user.lastName**. This chapter uses the formal notation because it's the same syntax used by JSP 2.0 and FreeMarker.

Velocity works by grabbing items from a *context* and displaying them on your page. Of course, you must put items into the context first. Putting items into the context is easy, but Spring makes it even easier.

The next section converts the MyUsers application from JSP to Velocity. You will start by configuring Velocity with Spring. This chapter requires that you have the following Velocity JARs in your classpath (*web/WEB-INF/lib*):

- *velocity-1.4.jar*
- *velocity-tools-view-1.1.jar*

USING VELOCITY IN MYUSERS

In the MyUsers application, SiteMesh is the page decorator. SiteMesh allows you to leave the JSP decoration intact and use a JSP-based decorator to *decorate* Velocity-powered pages. However, you may want to use Velocity for its decorator template as well. In this section, you'll start by configuring Velocity in the *action-servlet.xml* file. Then you'll modify SiteMesh to use a Velocity decorator.

VIEWRESOLVER CONFIGURATION

When you add Velocity to a web application, you usually have to add a *velocity.properties* file to the classpath. This file has settings in it to tell Velocity which **Resource-Loader** to use for loading templates. For convenience, Spring has a **Velocity-Configurer** class that allows you to specify a path to your templates (that is, pages) without configuring such a file.

1   Add the XML fragment in Listing 6.13 to *web/WEB-INF/action-servlet.xml*. This tells Velocity to load templates from your application's *WEB-INF /velocity* directory.

Listing 6.13

```
<bean id="velocityConfig"
    class="org.springframework.web.servlet.view.velocity
        .VelocityConfigurer">
    <property name="resourceLoaderPath" value="/"/>
</bean>
```

2   If you want more control of your **ResourceLoader** (for example, to load templates from a database), create a *velocity.properties* file. To load the file, specify a **configLocation** property and value on your **velocityConfig** bean. You can also specify the properties directly in the bean definition by replacing **configLocation** with properties. For more information on

using an alternative **ResourceLoader**, see Spring's *velocity.properties* documentation.

3 Declare the **VelocityViewResolver** as the **viewResolver** for your application. See Listing 6.14.

TIP: Be sure to comment out the **InternalResourceViewResolver** you used previously for JSPs.

Listing 6.14

```
<bean id="viewResolver"
    class="org.springframework.web.servlet.view.velocity
        .VelocityViewResolver">
    <property name="exposeSpringMacroHelpers" value="true"/>
    <property name="requestContextAttribute" value="rc"/>
    <property name="cache" value="true"/>
    <property name="prefix" value="/WEB-INF/velocity/"/>
    <property name="suffix" value=".vm"/>
</bean>
```

The first two properties in this definition, **exposeSpringMacroHelpers** and **requestContextAttribute**, are important. The first exposes macros for easy handling of forms and validation errors. The **requestContextAttribute** property is an alias to the **RequestContext** object. This object is useful for printing localized messages from the *messages.properties* file.

The **VelocityViewResolver** inherits a number of optional properties from its parent, the **AbstractTemplateViewResolver**. Table illustrates these properties and their descriptions. These properties are applicable for any **AbstractTemplateViewResolver** (such as the **FreeMarkerViewResolver**).

Table 6.2: `AbstractTemplateViewResolver` Properties

Property Name	Description	Default
`exposeRequestAttributes`	This property sets whether all request attributes are added to the model prior to merging with the template.	False
`exposeSessionAttributes`	This property sets whether all session attributes are added to the model prior to merging with the template.	False
`exposeSpringMacroHelpers`	This property sets whether to expose a **RequestContext** for use by Spring's macro library, under the name **springBind-RequestContext**.	True

To use Velocity with Spring, you must specify two bean definitions in your **-servlet.xml* file: `VelocityConfigurer` and `VelocityViewResolver`. Of course, there's a lot more work to do. You must create your Velocity templates and learn how to render error messages in VTL. In the MyUsers application, you must also learn how to do page decoration with SiteMesh's `Velocity Decorator`.

SITEMESH AND VELOCITY

The most difficult part of converting MyUsers to use Velocity instead of JSP has been configuring SiteMesh to use a `Velocity Decorator`. Fortunately, SiteMesh 2.1 added this functionality and it's now fairly easy.

1   Create a decorator similar to *web/decorators/default.jsp*; however, this one should use Velocity instead of JSP tags to pull in SiteMesh content. SiteMesh ships with a `VelocityDecoratorServlet` that pre-populates the context with several useful variables. See the following list:

- `${request}`: The `HttpServletRequest` object.
- `${response}`: The `HttpServletResponse` object.
- `${base}`: `request.getContextPath()`.
- `${title}`: Parsed page `<title>`.
- `${head}`: Parsed page `<head>`.
- `${body}`: Parsed page `<body>`.
- `${page}`: SiteMesh's internal `Page` object.

2   The *default.jsp* decorator in Listing 6.15 is rewritten as a `Velocity`
`Decorator`. Use these lines as a guide to create *web/decorators/default.vm*.
To save on space, ellipses represent blocks of text that don't require any
changes and therefore are not displayed here.

Notice that the VTL syntax is actually quite a bit cleaner than the JSP syntax (for
example, `<decorator:title default="MyUsers"/>` becomes simply
`${title}`).

TIP: Copy *web/decorators/default.jsp* to *web/decorators/default.vm* to prepare for the
following Velocity conversion.

Listing 6.15

```
<!DOCTYPE html PUBLIC "-//W3C//DTD XHTML 1.0 Transitional//EN"
    "http://www.w3.org/TR/xhtml1/DTD/xhtml1-transitional.dtd">

<%@ include file="/taglibs.jsp"%>

<html xmlns="http://www.w3.org/1999/xhtml" xml:lang="en">
<head>
    <title>${title}</title>
    <meta http-equiv="content-type"
        content="text/html; charset=utf-8"/>
    <link href="${base}/styles/global.css"
        type="text/css" rel="stylesheet"/>
    <link href="${base}/images/favicon.ico" rel="SHORTCUT ICON"/>
    ${head}
    ...
            <h1><span>Welcome to MyUsers</span></h1>
            <div id="logo" onclick="location.href='${base}'"
                onkeypress="location.href='${base}'"></div>
            <h2><span>Spring Rocks!</span></h2>
        </div>
        ...
        <div id="content">
            #parse("/messages.vm")
            ${body}
        </div>
    </div>

    <div id="supportingText">
        <div id="underground">
            $!{page.getProperty("page.underground")}
            </div>

        <div id="footer">
```

```
        . . .
      <a href="http://bobby.watchfire.com
          /bobby/bobbyServlet?URL=${request.requestURL}
              &amp;output=Submit&amp;gl=sec508&amp;test="
              title="Check the accessibility of this site
              according to U.S. Section 508">508</a> &middot;
      <a href="http://bobby.watchfire.com
          /bobby/bobbyServlet?URL=${request.requestURL}
              &amp;output=Submit&amp;gl=wcag1-aaa&amp;test="
              title="Check the accessibility of this site
              according to WAI Content Accessibility
              Guidelines 1">aaa</a>
  </div>
```

3   In the middle of this file, it parses and includes the *messages.vm* file. This file does not exist, so create it in the *web* directory. See Listing 6.16.

Listing 6.16

```
## Success Messages
#if ($message)
    <div class="message">${message}</div>
    ${request.session.removeAttribute("message")}
#end
```

4   Once you've created the Velocity template, configure SiteMesh to use it. Open *web/WEB-INF/decorators.xml* and change the default decorator's **page** attribute to refer to the *default.vm* file you just created. See Listing 6.17.

Listing 6.17

```
<decorators defaultdir="/decorators">
  <decorator name="default" page="default.vm">
    <pattern>/*</pattern>
  </decorator>
</decorators>
```

5   Configure the application to use SiteMesh's **VelocityDecoratorServlet** to parse the Velocity templates.

EDIT WEB.XML

In order for SiteMesh to properly parse the Velocity decorator, add a servlet definition and associated mapping to *web/WEB-INF/web.xml*. Add the XML in right after the **action** servlet declaration. See Listing 6.18.

Listing 6.18

```
<servlet>
    <servlet-name>sitemesh-velocity</servlet-name>
    <servlet-class>
        com.opensymphony.module.sitemesh.velocity
            .VelocityDecoratorServlet</servlet-class>
</servlet>

<servlet-mapping>
    <servlet-name>sitemesh-velocity</servlet-name>
    <url-pattern>*.vm</url-pattern>
</servlet-mapping>
```

These instructions are also available in SiteMesh's documentation.

CREATE VELOCITY TEMPLATES

The last step to converting from JSP to Velocity is to change all the JSP pages to use Velocity's VTL.

Copy the *WEB-INF/jsp* directory to *WEB-INF/velocity* and rename all the files to use a .vm extension. Your directory structure should be the same as the one in Figure 6.3.

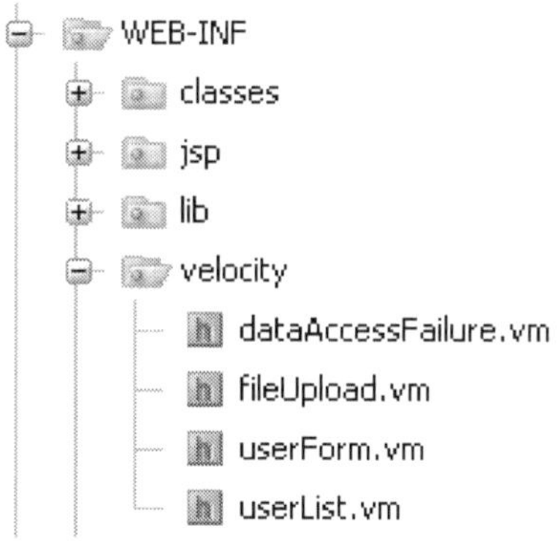

Figure 6.3: Project directory structure with Velocity templates

The following listings contain the code for the preceding Velocity templates and the changes that are necessary to make them work with Velocity. Special notes for each file are directly after the code. Any VTL code that you'll need in your templates is highlighted. First, see the userList.vm in Listing 6.19.

Listing 6.19

```
<title>MyUsers ~ User List</title>

<button onclick="location.href='editUser.html'">Add User</button>

<table class="list" id="userList">
<thead>
<tr>
    <th>${rc.getMessage("user.id")}</th>
    <th>${rc.getMessage("user.firstName")}</th>
    <th>${rc.getMessage("user.lastName")}</th>
</tr>
</thead>
<tbody>
#foreach ($user in $users)
#if ($velocityCount % 2 == 0) <tr class="even">
#else <tr class="odd">
#end
    <td><a href="editUser.html?id=${user.id}">${user.id}</a></td>
    <td>${user.firstName}</td>
    <td>${user.lastName}</td>
</tr>
#end
</tbody>
</table>
```

Notice the **${rc.getMessage()}** call to get localized messages from *web/WEB-INF/classes/messages.properties*. The **$velocityCount** variable is an internal Velocity value that's exposed when iterating. The userForm.vm is in Listing 6.20.

Listing 6.20

```
<title>MyUsers ~ User Details</title>

#springBind("user.*")
#if ($status.error)
<div class="error">
    #foreach ($error in $status.errorMessages)
        ${error}<br/>
    #end
</div>
#end

<p>Please fill in user's information below:</p>

<form method="post" action="editUser.html">
#springBind("user.id")
<input type="hidden" name="id" value="$!{status.value}"/>
```

```
<table>
<tr>
    <th>${rc.getMessage("user.firstName")}:</th>
    <td>
        #springBind("user.firstName")
        <input type="text" name="firstName"
            value="$!{status.value}"/>
        <span class="fieldError">${status.errorMessage}</span>
    </td>
</tr>
<tr>
    <th>${rc.getMessage("user.lastName")}:</th>
    <td>
        #springBind("user.lastName")
        <input type="text" name="lastName"
            value="$!{status.value}"/>
        <span class="fieldError">${status.errorMessage}</span>
    </td>
</tr>
<tr>
    <td></td>
    <td>
        <input type="submit" class="button"
            name="save" value="Save"/>
    #if ($user.id)
        <input type="submit" class="button"
            name="delete" value="Delete"/>
    #end
        <input type="submit" class="button"
            name="cancel" value="Cancel"/>
    </td>
</table>
</form>
```

Notice the **#springBind** macro call that exposes variables for each field. The exclamation point after the dollar sign (**$!{...}**) indicates that nothing should be printed if no value is found.

TIP: In this example, you could use **${status.expression}** for the **name** attribute of each input field, but using the name that's rendered by this expression has a shorter syntax.

These macros don't have a closing tag or ending statement like the **<spring:bind>** JSP tags require. The **#springBind** macro becomes available when you set the **exposeSpringMacroHelpers** property to **"true"** on the **viewResolver** bean.

Client-side validation with JavaScript and Commons Validator is only supported with JSPs.

VELOCITY FORM INPUT MACROS

In addition to the **#springBind** macro, several other macros simplify generating form input fields with Velocity. Using these macros, you can rewrite the *userForm.vm* with a much simpler syntax, as in Listing 6.21.

Listing 6.21

```
#set($springXhtmlCompliant = true)

<form method="post" action="#springUrl('editUser.html')">
#springFormHiddenInput("user.id" '')
<table>
<tr>
    <th><label for="firstName">
        #springMessage("user.firstName"):</label></th>
    <td>
        #springFormInput("user.firstName" 'id="firstName"')
        #springShowErrors("<br/>" "fieldError")
    </td>
</tr>
<tr>
    <th><label for="lastName">
        #springMessage("user.lastName"):</label></th>
    <td>
        #springFormInput("user.lastName" 'id="lastName"')
        #springShowErrors("<br/>" "fieldError")
    </td>
</tr>
```

TIP: The #set($springXhtmlCompliant = true) call at the beginning of this example is important if you want your elements to render with well-formed XHTML syntax.

The following list shows the form input macros that Spring provides for Velocity. The most up-to-date listing of these macros are in Spring's Reference Documentation — Chapter 13: Integrating View Technologies.

- **#springMessage($code)**: This macro outputs a string from a resource bundle based on a **$code** parameter.

- **#springMessageText($code $default)**: This macro is the same as **#springMessage**, but it allows a default value if **$code** not found in the resource bundle.

- **#springUrl($relativeUrl)**: This macro outputs a URL prefixed with **contextPath**.

- **#springFormInput($path $attributes)**: This macro outputs **<input type="text"/>** where the value is read from the **$path** and **$attributes**, which allows you to specify pass-through HTML attributes.

- **#springFormHiddenInput($path $attributes)**: This macro outputs **<input type="hidden"/>**.

- **#springFormPasswordInput($path $attributes)**: This macro outputs **<input type="password"/>**.

- **#springFormTextarea($path $attributes)**: This macro outputs **<textarea></textarea>**.

- **#springFormSingleSelect($path $options $attributes)**: This macro outputs **<select size="1"></select>**, where **$options** is a map of all available choices and the key in the map resolves to the **value** attribute of each **<option>**.

- **#springFormMultiSelect($path $options $attributes)**: This macro is the same as **#springSingleSelect**, except it has **<select multiple="multiple">**, which allows more than one option to be selected.

- **#springFormRadioButtons($path $options $separator $attributes)**: This macro outputs a set of radio buttons that allows a single selection.

- **#springFormCheckboxes($path $options $separator $attributes)**: This macro outputs a set of check boxes that allows zero or more options to be selected.

- **#springShowErrors($separator $classOrStyle)**: This macro outputs validation and conversion errors for a particular field.

NOTE: Velocity requires you to specify each argument when calling a macro, even if it's an empty **string** argument. For example, if you don't want to specify a **$classOrStyle** for the **#springShowErrors()** macro, you must use **#spring-ShowErrors("<br/>" "")**.

The fileUpload.vm is in Listing 6.22.

Listing 6.22

```
<h3>File Upload</h3>

#if ($model.filename)
<p style="font-weight: bold">
    Uploaded file (click to view):
```

```
    <a href="${model.url}">${model.filename}</a>
</p>
#end

<p>Select a file to upload:</p>
<form method="post" action="#springUrl('fileUpload.html')"
    enctype="multipart/form-data">
    <input type="file" name="file"/><br/>
    <input type="submit" value="Upload" class="button"
        style="margin-top: 5px"/>
</form>
```

The dataAccessFailure.vm is in Listing 6.23.

Listing 6.23

```
<h3>Data Access Failure</h3>
<p>
    ${exception}
</p>

<a href="${rc.contextPath}">&#171; Home</a>
```

This file does not have the exception's stack trace printed out in a comment like the JSP. Even with **${exception.printStackTrace()}** in a comment, the stack trace is never printed.

DEPLOY AND TEST

Now that you've told Spring to configure and use Velocity, configured SiteMesh to use a Velocity decorator, and converted all the JSPs to Velocity, it's time to test that everything worked. Start Tomcat and run **ant clean deploy reload**. Once the new context has restarted, run **ant test-web** to verify everything works.

> **WARNING:** If the test fails because a user is not found in the database, delete the database (**rm -r db**), restart Tomcat and try again. You can also add **<delete dir="db"/>** to the **delete** target.

SUMMARY OF VELOCITY

In this section, you learned how to use Velocity as an alternate view technology to JSP. Velocity has a much cleaner syntax than JSP (although JSP improved with version 2.0). Compilation is much faster than JSP when you first access a Velocity-backed template. With JSP, the initial load time can be a couple seconds, which is slightly painful when developing since you constantly have to wait. It's not something you notice until you've developed with Velocity and then go back to JSPs. The one downside to Velocity is that you can't use the rich set of tag libraries (for example, displaytag, oscache, etc.) that are available. However, a fast templating solution that allows you to use JSP tags is available: FreeMarker.

FREEMARKER

....

FreeMarker is an open source project hosted at reemarker.sourceforge.net. It is similar to Velocity in that it's a "template engine," which generates text output based on templates. The major difference between the two libraries is their template language syntax. FreeMarker is more robust, yet easier to work with. It also supports using JSP tag libraries in your templates (so you can use displaytag!). For more information on the differences between the two, see the FreeMarker vs. Velocity web page.

The next section converts the MyUsers application from Velocity to FreeMarker. Start by configuring FreeMarker with Spring. This chapter requires you to have FreeMarker's *freemarker.jar* file in your classpath (*web/WEB-INF/lib*).

NOTE: Spring requires FreeMarker version 2.3 or higher.

VIEWRESOLVER CONFIGURATION

1   Add a **configurer** bean definition to *web/WEB-INF/action-servlet.xml*. Comment out the **velocityConfig** bean as part of this exercise. See Listing 6.24.

Listing 6.24

```
<bean id="freemarkerConfig"
class="org.springframework.web.servlet.view.freemarker
    .FreeMarkerConfigurer">
    <property name="templateLoaderPath" value="/"/>
</bean>
```

Like the **VelocityConfigurer**, you can configure this class with a properties file (with a **configLocation** property pointing to the file). You can also set properties on the bean itself by specifying a **freemarkerSettings** list of properties.

2   Comment out the **velocityConfig** bean and the **viewResolver** bean, and add one for FreeMarker. The properties on this resolver are very similar to the Velocity version, the only difference being the **prefix** and the **suffix**. See Listing 6.25.

Listing 6.25

```
<bean id="viewResolver"
class="org.springframework.web.servlet.view.freemarker
   .FreeMarkerViewResolver">
   <property name="exposeSpringMacroHelpers" value="true"/>
   <property name="requestContextAttribute" value="rc"/>
   <property name="prefix" value="/WEB-INF/freemarker/"/>
   <property name="suffix" value=".ftl"/>
</bean>
```

Keep in mind that you can also expose request and session attributes using the **exposeRequestAttributes** and **exposeSessionAttributes** on this template resolver. This tutorial doesn't require them, but they have value.

SITEMESH AND FREEMARKER

Just like Velocity, SiteMesh has a *decorator servlet* specifically for FreeMarker called **FreeMarkerDecoratorServlet**. It pre-populates FreeMarker's data model with several context attributes. See the following list.

- **${base}**: **request.getContextPath()**
- **${title}**: Parsed page **<title>**
- **${head}**: Parsed page **<head>**
- **${body}**: Parsed page **<body>**
- **${page}**: SiteMesh's internal **Page** object

FreeMarker supports getting request parameters, request attributes and session variables, which is why you don't see **$req** and **$res** like you do with Velocity. These values are available in the templates through the variables **Request, Request-Parameters, Session**, and **Application** (for example, **${Session["user"]}**).

1   The Velocity decorator in Listing 6.26 is rewritten from the previous section using FreeMarker. The listing displays only the changed lines, so you don't have to copy the entire contents of the following file. Use these lines as a guide to create *web/decorators/default.ftl*. The variable references are the same as Velocity, but the conditional logic syntax is different.

TIP: Copy *web/decorators/default.vm* to *web/decorators/default.ftl* to prepare for the conversion.

Listing 6.26

```
    <div id="content">
        <#include "/messages.ftl"/>
        ${body}
    </div>
</div>

<div id="supportingText">
    <div id="underground">
    <#if page.getProperty("page.underground")?exists>
        ${page.getProperty("page.underground")}
    </#if>
    </div>
    ...
    <a href="http://bobby.watchfire.com
        /bobby/bobbyServlet?URL=${Request.requestURL}
            &amp;output=Submit&amp;gl=sec508&amp;test="
            title="Check the accessibility of this site
            according to U.S. Section 508">508</a> &middot;
    <a href="http://bobby.watchfire.com
        /bobby/bobbyServlet?URL=${Request.requestURL}
            &amp;output=Submit&amp;gl=wcag1-aaa&amp;test="
            title="Check the accessibility of this site
            according to WAI Content Accessibility
            Guidelines 1">aaa</a>
    ...
```

    2   Create the *web/messages.ftl* file with the contents in Listing 6.27:

Listing 6.27

```
<#-- Success Messages -->
<#if message?exists>
    <div class="message">${message}</div>
</#if>
```

    3   Change *web/WEB-INF/decorators.xml* to use the FreeMarker template as the default. See Listing 6.28.

Listing 6.28

```
<decorators defaultdir="/decorators">
    <decorator name="default" page="default.ftl">
        <pattern>/*</pattern>
    </decorator>
</decorators>
```

Notable differences between Velocity and FreeMarker are listed below:

- To check for a null value in Velocity, you simply write **#if (object.property)** to test for the existence of a value. With FreeMarker, you must append **?exists** to test for nulls.

- Velocity exposes the actual **HttpServletRequest** object, so you can call **${request.contextPath}** and **${request.requestURL}**. FreeMarker only exposes scoped attributes. Because of this, you can't simply remove messages from the session in the *messages.ftl* file.

FreeMarker has some limitations, which arguably make it a cleaner MVC implementation. The easiest and cleanest way to solve the issues above is to create a **ServletFilter** that searches for messages in the session, and if it finds them, it puts them in the request. This way, you can forget about removing them in a view page and let the filter do the work.

Listing 6.29 is a **MessageFilter.java** class to put in *src/org/appfuse/web*. The logic to set the **requestURL** in the request is to provide full links back to your application as part of the project's footer page.

Listing 6.29

```
package org.appfuse.web;

// use your IDE to organize imports

public class MessageFilter implements Filter {
    private static Log
        log = LogFactory.getLog(MessageFilter.class);

    public void doFilter(ServletRequest req, ServletResponse res,
                        FilterChain chain)
    throws IOException, ServletException {
        HttpServletRequest request = (HttpServletRequest) req;

        // grab messages from the session and put them into request
        // this is so they're not lost in a redirect
        Object message = request.getSession()
            .getAttribute("message");
        if (message != null) {
            request.setAttribute("message", message);
            request.getSession().removeAttribute("message");
        }

        // set the requestURL as a request attribute for templates
        // esp. freemarker, which doesn't allow
            request.getRequestURL()
```

```
    request.setAttribute("requestURL", request
        .getRequestURL());

    chain.doFilter(req, res);
}

public void init(FilterConfig filterConfig) {}

public void destroy() {}
}
```

4   Using this filter, you can eliminate any session removal logic in the all the
    messages templates (at *web/messages.**). To enable it, add a **`<filter>`** and
    `<filter-mapping>` to *web/WEB-INF/web.xml*. Put the **`<filter>`**
    declaration in Listing 6.30 just above the **`sitemesh`** filter.

Listing 6.30

```
<filter>
    <filter-name>messageFilter</filter-name>
    <filter-class>org.appfuse.web.MessageFilter</filter-class>
</filter>
```

5   Add the **`<filter-mapping>`** just above SiteMesh's filter-mapping, as in
    Listing 6.31.

Listing 6.31

```
<filter-mapping>
    <filter-name>messageFilter</filter-name>
    <url-pattern>/*</url-pattern>
</filter-mapping>
```

EDIT WEB.XML

To edit *web.xml* for SiteMesh, comment out the **`sitemesh-velocity`** servlet and
its mapping and add the **`sitemesh-freemarker`** servlet and mapping in
Listing 6.32.

Listing 6.32

```
<servlet>
    <servlet-name>sitemesh-freemarker</servlet-name>
    <servlet-class>
        com.opensymphony.module.sitemesh.freemarker.
            FreemarkerDecoratorServlet</servlet-class>
    <init-param>
        <param-name>TemplatePath</param-name>
```

```
            <param-value>/</param-value>
        </init-param>
        <init-param>
            <param-name>default_encoding</param-name>
            <param-value>ISO-8859-1</param-value>
        </init-param>
    </servlet>

    <servlet-mapping>
        <servlet-name>sitemesh-freemarker</servlet-name>
        <url-pattern>*.ftl</url-pattern>
    </servlet-mapping>
```

CREATE FREEMARKER TEMPLATES

The last step for implementing FreeMarker is to create page templates using FreeMarker's template language.

1   Copy the *WEB-INF/velocity* directory to *WEB-INF/freemarker* and rename all the files to use an *.ftl* extension. Your directory structure should be the same as the one in Figure 6.4.

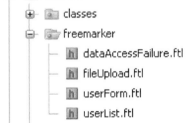

Figure 6.4: Project directory with FreeMarker templates

2   The following listings contain the code for the preceding FreeMarker templates and the changes that are necessary to make them work with Velocity. Special notes for each file are directly after the code. Any lines where the FreeMarker code is different from Velocity's VTL are underlined. See userList.ftl in Listing 6.33.

Listing 6.33

```
<title>MyUsers ~ User List</title>

<button onclick="location.href='editUser.html'">Add User</button>

<table class="list" id="userList">
```

```
<thead>
<tr>
    <th>${rc.getMessage("user.id")}</th>
    <th>${rc.getMessage("user.firstName")}</th>
    <th>${rc.getMessage("user.lastName")}</th>
</tr>
</thead>
<tbody>
<#list users as user>
<#if user index % 2 == 0> <tr class="even">
<#else> <tr class="odd">
</#if>
    <td><a href="editUser.html?id=${user.id}">${user.id}</a></td>
    <td>${user.firstName}</td>
    <td>${user.lastName}</td>
</tr>
</#list>
</tbody>
</table>
```

Similar to Velocity, the `${rc.getMessage()}` call gets localized messages from *web/WEB-INF/classes/messages.properties.* Listing 6.34 is userForm.ftl.

Listing 6.34

```
<#import "/spring.ftl" as spring/>

<title>MyUsers ~ User Details</title>

<@spring.bind "user.*"/>
<#if spring.status.error>
<div class="error">
    <#list spring.status.errorMessages as error>
        ${error}<br/>
    </#list>
</div>
</#if>

<p>Please fill in user's information below:</p>

<form method="post" action="editUser.html">
<@spring.bind "user.id"/>
<input type="hidden" name="id"
    value="${spring.status.value?default("")}"/>
<table>
<tr>
    <th><label for="firstName">
        ${rc.getMessage("user.firstName")}</label>:</th>
    <td>
        <@spring.bind "user.firstName"/>
```

```
        <input type="text" name="${spring.status.expression}"
            value="${spring.status.value?default("")}"/>
        <span class="fieldError">${spring.status.errorMessage}
            </span>
    </td>
</tr>
<tr>
    <th><label for="lastName">
        ${rc.getMessage("user.lastName")}</label>:</th>
    <td>
        <@spring.bind "user.lastName"/>
        <input type="text" name="${spring.status.expression}"
            value="${spring.status.value?default("")}"/>
        <span class="fieldError">${spring.status.errorMessage}
            </span>
    </td>
</tr>
<tr>
    <td></td>
    <td>
        <input type="submit" class="button"
            name="save" value="Save"/>
      <#if user.id?exists>
        <input type="submit" class="button" name="delete"
            value="Delete"/>
      </#if>
        <input type="submit" class="button" name="cancel"
            value="Cancel"/>
    </td>
</tr>
</table>
</form>
```

The most important thing to notice in this file is the first line where *spring.ftl* is imported. This file contains the **spring.bind** macro needed to expose a properties value.

You may also notice that each field is given a default by adding **?default('')** to the end of its expression.

These macros don't have a closing tag or ending statement like the **<spring:bind>** JSP tags require. The **<@spring.bind>** macro becomes available when you set the **exposeSpringMacroHelpers** property to **"true"** on the **viewResolver** bean.

Client-side validation with JavaScript and Commons Validator is only supported with JSPs.

FREEMARKER FORM INPUT MACROS

In addition to the `<@spring.bind>` macro, several other macros simplify generating form input fields with FreeMarker. Using these macros, you can rewrite the
userForm.ftl with a much simpler syntax, as in Listing 6.35.

Listing 6.35

```
<#assign xhtmlCompliant = true in spring>

<form method="post" action="<@spring.url '/editUser.html'/>">
<@spring.formHiddenInput "user.id"/>
<table>
<tr>
    <th><label for="firstName">
        <@spring.message "user.firstName"/></label>:</th>
    <td>
        <@spring.formInput "user.firstName", 'id="firstName"'/>
        <span class="fieldError">${spring.status.errorMessage}
            </span>
    </td>
</tr>
<tr>
    <th><label for="lastName">
        <@spring.message "user.lastName"/></label>:</th>
    <td>
        <@spring.formInput "user.lastName", 'id="lastName"'/>
        <span class="fieldError">${spring.status.errorMessage}
            </span>
    </td>
</tr>
```

TIP: The `<#assign xhtmlCompliant = true in spring>` call at the beginning of
this example is important if you want your elements to render with well-formed
XHTML syntax.

The following lists contains the form input macros that Spring provides for
FreeMarker. The most up-to-date listing of these macros is in Spring's Reference
Documentation — Chapter 13: Integrating View Technologies.

NOTE: The major difference between calling Velocity versus FreeMarker macros
is Velocity macro parameters are space-separated and FreeMarker macro parameters
are comma-separated.

- `<@spring.message $code/>`: This macro outputs a string from
  resource bundle based on `$code` parameter.

- **<@spring.messageText $code, $default/>**: This macro is the same as **<@spring.message/>**, but it allows a default value if **$code** not found in the resource bundle.

- **<@spring.url relativeUrl/>**: This macro outputs a URL prefixed with **contextPath**.

- **<@spring.formInput $path, $attributes, $fieldType/>**: This macro outputs **<input type="text"/>**, where the value is read from the **$path** and **$attributes**, which allows you to specify pass-through HTML attributes. The **$fieldType** can be specified to create hidden fields.

- **<@spring.formHiddenInput $path, $attributes/>**: This macro outputs **<input type="hidden"/>**.

- **<@spring.formPasswordInput $path, $attributes/>**: This macro outputs **<input type="password"/>**.

- **<@spring.formTextarea $path, $attributes/>**: This macro outputs **<textarea></textarea>**.

- **<@spring.formSingleSelect $path, $options, $attributes/>**: This macro outputs **<select size="1"></select>**, where **$options** is a map of all available choices and the key in the map resolves to the **value** attribute of each **<option>**.

- **<@spring.formMultiSelect $path, $options, $attributes/>**: This macro is the same as **<@spring.formSingleSelect/>**, except it has **<select multiple="multiple">**, which allows more than one option to be selected.

- **<@spring.formRadioButtons $path, $options, $separator, $attributes/>**: This macro outputs a set of radio buttons that allows a single selection.

- **<@spring.formCheckboxes $path, $options, $separator, $attributes/>**: This macro outputs a set of check boxes that allows zero or more options to be selected.

- **<@spring.showErrors $separator, $classOrStyle/>**: This macro outputs validation and conversion errors for a particular field.

NOTE: FreeMarker doesn't require you to specify each argument when calling a macro. You only have to pass in the arguments that have values. For example, if you don't want to specify a **$classOrStyle** for the **<@spring.showErrors>** macro, you can use **<@spring.showErrors "<br />"/>** instead of **<@spring.showErrors "<br />", ""/>**.

Listing 6.36 is fileUpload.ftl.

Listing 6.36

```
<#import "/spring.ftl" as spring/>

<h3>File Upload</h3>

<#if model?exists>
<p style="font-weight: bold">
    Uploaded file (click to view):
        <a href="${model.url}">${model.filename}</a>
</p>
</#if>

<p>Select a file to upload:</p>
<form method="post" action="<@spring.url '/fileUpload.html'/>"
    enctype="multipart/form-data">
    <input type="file" name="file"/><br/>
    <input type="submit" value="Upload" class="button"
        style="margin-top: 5px"/>
</form>
```

Listing 6.37 is dataAccessFailure.ftl.

Listing 6.37

```
<h3>Data Access Failure</h3>
<p>
    ${exception}
</p>

<a href="${rc.contextPath}">&#171; Home</a>
```

The code for this file is the same for FreeMarker and Velocity.

DEPLOY AND TEST

Now that you've told Spring to configure and use FreeMarker, configured SiteMesh to use a FreeMarker decorator, and converted all the pages to use FreeMarker, it's time to test that everything worked. Start Tomcat and run **ant clean deploy**. Once everything has started, run **ant test-web** to verify everything works.

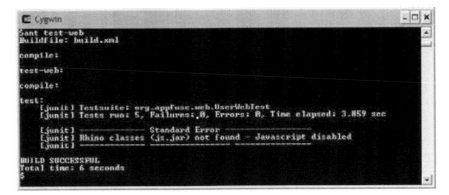

Figure 6.5: Running UserWebTest

JSP, Velocity, and FreeMarker are the dominant view choices when using Spring MVC. However, a few others can be quite useful. They are XSTL (for displaying and transforming XML), PDF, and Excel. In the next sections, you'll implement these to generate reports of the user list screen.

XSLT
∎∎

XSLT describes the process of combining XML and XSL to *transform* XML to another output. In most cases, this output is text-based, but you can also use XSL-FO to generate PDFs. Spring's XSLT views can be helpful if you're loading and presenting XML documents, or you can easily convert your model to XML.

Before creating an XSLT View, prepare the **UserController** class to handle rendering report views.

1   Open *UserControllerTest.java* in *test/org/appfuse/web* and add the test in Listing 6.38:

Listing 6.38

```
public void testGetUsersAsXML() throws Exception {
    UserController c =
        (UserController) ctx.getBean("userController");
    MockHttpServletRequest request = new MockHttpServletRequest();
    request.addParameter("report", "XML");
    ModelAndView mav =
        c.handleRequest(request, (HttpServletResponse) null);
    assertEquals(mav.getViewName(), "userListXML");
}
```

2   Open *UserController.java* in *src/org/appfuse/web* and add some logic to render a different view name if a **report** parameter is passed in. This logic will also render the Excel and PDF views covered later in this chapter. See Listing 6.39.

Listing 6.39

```
public ModelAndView handleRequest(HttpServletRequest request,
                                  HttpServletResponse response)
throws Exception {
    if (log.isDebugEnabled()) {
        log.debug("entering 'handleRequest' method...");
    }

    String viewName = "userList";
    if (request != null &&
        request.getParameter("report") != null) {
        viewName += request.getParameter("report");
    }

    return new ModelAndView(viewName, "users", mgr.getUsers());
}
```

3   The reports you're about to produce are simply going to contain the user's full name in a list format. To make this easier, add a **getFullName()** method the **User** class (in *src/org/appfuse/model*). See Listing 6.40.

Listing 6.40

```
public String getFullName() {
    return firstName + ' ' + lastName;
}
```

Now you're ready to create the view class.

CREATE THE VIEW CLASS

Before creating the class to convert the list of users to XML, create a class to test it.

1   In *test/org/appfuse/web*, create a **UserXMLViewTest** class that extends JUnit's **TestCase**. See Listing 6.41.

Listing 6.41

```
package org.appfuse.web;

// user your IDE to organize imports
```

```
public class UserXMLViewTest extends TestCase {
    private static Log log =
LogFactory.getLog(UserXMLViewTest.class);

    public void testXMLCreation() throws Exception {
        // setup a user to print out as XML
        User user = new User();
        user.setFirstName("James");
        user.setLastName("Strachan");
        List users = new ArrayList();
        users.add(user);
        Map model = new HashMap();
        model.put("users", users);

        // invoke the XsltView and call its 'createDomNode' method
        UserXMLView feed = new UserXMLView();
        Source source = feed.createXsltSource(model, "users",
                new MockHttpServletRequest(),
                new MockHttpServletResponse());
        Node node = ((DOMSource) source).getNode();
        assertEquals(node.getFirstChild().toString(),
                "<users><user>James Strachan</user></users>");
    }
}
```

2   In *src/org/appfuse/web*, create a **UserXMLView** class that extends
     AbstractXsltView and has the contents in Listing 6.42.

NOTE: The XML classes are from dom4j, which should be in your classpath.

Listing 6.42

```
package org.appfuse.web;

// use your IDE to organize imports

public class UserXMLView extends AbstractXsltView {
    protected Source createXsltSource(Map model, String rootName,
                                      HttpServletRequest request,
                                      HttpServletResponse response)
        throws Exception {
        Document doc = DocumentHelper.createDocument();
        Element root = doc.addElement(rootName);
        doc.setRootElement(root);

        List users = (List) model.get("users");
        for (Iterator it = users.iterator(); it.hasNext();) {
            User user = (User) it.next();
            root.addElement("user").addText(user.getFullName());
```

```
    }
    response.setContentType("text/xml");

    return new DOMSource(new DOMWriter().write(doc));
  }
}
```

3 Run **ant test -Dtestcase=UserXML** to verify this class is working as expected.

NOTE: In this example, you're going to modify this XML document to produce another XML document (that's why the response is set to be content type **"text /xml"**). If you were going to produce HTML in your XSL style sheet, you could eliminate this line.

---

4 Create a *users.xsl* file in *web/WEB-INF/xsl*. Add the XSL in Listing 6.43 to this document.

Listing 6.43

```
<?xml version="1.0"?>
<xsl:stylesheet version="1.0"
    xmlns:xsl="http://www.w3.org/1999/XSL/Transform">
    <xsl:output method="xml" omit-xml-declaration="no"/>

    <xsl:template match="/">
        <users>
            <xsl:for-each select="users/user">
                <user><xsl:value-of select="."/></user>
            </xsl:for-each>
        </users>
    </xsl:template>

</xsl:stylesheet>
```

5 Now that you have created all the view files, configure Spring to know about the **userListXML** view name. The easiest way to do this is to create a second **viewResolver** that uses **ResourceBundleViewResolver** to resolve its views. Since you already have a **viewResolver** bean for FreeMarker, you must give the new resolver a different **id**. Using **reportViewResolver** is a good solution: See Listing 6.44.

Listing 6.44

```
<bean id="reportViewResolver"
  class="org.springframework.web.servlet.view
   .ResourceBundleViewResolver">
   <property name="order" value="1"/></bean>
```

6   The **order** property specifies priorities of view resolvers. Add this same property to the viewResolver bean with a value of zero. The **ResourceBundleViewResolver** allows you to configure your view names, their classes, and their properties in a **ResourceBundle** (or properties file). By default, this file name is *views.properties*, and it should exist in your *WEB-INF/classes* directory. If you want to override the name of this file, specify a **basename** property on the **reportViewResolver** bean.

7   Create a *view.properties* file in *web/WEB-INF/classes* and fill it with the text in Listing 6.45:

Listing 6.45

```
userListXML.class=org.appfuse.web.UserXMLView
userListXML.stylesheetLocation=/WEB-INF/xsl/users.xsl
userListXML.root=users
```

DEPLOY AND TEST

You are now ready to deploy and test the application. Run **ant deploy reload populate** and load localhost:8080/myusers/users.html?report=XML into your browser. You should see something similar to Figure 6.6.

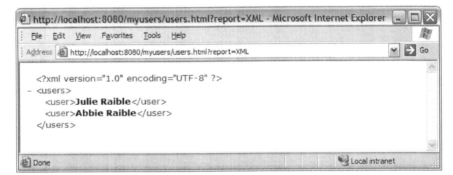

Figure 6.6: User list in XML format

One report is working; add reports for PDF and Excel, too. To make things easier, add a set of links to the current userList page. If you're still using FreeMarker, the file name is *userList.ftl* and it's located in *web/WEB-INF/freemarker*. Open it and add the HTML in Listing 6.46 to the top of the file, between the **<button>** and the **<table>**:

Listing 6.46

```
<p style="text-align: right; margin-bottom: -10px">
    <strong>Export Options:</strong>
    <a href="?report=XML">XML</a> &middot;
    <a href="?report=Excel">Excel</a> &middot;
    <a href="?report=PDF">PDF</a>
</p>
```

EXCEL

Excel documents are a useful way to export data for manipulation by users. If you simply need to output a list screen in Excel, I recommend using the display tag library (described earlier). If you need something more robust, then this section is for you. The next few steps show you how to build and send an Excel spreadsheet using Jakarta's POI library.

NOTE: If you downloaded and installed the *chapter6-jars.zip* file, you will already have *poi-2.5.1-final-20040804.jar* in your classpath. This JAR contains classes that are necessary to complete this exercise.

CREATE THE VIEW CLASS

First, create the view class.

1   Create a **UserExcelView** class in *src/org/appfuse/web*. This class should extend **AbstractExcelView** and contain the code in Listing 6.47:

Listing 6.47

```
package org.appfuse.web;

// use your IDE to organize imports

public class UserExcelView extends AbstractExcelView {

    protected void buildExcelDocument(Map model, HSSFWorkbook wb,
                                      HttpServletRequest req,
                                      HttpServletResponse resp)
    throws Exception {
```

```
HSSFSheet sheet = wb.createSheet("My Users");
sheet.setDefaultColumnWidth((short) 12);

List users = (List) model.get("users");

for (int i = 0; i < users.size(); i++) {
    HSSFCell cell = getCell(sheet, i, 0);
    setText(cell, ((User) users.get(i)).getFullName());
}
}
}
```

Notifying Spring that the **userListExcel** view exists is quite easy using the **ResourceBundleViewResolver**.

2   Open *web/WEB-INF/classes/views.properties* and add the line in Listing 6.48:

Listing 6.48

```
userListExcel.class=org.appfuse.web.UserExcelView
```

DEPLOY AND TEST

Run and test.

1   Run **ant deploy reload** and point your browser to localhost:8080/ myusers/users.html. You should see the screen in Figure 6.7.

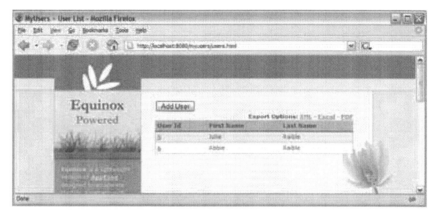

Figure 6.7: User list with export option links

2   Click on the **Excel** link at the top-right of the table. If you have Excel installed, it starts Excel and brings up a list of the current users. See Figure 6.8.

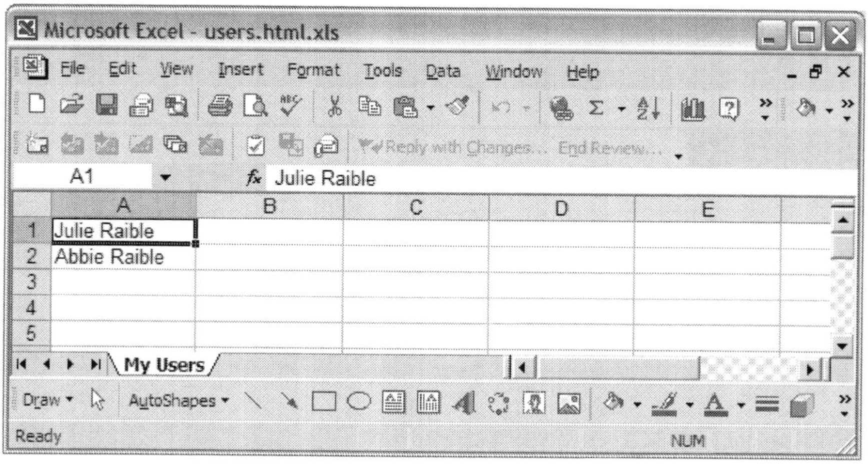

Figure 6.8: User list in Excel format

PDF

PDF documents are an excellent way to produce printable reports. In most MVC frameworks, you're required to use something like JasperReports to produce PDF output. With Spring, you simply create a subclass of **AbstractPdfView** and override the **buildPdfDocument()** method. This method returns an iText document that your browser can easily render.

> **NOTE:** If you downloaded and installed the *chapter6-jars.zip* file, you will already have *itext-1.3.jar* in your classpath. This JAR contains classes that are necessary to complete this exercise.

CREATE THE VIEW CLASS

First, create a view class.

1   Create a **UserPDFView** class in *src/org/appfuse/web*. Populate this class with the code in Listing 6.49.

Listing 6.49

```
package org.appfuse.web;

// use your IDE to organize imports

public class UserPDFView extends AbstractPdfView {

    protected void buildPdfDocument(Map model, Document doc,
```

```
                                    PdfWriter writer,
                                    HttpServletRequest req,
                                    HttpServletResponse resp)
        throws Exception {
            List users = (List) model.get("users");

            for (int i = 0; i < users.size(); i++) {
                String fullName = ((User) users.get(i)).getFullName();
                doc.add(new Paragraph(fullName));
            }
        }
    }
}
```

2 To notify Spring where the **userListPDF** view is, open *web/WEB-INF/ classes/views.properties* and add the line in Listing 6.50.

Listing 6.50

```
userListPDF.class=org.appfuse.web.UserPDFView
```

DEPLOY AND TEST

Run and test.

1 Run **ant deploy reload** and point your browser to localhost:8080/ myusers/users.html.

2 Click on the **PDF** link at the top-right of the table. This opens a PDF containing a list of the users' names.

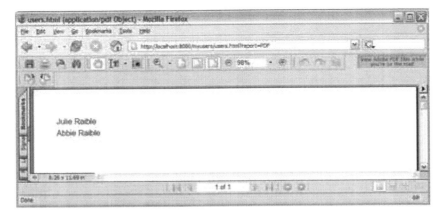

Figure 6.9: User list in PDF format

SUMMARY

This chapter explored the rich functionality offered in Spring's MVC framework. It showed you how to easily change from using JSP to Velocity without changing a single line of Java code. Then it showed you how to change that to FreeMarker by simply altering some XML files and re-working the templates a bit. You also learned how to use SiteMesh with Velocity and FreeMarker. The ability to use all of these J2EE templating engines with a highly configurable page decoration engine like Site-Mesh is a *very* powerful solution for quickly developing web applications. Spring makes it easy to switch from one to the other, so your templating technology of choice is not a hard-and-fast decision.

The ability to produce reports in PDF and Excel is another powerful and easy-to-use feature of Spring MVC. It's even nicer that these features are powered by solid and well-supported open source projects like iText and POI.

JASPERREPORTS

How to use JasperReports with Spring MVC

JasperReports is a powerful open source Java reporting tool that delivers many content types for printing. It currently supports PDF, HTML, XLS, CSV, and XML files. Unlike the view types in Chapter 6: View Options, JasperReports is designed for reporting and is an excellent tool for rendering printable pages.

ENVIRONMENT SETUP

To use JasperReports with your Spring MVC project, you'll need to download it and add its JAR to your project. In addition, it depends on a number of other projects, which are included in this chapter's download.

- *bsh-2.0b2.jar*
- *commons-beanutils.jar*
- *commons-collections.jar*
- *commons-digester.jar*
- *commons-logging.jar*
- *itext-1.3.jar*
- *jasperreports-0.6.7.jar*
- *jdt-compiler.jar*
- *poi-2.5.1-final-20040804.jar*

You only need the BeanShell JAR (*bsh-2.0b2.jar*) and *jdt-compiler.jar* if you plan to let Spring compile your JasperReport templates on-the-fly. The iText and POI JARs are only necessary if you plan to produce PDF and Excel reports.

NOTE: To use JasperReports 1.0.0 with iReport 0.5.0, copy all the JARs from the distribution's *lib* directory into iReport's *lib* directory.

CONFIGURATION

Spring contains five **View** implementations for JasperReports:

- **JasperReportsCsvView**
- **JasperReportsHtmlView**
- **JasperReportsPdfView**
- **JasperReportsXlsView**
- **JasperReportsMultiFormatView**

To use any of these views, you must configure a **ResourceBundleViewResolver** bean to map view names to view classes. The **ResourceBundleViewResolver** points to a properties file that defines a view's properties, such as *class* and *url*. A bean definition should already exist in your *web/WEB-INF/action-servlet.xml*. If it doesn't exist, add it using the code in Listing 7.1:

Listing 6.5.1

```
<bean id="viewResolver" class="org.springframework.web.servlet.view.
    ResourceBundleViewResolver">
    <property name="basename" value="views"/>
</bean>
```

The **basename** property refers to the name of a *.properties* file. In this example, a *views.properties* file should exist in your *web/WEB-INF/classes* directory.

In this exercise, you'll create a report that renders in CSV, Excel, HTML, and PDF. You can use one of these two ways to configure Spring MVC to render JasperReports:

- **Option 1:** In *views.properties*, specify each view name individually, along with the type of JasperReportView. In addition, specify a *url* property that points to the template that contains the layout data. Compiled JasperReport templates have a .jasper extension.

- **Option 2:** In *views.properties*, specify a *class* property that uses the **JasperReportsMultiFormatView**. This class allows you to render multiple formats from the same layout template. Like Option 1, configure a *url* property to point to the template.

NOTE: You can also create bean definitions in *web/WEB-INF/action-servlet.xml* for a particular view name. This technique is described in the *iReport issues* section.

To use Option 1, create (or add to) a *views.properties* file in *web/WEB-INF/classes* and add the following individual view configurations for each content-type. See Listing 7.2.

Listing 6.5.2

```
simpleReportHtml.class=org.springframework.web.servlet.view.
    jasperreports.JasperReportsHtmlView
simpleReportHtml.url=/WEB-INF/reports/simpleReport.jasper

simpleReportCsv.class=org.springframework.web.servlet.view
    .jasperreports.JasperReportsCsvView
simpleReportCsv.url=/WEB-INF/reports/simpleReport.jasper

simpleReportExcel.class=org.springframework.web.servlet.view.
    jasperreports.JasperReportsXlsView
simpleReportExcel.url=/WEB-INF/reports/simpleReport.jasper

simpleReportPdf.class=org.springframework.web.servlet.view
    .jasperreports.JasperReportsPdfView
simpleReportPdf.url=/WEB-INF/reports/simpleReport.jasper
```

Option 2 allows you to simplify your configuration. Rather than specifying a view definition for each content-type, you can specify a single view definition for *all* content-types. The **JasperReportsMultiFormatView** allows you to do this and it is much easier to configure. See Listing 7.3.

Listing 6.5.3

```
simpleReport.class=org.springframework.web.servlet.view
    .jasperreports.JasperReportsMultiFormatView
simpleReport.url=/WEB-INF/reports/simpleReport.jasper
```

NOTE: It is possible to have Spring automatically compile the *.jrxml* file into a *.jasper* file. However, it is more efficient to precompile the report as part of your build process.

CREATING THE REPORT

While it is possible to learn how JasperReports uses an XML-based template to control its content, it is far more efficient to use open source GUI tools like Jasper-Assistant or iReport to generate them. The following steps illustrate how to use iReport to create a report.

1   Download iReport from ireport.sourceforge.net.

2   The default *classic.xml* template is modified to work around missing image and white-on-white font issues with iReport. You can download it from sourcebeat.com/downloads/splive/classicC.xml. After downloading, back up the existing *iReport-0.5.0/templates/classicC.xml* file and copy this template into the *iReport-0.5.0/templates* subdirectory.

3   Run *iReport.bat* (or *iReport.sh* on Unix) to start iReport.

WARNING: On Windows, you may need to copy *tools.jar* from your JDK into the iReport installation's *lib* directory.

---

4   Start the HSQL database in standalone mode by executing *hsql.bat* (or *hsql.sh* for UNIX) from the *bin* directory in the MyUsers project. See Figure 7.1.

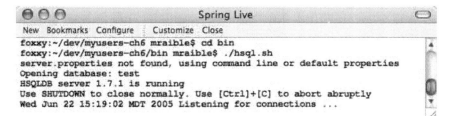

Figure 6.5.1: Starting up HSQL

5   After iReport has started, select **Connections / Datasources** from the **Datasource** menu. A dialog box displays, and you can select **New** to add a new data source. Enter the following settings:

- Name: `myusers-hsql-server`
- JDBC Driver: `org.hsqldb.jdbcDriver`
- JDBC URL: `jdbc:hsqldb:hsql://localhost`
- Username: `sa`
- No password

See Figure 7.2.

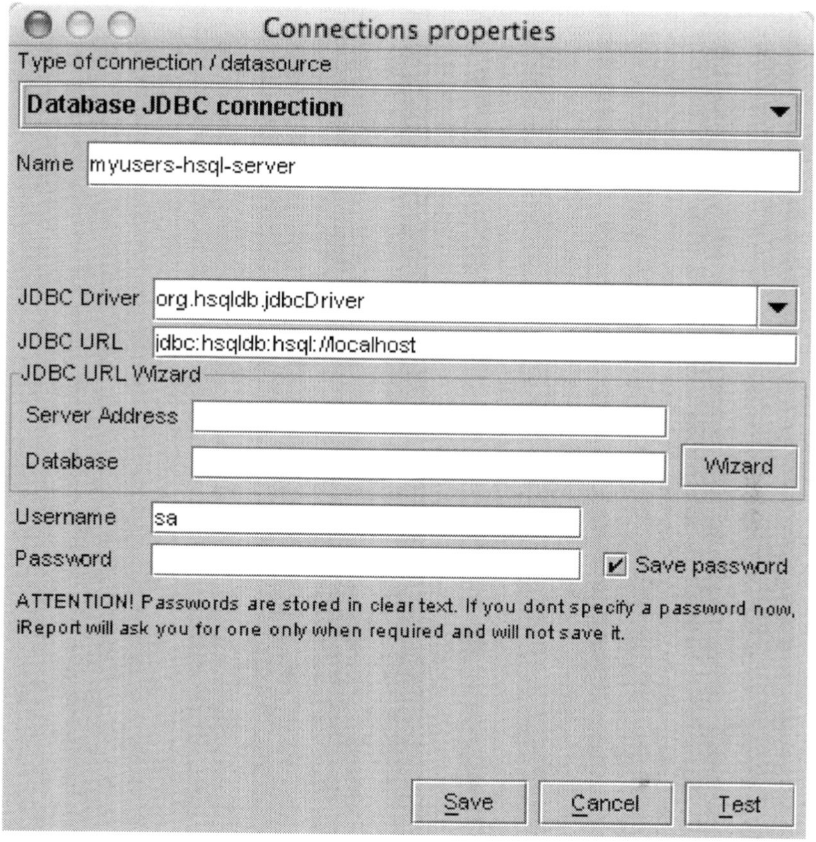

Figure 6.5.2: iReport datasource dialog box

Click the **Test** button to ensure your settings are correct and you can connect to the database.

6   Create a report by selecting **Report Wizard** from the **File** menu. See Figure 7.3.

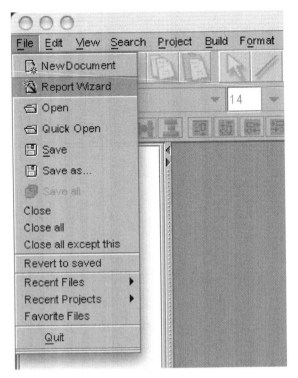

Figure 6.5.3: Report wizard

7   The wizard displays in a series of steps. Step 1 prompts you for the SQL query to retrieve data. Enter `select * from app_user order by last_name, first_name` and click **Next**. See Figure 7.4.

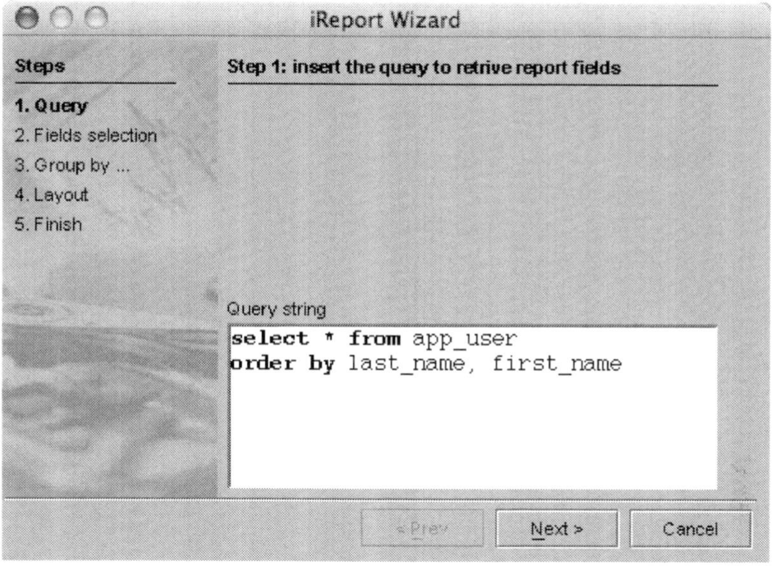

Figure 6.5.4: Specify SQL query

8   Step 2 prompts you to choose the fields to display on the report. Select the **FIRST_NAME** and **LAST_NAME** fields and move them from the left pane to the right pane. Click **Next** to continue. See Figure 7.5.

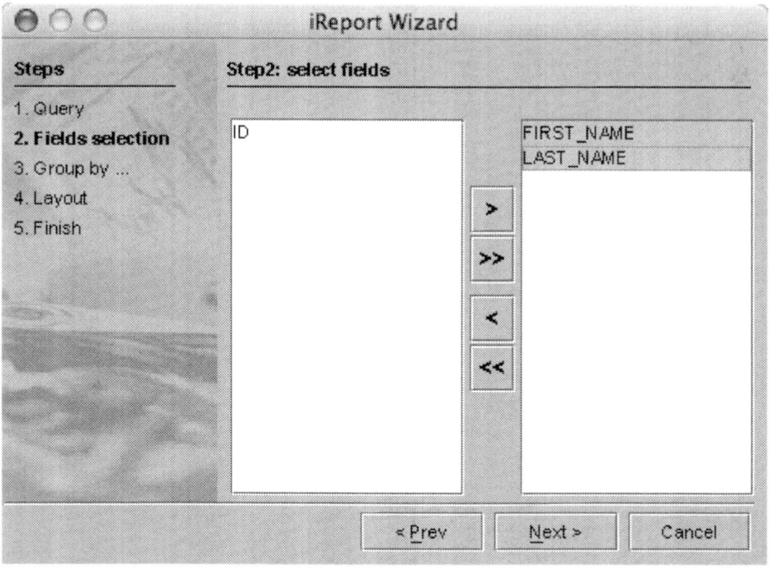

Figure 6.5.5: Select report fields

9 Step 3 prompts you for your group by criteria. Select **LAST_NAME** for Group 1 and leave Group 2 blank. Click **Next** to continue. See Figure 7.6.

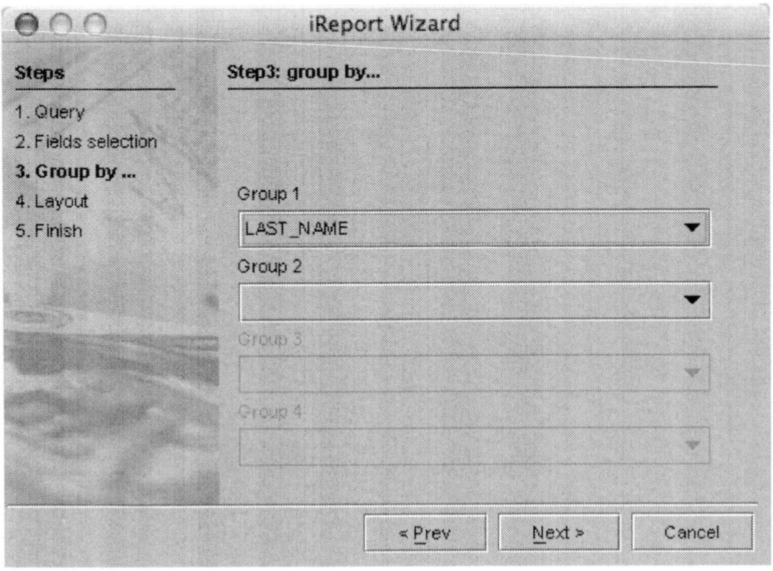

Figure 6.5.6: Group by dialog box

10 Step 4 prompts you to choose the layout and report format. Choose **Columnar** and **classicC.xml**. Click **Next** to continue. See Figure 7.7.

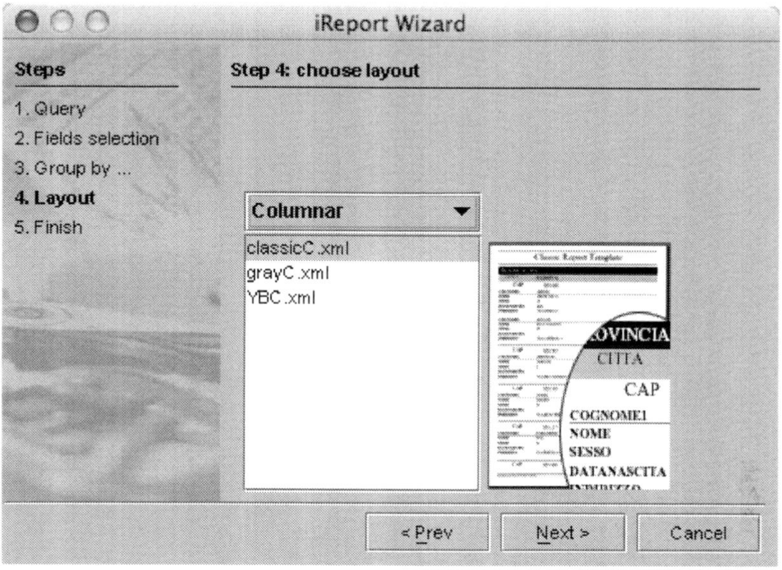

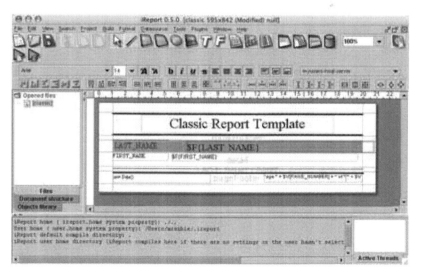

Figure 6.5.7: Layout dialog box

11 Step 5 shows you a **Finish** dialog. Click **Finish** to complete the wizard.

12 The report layout should now display, allowing you to manipulate the elements. See Figure 7.8.

Figure 6.5.8: Report layout

13 Run the report using a connection. There is a button with a green triangle and a blue database icon in the top right corner that allows you to do this. See Figure 7.9.

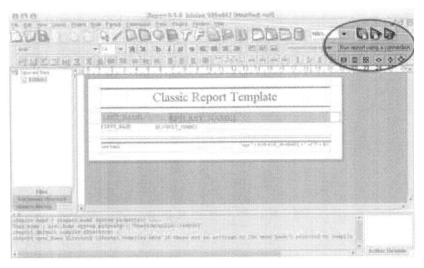

Figure 6.5.9: Run report using a connection

14 When prompted, save the report as *users.jrxml* in the *myusers/web/WEB-INF/reports* directory (you will have to create this directory). See Figure 7.10.

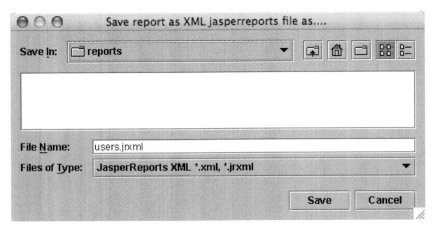

Figure 6.5.10: Save report

15 After saving the report, iReport displays a preview of your report. At this point, you can change the look and feel of the report as much as you like. See Figure 7.11.

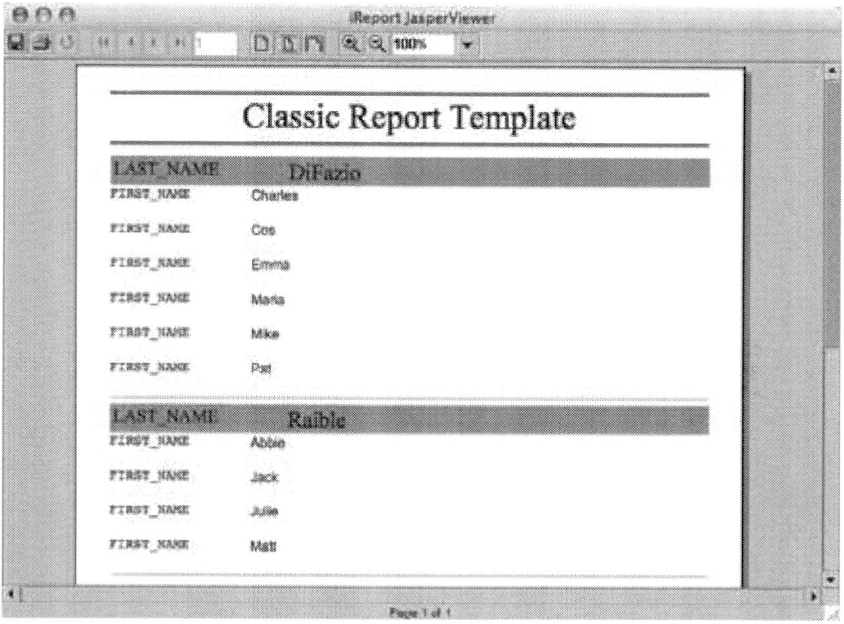

Figure 6.5.11: Previewing the report

INTEGRATING JASPERREPORTS INTO MYUSERS

1 In the MyUsers project's *build.xml* file, define JasperReports' **JRAntCompileTask**, as well as targets to compile and view reports. Precompiling the report minimizes the memory usage on the server. See Listing 7.4.

Listing 6.5.4

```
<property name="report.dir" value="${web.dir}/WEB-INF/reports"/>

<target name="jrc" description="compile jasperreports">
    <taskdef name="jrc"
        classname="net.sf.jasperreports.ant.JRAntCompileTask">
        <classpath refid="classpath"/>
    </taskdef>

    <mkdir dir="${build.dir}/temp"/>
```

```
        <jrc destdir="${report.dir}" xmlvalidation="true"
            tempdir="${build.dir}/temp" keepjava="true">
            <classpath refid="classpath"/>
            <src>
                <fileset dir="${report.dir}" includes="**/*.jrxml"/>
            </src>
        </jrc>
    </target>
```

2   Make the **war** and **deploy** targets depend on the **jrc** target. See
Listing 7.5.

Listing 6.5.5

```
<target name="war" depends="compile,jrc"
    description="Packages app as WAR">
...
<target name="deploy" depends="compile,jrc"
    description="Deploy application">
```

The following steps show you how to use **JasperReportsMultiFormatView** to
render a report listing the current users in your project's database.

3   Add a **<servlet-mapping>** to *web/WEB-INF/web.xml* so any URLs with
"**/reports/**" in them will map to Spring's **DispatcherServlet**. Add
the code in Listing 7.6 after the **.html* mapping.

Listing 6.5.6

```
<servlet-mapping>
    <servlet-name>action</servlet-name>
    <url-pattern>/reports/*</url-pattern>
</servlet-mapping>
```

4   Create a controller that can determine and pass the desired format to the
view class. The format is passed to the view as part of the model. Creating
a controller that extends **MultiActionController** allows you to do this
easily. See Listing 7.7.

Listing 6.5.7

```
public class ReportController extends MultiActionController {
    private Log log = LogFactory.getLog(ReportController.class);

    /**
     * Determine the view format (html, pdf, csv, xls) from the
     * extension the view will bind the datasource.
     */
```

```java
public ModelAndView viewReport(HttpServletRequest request,
                               HttpServletResponse response)
throws Exception {

    String uri = request.getRequestURI();
    String format = "html";
    try {
        format = uri.substring(uri.lastIndexOf(".") + 1);
    } catch (IndexOutOfBoundsException e) {
        // ignore - html format will be used
    }
    log.debug("using format: " + format);

    Map model = new HashMap();
    model.put("format", format);

    return new ModelAndView("reportView", model);
}
}
```

The **JasperReportsMultiFormatView** keys off the **format** key in the model to determine which format it should use. See the default mapping keys and their corresponding view classes in the following list.

- csv: **JasperReportsCsvView**
- html: **JasperReportsHtmlView**
- pdf: **JasperReportsPdfView**
- xls: **JasperReportsXlsView**

5 In *web/WEB-INF/classes/views.properties*, add the **reportView** view name you specified in the **ReportController** class. See Listing 7.8.

Listing 6.5.8

```
reportView.class=org.springframework.web.servlet.view.jasperreports.
    JasperReportsMultiFormatView
reportView.url=/WEB-INF/reports/users.jasper
reportView.jdbcDataSource(ref)=dataSource
```

Specifying the **jdbcDataSource** as a bean reference is optional. Another option is to put a **java.util.Collection** or **JRDataSource** into your model, in the **ReportController**. Spring will use the first of these it finds, but if you're using iReport — and configuring it to talk to a data source — specifying the **jdbcData-Source** is the easiest way to hook Spring and JasperReports together.

6 Create a **reportController** bean definition in *web/WEB-INF/action-servlet.xml*. See Listing 7.9.

Listing 6.5.9

```
<bean id="reportController" class="org.appfuse.web.ReportController">
    <property name="methodNameResolver" ref="resolver"/>
</bean>
```

7   Create a bean definition named "**resolver**" for the **reportController**
    bean's **methodNameResolver** property. This bean utilizes a **Proper-
    tiesMethodNameResolver** to handle the URL mapping to the
    appropriate method. In this example, when */reports/userReport.html* is
    referenced the **viewReport()** method of the **reportController** is
    called. See Listing 7.10.

Listing 6.5.10

```
<bean id="resolver"
    class="org.springframework.web.servlet.mvc.multiaction
        .PropertiesMethodNameResolver">
    <property name="mappings">
        <props>
            <prop key="/userReport.*">viewReport</prop>
        </props>
    </property>
</bean>
```

NOTE: The reason you don't need "**/reports/**" in the property key is that
/reports/ is already mapped in *web.xml* — and therefore redundant. You only need to
specify the servlet path after */reports*.

---

8   Modify the **urlMapping** bean in *web/WEB-INF/action-servlet.xml* to map
    URLs with "**/userReport**" in them to the **reportController** bean. See
    Listing 7.11.

Listing 6.5.11

```
<prop key="/userReport.*">reportController</prop>
```

9   Run **ant deploy**, start Tomcat, and navigate to localhost:8080/myusers/
    reports/userReport.pdf in your browser.

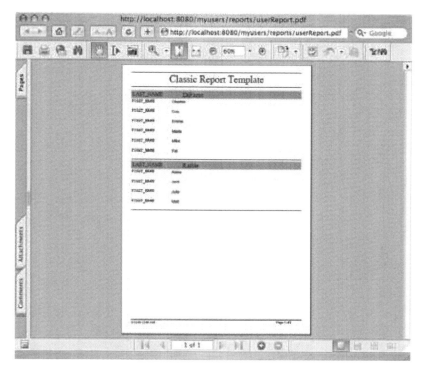

Figure 6.5.12: View user report as PDF in browser

To see other report formats, try the following URLs:

- localhost:8080/myusers/reports/userReport.csv
- localhost:8080/myusers/reports/userReport.html
- localhost:8080/myusers/reports/userReport.xls

When viewing the previous URLs, you might notice that the HTML page renders in your browser, complete with SiteMesh decoration. To exclude reports from being decorated, complete the following two steps:

1 Edit *web/WEB-INF/sitemesh.xml* and add the line in Listing 7.12 just after the **<sitemesh>** element at the beginning of the file:

Listing 6.5.12

```
<excludes file="/WEB-INF/decorators.xml"/>
```

2 Edit *web/WEB-INF/decorators.xml* and add an **<excludes>** block after the initial **<decorators>** element. See Listing 7.13.

Listing 6.5.13

```
<excludes>
    <pattern>/reports*</pattern>
    <pattern>/images/px</pattern>
</excludes>
```

The second pattern exclusion is to stop the processing of the *px* image that you'll add in the next step. The reason the first pattern doesn't pick it up is that there's no file extension to set the content-type.

3   Run `ant deploy reload` (with Tomcat running) and try viewing the report again. See Figure 7.13. This time, it should not be decorated. The missing images problem you see in Figure 7.13 is solved in the next section.

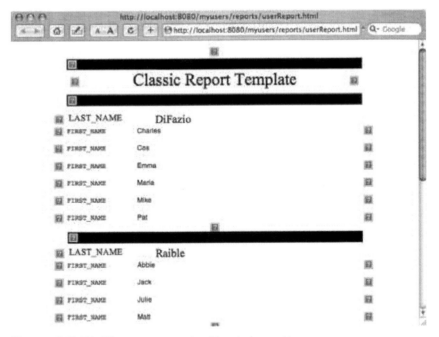

Figure 6.5.13: View user report without decoration

IREPORT ISSUES

The default installation of iReport has some issues with exporting HTML and Excel reports. Both report types render the report text in a white font on a white background, so you can't read anything. The second problem is the missing image problem you saw in Figure 7.13.

WHITE FONT ON WHITE BACKGROUND

With the default template, JasperReports is unable to locate the font for HTML and Excel reports so it defaults to the first one it can find. Often, it does not have the font for the specified point size and therefore does not render it.

This problem was fixed near the beginning of this chapter when you replaced the default *classicC.xml*. If you didn't replace this template, you would have seen the problem. The modified template matches up the template's font names for both HTML and PDF.

MISSING LAYOUT IMAGE

The missing image problem is because JasperReports looks for a *nullpx* image to help lay out the report. To fix this issue, complete the following steps:

1   Download the missing image from sourcebeat.com/downloads/splive /nullpx. Rename it to *px* and place it the *images* directory.

2   Rather than configuring the **reportView** bean's attributes in *web/WEB-INF/classes/view.properties*, create the definition in *web/WEB-INF/action-servlet.xml*.

   a   Comment out the attributes in your *view.properties* file. See Listing 7.14.

Listing 6.5.14

```
#reportView.class=org.springframework.web.servlet.view
    .jasperreports.JasperReportsMultiFormatView
#reportView.url=/WEB-INF/reports/users.jasper
#reportView.jdbcDataSource(ref)=dataSource
```

   b   Add a **reportView** bean definition to *action-servlet.xml* and add an **exporterParameters** property with a map that sets the path to your report images. See Listing 7.15.

Listing 6.5.15

```
<bean id="reportView" class="org.springframework.web.servlet.view
    .jasperreports.JasperReportsMultiFormatView">
    <property name="url" value="/WEB-INF/reports/users.jasper"/>
    <property name="jdbcDataSource" ref="dataSource"/>
    <property name="exporterParameters">
        <map>
```

```
                    <entry key="net.sf.jasperreports.engine.export
                       .JRHtmlExporterParameter.IMAGES_URI"
                       value="/myusers/images/"/>
            </map>
        </property>
    </bean>
```

3   Run **ant deploy reload** and go to localhost:8080/myusers/reports
/userReport.html. This time, the report should render correctly. See
Figure 7.14.

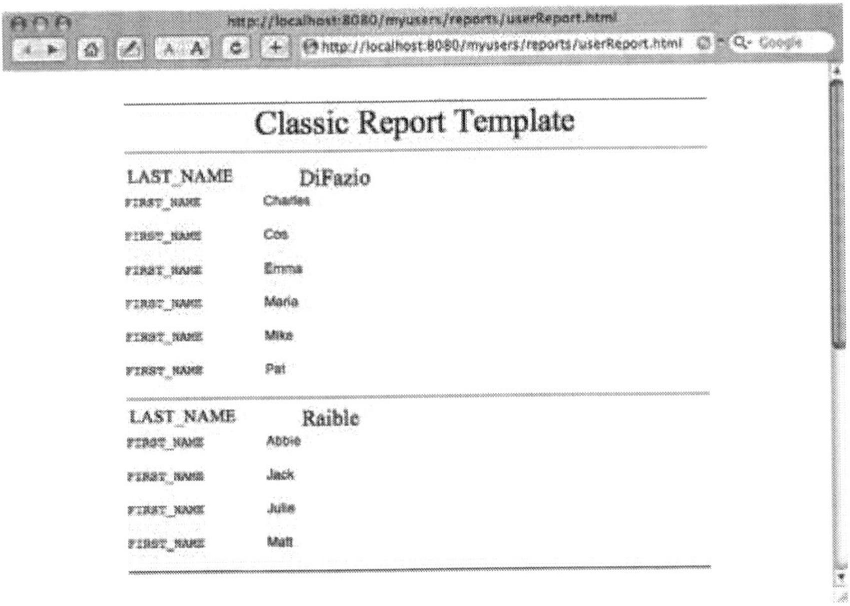

Figure 6.5.14: HTML user report with layout image

OTHER ISSUES

A couple of other issues existed in the default *classicC.xml* template:

- The default size of the detail column header had to be adjusted; it
  originally spanned the line and overwrote the detail data (**firstname**, in
  this example).

- The background and foreground colors for the group header and group
  value (**lastname**) had to be revised.

You could have fixed these problems manually for each report by using the GUI
builder to make the adjustments. It is also possible to edit all the *.jrxml* files that are

generated. Since this task would have to be repeated for every report generated, an improved *classicC.xml* template has been provided.

SUMMARY
....

Using iReport and JasperReports with Spring MVC is an easy way to create HTML, CSV, Excel, and PDF-based reports. iReport makes it easy to create reports, and Spring MVC makes it easy to integrate JasperReports. You can easily configure reports to render as one specific content type, or you can use **JasperReports-MultiFormatView** to export all content types.

PERSISTENCE STRATEGIES: HIBERNATE, iBATIS, JDBC, JDO, AND OJB

. . . .

How to integrate five popular persistence frameworks into your application

Hibernate is quickly becoming a popular choice for persistence in Java applications, but sometimes it doesn't fit. If you have an existing database schema — or even pre-written SQL — sometimes it's better to use JDBC or iBATIS (which supports externalized SQL in XML files). This chapter refactors the MyUsers application to support both JDBC and iBATIS as persistence framework options. It also implements the **UserDAO** *using JDO and OJB to showcase Spring's excellent support for these frameworks.*

OVERVIEW

Most modern applications talk to databases to load and store their information. Persistence is the process of retrieving, saving, and deleting data from a data store (usually a relational database). Persistence is a critical feature in web applications for loading and displaying information. For many years, this has been the ugly part of Java. You *could* use JDBC, and it usually works across database vendors. After all, the point of the JDBC API is to provide a *standard* for accessing databases from Java. However, JDBC is difficult to write, especially for a newcomer. It requires developers to catch exceptions and close connections in a final block, which many Java rookies forget to do. Additionally, the exceptions thrown by different JDBC Driver vendors are not standard, so an error code on one server might mean something completely different on another server.

With the advent of Spring's persistence support, many of the issues with JDBC disappear. Its JDBC framework converts JDBC's checked exceptions to a common hierarchy of RuntimeExceptions. These exceptions provide precise information about what went wrong, which is much better than **SQLException** reports. It uses closures to handle closing database connections, and it includes a set of common SQL error codes for numerous database types.

TIP: A *closure* is an object that's represented as a block of code within a method. You can use this object like any Java object, such as parameters and variables. For more information, see the Java Glossary (mindprod.com/jgloss/closure.html). Charles Miller also has a tutorial on closures and Java at fishbowl.pastiche.org /2003/05/16/closures_and_java_a_tutorial.

Spring provides support classes for numerous other persistence frameworks, including Hibernate, iBATIS, JDO, and OJB. It even uses a common methodology in its support, further simplifying the learning curve from one framework to the other. If you learn how to use Spring's Hibernate support, it's very easy to use Spring's iBATIS or JDO APIs.

In this chapter, you will learn more about Spring's Hibernate support and how MyUsers uses Hibernate. From there, you will implement DAOs using iBATIS, Spring JDBC, JDO, and OJB. By the end of this chapter, you will know how to use these technologies and configure them with the Spring Framework. The purpose of this chapter is to briefly introduce persistence options with Spring and how to configure them. You will not learn how to solve complicated persistence problems with each framework. Please consult the framework's respective project page for that information.

NOTE: Transactions will be covered in *Chapter 11: Transactions.*

Spring has a common theme when it comes to persistence:

- Provide easy configuration using dependency injection.
- Provide base DaoSupport classes for the popular persistence frameworks, including Hibernate, JDBC, iBATIS, JDO, and OJB.
- Convert the checked exceptions for the different frameworks to a common exception hierarchy, relieving your upper-level classes of the specifics of the persistence layer. Figure 8.1[1] illustrates this hierarchy.
- Provide easy-to-use *Template* classes that reduce many DAO methods to one-liners. These templates can be used standalone or obtained from the DaoSupport parent classes.
- Open and close any necessary resources (such as database connections) for you.

---

1. Diagram modeled from the one found at www.springframework.org/docs/reference/ dao.html.

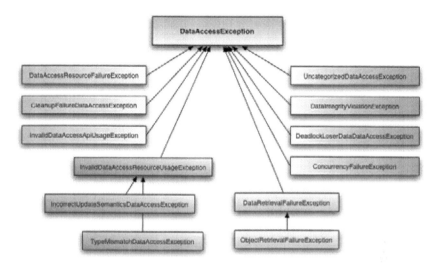

Figure 7.1: `DataAccessException` hierarchy

The code in this chapter should be easy to test because you already have a **User-DAOTest** that does not contain any Hibernate-specific code. This test will verify your implementations. Each persistence framework section will show you how to configure the respective framework with Spring, and how to implement the **UserDAO**.

PREPARING FOR THE EXERCISES

The best way to learn is to follow along with the exercises in this chapter. The easiest way to do this is to download the **MyUsers Chapter 7** bundle from source-beat.com/downloads. This project tree is the result of exercises in *Chapter 6: View Options* and contains all the JARs you will use in this chapter. The *Configuration* subtopic of each section describes the dependencies each project needs. You can use this chapter as a reference for integrating these principles into your own applications.

In this chapter's example, you must change the way that the MyUsers application loads context files. Rather than just loading *applicationContext.xml*, the tests and *web.xml* have been changed to load *applicationContext*.xml*. This is for convenience. When creating context files for each persistence option, it's easier to specify a wildcard to match the filename. Otherwise, you'd have to change the tests and *web.xml* each time you switched persistence layers.

The following files are affected by this change:

- *test/org/appfuse/dao/BaseDAOTestCase.java*

- *test/org/appfuse/service/UserManagerTest.java*
- *test/org/appfuse/web/UserControllerTest.java*
- *test/org/appfuse/web/UserFormControllerTest.java*
- *web/WEB-INF/web.xml*

In this chapter's exercises, you'll be creating a different context file for each persistence frameworks. This file will contain bean definitions for each DAO implementation, as well as any **DataSource**-related settings. The baseline *applicationContext.xml* for this chapter has been modified to remove the Hibernate-specific settings, removing the following beans:

- **dataSource**
- **sessionFactory**
- **transactionManager**
- **userDAO**

The userManager, userManagerTarget, and userValidator are the only remaining bean definitions.

HIBERNATE

Hibernate is an open source Object/Relational Mapping (ORM) solution. ORM is the technique of mapping an Object model to a Relational model (usually represented by a SQL database). Hibernate was created in late 2001 by Gavin King and a handful of other developers. Since then, Hibernate has become a very popular persistence framework in the Java community. It's become so popular that the next version of EJB (3.0) is using Hibernate as a source of good ideas. The reasons for its popularity are mainly due to its good documentation, ease of use, excellent features, and smart project management. Hibernate's license is LGPL, which means you can use it for free as long as you don't modify its source code. More information on its license is available on the Hibernate web site.

Hibernate frees you from hand-coding JDBC. Rather than using SQL and JDBC, you can use domain objects (which are usually POJOs) and simply create XML-based *mapping files*. These files indicate which fields (in an object) map to which columns (in a table). Hibernate has a powerful query language called Hibernate Query Language (HQL). This language allows you to write SQL, but also use object-oriented semantics. One of the best parts about its query language is you can literally guess at its syntax and get it right.

Hibernate's Session interface is similar to a database connection in that you must open and close it at appropriate times to avoid errors and memory leaks. One of the biggest advantages of using Spring with Hibernate is that you don't have to manage opening and closing these Sessions — everything just works. In addition, Spring simplifies transactions with Hibernate and allows you to set transaction semantics declaratively (in XML).

NOTE: Spring's Hibernate 3 support classes are located in the `org.spring-framework.orm.hibernate3` and `org.springframework.orm.hibernate3.support` packages.

Although *Chapter 2: Spring Quick-Start Tutorial* covers integrating Hibernate into MyUsers, this chapter covers it as well to provide a single chapter describing Spring's persistence support. In addition, this chapter covers Hibernate 3, whereas *Chapter 2: Spring Quick-Start Tutorial* used Hibernate 2. If you'd like to see a version of this chapter that covers Hibernate 2, please download a version of this book from before October 2005. If you downloaded the *myusers-ch7* bundle, the Hibernate configurations are eliminated so you can start with a clean slate.

DEPENDENCIES

Hibernate has a number of third-party libraries it depends on. All of these are available as part of the Hibernate download. The following JARs are included in the MyUsers download as part of Hibernate 3.0.5. They are all required, except for the ones marked optional.

- `hibernate3.jar` — Hibernate core
- `c3p0-0.8.5.2.jar` — Basic connection pool for running unit tests
- `commons-collections.jar` — Enhanced Collections library
- `cglib-2.1.jar` — Code Generation Library for generating proxies for persistent classes
- `dom4j-1.6.jar` — XML library for parsing configuration and mapping files
- `ehcache-1.1.jar` — A pure Java, in-process cache; the default cache for Hibernate
- `jta.jar` — Java Transaction API
- (optional) `oscache-2.1.jar` and (cluster-aware) `swarmcache-1.0rc2.jar` — Alternative caching implementations

---

NOTE: The primary difference between Hibernate 2 and Hibernate 3 is that the package name changed from *net.sf.hibernate.** to *org.hibernate.**. From a Spring perspective, the main difference is the package name as well; use `org.springframework.orm.hibernate` for Hibernate 2 and `org.springframework.orm.hibernate3` for Hibernate 3. In addition to these changes, Hibernate 3 changed most of its exceptions from checked to runtime.

CONFIGURATION

To make your objects persistable with Hibernate, first create a mapping file. (This chapter assumes you have already created a **User** POJO in *src/org/appfuse/model*, with **id**, **firstName** and **lastName** properties.)

1   In the *src/org/appfuse/model* directory, create a *User.hbm.xml* file with the contents in Listing 8.1:

Listing 7.1

```
<?xml version="1.0" encoding="UTF-8"?>
<!DOCTYPE hibernate-mapping PUBLIC
    "-//Hibernate/Hibernate Mapping DTD 3.0//EN"
    "http://hibernate.sourceforge.net/hibernate-mapping-3.0.dtd">

<hibernate-mapping>
    <class name="org.appfuse.model.User" table="app_user">

        <id name="id" column="id" unsaved-value="0">
            <generator class="increment"/>
        </id>
        <property name="firstName" column="first_name"
            not-null="true"/>
        <property name="lastName" column="last_name"
            not-null="true"/>

    </class>
</hibernate-mapping>
```

In the above mapping, the **<id>** element uses **increment** to indicate *max value + 1* for the generated primary key. The generator type of **increment** is not recommended for a cluster. Fortunately, Hibernate has many other options.

NOTE: If you're using JDK 5, you can use Hibernate annotations as an alternative to the above mapping file. You will need to download the Hibernate annotations distribution and copy *hibernate-annotations.jar* and *ejb-3.0-edr2.jar* into your classpath. Annotations are covered later in this chapter.

---

2   Create an *applicationContext-hibernate.xml* file in the *web/WEB-INF* directory and add a bean definition for a **DataSource**. You can use the existing *applicationContext-empty.txt* as a template. This file should have the *spring-beans.dtd* and root **<beans>** element defined before the bean definition.

The **dataSource** bean in Listing 8.2 uses an HSQLDB database, which is a pure Java database that runs from a simple *hsqldb.jar* file in the *web/WEB-INF/lib* directory. Later, you'll change this to use MySQL to see how easy it is to change databases.

Listing 7.2

```
<bean id="dataSource"
    class="org.springframework.jdbc.datasource
        .DriverManagerDataSource">
    <property name="driverClassName"
        value="org.hsqldb.jdbcDriver"/>
    <property name="url" value="jdbc:hsqldb:db/appfuse"/>
    <property name="username" value="sa"/>
    <property name="password" value=""/>
</bean>
```

The **DriverManagerDataSource** is a simple **DataSource** that configures a JDBC Driver via bean properties. You can also configure a JNDI **DataSource** if you'd rather use your container's pre-configured **DataSource**. For example, a common strategy is to use the **DriverManagerDataSource** for testing, and the JNDI **DataSource** (Listing 8.3) for production.

NOTE: *Chapter 9: Testing Spring Applications* shows how to mock the JNDI **Data-Source** and use the configuration below for both testing and production.

Listing 7.3

```
<bean id="dataSource"
    class="org.springframework.jndi.JndiObjectFactoryBean">
    <property name="jndiName" name="java:comp/env/jdbc/appfuse">
</bean>
```

Most web applications talk to databases using the same user name and password (as configured in the connection pool). However, some databases have more rigorous security in place and require users to log in with their personal user name and password when they invoke the **getConnection()** method. If you have this type of environment, you might want to use the **UserCredentialsDataSourceAdapter** class to wrap your **dataSource** bean. This proxy class allows you to optionally set a user name and password for a connection. If no user name is specified, this proxy simply calls the standard **getConnection()** of the target **DataSource** (instead of **getConnection(username, password)**). See Listing 8.4.

Listing 7.4

```
<bean id="dataSource"
    class="org.springframework.jdbc.datasource
        .UserCredentialsDataSourceAdapter">
    <property name="targetDataSource">
        <bean class="org.springframework.jndi.JndiObjectFactoryBean">
            <property name="jndiName
```

```
                value="java:comp/env/jdbc/myusers"/>
        </bean>
    </property>
    <property name="username" value="root"/>
    <property name="password" value=""/>
</bean>
```

After configuring your **dataSource** bean to use the **UserCredentialsData-SourceAdapter**, you can pass in individual user names and passwords using calls as in Listing 8.5:

Listing 7.5

```
ApplicationContext ctx = ...
UserCredentialsDataSourceAdapter ds =
    (UserCredentialsDataSourceAdapter)ctx.getBean("dataSource");
ds.removeCredentialsFromCurrentThread();
ds.setCredentialsForCurrentThread(username, password);
```

TIP: If you want to make a call like the one above in your services or data layer, using Acegi Security can greatly simplify things. It includes a feature whereby it sets the current user's credentials in a **ThreadLocal**. This makes it easy to retrieve a user's information in any layer.

---

3   Add a **sessionFactory** bean definition, which depends on the previous **dataSource** bean and the mapping file. The **hibernate.dialect** property will change based on the database, and the **hibernate.hbm2ddl .auto** property creates the database on-the-fly when the application starts. You might notice that the **dataSource** reference has changed (from previous chapters) to use **<ref bean>** rather than **<ref local>**. This is so you can configure the **dataSource** bean in separate file, possibly switching a testing version with an in-container version. See Listing 8.6.

Listing 7.6

```
<bean id="sessionFactory"
    class="org.springframework.orm.hibernate3
        .LocalSessionFactoryBean">
    <property name="dataSource" ref="dataSource"/>
    <property name="mappingResources">
        <list>
            <value>org/appfuse/model/User.hbm.xml</value>
        </list>
    </property>
    <property name="hibernateProperties">
        <props>
```

```
        <prop key="hibernate.dialect">
            org.hibernate.dialect.HSQLDialect</prop>
        <prop key="hibernate.hbm2ddl.auto">create</prop>
    </props>
  </property>
</bean>
```

As an alternative to specifying each individual mapping file, use the **mappingJar-Locations** or **mappingDirectoryLocations** properties to refer to a JAR file or directory. You can also use a *hibernate.cfg.xml* file to specify your settings and point to it using a **configLocation** property.

TIP: Whenever you have a **java.util.Properties** dependency type, you can use a **<props>** element (as shown for the **hibernateProperties** property). You can also use a **<value>**, which allows you to write less XML to achieve the same result. See Listing 8.7.

Listing 7.7

```
<property name="hibernateProperties">
    <value>
        hibernate.dialect=org.hibernate.dialect.HSQLDialect
        hibernate.hbm2ddl.auto=create
    </value>
</property>
```

---

4   Add a **transactionManager** bean definition that uses Spring's **HibernateTransactionManager** class. This class's Javadocs describe it best: "This class binds a Hibernate Session from the specified factory to the thread, potentially allowing for one thread Session per factory." **SessionFactoryUtils** and **HibernateTemplate** are aware of thread-bound sessions and will participate in such transactions automatically. Using either is required for Hibernate access code that needs to support a transaction-handling mechanism. See Listing 8.8.

Listing 7.8

```
<bean id="transactionManager"
    class="org.springframework.orm.hibernate3
        .HibernateTransactionManager">
    <property name="sessionFactory" ref="sessionFactory"/>
</bean>
```

The **UserHibernateDAO** or **UserDAOTest** do not use this bean specifically, but the **userManager** bean's definition references it. *Chapter 9: Testing Spring Applications* and the *JDO* section in this chapter show you how to utilize transactions in your DAO tests.

5   Create a **UserDAOHibernate.java** class in *src/org/appfuse/dao/hibernate* (you will need to create this directory/package). This file extends **HibernateDaoSupport** and implements **UserDAO**. See Listing 8.9.

Listing 7.9

```
package org.appfuse.dao.hibernate;

// use your IDE to organize imports

public class UserDAOHibernate extends HibernateDaoSupport
    implements UserDAO {

    public List getUsers() {
        return getHibernateTemplate().find("from User");
    }

    public User getUser(Long id) {
        User user = (User) getHibernateTemplate().get(User.class, id);
        if (user == null) {
            throw new ObjectRetrievalFailureException(
                User.class, id);
        }
        return user;
    }

    public void saveUser(User user) {
        getHibernateTemplate().saveOrUpdate(user);
    }

    public void removeUser(Long id) {
        Object user = getHibernateTemplate().load(User.class, id);
        getHibernateTemplate().delete(user);
    }
}
```

6   Add a bean definition for the **userDAO** to *applicationContext-hibernate.xml*. See Listing 8.10.

Listing 7.10

```
<bean id="userDAO" class="org.appfuse.dao.hibernate
  .UserDAOHibernate">
  <property name="sessionFactory" ref="sessionFactory"/>
</bean>
```

In the **UserDAOHibernate** class, **HibernateTemplate** does most of the work. Using templates to handle persistence calls is a common theme among Spring DAO support classes. Also note the following items in the **UserDAOHibernate.java** class:

- The **getUser()** method uses **HibernateTemplate().get()**, which returns null if it finds no matching objects. The alternative is to use **HibernateTemplate().load()**, which throws an exception if it finds no objects. **HibernateTemplate.load()** is used in the **removeUser()** method, but you could easily use **get()** instead.

- The **getUser()** method throws an **ObjectRetrievalFailureException** when it finds no user.

- It has no checked exceptions. You will likely end up writing a fair amount of try/catch statements with Hibernate.

A **logger** variable is already defined in **HibernateDaoSupport**, allowing for easy logging in subclasses. For example, add the code in Listing 8.11 to the end of the **saveUser()** method.

Listing 7.11

```
if (logger.isDebugEnabled()) {
    logger.debug("User's id set to: " + user.getId());
}
```

NOTE: In this example, the **UserDAOHibernate** class is specific to the **User** entity object. If you're creating a large application with Hibernate, it might make sense to create a generic DAO that can handle any type of object. If you're using JDK 5, you can write a type-safe generic DAO using the Generics feature of JDK 5. If you're using a version of JDK earlier than JDK 5, you can still write a generic DAO, but you'll have to cast your returned objects to their real type (if you need to call specific methods). Below are links with code for each of the generic DAO types.

- JDK 5: blog.hibernate.org/cgi-bin/blosxom.cgi/2005/09/08#genericdao
- JDK 1.4.2: static.appfuse.org/api/org/appfuse/dao/hibernate/BaseDAOHibernate.java.html

TEST IT!

The `UserDAOTest.testGetUsers()` method in this chapter's download is different from previous chapters. The new method is below. It removes assertions that checked for an empty database table before the test and a single record after the test. The reason for this is that the `hibernate.hbm2ddl.auto` property (on the `sessionFactory` bean) to `update`. This changes Hibernate's behavior and updates the schema when the Java Virtual Machine (JVM) starts (rather than creating it each time). The primary motivation for this is other frameworks don't easily create/delete tables, and you want to have a consistent unit test. See Listing 8.12.

Listing 7.12

```
public void testGetUsers() {
    user = new User();
    user.setFirstName("Rod");
    user.setLastName("Johnson");
    dao.saveUser(user);

    List users = dao.getUsers();
    assertTrue(users.size() >= 1);
    assertTrue(users.contains(user));
}
```

7   Run **ant test -Dtestcase=UserDAO**. Your results should be similar to Figure 8.2.

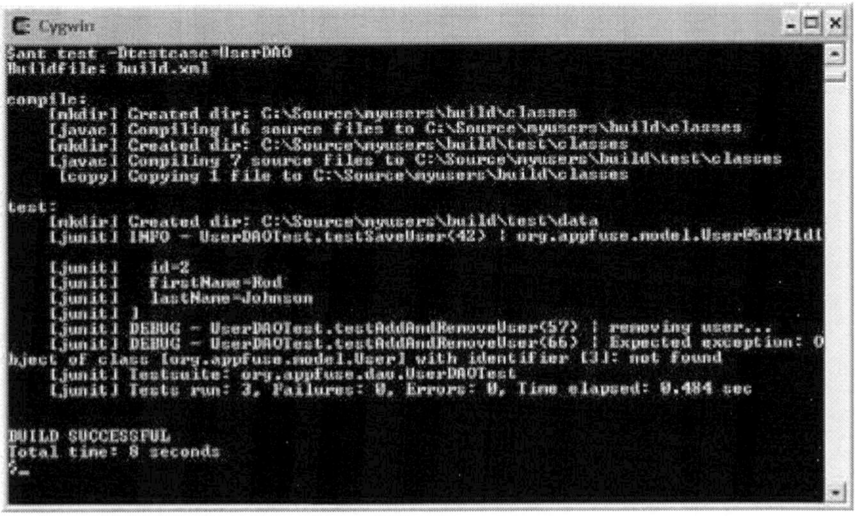

Figure 7.2: Running `UserDAOTest` for Hibernate

The warning you see in this screenshot is normal — it's merely EHCache's way of reminding you that it needs to be configured. EHCache is the default caching engine in Hibernate; you'll configure it with an *ehcache.xml* file in the *Caching* section.

HIBERNATE ANNOTATIONS

As an alternative to mapping files, Hibernate 3 allows you to use annotations to define how an object maps to a table. To use Hibernate annotations, you must have *hibernate-annotations.jar* and *ejb-3.0-edr2.jar* in your classpath. These have already been added to the classpath for this chapter. You may need to modify your IDE to use JDK 5.0 so it understands annotations.

Complete the following steps to modify the **User** class to use annotations.

1   Open **User.java** and add annotations to it.

Just above the class name, add **@Entity** and **@Table** and specify the table name that the entity will be bound to. You will need to import these annotations into your class as well. See Listing 8.13.

Listing 7.13

```
import javax.persistence.Entity;
import javax.persistence.Table;

@Entity
@Table(name="app_user")
public class User ...
```

2   Add the **@Id** annotation just above the **getId()** method. You will need to import **javax.persistence.GeneratorType** and **javax.persistence.Id** as part of this change. See Listing 8.14.

Listing 7.14

```
@Id @GeneratedValue(strategy=GenerationType.AUTO)
public Long getId() {
```

3   Map the **firstName** and **lastName** properties to their respective columns and import javax.persistence.Column so your class compiles. All properties in a class are assumed to be columns in the table, and the methods without explicitly defined column names are defaulted to the property name (for example, **firstName**). See Listing 8.15.

Listing 7.15

```
@Column(name="first_name")
public String getFirstName() {

    . . .

@Column(name="last_name")
public String getLastName() {
```

4 For properties you *don't* want persisted, add an **@Transient** annotation to their **get** method. See Listing 8.16.

Listing 7.16

```
@Transient
public String getFullName() {
```

5 Change your **sessionFactory** bean (in *web/WEB-INF/applicationContext-hibernate.xml*) to use **AnnotationSessionFactoryBean**. Rather than specifying a **resource** attribute, use **class**. See Listing 8.17.

Listing 7.17

```
<bean id="sessionFactory"
    class="org.springframework.orm.hibernate3.annotation.
    AnnotationSessionFactoryBean">
    <property name="dataSource" ref="dataSource"/>
    <property name="annotatedClasses">
        <list>
            <value>org.appfuse.model.User</value>
        </list>
    </property>
    <property name="hibernateProperties">
        <value>
            hibernate.dialect=org.hibernate.dialect.MySQLDialect
            hibernate.hbm2ddl.auto=update
        </value>
    </property>
</bean>
```

6 After making all of these changes, you should be able to successfully run **ant test-dao -Dtestcase=UserDAO**.

For more information about using annotations with Hibernate, see the Hibernate Annotations project.

HSQL CONFIGURATION

In previous chapters, using **hibernate.hbm2ddl.auto=update** worked well for both creating the database and retaining its data while testing. However, this setup works with only Hibernate 2.x and HSQL 1.7.1. If you're using Hibernate 3 with HSQLDB (this chapter uses version 1.8.0), **update** won't create the database or tables for you. To work around this limitation, you have a few options:

1 Use **create** instead of **update**. This configuration will always cause your database to be clean when running tests. The downside is that you'll never be able to retain any data.

2 Change the in-memory JDBC URL so that it is a server URL and then manually start HSQLDB and create the tables before running tests or starting Tomcat.

3 Use a different database server (MySQL or PostgreSQL are good open source options).

MySQL CONFIGURATION

Switching from HSQLDB to MySQL is quite easy. Thanks to Spring, it's just a matter of configuration settings.

1 Make sure MySQL is installed and running.

2 In *applicationContext-hibernate.xml*, change the **dataSource** bean's properties to the properties in Listing 8.18:

Listing 7.18

```
<bean id="dataSource"
    class="org.springframework.jdbc.datasource
        .DriverManagerDataSource">
    <property name="driverClassName"
        value="com.mysql.jdbc.Driver"/>
    <property name="url" value="jdbc:mysql://localhost/myusers"/>
    <property name="username" value="root"/>
    <property name="password" value=""/>
</bean>
```

A user name of **root** and empty password are the default installation settings. You may need to adjust them for your installation.

TIP: You can use a **PropertyPlaceHolderConfigurer** bean to set the previous property values from a properties file. This is covered in *Chapter 9: Testing Spring Applications.*

> **3** Change the **sessionFactory** bean's **hibernate.dialect** property to MySQL, as in Listing 8.19:

Listing 7.19

```
<property name="hibernateProperties">
    <value>
        hibernate.dialect=org.hibernate.dialect.MySQLDialect
        hibernate.hbm2ddl.auto=update
    </value>
</property>
```

> **4** Create the *myusers* database before running unit tests or starting Tomcat. See Listing 8.20.

Listing 7.20

```
mysqladmin -u root -p create myusers
```

Optionally, change the **driver, url** and **userid** properties in the **populate** target of *build.xml* if you want to use that target with MySQL.

> **5** Run **ant test -Dtestcase=UserDAO**. The results should be the same as in Figure 8.2.

CACHING

A powerful feature in persistence frameworks is the ability to *cache* data and avoid constant trips to the database. The Hibernate **Session** object is a transaction-level cache of persistent data, but it doesn't handle per-class or collection-by-collection caching at the JVM or cluster level. However, it does support plugging in both JVM or clustered caches (also called *second-level* caches). For a complete list of supported caches, see Hibernate's Second Level Cache documentation at www.hibernate.org/hib_docs/reference/en/html/performance.html#performance-cache.

The following example shows how to configure the EHCache for JVM-level caching.

> **NOTE:** EHCache is the default cache, so you don't need to configure a **hibernate.cache.provider_class** setting in *applicationContext-hibernate.xml*.

> **1** The simplest way to enable caching for an object is to add a **<cache>** tag to its mapping file. To do this with the **User** object, add a **<cache>** element to the *User.hbm.xml* file in *src/org/appfuse/model*. Optional values are **read-write** and **read-only**. You should use the second option only if you're referring to an object or table that rarely changes. See Listing 8.21.

Listing 7.21

```
<class name="org.appfuse.model.User" table="app_user">
    <cache usage="read-write"/>
    <id name="id" column="id" unsaved-value="0">
```

2 (Optional) Create settings in EHCache's configuration file for this class.
   Create an *ehcache.xml* file in *web/WEB-INF/classes* and fill it with the XML
   in Listing 8.22:

Listing 7.22

```
<ehcache>
    <!-- Only needed if overFlowToDisk="true" -->
    <diskStore path="java.io.tmpdir"/>
    <!-- Required element -->
    <defaultCache
        maxElementsInMemory="10000"
        eternal="false"
        timeToIdleSeconds="120"
        timeToLiveSeconds="120"
        overflowToDisk="true"/>

    <!-- Cache settings per class -->
    <cache name="org.appfuse.model.User"
        maxElementsInMemory="1000"
        eternal="false"
        timeToIdleSeconds="300"
        timeToLiveSeconds="600"
        overflowToDisk="true"/>
</ehcache>
```

3 To prove that your **User** object is being cached, turn on debug logging for
   EHCache in *web/WEB-INF/classes/log4j.xml*. See Listing 8.23.

Listing 7.23

```
<logger name="net.sf.ehcache">
    <level value="DEBUG"/>
</logger>
```

4 Run **ant test -Dtestcase=UserDAO**. Your results should be similar to
   Figure 8.3.

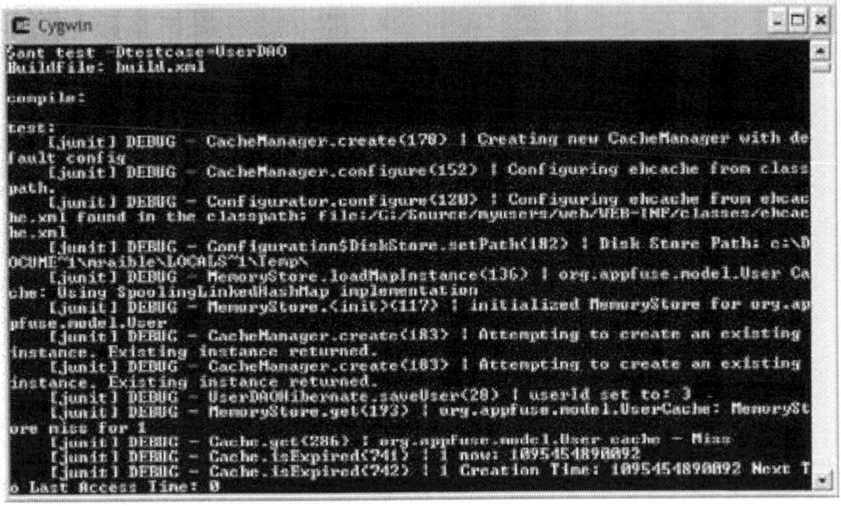

Figure 7.3: Running `UserDAOTest` with EHCache enabled

The Hibernate reference documentation has more information on using and configuring Second Level Caches. In general, caching is something that you shouldn't configure for your application until you've tuned your database (that is, with indexes). This cache implementation is for demonstration purposes only.

LAZY-LOADING DEPENDENT OBJECTS

One of Hibernate's many features is the ability to *lazy-load* dependent objects. For example, if a list of users refers to a collection of roles objects, you probably don't need the roles loaded to display the list of users. By marking the roles collection with `lazy-load="true"`, they won't be loaded until you try to do something with them (usually in the UI).

TIP: Hibernate 3.x uses `lazy-load="true"` by default, whereas Hibernate 2.x uses `lazy-load="false"` by default.

To use this feature with Spring, configure the `OpenSessionInViewFilter` in your application. This will open a session when a particular URL is first requested, and close it when the page finishes loading. To enable this feature, add the XML in Listing 8.24 to *web.xml*.

Listing 7.24

```
<filter>
    <filter-name>hibernateFilter</filter-name>
    <filter-class>
        org.springframework.orm.hibernate3.support
            .OpenSessionInViewFilter
    </filter-class>
</filter>
<filter-mapping>
    <filter-name>hibernateFilter</filter-name>
    <url-pattern>*.html</url-pattern>
<filter-mapping>
```

As an alternative to configuring a filter in your *web.xml*, you can also use Spring's `OpenSessionInViewInterceptor`. Using this interceptor in conjunction with your Spring MVC controllers is as simple as adding it as an interceptor in your *action-servlet.xml* file. See Listing 8.25.

Listing 7.25

```
<bean id="urlMapping"
    class="org.springframework.web.servlet.handler
        .SimpleUrlHandlerMapping">
    <property name="interceptors">
        <list>
            <ref bean="openSessionInViewInterceptor"/>
        </list>
    </property>
    <property name="mappings">
    ...
</bean>

<bean name="openSessionInViewInterceptor"
    class="org.springframework.orm.hibernate3.support
        .OpenSessionInViewInterceptor">
    <property name="sessionFactory" ref="sessionFactory"/>
</bean>
```

Using this feature may cause the following error when running DAO unit tests:

```
[junit] net.sf.hibernate.LazyInitializationException:
Failed to lazily initialize a collection - no session or session
was closed
```

To fix this, add the code in Listing 8.26 to the `setUp()` and `tearDown()` methods of your test, or use Spring's `AbstractTransactionalDataSourceSpringContextTests` as your parent class.

Listing 7.26

```
protected void setUp() throws Exception {
    // the following is necessary for lazy loading
    sf = (SessionFactory) ctx.getBean("sessionFactory");
    // open and bind the session for this test thread.
    Session s = sf.openSession();
        TransactionSynchronizationManager
            .bindResource(sf, new SessionHolder(s));

    // setup code here
}

protected void tearDown() throws Exception {
    // unbind and close the session.
    SessionHolder holder = (SessionHolder)
        TransactionSynchronizationManager.getResource(sf);
    Session s = holder.getSession();
    s.flush();
    TransactionSynchronizationManager.unbindResource(sf);
    SessionFactoryUtils.closeSessionIfNecessary(s, sf);

    // teardown code here
}
```

While using this open session-in-view pattern is a well-known Hibernate session handling idiom, some Spring developers advocate initializing all necessary data in the service layer. Loading everything at once is more efficient and guarantees the same data for all clients. This is especially important when working with services for remote clients, such as web services or EJBs.

If you're interested in implementing your Hibernate DAOs without Spring's helper classes, you can do this easily using the **sessionFactory.getCurrentSession()** call (added in Hibernate 3.0.1). Using Spring with Hibernate vastly simplifies Hibernate 2.x, but many of the features from Spring were rolled into Hibernate 3.x. Nevertheless, Spring's declarative transactions and generic data access exceptions make working with Hibernate much simpler.

Other tips and tricks for Hibernate are available on the Hibernate web site.

STORED PROCEDURES

Stored procedures can be very useful for processing data quickly and efficiently in your database. If you have an operation that needs to update multiple tables, using stored procedures is an excellent way to do this. This section will not describe how to write stored procedures, but rather how to execute them using Hibernate. A new feature in Hibernate 3 is the ability to customize the SQL statements that manipulate a domain object, as well as supporting stored procedures.

In order to use custom SQL or stored procedures when fetching and persisting objects with Hibernate, you can use the **\<sql-insert\>**, **\<sql-update\>** and **\<sql-delete\>** elements. An example is shown in Listing 8.27:

Listing 7.27

```
<class name="org.appfuse.model.User" table="app_user">
    <id name="id" column="id" unsaved-value="0">
        <generator class="increment"/>
    </id>
    <property name="firstName" column="first_name"/>
    ...
    <sql-insert>
        insert into app_user (firstName, id) values (?, ?)
    </sql-insert>
    <sql-update>
        update app_user set firstName=? where id=?
    </sql-update>
    <sql-delete>
        delete from app_user where id=?
    </sql-delete>
</class>
```

The **?** placeholders in the SQL are populated in the same order they appear (as properties) in the mapping definition. The **id** column always appears last in the list of properties. Currently, named parameters aren't supported, but it's likely they will be in a future release. In order to use a stored procedure in one of the aforementioned elements, you can set the callable attribute to true, and then use the name of a stored procedure instead of SQL. Listing 8.28 is an example:

Listing 7.28

```
<sql-insert callable="true">
    {call createUser (?, ?)}
</sql-insert>
```

You can also map the results of a stored procedure to one of your objects. See Listing 8.29.

Listing 7.29

```
<sql-query name="selectAllUsers_SP" callable="true">
    <return alias="u" class="User">
        <return-property name="firstName" column="first_name"/>
```

```
            <return-property name="lastName" column="last_name"/>
        </return>
            { ? = call selectAllUsers() }
    </sql-query>
```

More information on using stored procedures with Hibernate is available at
www.hibernate.org/hib_docs/v3/reference/en/html_single/#sp_query.

COMMUNITY AND SUPPORT

The Hibernate community is a vibrant one. In addition to having good documentation and well-supported user forums, it is very popular with tens of thousands of
developers. It releases early and often, and downloads average 30,000 per release.
The Hibernate web site has a list of Who Uses Hibernate. Commercial Support and
Training are also available.

iBATIS

The iBATIS Data Mapper framework is an open source persistence framework that
allows you to use your model objects with a relational database. In contrast to
Hibernate, you write SQL, much like you would with JDBC. You do this in a very
simple XML file, allowing abstraction of SQL from Java classes. iBATIS is not an
ORM; rather, it is a *data mapper*. In Martin Fowler's Patterns of Enterprise Application Architecture, he describes two patterns: Data Mapper and Metadata Mapping.
The difference is that ORMs (metadata mappers) map classes to tables; iBATIS
(Data Mapper) maps inputs and outputs to an interface (for example, SQL interface
to an RDBMS). An ORM solution works well when you have control of your database. A Data Mapper like iBATIS works well when the database is heavily normal-
ized and you need to pull from several tables to populate an object.

iBATIS is the name of a open source project started by Clinton Begin in 2001.
Clinton had a few products, but none of them gained much recognition until the
.NET Pet Shop was released, claiming that .NET was superior to Java in developer
productivity and performance. Microsoft published a paper claiming that .NET's
version of Sun's PetStore was 10 times faster and 4 times more productive.
Knowing this wasn't the case, Clinton responded with JPetStore 1.0 in July 2002.
Not only did this application have fewer lines of code and a better design than its
.NET counterpart, but Clinton implemented it over a few weeks in his spare time!

Clinton's goals while writing JPetStore were to argue the points of good design,
code quality, and productivity. The original .NET Pet Shop had a horrible design
with much of the business logic contained in stored procedures, whereas JPetStore
had a clean and efficient persistence framework.

This framework quickly drew the attention of the open source community. Today, iBATIS refers to the "iBATIS Database Layer," which consists of a DAO framework and a SQL Map framework. Spring supports the iBATIS SQL Maps by providing helper classes to easily configure and use them. Furthermore, the Spring project includes JPetStore as one of its sample applications, rewriting many of its pieces to use Spring features.

iBATIS is a "sleeper project" in the open source community. Not many folks know about it, but those who do really like it. Perhaps the Spring supporting classes will boost its popularity.

IBATIS's license is Apache, which means you can use it freely as long as your end-user documentation states that your product contains software developed by the Apache Software Foundation. You can modify the code, but then you can no longer distribute it under the Apache name without permission.

iBATIS is an excellent persistence framework to use with existing or legacy databases. You can easily migrate a JDBC-based application to iBATIS (most of the work involves extracting the SQL out of Java classes and into Java files). Not only is iBATIS fast and efficient, but it doesn't hide SQL, which is one of the most powerful and oldest languages today. Using iBATIS's *SQL Maps*, developers write SQL in XML files and populates objects based on the results of those queries. Much like the Spring/Hibernate combination, iBATIS DAOs require very few lines of code in each method.

In my experience, I've found the following qualities to be true of iBATIS:

* Easy to learn

* Queries are extremely efficient

* Easy transition because of pre-existing SQL

* Just as fast (if not faster) than Hibernate

* Writing iBATIS DAOs is similar to writing Hibernate DAOs

NOTE: iBATIS's `sqlMapClient` is similar to Hibernate's `Session` and JDBC's `Connection`. Spring's iBATIS support classes are located in the `org.spring-framework.orm.ibatis` and `org.springframework.orm.ibatis.support` packages.

DEPENDENCIES

For J2SE 1.4, iBATIS has only one third-party dependency: Commons Logging. For J2SE 1.3, see the *jar-dependencies.txt* file included in the download. Below are the JARs included in the MyUsers download as part of iBATIS 2.1.5. Spring supports both iBATIS 1.x and 2.x; the main difference is the word `Client` on the 2.x classes. This section only covers 2.x.

- **ibatis-common-2.jar** — common classes
- **ibatis-sqlmap-2.jar** — required for SQL Maps 2.0
- **commons-logging.jar** — Logging framework that provides ultra-thin bridge between different logging libraries
- **(optional) cglib-2.1.jar** — Code Generation Library that enables runtime byte-code enhancement for optimized JavaBean property access and enhanced lazy loading.

CONFIGURATION

To integrate iBATIS you must create a SQL Map for the **User** object. A SQL Map is an XML file that contains SQL statements to *map* a query's inputs and outputs to objects. In order to avoid conflicts among bean names, rename the *applicationContext-hibernate.xml* file (in *web/WEB-INF*) to *applicationContext-hibernate.xml.txt*. This will prevent Spring from loading it.

1   In the *src/org/appfuse/model* directory, create a file named *UserSQL.xml* with the contents in Listing 8.30.

Listing 7.30

```xml
<?xml version="1.0" encoding="UTF-8"?>
<!DOCTYPE sqlMap PUBLIC "-//iBATIS.com//DTD SQL Map 2.0//EN"
    "http://www.ibatis.com/dtd/sql-map-2.dtd">

<sqlMap namespace="UserSQL">
    <insert id="addUser" parameterClass="org.appfuse.model.User">
        insert into app_user (id, first_name, last_name)
        values (#id#, #firstName#, #lastName#)
        <selectKey resultClass="java.lang.Long" keyProperty="id" >
            select last_insert_id()
        </selectKey>
    </insert>

    <update id="updateUser" parameterClass="org.appfuse.model
        .User">
        update app_user set first_name = #firstName#,
        last_name = #lastName#
        where id = #id#
    </update>

    <select id="getUser" parameterClass="java.lang.Long"
            resultClass="org.appfuse.model.User">
        select id, first_name as firstName, last_name as lastName
        from app_user where id=#id#
    </select>
```

```
<select id="getUsers" resultClass="org.appfuse.model.User">
    select id, first_name as firstName, last_name as lastName
    from app_user
</select>

<delete id="deleteUser" parameterClass="java.lang.Long">
    delete from app_user where id = #id#
</delete>
</sqlMap>
```

In this file, you can see that different elements (**<insert>**, **<update>**, **<select>**, **<delete>**) indicate database operations. Note that each element can optionally specify a **parameterClass** or **resultClass** attribute. Dynamic variables are enclosed in **#value#** and indicate properties in the **parameterClass**.

2   Create a *sql-map-config.xml* file in *src/org/appfuse/dao/ibatis* (you must create this directory) that indicates the location of the *UserSQL.xml* SQL Map. See Listing 8.31.

Listing 7.31

```
<?xml version="1.0" encoding="UTF-8"?>
<!DOCTYPE sqlMapConfig PUBLIC
    "-//iBATIS.com//DTD SQL Map Config 2.0//EN"
    "http://www.ibatis.com/dtd/sql-map-config-2.dtd">

<sqlMapConfig>
    <settings enhancementEnabled="true" maxTransactions="5"
        maxRequests="32" maxSessions="10"/>

    <sqlMap resource="org/appfuse/model/UserSQL.xml"/>
</sqlMapConfig>
```

See iBATIS's Documentation (a PDF download from prdownloads.sourceforge .net/ibatisdb/iBATIS-SqlMaps-2.pdf?) for more information on the **<settings>** element. The values shown here should be sufficient for most applications.

3   Create an *applicationContext-ibatis.xml* file in the *web/WEB-INF* directory and add a **dataSource** bean definition. The **dataSource** bean in Listing 8.32 uses the MySQL database you configured in the *MySQL configuration* section.

Listing 7.32

```
<?xml version="1.0" encoding="UTF-8"?>
<!DOCTYPE beans PUBLIC "-//SPRING//DTD BEAN//EN"
    "http://www.springframework.org/dtd/spring-beans.dtd">
```

```
<beans>
    <bean id="dataSource"
        class="org.springframework.jdbc.datasource
            .DriverManagerDataSource">
        <property name="driverClassName"
            value="com.mysql.jdbc.Driver"/>
        <property name="url"
            value="jdbc:mysql://localhost/myusers"/>
        <property name="username" value="root"/>
        <property name="password" value=""/>
    </bean>
    <!-- Add bean definitions here -->
</beans>
```

4 Add a `sqlMapClient` bean definition to integrate iBATIS with Spring. See Listing 8.33.

Listing 7.33

```
<bean id="sqlMapClient"
    class="org.springframework.orm.ibatis
        .SqlMapClientFactoryBean">
    <property name="configLocation">
        <value>classpath:/org/appfuse/dao/ibatis
            /sql-map-config.xml</value>
    </property>
    <property name="dataSource" ref="dataSource"/>
</bean>
```

5 Add a `transactionManager` bean definition that uses a `DataSource-TransactionManager`. This `PlatformTransactionManager` implementation binds a JDBC connection from the specified `DataSource` to the thread, potentially allowing for one thread connection per data source. See Listing 8.34.

NOTE: The primary reason you need a bean named `transactionManager` is that the `userManager` bean references a bean with that name for handling declarative transactions.

Listing 7.34

```
<bean id="transactionManager"
    class="org.springframework.jdbc.datasource
        .DataSourceTransactionManager">
        <property name="dataSource" ref="dataSource"/>
</bean>
```

6   Create a **UserDAOiBatis.java** class in *src/org/appfuse/dao/ibatis*. This file extends **SqlMapClientDaoSupport** and implements **UserDAO**. See Listing 8.35.

Listing 7.35

```java
package org.appfuse.dao.ibatis;

// use your IDE to organize imports

public class UserDAOiBatis extends SqlMapClientDaoSupport
    implements UserDAO {

    public List getUsers() {
        return getSqlMapClientTemplate()
            .queryForList("getUsers", null);
    }

    public User getUser(Long id) {
        User user = (User) getSqlMapClientTemplate()
            .queryForObject("getUser", id);

        if (user == null) {
            throw new ObjectRetrievalFailureException
                (User.class, id);
        }

        return user;
    }

    public void saveUser(User user) {
        if (user.getId() == null) {
          // Use iBatis's <selectKey> feature,
              which is db-specific
          Long id = (Long) getSqlMapClientTemplate()
              .insert("addUser", user);
          user.setId(id);
          logger.info("new User id set to: " + id);
        } else {
            getSqlMapClientTemplate().update("updateUser", user);
        }
    }

    public void removeUser(Long id) {
        getSqlMapClientTemplate().update("deleteUser", id);
    }
}
```

7   Add a **userDAO** bean definition to *applicationContext-ibatis.xml*. The example in Listing 8.36 uses the **autowire** attribute rather than specifying the **sqlMapClient** property. When using autowire, it's a good idea to specify the injected dependencies in a comment.

Listing 7.36

```
<bean id="userDAO" autowire="byName"
    class="org.appfuse.dao.ibatis.UserDAOiBatis"/>
    <!-- injected property: sqlMapClient -->
```

NOTE: In Spring versions prior to 1.0.2, beans that subclassed **SqlMapClient-DaoSupport** required a **dataSource** property be set in their bean definition. In 1.0.2, a **dataSource** property was added to **SqlMapClientFactoryBean** as an alternative to per-DAO **DataSource** references. Setting a **dataSource** on the **SqlMapClientFactoryBean** is necessary if you want to use iBATIS's lazy-loading feature.

8   The **app_user** table created by Hibernate does not allow nulls in the **id** column. With iBATIS, it's easiest to insert nulls for primary keys and retrieve the generated id back from the database. To do this, drop and re-create the **app_user** table.

a   Log in to MySQL by typing **mysql -u root -p myusers** from the command line.

b   Execute **drop table app_user**.

c   Execute the SQL statement in Listing 8.37.

Listing 7.37

```
create table app_user (id bigint not null auto_increment,
first_name varchar(50), last_name varchar(50),
primary key (id));
```

TEST IT!

Run **ant clean test -Dtestcase=UserDAO**. The output from this test should be similar to the **UserDAOHibernate** class.

CACHING

iBATIS supports many caching strategies for SQL Maps. To add a caching strategy to the *UserSQL.xml* file, add the **<cacheModel>** element in Listing 8.38:

Listing 7.38

```
<sqlMap namespace="UserSQL">

<cacheModel id="userCache" type="LRU">
    <flushInterval hours="24"/>
    <property name="size" value="1000"/>
</cacheModel>

<insert id="addUser" parameterClass="org.appfuse.model.User">
```

Add a **cacheModel** attribute to any **<select>** statements. For example, add it to the **getUser** statement. See Listing 8.39.

Listing 7.39

```
<select id="getUser" parameterClass="java.lang.Long"
    resultClass="org.appfuse.model.User"
    cacheModel="userCache">
    select id, first_name as firstName, last_name as lastName
    from app_user where id=#id#;
</select>
```

RETRIEVING GENERATED PRIMARY KEYS

The **addUser** statement uses a database-specific means to retrieve the generated primary key. The **<selectKey>** element allows you to retrieve generated primary keys quite easily. See Listing 8.40.

Listing 7.40

```
<insert id="addUser" parameterClass="org.appfuse.model.User">
    insert into app_user (id, first_name, last_name)
    values (#id#, #firstName#, #lastName#);
    <selectKey resultClass="java.lang.Long" keyProperty="id">
        select last_insert_id();
    </selectKey>
</insert>
```

The problem with this approach is that it's database-specific. Using **select last_insert_id()** will only work with MySQL. This shows how the SQL standard allows variations and is not a *true* standard. A good ORM tool like Hibernate or JDO does this transparently for you.

NOTE: If you'd like to try switching back to HSQLDB at this point, simply change the **<selectKey>** statement to **call identity();** Also change the **dataSource** bean appropriately. Run **ant browse** and drop/re-create the **app_user** table. The SQL script in Listing 8.41 will help you with the table.

Listing 7.41

```
create table app_user
    (id integer identity, first_name varchar(50),
last_name varchar(50));
```

As an alternative, you can use a Spring class to generate the primary key for you. For example, to use the **MySQLMaxValueIncrementer**, perform the following steps:

1   Comment out the **<selectKey>** element in *UserSQL.xml*.

2   Change the **save()** method to the code in Listing 8.42:

Listing 7.42

```
public void saveUser(User user) {
    if (user.getId() == null) {
        MySQLMaxValueIncrementer incrementer =
            new MySQLMaxValueIncrementer(
                getDataSource(), "user_sequence", "value");
        Long id = new Long(incrementer.nextLongValue());
        user.setId(id);

        getSqlMapClientTemplate().insert("addUser", user);
        logger.info("new User id set to: " + id);
    } else {
        getSqlMapClientTemplate().update("updateUser", user);
    }
}
```

3   Create the **user_sequence** table to allow the retrieval of primary keys. See Listing 8.43.

Listing 7.43

```
create table user_sequence (value bigint auto_increment,
    primary key (value));
insert into user_sequence values(0);
```

If you clean and run the **UserDAOTest**, all your tests should pass.

WARNING: If your tests do not pass and you get duplicate-entry errors, log in to MySQL and execute **delete from app_user** to delete all user records.

The problem with putting the **MySQLMaxValueIncrementer** into your class is now you've hard-coded your DAO to depend on MySQL. Having the **select last_insert_id()** statement seems more configurable since it was in XML. Refactor this class to use dependency injection.

1   Add an **incrementer** variable of type **DataFieldMaxValueIncremen-ter** and setter to the **UserDAOHibernate** class. See Listing 8.44.

Listing 7.44

```
private DataFieldMaxValueIncrementer incrementer;

public void setIncrementer
    (DataFieldMaxValueIncrementer incrementer) {
    this.incrementer = incrementer;
}
```

2   Change the **saveUser()** method to use this incrementer. Just delete the three lines that initialize the incrementer.

3   Configure the incrementer as a bean in *web/WEB-INF/applicationContext-ibatis.xml*. Since **userDAO** autowires by name, this property will be injected by Spring. See Listing 8.45.

Listing 7.45

```
<bean id="incrementer" class="org.springframework.jdbc.support
    .incrementer.MySQLMaxValueIncrementer">
    <property name="dataSource" ref="dataSource"/>
    <property name="incrementerName" value="user_sequence"/>
    <property name="columnName" value="value"/>
</bean>
```

4   Run **ant test -Dtestcase=UserDAO**.

iBATIS doesn't support JDBC 3.0's **getGeneratedKeys()** method, so you must use one of the above methods to generate primary keys. Of course, you can also **select max(id)** and increment the primary key yourself.

STORED PROCEDURES

When using iBATIS, you can execute stored procedures by using the **<procedure>** statement element in your SQL mapping file. Listing 8.46 shows calling a stored procedure with output parameters.

Listing 7.46

```
<parameterMap id="swapParams" class="map">
    <parameter property="firstName" jdbcType="VARCHAR"
        javaType="java.lang.String" mode="INOUT"/>
    <parameter property="lastName" jdbcType="VARCHAR"
        javaType="java.lang.String" mode="INOUT"/>
</parameterMap>

<procedure id="swapNames" parameterMap="swapParams">
    {call swap_names (?, ?)}
</procedure>
```

Calling this procedure would swap the names in the database table, as well as in the parameter map. When using output parameters, as in this example, the mode attribute can be set to **INOUT** or **OUT**.

COMMUNITY AND SUPPORT

Developers who use iBATIS tend to be very happy with it. It has clean and concise documentation and tutorials. The documentation is a mere 53 pages and the tutorial is only 9 pages! In my experience, this is a framework you can learn and use in the same day. IBATIS's mailing list information can be found at ibatis.apache.org/mailinglists.html.

SPRING JDBC

If you've written JDBC code before, you know that it can be tedious. Not only do you have to set up Connections, Statements, and ResultSets, but you have to close them after you've retrieved your data. Closing resources in JDBC code is an area that many new developers don't know how to do properly. They tend to forget to use the *finally* block, even though it's a basic JDBC code pattern.

As you've seen in the previous examples, Spring removes the open/close resource responsibility from the developer. It manages these operations for you, allowing you to write application code rather than infrastructure code. Spring's JDBC core is an abstraction on top of J2SE's JDBC that allows you to write a minimal amount of code to retrieve, save and delete your data.

Four packages make up the JDBC abstraction framework: **core**, **datasource**, **object**, and **support**. The functionality of each package is below:

- `org.springframework.jdbc.core`: Core classes, **JdbcTemplate**, and **JdbcDaoSupport** convenience class

- `org.springframework.jdbc.datasource`: Classes for easy **DataSource** access and basic **DataSource** implementations

- `org.springframework.jdbc.object`: Classes for corresponding to database queries, updates, and stored procedures as thread-safe reusable objects

- `org.springframework.jdbc.support`: SQLException translation, **DataFieldMaxValueIncrementer** implementations, and support classes for `jdbc.core` and `jdbc.object`

In this section, you will use **JdbcTemplate** and **JdbcDaoSupport**. The names are similar to the **Template** and **DaoSupport** classes you used with Hibernate and iBATIS. This section will not cover **SQLException** translation because you rarely need to do it yourself. The classes are used internally and a number of default translations are built-in for the following databases: DB2, HSQL, SQL Server, MySQL, Oracle, Informix, PostgreSQL, and Sybase. You can find a complete list of error code to exception mappings in the *jdbc/support/sql-error-codes.xml* file.

MAPPING RESULTSSETS TO OBJECTS

Similar to Hibernate and iBATIS, Spring JDBC requires you to map results from a query to your POJOs. With Hibernate and iBATIS, you did this using XML. With Spring JDBC, you must do this programmatically. You don't necessarily *have* to map results to objects; you can simply return maps of your data. For instance, the code in Listing 8.47 returns a map with each entry as a row:

Listing 7.47

```
public List getList() {
    return getJdbcTemplate().queryForList
        ("select * from tablename");
}
```

In most cases, however, you'll want to map these results to a **List** of objects. To do this with Spring JDBC, use a **MappingSqlQuery** class to convert each row of the JDBC **ResultSet** to an object. Listing 8.48 is an example of this type of class retrieving a list of users in the MyUsers application:

Listing 7.48

```
public class UsersQuery extends MappingSqlQuery {
    public UsersQuery(DataSource ds) {
        super(ds, "SELECT * FROM app_user");
        compile();
    }
```

```
        protected Object mapRow(ResultSet rs, int rowNum)
        throws SQLException {
            User user = new User();
            user.setId(new Long(rs.getLong("id")));
            user.setFirstName(rs.getString("first_name"));
            user.setLastName(rs.getString("last_name"));
            return user;
        }
    }
```

When extending **MappingSqlQuery**, you must override the **mapRow(ResultSet rs, int rowNum)** method. Use the **UsersQuery** class to get a list of **User** objects. See Listing 8.49.

Listing 7.49

```
    public List getUsers() {
        return new UsersQuery(getDataSource()).execute();
    }
```

Declare parameters on your query by using the **declareParameter()** method of **MappingSqlQuery**. See Listing 8.50.

Listing 7.50

```
    public UserQuery(DataSource ds) {
        super(ds, "SELECT * FROM app_user WHERE id = ?");
        super.declareParameter(
            new SqlParameter("id", Types.INTEGER));
        compile();
    }
```

Pass in the **id** parameter using an **Object** array, as in Listing 8.51:

Listing 7.51

```
    public User getUser(Long id) {
        List users = new UserQuery(getDataSource())
                        .execute(new Object[]{id});
        if (users.isEmpty()) {
            throw new ObjectRetrievalFailureException
                (User.class, id);
        }
        return (User) users.get(0);
    }
```

RowSets

As of Spring 1.2, you can use JDBC's **RowSet** concept with Spring JDBC. A **RowSet** object contains a set of rows from a result set or some other source of tabular data, like a file or spreadsheet. Because a **RowSet** object follows the Java-Beans model for properties and event notification, it is a JavaBeans component that can be combined with other components in an application. The **SqlRowSet** class allows for disconnected result sets with Spring exceptions. Listing 8.52 is a very simple example of using a **RowSet** with Spring JDBC:

Listing 7.52

```
SqlRowSet rset = getJdbcTemplate().queryForRowSet(
    "select id, name from mytest where id > ? and name < ?",
    new Object[] {new Long(1), "Z"});

int i = 0;
while (rset.next()) {
    i++;
    System.out.println("Row" + i + " " + rset.getString(2));
}
```

Executing update queries

Mapping **ResultSets** to objects helps you retrieve data, but it doesn't help you update it. For that, use a **SqlUpdate** class to create a reusable object for updating rows. Listing 8.53 is an example:

Listing 7.53

```
public class UserUpdate extends SqlUpdate {
    public UserUpdate(DataSource ds) {
        super(ds, "INSERT INTO app_user
            (id, first_name, last_name) values (?, ?, ?)");
        declareParameter(new SqlParameter("id", Types.BIGINT));
        declareParameter
            (new SqlParameter("first_name", Types.VARCHAR));
        declareParameter
            (new SqlParameter("last_name", Types.VARCHAR));
        compile();
    }
}
```

Call this class using the example code in Listing 8.54:

Listing 7.54

```
Object[] params =
    new Object[] {user.getId(), user.getFirstName(),
        user.getLastName()};
    new UserUpdate(getDataSource()).update(params);
```

Another, less verbose option is to use the **update()** method of **JdbcTemplate**.
See Listing 8.55.

Listing 7.55

```
getJdbcTemplate().update(
    "UPDATE app_user SET first_name = ?,
        last_name = ? WHERE id = ?",
    new Object[] {user.getFirstName(), user.getLastName(),
        user.getId()});
```

Finally, you don't need to implement a full **SqlUpdate** class; simply declare one in-
line within a method, as in Listing 8.56.

Listing 7.56

```
String sql = "INSERT INTO app_user (id, first_name, last_name) ";
    sql += "values (?, ?, ?)";
SqlUpdate su = new SqlUpdate(getDataSource(), sql);
su.declareParameter(new SqlParameter("id", Types.BIGINT));
su.declareParameter
    (new SqlParameter("first_name", Types.VARCHAR));
su.declareParameter(new SqlParameter("last_name",
Types.VARCHAR));
su.compile();

Object[] params = new Object[]
    {user.getId(), user.getFirstName(), user.getLastName()};

su.update(params);
```

RETRIEVING GENERATED PRIMARY KEYS

JDBC 3.0, which is part of J2SE 1.4, specifies that a JDBC 3.0-compliant driver has
to implement the **java.sql.Statement.getGeneratedKeys()** method. This
method is to retrieve generated keys from databases (for example, calling **select
last_insert_id();** from MySQL). The MySQL driver in MyUsers is JDBC 3.0-
compliant.

To take advantage of retrieving generated keys with Spring JDBC, use a **KeyHolder** as a second parameter to the **SqlUpdate.update()** method. In addition, you'll need to call **setReturnGeneratedKeys(true)** on **SqlUpdate**. See Listing 8.57.

Listing 7.57

```
KeyHolder keys = new GeneratedKeyHolder();
su.setReturnGeneratedKeys(true);
su.update(params, keys);
user.setId(new Long(keys.getKey().longValue()));
```

For non-compliant JDBC Drivers, use the **DataFieldMaxValueIncrementer** strategy as described on page 248.

DEPENDENCIES

Since Spring JDBC is part of Spring, it has no third-party dependencies like the other libraries. If you only want to use the JDBC functionality of Spring, use *spring-dao.jar* (rather than the all-encompassing *spring.jar*) in your application.

CONFIGURATION

Spring JDBC has no *mapping files* or *sql maps*, so it's simple to configure in the MyUsers application.

   1   Create an *applicationContext-jdbc.xml* file in the *web/WEB-INF* directory and add a bean definition for **dataSource**. Be sure to rename the previous *applicationContext-ibatis.xml* to *applicationContext-ibatis.xml.txt*. See Listing 8.58.

NOTE: You may want to duplicate the iBATIS version of this file and all beans except **dataSource**.

Listing 7.58

```
<bean id="dataSource"
    class="org.springframework.jdbc.datasource
        .DriverManagerDataSource">
    <property name="driverClassName"
        value="com.mysql.jdbc.Driver"/>
    <property name="url" value="jdbc:mysql://localhost/myusers"/>
    <property name="username" value="root"/>
    <property name="password" value=""/>
</bean>
```

   2   Add a transaction manager, as in Listing 8.59.

Listing 7.59

```
<bean id="transactionManager"
    class="org.springframework.jdbc.datasource
        .DataSourceTransactionManager">
    <property name="dataSource" ref="dataSource"/>
</bean>
```

3 Create a **UserDAOJdbc.java** class in *src/org/appfuse/dao/jdbc*. This file extends **JdbcDaoSupport** and implements **UserDAO**. See Listing 8.60.

Listing 7.60

```
package org.appfuse.dao.jdbc;

// use your IDE to organize imports

public class UserDAOJdbc extends JdbcDaoSupport
    implements UserDAO {

    public List getUsers() {
        return new UsersQuery(getDataSource()).execute();
    }

    public User getUser(Long id) {
        List users = new UserQuery(getDataSource())
                        .execute(new Object[]{id});
        if (users.isEmpty()) {
            throw new ObjectRetrievalFailureException
                (User.class, id);
        }
        return (User) users.get(0);
    }

    public void saveUser(User user) {
        if (user.getId() == null) {
            String sql = "INSERT INTO app_user (id, first_name, ";
                sql += " last_name) values (?, ?, ?)";
            SqlUpdate su = new SqlUpdate(getDataSource(), sql);
            su.declareParameter
                (new SqlParameter("id", Types.BIGINT));
            su.declareParameter
                (new SqlParameter("first_name", Types.VARCHAR));
            su.declareParameter
                (new SqlParameter("last_name", Types.VARCHAR));
            su.compile();

            Object[] params = new Object[]
```

```
                {user.getId(), user.getFirstName(),
                    user.getLastName()};

            KeyHolder keys = new GeneratedKeyHolder();
            su.setReturnGeneratedKeys(true);
            su.update(params, keys);
          user.setId(new Long(keys.getKey().longValue()));


            if (logger.isDebugEnabled()) {
                logger.info("user's id is: " + user.getId());
            }
        } else {
            getJdbcTemplate().update
                ("UPDATE app_user SET first_name =
                    ?, last_name = ? WHERE id = ?",
                new Object[] {user.getFirstName(),
                    user.getLastName(),
                            user.getId()});
        }
    }

    public void removeUser(Long id) {
        getJdbcTemplate().update
            ("DELETE FROM app_user WHERE id = ?",
                            new Object[] {id});
    }

    // Query to get a single User
    class UserQuery extends MappingSqlQuery {
        public UserQuery(DataSource ds) {
            super(ds, "SELECT * FROM app_user WHERE id = ?");
            super.declareParameter
                (new SqlParameter("id", Types.INTEGER));
            compile();
        }

        protected Object mapRow(ResultSet rs, int rowNum)
        throws SQLException {
            User user = new User();
            user.setId(new Long(rs.getLong("id")));
            user.setFirstName(rs.getString("first_name"));
            user.setLastName(rs.getString("last_name"));
            return user;
        }
    }

    // Query to get a list of User objects
    class UsersQuery extends MappingSqlQuery {
        public UsersQuery(DataSource ds) {
```

```
                super(ds, "SELECT * FROM app_user");
                compile();
            }

            protected Object mapRow(ResultSet rs, int rowNum)
            throws SQLException {
                User user = new User();
                user.setId(new Long(rs.getLong("id")));
                user.setFirstName(rs.getString("first_name"));
                user.setLastName(rs.getString("last_name"));
                return user;
            }
        }
    }
```

This class has a lot more lines of code than the previous two. However, it does not require any configuration files. The **UserQuery** and **UsersQuery** classes are inner classes, but could just as easily be refactored into their own *.java* files.

4   Add a **userDAO** bean to the *applicationContext-jdbc.xml* file in the *web/WEB-INF* directory. See Listing 8.61.

Listing 7.61

```
<bean id="userDAO" class="org.appfuse.dao.jdbc.UserDAOJdbc">
    <property name="dataSource" ref="dataSource"/>
</bean>
```

TEST IT!

To ensure a clean database, drop and re-create the **app_user** table.

1   Log in to MySQL by typing **mysql -u root -p myusers** from the command line.

2   Execute **drop table app_user;**.

3   Execute the statement in Listing 8.62:

Listing 7.62

```
create table app_user (id bigint not null auto_increment,
first_name varchar(50), last_name varchar(50),
    primary key (id));
```

4   Run **ant test -Dtestcase=UserDAO**.

STORED PROCEDURES

Spring JDBC makes it very easy to call stored procedures using its `StoredProcedure` class. While stored procedures are not part of the core SQL standard, most database vendors support them. To call a stored procedure with Spring, you can subclass the **StoredProcedure** class. This class has an **execute()** method that takes a **Map** of input parameters as its only argument. The results are also returned using a **Map**, which contains one entry per output parameter. In the class you write, you'll typically define an **execute()** method that has a parameter signature that matches the stored procedure. Listing 8.63 is an example that calls an **add_user** stored procedure that returns a primary key.

Listing 7.63

```
public class AddUser extends StoredProcedure {
    private static final String ADD_USER_SQL = "add_user";

    public AddUser(DataSource ds) {
        super(ds, ADD_USER_SQL);
        declareParameter(new SqlParameter("firstName",
                         Types.VARCHAR));
        declareParameter(new SqlParameter("lastName",
                         Types.VARCHAR));
        declareParameter(new SqlOutParameter("new_user_id",
                         Types.INTEGER));
        compile();
    }

    public int execute(String firstName, String lastName) {
        Map in = new HashMap();
        in.put("firstName", firstName);
        in.put("lastName", lastName);
        Map out = execute(in);
        if (out.size() > 0) {
            return ((Integer) out.get("new_user_id")).intValue();
        } else {
            return 0;
        }
    }
}
```

Now that you have all of the logic encapsulated in the **AddUser** class, you can very easily create it and call its **execute()** method. The **execute()** method shown in Listing 8.64 is from the **StoredProcedure** class.

Listing 7.64

```
AddUser sp = new AddUser(dataSource);
int userId = sp.execute(firstName, lastName);
```

COMMUNITY AND SUPPORT

Spring's JDBC framework is a clean abstraction on top of JDBC. It frees you from opening and closing resources and works great for batch processing large amounts of data. Spring's reference documentation is a good resource for learning more about it, and Spring's Data Access Support Forum at forum.springframework.org/forumdisplay.php?f=27 is a great place to get your questions answered.

Commercial support for Spring and its JDBC framework is available through Interface21 at www.springframework.com/company.

JDO
....

JDO is a Java standard, which means it was developed as part of the Java Community Process. As a standard, it's not an actual product, but a specification of how the product should be built. The goals of JDO are described best in section 1.1 (Overview) of the JDO 2.0 specification.

> "There are two major objectives of the JDO architecture: first, to
> provide application programmers a transparent Java-centric view of
> persistent information, including enterprise data and locally stored
> data; and second, to enable pluggable implementations of datastores
> into application servers."

This section covers how to use Spring to configure and use your JDO implementation, which may be from your app server vendor, or from an open source provider like JPOX or ObjectWeb's Speedo. These examples use JPOX because it is the open source Reference Implementation for JDO 2.0.

NOTE: Spring's JDO support classes are located in the `org.springframe-work.orm.jdo` and `org.springframework.orm.jdo.support` packages.

JDO AND PRIMARY KEYS

JDO handles primary keys (also called *object ids*) very differently from other persistence options. This is because JDO is designed for both object databases and relational databases. In most cases, you'll be working with a relational database and will therefore want to use *application* identity. However, if you're prototyping an application, it might be easier to use *database* identity and not worry about primary keys. Table is a list of the different identity types in the JDO specification.

Table 7.1: Identity Types in the JDO Specification

Identity Type	JDO-Controlled Schema	Existing Schema
datastore	#1. Generates tables; adds a primary key and defines its value	#2. Allows you to configure classes to map to existing tables and define the primary key column name
application	#3. Generates tables; allows you to define classes for primary keys	#4. Maps to existing tables; allows you to define classes for primary keys

JDO IDENTITY TYPES

The purpose of the *datastore* identity type is to let the JDO completely handle the primary key. For example, to use the **User** object with type #1, remove the **id** field and its access method, as JDO does not use them. This creates its own column (**user_id**) in the database and its own table (**user**). The assumption is that you don't need to know the primary key in your action.

With type #2, you can define a column name that matches the **id** property in **User**, but the database won't populate it when you persist the object. In other words, it won't tell you what the generated primary key is.

If you want to know the primary key, you must use the *application* identity type. Using this option, you can still have your tables generated for you (type #3), or you can use **MetaData** (which is really a mapping file similar to Hibernate's) to specify a table name (type #4). To use application identity, you must specify a primary key class. In MyUsers, the **UserDAOTest.testSaveUser()** method verifies that the primary key was assigned. See Listing 8.65.

Listing 7.65

```
public void testSaveUser() throws Exception {
    user = new User();
    user.setFirstName("Rod");
    user.setLastName("Johnson");

    dao.saveUser(user);
    assertTrue("primary key assigned", user.getId() != null);
    log.info(user);
    assertTrue(user.getFirstName() != null);
}
```

Because of this, the JDO implementation of **UserDAO** will use *application* identity.

DEPENDENCIES

This example uses JPOX version 1.1.0-beta-4, which is an implementation of JDO 2.0. Below are the JARs that are included in the MyUsers download as part of JPOX.

- **bcel-5.1jar** — Byte-Code Engineering Library enhances the classes with byte-code

- **jdo-2.0-snapshot7.jar** — Apache JDO API. The definition of the JDO interface.

- **jpox-enhancer-1.1.0-beta-4.jar** — JPOX byte-code Enhancer enhances classes before running a JDO-enabled application with JPOX

- **jpox-1.1.0-beta-4.jar** — Core JPOX classes

- **log4j-1.2.11.jar** — Logging framework. Used for logging within JPOX.

CONFIGURATION

JDO requires a little more setup than the other frameworks. You must add an extra step to the build process that *enhances* your persistable objects. To avoid conflicts with the previous section on iBATIS, rename the *applicationContext-jdbc.xml* file (in *web/WEB-INF*) to *applicationContext-jdbc.xml.txt*. This will prevent it from being loaded.

NOTE: The JPOX implementation for this example is a beta release of JDO 2.0. The 2.0 specification has a proposed final draft available from the JSR 243 web site at www.jcp.org/en/jsr/detail?id=243.

---

1   Open the *build.xml* file in MyUsers and add the **enhance** target in Listing 8.66 just before the **test** target.

Listing 7.66

```
<target name="enhance" description="JPOX enhancement"
    depends="compile">
    <taskdef name="jpoxenhancer"
        classname="org.jpox.enhancer.tools.EnhancerTask"
        classpathref="classpath"/>

<jpoxenhancer dir="${build.dir}/classes" failonerror="true"
    fork="true">
    <classpath>
        <path refid="classpath"/>
```

```
        <path location="${build.dir}/classes"/>
        <path location="web/WEB-INF/classes"/>
    </classpath>
</jpoxenhancer>
</target>
```

Change the **test** and **deploy** targets to depend on **enhance**. See Listing 8.67.

Listing 7.67

```
<target name="test" depends="enhance"
    description="Runs JUnit tests">
...
<target name="war" depends="enhance"
    description="Packages app as WAR">
```

2   Create a metadata file to map the **User** object to the **app_user** table. In
    the *org/appfuse/model* directory, create a file named *package.jdo* with the
    contents in Listing 8.68:

Listing 7.68

```
<?xml version="1.0"?>
<!DOCTYPE jdo PUBLIC
    "-//Sun Microsystems, Inc.//DTD Java Data Objects Metadata 2.0
        //EN"
    "http://java.sun.com/dtd/jdo_2_0.dtd">
<jdo>
    <package name="org.appfuse.model">
        <class name="User"
            identity-type="application" detachable="true"
                table="app_user">
            <field name="id" primary-key="true" value-
strategy="native"/>
            <field name="firstName">
                <column name="first_name"
                    jdbc-type="VARCHAR" length="50"/>
            </field>
            <field name="lastName">
                <column name="last_name"
                    jdbc-type="VARCHAR" length="50"/>
            </field>
        </class>
    </package>
</jdo>
```

Most of the items in this class are self-explanatory. You can see where the table
name, columns and sizes are set, and how each field is defined as a column in the

User class. Note that the *package.jdo* file can hold metadata for all the classes in the **org.appfuse.model** package (defined by the **<package>** element).

You might notice that the **<class>** element has a **detachable="true"** attribute. This is used to indicate that the class can be used and modified outside of a transaction (for instance, in a web application).

The **value-strategy="native"** attribute on the **id** field is an indicator to use a database's default strategy for generating primary keys. There are many ways to control how primary keys are generated. For more information, please see JPOX's documentation.

3   In order to copy and package the *package.jdo* file with the war, modify the **compile** target in *build.xml* to include *.jdo files. See Listing 8.69.

Listing 7.69

```
<!-- Copy XML files to ${build.dir}/classes -->
<copy todir="${build.dir}/classes">
    <fileset dir="${src.dir}" includes="**/*.xml"/>
    <!-- Copy JDO mapping files -->
    <fileset dir="${src.dir}" includes="**/*.jdo"/>
</copy>
```

4   Run **ant clean enhance** to see the metadata enhance the **org.appfuse .model.User** class. You should see something similar to Figure 8.4.

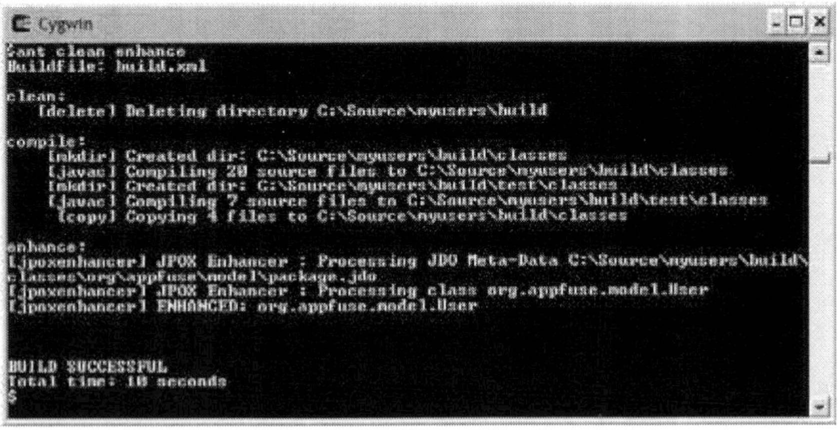

Figure 7.4: Running the JPOX enhancer

5   Create an *applicationContext-jdo.xml* file (using *applicationContext-empty.txt* as a template) in *web/WEB-INF*. Add the following **persistenceManager-**

Factory bean definition that uses the **LocalPersistenceManager-FactoryBean**. See Listing 8.70.

Listing 7.70

```
<bean id="persistenceManagerFactory"
    class="org.springframework.orm.jdo
        .LocalPersistenceManagerFactoryBean">
    <property name="jdoProperties">
        <props>
            <prop key="javax.jdo.PersistenceManagerFactoryClass">
                org.jpox.PersistenceManagerFactoryImpl
            </prop>
            <prop key="javax.jdo.option.ConnectionDriverName">
                com.mysql.jdbc.Driver
            </prop>
            <prop key="javax.jdo.option.ConnectionUserName">root
                </prop>
            <prop key="javax.jdo.option.ConnectionPassword">
                </prop>
            <prop key="javax.jdo.option.ConnectionURL">
                jdbc:mysql://localhost/myusers
            </prop>
            <prop key="javax.jdo.option.NontransactionalRead">true
                </prop>
            <prop key="javax.jdo.option.RetainValues">true</prop>
            <prop key="org.jpox.autoCreateSchema">true</prop>
            <prop key="org.jpox.identifier.case">LowerCase</prop>
            <prop key="org.jpox.validateTables">false</prop>
        </props>
    </property>
</bean>
```

There are two properties in this bean you should take note of. The first is **javax.jdo.option.RetainValues**; if you don't specify this property, or use a value of **"false"**, all values but the primary key will be cleared after a commit. The second property is **org.jpox.identifier.case**; this property is used to control the case of automatically generated tables. If you don't specify this value, the underlying database's default case will be used. By setting it to **LowerCase**, you can guarantee your tables and column names will be created with lowercase names.

6 Add a **transactionManager** bean definition that uses a **JdoTransactionManager**. This binds a JDO **PersistenceManager** from the specified factory to the thread, potentially allowing for one thread **PersistenceManager** per factory. See Listing 8.71.

Listing 7.71

```
<bean id="transactionManager"
    class="org.springframework.orm.jdo.JdoTransactionManager">
    <property name="persistenceManagerFactory"
        ref="persistenceManagerFactory"/>
</bean>
```

7   Create a **UserDAOJdo.java** class in *src/org/appfuse/dao/jdo* (you must create this directory). This class extends **JdoDaoSupport** and implements **UserDAO**. See Listing 8.72.

Listing 7.72

```
package org.appfuse.dao.jdo;

// user your IDE to organize imports

public class UserDAOJdo extends JdoDaoSupport
    implements UserDAO {

    public List getUsers() {
        Collection users = getJdoTemplate().find(User.class);
        users = getPersistenceManager().detachCopyAll(users);
        return new ArrayList(users);
    }

    public User getUser(Long id) {
        User user = (User)
getJdoTemplate().getObjectById(User.class, id);
        if (user == null) {
            throw new ObjectRetrievalFailureException
                (User.class, id);
        }
        return (User) getPersistenceManager().detachCopy(user);
    }

    public void saveUser(User user) {
        if (user.getId() == null) {
            getJdoTemplate().makePersistent(user);
        } else {
            getPersistenceManager().attachCopy(user, true);
        }
    }

    public void removeUser(Long id) {
```

```
            getJdoTemplate().deletePersistent(
                getJdoTemplate().getObjectById(User.class, id));
    }
}
```

8   Add a **userDAO** bean definition to *applicationContext-jdo.xml*. See Listing 8.73.

Listing 7.73

```
<bean id="userDAO" class="org.appfuse.dao.jdo.UserDAOJdo">
    <property name="persistenceManagerFactory"
        ref="persistenceManagerFactory"/>
</bean>
```

TEST IT!

To ensure a clean database, as well as to allow JPOX to create tables for you, drop the **app_user** table.

1   Log in to MySQL by typing **mysql -u root -p myusers** from the command line.

2   Execute **drop table app_user;**.

3   Testing this class isn't as simple as previous examples. JDO requires a transaction for any write operations, unless you specifically indicate that it doesn't need one. If you run **ant test -Dtestcase=UserDAO**, you will see a stack trace in your console complaining that a transaction isn't active. See Figure 8.5.

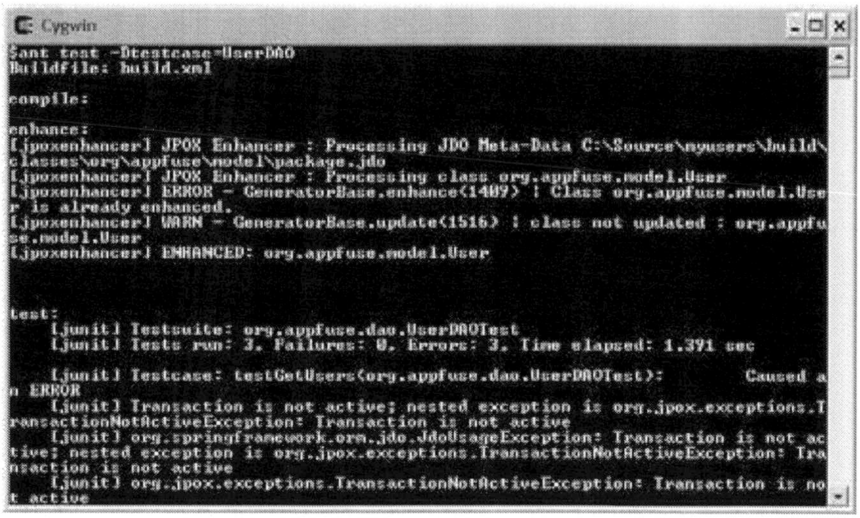

Figure 7.5: Running `UserDAOTest` for JDO without transactions

The JDO specification describes how you can turn off transactions by setting `javax.jdo.option.NontransactionalWrite` to *true*, but JPOX doesn't support this feature (yet). In reality, you *do* want the save operation to participate in a transaction. If you don't have an active transaction, you must create one, which is why the **userManager** bean has a **PROPOGATION_REQUIRED** transaction attribute on its **save*** methods.

In the normal course of the application, the **save** methods in the **UserManager** will participate in a transaction, so the only issue is in the **UserDAOTest**. To prove the issue is with this class and not the **UserDAOJdo**, run **ant test -Dtestcase=User-Manager**.

The easiest way to fix this is to override the definition of **userDAO** and wrap it with declarative transactions.

1   Create a file named *applicationContext-test.xml* in *test/org/appfuse/dao*. Put the XML in Listing 8.74 into this file:

Listing 7.74

```
<?xml version="1.0" encoding="UTF-8"?>
<!DOCTYPE beans PUBLIC "-//SPRING//DTD BEAN//EN"
    "http://www.springframework.org/dtd/spring-beans.dtd">

<beans>
    <!-- userDAO for testing UserDAOJdo -->
    <bean id="userDAO"
```

```
        class="org.springframework.transaction.interceptor
            .TransactionProxyFactoryBean">
        <property name="transactionManager"
            ref="transactionManager"/>
        <property name="target">
            <bean class="org.appfuse.dao.jdo.UserDAOJdo"
                autowire="byName"/>
        </property>
        <property name="transactionAttributes">
            <props>
                <prop key="*">PROPAGATION_REQUIRED</prop>
            </props>
        </property>
    </bean>
</beans>
```

2   Change the **setUp()** method in **UserDAOTest** to load this file before grabbing the **userDAO**. See Listing 8.75.

Listing 7.75

```
protected void setUp() throws Exception {
    String[] paths =
        {"/org/appfuse/dao/applicationContext-test.xml"};
    ctx = new ClassPathXmlApplicationContext(paths, ctx);
    dao = (UserDAO) ctx.getBean("userDAO");
}
```

3   Improve the **compile** target in *build.xml* to copy this file into the test classpath. See Listing 8.76.

Listing 7.76

```
        <!-- Copy JDO mapping files -->
        <fileset dir="${src.dir}" includes="**/*.jdo"/>
    </copy>
    <!-- Copy overriding test files -->
    <copy todir="${test.dir}/classes">
        <fileset dir="${test.src}" includes="**/*.xml"/>
    </copy>
</target>
```

4   Run **ant test -Dtestcase=UserDAO**. Your results should be similar to the results in Figure 8.6.

Figure 7.6: Running `UserDAOTest` for JDO with incorrect `User.equals()` method

5   This test should fail with an **AssertionFailedError** on line 32 of **UserDAOTest**. Line 32 is the last line in the **testGetUsers()** method. See Listing 8.77.

Listing 7.77

```
public void testGetUsers() {
    user = new User();
    user.setFirstName("Rod");
    user.setLastName("Johnson");
    dao.saveUser(user);

    List users = dao.getUsers();
    assertTrue(users.size() >= 1);
    assertTrue(users.contains(user));
}
```

The reason this assertion is failing is because the **User** object created at the beginning of the test does not match the one returned by the DAO. This is because the **equals()** method in **User.java** is inherited from **BaseObject**, which uses reflection to determine if all properties are equal. Because JDO enhances this class, the properties can be different.

The easiest way to make this test pass is to override the **equals()** method in **User.java** to determine equality based on the primary key. Add the method in Listing 8.78 to the bottom of *src/org/appfuse/model/User.java*:

Listing 7.78

```
public boolean equals(Object o) {
    if (this == o) return true;
    if (!(o instanceof User)) return false;

    final User user = (User) o;

    if (id != null ? !id.equals(user.getId()) :
        user.getId() != null) return false;

    return true;
}
```

6   Now if you run **ant test -Dtestcase=UserDAO**, all tests should pass. See Figure 8.7.

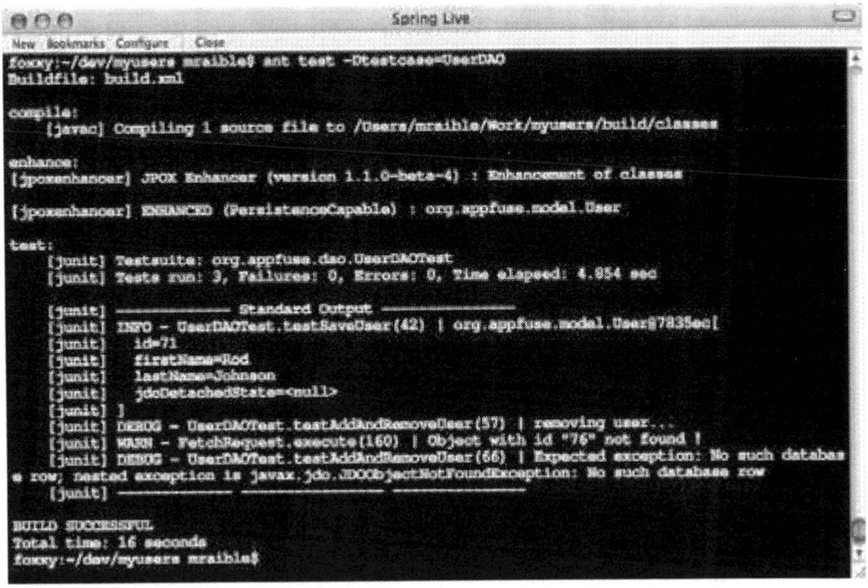

Figure 7.7: Running `UserDAOTest` for JDO with corrected `User.equals()` method

CACHING

See JPOX's web site for information on its caching support.

COMMUNITY AND SUPPORT

JDO is a standard, so unlike the other persistence options, it's likely that many vendors will create JDO-compliant products. Many good books on JDO are available. As you may have noticed from this short tutorial, it's not as refined as the other options; it requires an *enhancement* step that the other frameworks don't. The JPOX project has user forums and good documentation and seems to be one of the few that offers JDO 2.0 support. They've also published a "JPOX with Spring" tutorial (jroller.com/page/raible/home/spring_jpox_tutorial).

Kodo JDO is a commercial implementation of JDO by SolarMetric. Along with their product, they offer commercial support and training. They also have a sample application for download that uses Spring and Kodo JDO.

OJB

ObJectRelationalBridge (OJB) is an Apache project that is very similar to Hibernate. In fact, its description is quite similar: An ORM tool that allows transparent persistence for Java objects against relational databases. Because of this similarity, this chapter doesn't describe how it works. You can find a complete feature list on OJB's web site.

This section covers how to configure and use OJB with Spring.

> **NOTE:** Spring's OJB support classes are located in the `org.springframe-work.orm.ojb` and `org.springframework.orm.ojb.support` packages.

DEPENDENCIES

This example uses OJB version 1.0.3. Below are the JARs included in the MyUsers download as part of OJB.

* `commons-dbcp.jar` and `commons-pool.jar` — Connection pool implementation
* `db-ojb-1.0.3.jar` — Core OJB classes

CONFIGURATION

The first step to integrating OJB is to create a repository file that maps objects to tables.

1   Create a new file named *repository.xml* and put it the *src/org/appfuse/model* directory.

Listing 7.79

```
<descriptor-repository version="1.0">
    <jdbc-connection-descriptor jcd-alias="dataSource"
        default-connection="true" useAutoCommit="1" platform="MySQL">
        <sequence-manager
            className="org.apache.ojb.broker.util.sequence
                .SequenceManagerNativeImpl"/>
    </jdbc-connection-descriptor>

    <class-descriptor class="org.appfuse.model.User"
table="app_user">
        <field-descriptor name="id" column="id" primarykey="true"
            autoincrement="true" access="readonly"/>
        <field-descriptor name="firstName" column="first_name"/>
        <field-descriptor name="lastName" column="last_name"/>
    </class-descriptor>
</descriptor-repository>
```

The first part of this file describes the JDBC connection information (`<jdbc-connection-descriptor>`). The platform helps OJB figure out how it should retrieve primary keys, so it's important that it match your database. The **jcd-alias** attribute points to a **dataSource** bean that you need to define.

2   Create an *applicationContext-ojb.xml* file in the *web/WEB-INF* directory. While you're in that directory, rename *applicationContext-jdo.xml* to *applicationContext-jdo.xml.txt*. Also change the dependencies in *build.xml* so the **test** and **war** targets don't depend on **enhance**. Add the **dataSource** bean definition as in Listing 8.80:

Listing 7.80

```xml
<?xml version="1.0" encoding="UTF-8"?>
<!DOCTYPE beans PUBLIC "-//SPRING//DTD BEAN//EN"
    "http://www.springframework.org/dtd/spring-beans.dtd">

<beans>
    <bean id="dataSource"
        class="org.springframework.jdbc.datasource
            .DriverManagerDataSource">
        <property name="driverClassName"
            value="com.mysql.jdbc.Driver"/>
        <property name="url"
            value="jdbc:mysql://localhost/myusers"/>
        <property name="username" value="root"/>
        <property name="password" value=""/>
    </bean>
</beans>
```

3   Add a **transactionManager** bean definition that uses a **Persistence- BrokerTransactionManager**. This transaction manager is similar to the others; it binds an OJB **PersistenceBroker** from the specified key to the thread. **PersistenceBrokerTemplate** is aware of thread-bound persistence brokers and participates in such transactions automatically. See Listing 8.81.

Listing 7.81

```xml
<bean id="transactionManager"
    class="org.springframework.orm.ojb
        .PersistenceBrokerTransactionManager"/>
```

4   Add an **ojbConfigurer** bean. When the **LocalOjbConfigurer** class is initialized, it exposes Spring's **BeanFactory** to OJB so it can use the Spring-managed **DataSource**. See Listing 8.82.

Listing 7.82

```
<bean id="ojbConfigurer"
    class="org.springframework.orm.ojb.support.LocalOjbConfigurer"/>
```

5   Configure OJB to recognize Spring's **dataSource** bean. Do this by overriding a few settings in the default **OJB.properties**.

     a   Download the default *OJB.properties* file and put it in *web/WEB-INF/ classes*. Be sure it's named *OJB.properties*.

     b   Change **repositoryFile** to the code in Listing 8.83:

Listing 7.83

```
repositoryFile=org/appfuse/model/repository.xml
```

     c   Change **ConnectionFactoryClass** to the code in Listing 8.84 to allow a Spring-defined **DataSource**:

Listing 7.84

```
ConnectionFactoryClass=org.springframework.orm.ojb.support
    .LocalDataSourceConnectionFactory
```

6   Create a **UserDAOOjb.java** class in *src/org/appfuse/dao/ojb* (you must create this directory). This class extends **PersistenceBrokerDaoSupport** and implements **UserDAO**. See Listing 8.85.

Listing 7.85

```
package org.appfuse.dao.ojb;

// organize imports with your IDE

public class UserDAOOjb extends PersistenceBrokerDaoSupport
    implements UserDAO {

    public List getUsers() {
        return new ArrayList(getPersistenceBrokerTemplate().
            getCollectionByQuery
                (new QueryByCriteria(User.class)));
    }

    public User getUser(Long id) {
        Criteria criteria = new Criteria();
        criteria.addEqualTo("id", id);
        User user = (User) getPersistenceBrokerTemplate()
```

```
                    .getObjectByQuery(new QueryByCriteria
                        (User.class, criteria));
            if (user == null) {
                throw new ObjectRetrievalFailureException
                    (User.class, id);
            }
            return user;
        }

        public void saveUser(User user) {
            getPersistenceBrokerTemplate().store(user);
        }

        public void removeUser(Long id) {
            getPersistenceBrokerTemplate().delete(getUser(id));
        }
    }
```

7 Add this class as the **userDAO** in *web/WEB-INF/applicationContext-ojb.xml*.
See Listing 8.86.

Listing 7.86

```
<bean id="userDAO" class="org.appfuse.dao.ojb.UserDAOOjb"/>
```

8 The **app_user** table created by JDO does not allow nulls in the **id**
column. With OJB, it's easiest to insert nulls for primary keys and retrieve
the generated id back from the database. To do this, drop and re-create the
app_user table.

  a Log in to MySQL by typing **mysql -u root -p myusers** from the
command line.

  b Execute **drop table app_user;**.

  c Execute the SQL statement in Listing 8.87:

Listing 7.87

```
create table app_user (id bigint not null auto_increment,
first_name varchar(50), last_name varchar(50),
    primary key (id));
```

TEST IT!

Before you run the **UserDAOTest**, change its **setUp()** method so it doesn't override the **userDAO** you just created. Listing 8.88 is a **setUp()** method that eliminates
loading the transaction-wrapped DAO for JDO.

Listing 7.88

```
protected void setUp() throws Exception {
    //String[] paths =
        {"/org/appfuse/dao/applicationContext-test.xml"};
    //ctx = new ClassPathXmlApplicationContext(paths, ctx);
    dao = (UserDAO) ctx.getBean("userDAO");
}
```

You can also simply change the **class** attribute of the **target** bean in *application-Context-test.xml*. See Listing 8.89.

Listing 7.89

```
<property name="target">
    <bean class="org.appfuse.dao.ojb.UserDAOOjb"/>
</property>
```

9   Run **ant test -Dtestcase=UserDAO**. If you've used the first option (commenting out lines in **setUp()**), you'll see this warning: "No running tx found." The second option will eliminate this warning.

NOTE: With OJB, you won't need the **enhance** target in *build.xml* anymore. You can remove it, as well as modify the **test** and **deploy** to depend on **compile** instead of **enhance**.

CACHING

See OJB's web site for information on its caching support.

COMMUNITY AND SUPPORT

OJB 1.0 was released on June 30, 2004 and three updates to that release have been released since. It's an Apache project with a fair amount of real-world implementations. For support, your best option is to use its mailing lists. The OJB web site also has excellent documentation.

SUMMARY
. . . .

This chapter explored the different persistence options that Spring supports: Hibernate, iBATIS SQL Maps, its own JDBC abstraction, JDO and OJB. You saw how Spring configures each one in the MyUsers application. It is my opinion that Hibernate and iBATIS are the best tools to use for persistence.

Hibernate makes it easy to persist objects using simple mapping files, and you can even use XDoclet to generate the mapping files for you. iBATIS is ideal if you have an existing, complicated schema or legacy database, or if you simply prefer writing your own SQL.

This chapter has shown how powerful Spring is as a configuration tool and loose-coupling promoter. Of the five persistence frameworks, you only had to change the **UserDAOTest** for one. Not only does Spring promote good design, it makes good design a lot easier to use.

TESTING SPRING APPLICATIONS

How Spring makes testing easier

This chapter covers how to use test-driven development (TDD) to create high-quality, well-tested, Spring-based applications. You will learn how to test your components using tools such as Easy-Mock, jMock, and DbUnit. For the controllers, you will learn how to use Cactus for in-container testing and Spring mocks for out-of-container testing. Last, you will learn how to use jWebUnit and Canoo's WebTest for testing the web interface.

OVERVIEW

Using TDD is the best way to produce high-quality code. Not only do you think about how your application is supposed to work as you're writing the test (from your user's API's perspective), but you actually *design* the contracts that your application is supposed to fulfill. If your tests don't pass as you expect, then you have a problem with your test or your implementation. If your tests do as expected in that contract, you must modify your implementation to produce that expectation. See Figure 9.1.

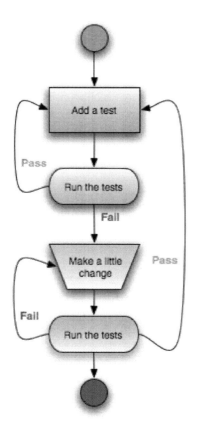

Figure 8.1: The *test-first develop-ment* methodology

Using the *test-first* development meth-odology, the developer writes one test to verify a specific behavior of the problem at hand. Next, the developer writes the simplest code that will make that test pass. This process is repeated by adding a test and then writing the code to make this new test pass until everything has been tested. The devel-oper continues to take baby steps to get the test to pass or fail during devel-opment. The diagram[1] in Figure 9.1 illustrates this technique.

While test-driven and test-first tech-niques are similar, the most important aspect is that the process of writing tests forces you to consider how your classes behave. Test-first advocates a more rigorous system of small steps.

In this chapter, you will learn how to use testing technologies to develop Spring applications faster and more efficiently. By employing test-first development, you can virtually elimi-nate the trial-and-error procedures that are common with developing browser-based applications. You can also gain confidence in your code and add regular automation to ensure that no one "broke the build."

Developing software that you can test easily is a very liberating experience because it allows you to find out quickly whether something worked.

---

1) The diagram in Figure 9.1 is based on one in Scott W. Ambler's Test Driven Development essay.

Spring makes it easy to write testable software. Its IoC container gives you the freedom to set dependencies on classes any way you like. You can load Spring's **Application-Context** in your test and use your beans like your application does, or you can set a bean's dependencies using mock objects. This chapter explores both techniques and shows you how to use tools like EasyMock and jMock to create mock versions of your classes on the fly. You will also see how to use DbUnit to load data in a database before testing.

NOTE: A mock object is a fake and simplistic version of a real object. For instance, you can use mocks to imitate the Servlet API so you can run tests outside of a servlet container.

For testing the controllers in your application, you will learn how to use StrutsTest-Case, Spring Mocks, and Cactus. For testing the view layer, you will learn how to use jWebUnit and Canoo WebTest.

JUNIT

JUnit has quickly become the de facto standard for TDD in Java. It's an easy framework to use, and most modern IDEs support it. If you don't use an IDE, you probably use Ant, which is also easy to use with a **<junit>** task. In this chapter, you will use JUnit to write most of your tests. If you're not using JUnit directly, you'll be using an extension. For example, DbUnit, Cactus, and StrutsTestCase are all JUnit extensions.

A basic JUnit test simply contains a **testXXX()** method, where **XXX** is a descriptive name of what the test does. It's important to use a name that describes the test accurately. For example, if you have an object that allows results to be filtered, **test-GetUsersWithNoFiltering()** is better than the more generic **testGetUsers()**. The example in Listing 9.1 demonstrates a simple JUnit test:

Listing 8.1

```
package org.appfuse.dao;

import junit.framework.TestCase;
import org.appfuse.model.User;

public class SimpleTest extends TestCase {

    public void testGetFullName() {
        User user = new User();
        user.setFirstName("Jack");
```

```
        user.setLastName("Raible");
        assertEquals("Jack Raible", user.getLastName());
    }
}
```

Running this test results in a failure because you're getting the last name rather than the full name. Running your tests with failures first is important to make sure they meet your expectations. Changing **assertEquals()** to the following snippet will yield a passing test:

assertEquals("Jack Raible", user.getFullName());

Optional methods to implement in a JUnit test include **setUp()**, **tearDown()**, and **main(String[])**. Using **setUp()** and **tearDown()** are useful for creating a testing environment, then tearing down that environment *before running the next test*. These methods are called before and after each **testXXX()** method. If you have testwide setup procedures, you should implement those in a static initialization block or use JUnit's **TestSetup** class.

It is necessary to implement the **main(String[])** to run a JUnit test from the command line using the **java** command. However, with modern IDE and Ant support, you may never need to implement this method. To prove it, remove the **main(String[])** from the **UserDAOTest** in MyUsers; your tests will continue to run.

In the Java Community, using TDD has increasingly become the norm, especially among open-source developers. The projects with a rich test suite typically gain more credibility from other developers. However, there is a philosophical difference of *how* one should do TDD. Many advocate the use of Mock Objects, or mocks, while others think integration testing is good enough.

This chapter often refers to *unit tests*. You may not agree that it's a *unit* test but rather an *integration test*. J. B. Rainsberger said it best in the book JUnit Recipes:

"The testing that programmers do is generally called unit testing, but we prefer not to use this term. It is overloaded and overused, and it causes more confusion than it provides clarity. As a community, we cannot agree on what a unit is — is it a method, a class, or a code path? If we cannot agree on what unit means, then there is little chance we will agree on what unit testing means."

This chapter shows you two types of testing: *mock testing* and *integration testing*. Let's take a brief look at the philosophies behind them.

MOCK TESTING

Mock testing is the process of isolating your test case to test a single unit of work, most often a class. Using mocks, you can test your class in isolation, without reliance on any of its dependencies. In the instance of a business façade (or Manager), you would *mock* its dependent DAO. This allows you to test the business façade for its specific functionality, not including the DAO's functionality.

A mock is typically a *stub* (a minimal test-only class you write yourself) or a *dynamic mock*. Dynamic mocks are a slick way of setting *expectations* on a class or interface. With dynamic mocks, you can create an instance of your class on the fly and write code to set expected behavior. The general rule for using mocks is "only mock types that you can change" or "only mock APIs that are yours."

INTEGRATION TESTING

Integration testing is the process of testing your classes in their normal environment with all of their dependencies intact. The main disadvantages of integration testing are *speed* and *non-isolated tests*. For example, for a business façade test that depends on its real DAO, you must establish a database connection to retrieve actual data. By coding and running non-isolated tests, you're writing tests that depend on your environment, which really has nothing to do with your test.

There is a place for both types of tests. Dynamic mocks are great for team development, where different developers are responsible for different layers. For instance, if developer Bruce is responsible for the DAO layer, and developer James is responsible for the business logic layer, they have no reason to be dependent on each other's implementations. Bruce can provide James with interfaces, and James can create mocks of these in order to test his code in isolation. Then it doesn't matter if Bruce takes longer to deliver his DAO implementation.

If you're working on a small team or alone, integration tests will probably suffice. Of course, this means you will have to develop your application in a specific order, where dependencies are coded first so implementations that depend on them can run properly.

A properly designed application has integration tests in the database layer, mock tests in the business and web layers, and integration tests in the UI. Of course, this all depends on how complicated each layer is. For the database layer, it's important to test that its interaction with your underlying datastore works. There's no reason to mock the database connection or Spring-supplied `Template`. These are framework-level components and shouldn't be a concern of your application. Once your DAOs return the expected results, it's pointless to verify this again in the business layer. Therefore, you can mock the DAOs in the business (or service) layer and concentrate on testing your business logic.

In the web tier, particularly with MVC controllers and regardless of web framework, it's helpful to mock a J2EE container environment. Mocks can impersonate requests, responses, and other servlet-related classes, allowing you to run your tests out of container, which is often much faster. Using real business objects versus mocks in your controller tests is a matter of taste at that point. Testing them in isolation is usually a good idea, since the important functionality in controllers is controlling which views are returned for specific inputs.

The UI layer is the best place to test the full stack of integrated functionality. Testing the UI layer involves shadowing the actions a user would take when using your application: clicking links, entering data, clicking buttons, etc. These tests don't talk to your classes directly but perform browser actions. They typically pull HTML from a URL, parse it, and submit request parameters based on your test code. The frameworks for UI testing make this very simple so you can write one-liners to submit forms, enter data, and verify page titles or text.

Now that you understand the different strategies of testing, let's look at some specific examples in the context of the MyUsers application. In this chapter, like previous ones, you can follow along and do the examples as you go. The easiest way to do this is to download the **MyUsers Chapter 8** bundle from sourcebeat.com/downloads. This project tree is the result of *Chapter 8: Persistence Strategies: Hibernate, iBATIS, JDBC, JDO, and OJB* exercises. It also contains all the JARs you will need in this chapter in its *web/WEB-INF/lib* directory. Each section notes new JARs you might need, so you can use this chapter as a reference for integrating these principles into your own applications.

In *Chapter 8: Persistence Strategies: Hibernate, iBATIS, JDBC, JDO, and OJB*, you integrated a number of persistence strategies. If you completed all the exercises in the chapter, your MyUsers application should be using OJB, since that was the last strategy explored. Since Hibernate is the most popular persistence framework used with Spring, this chapter has Hibernate enabled by default. If you'd like to change your application to use a different framework, follow the specific section for that framework. Here are a few things to remember if you decide to switch from OJB to something else:

- JDO requires modifications to *build.xml* so **enhance** is called by the **test** and **war** targets. You may also have to change **UserDAOTest** so it loads *applicationContext-test.xml*.

- You may need to drop the **app_user** table and re-create it (see the instructions for each DAO type).

If you have issues with switching DAOs, feel free to email the author at mattr@sourcebeat.com, ask a question on the Spring Live Forum at www.javalobby.org/forums/forum.jspa?forumID=174, or enter an issue in the Spring Live Issue Tracker (provided by Atlassian) at issues.sourcebeat.com/browse/SPL.

TESTING THE DATABASE LAYER

As mentioned earlier, it's best to test your DAOs directly against your database. This ensures that your persistence framework works as you want. Testing a database layer involves retrieving, adding, updating, and removing data using your application-specific classes. Review the **UserDAOTest** in Listing 9.2, which you created in *Chapter 2: Spring Quick-Start Tutorial*.

Listing 8.2

```
package org.appfuse.dao;

// use your IDE to organize imports

public class UserDAOTest extends BaseDAOTestCase {
    private User user = null;
    private UserDAO dao = null;

    protected void setUp() throws Exception {
        super.setUp();
        dao = (UserDAO) ctx.getBean("userDAO");
    }

    protected void tearDown() throws Exception {
        super.tearDown();
        dao = null;
    }

    public void testGetUsers() {
        // add a record so we have something to work with
        user = new User();
        user.setFirstName("Rod");
        user.setLastName("Johnson");
        dao.saveUser(user);

        List users = dao.getUsers();
        assertTrue(users.size() >= 1);
        assertTrue(users.contains(user));
    }

    public void testSaveUser() throws Exception {
        user = new User();
        user.setFirstName("Rod");
        user.setLastName("Johnson");

        dao.saveUser(user);
        assertNotNull(user.getId());
        log.info(user);
        assertTrue(user.getFirstName() != null);
```

```
        }

        public void testAddAndRemoveUser() throws Exception {
            user = new User();
            user.setFirstName("Bill");
            user.setLastName("Joy");

            dao.saveUser(user);

            assertNotNull(user.getId());
            assertEquals("Bill", user.getFirstName());

            if (log.isDebugEnabled()) {
                log.debug("removing user...");
            }

            dao.removeUser(user.getId());

            try {
                user = dao.getUser(user.getId());
                fail("User found in database");
            } catch (DataAccessException dae) {
                log.debug("Expected exception: " + dae.getMessage());
                assertTrue(dae != null);
            }
        }
    }
```

This class is an integration test because it depends on Spring's **ApplicationContext** to retrieve the **UserDAO** implementation class, with all its dependencies set. The **ApplicationContext** is initialized using **ClassPathXmlApplicationContext** in the **BaseDAOTestCase**, which this class extends. See Listing 9.3.

Listing 8.3

```
    protected ApplicationContext ctx = null;

    public BaseDAOTestCase() {
        String[] paths = { "/WEB-INF/applicationContext*.xml" };
        ctx = new ClassPathXmlApplicationContext(paths);
    }
```

In addition to the **ClassPathXmlApplicationContext**, you can use the **FileSystemXmlApplicationContext** class to load your context files. Both of these classes allow the Ant-style syntax (**.xml*) to load any resources that match the specified pattern. If you'd rather load context files using that class, you could refactor the above code to the match Listing 9.4:

Listing 8.4

```
public BaseDAOTestCase() {
    String[] paths = { "web/WEB-INF/applicationContext*.xml" };
    ctx = new FileSystemXmlApplicationContext(paths);
}
```

The advantage of using **ClassPathXmlApplicationContext** is that your files don't have to be in a precise location; they just have to be in your classpath. This chapter uses /*WEB-INF/applicationContext*.xml* instead of /*applicationContext*.xml* because the first is in the classpath and the second isn't. The classpath is set in both the Eclipse .classpath file and the Ant build file.

The Eclipse setting in the *.classpath* file is listed below:

```
<classpathentry excluding="WEB-INF/classes/"
    kind="src" path="web"/>
```

The Ant setting in the **test** target is listed in Listing 9.5:

Listing 8.5

```
<classpath>
    <path refid="classpath"/>
    <path location="${build.dir}/classes"/>
    <path location="${test.dir}/classes"/>
    <path location="web/WEB-INF/classes"/>
    <path location="web"/>
</classpath>
```

Using /*WEB-INF/applicationContext*.xml* is also helpful because *action-servlet.xml* refers to validator resource files using this path, requiring the *web* folder to be in the classpath when testing classes use that file. When you refactor your controller tests to be self-contained unit tests, you will no longer need to load the context, freeing you to change this path.

TESTING CLASSES PROVIDED BY SPRING

To simplify integration testing, Spring provides a number of classes in its **org.springframework.test** package. These classes are only available if you include *spring-mock.jar* in your classpath (the project for this chapter already contains this file). The classes within this package are abstract and designed to be extended. They contain the following functionality:

- **ApplicationContext** caching
- Dependency injection for test classes (using autowiring)

- Transaction management for testing scenarios (rollback after test method exits)
- Inherited instance variables for testing

APPLICATIONCONTEXT CACHING

The two most-used classes in **org.springframework.test** are **AbstractDependencyInjectionSpringContextTests** and **AbstractTransactionalDataSourceSpringContextTests**. Both of these classes allow you to load context files by implementing a **String[] getConfigLocations()** method. See Listing 9.6.

Listing 8.6

```
protected String[] getConfigLocations() {
    return new String[] {"/applicationContext*.xml"};
}
```

Once you load the context files, Spring caches them for subsequent test executions. This makes test execution much faster, especially if you're using JUnit and loading your context files before each test run. You can force reloading of the context files by calling **setDirty()**.

Another feature of these classes is they tighten up the JUnit API. When writing normal JUnit **TestCase** subclasses, you must implement **void setUp()** and **void tearDown()** for instantiating and destroying objects before and after each test. While this works, if you have a parent **TestCase**, it's easy to forget you need to call **super.setUp()** and **super.tearDown()** in your methods. Spring's JUnit extensions eliminate this problem by making **setUp()** and **tearDown()** final and requiring you to override **onSetUp()** and **onTearDown()** instead.

TIP: If you're using JDK 5, the **@Override** annotation allows you to verify that you're overriding a parent class. If you misspell **onSetup()**, it won't be called. Using this annotation will prevent this from happening.

DEPENDENCY INJECTION FOR TEST CLASSES

In addition to caching and loading your context files, these classes allow you to do dependency injection in your tests. This means that instead of calling **ctx.getBean("beanName")** in your **setUp()** method, you can simply add a setter to your test class. See Listing 9.7.

Listing 8.7

```
private UserManager userManager;

public void setUserManager(UserManager userManager) {
    this.userManager = userManager;
}
```

In this example, Spring will use its autowiring feature to set the **UserManager** dependency. It uses *autowire by type* by default, which can be problematic if you have multiple implementations of an interface. For this reason, it's recommended that you change the autowiring mode to *by name*. See Listing 9.8.

Listing 8.8

```
protected String[] getConfigLocations() {
    setAutowireMode(AUTOWIRE_BY_NAME);
    return new String[] {"/applicationContext*.xml"};
}
```

If you don't do dependency injection in your tests, simply don't add **set** methods to your test class. You can also extend **AbstractSpringContextTests**, which allows you to load and cache context files but perform no dependency injection.

TRANSACTION MANAGEMENT FOR TESTING SCENARIOS

Transaction management is an important feature provided by Spring. Being able to leverage this feature in tests can make your classes much easier to test. The **AbstractTransactionalDataSourceSpringContextTests** is not only one of the longest class names in Spring, it's one of the most useful classes, too.

If you extend this class, a transaction will automatically be created and rolled back for each test method. This means you can delete records from a database, insert 1,000 rows, or do whatever you like. After you're done, your database will be returned to the state it started in. In fact, your database is never really altered, but your test case thinks it is because it's reading the state of what happens in that transaction.

This class exposes a **deleteFromTables(String [])** that allows you to clear table data before your tests run. It also exposes a **jdbcTemplate** variable that you can use to query your database while your test is running. This variable is instantiated with a **DataSource** that's set via **setDataSource()**. It's important to note that this class is only designed to work with a single database, but you can easily work with two by adding an additional method to set your second **DataSource** and create a second **JdbcTemplate** from it.

By wrapping tests with transactions, you can avoid Hibernate's `LazyInitializa-tionException` from being thrown because your session will stay open. Also, using this class will allow you to easily test your DAOs that require a transaction be present (for example, classes that extend JdoDaoSupport). Rolling back transactions is the default behavior, but you can change that. If you call `setComplete()` in your test, it will cause the transaction to commit instead of rolling back. You can also use the `endTransaction()` method to roll back a transaction before a test method exits, followed by `startNewTransaction()` if you'd like to start a new one. Of course, if you call `setComplete()` before `endTransaction()`, it will commit the transaction instead.

This functionality is useful if you want to test the behavior of "disconnected" data objects, such as Hibernate-mapped POJOs that are used in your web (or remoting) outside a transaction. Often, lazy-loading errors are discovered only through UI testing; if you call `endTransaction()`, you can ensure correct operation of the UI without actually testing the UI.

If you need to implement setup or tear down behavior with this class, you'll want to implement `onSetUpBeforeTransaction()`, `onSetUpInTransaction()`, or the similarly named `onTearDown` methods. The `onSetUp()` and `onTearDown()` methods are declared final in `AbstractTransactionalDataSourceSpringContextTests`.

INHERITED INSTANCE VARIABLES FOR TESTING

By extending one of Spring's classes for JUnit, you gain access to some variables, which are listed below:

- `logger`: Commons Logging logger for subclasses.

- `applicationContext`: The `ConfigurableApplicationContext` instantiated by context files specified in `getConfigLocations()`.

- `jdbcTemplate`: Exposed by `AbstractTransactionalDataSource-SpringContextTests`, and therefore only available when inheriting from it. This variable can be useful for querying the state of your database during a test's execution.

There's no better way to learn than by implementing your new-found knowledge. Refactoring the `BaseDAOTestCase` and `UserDAOTest` is really quite easy.

1   Open *test/org/appfuse/dao/BaseDAOTestCase.java*. Modify it so it extends `AbstractTransactionalDataSourceSpringContextTests` and implements the `getConfigLocations()` method. See Listing 9.9.

Listing 8.9

```
public class BaseDAOTestCase extends
    AbstractTransactionalDataSourceSpringContextTests {
    protected final Log log = logger;

    protected String[] getConfigLocations() {
        return new String[]
            {"/WEB-INF/applicationContext*.xml"};
    }
}
```

2   Refactor **UserDAOTest.java** to remove its **setUp()** and **tearDown()**
    methods, as well as expose the **UserManager** for dependency injection.
    See Listing 9.10.

Listing 8.10

```
public class UserDAOTest extends BaseDAOTestCase {
    private User user;
    private UserDAO dao;

    public void setUserDAO(UserDAO userDAO) {
        this.dao = userDAO;
    }
```

3   Run the **UserDAOTest** using your IDE or with Ant by running **ant test
    -Dtestcase=UserDAO**.

DbUnit
. . . .

DbUnit is a testing framework useful for putting a database in a known state before
running tests. DbUnit has a single JAR that you need in your classpath: *dbunit-2.1.jar.*
This is included in the MyUsers download.

In the **UserDAOTest**, a record is added in the **testGetUsers()** method. Refactor
this class to use DbUnit to load a record before running the test. You must first
create some sample data with which to populate the database. A number of *datasets*
are available to use with DbUnit, but the easiest is the **XmlDataSet**.

NOTE: The following example assumes you haven't changed **BaseDAOTestCase**
to extend **AbstractTransactionalDataSourceSpringContextTests**, which
gives you similar functionality to DbUnit. You can read more about a comparison
between the two at tinyurl.com/zh52o. The assumed **BaseDAOTestCase** is as
follows in Listing 9.11:

Listing 8.11

```
public class BaseDAOTestCase extends TestCase {
    protected final Log log = LogFactory.getLog(getClass());
    protected ApplicationContext ctx = null;

    public BaseDAOTestCase() {
        String[] paths = {"/WEB-INF/applicationContext*.xml"};
        ctx = new ClassPathXmlApplicationContext(paths);
    }
}
```

1   Create a *sample-data.xml* file in *test/ data* (you must create this directory).
    Populate it with the XML in Listing 9.12.

Listing 8.12

```
<?xml version="1.0" encoding="utf-8"?>
<dataset>
  <table name='app_user'>
    <column>id</column>
    <column>first_name</column>
    <column>last_name</column>
    <row>
      <value>1</value>
      <value>Rod</value>
      <value>Johnson</value>
    </row>
  </table>
</dataset>
```

2   With DbUnit, you can extend its **DatabaseTestCase** or use your own
    TestCase. It's easier to use your own **TestCase** than to change the
    parent class. Add the two variables in Listing 9.13 as member variables of
    the **BaseDAOTestCase** class:

Listing 8.13

```
private IDatabaseConnection conn = null;
private IDataSet dataSet = null;
```

3   Create a **setUp()** method to clear out the database for any tables specified
    in the *sample-data.xml* file. See Listing 9.14.

Listing 8.14

```
protected void setUp() throws Exception {
    DataSource ds = (DataSource) ctx.getBean("dataSource");
    conn = new DatabaseConnection(ds.getConnection());
    dataSet = new XmlDataSet(new FileInputStream(
                            "test/data/sample-data.xml"));
    // clear table and insert only sample data
    DatabaseOperation.CLEAN_INSERT.execute(conn, dataSet);
}
```

4   Add logic in the **tearDown()** method to close the connection and delete any added data. See Listing 9.15.

Listing 8.15

```
protected void tearDown() throws Exception {
    // clear out database
    DatabaseOperation.DELETE.execute(conn, dataSet);
    conn.close();
    conn = null;
}
```

5   Alter **UserDAOTest** so the **setUp()** and **tearDown()** methods call **super.setUp()** and **super.tearDown()**. See Listing 9.16.

Listing 8.16

```
protected void setUp() throws Exception {
    super.setUp();
    dao = (UserDAO) ctx.getBean("userDAO");
}

protected void tearDown() throws Exception {
    super.tearDown();
    dao = null;
}
```

6   Change the **getUsers()** method to verify only one record is in the database, and it's the one DbUnit entered. See Listing 9.17.

Listing 8.17

```
public void testGetUsers() {
    List users = dao.getUsers();
```

```
                assertTrue(users.size() == 1);
                User user = (User) users.get(0);
                assertEquals("Rod Johnson", user.getFullName());
    }
```

Running **ant test -Dtestcase=UserDAO** should yield "BUILD SUCCESSFUL," and the **app_user** table should be empty in the database.

Ant is another way to use DbUnit in your application. You can configure a target that loads the database before running your tests. AppFuse uses this strategy; see its *build.xml* file and the **db-load** target for an example. This is useful because you can run a block of tests with predefined data rather than reloading the data for each test. The advantage of using this strategy is your suite of tests will run faster since the database isn't reset before each test is run. An advantage of using DbUnit directly in your classes is you can run your tests in an IDE without Ant dependencies.

DATABASE SWITCHING

Using Spring to configure your database connection makes it easy to swap the database with which you test your code. For example, you could use an HSQL database for unit tests and switch to a DB2 database for production. In most cases, it's a good idea to test against your production database, but if your developers use PowerBooks, DB2 doesn't have an install for Mac OS X.

One way to configure database switching is to use two properties files. Most of Spring's sample applications (in *CVS/samples*) use this strategy. By defining a **propertyConfigurer** bean (with class **PropertyPlaceholderConfigurer**), you can configure your **dataSource** bean's properties with Ant-style placeholders: **${...}**. This allows you to refer to test settings and production settings. It also allows you to share your database configuration between your Spring configuration files and your *build.xml* file. To configure a properties file with your database settings in MyUsers, complete the following steps:

1   Modify your current DAO strategy's XML file. This should be *applicationContext-hibernate.xml*. Replace the **dataSource** bean's property values with Ant-style properties, as in Listing 9.18.

Listing 8.18

```
<bean id="dataSource"
    class="org.springframework.jdbc.datasource
        .DriverManagerDataSource">
    <property name="driverClassName"
        value="${jdbc.driverClassName}"/>
    <property name="url" value="${jdbc.url}"/>
    <property name="username" value="${jdbc.username}"/>
    <property name="password" value="${jdbc.password}"/>
</bean>
```

2   Create a *jdbc.properties* file in the *web/WEB-INF/classes* directory. See
    Listing 9.19.

Listing 8.19

```
jdbc.driverClassName=com.mysql.jdbc.Driver
jdbc.url=jdbc:mysql://localhost/myusers
jdbc.username=root
jdbc.password=
```

3   Add a **PropertyPlaceHolderConfigurer** bean to *web/WEB-INF/*
    applicationContext.xml. The commented out section at the bottom of this
    definition shows you how to use a single **location** property as an
    alternative to the **locations** property. See Listing 9.20.

Listing 8.20

```
<bean id="propertyConfigurer"
    class="org.springframework.beans.factory.config
       .PropertyPlaceholderConfigurer">
    <property name="location" value="classpath:jdbc.properties"/>
</bean>
```

To specify multiple properties files for loading, use the **locations**
property instead of **location**, as in Listing 9.21.

Listing 8.21

```
<property name="locations">
    <list>
        <value>classpath:jdbc.properties</value>
        <value>classpath:mail.properties</value>
    </list>
</property>
```

4   To expose *jdbc.properties* to *build.xml,* add it as a properties file at the top of
    build.xml, as in Listing 9.22.

Listing 8.22

```
<property file="build.properties"/>
<property file="web/WEB-INF/classes/jdbc.properties"/>
```

5   Change the **populate** target's **<sql>** task to use the format in
    Listing 9.23.

Listing 8.23

```
<sql driver="${jdbc.driverClassName}" url="${jdbc.url}"
     userid="${jdbc.username}" password="${jdbc.password}">
```

OVERRIDING BEANS FOR TESTS

If you have DAOs with methods that require transactions be wrapped around them (and you don't want to use **AbstractTransactionalDataSourceSpringContextTests**), you can define beans specifically for unit tests. This was done in *Chapter 8: Persistence Strategies: Hibernate, iBATIS, JDBC, JDO, and OJB* for the JDO DAO because JDO requires that any **makePersistent()** calls are inside a transaction. Using Spring's declarative transactions in your test is much easier than using transactions. If you're still using the OJB DAO, you may have received several warning messages about no running transaction. See Figure 9.2.

Figure 8.2: Running **UserDAOTest** against **UserDAOojb**

To fix this, create a bean definition just for testing, and override the regular **userDAO** by loading this definition in **UserDAOTest**.

1   In *test/org/appfuse/dao*, create an *applicationContext-test.xml* file with a transaction-wrapped **userDAO** bean. See Listing 9.24.

Listing 8.24

```xml
<?xml version="1.0" encoding="UTF-8"?>
<!DOCTYPE beans PUBLIC "-//SPRING//DTD BEAN//EN"
    "http://www.springframework.org/dtd/spring-beans.dtd">

<beans>
    <!-- userDAO for testing UserDAOJdo -->
    <bean id="userDAO"
        class="org.springframework.transaction.interceptor
            .TransactionProxyFactoryBean">
        <property name="transactionManager"
            ref="transactionManager"/>
        <property name="target">
            <bean class="org.appfuse.dao.ojb.UserDAOOjb"
                autowire="byName"/>
        </property>
        <property name="transactionAttributes">
            <props>
                <prop key="*">PROPAGATION_REQUIRED</prop>
            </props>
        </property>
    </bean>
</beans>
```

2   Refactor the **setUp()** method of **UserDAOTest** to load this file before each test. See Listing 9.25.

Listing 8.25

```java
protected void setUp() throws Exception {
    super.setUp();
    String[] paths =
            {"/org/appfuse/dao/applicationContext-test.xml"};
    ctx = new ClassPathXmlApplicationContext(paths, ctx);
    dao = (UserDAO) ctx.getBean("userDAO");
}
```

3   Now the **UserDAOTest** should run (**ant test -Dtestcase=UserDAO**) without the transactions warning.

NOTE: You won't use this test configuration in the **UserManagerTest** since the **userManager** bean is already wrapped in transactions.

USE JNDI DATASOURCE IN TESTS

As mentioned previously, you can define two different **dataSource** beans for testing and production. The production bean will likely be a **DataSource** that's looked up via JNDI. An example definition is in Listing 9.26:

Listing 8.26

```
<bean id="dataSource"
    class="org.springframework.jndi.JndiObjectFactoryBean">
    <property name="jndiName" value="java:comp/env/jdbc/myusers"/>
</bean>
```

To use this bean in your tests, use Spring's JNDI mocks to bind this to a simple JNDI implementation. See Listing 9.27.

Listing 8.27

```
try {
    SimpleNamingContextBuilder builder =
        SimpleNamingContextBuilder.emptyActivatedContextBuilder();

    DriverManagerDataSource ds = new DriverManagerDataSource();
        ds.setDriverClassName("com.mysql.jdbc.Driver");
        ds.setUrl("jdbc:mysql://localhost/myusers");
        ds.setUsername("root");
        ds.setPassword("");
    builder.bind("java:comp/env/jdbc/myusers", ds);
} catch (NamingException ne) {
    // do nothing, test will fail on its own
}
```

To try this, put the JNDI **DataSource** in *applicationContext-test.xml* and add the context build code (above) to the beginning of the static initialization block in **BaseDAOTestCase.java**. For the **DriverManagerDataSource** properties above, you could also use a **ResourceBundle** to pull the information from *jdbc.properties*.

To use a JNDI **DataSource** in Tomcat, replace the **dataSource** bean in your DAO context file with the JNDI one configured in your container appropriately. Below are instructions for Tomcat 5.5.x:

1   Create a *myusers.xml* file in *$CATALINA_HOME/conf/Catalina/localhost* and populate it with the XML in Listing 9.28:

Listing 8.28

```
<Context path="/myusers" docBase="myusers" reloadable="true">
    <Resource name="jdbc/myusers" auth="Container"
            type="javax.sql.DataSource"
            maxActive="100" maxIdle="30" maxWait="10000"
            driverClassName="com.mysql.jdbc.Driver"
            username="root" password=""
            url="jdbc:mysql://localhost/myusers"
            defaultAutoCommit="true"/>
</Context>
```

2   Copy the MySQL JDBC Driver (*mysql-connector-java-3.1.12-bin.jar*) from *web/WEB-INF/lib* to *$CATALINA_HOME/common/lib*.

3   Add the XML fragment in Listing 9.29 to the bottom of *web/WEB-INF /web.xml*.

Listing 8.29

```
<resource-ref>
    <description>Connection Pool</description>
    <res-ref-name>jdbc/myusers</res-ref-name>
    <res-type>javax.sql.DataSource</res-type>
    <res-auth>Container</res-auth>
</resource-ref>
```

Now if you run **ant deploy** and stop/start Tomcat, everything should work as before.

TESTING THE SERVICE LAYER

In the last section, you learned how to test your DAO implementations against a database. This is important for your database layer to verify that what you put into the database is the same thing that comes out of it. However, once you have your DAOs tested and verified, you don't have much reason to use them in your service layer tests.

Spring not only promotes interface-based design, but it doesn't put any restrictions on how you write your unit tests. As the previous section demonstrates, you can easily load your context files in your tests and interact with your beans just as you would in a production environment. This is an important concept that is often overlooked. Many folks get caught up in mocking everything, which is great for test isolation, but they forget to test how the application's layers interact with each other.

You should always try to use integration tests first by loading the context in your test and operating on your beans accordingly. This is because it's easy to set up and it tests your *real* code, not a fake object. However, this approach can break down in two instances:

- You're working on a team and each developer is responsible for different layers. You don't want to wait for an implementation before writing tests for a parent layer.

- Your application context files grow so large that they take several seconds to load and initialize their beans.

To work around these issues, use mocks to simulate dependencies of your class.

USING MOCKS FOR DAO OBJECTS

This section refactors the **UserManagerTest** to use mocks for the **UserDAO**. There are two types of mocks: *stubs*, which you create yourself, and *dynamic mocks*, which allow you to implement classes on the fly. In the process of creating dynamic mocks, the developer is responsible for setting expected results when methods are called. Dynamic mocks are typically easier to use and don't litter your source tree with a second set of classes to maintain.

EASYMOCK

EasyMock is a project that provides mocks for interfaces in JUnit tests by generating them using Java's proxy mechanism. A class extension is also available to mock implementation classes. To use EasyMock in a test, perform the following steps:

1   Create a **MockControl** for the interface you would like to simulate.

2   Get the mock from the **MockControl**.

3   Specify the behavior of the mock (record state).

4   Activate the mock with the control (replay state).

5   Execute the methods you want to test.

6   Verify that the methods were called as expected.

The code in Listing 9.30 illustrates these setups:

Listing 8.30

```
private UserManagerImpl mgr = new UserManagerImpl();
private MockControl control;
private UserDAO mockDAO;

protected void setUp() throws Exception {
```

```
    // Create a MockControl
        control = MockControl.createControl(UserDAO.class);
        // Get the mock
        mockDAO = (UserDAO) control.getMock();

        // Set required dependencies
        mgr.setValidator(new UserValidator());
        mgr.setUserDAO(mockDAO);
    }

        protected void testGetUser() {
            // Set expected behavior
        mockDAO.removeUser(new Long(1));
        control.setVoidCallable();

        // Active the mock
        control.replay();

        // Execute method to test
        mgr.removeUser("1");

        // Verify methods called
        control.verify();
    }
}
```

This code never uses an implementation of the **UserDAO**. Rather, a mock is created from its interface and a dynamic implementation is created using EasyMock.

In the MyUsers application, the **UserManagerTest** integration test already exists for the middle tier. This class loads *applicationContext.xml* files and uses the beans as you would normally in your application. Refactoring this class to use EasyMock is easy and will run much faster in the long run. You might as well keep your original **UserManagerTest** around, since it will continue to serve as a good integration test.

Create a new class named **UserManagerEMTest** in *test/org/appfuse/service/impl*. This class does not contain any Spring dependencies in this example and has the same basic functionality as **UserManagerTest**. The main difference is this class is isolated (thanks to mocks) and will run very quickly. It has the code in Listing 9.31:

Listing 8.31

```
package org.appfuse.service.impl;

// use your IDE to organize imports

public class UserManagerEMTest extends TestCase {
    private final Log
        log = LogFactory.getLog(UserManagerEMTest.class);
    private UserManagerImpl mgr = new UserManagerImpl();
```

```
private MockControl control;
private UserDAO mockDAO;

protected void setUp() throws Exception {
    control = MockControl.createControl(UserDAO.class);
    mockDAO = (UserDAO) control.getMock();
    mgr.setValidator(new UserValidator());
    mgr.setUserDAO(mockDAO);
}

public void testAddAndRemoveUser() throws Exception {
    User user = new User();
    user.setFirstName("Easter");
    user.setLastName("Bunny");

    // set expected behavior on dao
    mockDAO.saveUser(user);
    control.setVoidCallable();

    // switch from record to playback
    control.replay();

    user = mgr.saveUser(user);
    assertEquals("Easter Bunny", user.getFullName());
    control.verify();

    log.debug("removing user...");

    // set userId since Hibernate doesn't do it
    String userId = "1";
    user.setId(new Long(userId));

    // reset to record state
    control.reset();
    mockDAO.removeUser(new Long(1));
    control.setVoidCallable();
    control.replay();

    mgr.removeUser(userId);

    control.verify();

    try {
        // reset to record state
        control.reset();
        control.expectAndThrow(mockDAO.getUser(user.getId()),
                new ObjectRetrievalFailureException(
                    User.class, user.getId()));
        // switch to playback
        control.replay();
```

```
            user = mgr.getUser(userId);

            control.verify();
            fail("User '" + userId + "' found in database");
        } catch (DataAccessException dae) {
            log.debug("Expected exception: " + dae.getMessage());
            assertNotNull(dae);
        }
    }
}
```

Run this test using **ant test -Dtestcase=UserManagerEM**. The speed difference is substantial between this test and **UserManagerTest**; the **UserManagerEM** executes in 0.172 seconds, while the **UserManagerTest** takes 1.59 seconds.

jMock

jMock is another open-source project that produces dynamic mocks. jMock has a slightly different approach to mocking than EasyMock. It requires you to subclass **MockObjectTestCase**. This class performs method invocation verification and provides the syntactic sugar that makes jMock tests easy to read. To use jMock in a test, perform the following steps:

1   Create a **Mock** for the interface you would like to simulate

2   Set expected behavior on the mock.

3   Execute methods you want to test.

4   Verify expectations.

The code in Listing 9.32 is a simple example of the preceding steps:

Listing 8.32

```
private UserManagerImpl mgr = new UserManagerImpl();
private Mock mockDAO;

protected void setUp() throws Exception {
    // Create a Mock
    mockDAO = new Mock(UserDAO.class);


    // Set dependencies
    mgr.setValidator(new UserValidator());
    mgr.setUserDAO((UserDAO) mockDAO.proxy());
}

protected void testGetUser() {
    // Set expected behavior
```

```
mockDAO.expects(once()).method("getUser")
        .with( eq(new Long(1)));


// Execute method to test
mgr.removeUser("1");


// Verify expectations
mockDAO.verify();

}
```

jMock's syntax is a bit cleaner, but its expectations syntax is more complicated. A differentiating feature of jMock is the ability to write custom stubs to simulate side effects of calling methods. For instance, in the **UserDAOHibernate.saveUser()**, the **User** object is assigned an **id** by Hibernate (if one doesn't exist).

To mimic this same functionality when mocking **UserDAO**, create an **AssignId-Stub** class in *test/org/appfuse/service/impl*. The code for this class contains logic that merely sets a random **Long** as the id on the **User** object. See Listing 9.33.

Listing 8.33

```
package org.appfuse.service.impl;

// use your IDE to organize imports

public class AssignIdStub implements Stub {

    public StringBuffer describeTo(StringBuffer buffer) {
        return buffer.append("assigns random id to an object");
    }

    public Object invoke(Invocation invocation) throws Throwable {
        Long id = new Long(new Random().nextInt(10));
        ((User) invocation.parameterValues.get(0)).setId(id);

        return null;
    }
}
```

Create a **UserManagerJMTest** class in this same directory. See Listing 9.34.

Listing 8.34

```
package org.appfuse.service.impl;

// use your IDE to organize imports

public class UserManagerJMTest extends MockObjectTestCase {
    private final Log
        log = LogFactory.getLog(UserManagerJMTest.class);
    private UserManagerImpl mgr = new UserManagerImpl();
    private Mock mockDAO;

    protected void setUp() throws Exception {
        mockDAO = new Mock(UserDAO.class);
        mgr.setValidator(new UserValidator());
        mgr.setUserDAO((UserDAO) mockDAO.proxy());
    }

    public void testAddAndRemoveUser() throws Exception {
        User user = new User();
        user.setFirstName("Easter");
        user.setLastName("Bunny");

        // set expected behavior on dao
        mockDAO.expects(once()).method("saveUser")
                .with( same(user) ).will(assignId());

        user = mgr.saveUser(user);

        // verify expectations
        mockDAO.verify();

        assertEquals("Easter Bunny", user.getFullName());

        assertNotNull(user.getId());

        log.debug("removing user...");

        String userId = user.getId().toString();

        mockDAO.expects(once()).method("removeUser")
                .with( eq(new Long(userId)) );

        mgr.removeUser(userId);

        // verify expectations
        mockDAO.verify();

        try {
            // set expectations
```

```
                   Throwable ex =
                       new ObjectRetrievalFailureException(
                           User.class, user.getId());

                   mockDAO.expects(once()).method("getUser")
                           .with( eq(new Long(userId)))
                           .will(throwException(ex));

                   user = mgr.getUser(userId);

                   // verify expectations
                   mockDAO.verify();
                   fail("User '" + userId + "' found in database");
               } catch (DataAccessException dae) {
                   log.debug("Expected exception: " + dae.getMessage());
                   assertNotNull(dae);
               }
           }
       }

       private Stub assignId() {
           return new AssignIdStub();
       }
   }
```

Run this test with **ant test -Dtestcase=UserManagerJM**. The test should run as fast as the EasyMock test, and its output should resemble Figure 9.3.

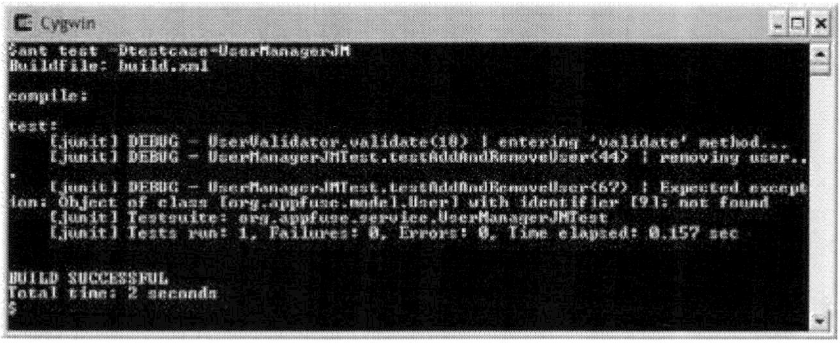

Figure 8.3: Running `UserManagerJMTest`

This section has shown you how to do true unit tests on your business façades and how using mocks in your testing strategy can greatly reduce the amount of time for tests to run.

In these tests, the **UserManagerImpl** class was instantiated with its default constructor, and a mock object simulated its interactions with the **UserDAO**. Spring was not in any of the mock tests, proving that it's nonevasive. Spring's JavaBeans philosophy for setter-based dependency injection made it easy to set whatever dependencies you wanted.

If you'd like to learn more about the differences between jMock and EasyMock, the jMock web site has a detailed comparison. jMock is more flexible, but its API can be a bit difficult to understand. Since it requires you extend its `MockObjectTestCase`, you cannot always use it. jMock has a much more active mailing list, but EasyMock enjoys the benefits of being released first and used more widely.

TESTING THE WEB LAYER

Testing the web layer in an application is the most important part of an application test suite. By properly testing your controllers, you verify the control flow of your application and determine if inputs will return the expected outputs. In Spring MVC, inputs are requests and outputs are `ModelAndView` objects returned by controller methods. Spring Mocks allow you to easily mimic requests and verify results. You can test in-container with Cactus.

While testing controllers is important, testing the view by interacting with the User Interface (UI) is usually the best way to be sure your application works properly. You may have a Quality Assurance (QA) department that does this for you. However, it's easy to write tests for the UI using jWebUnit and Canoo WebTest, both of which are simplifications of HttpUnit. HttpUnit emulates the relevant portions of a browser's behavior, including form submission, JavaScript, basic http authentication, cookies, and automatic page redirection. It allows Java test code to examine returned pages as text, XML DOM, or containers of forms, tables, and links. Tests that interact with the UI are great integration tests to verify all layers of your application. Of course, they won't verify that colors, fonts, and position are correct; that will always need a human eye to test.

You can automate all of the tests mentioned in this chapter. That is, you can test them without human interaction. This ability enables a healthy continuous build mechanism that you will explore in this chapter.

TESTING CONTROLLERS

In *Chapter 4: Spring's MVC Framework*, you created JUnit tests for the two main controllers in MyUsers: `UserController` and `UserFormController`. In this section, you will refactor those tests to be independent of Spring's `Application-Context`. Instead, you will use EasyMock and jMock to mock your controller's dependencies.

You will create Cactus tests to see how to test controllers in-container. You will learn how to use mocks in many of these tests to isolate your tests and make them true unit tests (they only test a single class). You will also learn how to write a test for the **FileUploadController** and test the email it sends using Dumbster.

NOTE: Dumbster is a fake SMTP server for unit and system testing applications that send email messages. It responds to all standard SMTP commands but does not deliver messages to the user. The messages are stored within Dumbster for later extraction and verification.

SPRING MOCKS

Spring Mocks is a general name for the mock classes that Spring distributes for testing JNDI and controllers. These classes were originally used internally by Spring to test the framework itself. As developers tested Spring's controllers with mocks (specifically, Mock Object's Servlet API), it became apparent that Mock Objects did not provide rich enough functionality. In June 2002, Spring developers realized that their mocks were actually quite feature-rich, and they began releasing them as part of the distribution (since 1.0.2).

One of the best things about Spring Mocks is that the classes are for mocking the Servlet API and aren't tied to Spring at all. This means you could easily use them to test other controllers, such as WebWork. Struts, Spring, and WebWork. Struts has support for testing via **StrutsTestCase**, Spring has its mocks, and WebWork can be tested using regular JUnit tests. A later chapter will implement WebWork, Tapestry, and JSF in MyUsers. Unlike the request/response web frameworks, Tapestry and JSF are component- and event-driven web frameworks. They often depend on JavaScript and currently don't have much support for unit testing their controller components.

TESTING CONTROLLERS

Listing 9.35 is the **UserControllerTest** that you created in *Chapter 4: Spring's MVC Framework*:

Listing 8.35

```
package org.appfuse.web;

// use your IDE to organize imports

public class UserControllerTest extends TestCase {
    private Log log = LogFactory.getLog(UserControllerTest.class);
    private XmlWebApplicationContext ctx;

    public void setUp() {
        String[] paths = {"/WEB-INF/applicationContext*.xml",
                          "/WEB-INF/action-servlet.xml"};
```

```
        ctx = new XmlWebApplicationContext();
        ctx.setConfigLocations(paths);
        ctx.setServletContext(new MockServletContext(""));
        ctx.refresh();
    }

    public void testGetUsers() throws Exception {
        UserController c =
            (UserController) ctx.getBean("userController");
        ModelAndView mav =
            c.handleRequest((HttpServletRequest) null,
                            (HttpServletResponse) null);
        Map m = mav.getModel();
        assertNotNull(m.get("users"));
        assertEquals(mav.getViewName(), "userList");
    }
}
```

This class makes use of two Spring Mocks: **MockHttpServletRequest** and **Mock-ServletContext**. It loads context files and grabs the beans from the initialized **XmlWebApplicationContext**. This works well but is more of an integration test rather than a unit test. This is because Spring has already wired the **UserController** and all its dependent objects. In order to create a unit test, you must remove any trace of an **ApplicationContext** and set the dependencies manually in the unit test.

To refactor this test to use EasyMock, create a **UserControllerEMTest.java** class in *test/org/appfuse/web*. This class extends JUnit's **TestCase** class. See Listing 9.36.

Listing 8.36

```
package org.appfuse.web;

// use your IDE to organize imports

public class UserControllerEMTest extends TestCase {
    private MockControl control = null;
    private UserManager mockManager = null;
    private UserController c = new UserController();

    protected void setUp() throws Exception {
        control = MockControl.createControl(UserManager.class);
        mockManager = (UserManager) control.getMock();
        c.setUserManager(mockManager);
    }

    public void testGetUsers() throws Exception {
        // set expected behavior on manager
```

```
        mockManager.getUsers();
        control.setReturnValue(new ArrayList());

        // switch from record to playback
        control.replay();

        ModelAndView mav =
            c.handleRequest((HttpServletRequest) null,
                            (HttpServletResponse) null);
        Map m = mav.getModel();
        assertNotNull(m.get("users"));
        assertEquals("userList", mav.getViewName());

        // verify getUsers() was called on manager
        control.verify();
    }
}
```

To run this test, execute **ant test -Dtestcase=UserControllerEM**. Your console output should resemble Figure 9.4.

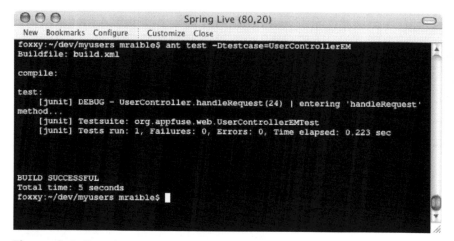

Figure 8.4: Running `UserControllerEMTest`

This test runs *much* faster than the previous one. To compare, run **ant test -Dtestcase=UserControllerTest** and compare the "Time elapsed" value. On my 1.33Mhz/512RAM PowerBook, there's quite a difference: 0.223 seconds for the mocked test and 6.455 seconds for the non-mock version. See Figure 9.5.

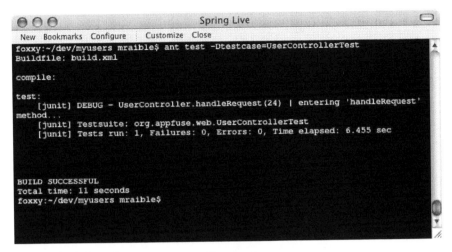

Figure 8.5: Running `UserControllerTest`

You've created an EasyMock version of `UserControllerTest`; now create a jMock version. Create a new `UserControllerJMTest.java` class in *test/org /appfuse/web*. This class extends jMock's `MockObjectTestCase`. See Listing 9.37.

Listing 8.37

```java
package org.appfuse.web;

// use your IDE to organize imports

public class UserControllerJMTest extends MockObjectTestCase {
    private UserController c = new UserController();
    private Mock mockManager = null;

    protected void setUp() throws Exception {
        mockManager = new Mock(UserManager.class);
        c.setUserManager((UserManager) mockManager.proxy());
    }

    public void testGetUsers() throws Exception {
        // set expected behavior on manager
        mockManager.expects(once()).method("getUsers")
                    .will(returnValue(new ArrayList()));

        ModelAndView mav =
            c.handleRequest((HttpServletRequest) null,
                            (HttpServletResponse) null);
        Map m = mav.getModel();
        assertNotNull(m.get("users"));
        assertEquals("userList", mav.getViewName());
```

```
            // verify expectations
            mockManager.verify();
        }
    }
```

Run this test using **ant test -Dtestcase=UserControllerJM**.

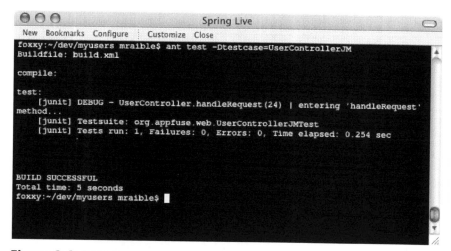

Figure 8.6: Running `UserControllerJMTest`

TESTING FORMCONTROLLERS

Testing form classes, which extend `SimpleFormController`, is much like testing classes that implement `controller`. The major difference is that `FormControllers` do more; for example, they validate data, set messages, and use request parameters. The test for `UserFormController` (from *Chapter 4: Spring's MVC Framework*) is listed below. It verifies that no validation errors occur in its `testSave()` method and that a success message is set. See Listing 9.38.

Listing 8.38

```java
package org.appfuse.web;

// use your IDE to organize imports

public class UserFormControllerTest extends TestCase {
    private static Log log =
        LogFactory.getLog(UserFormControllerTest.class);
    private XmlWebApplicationContext ctx;
    private UserFormController c;
    private MockHttpServletRequest request;
    private ModelAndView mv;
```

```
    private User user;

    public void setUp() {
        String[] paths = {"/WEB-INF/applicationContext*.xml",
                          "/WEB-INF/action-servlet.xml"};
        ctx = new XmlWebApplicationContext();
        ctx.setConfigLocations(paths);
        ctx.setServletContext(new MockServletContext(""));
        ctx.refresh();
        c = (UserFormController) ctx.getBean("userFormController");
        // add a test user to the database
        UserManager mgr = (UserManager) ctx.getBean("userManager");
        user = new User();
        user.setFirstName("Matt");
        user.setLastName("Raible");
        user = mgr.saveUser(user);
    }

    public void tearDown() {
        ctx = null;
        c = null;
        user = null;
    }

    public void testEdit() throws Exception {
        log.debug("testing edit...");
        request = new MockHttpServletRequest("GET", "/editUser.html");
        request.addParameter("id", user.getId().toString());
        mv = c.handleRequest(request, new MockHttpServletResponse());
        assertEquals("userForm", mv.getViewName());
    }

    public void testSave() throws Exception {
        request = new MockHttpServletRequest("POST", "/editUser.html");
        request.addParameter("id", user.getId().toString());
        request.addParameter("firstName", user.getFirstName());
        request.addParameter("lastName", "Updated Last Name");
        mv = c.handleRequest(request, new MockHttpServletResponse());
        Errors errors =
            (Errors) mv.getModel()
                .get(BindException.MODEL_KEY_PREFIX + "user");
        assertNull(errors);
        assertNotNull(request.getSession().getAttribute("message"));
    }

    public void testRemove() throws Exception {
        request = new MockHttpServletRequest("POST", "/editUser.html");
        request.addParameter("delete", "");
        request.addParameter("id", user.getId().toString());
```

```
        mv = c.handleRequest(request, new MockHttpServletResponse());
        assertNotNull(request.getSession().getAttribute("message"));
    }
}
```

While this test works, it takes several seconds to run (10.2 on my PowerBook). Refactoring it to remove Spring dependencies and use jMock will speed things up dramatically.

To refactor this class, create a new **UserFormControllerJMTest.java** class in the *test/org/appfuse/web* directory. This class extends **MockObjectTestCase** and contains the code in Listing 9.39:

Listing 8.39

```
package org.appfuse.web;

// use your IDE to organize imports

public class UserFormControllerJMTest extends MockObjectTestCase {
    private Log log =
        LogFactory.getLog(UserFormControllerJMTest.class);
    private UserFormController c = new UserFormController();
    private MockHttpServletRequest request = null;
    private ModelAndView mv = null;
    private User user = new User();
    private Mock mockManager = null;

    protected void setUp() throws Exception {
        super.setUp();
        mockManager = new Mock(UserManager.class);

        // manually set properties (dependencies)
        //     on userFormController
        c.setUserManager((UserManager) mockManager.proxy());
        c.setFormView("userForm");

        // set context with messages avoid NPE when controller calls
        // getMessageSourceAccessor().getMessage()
        StaticApplicationContext ctx = new StaticApplicationContext();
        Map properties = new HashMap();
        properties.put("basename", "messages");
        ctx.registerSingleton("messageSource",
                              ResourceBundleMessageSource.class,
                              new MutablePropertyValues(properties));
        ctx.refresh();
        c.setApplicationContext(ctx);

        // setup user values
        user.setId(new Long(1));
```

```
        user.setFirstName("Matt");
        user.setLastName("Raible");
    }

    public void testEdit() throws Exception {
        log.debug("testing edit...");

        // set expected behavior on manager
        mockManager.expects(once()).method("getUser")
                .will(returnValue(new User()));

        request = new MockHttpServletRequest("GET", "/editUser.html");
        request.addParameter("id", user.getId().toString());
        mv = c.handleRequest(request, new MockHttpServletResponse());
        assertEquals("userForm", mv.getViewName());
        // The getCommandName() method is available in Spring 1.1.1+
        User editUser = (User) mv.getModel().get(c.getCommandName());
        assertEquals(editUser.getFullName(), "Matt Raible");

        // verify expectations
        mockManager.verify();
    }

    public void testSave() throws Exception {
        // set expected behavior on manager
        // called by formBackingObject()
        mockManager.expects(once()).method("getUser")
                .will(returnValue(user));

        User savedUser = user;
        savedUser.setLastName("Updated Last Name");
        // called by onSubmit()
        mockManager.expects(once()).method("saveUser")
                .with(eq(savedUser));

        request = new MockHttpServletRequest("POST", "/editUser.html");
        request.addParameter("id", user.getId().toString());
        request.addParameter("firstName", user.getFirstName());
        request.addParameter("lastName", "Updated Last Name");
        mv = c.handleRequest(request, new MockHttpServletResponse());
        Errors errors =
            (Errors) mv.getModel().get(BindException.MODEL_KEY_PREFIX
                                    + "user");
        assertNull(errors);
        assertNotNull(request.getSession().getAttribute("message"));

        // verify expectations
        mockManager.verify();
    }
```

```
public void testRemove() throws Exception {
    // set expected behavior on manager
    // called by formBackingObject()
    mockManager.expects(once()).method("getUser")
                .will(returnValue(user));
    // called by onSubmit()
    mockManager.expects(once()).method("removeUser").with(eq("1"));

    request = new MockHttpServletRequest("POST", "/editUser.html");
    request.addParameter("delete", "");
    request.addParameter("id", user.getId().toString());
    mv = c.handleRequest(request, new MockHttpServletResponse());
    assertNotNull(request.getSession().getAttribute("message"));

    // verify expectations
    mockManager.verify();
}
}
```

In the above class's **setUp()** method, Spring's **StaticApplicationContext** provides a convenient way to add and use beans in unit tests. Its **register-Singleton()** method registers the **messages.properties** file for accessing messages. Without doing this, it would throw a **NullPointerException** when the **FormController** tries to access the **messageSource** bean. You could also use the **StaticMessageSource** class for adding messages programmatically in your tests. More information on using these classes in your tests is available in Spring's **StaticApplicationContextTests**.

TIP: Spring's internal tests are an excellent source of information on how to write your own unit tests.

CACTUS

This section uses Cactus to test controllers in their deployed environment. Cactus is an extension of JUnit for unit testing server-side Java code.

To use Cactus for testing controllers, modify MyUser's *build.xml* by adding a **test-cactus** target, as in Listing 9.40.

Listing 8.40

```
<target name="test-cactus" depends="war"
    description="Runs Cactus tests in-container">

    <!-- Define Cactus Tasks -->
    <taskdef resource="cactus.tasks" classpathref="classpath"/>

    <cactifywar srcfile="${dist.dir}/${webapp.name}.war"
```

```
            destfile="${dist.dir}/${webapp.name}-cactus.war">
            <classes dir="${test.dir}/classes"/>
            <classes dir="test" includes="cactus.properties"/>
            <!-- If you use EasyMock or Spring Mocks in a Cactus test
                 it needs to be included in the WAR -->
            <lib dir="web/WEB-INF/lib" includes="*mock.jar"/>
            <servletredirector/>
        </cactifywar>

        <mkdir dir="${test.dir}/data/tomcat"/>

        <cactus warfile="${dist.dir}/${webapp.name}-cactus.war"
            printsummary="yes" failureproperty="tests.failed">
            <classpath>
                <path refid="classpath"/>
                <path location="${build.dir}/classes"/>
                <path location="${test.dir}/classes"/>
            </classpath>
            <containerset>
                <tomcat5x dir="${tomcat.home}" if="tomcat.home"
                    port="8080" todir="${test.dir}/data/tomcat"/>
            </containerset>
            <formatter type="xml"/>
            <formatter type="brief" usefile="false"/>
            <batchtest todir="${test.dir}/data" if="testcase">
                <fileset dir="${test.dir}/classes">
                    <include name="**/*${testcase}*"/>
                    <exclude name="**/*TestCase.class"/>
                </fileset>
            </batchtest>
            <batchtest todir="${test.dir}/data" unless="testcase">
                <fileset dir="${test.dir}/classes">
                    <include name="**/*Cactus*Test.class*"/>
                </fileset>
            </batchtest>
        </cactus>
        <fail if="tests.failed">Cactus test(s) failed.</fail>
    </target>
```

The **<cactifywar>** task at the beginning of this listing is responsible for modifying the *web.xml* and WAR files so Cactus can test it. A **<tomcat5x>** task is in the middle of this target. This task specifies the container in which to run the tests. See Cactus's project site for more information on its Ant integration and the list of supported containers for the **<cactus>** task.

Now that you've set up Cactus, create a **UserCactusTest.java** class in *test/org /appfuse/web*. This class extends **ServletTestCase**. This first version manually creates the **UserController** and **UserFormController** and then sets their necessary dependencies (**UserManager** and context for **messageSource** bean).

The `ApplicationContext` for this test is retrieved from the `ServletContext`, not initialized from the `ClassPathXmlApplicationContext`. This is because the test will be running in the context of the application, and Spring's application context is initialized by the `ContextLoaderListener` in *web.xml*. See Listing 9.41.

Listing 8.41

```
package org.appfuse.web;

// use your IDE to organize imports

public class UserCactusTest extends ServletTestCase {
    private UserController list = new UserController();
    private UserFormController form = new UserFormController();

    protected void setUp() throws Exception {
        super.setUp();
        ApplicationContext ctx =
            WebApplicationContextUtils
                .getRequiredWebApplicationContext(
                    session.getServletContext());
        UserManager userManager =
            (UserManager) ctx.getBean("userManager");
        list.setUserManager(userManager);
        form.setUserManager(userManager);

        // needed to prevent NPE with getMessageSourceAccessor()
        StaticApplicationContext staticCtx =
            new StaticApplicationContext();
        Map properties = new HashMap();
        properties.put("basename", "messages");
        staticCtx.registerSingleton("messageSource",
                            ResourceBundleMessageSource.class,
                            new MutablePropertyValues(properties));
        staticCtx.refresh();
        form.setApplicationContext(staticCtx);
    }

    public void beginAddUser(WebRequest wRequest) {
        wRequest.addParameter("firstName", "Dion", "post");
        wRequest.addParameter("lastName", "Almaer", "post");
    }

    public void testAddUser() throws Exception {
        form.handleRequest(request, response);
        assertNotNull(request.getSession().getAttribute("message"));
    }

    public void testUserList() throws Exception {
        ModelAndView mav = list.handleRequest(request, response);
```

```
        Map m = mav.getModel();
        assertNotNull(m.get("users"));
        assertEquals("userList", mav.getViewName());
    }
}
```

Create a *cactus.properties* file in the *test* directory. Cactus requires the information in Listing 9.42 to run its servlet tests:

Listing 8.42

```
# Web app Context under which our application to test runs
cactus.contextURL=http://localhost:8080/myusers-cactus

# Default Servlet Redirector Name. Used by ServletTestCase test cases.
cactus.servletRedirectorName=ServletRedirector
```

Run this test by executing **ant test-cactus -Dtestcase=UserCactusTest**.

Also, if you choose, you can mock the **UserManager** with EasyMock. The following **UserCactusEMTest** class illustrates this technique. You *cannot* use jMock with Cactus because both of them require you to extend their **TestCase** classes. See Listing 9.43.

Listing 8.43

```
package org.appfuse.web;

// user your IDE to organize imports

public class UserCactusEMTest extends ServletTestCase {
    private UserController list = new UserController();
    private UserFormController form = new UserFormController();
    private MockControl control = null;
    private UserManager mockManager = null;

    protected void setUp() throws Exception {
        control = MockControl.createControl(UserManager.class);
        mockManager = (UserManager) control.getMock();
        list.setUserManager(mockManager);
        form.setUserManager(mockManager);

        // needed to prevent NPE with getMessageSourceAccessor()
        StaticApplicationContext staticCtx =
            new StaticApplicationContext();
        Map properties = new HashMap();
        properties.put("basename", "messages");
        staticCtx.registerSingleton("messageSource",
                            ResourceBundleMessageSource.class,
```

```
                                new MutablePropertyValues(properties));
            staticCtx.refresh();
            form.setApplicationContext(staticCtx);
        }

        public void beginAddUser(WebRequest wRequest) {
            wRequest.addParameter("firstName", "Dion", "post");
            wRequest.addParameter("lastName", "Almaer", "post");
        }

        public void testAddUser() throws Exception {
            // set expected behavior on manager
            User user = new User();
            user.setFirstName("Dion");
            user.setLastName("Almaer");
            mockManager.saveUser(user);
            control.setReturnValue(user);

            // switch from record to playback
            control.replay();

            form.handleRequest(request, response);

            // verify saveUser() was called
            control.verify();
            assertTrue(request.getSession()
                        .getAttribute("message") != null);
        }

        public void testUserList() throws Exception {
            // set expected behavior on manager
            control.expectAndReturn(mockManager.getUsers(),
                            new ArrayList());
            // switch from record to playback
            control.replay();

            ModelAndView mav = list.handleRequest(request, response);

            // verify getUsers() was called
            control.verify();

            Map m = mav.getModel();
            assertNotNull(m.get("users"));
            assertEquals(mav.getViewName(), "userList");
        }
    }
}
```

To run this test, execute **ant test-cactus -Dtestcase=UserCactusEM**.

Running Cactus tests requires quite a bit of time since it has to parse/modify the WAR and start/stop the container; therefore, using mocks is unlikely to increase your test performances. However, they are still helpful for isolating your test in the container.

TESTING FILE UPLOAD AND EMAIL

As promised in *Chapter 5: Advanced Spring MVC*, you will now learn how to test the **FileUploadController** class. This class is responsible for uploading files and sending a notification email.

1   In *test/org/appfuse/web*, create a **FileUploadControllerTest** that extends JUnit's **TestCase**. The code in Listing 9.44 represents the contents of this class with a **setUp()** method to initialize the context files:

Listing 8.44

```
package org.appfuse.web;

// organize imports using your IDE

public class FileUploadControllerTest extends TestCase {
    private final Log log =
        LogFactory.getLog(FileUploadControllerTest.class);
    private XmlWebApplicationContext ctx = null;
    private FileUploadController fileUpload = null;

    public void setUp() {
        String[] paths = {"/WEB-INF/applicationContext*.xml",
                          "/WEB-INF/action-servlet.xml"};
        ctx = new XmlWebApplicationContext();
        ctx.setConfigLocations(paths);
        ServletContext servletContext =
            new MockServletContext("file:web");

        ctx.setServletContext(servletContext);
        ctx.refresh();
        fileUpload = (FileUploadController)
            ctx.getBean("fileUploadController");

        // Create a mailSender that'll use Dumbster's ports
        JavaMailSenderImpl mailSender = new JavaMailSenderImpl();
        mailSender.setHost("localhost");
        mailSender.setPort(2525);
        fileUpload.setMailSender(mailSender);
    }

    // continued below
```

This **setUp()** method contains unique configurations. First, the **MockServlet-Context** is initialized using **file:web**. A **ResourceLoader** class uses this value to determine the root of the web application. Without this, the following variable assignment in **FileUploadController** will fail. See Listing 9.45.

Listing 8.45

```
String uploadDir = getServletContext().getRealPath("/upload/");
```

Second, **setUp()** contains a custom **mailSender** bean that sends email on a non-standard port (2525; 25 is standard). This is so you can use Dumbster. You will use Dumbster to start and stop an SMTP server on port 2525 before and after running the **FileUploadControllerTest**.

NOTE: This example uses port 2525 to avoid conflicts with a server that might be running on port 25.

2   Finish the test by adding the **testUpload()** method in Listing 9.46:

Listing 8.46

```
public void testUpload() throws Exception {
    log.debug("testing upload...");
    MockHttpServletRequest request =
        new MockHttpServletRequest("POST", "/fileUpload.html");

    MockCommonsMultipartResolver resolver =
        new MockCommonsMultipartResolver();

    request.setContentType("multipart/form-data");
    request.addHeader("Content-type", "multipart/form-data");
    assertTrue(resolver.isMultipart(request));
    MultipartHttpServletRequest multipartRequest =
        resolver.resolveMultipart(request);

    // setup a simple mail server using Dumbster
    SimpleSmtpServer server = SimpleSmtpServer.start(2525);

    ModelAndView mav =
        fileUpload.handleRequest(multipartRequest,
                                new MockHttpServletResponse());

    server.stop();
    // the getRecieved() method is spelled wrong in the API. ;-)
    assertEquals(1, server.getReceivedEmailSize());

    log.debug("model: " + mav.getModel());
```

```
        assertNotNull(request.getSession().getAttribute("message"));

        // ensure the file got uploaded
        Resource uploadedFile =
            ctx.getResource("file:web/upload/test.xml");
        assertTrue(uploadedFile.exists());

        // delete the upload directory
        Resource uploadDir = ctx.getResource("file:web/upload");
        uploadedFile.getFile().delete();
        uploadDir.getFile().delete();
        assertFalse(uploadDir.exists());
    }

    public static class MockCommonsMultipartResolver
        extends CommonsMultipartResolver {

        protected FileUpload newFileUpload(FileItemFactory factory) {
            return new ServletFileUpload() {
                public List parseRequest(HttpServletRequest request) {
                    if (request instance of MultipartHttpServletRequest)
                    {
                        throw new IllegalStateException(
                            "Already a multipart request");
                    }
                    List fileItems = new ArrayList();
                    MockFileItem fileItem =
                        new MockFileItem("file", "text/html",
                                         "test.xml", "<root/>");
                    fileItems.add(fileItem);
                    return fileItems;
                }
            };
        }
    }
}
}
```

The **MockCommonsMultipartResolver** class in this test refers to a **MockFile-Item** class. This class mimics an uploaded file. The *MockFileItem.java* file is included in the download for this chapter; it's also available in Spring's **CommonsMultipart-ResolverTests** class. You can implement it as an inner class like the Spring test does; this example extracts it out in the interest of saving space.

3   Run this test using **ant test -Dtestcase=FileUploadController**. The test's output should resemble Figure 9.7.

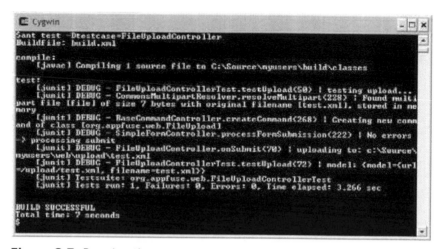

Figure 8.7: Running the `FileUploadControllerTest`

From all of the examples in this section, you can see that many options for testing controllers are available. The simplest way to write controller tests is to initialize a context in your test class, retrieve your controllers (using `ctx.getBean("controllerName")`), and execute methods on them. This technique allows Spring to wire the controller's dependencies. Using mocks requires a little more work because you must know your controller's dependencies. You also must be aware what methods will be called on your mocked object. The advantage is you'll know exactly what your controller depends on and how it interacts with those dependencies.

TESTING VIEWS

In *Chapter 6: View Options*, you created a jWebUnit test (**UserWebTest**) that inter-acted with links and buttons to verify the functionality of the UI. jWebUnit is a nice framework for testing views because it allows you to write your tests in Java. This section modifies the **test-web** target in *build.xml* so that Tomcat starts and stops before any jWebUnit tests run. You will also change the current test to switch locales and verify text against *messages.properties* rather than hard coding it in the class. Finally, you will use Canoo WebTest as an alternative method of testing the UI. WebTest is friendlier to non-programmers because tests are written in an Ant build file using XML.

The tests in this section are commonly referred to as *integration tests*. They verify that all the layers are integrated properly by navigating the UI as a user would in a browser. Both jWebUnit and Canoo WebTest support JavaScript testing. This means that if you have an **onclick** handler on a button and you specify to click this button, the JavaScript call will execute.

jWebUnit

Before you change the **UserWebTest** in MyUsers, review its source. The constructor or the **setUp()** method should always contain a call to **setBaseUrl()** to point the test case to the application. Since jWebUnit refers to submit buttons by name, you must specify a name attribute on your buttons. If you want to test tables and their data, you must specify an id attribute on your tables. MyUsers should already contain all the necessary names and ids. See Listing 9.47.

Listing 8.47

```
package org.appfuse.web;

// use your IDE to organize imports

public class UserWebTest extends WebTestCase {

    public UserWebTest(String name) {
        super(name);
        getTestContext().setBaseUrl("http://localhost:8080/myusers");
    }

    public void testWelcomePage() {
        beginAt("/");
        assertTitleEquals("MyUsers ~ Welcome");
    }

    public void testAddUser() {
        beginAt("/editUser.html");
        assertTitleEquals("MyUsers ~ User Details");
        setFormElement("firstName", "Spring");
        setFormElement("lastName", "User");
        submit("save");
        assertTextPresent("saved successfully");
    }

    public void testListUsers() {
        beginAt("/users.html");

        // check that table is present
        assertTablePresent("userList");

        //check that a set of strings are present somewhere in table
        assertTextInTable("userList",
                        new String[] {"Spring", "User"});
    }

    public void testEditUser() {
        beginAt("/editUser.html?id=" + getInsertedUserId());
```

```
            assertFormElementEquals("firstName", "Spring");
            submit("save");
            assertTitleEquals("MyUsers ~ User List");
        }

    public void testDeleteUser() {
            beginAt("/editUser.html?id=" + getInsertedUserId());
            assertTitleEquals("MyUsers ~ User Details");
            submit("delete");
            assertTitleEquals("MyUsers ~ User List");
        }

    /**
      * Convenience method to get the id of the inserted user
      * Assumes last inserted user is "Spring User"
      */
    protected String getInsertedUserId() {
            beginAt("/users.html");
            assertTablePresent("userList");
            assertTextInTable("userList", "Spring");
            String[][] tableCellValues =
                    getDialog().getSparseTableBySummaryOrId("userList");
            return tableCellValues[tableCellValues.length-1][0];
        }
    }
```

In order to internationalize this test, you first must internationalize the titles in
MyUsers. Currently, they are hard-coded into their respective templates.

    1   Create entries in *messages.properties*, as in Listing 9.48.

Listing 8.48

```
# Page titles
index.title=MyUsers ~ Welcome
userList.title=MyUsers ~ User List
userForm.title=MyUsers ~ User Details
```

    2   The download for this chapter uses FreeMarker templates for the view, so
you must edit the FreeMarker templates:

- web/WEB-INF/freemarker/userList.ftl:

  ```
  <title>${rc.getMessage("userList.title")}</title>
  ```

- web/WEB-INF/freemarker/userForm.ftl:

  ```
  <title>${rc.getMessage("userForm.title")}</title>
  ```

- web/index.ftl:

  ```
  <title>${rc.getMessage("index.title")}</title>
  ```

The welcome page (*index.ftl*) requires a bit more work to resolve the **rc** variable. In the download for this chapter, *index.ftl* is located in the web directory and configured as a welcome-file in *web.xml*. It's not easy to expose the *messages.properties* file to the SiteMesh Servlet, which parses *index.ftl*, however, you can work around this issue by putting *index.ftl* with the rest of the templates and using Paul Tuckey's **UrlRewriteFilter** to resolve it as the welcome page. Below are the steps to make this change:

1   Move *index*.ftl to *web/WEB-INF/freemarker*.

2   Add **/index.html** as a URL to the **urlMapping** bean in *web/WEB-INF/ action-servlet.xml*.

    `<prop key="/index.html">filenameController</prop>`

3   To make this the welcome file, use the **UrlRewriteFilter**. To configure it, declare it as a filter in *web/WEB-INF/web.xml*. See Listing 9.49.

Listing 8.49

```
<filter>
    <filter-name>rewriteFilter</filter-name>
    <filter-class>
        org.tuckey.web.filters.urlrewrite.UrlRewriteFilter
    </filter-class>
</filter>
```

4   After the **sitemesh** filter-mapping, add a **filter-mapping** for this filter, as in Listing 9.50.

Listing 8.50

```
<filter-mapping>
    <filter-name>rewriteFilter</filter-name>
    <url-pattern>/*</url-pattern>
</filter-mapping>
```

5   The *urlrewrite.xml* file in *web/WEB-INF* should already have the following XML in it to complete the redirect. See Listing 9.51.

Listing 8.51

```
<urlrewrite>
    <rule>
        <from>/$</from>
        <to type="forward">index.html</to>
    </rule>
    <rule>
```

```
            <from>/index.ftl</from>
            <to type="forward">index.html</to>
        </rule>
    </urlrewrite>
```

NOTE: Use these same steps to alter the Velocity templates. For JSP, use JSTL's `<fmt:message>` tag in the `<title>` tags.

At this point, start Tomcat and run **ant clean deploy test-web** to verify that this change worked. After verifying that it worked, modify this class to take advantage of jWebUnit's internationalization capabilities. Namely, it has the ability to set a **ResourceBundle** and verify titles and text based on key names rather than text values. More information on this feature and others is available in jWebUnit's QuickStart Guide.

The main difference between the following class and the previous un-internationalized class is that the **testAddUser()** method verifies the resulting page's title rather than the success message text. This is because the success message gets the new user's name substituted into its final output and, therefore, the key's value is different from the value displayed. A patch for jWebUnit to allow testing keys with dynamic values is available.

Changed code is underlined in Listing 9.52, and previous assertions are commented out:

Listing 8.52

```
package org.appfuse.web;

import java.util.List;
import java.util.Locale;

import net.sourceforge.jwebunit.WebTestCase;

import org.apache.commons.logging.Log;
import org.apache.commons.logging.LogFactory;
import org.appfuse.dao.UserDAO;
import org.appfuse.model.User;
import org.springframework.context.ApplicationContext;
import org.springframework.context.support
    .ClassPathXmlApplicationContext;

public class UserWebTest extends WebTestCase {

    public UserWebTest(String name) {
        super(name);
        getTestContext().setBaseUrl("http://localhost:8080/myusers");
        getTestContext().setResourceBundleName("messages");
```

```
        getTestContext().setLocale(Locale.ENGLISH);
    }

    public void testWelcomePage() {
        beginAt("/");
        //assertTitleEquals("MyUsers ~ Welcome");
        assertTitleEqualsKey("index.title");
    }

    public void testAddUser() {
        beginAt("/editUser.html");
        //assertTitleEquals("MyUsers ~ User Details");
        assertTitleEqualsKey("userForm.title");
        setFormElement("firstName", "Spring");
        setFormElement("lastName", "User");
        submit("save");
        //assertTextPresent("saved successfully");
        assertTitleEqualsKey("userList.title");
    }

    public void testListUsers() {
        beginAt("/users.html");

        // check that table is present
        assertTablePresent("userList");

        //check that a set of strings are present somewhere in table
        assertTextInTable("userList",
                        new String[] {"Spring", "User"});
    }

    public void testEditUser() {
        beginAt("/editUser.html?id=" + getInsertedUserId());
        assertFormElementEquals("firstName", "Spring");
        submit("save");
        //assertTitleEquals("MyUsers ~ User List");
        assertTitleEqualsKey("userList.title");
    }

    public void testDeleteUser() {
        beginAt("/editUser.html?id=" + getInsertedUserId());
        //assertTitleEquals("MyUsers ~ User Details");
        assertTitleEqualsKey("userForm.title");
        submit("delete");
        //assertTitleEquals("MyUsers ~ User List");
        assertTitleEqualsKey("userList.title");
    }

    /**
     * Convenience method to get the id of the inserted user
```

```
 * Assumes last inserted user is "Spring User"
 */
protected String getInsertedUserId() {
    beginAt("/users.html");
    assertTablePresent("userList");
    assertTextInTable("userList", "Spring");
    String[][] tableCellValues =
            getDialog().getSparseTableBySummaryOrId("userList");
    return tableCellValues[tableCellValues.length-1][0];
}
}
```

To test this class using a different locale (and *messages.properties* file), follow these steps:

1   Duplicate the *messages.properties* file and name it *message_de.properties*. Change some of the title values so you know it's using the new message bundle.

2   Change the **setLocale()** call in the constructor to set the locale to German.

```
getTestContext().setLocale(Locale.GERMAN);
```

This will load the German messages file, but it will *not* set the locale for the request. This has been reported as a bug in jWebUnit. To work around this bug, set the **Accept-Language** header as part of the underlying HttpUnit WebClient:

```
getTestContext().getWebClient()
        .setHeaderField("Accept-Language", "de");
```

3   Run the test using **ant deploy reload test-web**.

Automate starting Tomcat

The current setup for running jWebUnit tests requires you to start Tomcat before running the tests. To alleviate this pain, add a new target to *build.xml* that automates the startup and shutdown of Tomcat before and after running the test. Cargo is an open-source project started by Vincent Massol, who also created Cactus. It provides a Java API and Ant tasks to start, stop, and configure Java containers. Since the Cargo JAR is already included in this chapter's download, you must simply add the following target to *build.xml*. See Listing 9.53.

Listing 8.53

```
<target name="test-tomcat" depends="war"
    description="Starts Tomcat, runs jWebUnit tests, stops Tomcat">

    <taskdef resource="cargo.tasks">
        <classpath>
            <!-- To workaround the fact that Cactus uses Cargo 0.5 -->
            <fileset dir="${web.dir}/WEB-INF/lib"
```

```
                includes="cargo*0.8*.jar"/>
        </classpath>
    </taskdef>

    <cargo containerId="tomcat5x" home="${tomcat.home}"
        output="${test.dir}/cargo.log" action="start" wait="false">
        <configuration home="${test.dir}/${cargo.server}">
            <deployable type="war"
                file="${basedir}/${dist.dir}/${webapp.name}.war"/>
        </configuration>
    </cargo>

    <antcall target="test-web"/>
</target>
```

Now you should be able to stop Tomcat and run **ant test-tomcat** to run the UserWebTest in Tomcat without manually starting it.

CANOO WEBTEST

Canoo WebTest is a free open-source tool for automating web application tests. It's similar to jWebUnit, except you write its tests using XML and execute them using Ant. One differentiating feature is the ability to test the content and properties of PDF files, Excel files, and email messages and attachments. In order to add Canoo WebTest tests to MyUsers, complete the following steps:

1   Add links to the *userList.ftl* page in *web/WEB-INF/*freemarker so that you can bring up a PDF by just clicking on the **PDF** link. Put the HTML in Listing 9.54 just after the **Add User** button.

Listing 8.54

```
<p style="text-align: right; margin-bottom: -10px">
<strong>Export Options:</strong>
    <a href="?report=XML">XML</a> &middot;
    <a href="?report=Excel">Excel</a> &middot;
    <a href="?report=PDF">PDF</a>
</p>
```

2   Add a **test-canoo** target to *build.xml*, as in Listing 9.55.

Listing 8.55

```
<target name="test-canoo" depends="deploy"
    description="Runs Canoo WebTests in Tomcat to test JSPs">

    <taskdef file="webtestTasks.properties">
        <classpath>
```

```
                <path refid="classpath"/>
                <!-- for log4j.xml -->
                <path location="web/WEB-INF/classes"/>
            </classpath>
        </taskdef>

        <mkdir dir="${test.dir}/data"/>
        <!-- Delete old results file if it exists -->
        <delete file="${test.dir}/data/web-tests-result.xml"/>

        <property name="testcase" value="run-all-tests"/>
        <ant antfile="test/web-tests.xml" target="${testcase}"/>
    </target>
```

3   Create a *config.xml* file in the *test* directory and add the XML in Listing 9.56
     to it:

Listing 8.56

```
    <config host="localhost" port="8080"
        protocol="http" basepath="${webapp.name}"
        resultpath="${test.dir}/data"
        resultfile="web-tests-result.xml"
        summary="true" saveresponse="true"/>
```

4   Create a *web-tests.xml* file in the *test* directory with the structure in
     Listing 9.57.

Listing 8.57

```
<!DOCTYPE project [
    <!ENTITY config SYSTEM "file:./config.xml">
]>
<project basedir="." default="run-all-tests">
    <!-- Include messages.properties so we can test against
        keys, rather than values -->
    <property file="web/WEB-INF/classes/messages.properties"/>

    <!-- runs all targets -->
    <target name="run-all-tests" depends="UserTests"
        description="Call and executes all test cases (targets)">
        <echo>All UserTests passed!</echo>
    </target>

    <!-- Verify adding a user, viewing and deleting a user works -->
    <target name="UserTests"
        description="Adds a new user profile">
        <webtest name="userTests">
            &config;
```

```
            <steps>
                <!-- View add screen -->
                <invoke url="/editUser.html"/>
                <verifytitle text="${userForm.title}"/>
                <!-- Enter data and save -->
                <setinputfield name="firstName" value="Test"/>
                <setinputfield name="lastName" value="Name"/>
                <clickbutton label="Save"/>
                <!-- View user list -->
                <verifytitle text="${userList.title}"/>
                <!-- Verify PDF contains new user -->
                <clicklink label="PDF"/>
                <verifyPdfText text="Test Name"/>
                <!-- Delete first user in table -->
                <invoke url="/users.html"/>
                <clicklink href="editUser.html"/>
                <verifytitle text="${userForm.title}"/>
                <clickbutton label="Delete"/>
                <verifytitle text="${userList.title}"/>
            </steps>
        </webtest>
    </target>
</project>
```

This file's **UserTests** target contains the tasks to test the various operations on the MyUsers UI. In the middle of the target is a call to bring up the PDF and verify the newly added user.

WARNING: If the rendering of the PDF doesn't work for your application, make sure the **viewResolver2** bean in *action-servlet.xml* contains the following property:

```
<property name="order" value="1"/>
```

If you get errors about log4j, make sure the XML in Listing 9.58 is in your *log4j.xml* file (in *web/WEB-INF/classes*):

Listing 8.58

```
<logger name="com.canoo">
    <level value="WARN"/>
</logger>
```

5   Run **ant deploy**, start Tomcat, and then run **ant test-canoo**. All tests should pass, and you will see a console output similar to Figure 9.8.

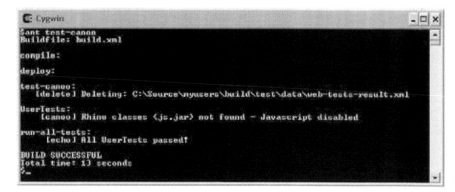

Figure 8.8: Running the Canoo WebTest tests

AUTOMATE STARTING TOMCAT

Just like with jWebUnit, it's easy to automate the startup and shutdown of Tomcat before and after running Canoo tests. Use the Cargo API again, and add the following **test-view** target to *build.xml*. See Listing 9.59.

Listing 8.59

```
<target name="test-view" depends="war"
    description="Starts Tomcat, runs WebTest tests, stops Tomcat">

    <taskdef resource="cargo.tasks">
        <classpath>
            <fileset dir="${web.dir}/WEB-INF/lib"
                includes="cargo*0.8*.jar"/>
        </classpath>
    </taskdef>

    <cargo containerId="tomcat5x" home="${tomcat.home}"
        output="${test.dir}/cargo.log" action="start" wait="false">
        <configuration home="${test.dir}/${cargo.server}">
            <deployable type="war"
                file="${basedir}/${dist.dir}/${webapp.name}.war"/>
        </configuration>
    </cargo>

    <antcall target="test-canoo"/>
</target>
```

If Tomcat isn't running, you should be able to test this target by running **ant test-view**.

> TIP: The Canoo WebTest team keeps a weblog of tips related to this project.

From this brief overview of jWebUnit and Canoo's WebTest, you should know enough about how each one works to use in your projects. Many developers don't know it's possible to automate UI tests, and both of these tools can save you a lot of time. Of course, you must still often look at your UI in a browser to tweak colors, fonts, and positioning.

SUMMARY

This chapter covered a lot of information on how to test Spring, as well as how to write unit tests in general. You learned how to use JUnit, DbUnit, EasyMock, jMock, Spring Mocks, Cactus, jWebUnit, and Canoo's WebTest. For the database layer, you saw how it's best to talk directly to a running database and verify that your DAOs are operating as they should. It also described techniques for overriding beans for tests (for example, to wrap transactions around a DAO implementation).

In the business façade layer, demonstrations were given of using EasyMock and jMock, both of which greatly simplify mocking objects. The best strategy for deciding what to mock is to never mock APIs that aren't yours. Since the **UserDAO** interface and its implementations are classes you've created, it makes sense to mock it in the **UserManagerTest** unit test. Using mocks provides a convenient way to isolate a test and in most cases makes your tests run much faster.

In the web layer, you learned how to use jWebUnit to write a Java-based test for verifying the UI's features. Canoo's WebTest demonstrated the same testing functionality, but with Ant/XML instead of Java. The new Cargo project showed how you can easily start and stop Tomcat as part of running your tests.

This chapter did not cover testing rich clients (for example, SWT or Swing applications), mainly because the Spring Rich has not been released at the time of this writing. Also, there seems to be a lack of tools for testing these types of applications.

Testing is an important part of developing any software. This chapter has provided you with the tools and techniques you need to use TDD in your projects to produce high-quality software.

AOP

What is AOP and how can Spring make it easier?

Aspect-Oriented Programming (AOP) has received a lot of attention in the Java community in the last couple of years. What is AOP and how can it help you in your applications? This chapter will cover the basics of AOP and provide some useful examples of how AOP might help you.

OVERVIEW

If you're active in the Java community, you've probably heard of Aspect-Oriented Programming (AOP). While AOP has been around for several years, it has only recently gained attention. This is likely because many Java-based frameworks are now available to ease the use of AOP.

The most basic definition of AOP is "it's a way of removing code duplication." Java is an Object-Oriented (OO) language. It allows you to create applications and their objects in a hierarchical fashion. However, it doesn't offer an easy way to remove code duplication among classes that aren't in the same hierarchy. In this chapter, you will learn how to use AOP to modify the MyUsers application to use AOP for controlling logging, caching, transactions, and email.

An application typically has two types of concerns: *core concerns* and *crosscutting concerns*. Core concerns relate to application functionality, while crosscutting concerns are system-wide. Modules created to manage these crosscutting concerns are known as *aspects* — hence the name *Aspect*-Oriented Programming.

AOP is simply a way to modularize crosscutting concern logic from your classes and abstract them into application-wide concerns, such as logging, security, and transactions. By writing generic AOP classes, you can easily apply these concerns in other projects. Using Spring's IoC container, you can configure these classes and package them as a JAR to include in your projects.

In Spring terms, an aspect is typically an *interceptor* configured to inspect method calls. During inspection, this interceptor can do many things: It can log that the method is being called, modify the returned objects, or send notifications. Servlet

Filters are a form of AOP that offers the ability to perform pre- and post-processing of servlet invocations.

The Java community's consensus on AOP seems to be "only factor concerns into AOP that your system can live without." In other words, if it's something vitally important to your application, such as business logic, it should remain in your application's code. This is because AOP configuration and code is not highly visible. With Spring, you must examine an XML file to see what interceptors are applied to which methods. New developers may not be aware of this and spend hours trying to figure out why certain behavior (performed by interceptors) is happening. If you need to the see the functionality in your class, it shouldn't be in an aspect.

AOP helps you in terms of what you *should* see versus what you *shouldn't* see. For example, it's better to have Spring handle transaction-handling code than to see or write it yourself. This works especially well in an environment with junior and senior developers; the experienced developers can hide aspects from the junior developers.

This chapter is for new users of AOP. Entire books are available on AOP, and the information in them is beyond the scope of this book. I recommend *AspectJ in Action* by Ramnivas Laddad. Its first chapter provides an excellent introduction to AOP.

In this chapter, like previous ones, you can follow along and do the examples as you read the chapter. The easiest way to do this is to download the **MyUsers Chapter 9** bundle from sourcebeat.com/downloads. This project tree is the result of exercises in *Chapter 9: Testing Spring Applications*. It also contains all the JARs you will need for this chapter in the web/WEB-INF/lib directory. Each section has a list of new JARs you may need for each new technology. You can use this chapter as a reference for integrating these principles into your own applications.

NOTE: If you have any issues downloading or running these examples, email me at mattr@sourcebeat.com or enter an issue in the Spring Live Issue Tracker at issues.sourcebeat.com/secure/Dashboard.jspa.

LOGGING EXAMPLE
. . . .

For debugging purposes, it makes sense to add log messages to the beginning and end of methods. Spring makes this very easy, and it doesn't require any coding (only XML).

NOTE: In order to apply interceptors to beans, configure them as proxied classes. This is so JDK dynamic proxies can create implementations of interfaces at runtime. This section covers the different AOP implementation options after the following logging examples.

Spring ships with a `SimpleTraceInterceptor` that you can add as an interceptor to your proxied beans. In MyUsers, the **userManager** bean is already proxied using `TransactionProxyFactoryBean`, so adding an interceptor is easy.

1   Open the *applicationContext.xml* file in *web/WEB-INF* and add a `loggingInterceptor` bean, as in Listing 10.1.

Listing 9.1

```
<bean id="loggingInterceptor"
    class="org.springframework.aop.interceptor
      .SimpleTraceInterceptor"/>
```

2   Add a **preInterceptors** property to the **userManager** bean with this interceptor. See Listing 10.2.

Listing 9.2

```
<property name="preInterceptors">
    <list>
        <ref bean="loggingInterceptor"/>
    </list>
</property>
```

3   Add a logger to *web/WEB-INF/classes/log4j.xml* to show log output from `SimpleTraceInterceptor`. See Listing 10.3.

Listing 9.3

```
<logger name="org.springframework.aop.interceptor">
    <level value="DEBUG"/>
</logger>
```

4   Run **ant test -Dtestcase=UserManagerTest**. Your results should resemble Figure 10.1.

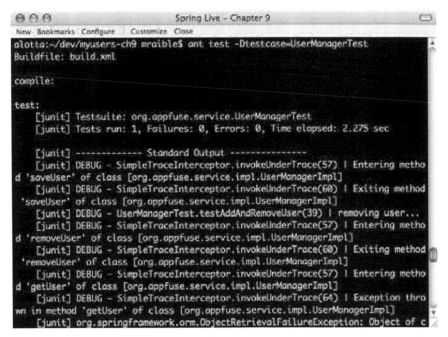

Figure 9.1: Logging from the `SimpleTraceInterceptor`

If you look at the source of `SimpleTraceInterceptor`, you can see how simple AOP can be. The `org.springframework.aop.interceptor` package contains a number of other interceptors that you may find useful in your projects.

This simple example is a brief introduction to AOP. Before diving into more intricate examples, it's important to be familiar with AOP terminology.

DEFINITIONS AND CONCEPTS

AOP, much like other programming paradigms, has its own vocabulary. The following list defines a number of the words and phrases you may encounter when reading about or working with AOP. These definitions are not Spring-specific.

- Concern: A particular issue, concept, or area of interest for an application. Examples include transaction management, persistence, logging, and security.

- Crosscutting concern: A concern in which the implementation cuts across many classes. These are often difficult to implement and maintain with OOP.

- Aspect: The modularization of a crosscutting concern; implemented by gathering and isolating code.

- Join point: A point during the execution of a program or class. In Spring's AOP implementation, a join point is always a method invocation. Other examples include accessing fields, where read or write access occurs on an instance variable, and exception handling.

- Advice: An action taken at a particular join point. Different types of advice in Spring include around, before, throws, and after returning. Of these, around is the most powerful, as you can define an action before and after a method is invoked.

- Pointcuts: A set of join points specifying when an advice should fire. Pointcuts often use regular expressions or wildcard syntax. See the *Pointcuts* section for more information.

- Introduction: Adds fields or methods to an advised class. Spring allows you to introduce new interfaces to any advised object. For example, you could use an introduction to make any object implement an **IsModified** interface to simplify caching.

- Weaving: Assembles aspects to create an advised object. This can be done at compile time or at runtime. See the *Weaving strategies* section for more information.

- Interceptor: An AOP implementation strategy, where a chain of interceptors may exist for a particular join point.

- AOP proxy: An object created by the AOP framework, including advice. In Spring, an AOP proxy is a JDK dynamic proxy or a CGLIB (Code Generation Library) proxy.

- Target object: An object containing the join point. In frameworks using interception, it's the object instance at the end of an interceptor chain. Also called an *advised* or *proxied* object.

POINTCUTS

Pointcuts are an important part of AOP. They enable you to specify when and where to invoke interceptors (advice). In a sense, they're often similar to declarative validation, but rather than specifying a field to validate, you specify a method to inspect. In Table 9.1, pointcuts are defined as "a set of join points specifying when an [interceptor] should fire." Since Spring only supports *method invocation* join points, a pointcut is just a declaration of methods to which an interceptor should be applied.

The easiest way to define pointcuts in Spring AOP is using regular expressions in a context file. The following example defines a pointcut for data manipulation operations. See Listing 10.4.

Listing 9.4

```
<bean id="dataManipulationPointcut"
    class="org.springframework.aop.support.JdkRegexpMethodPointcut">
    <property name="patterns">
        <list>
            <value>.*save.*</value>
            <value>.*remove.*</value>
        </list>
    </property>
</bean>
```

This pointcut intercepts methods that start with *save* or *remove*.

NOTE: The preceding `JdkRegexpMethodPointcut` class requires J2SE 1.4, which has built-in regular expression support. You can also use the `Perl5Regexp-MethodPointcut`, which requires Jakarta ORO (included in MyUsers) if you're using J2SE 1.3.

In most cases, you won't need to define individual pointcuts like the preceding one. Rather, Spring provides *advisor* classes that encapsulate interceptors and pointcuts in the same bean definition.

For regular expression pointcuts, you can use the `RegexpMethodPointcutAd-visor`. The example in Listing 10.5 shows a `RegularExpressionPointcutAd-vice` that triggers a `NotificationInterceptor` when a user's information is saved.

Listing 9.5

```
<bean id="notificationAdvisor"
    class="org.springframework.aop.support
        .RegexpMethodPointcutAdvisor">
    <property name="advice" ref="notificationInterceptor"/>
    <property name="pattern" value=".*saveUser"/>
</bean>
```

Currently, the `RegexpMethodPointcutAdvisor` only supports Perl5 pointcuts, meaning that you must have *jakarta-oro.jar* in your classpath if you want to use it. A complete list of pointcuts and their useful advisors are available in the `org.springframework.aop.support` package.

WEAVING STRATEGIES

Weaving is the process of applying aspects to target objects. The following list shows the primary strategies for implementing AOP, ordered from simplest to most sophisticated.

* JDK Dynamic Proxies
* Dynamic Byte-Code Generation
* Custom Class Loading
* Language Extensions

The following sections describe each of these weaving strategies in detail.

JDK DYNAMIC PROXIES

Dynamic proxies is a feature built into J2SE 1.3+. It allows you to create an implementation of one or more interfaces on the fly. Dynamic proxies are built into the JDK, eliminating the risk of strange behavior in various environments. Their one limitation is they can't proxy classes, only interfaces. If you've designed your application correctly with interfaces, this shouldn't be an issue.

There is some reflection overhead when using dynamic proxies, but the performance impact is negligible in J2SE 1.4+ JVMs. Spring uses dynamic proxies by default when proxying against interfaces. The dynaop project uses this strategy when proxying interfaces.

For more information on dynamic proxies, see the Java 2 SDK documentation.

DYNAMIC BYTE-CODE GENERATION

Spring uses dynamic byte-code generation when proxying against classes. A popular tool for this is CGLIB. It intercepts methods by generating subclasses dynamically. These subclasses override parent methods and have hooks to invoke interceptor implementations. Hibernate uses CGLIB extensively, and it has been proven to be a very stable solution in J2EE environments.

One limitation is that dynamic subclasses cannot override and proxy **final** methods.

CUSTOM CLASS LOADING

Using a custom class loader allows you to advise all instances of created classes. This can be quite powerful, since it gives you the opportunity to change the behavior of the **new** operator. JBoss AOP and AspectWerkz use this approach, loading classes and weaving in their advice behavior as defined in XML files.

The main danger in this approach is J2EE servers must typically control the class-loading hierarchy. What works on one server may not work on another.

LANGUAGE EXTENSIONS

AspectJ is the pioneering framework of AOP in Java. Rather than using a simple strategy for weaving in aspects, it contains language extensions and its own compiler for using them.

While AspectJ is a powerful and mature AOP implementation, its syntax is complex. However, AOP itself is not very intuitive, so trying to implement with a new language can be difficult. Another limitation of this approach is the learning curve associated with a new language. However, if you want the full power of AOP, including field-level interception, AspectJ will prove to be useful.

Spring takes a pragmatic "80/20 rule" approach to its AOP implementation. Rather than trying to satisfy *everyone's* needs, it solves the most common ones and leaves the rest to more specialized AOP frameworks. In Spring 2.0, much tighter integration with AspectJ was added, including support for AspectJ's pointcut language in Spring context files.

CONVENIENT PROXY BEANS

As mentioned earlier, in order to apply advice to beans defined in a context file, they must be proxied. Spring contains a number of support classes (or proxy beans) to make proxying easier. The first is the **ProxyFactoryBean**, which allows you to specify beans to proxy and interceptors to apply. The example in Listing 10.6 uses this bean to create a proxy of a business object.

Listing 9.6

```
<bean id="businessObject"
    class="org.springframework.aop.framework.ProxyFactoryBean">
    <property name="target">
        <bean class="org.appfuse.service.BusinessObject"/>
    </property>
    <property name="interceptorNames">
        <list><value>loggingInterceptor</value></list>
    </property>
</bean>
```

This example uses an *inner-bean* in the **target** property's value. This is a convenient way to hide a business object behind a proxy, so it will always be advised when grabbed from the **ApplicationContext**.

The **TransactionProxyFactoryBean** is the most useful and most used proxy bean. It enables you to use AOP to define transactions declaratively on target objects. This useful feature was previously only available with EJB Container-Managed Transactions (CMTs). The *Practical AOP examples* section describes the usage of this bean.

AUTOPROXY BEANS

The aforementioned Proxy Beans provide easy manipulation of single beans, but what if you want to proxy multiple beans, or all beans in a context? Spring provides two classes in the `org.springframework.aop.framework.autoproxy` package that simplify this procedure.

The first is the `BeanNameAutoProxyCreator`, which enables you to specify a list of bean names as a property. This property supports literals (actual bean names) and wildcards like `*Manager`. You can set interceptors using the `interceptorNames` property. See Listing 10.7.

Listing 9.7

```
<bean id="managerProxyCreator"
    class="org.springframework.aop.framework.autoproxy
        .BeanNameAutoProxyCreator">
    <property name="beanNames" value="*Manager"/>
    <property name="interceptorNames">
        <list>
            <value>loggingInterceptor</value>
        </list>
    </property>
</bean>
```

The second, more generic, multiple bean proxy creator is the `DefaultAdvisorAutoProxyCreator`. To use this proxy bean, simply define it in your context file. See Listing 10.8.

Listing 9.8

```
<bean id="autoProxyCreator"
    class="org.springframework.aop.framework.autoproxy
        .DefaultAdvisorAutoProxyCreator"/>
```

Unlike the `BeanNameAutoProxyCreator`, you cannot specify interceptors to apply. Rather, it will inspect any advisors you have in this file and figure if their pointcuts make them applicable to other beans. For more information on advisors, see Spring's reference documentation. This is also a useful resource for other auto-proxy examples.

PRACTICAL AOP EXAMPLES

This section contains several examples of using AOP to manage crosscutting concerns in your application. The concerns include transactions, caching, and event notification.

TRANSACTIONS

Specifying that operations should occur within a transaction can often result in a lot of duplication in your DAOs. Using transactions the traditional way requires many calls to **tx.begin()** and **tx.commit()** in data manipulation methods. Spring and AOP can consolidate transaction concerns into a single location and configuration.

You might not have been aware, but you've been using AOP in the MyUsers application since *Chapter 2: Spring Quick-Start Tutorial*. The ability to declaratively specify transaction attributes on the **userManager** bean is supported by Spring's AOP and the **TransactionProxyFactoryBean**. Listing 10.9 shows a refactored version of the **userManager** bean — this time using a *transaction template* bean and an inner-bean.

Listing 9.9

```
<bean id="txProxyTemplate" abstract="true"
    class="org.springframework.transaction.interceptor
        .TransactionProxyFactoryBean">
    <property name="transactionManager" ref="transactionManager"/>
    <property name="transactionAttributes">
        <props>
            <prop key="save*">PROPAGATION_REQUIRED</prop>
            <prop key="remove*">PROPAGATION_REQUIRED</prop>
            <prop key="*">PROPAGATION_REQUIRED,readOnly</prop>
        </props>
    </property>
    <property name="preInterceptors">
        <list>
            <ref bean="cacheInterceptor"/>
        </list>
    </property>
</bean>

<bean id="userManager" parent="txProxyTemplate">
    <property name="target">
        <bean class="org.appfuse.service.impl.UserManagerImpl">
            <property name="userDAO" ref="userDAO"/>
            <property name="validator" ref="userValidator"/>
        </bean>
    </property>
</bean>
```

Chapter 11: Transactions covers declarative transactions and handling their exceptions and rollbacks in more detail.

CACHING IN THE MIDDLE TIER

Another good example of a crosscutting concern is caching data. The main reason for adding a cache is to improve performance, especially if fetching data is a costly operation. Most of the frameworks covered in *Chapter 9: Testing Spring Applications* have their own caching solutions; however, caching is a practical crosscutting concern.

Since your motivation behind caching is to improve performance, add a test to **UserManagerTest** to test the performance of **UserManagerImpl**. Put the code in Listing 10.10 in *test/org/appfuse/service/UserManagerTest.java*.

NOTE: The **StopWatch** class in this test is a utility class for timing tasks like this.

Listing 9.10

```
public void testGetUserPerformance() {
    user = new User();
    user.setFirstName("Easter");
    user.setLastName("Bunny");

    user = mgr.saveUser(user);

    String name = "getUser";
    StopWatch sw = new StopWatch(name);
    sw.start(name);
    log.debug("Begin timing of method '" + name + "'");

    for (int i=0; i < 200; i++) {
        mgr.getUser(user.getId().toString());
    }

    sw.stop();
    log.info(sw.shortSummary());
    log.debug("End timing of method '" + name + "'");
}
```

Running **ant test -Dtestcase=UserManagerTest** (with no interceptors configured in *applicationContext.xml*) should yield results similar to Figure 10.2. In this initial test, fetching the same user took about 10 seconds.

WARNING: If you use **-Dtestcase=UserManager** (without the **Test** suffix), it will run the mock tests you created in *Chapter 9: Testing Spring Applications*. Since these tests isolate the **UserManager** from Spring, they won't demonstrate applying inter-ceptors to be defined in the *applicationContext.xml* file.

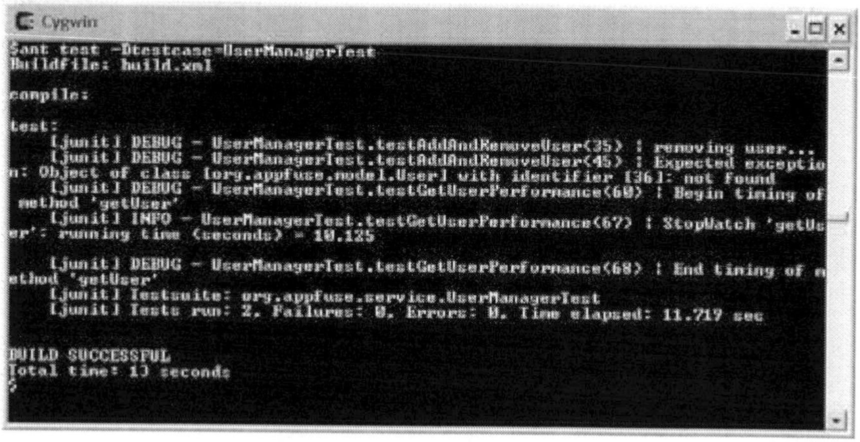

Figure 9.2: Logging output from **StopWatch**

In order to improve performance, add a simple cache to the **UserManagerImpl**. The basic requirements for this cache are as follows:

- Whenever you fetch objects from the database, put them into the cache (which is a simple **HashMap** in this example).

- When the **save()** or **delete()** methods are called, remove objects from the cache.

In the MyUsers application, you can implement the basic (non-AOP) solution by adding a **BaseManager** (in the **org.appfuse.service.impl** package) from which all manager implementations extend. See Listing 10.11.

Listing 9.11

```
package org.appfuse.service.impl;

// use your IDE to organize imports

public class BaseManager {
    // Adding this log variable will allow children to re-use it
    protected final Log log = LogFactory.getLog(getClass());
    protected Map cache;

    protected void putIntoCache(String key, Object value) {
        if (cache == null) {
            cache = new HashMap();
        }
```

```
        cache.put(key, value);
    }

    protected void removeFromCache(String key) {
        if (cache != null) {
            cache.remove(key);
        }
    }
}
```

To modify the **UserManagerImpl** to use this cache, make it extend **BaseManager**, then add calls to the cache in each method. The example in Listing 10.12 is a simple version of **UserManagerImpl** before adding these calls.

Listing 9.12

```
public User getUser(String userId) {
    return dao.getUser(Long.valueOf(userId));
}

public User saveUser(User user) {
    dao.saveUser(user);
    return user;
}

public void removeUser(String userId) {
    dao.removeUser(Long.valueOf(userId));
}
```

After adding these methods, they become much more verbose. See Listing 10.13.

Listing 9.13

```
public User getUser(String userId) {
    // check cache for user
    User user = (User) cache.get(userId);
    if (user == null) {
        // user not in cache, fetch from database
        user = dao.getUser(Long.valueOf(userId));
        super.putIntoCache(userId, user);
    }
    return user;
}

public User saveUser(User user) {
    dao.saveUser(user);
    // update cache with saved user
    super.putIntoCache(String.valueOf(user.getId()), user);
    return user;
```

```
        }

        public void removeUser(String userId) {
            dao.removeUser(Long.valueOf(userId));
            // remove user from cache
            super.removeFromCache(userId);
        }
```

Running **ant test -Dtestcase=UserManagerTest** increases the performance. In Figure 10.3, the running time is 9 seconds.

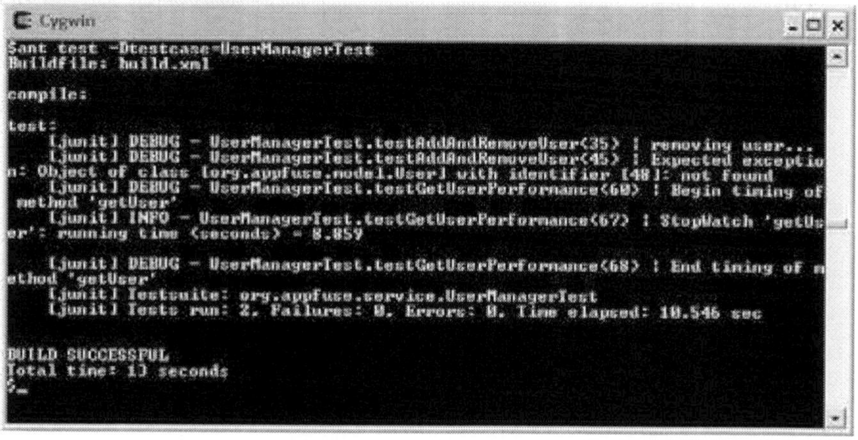

Figure 9.3: Running `UserManagerTest` with programmatic caching

While adding these calls to add/remove from the cache is easy with a simple application like MyUsers, it will become increasingly difficult with a larger application. You will have to remember to add these methods to each Manager. Since caching is not a core concern of the application, you shouldn't really be concerned with it.

By using AOP, you can remove these method calls and *intercept* the appropriate methods to use the cache. Furthermore, by abstracting the caching away from your code, it allows you to concentrate on writing the business logic.

To add a caching interceptor, perform the following steps:

1   Create a **CacheInterceptor** class in the **org.appfuse.aop** package (you must create this). Populate it with the code in Listing 10.14.

Listing 9.14

```
package org.appfuse.aop;

// use your IDE to organize imports
```

```java
public class CacheInterceptor implements MethodInterceptor {

    public Object invoke(MethodInvocation invocation)
        throws Throwable {
        String name = invocation.getMethod().getName();
        Object returnValue;

        // check cache before executing method
        if (name.indexOf("get") > -1 && !name.endsWith("s")) {
            String id = (String) invocation.getArguments()[0];
            returnValue = cache.get(id);
            if (returnValue == null) {
                // user not in cache, proceed
                returnValue = invocation.proceed();
                putIntoCache(id, returnValue);
                return returnValue;
            }
        } else {
            returnValue = invocation.proceed();

            // update cache after executing method
            if (name.indexOf("save") > -1) {
                Method getId =
                    returnValue.getClass()
                        .getMethod("getId", new Class[]{});
                Long id = (Long) getId.invoke(returnValue,
                                          new Object[]{});
                putIntoCache(String.valueOf(id), returnValue);
            } else if (name.indexOf("remove") > -1) {
                String id = (String) invocation.getArguments()[0];
                removeFromCache(String.valueOf(id));
            }
        }
        return returnValue;
    }

    protected Map cache;

    protected void putIntoCache(String key, Object value) {
        if (cache == null) {
            cache = new HashMap();
        }
        cache.put(key, value);
    }

    protected void removeFromCache(String key) {
        if (cache != null) {
```

```
            cache.remove(key);
        }
    }
}
```

2 Add a `cacheInterceptor` bean to *applicationContext.xml* (in *web/WEB-INF*). See Listing 10.15.

Listing 9.15

```
<bean id="cacheInterceptor" class="org.appfuse.aop
    .CacheInterceptor"/>
```

3 Replace the `loggingInterceptor` with the `cacheInterceptor` on the `userManager` bean. See Listing 10.16.

Listing 9.16

```
<property name="preInterceptors">
    <list>
        <ref bean="cacheInterceptor"/>
    </list>
</property>
```

Running **ant test -Dtestcase=UserManagerTest** results in a dramatic performance increase. See Figure 10.4.

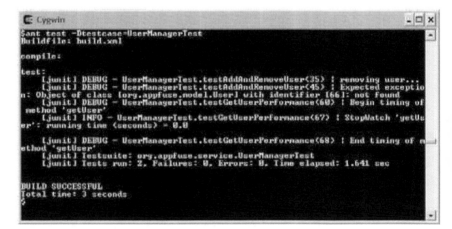

Figure 9.4: Running `UserManagerTest` with AOP-based caching

Using a *caching aspect*, you've reduced the performance to zero seconds! The reason for the dramatic increase in performance is the `CacheInterceptor` returns the data before almost all of the method invocations on `UserManagerImpl`.

The caching example provided here is very simplistic. For a more robust caching implementation, refer to Pieter Coucke's Spring AOP Cache (opensource.atlassian.com/confluence/spring/pages/viewpage.action?pageId=653) or using Spring and EhCache (opensource.atlassian.com/confluence/spring/display/DISC/Caching+the+result+of+methods+using+Spring+and+EHCache).

EVENT NOTIFICATION

If you're developing a web application that's open to the public, you might want to be aware when new users sign up. This can be particularly useful if you want to examine the user's information before authorizing an account. In the following example, you'll create a `NotificationInterceptor` and configure it to send an email when a new user registers.

1   Modify the `UserManagerTest` to use Dumbster to ensure that a message is sent when a new user registers. Only relevant sections are included below. The new code in this class is underlined. After adding this, run **ant test -Dtestcase=UserManagerTest** to ensure it fails. See Listing 10.17.

Listing 9.17

```
protected void setUp() throws Exception {
    String[] paths = {"/WEB-INF/applicationContext*.xml"};
    ctx = new ClassPathXmlApplicationContext(paths);
    mgr = (UserManager) ctx.getBean("userManager");

    // Modify the mailSender bean to use Dumbster's ports
    JavaMailSenderImpl mailSender =
        (JavaMailSenderImpl) ctx.getBean("mailSender");
    mailSender.setPort(2525);
}

public void testAddAndRemoveUser() throws Exception {
    user = new User();
    user.setFirstName("Easter");
    user.setLastName("Bunny");

    // setup a simple mail server using Dumbster
    SimpleSmtpServer server = SimpleSmtpServer.start(2525);

    user = mgr.saveUser(user);

    server.stop();
```

```
            assertEquals(1, server.getReceivedEmailSize());
            SmtpMessage sentMessage =
                (SmtpMessage) server.getReceivedEmail().next();
            assertTrue(sentMessage.getBody()
                .indexOf("Easter Bunny") != -1);
            log.debug(sentMessage);

            assertNotNull(user.getId());
            ...
    }
    public void testGetUserPerformance() {
        user = new User();
        user.setFirstName("Easter");
        user.setLastName("Bunny");

        // setup a simple mail server using Dumbster
        SimpleSmtpServer server = SimpleSmtpServer.start(2525);

        user = mgr.saveUser(user);

        server.stop();

        ...
    }
```

2   Create a **NotificationInterceptor** class in *src/org/appfuse/aop*.
    Populate it with the code in Listing 10.18.

Listing 9.18

```
package org.appfuse.aop;

// organize imports using your IDE

public class NotificationInterceptor implements MethodInterceptor {
    private final Log log =
        LogFactory.getLog(NotificationInterceptor.class);
    private MailSender mailSender;
    private SimpleMailMessage message;

    public void setMailSender(MailSender mailSender) {
        this.mailSender = mailSender;
    }

    public void setMessage(SimpleMailMessage message) {
        this.message = message;
    }

    public Object invoke(MethodInvocation invocation)
        throws Throwable {
```

```
            User user = (User) invocation.getArguments()[0];
            Object returnValue = null;

            if (user.getId() == null) {
                returnValue = invocation.proceed();
                StringBuffer sb = new StringBuffer(100);
                sb.append("User added: ");
                sb.append(user.getFirstName() + " " + user.getLastName());
                message.setText(sb.toString());
                mailSender.send(message);
            } else {
                invocation.proceed();
            }

            return returnValue;
    }
}
```

3 Configure this interceptor and its dependent beans (**MailSender** and **SimpleMailMessage**) in *web/WEB-INF/applicationContext.xml*. See Listing 10.19.

WARNING: Be sure to change the email address in the **to** property of the following **accountMessage** bean. If you don't, the test will fail.

Listing 9.19

```xml
<bean id="notificationInterceptor"
    class="org.appfuse.aop.NotificationInterceptor">
    <property name="mailSender" ref="mailSender"/>
    <property name="message" ref="accountMessage"/>
</bean>

<bean id="mailSender"
    class="org.springframework.mail.javamail.JavaMailSenderImpl">
    <property name="host" value="localhost"/>
</bean>

<bean id="accountMessage" singleton="false"
    class="org.springframework.mail.SimpleMailMessage">
    <property name="to">
        <value><![CDATA[MyUser Admin <youremailhere>]]></value>
    </property>
    <property name="from">
        <value><![CDATA[MyUsers <mattr@sourcebeat.com>]]></value>
    </property>
    <property name="subject" value="MyUsers Account Information"/>
</bean>
```

4   Configure this interceptor in an advisor to be fired using the
RegexpMethodPointcutAdvisor class. See Listing 10.20.

Listing 9.20

```
<bean id="notificationAdvisor"
    class="org.springframework.aop.support
        .RegexpMethodPointcutAdvisor">
    <property name="advice" ref="notificationInterceptor"/>
    <property name="pattern" value=".*saveUser"/>
</bean>
```

5   Add the **notificationAdvisor** bean to the list of **preInterceptors**
on the **userManager** bean. I recommend commenting out the other
examples. See Listing 10.21.

Listing 9.21

```
<property name="preInterceptors">
    <list>
        <!--ref bean="loggingInterceptor"/-->
        <!--ref bean="cacheInterceptor"/-->
        <ref bean="notificationAdvisor"/>
    </list>
</property>
```

6   Save all your files and run **ant test -Dtestcase=UserManagerTest**.
Your console output should be similar to Figure 10.5.

```
 ● ● ●                 Spring Live - Chapter 9 (80,34)
 New  Bookmarks  Configure     Customize  Close
foxxy:~/dev/myusers-ch9 mraible$ ant test -Dtestcase=UserManagerTest
Buildfile: build.xml

compile:
    [javac] Compiling 1 source file to /Users/mraible/workspace/myusers-ch9/buil
d/classes

test:
    [junit] DEBUG - NotificationInterceptor.invoke(28) | detected new user...
    [junit] DEBUG - UserManagerTest.testAddAndRemoveUser(48) | From: MyUsers <ma
ttr@sourcebeat.com>
    [junit] Subject: MyUsers Account Information
    [junit] To: MyUser Admin <mattr@sourcebeat.com>
    [junit] Content-Type: text/plain; charset=us-ascii
    [junit] Mime-Version: 1.0
    [junit] Content-Transfer-Encoding: 7bit
    [junit] Message-ID: <1430135.1096055161521.JavaMail.mraible@foxxy.local>

    [junit] A new account has been created for Easter Bunny.
    [junit] View this users information at:      http://localhost:8080/myusers/ed
itUser.html?id=122

    [junit] DEBUG - UserManagerTest.testAddAndRemoveUser(53) | removing user...
    [junit] DEBUG - UserManagerTest.testAddAndRemoveUser(63) | Expected exceptio
n: Object of class [org.appfuse.model.User] with identifier [122]: not found
    [junit] Testsuite: org.appfuse.service.UserManagerTest
    [junit] Tests run: 1, Failures: 0, Errors: 0, Time elapsed: 5.206 sec


BUILD SUCCESSFUL
Total time: 11 seconds
foxxy:~/dev/myusers-ch9 mraible$ █
```

Figure 9.5: Running `UserManagerTest` with `NotificationInterceptor`

Using a setup like this, you could easily add notifications based on values or conditions.

These examples are a good introduction to AOP and how to use it in your application. Some other examples of where you might use AOP in your applications include:

* Resource pooling
* Thread pooling
* XSLT style sheet caching
* Authentication and authorization

Examples and code for implementing these are available in *AspectJ in Action*.

AOP is very powerful, and new users should be careful when introducing it into their codebase. Two good ways to get into AOP and learn more about it are listed below:

* Via recipe: Copy and paste code from books or articles.

- Non-production: You don't have to use all of AOP's features at once. It has an incremental curve. You can start using it in development (for example, the Logging/Tracing example), then you can move into having items that check on policy or help with testing. Once you get comfortable, you can start using it in production.

While AOP might not be for everyone, it has a place for creating modular, maintainable Java applications.

SUMMARY

AOP has been around for several years, but only recently has it gained so much popularity in the Java arena. This is likely due to the many open-source frameworks for implementing AOP. At the time of this writing, these include AspectJ, dynaop, JAC, JBoss AOP, and Spring AOP.

Spring provides a simple-to-use API for AOP, and it integrates well with other AOP frameworks, particularly AspectJ. In October 2005, the lead developer of AspectJ, Adrian Colyer, became an Interface21 employee and Spring developer. This has lead to much tighter integration between Spring and AspectJ. Spring 2.0 allows you to use AspectJ's pointcut expression language in your context files. AspectJ 5 also allows you to wire up your aspects using Spring and annotations.

In this chapter, you learned about the different concepts in AOP, from *aspects* to *pointcuts* to *weaving*. After defining the verbiage in AOP, the different implementation strategies were explored. JDK Dynamic Proxies and byte-code manipulation are the most popular weaving strategies used in the aforementioned AOP frameworks. AspectJ is the most mature and sophisticated AOP implementation, providing its own language and compiler for integrating aspects and classes. Finally, you learned how to write aspects and advisors in the MyUsers application to implement logging, caching, transactions, and event notification.

TRANSACTIONS

Using declarative and programmatic transactions with Spring

Transactions are an important part of J2EE, allowing you to view several database calls as one and roll them back if they don't all succeed. One of the most highlighted features of EJBs is declarative transactions. This chapter demonstrates how Spring simplifies using declarative and programmatic transactions.

OVERVIEW

Java applications often run as distributed applications, allowing multiple applications (or clients) to appear as one. To the user, they seem like one system even though many users may be accessing, updating, and deleting the same data. Transactions guarantee that data stays consistent among users.

Transactions often occur at the business service level of an application. This is because business logic typically involves a number of steps (or data operations) that should appear as one unit of work. Figure 11.1 illustrates how a transaction might look in a stock trading application.

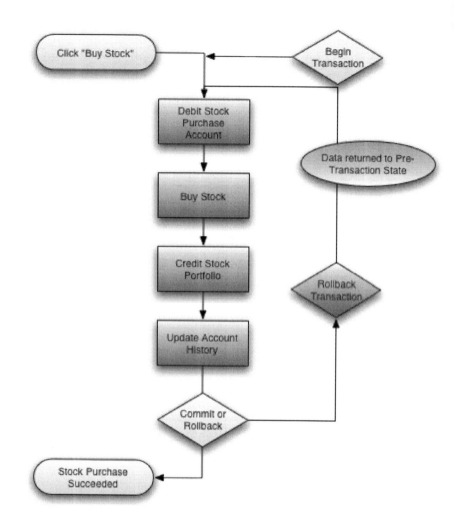

Figure 10.1: Stock purchase transaction example

The blue rectangles represent the four steps that compose an indivisible unit of work; they complete in the same transaction or not at all. The four properties of transactions are commonly known as ACID[1]:

* Atomicity: Each step in the sequence of actions performed within the boundaries of a transaction must complete successfully or all work must roll back.

---

1. Definitions are from Martin Fowler's "Patterns of Enterprise Application Architecture."

- Consistency: A system's resources must be in a consistent, noncorrupt state at both the start and the completion of a transaction.

- Isolation: The result of an individual transaction must not be visible to any other open transactions until that transaction commits successfully.

- Durability: Any result of a committed transaction must be made permanent. This translates to "Must survive a crash of any sort."

Using transactions in your Spring-based application will guarantee trustworthy data and allow you to concentrate on writing business logic. With traditional J2EE containers, you have two choices for managing transaction boundaries: programmatically grab a `UserTransaction` from JNDI and call `UserTransaction.begin()`, `UserTransaction.commit()`, or `UserTransaction.rollback()`; or use Container-Managed Transactions (CMTs). To use CMTs, you would define transactional attributes for each EJB method in the deployment descriptor and let the container decide when to begin and end a transaction.

You can set transaction behavior in CMTs and Spring by defining *propagation behavior*. Propagation behavior tells the container how to handle the creation of new transactions and the propagation of existing transactions. There are six options:

- Required: Execute within a current transaction; create a new one if none exists.

- Supports: Execute within a current transaction; execute without a transaction if none exists.

- Mandatory: Execute within a current transaction; throw an exception if none exists.

- Requires New: Create a new transaction; suspend the current transaction if one exists.

- Not Supported: Execute without a transaction; suspend the current transaction if one exists.

- Never: Execute without a transaction; throw an exception if a transaction exists.

The default behavior is *required*, which is often the most appropriate. In addition to propagation behavior, you can set a read-only hint. Various resources can use this to optimize for a read-only transaction. For example, the resource can send you to a slave database server instead of a master if all you're doing is reading data.

With CMTs, you can set propagation behaviors using *transaction attribute* values in a deployment descriptor or programmatically in code. Spring supports this same methodology by allowing you to define transaction attributes programmatically or in XML. Furthermore, you can write source-level metadata to define transaction behavior (using Commons Attributes and JDK 5 Annotations). The available transaction attributes are listed below:

- **TX_BEAN_MANAGED** (indicates programmatic transaction demarcation)
- **TX_NOT_SUPPORTED**
- **TX_REQUIRED**
- **TX_REQUIRES_NEW**
- **TX_SUPPORTS**
- **TX_MANDATORY**
- **TX_NEVER**

Spring has a similar set of propagation attributes as part of its **TransactionDefinition** interface:

- **PROPAGATION_NOT_SUPPORTED**
- **PROPAGATION_REQUIRED**
- **PROPAGATION_REQUIRES_NEW**
- **PROPAGATION_SUPPORTS**
- **PROPAGATION_MANDATORY**
- **PROPAGATION_NEVER**

It also has a new attribute that allows you to use nested transactions, which can have their own unique rollback rules:

- **PROPAGATION_NESTED**: Execute within a nested transaction if a current transaction exists, or fallback to **PROPAGATION_REQUIRED**.

Transactions are great for ensuring your processes complete (or roll back), but they also help to isolate data modified by the processes. The *isolation level* describes how visible the updated data is to other transactions. When a transaction's data is not visible by other transactions, it's called *full transaction isolation,* or a *serializable transaction.* While this is a nice concept, it can be performance intensive. Using a less restrictive isolation level will help achieve better performance. The SQL standard defines four levels of isolation:

- Serializable: Transactions can execute concurrently with the same results as executing them separately.
- Repeatable read: Allows *phantoms.* Phantoms occur when rows are added to the database, but the reader only picks up some of them.
- Read committed: Allows *unrepeatable reads.* An unrepeatable read occurs when a transaction sees different result sets from the same query while it is in progress.

- Read uncommitted: Allows *dirty reads*. A dirty read occurs when a reader can see the data that another transaction hasn't committed yet.

Using a serializable isolation level is the best choice to ensure the accuracy of your data; however, it's also the slowest. Well-designed applications use different isolation levels for different transactions. When performance is more important than data integrity, I recommend a lower isolation level.

NOTE: Most performance bottlenecks result from untuned SQL queries and a lack of proper indexes. Concentrate on tuning your database before worrying about your transaction isolation levels.

Table 11.1 illustrates the isolation levels and the inconsistent read errors that each allows.

Table 10.1: Isolation levels and read errors

Top of Form

Isolation Level	Phantom	Unrepeatable Read	Dirty Read
Serializable	No	No	No
Repeatable Read	Yes	No	No
Read Committed	Yes	Yes	No
Read Uncommitted	Yes	Yes	Yes

Bottom of Form

J2EE TRANSACTION MANAGEMENT

J2EE developers traditionally have had two choices for managing transactions: *Locally* or *globally*. Local transactions are specific to a resource (for example, a database), while global transactions typically rely on a transaction manager using the Java Transaction API (JTA). Global transactions have the ability to span resources (usually databases). While global transactions are useful, local transactions are sufficient in most cases. Spring makes it easier to use both local and global transactions. You can simply use its IoC container to inject the transaction manager you want to use.

Before diving into using Spring to manage transactions, read the J2EE BluePrints' explanation of JTA and transactions in J2EE:

"A JTA transaction is a transaction managed and coordinated by the J2EE platform. A J2EE product is required to support JTA transactions as defined in the J2EE specification. A JTA transaction can span multiple components and enterprise information systems. A transaction is propagated automatically between components and to enterprise

information systems accessed by components within the transaction. For example, a JTA transaction may comprise a servlet or JSP page accessing multiple enterprise beans, some of which access one or more resource managers.[2] "

Using CMTs is an easy way to interface with a container's global transaction management service, but you can also use JTA directly in your application by grabbing transaction-aware resources and JTA transaction objects from JNDI.

A spec-compliant J2EE application server must have a transaction manager that is capable of handling distributed transactions. This allows J2EE developers to worry about writing code, not how transactions will be applied to various resources. In fact, since resources are configured on a per-container basis, J2EE applications don't contain any information about distributed transactions. The container is responsible for handling all transactions and can (optionally) optimize single resource transactions.

The J2EE specification recommends that J2EE containers support the 2 Phase Commit (2PC) protocol according to the X/Open XA specification. Using this protocol allows an XA transaction coordinator to conduct the processing rather than the resource itself.

> **TIP:** Mike Spille has an in-depth article covering how 2 Phase Commit works in J2EE at jroller.com/page/pyrasun?catname=/XA.

To configure resources to participate in a container's 2PC process, they must be *XA-aware*. This means you should set up a JNDI **DataSource** using a **javax.sql.XADataSource** implementation (usually provided with your JDBC Driver). Most containers allow non-XA-aware data sources to participate in global transactions, but they won't have the 2PC capability, which may cause strange behavior.

Other options for configuring XA-aware resources include using the J2EE Connector Architecture (JCA) and obtaining JTA's internal **javax.transaction .TransactionManager**. You can use the **TransactionManager** object to register callbacks to retrieve information about global JTA transactions.

MANAGING TRANSACTIONS WITH SPRING

Spring's transaction API allows you to use transactions quite easily. This is different from J2EE, where you must look up a **UserTransaction** from JNDI for programmatic transactions or use EJBs for declarative transactions. The nice thing about using Spring's API is that you don't lose anything that J2EE gives you; Spring just

---

2. From the J2EE BluePrints.

makes it simpler. You can still use JTA (with a **JtaTransactionManager**) or hook into your container's underlying transaction manager. The different transaction managers provided by Spring are covered in the *Spring transaction managers* section.

TRANSACTION MANAGER CONCEPTS

Spring has a rich infrastructure to implement and control transactions in a J2EE (or J2SE) environment. It all starts with its **PlatformTransactionManager** interface, diagrammed in Figure 11.2.

```
                         <<interface>>
                   PlatformTransactionManager
getTransaction(definition: TransactionDefinition) : TransactionStatus
commit(status: TransactionStatus) : void
rollback(status: TransactionStatus) : void
```

Figure 10.2: **PlatFormTransactionManager** interface

In most cases, you won't need to use this interface directly. Rather, you'll use the **TransactionTemplate** class for programmatic transaction demarcation or the **TransactionInterceptor** for declarative transactions with AOP. Both of these strategies interact with a PlatformTransactionManager and read from a **TransactionDefinition**.

The TransactionDefinition interface declares transaction settings such as propagation behavior, isolation levels, and timeout settings. The **DefaultTransactionDefinition** class is an implementation of TransactionDefinition with sensible default values (**PROPAGATION_REQUIRED, ISOLATION_DEFAULT, TIMEOUT_DEFAULT, readOnly=false**). It is the base class for both **TransactionTemplate** and **DefaultTransactionAttribute** (for declarative definitions). The UML diagram[3] in Figure 11.3 illustrates how all these interfaces and implementations fit into Spring's transaction infrastructure.

---

3. This UML diagram is based on one found in J2EE Development without EJB (page 242).

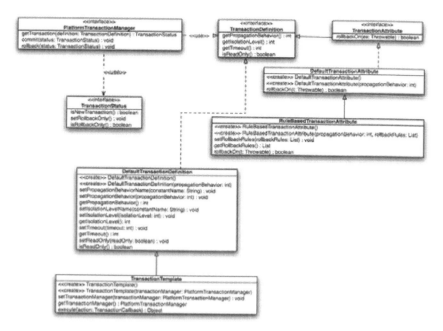

Figure 10.3: Spring Framework transaction infrastructure

NOTE: See a larger version of this diagram on the SourceBeat web site at www.sourcebeat.com/downloads.

The *Programmatic transactions* section demonstrates how to use the **Transaction-Template** class to demarcate transactions in your Java code. You'll also learn how to configure declarative transactions in a context file and in the source using metadata. Finally, you'll enhance the transaction attributes on the **userManager** bean to set some rollback rules when certain exceptions occur.

PREPARING FOR THE EXERCISES

In order to follow along and do the examples in this chapter, you must download the **MyUsers Chapter 10** bundle from sourcebeat.com/downloads. This source code is the result of **Chapter 9** exercises and contains all the JARs you will use here.

In this chapter, you can use any database you like; most of them have transactional capabilities. Instructions for installing and configuring MySQL and PostgreSQL are provided below. The download for this chapter is configured for MySQL.

> **NOTE:** If you're looking for another embeddable database such as HSQLDB, check out Derby (formerly IBM's Cloudscape), which recently became an open-source Apache project.

The JDBC drivers for all three databases are included in *web/WEB-INF/lib*. The screenshots and error messages displayed in these examples use PostgreSQL 8.1.

MYSQL

Chapter 8: Persistence Strategies: Hibernate, iBATIS, JDBC, JDO, and OJB demonstrates how to switch from using an HSQL database to using MySQL. By default, MySQL 4.0.x creates non-transactional tables. You must create tables of type **InnoDB** to use transactions and their rollbacks successfully. The following steps illustrate how to configure a transaction-aware MySQL database for this chapter.

1   If you have a *myusers* database from previous chapters, drop and re-create it.

•   Command line: Log in using **mysql**. Execute **drop database myusers; create database myusers**.

•   Windows: Use the MySQL Administrator application.

•   Mac OS X: Use MySQL Administrator or CocoaMySQL.

2   Configure *web/WEB-INF/classes/jdbc.properties* to point to this database. See Listing 11.1.

Listing 10.1

```
jdbc.driverClassName=com.mysql.jdbc.Driver
jdbc.url=jdbc:mysql://localhost/myusers
jdbc.username=root
jdbc.password=
```

3   Modify *web/WEB-INF/applicationContext-hibernate.xml* to use Hibernate's **MySQLInnoDBDialect**. See Listing 11.2.

Listing 10.2

```
<property name="hibernateProperties">
    <value>
        hibernate.dialect=org.hibernate.dialect
            .MySQLInnoDBDialect
        hibernate.hbm2ddl.auto=create
    </value>
</property>
```

4 Because you're using Hibernate and the `hibernate.hbm2ddl.auto` property is set to `create`, the database tables will be created when the JVM starts up. To verify that everything works, run `ant test -Dtestcase=UserDAO`.

POSTGRESQL

PostgreSQL is a popular open-source database that supports transactions out of the box, as most databases do. To install it for these exercises, perform the following steps:

1 Download the PGInstaller program for PostgreSQL. For Mac OS X, Marc Liyanage provides a nice installer package, or you can use Fink to install it. Many Linux distributions come with PostgreSQL pre-installed.

2 To create the *myusers* database, use the following instructions:

• For Windows, use the PG3Admin tool in the installed directory (in *C:\Program Files\PostgreSQL\8.1\pgAdmin III*). Add a server, right-click on the databases node, and create a new database called *myusers*. Designate the postgres user as the database owner, or create a new user to own this database.

• For UNIX or Linux, log in to PostgreSQL by typing `psql template1 postgres` from the command line. Execute `create database myusers owner postgres`. If you're using Mac OS X, PostMan Query is a nice GUI tool.

3 Configure *web/WEB-INF/classes/jdbc.properties* to point to this database. See Listing 11.3.

Listing 10.3

```
jdbc.driverClassName=org.postgresql.Driver
jdbc.url=jdbc:postgresql://localhost/myusers
jdbc.username=postgres
jdbc.password=postgres
```

4 Configure *web/WEB-INF/applicationContext-hibernate.xml* to use Hibernate's `PostgreSQLDialect`. See Listing 11.4.

Listing 10.4

```
hibernate.dialect=org.hibernate.dialect.PostgreSQLDialect
```

> **NOTE:** PostgreSQL does not have a default password like MySQL does, so be sure this matches the one you configured for your installation.

5 Because you're using Hibernate, and the `hibernate.hbm2ddl.auto` property is set to create, the database tables will be created when the JVM starts up. To verify that everything works, run **ant test -Dtestcase =UserDAO**.

MODIFY USERMANAGER SO ROLLBACK OCCURS

The download for this chapter has a few changes in order to demonstrate transactions:

- The `hibernate.hbm2ddl.auto` property (on the **sessionFactory** bean) is set to **create** so the database will be wiped clean every time and leftover data will not interfere with the tests.

- The **UserManagerTest** has only a **testAddUser()** test. See Listing 11.5.

Listing 10.5

```
public void testAddUser() throws Exception {
    user = new User();
    user.setFirstName("Easter");
    user.setLastName("Bunny");

    mgr.saveUser(user);

    assertNotNull(user.getId());
}
```

- All code associated with caching a user (in **UserManagerImpl.java**) has been removed. In addition, the **saveUser()** method's signature has been changed from **public User saveUser()** to **public void saveUser()** since it has the same effect.

- Any transactions associated with the **userManager** bean are removed. It is a simple POJO with no special behavior. See Listing 11.6.

Listing 10.6

```
<bean id="userManager"
    class="org.appfuse.service.impl.UserManagerImpl">
    <property name="userDAO" ref="userDAO"/>
</bean>
```

The changes in Listing 11.6 make it easier to test when inserts succeed and fail. To prove that transactions are working and rolling back as expected, make a few modifications to the MyUsers application.

1   Modify the **app_user** table to require that the **last_name** column be unique. You can do this by adding **unique="true"** to the **lastName** property in *src/org/appfuse/model/User.hbm.xml*. See Listing 11.7.

Listing 10.7

```
<property name="lastName" column="last_name" not-null="true"
    unique="true"/>
```

2   Modify the **saveUser()** method in the **UserManagerImpl** class so it inserts multiple records. On the third insert, it should fail because it's trying to insert a record with the same last name as the first record. See Listing 11.8.

Listing 10.8

```
public void saveUser(User user) {
    String lastName = user.getLastName();
    for (int i=0; i < 3; i++) {
        user.setId(null);
        user.setLastName(lastName + i);
        // make the last one a duplicate record
        if (i == 2) {
            user.setLastName(lastName + 0);
        }
        log.debug("entering record " + user);
        dao.saveUser(user);
    }
}
```

3   Run **ant test -Dtestcase=UserManagerTest**; the last record should fail to insert as seen in Figure 11.4.

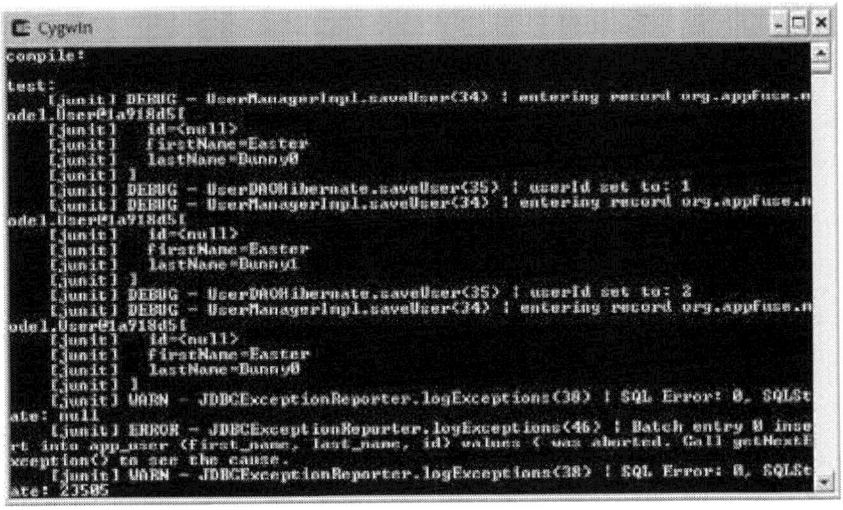

Figure 10.4: `UserManagerTest` results

Now you can see the problem you're going to solve with transactions: The `saveUser()` method failed on the last record, but the first two records were added to the database regardless (see Figure 11.5 for a visual).

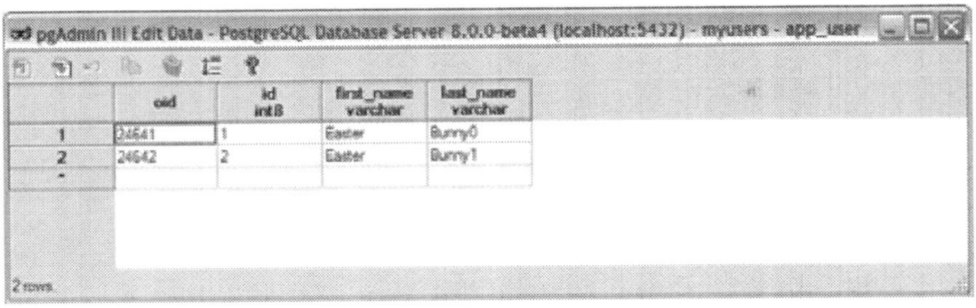

Figure 10.5: Data view with failing transactions

The next several sections demonstrate how to use transactions to ensure the processes that occur in `saveUser()` are `atomic`. All of them should succeed, or none of them should succeed.

PROGRAMMATIC TRANSACTIONS

Spring's Transaction API makes it easy to use transactions in your code. With traditional J2EE, the only way to do this is to use the `UserTransaction` object, which you have to look up from JNDI. Not only is it a pain to look up this object from JNDI, but you have to catch a ridiculous amount of exceptions that may be thrown when looking up and using a `UserTransaction`. Here's an example of using such a

transaction strategy in the **UserManagerImpl.saveUser()** method. See
Listing 11.9.

Listing 10.9

```
public void saveUser(User user) {

    UserTransaction tx = null;
    try {
        InitialContext ctx = new InitialContext();
        tx = (javax.transaction.UserTransaction)
        ctx.lookup( "java:comp/UserTransaction" );

        // begin transaction
        tx.begin();
        dao.saveUser(user);

        // commit transactions
        tx.commit();
    } catch (NamingException ne) {
        log.error("NamingException occurred: " + ne.getMessage());
    } catch (SystemException se) {
        log.error("SystemException occurred: " + se.getMessage());
    } catch (NotSupportedException nse) {
        log.error("NotSupported!");
    } catch (SecurityException e) {
        log.error("How many of these are there?");
        e.printStackTrace();
    } catch (IllegalStateException e) {
        log.error("Is this the longest catch block ever?");
        e.printStackTrace();
    } catch (RollbackException e) {
        e.printStackTrace();
    } catch (HeuristicMixedException e) {
        e.printStackTrace();
    } catch (HeuristicRollbackException e) {
        e.printStackTrace();
    }
}
```

You could put all of this try/catch logic in a parent or helper class (or just catch
Exception), but it's still a lot of code for wrapping a simple transaction around a
method. This example doesn't even contain the rollback logic you need when the
commit fails! One of the worst parts about the preceding system is that it's difficult
to unit test. You have to run your code in a container or use some mock JNDI
setup.

The preceding code also requires you to have a transaction manager installed and
configured for your application server; otherwise, the JNDI lookup will fail. While

most J2EE containers with EJB have this, servlet containers like Tomcat require you to install a transaction manager.

TRANSACTIONTEMPLATE

With Spring, not only is the code less verbose, but there are no exceptions to catch. Spring gives you two ways to demarcate transactions in your Java code: **PlatformTransactionManager** and **TransactionTemplate**. The most common choice is the **TransactionTemplate** class. This class has a central **execute()** method and uses a *callback* approach to relieve you from grabbing and releasing resources, as well as any try/catch logic.

You can use two types of callbacks with **TransactionTemplate**: a **TransactionCallback** class, which allows you to return a value from the **execute()** method, and a **TransactionCallbackWithoutResult** class, which is perfect for the **void saveUser()** method.

In order to use a **TransactionTemplate**, you must have a transaction manager available. The transaction manager should always be configured in a context file and then passed to your business object for usage.

The following steps detail how to use a **TransactionTemplate** in the **UserManagerImpl** class:

1   Edit the **userManager** bean mapping and add a property for **transactionManager**. Set it to refer to the **transactionManager** bean. See Listing 11.10.

Listing 10.10

```
<bean id="userManager"
    class="org.appfuse.service.impl.UserManagerImpl">
    <property name="transactionManager" ref="transactionManager"/>
    <property name="userDAO" ref="userDAO"/>
</bean>
```

2   The **transactionManager** bean is already defined in *web/WEB-INF/application-Context-hibernate.xml* and refers to a **HibernateTransactionManager**.

3   Add a private **transactionTemplate** variable and a **transactionManager** setter in **UserManagerImpl** for the **PlatformTransactionManager**. In this method, configure the **TransactionTemplate**. See Listing 11.11.

Listing 10.11

```
private TransactionTemplate txTemplate;

public void setTransactionManager
    (PlatformTransactionManager txManager)
{
    this.txTemplate = new TransactionTemplate(txManager);
    // set propagation behavior, isolation level etc. template
    // we don't need to since REQUIRED is the default
}
```

4   Refactor the **saveUser()** method to use the transaction template. See Listing 11.12.

Listing 10.12

```
public void saveUser(final User user) {
    txTemplate.execute(new TransactionCallbackWithoutResult() {
        public void doInTransactionWithoutResult
            (TransactionStatus status) {
            // do business logic
            String lastName = user.getLastName();

            for (int i = 0; i < 3; i++) {
                // can't just set user.id to null or Hibernate
                // complains that identifier was changed
                User u = new User();
                u.setFirstName(user.getFirstName());
                u.setLastName(user.getLastName() + i);

                // make the last one a duplicate record
                if (i == 2) {
                    u.setLastName(lastName + 0);
                }

                if (log.isDebugEnabled()) {
                    log.debug("entering record " + u);
                }

                dao.saveUser(u);
            }
        }
    });
}
```

Run **ant test -Dtestcase=UserManagerTest**; you'll get the same errors you saw in Figure 11.4, but a transaction will cause this method to execute an all-or-nothing process. The **app_user** table should be empty.

TIP: To turn on more verbose logging of Spring's transaction handling, add the following code to *web/WEB-INF/classes/log4j.xml*. See Listing 11.13.

Listing 10.13

```
<logger name="org.springframework.transaction">
    <level value="DEBUG"/>
</logger>
```

PLATFORMTRANSACTIONMANAGER

The other way to demarcate transactions programmatically is to use the **Plat-formTransactionManager** directly. The problem with this approach is that you must manage the logic to roll back the transaction when an exception is thrown. To use the **PlatformTransactionManager**, follow these steps:

1   As in the **TransactionTemplate** example, set the **PlatformTrans-actionManager** as a variable in your **UserManagerImpl** class. See Listing 11.14.

Listing 10.14

```
private PlatformTransactionManager transactionManager;

public void setTransactionManager
    (PlatformTransactionManager txManager) {
    this.transactionManager = txManager;
}
```

2   Refactor the **saveUser()** method so it catches a **DataAccessException** and rolls back appropriately. See Listing 11.15.

Listing 10.15

```
public void saveUser(final User user) {
    DefaultTransactionDefinition txDef =
        new DefaultTransactionDefinition();
    // set propagation behavior, isolation level etc. template
    // we don't need to since REQUIRED (the default)
        is good enough
```

```
      TransactionStatus status =
          transactionManager.getTransaction(txDef);

      try {
          // do business logic
          String lastName = user.getLastName();

          for (int i = 0; i < 3; i++) {
              // can't just set user.id to null or Hibernate
              // complains that identifier was changed
              User u = new User();
              u.setFirstName(user.getFirstName());
              u.setLastName(user.getLastName() + i);

              // make the last one a duplicate record
              if (i == 2) {
                  u.setLastName(lastName + 0);
              }

              if (log.isDebugEnabled()) {
                  log.debug("entering record " + u);
              }

              dao.saveUser(u);
          }
      } catch (DataAccessException ex) {
          transactionManager.rollback(status);
          throw ex;
      }
      transactionManager.commit(status);
  }
```

The **TransactionTemplate** requires less code, but the **PlatformTransaction-Manager** allows you to use any existing exception handling logic. Using a **Transac-tionTemplate** is the recommended approach. Both approaches allow you to test your code easily without running it inside a J2EE container.

Programmatic transactions are nice, but they require a fair amount of code. In the last example, the business logic takes up 20 lines of code (LOC), while the entire method is 34 LOC. Using declarative and source-level metadata to specify transaction attributes allows you to reduce your methods to contain only the business logic, without needing any knowledge of transactions.

DECLARATIVE TRANSACTIONS

Declarative transactions describe the ability to specify transaction attributes using XML and metadata. Rather than *programming* the behavior directly by wrapping your code, you *declare* the behavior. The primary advantage of this approach is that, for the most part, your code is not aware of its transactional behavior. It also leads to less typing and promotes reusability of transaction attributes across multiple objects.

AOP WITH TRANSACTIONPROXYFACTORYBEAN

The first and most common way of performing declarative transactions with Spring is to wrap your object with a **TransactionProxyFactoryBean**. Its Javadocs describe its function:

"This class is intended to cover the typical case of declarative transaction demarcation: namely, wrapping a (singleton) target object with a transactional proxy, proxying all the interfaces that the target implements."

You used this technique in previous chapters. To continue, follow the steps below:

1   Change the **UserManagerImpl.saveUser()** method to contain only the business logic. You can also remove any **TransactionManager/ Template** variables and methods. See Listing 11.16.

Listing 10.16

```
public void saveUser(final User user) {
    // do business logic
    String lastName = user.getLastName();

    for (int i = 0; i < 3; i++) {
        // can't just set user.id to null or Hibernate
        // complains that identifier was changed
        User u = new User();
        u.setFirstName(user.getFirstName());
        u.setLastName(user.getLastName() + i);

        // make the last one a duplicate record
        if (i == 2) {
            u.setLastName(lastName + 0);
        }

        if (log.isDebugEnabled()) {
            log.debug("entering record " + u);
        }

        dao.saveUser(u);
    }
}
```

2   Change the **userManager** bean definition to wrap **UserManagerImpl** with a **TransactionProxyFactoryBean**. The **target** attribute points to the class to which you want to apply transactional behavior. See Listing 11.17.

NOTE: Lines 2 and 3 in the following listing should be on the same line. To fit them into the width of this page, the line has been broken.

Listing 10.17

```
<bean id="userManager"
        class="org.springframework.transaction.interceptor
          .TransactionProxyFactoryBean">
    <property name="transactionManager" ref="transactionManager"/>
    <property name="target" ref="userManagerTarget"/>
    <property name="transactionAttributes">
        <props>
            <prop key="save*">PROPAGATION_REQUIRED</prop>
            <prop key="remove*">PROPAGATION_REQUIRED</prop>
            <prop key="*">PROPAGATION_REQUIRED,readOnly</prop>
        </props>
    </property>
</bean>

<bean id="userManagerTarget"
    class="org.appfuse.service.impl.UserManagerImpl">
    <property name="userDAO" ref="userDAO"/>
</bean>
```

TIP: If you receive an error similar to "Write operations are not allowed in read-only mode," make sure you don't have a **readOnly** hint set for that method.

The **transactionsAttributes** properties are set using a **Properties** format specified in the **NameMatchTransactionAttributeSource** class. This format is smart enough to know how the propagation behavior, isolation level, and other attributes map to a **TransactionDefinition**.

The problem with this example is the **userManagerTarget** bean is exposed to developers, and it's possible for someone to use the **UserManagerImpl** class without transactional behavior. To avoid this situation, you can make the **userManagerTarget** into an *anonymous inner-bean* so that no one can retrieve it from the **ApplicationContext**. The example in Listing 11.18 demonstrates this safety measure:

Listing 10.18

```
<bean id="userManager"
    class="org.springframework.transaction.interceptor
        .TransactionProxyFactoryBean">
    <property name="transactionManager" ref="transactionManager"/>
    <property name="target">
        <bean class="org.appfuse.service.impl.UserManagerImpl">
```

```
            <property name="userDAO" ref="userDAO"/>
        </bean>
    </property>
    <property name="transactionAttributes">
        <props>
            <prop key="save*">PROPAGATION_REQUIRED</prop>
            <prop key="remove*">PROPAGATION_REQUIRED</prop>
            <prop key="*">PROPAGATION_REQUIRED,readOnly</prop>
        </props>
    </property>
</bean>
```

The **transactionAttributes** property specifies propagation behavior, isolation levels, read-only hints, and rollback behavior. Using the settings above will result in using the **ISOLATION_DEFAULT** isolation level, as evidenced by Figure 11.6:

Figure 10.6: Logging from **UserManagerTest**

You can easily change the isolation level by adding one of the five levels to a method's transaction definition. See Listing 11.19.

Listing 10.19

```
<prop key="save*">PROPAGATION_REQUIRED,ISOLATION_REPEATABLE_READ
    </prop>
```

This trick will only work if your transaction manager supports the specified isolation level. The **HibernateTransactionManager** does not support repeatable read, but it does support serializable. See Figure 11.7 to see what happens when you try to use a repeatable read isolation level with Hibernate.

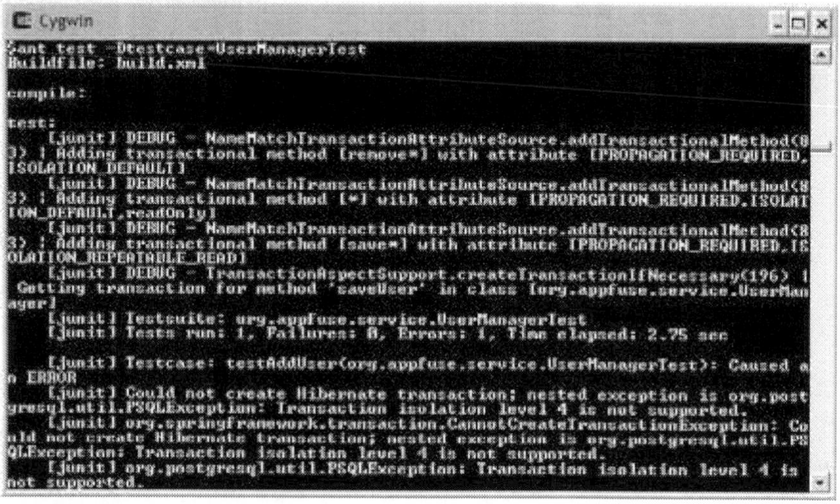

Figure 10.7: Hibernate does not support repeatable read

I recommend using **ISOLATION_DEFAULT**, which uses the underlying database's default.

ROLLBACK RULES AND EXCEPTIONS

In addition to setting propagation behavior and read-only hints, you can set conditions on which to roll back. This is an advantage over CMTs, where you can only specify **setRollbackOnly()**.

To specify *rollback rules*, add exception names to the transaction attribute. A minus (-) prefix indicates you want to force a rollback, and a plus (+) prefix indicates you want to commit anyway. By default, any runtime exceptions are rolled back. To indicate that you want to continue committing when your business logic throws a **UserExistsException**, change the **save*** method's behavior to the behavior in Listing 11.20:

Listing 10.20

```
<prop key="save*">PROPAGATION_REQUIRED,+UserExistsException</prop>
```

TRANSACTION TEMPLATE BEAN

The configuration you currently have for the **userManager** bean can become quite verbose if you start adding many objects with similar transaction attributes. To combat this, you can use a *transaction template bean* to specify attributes for all beans that inherit it. Previous chapters use this strategy, and it is described in detail on Colin Sampaleanu's weblog. This strategy is the recommended strategy for configuring your applications.

Using a template bean for transactions involves two steps:

1   Create a bean definition in your context file that acts as a template for other beans. Make sure this bean has **abstract="true"** as part of its bean definition. See Listing 11.21.

Listing 10.21

```
<bean id="txProxyTemplate" abstract="true"
    class="org.springframework.transaction.interceptor
        .TransactionProxyFactoryBean">
    <property name="transactionManager" ref="transactionManager"/>
    <property name="transactionAttributes">
        <props>
            <prop key="save*">PROPAGATION_REQUIRED</prop>
            <prop key="remove*">PROPAGATION_REQUIRED</prop>
            <prop key="*">PROPAGATION_REQUIRED,readOnly</prop>
        </props>
    </property>
</bean>
```

2   When you create beans to which you want to apply this template, refer to the id of the template bean using the **parent** attribute. Then define the class as an inner-bean in the **target** property. See Listing 11.22.

Listing 10.22

```
<bean id="userManager" parent="txProxyTemplate">
    <property name="target">
        <bean class="org.appfuse.service.impl.UserManagerImpl">
            <property name="userDAO" ref="userDAO"/>
        </bean>
    </property>
</bean>
```

TRANSACTIONATTRIBUTESOURCE

Another option for configuring a declarative transaction is to specify a bean that refers to the **NameMatchTransactionAttributeSource** class and defines the methods and their behaviors. This strategy isn't as clean as a template bean because it still requires you to wrap all your beans with a **TransactionProxyFactory-Bean**.

To use this approach, complete the following steps:

1   Create a bean definition that describes the transaction attributes. See
     Listing 11.23.

Listing 10.23

```
<bean name="txAttributes"
        class="org.springframework.transaction.interceptor
            .NameMatchTransactionAttributeSource">
    <property name="properties">
        <props>
            <prop key="save*">PROPAGATION_REQUIRED</prop>
            <prop key="remove*">PROPAGATION_REQUIRED</prop>
            <prop key="*">PROPAGATION_REQUIRED,readOnly</prop>
        </props>
    </property>
</bean>
```

2   Create your transaction-wrapped bean definition with a reference to this
     bean in the **transactionAttributeSource** property. As in
     Listing 11.24.

Listing 10.24

```
<bean id="userManager"
        class="org.springframework.transaction.interceptor
            .TransactionProxyFactoryBean">
    <property name="transactionManager" ref="transactionManager"/>
    <property name="target">
        <bean class="org.appfuse.service.impl.UserManagerImpl">
            <property name="userDAO" ref="userDAO"/>
        </bean>
    </property>
    <property name="transactionAttributeSource" ref="txAttributes"/>
</bean>
```

More details about this strategy are available on Chris Winter's weblog at
www.cwinters.com/news/display/?news_id=3149.

BEANNAMEAUTOPROXYCREATOR

The final option for configuring declarative transactions is to use a **BeanNameAuto-
ProxyCreator**. This strategy allows you to specify a list of bean names to which to
apply a set of transaction attributes. An example configuration is in Spring's reference documentation. In addition to this strategy, you can use source-level metadata
to create proxies automatically.

SOURCE-LEVEL METADATA

In addition to specifying transaction behavior in XML, you can declare it directly in your classes. You can do this two ways in Spring: using Commons Attributes or using JDK 5 Annotations. Both strategies solve the same problem, but Commons Attributes will work on JDK 1.2 and later. Both strategies allow you to eliminate the **TransactionProxyFactoryBean**. Beans that contain transaction attributes will be automatically intercepted to wrap them with declarative transaction management. Commons Attributes is not covered in this section because it doesn't seem to be used by many Spring users. For more information regarding Spring support for Commons Attributes, see *Chapter 25. Annotations and Source Level Metadata Support* in the Spring documentation.

USING JDK 5.0 ANNOTATIONS

If you're using JDK 5, you can also use JDK 5 annotations. To use JDK 5 annotations in the MyUsers project, perform the following steps:

1 Remove **target="1.4" source="1.4"** from the javac tasks in the **compile** target in *build.xml*.

2 Change the **transactionAttributeSource** bean in *web/WEB-INF/applicationContext.xml* to use the annotations implementation in Listing 11.25.

Listing 10.25

```
<bean id="transactionAttributeSource"
    class="org.springframework.transaction.annotation
        .AnnotationTransactionAttributeSource"
    autowire="constructor"/>
```

3 Delete the **txAttributes** bean because you no longer need it.

4 Add an **@Transactional** annotation to the **saveUser()** method. You'll need to import **org.springframework.transaction.annotation.Transactional** to use this annotation. Annotations do not go inside javadoc tags. See Listing 11.26.

Listing 10.26

```
@Transactional
public void saveUser(final User user) {
```

5 Run **ant test -Dtestcase=UserManagerTest** and verify that the **app_user** table is empty.

You can put the preceding annotation at the class level if you want it to apply to all methods. To see the available properties you can set on the `@Transactional` annotation, see *Chapter 9, section 9.5.6* in the Spring documentation.

SPRING TRANSACTION MANAGERS

This chapter has explored many ways to use transactions with Spring. For all of the examples, you had to configure a `PlatformTransactionManager` implementation in a context file. This section covers the available transaction manager implementations and when you should use them.

DATASOURCETRANSACTIONMANAGER

The `DataSourceTransactionManager` is useful when using a single JDBC `Data-Source`. It binds a JDBC connection from the `DataSource` to the thread and supports custom isolation levels and timeouts. If you're using JDBC 3.0, the `DataSourceTransactionManager` supports nested transactions via JDBC 3.0 savepoints.

This implementation is an alternative to `JtaTransactionManager` when using a single database. Switching between this implementation and JTA is really just a matter of configuration. You only need the JTA manager if you must support more than one database or if you want to use your app server's transaction manager.

I recommend using this transaction manager with iBATIS and Spring JDBC.

HIBERNATETRANSACTIONMANAGER

The `HibernateTransactionManager` is designed for use with a single Hibernate `SessionFactory`. It binds a `Session` from the factory to the thread. The Hibernate helper classes (`SessionFactoryUtils` and `HibernateTemplate`) are aware of thread-bound sessions and participate in their transactions automatically. Like the `DataSourceTransactionManager`, this implementation supports JDBC 3.0 savepoints and allows you to set custom isolation levels and timeouts.

If you need support for spanning transactions across resources, you can change your configuration to use a `JtaTransactionManager`. You can also use the Hibernate JCA connector for direct container integration. Unfortunately, there doesn't seem to be any documentation on using or configuring Hibernate JCA.

JDOTRANSACTIONMANAGER

The `JdoTransactionManager` is designed for use with a single JDO `PersistanceManagerFactory`. Like the previous two, this implementation binds a `PersistenceManager` from the factory to the thread. `PersistenceManagerFactoryUtils` and `JdoTemplate` are aware of thread-bound transactions and participate accordingly. This implementation is most effective when JDO is the primary means of transactional data access. It supports JDBC 3.0 savepoints, as long as your JDBC driver supports them.

You must use `JtaTransactionManager` if you want to talk transactionally to multiple resources. However, you will likely have to configure your JDO implementation to participate in JTA transactions.

JTATRANSACTIONMANAGER

The `JtaTransactionManager` is the preferred implementation if you handle distributed transactions or transactions on a J2EE Connector (registered via JCA). For single resources, the aforementioned transaction managers should suit your needs.

With the JTA implementation, transaction synchronization is on by default. This synchronization allows data access support classes to register resources as closed when the transaction commits. Spring's support classes for JDBC, Hibernate, and JDO all perform these registrations when the resources are opened within a transaction. Standard JTA does not guarantee that opened resources will be closed, so this is a nice feature of Spring's JTA implementation. For advanced usage, including how to suspend transactions with certain app servers, please see this class's javadocs.

PERSISTENCEBROKERTRANSACTIONMANAGER

The `PersistenceBrokerTransactionManager` is appropriate when using OJB for your data access layer. It binds an OJB PersistenceBroker from the specified key to a thread. `OjbFactoryUtils` and `PersistenceBrokerTemplate` are aware of thread-bound persistence brokers and automatically participate in transactions. Like the other implementations, you should use the `JtaTransactionManager` when you need to access multiple resources in a transaction.

SUMMARY

The ability to manage transactions easily and efficiently in Spring is one of its best features. Not only is it easy, but many options are available. You can ease the pain of looking up `UserTransaction` from JNDI and use the `PlatformTransaction-Manager` directly. To simplify and eliminate the need to handle exceptions, you can use a `TransactionTemplate` and its callbacks or you can use declarative transactions in an XML file. Furthermore, you can even use source-level metadata with Commons Attributes and JDK 5.0 annotations.

One of the greatest benefits of J2EE is the ability to create transactional enterprise systems. Before Spring, you had to run your application in a full-blown application server to implement transactions and you had to use EJBs if you wanted to use declarative transactions. By using Spring, you can define transactions for any POJO and choose when you want to *scale up*. For most applications, using a single **Data-Source** and an appropriate transaction manager is all you need. A powerful database will often handle any performance enhancements you might get from spreading the load across multiple databases. However, you still have the option of using multiple **DataSources** and simply changing the transaction manager implementation to use **JtaTransactionManager**.

WEB FRAMEWORK INTEGRATION

Integrating Spring with four popular web frameworks

Spring has its own web framework, but it also integrates well with other frameworks. This capability allows you to leverage your existing knowledge and still use Spring to manage your business objects and data layer. This chapter explores Spring integration with four popular web frameworks: JSF (JavaServer Faces), Struts, Tapestry, and WebWork.

OVERVIEW

Choosing a web framework is a controversial subject in the Java community. Many developers are proficient in a specific framework and, therefore, disagree about which framework is the best. However, if you're a Java web developer and you only know one web framework, you're selling yourself short. You're limiting your opportunities, and you should diversify your investments. By learning more than one framework, your portfolio of skills will be more valuable, and you might even gain some insight on how to do things easier in your preferred framework.

Spring has its own web framework, yet it supports many others. It has built-in support for JSF and Struts, and it's easy to integrate Spring with Tapestry and WebWork. This chapter briefly describes each of these frameworks and how to integrate them with Spring. It shows you how to configure validation for each of them, and it covers programmer testing strategies. It also covers view options, such as Velocity and JSP and shows how to convert complex types, like dates.

CHAPTER EXERCISES

This chapter is a little different from previous chapters in that the code is written using Equinox 1.6 rather than built on the MyUsers application. The advantage of this is you don't have a lot of unused JARs in *web/WEB-INF/lib*, and you'll only have code that's actually used in your source tree. All of the example exercises in this chapter are contained in *Appendix A: Examples and References*.

The JSF, Tapestry, and WebWork sections offer examples on how to write a simple application that has the same functionality as the one described in *Chapter 2: Spring*

Quick-Start Tutorial and *Chapter 4: Spring's MVC Framework*. Basically, it just does CRUD on a database with master/detail screens.

The examples show you how to write tests, implement validation, set up internationalization, and display success messages. They do not cover authenticating, authorizing, or uploading files. If you're interested in these topics, check out AppFuse, which has all of these features implemented.

To do the JSF, Tapestry, and WebWork exercises in this chapter, download the **Chapter 11** bundle from sourcebeat.com/downloads. This file contains projects that are stripped-down versions of the completed code in Equinox 1.6. The Struts section has no bundle or exercises because it was covered in *Chapter 2: Spring Quick-Start Tutorial*.

The downloads show you how to create an application from scratch with each framework. This chapter does not aim to be a complete reference for JSF, Struts, Tapestry, or WebWork, however. Its main goal is to introduce you to each framework and show you how to use them with Spring. Each section contains additional resources to help you learn more about each framework, as well as tips and tricks for developing with them.

INTEGRATING SPRING INTO WEB APPLICATIONS

The easiest way to integrate Spring into an existing web application is to declare the **ContextLoaderListener** in your *web.xml* and use a **contextConfigLocation** **<context-param>** to set which context files to load. The downloads for this chapter already have this configured, but the code here is for review.

The **<context-param>** is in Listing 12.1:

Listing 11.1

```
<context-param>
    <param-name>contextConfigLocation</param-name>
    <param-value>/WEB-INF/applicationContext*.xml</param-value>
</context-param>
```

See the **<listener>** in Listing 12.2:

Listing 11.2

```
<listener>
    <listener-class>
        org.springframework.web.context.ContextLoaderListener
    </listener-class>
</listener>
```

> **NOTE:** Listeners were added to the Servlet API in version 2.3. If you have a Servlet 2.2 container, you can use the **ContextLoaderServlet** to achieve this same functionality.

If you don't specify the **contextConfigLocation** context parameter, the **ContextLoaderListener** will look for a */WEB-INF/applicationContext.xml* file to load. Once the context files are loaded, Spring creates a **WebApplicationContext** object based on the bean definitions and puts it into the **ServletContext**.

All Java web frameworks are built on top of the Servlet API, so you can use the code to get the **ApplicationContext** that Spring created in Listing 12.3.

Listing 11.3

```
WebApplicationContext ctx =
    WebApplicationContextUtils.getWebApplicationContext
        (servletContext);
```

A common way to get the **ServletContext** object in your web framework of choice is to use this code. See Listing 12.4.

Listing 11.4

```
ServletContext servletContext =
    request.getSession().getServletContext();
```

The **WebApplicationContextUtils** class is for convenience, so you don't have to remember the name of the **ServletContext** attribute. Its **getWebApplicationContext()** method will return **null** if an object doesn't exist under the **WebApplicationContext.ROOT_WEB_APPLICATION_CONTEXT_ATTRIBUTE** key. Rather than risk getting **NullPointerExceptions** in your application, it's better to use the **getRequiredWebApplicationContext()** method. This method throws an exception when the **ApplicationContext** is missing.

> **NOTE:** If you've configured your application properly, the **ApplicationContext** should always be available in the **ServletContext**.

Once you have a reference to the **WebApplicationContext**, you can retrieve beans by their name or type. Most developers retrieve beans by name then cast them to one of their implemented interfaces.

Fortunately, most of the frameworks in this chapter have simpler ways of looking up beans. Not only do they make it easy to get beans from the **BeanFactory**, but they also allow you to use dependency injection on their controllers. Each framework section has more detail on its specific integration strategies.

JAVASERVER FACES

JavaServer Faces (JSF) is a component-based, event-driven web framework. According to Sun Microsystems' JSF Overview, JSF technology includes:

- A set of APIs for representing UI components and managing their state, handling events and input validation, defining page navigation, and supporting internationalization and accessibility

- A JavaServer Pages (JSP) custom tag library for expressing a JavaServer Faces interface within a JSP page

Figure 12.1[1] shows how JSF fits into a web application's architecture.

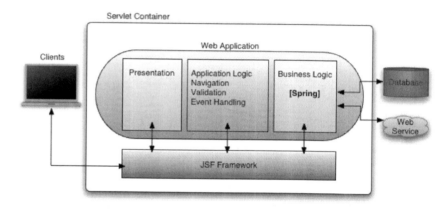

Figure 11.1: JSF with Spring

One of JSF's prominent features is the ability to wire client-generated events to server-side event handlers. For example, when a user clicks a link or a button, a specific method in a class can be called. These methods can be *listeners* or *actions*. Listeners typically alter the state of a page-backing Java class, or *managed bean*. They can alter the JSF lifecycle, but they do not typically control navigation. Actions are no-argument methods that return a string that signifies where to go next. Returning null from an action means "Stay on the same page."

The JSF lifecycle consists of six phases:

1 Restore view: Re-creates the server-side component tree when you revisit a JSF page.

---

1. Diagram based on the one on page 23 of Core JavaServer Faces. (Geary, David and Horstmann, Cay. Core JavaServer Faces. Sun Microsystems Press, 2004.)

2   Apply request values: Copies request parameters into submitted values components.

3   Process validations: Converts submitted values and validates them.

4   Update model values: Copies converted and validated values to model objects.

5   Invoke application: Invokes listeners and actions for command components. (You typically use actions to call your Spring beans to manage business logic and persistence.)

6   Render response: Saves the state and loads the next view

Figure 12.2[2] illustrates the phases in a JSF application, from request to response.

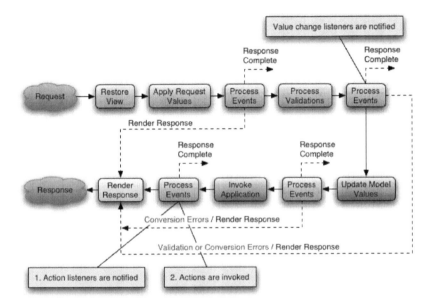

Figure 11.2: JSF lifecycle .

The navigation in JSF applications is determined by a number of *navigation rules* in a *WEB-INF/faces-config.xml* file. This file contains a number of additional settings:

*   **ResourceBundle** names and supported locales
*   Custom **VariableResolvers**

---

2. Diagram based on the one from page 274 of Core JavaServer Faces. (Geary, David and Horstmann, Cay. *Core JavaServer Faces*. Sun Microsystems Press, 2004.)

- Managed beans and their properties

Many of the settings related to your JSF framework will be contained in this file. Listing 12.5 is a trimmed-down version of the *faces-config.xml* you will be writing in this section.

Listing 11.5

```xml
<?xml version="1.0"?>
<!DOCTYPE faces-config PUBLIC
    "-//Sun Microsystems, Inc.//DTD JavaServer Faces Config 1.1//EN"
    "http://java.sun.com/dtd/web-facesconfig_1_1.dtd">

<faces-config>
    <!-- Spring VariableResolver for JSF -->
    <application>
        <variable-resolver>
            org.springframework.web.jsf.DelegatingVariableResolver
        </variable-resolver>
        <locale-config>
            <default-locale>en</default-locale>
            <supported-locale>en</supported-locale>
            <supported-locale>es</supported-locale>
        </locale-config>
        <message-bundle>messages</message-bundle>
    </application>

    <navigation-rule>
        <from-view-id>/userList.jsp</from-view-id>
        <navigation-case>
            <from-outcome>add</from-outcome>
            <to-view-id>/userForm.jsp</to-view-id>
        </navigation-case>
    </navigation-rule>

    <managed-bean>
        <managed-bean-name>userList</managed-bean-name>
        <managed-bean-class>org.appfuse.web.UserList
            </managed-bean-class>
        <managed-bean-scope>request</managed-bean-scope>
        <managed-property>
            <property-name>userManager</property-name>
            <value>#{userManager}</value>
        </managed-property>
    </managed-bean>
</faces-config>
```

JSF is a web framework and doesn't provide an API for managing business logic or persistence logic. However, Spring has a **DelegatingVariableResolver** class that provides transparent dependency injection for JSF applications. In the *faces-config.xml* file, the **userManager** bean from *web/WEB-INF/applicationContext.xml* is set on the **UserList** class the same way you'd set it on a normal Spring-managed bean — by adding a **setUserManager()** method. See Listing 12.6.

Listing 11.6

```
<managed-property>
    <property-name>userManager</property-name>
    <value>#{userManager}</value>
</managed-property>
```

Unlike the other frameworks, JSF is really a *specification*, which is a set of rules and requirements for a *JSF implementation*. JSF implementations are the code that supports the JSF specification. At the time of this writing, two free JSF implementations are available:

- Sun's Reference Implementation, hosted at javaserverfaces.dev.java.net.
- Apache's MyFaces implementation, hosted at incubator.apache.org/myfaces.

INTEGRATING JSF WITH SPRING

The primary way to integrate your Spring beans with your JSF application is to use Spring's **DelegatingVariableResolver**. To configure this variable resolver for the Equinox-JSF application, open *web/WEB-INF/faces-context.xml*. After the opening **<faces-config>** element, add the **<application>** element in Listing 12.7.

Listing 11.7

```
<faces-config>
    <application>
        <variable-resolver>
            org.springframework.web.jsf.DelegatingVariableResolver
        </variable-resolver>
        <locale-config>
            <default-locale>en</default-locale>
            <supported-locale>en</supported-locale>
            <supported-locale>es</supported-locale>
        </locale-config>
        <message-bundle>messages</message-bundle>
    </application>
```

By specifying Spring's variable resolver, you can configure Spring beans as managed properties of your managed beans. The **DelegatingVariableResolver** will first delegate value lookups to the default resolver of the underlying JSF implementation and then to Spring's root `WebApplicationContext`. This allows you to easily inject dependencies into your JSF-managed beans.

Managed beans are defined in the *web/WEB-INF/faces-config.xml* file. Listing 12.8 is an example where `#{userManager}` is a bean that's retrieved from Spring's `Bean-Factory`.

Listing 11.8

```
<managed-bean>
    <managed-bean-name>userList</managed-bean-name>
    <managed-bean-class>org.appfuse.web.UserList</managed-bean-class>
    <managed-bean-scope>request</managed-bean-scope>
    <managed-property>
        <property-name>userManager</property-name>
        <value>#{userManager}</value>
    </managed-property>
</managed-bean>
```

The `DelegatingVariableResolver` is the recommended strategy for integrating JSF and Spring. However, you can also use the JSF-Spring project on SourceForge if you need more features. According to this project's home page, the latest release is compatible with JSF 1.1 and Spring 1.2.6.

A custom `VariableResolver` works well when mapping your properties to beans in *faces-config.xml*, but at times you may need to grab a bean explicitly. The `Faces-ContextUtils` class makes this easy. It's similar to `WebApplicationContex-tUtils` except that it takes a `FacesContext` parameter rather than a `ServletContext` parameter. See Listing 12.9.

Listing 11.9

```
ApplicationContext ctx =
        FacesContextUtils.getWebApplicationContext(
                        FacesContext.getCurrentInstance());
```

VIEW OPTIONS

JSP is the only view technology supported by JSF out of the box. However, it does have extension points for using other technologies to configure the UI. Hans Bergsten explains how to do this in his article "Improving JSF by Dumping JSP." Facelets is a technology that solves many of the problems that JSP has with JSF. Equinox 1.7 and AppFuse 1.9.4 both use Facelets instead of JSP in their JSF option.

For more information about the role of JSPs in JSF, see Kito Mann's article "Getting around JSF: The Role of JSP." To learn more about JSP in general, see Pro JSP, Third Edition (Apress), which I contributed to.

One of the nicest things about JSF is that it's an API designed for extension. Because it is a component-based framework, it encourages companies and developers to create and share components. See the following list of freely available JSF components:

- MyFaces Tomahawk Components (open source — Apache License)
- ICEfaces Community Edition (free — not open source)
- Oracle ADF Faces Components (donated to MyFaces; name changed to Trinidad)

JSF AND SPRING CRUD EXAMPLE

See *Appendix A: Examples and References* for a tutorial about creating a JSF application using Spring for its middle tier and Hibernate for the back end.

STRUTS

Struts is the *de facto* web framework for Java applications, mainly because it was one of the first to be released in June 2001. Invented by Craig McClanahan, Struts is an open-source project hosted by the Apache Software Foundation. It greatly simplified the JSP/servlet programming paradigm and won over many developers who were using proprietary frameworks. It simplified the programming model, it was open source, and it had a large community, which allowed the project to grow and become popular among Java web developers.

Figure 12.3 shows how Struts fits into a web application's architecture.

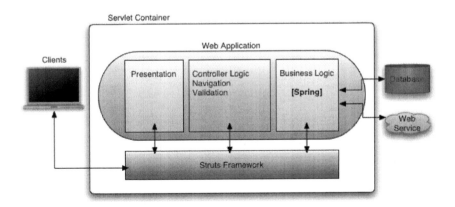

Figure 11.3: Struts with Spring

Struts doesn't have a lifecycle in its actions (also called *controllers*). That is, an action typically has a single point of entry, or a *method*, that's invoked by the framework. This is in sharp contrast to Spring MVC, particularly its `SimpleFormController`. Spring allows you to override a number of methods to control value binding, validation, and form processing on a per-form basis. With Struts, you must subclass `ActionServlet` or create a custom `RequestProcessor` to override this behavior.

However, five basic steps occur before and after that method invocation:

1 Populate `ActionForm`: Struts calls a `reset()` method for the `ActionForm` and populates it with request parameters for the specified `Action`. The `Action`-to-`ActionForm` mapping (also called action-mapping) is defined in an application's /*WEB-INF*/*struts-config.xml* file.

2 Process validations: If the action-mapping has `validate="true"`, the Struts validator first performs validation (if configured) and then calls the `validate()` method of the `ActionForm`. The `ActionForm` must subclass `ValidatorForm` for this process to work.

3 Create `Action`: The `ActionServlet` creates the action class mapped to the specified URL.

4 Invoke method: Struts invokes the `execute()` method for the `Action`. Struts has many `Action` classes you can subclass, so this method name may vary.

5 Forward to view: A Struts `Action` must return an `ActionForward`, which is a thin wrapper around a URL. An `ActionForward` is configured in the *struts-config.xml* file.

Figure 12.4 shows the lifecycle phases in a Struts application — from request to response.

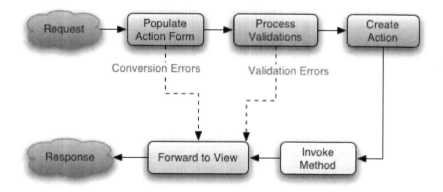

Figure 11.4: Struts lifecycle

Struts actions are typically multithreaded. That is, multiple clients will share class variables. For this reason, Struts advocates putting all your instance variables in methods. Using the Spring plug-in for Struts allows you to change this behavior and create new actions for each request.

The actions created in a Struts application are all subclasses of the Struts **Action** class. When extending **Action**, you must implement its **execute()** method, which uses the signature in Listing 12.10:

Listing 11.10

```
public ActionForward execute(ActionMapping mapping,
                             ActionForm form,
                             HttpServletRequest request,
                             HttpServletResponse response)
throws Exception;
```

In addition to the **Action** class, you can extend a number of other classes. The choice is usually based on your desired behavior. The following actions are the most common ones. Spring has subclasses for all of these classes to simplify Struts-Spring integration.

- **Action**: Displays data or processes a specific type of request.
- **DispatchAction**: Allows for more than one processing method, where the method name is indicated by a request parameter. Requires JavaScript for multiple buttons on a form.
- **LookupDispatchAction**: Similar to the **DispatchAction**, but maps **ResourceBundle** keys to method names. Good for forms with multiple buttons.
- **MappingDispatchAction**: Allows the method name to be specified in the action-mapping in *struts-config.xml*.

INTEGRATING STRUTS WITH SPRING

To integrate your Struts application with Spring, you have two options:

- Configure Spring to manage your actions as beans, using the **ContextLoaderPlugIn**, and set their dependencies in a Spring context file.
- Subclass Spring's **ActionSupport** classes and grab your Spring-managed beans explicitly using a **getWebApplicationContext()** method.

CONTEXTLOADERPLUGIN

The `ContextLoaderPlugin` is a Struts 1.1+ plug-in that loads a Spring context file for the Struts `ActionServlet`. This context refers to the root `WebApplication-Context` (loaded by the `ContextLoaderListener`) as its parent. The default name of the context file is the name of the mapped servlet plus *-servlet.xml*. If `ActionServlet` is defined in *web.xml* as `<servlet-name>action</servlet-name>`, the default is */WEB-INF/action-servlet.xml*.

To configure this plug-in, add the XML in Listing 12.11 to the plug-ins section near the bottom of the *struts-config.xml* file:

Listing 11.11

```
<plug-in
   className="org.springframework.web.struts.ContextLoaderPlugIn">
   <set-property property="contextConfigLocation"
      value="/WEB-INF/applicationContext-hibernate.xml,
             /WEB-INF/applicationContext.xml,
             /WEB-INF/action-servlet.xml"/>
</plug-in>
```

This example doesn't rely on the `ContextLoaderListener` to load the *application-Context-hibernate.xml* and *applicationContext.xml* files because `StrutsTestCase` doesn't initialize `<listener>` entries in *web.xml*. By specifying each context file in the plug-in, your `StrutsTestCase` tests will have access to all your Spring-managed beans.

CAUTION: The `StrutsTestCase` `ServletContextSimulator` does not support the `getResourcePaths()` method that Spring uses to load files with a wildcard, such as */WEB-INF/applicationContext*.xml*. You must explicitly set each context file if you plan on using StrutsTestCase to test your actions.

After configuring this plug-in in *struts-config.xml*, you can configure your action to be managed by Spring. Spring provides two ways to do this:

- Override the default `RequestProcessor` in Struts with Spring's `DelegatingRequestProcessor`.

- Use the `DelegatingActionProxy` class in the `type` attribute of your `<action-mapping>`.

Both of these methods allow you to manage your actions and their dependencies in the *action-context.xml* file. The bridge between the action in *struts-config.xml* and *action-servlet.xml* is built with the action-mapping's path and the bean's name. If you have the code in Listing 12.12 in your *struts-config.xml* file:

Listing 11.12

```
<action path="/users" .../>
```

You must define that action's bean with the **"/users"** name in *action-servlet.xml*. See Listing 12.13.

Listing 11.13

```
<bean name="/users" .../>
```

DELEGATINGREQUESTPROCESSOR

To configure the **DelegatingRequestProcessor** in your *struts-config.xml* file, override the **processorClass** property in the **<controller>** element. These lines follow the **<action-mapping>** element. See Listing 12.14.

Listing 11.14

```
<controller>
    <set-property property="processorClass"
        value="org.springframework.web.struts
            .DelegatingRequestProcessor"/>
</controller>
```

After adding this setting, your action will automatically be looked up in Spring's context file, no matter what the type. In fact, you don't even need to specify a type. The snippets in Listing 12.15 and Listing 12.16 will work:

Listing 11.15

```
<action path="/user" type="org.appfuse.web.UserAction"/>
```

Listing 11.16

```
<action path="/user"/>
```

If you're using the "modules" feature in Struts, your bean names must contain the module prefix. For example, an action defined as **<action path="/user"/>** with the module prefix **"admin"** requires a bean name with **<bean name="/admin/ user"/>**.

CAUTION: If you're using Tiles in your Struts application, you must configure your **<controller>** with the **DelegatingTilesRequestProcessor**.

DELEGATINGACTIONPROXY

If you have a custom **RequestProcessor** and can't use the **DelegatingTiles-Request-Processor**, you can use the **DelegatingActionProxy** as the **type** in your **action-mapping**. *Chapter 2: Spring Quick-Start Tutorial* used it as presented in Listing 12.17:

Listing 11.17

```
<action path="/user"
    type="org.springframework.web.struts.DelegatingActionProxy"
    name="userForm" scope="request" parameter="method"
    validate="false">
        <forward name="list" path="/userList.jsp"/>
        <forward name="edit" path="/userForm.jsp"/>
</action>
```

The bean definition in *action-servlet.xml* remains the same, whether you use a custom **RequestProcessor** or the **DelegatingActionProxy**.

Defining your action in a context file enables you to use Spring's IoC features, as well as instantiate new actions for each request. To use this feature, add **singleton="false"** to your action's bean definition. See Listing 12.18.

Listing 11.18

```
<bean name="/user" singleton="false" autowire="byName"
    class="org.appfuse.web.UserAction"/>
```

This allows you to put member variables in your class, since each user will get its own instance. The performance cost to create new instances is minimal, and many web frameworks, including JSF and WebWork, use this approach for their controllers.

If you don't want to maintain two XML files for your actions, use XDoclet to generate the XML for you, or use Spring's **ActionSupport** classes.

ACTIONSUPPORT CLASSES

As previously mentioned, you can retrieve the **WebApplicationContext** from the **ServletContext** using the **WebApplicationContextUtils** class. An easier way is to extend Spring's **Action** classes. For example, instead of subclassing the **Action** class in Struts, you can subclass Spring's **ActionSupport** class.

Spring's **ActionSupport** class provides additional convenience methods, like **getWebApplicationContext()**. Listing 12.19 is an example of how you might use this in an action:

Listing 11.19

```
public class UserAction extends DispatchActionSupport {

    public ActionForward execute(ActionMapping mapping,
                                 ActionForm form,
                                 HttpServletRequest request,
                                 HttpServletResponse response)
        throws Exception {
        if (log.isDebugEnabled()) {
            log.debug("entering 'delete' method...");
        }

        WebApplicationContext ctx = getWebApplicationContext();
        UserManager mgr = (UserManager) ctx.getBean("userManager");

        // talk to manager for business logic

        return mapping.findForward("success");
    }
}
```

Spring includes subclasses for all of the standard Struts actions — the Spring versions merely have *Support* appended to the name: **ActionSupport**, **DispatchActionSupport**, **LookupDispatchActionSupport**, and **MappingDispatchActionSupport**.

Use the approach that best suits your project. Subclassing makes your code more readable, and you know exactly how your dependencies are resolved. However, plug-ins allow you to easily add new dependencies in your context XML file. Either way, Spring provides some nice options for integrating the two frameworks.

VIEW OPTIONS

JavaServer Pages are the default view technology for Struts applications. However, other options are available. Velocity and its VelocityStruts subproject allow you to use Velocity templates as an alternative to JSP, or with JSPs in the same application. You can also use XML and XSLT. Two open-source projects exist to help make this easier: StrutsCX and Struts for Transforming XML with XSL (stxx). However, these projects haven't been maintained in quite some time, so use them with caution as there might not be a lot of support available.

STRUTS AND SPRING CRUD EXAMPLE

Please see *Chapter 2: Spring Quick-Start Tutorial* for a tutorial about creating a Struts application with Spring for its middle-tier and Hibernate for the back end. The tutorial in that chapter gives you a good idea of how to develop a Struts application with Spring.

TAPESTRY

Tapestry is a component-based framework for developing web applications. Unlike many Java web frameworks, Tapestry uses a component object model similar to traditional GUI frameworks. According to Howard Lewis Ship, the founder of Tapestry:

"A component is an object that fits into an overall framework; the responsibilities of the component are defined by the design and structure of the framework. A component is a component, and not simply an object, when it follows the rules of the framework. These rules can take the form of classes to inherit from, naming conventions (for classes or methods) to follow, or interfaces to implement. Components can be used within the context of the framework. The framework will act as a container for the component, controlling when the component is instantiated and initialized, and dictating when the methods of the component are invoked."[3]

Figure 12.5 shows how Tapestry fits into a web application's architecture:

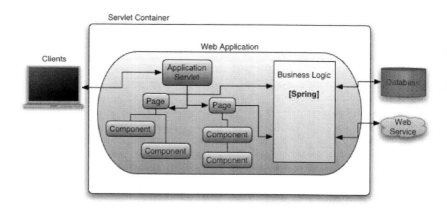

Figure 11.5: Tapestry with Spring

Tapestry's component model allows you to have a very high level of reuse within and between projects. You can package components in JAR files and distribute them among teams and developers.

Tapestry tries to hide the Servlet API from developers. In fact, learning Tapestry is often characterized as an "unlearning" process. GUI programmers typically have an

---

3. Lewis Ship, Howard. *Tapestry in Action.* Greenwich, CT: Manning Publications Co., 2004.

easier time adjusting to the way things work in Tapestry because it operates in terms of objects, methods, and properties rather than in URLs and query parameters. All of the URL building, page dispatching, and method invocation happens transparently.

Other benefits of Tapestry include line-precise error reporting and easy-to-use HTML templates. While other frameworks use external templating systems, Tapestry has its own templating system. Tapestry templates are often HTML files, but they can also be WML or XML. You can hook into these templates by using Tapestry-specific attributes on existing HTML elements.

About 90% of a template is regular HTML markup. This HTML has tags that work as placeholders for Tapestry components. These tags are recognized by a **jwcid** attribute. JWC is short for Java Web Component. Listing 12.20 is an example using the **Insert** component[4]:

Listing 11.20

```
<span jwcid="@Insert" value="ognl:user.name">Joe User</span>
```

This special template language allows you to edit HTML templates using a WYSIWYG HTML editor and to view them using a browser. Graphic designers and HTML developers can easily edit dynamic pages in your web application.

When you submit a form in Tapestry, the framework executes six basic steps:

1   Initialize **Page** class: Creates the **Page** class or retrieves it from a pool if it were already initialized. Tapestry sets all persistent page properties.

2   Invoke **pageBeginRender()** method: Invokes the **pageBeginRender()** method just before the page renders a response. This step allows you to set or initialize certain page properties.

3   Populate page properties: Populates the properties of the **Page** class based on expressions in the HTML template.

4   Invoke listener methods: Invokes the page's listener methods. It invokes a Submit component's listener method first, then the Form component's listener method. Submit components are usually buttons, but you can also use ImageSubmit and LinkSubmit to achieve similar functionality.

5   Activate next page: The developer activates the next page in the listener method.

---

4. A complete list of Tapestry components is available at tapestry.apache.org/tapestry3/doc/ ComponentReference/index.html.

6   Invoke **pageBeginRender** () method: Invokes the **pageBeginRender** () method after a successful render of the page. This step allows the objects to release any resources they needed during the render.

NOTE: A **pageEndRender** () method also exists, but it's rarely used. An empty implementation is provided for you.

Figure 12.6 illustrates the phases of a form submitted in Tapestry.

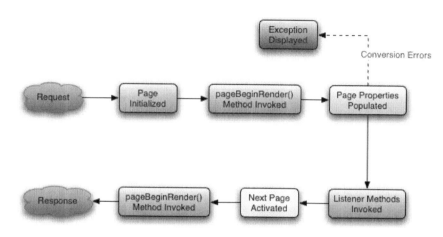

Figure 11.6: Tapestry lifecycle

Unlike a web framework that uses stateless servlets for controllers, Tapestry's page classes are stateful JavaBeans. For every page view in a Tapestry application, there is an associated page-specification XML file, an HTML template, and a Java class that extends **BasePage** (creating a Java class is optional). Constructing a new instance of a page requires a fair amount of work:

1   Load and parse the page specification.
2   Dynamically load and parse a subclass of the page.
3   Instantiate the page.
4   Locate, parse, extend, and instantiate each component of the page.
5   Read and apply the page's template to the page.
6   Components within templates must find their templates and parse/apply them.

All of this can require a lot of processing power; therefore, the page instances are gathered in a central page pool, much like a database connection pool. Each request gets its own page instance, which is cached for the duration of the request. This allows for a very efficient use of resources and fast page-loads in Tapestry applications.

INTEGRATING TAPESTRY WITH SPRING

Spring does not provide support for Tapestry as it does for JSF and Struts. However, there is a tapestry-spring project on JavaForge that provides easy integration. After including the *tapestry-spring.jar* in your classpath, you can use Tapestry's dependency injection feature.

The following steps show you how to expose a dependency in your page class and wire it up in a page-specification file.

1   In your page class, add an abstract **getter** for the Spring bean you want to access. See Listing 12.21.

Listing 11.21

```
package org.appfuse.web;

import org.appfuse.service.UserManager;

public abstract class UserList extends BasePage {
    public abstract UserManager getUserManager();
}
```

2   Wire the dependency in your page class using the syntax in Listing 12.22 in your page-specification file:

Listing 11.22

```
<inject property="userManager" type="spring" object="userManager"/>
```

If you're using Java 5 and Tapestry's annotation support, you can also use the **@InjectSpring** annotation to inject your dependencies.

See the *Tapestry and Spring CRUD example* section in *Appendix A: Examples and References* to learn how to inject Spring-managed beans into your page classes.

TIP: Hivemind is an IoC container much like Spring. Tapestry 4.x uses Hivemind to wire together its internal services.

VIEW OPTIONS

Tapestry does not have any alternative templating engines. However, it does support XML and WML from its templates.

TAPESTRY AND SPRING CRUD EXAMPLE

Please see *Appendix A: Examples and References* for a tutorial about creating a Tapestry application that uses Spring for the middle tier and Hibernate for the back end.

WEBWORK

WebWork is a web framework designed with simplicity in mind. It's built on top of XWork, which is a generic command framework. XWork also has an IoC container, but it isn't as full-featured as Spring and won't be covered in this section. As of WebWork 2.2, Spring was changed to be the default IoC container for WebWork. WebWork controllers are called *actions*, mainly because they must implement the **Action** interface. The **ActionSupport** class implements this interface, and it is the most common parent class for WebWork actions.

NOTE: WebWork was recently merged with Struts to become Struts 2. The first release of this project was on September 27, 2006.

Figure 12.7 shows how WebWork fits into a web application's architecture.

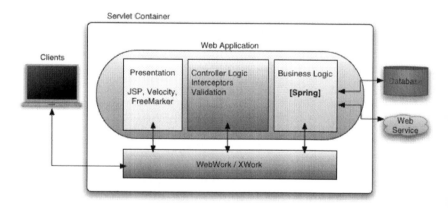

Figure 11.7: WebWork with Spring

WebWork actions typically contain methods for accessing model properties and methods for returning strings. These strings are matched with "result" names in an *xwork.xml* configuration file.

The actions you develop in a WebWork application look similar to the ones you develop in a JSF application. Actions typically have a single **execute()** method, but you can easily add multiple methods and control execution on a URL basis.

Listing 12.23 is a simple action example and its associated configuration in *xwork.xml*.

Listing 11.23

```
public class UserAction extends ActionSupport {
    private UserManager mgr = null;
    private List users;

    public void setUserManager(UserManager userManager) {
        this.mgr = userManager;
    }

    public List getUsers() {
        return users;
    }

    public String execute() {
        users = mgr.getUsers();
        return SUCCESS;
    }
}

<action name="users" class="org.appfuse.web.UserAction">
    <result name="success" type="dispatcher">userList.jsp
        </result>
</action>
```

Much like the Spring MVC, WebWork uses *interceptors* to intercept the request and response process. This is much like servlet filters, except you can talk directly to the action. WebWork uses interceptors in the framework itself. A number of them initialize the action, prepare it for population, set parameters on it, and handle any conversion errors. Listing 12.24 is the default stack of interceptors for each request:

Listing 11.24

```
<interceptor-stack name="defaultStack">
    <interceptor-ref name="servlet-config"/>
    <interceptor-ref name="prepare"/>
    <interceptor-ref name="static-params"/>
    <interceptor-ref name="params"/>
    <interceptor-ref name="conversionError"/>
</interceptor-stack>
```

These interceptors are a part of every request and help to define WebWork's life-cycle. You can override the list above on a per-action basis. When you submit a form, it usually configures validation, routes the user, and shows errors (workflow).

Two interceptors take care of this: `ValidationInterceptor` and `DefaultWork-FlowInterceptor`. The WebWork's lifecycle has seven steps:

1 Configure and prepare: Prepares null values for population; reads configuration for `Action` class.

2 Create action: Creates the `Action` class (one per request).

3 Set parameters and populate action: Converts request parameters into meaningful values in the `ValueStack` and sets properties on the `Action` class.

4 Convert types: Converts strings into the object types specified on the `Action`. If errors occur, it forwards to the inputting page.

5 Process validations: If the `Action` has validation rules defined, it processes them. If errors occur, it forwards to the inputting page.

6 Invoke method: Invokes the `execute()` method or otherwise specified method.

7 Forward to view: Forwards to a JSP, Velocity, or FreeMarker view.

Figure 12.8 shows the phases in a WebWork application, from request to response.

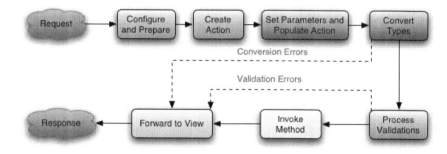

Figure 11.8: WebWork lifecycle

INTEGRATING WEBWORK WITH SPRING

Making WebWork aware of Spring is simply a matter of configuring your *webwork.properties* file (located in *WEB-INF/classes*) with the entry in Listing 12.25.

Listing 11.25

```
webwork.objectFactory=spring
```

By default, this uses autowire by name, but you can change it to autowire by the other supported strategies: type, auto, or constructor. Once you've configured

WebWork to use Spring for dependency injection, you can wire up your actions using the following steps:

1   Configure your WebWork action in a Spring context file (for example, *WEB-INF/action-servlet.xml*). The name of this file doesn't matter; it just needs to be loaded by the `ContextLoaderListener`. Wire your dependencies like you normally would with Spring. See Listing 12.26.

Listing 11.26

```
<bean id="userAction" class="org.appfuse.web.UserAction"
    singleton="false">
    <property name="userManager" ref="userManager"/>
</bean>
```

2   In *xwork.xml*, change the class attribute of your action to match the bean's `id` (using the bean's **name** attribute will also work). See Listing 12.27.

Listing 11.27

```
<action name="users" class="userAction" method="list">
    <result name="success">userList.jsp</result>
</action>
```

This technique also allows you to configure interceptors in Spring.

VIEW OPTIONS

WebWork supports FreeMarker, JSP, JasperReports, Tiles, Velocity, and JSF as view technologies. Yes, that's right — I said JSF. Don Brown has an explanation of how Struts 2 will support JSF on his blog. For more information about configuring and using these technologies, please see WebWork's Tutorials or Struts 2 Tutorials. For a history of Struts 2 and how it came to be, see Don Brown's blog entry "My History of Struts 2"[5].

A unique feature of WebWork's JSP tags is they use FreeMarker templates for constructing the HTML. This makes it very easy to change the default HTML produced by the tags. AppFuse has examples of this in its WebWork version, in the *web/template* directory.

---

5. oreillynet.com/onjava/blog/2006/10/my_history_of_struts_2.html

WebWork and Spring CRUD example

Please see *Appendix A: Examples and References* for a tutorial about creating a WebWork application that uses Spring for the middle tier and Hibernate for the back end.

FRAMEWORK COMPARISON

Now that you've seen how to integrate Spring with JSF, Struts, Tapestry, and WebWork, you must choose one. Choosing a web framework is often a personal choice based on your production needs or experience. Table features the strengths and weaknesses of each framework. This information is based on my experience of working with each one. Note that I'm a long-time Struts developer, so I may be a bit biased.

Table 11.1: Frameworks: Their Strengths and Weaknesses

Framework	Strengths	Weaknesses
Struts	• Longevity — One of the first and still the most widely used. • Good documentation and lots of books/ examples. • Full-featured JSP Tag Library for working with forms. • `StrutsTestCase` makes integration tests easy.	• `ActionForms` — All other frameworks allow direct communication with model objects. • Difficult to isolate actions for true unit testing.
JSF	• Standard web framework for J2EE, which will gather the backing of many vendors. • A view-based framework and not necessarily tied to HTML. • Fast and easy to develop with if you're familiar with Struts and JSP.	• Very new and still a bit immature, especially when used with JSP. • "Tag soup" - Many JSPs don't contain a single line of HTML. • Writing HTML in components/Java seems like a step backward.

Table 11.1: Frameworks: Their Strengths and Weaknesses

Framework	Strengths	Weaknesses
JSF	• Easy to integrate and use navigation feature. • Component-based framework, which leads to high reusability between projects.	• Too focused on tools vendors rather than on developers.
Spring MVC	• Has a lifecycle that allows easy overriding of controller behavior. • JSP tags allow full control over HTML. • Wizard-type form support is built in. • Supports interceptors and uses IoC. • Supports the most view options. • Easy integration with Spring middle tier.	• JSP tags require more lines of code for input controls. • Not as popular as the other frameworks (but growing).
Tapestry	• HTML templates support WYSIWYG and allow designers to easily interact with developers. • API will be familiar to GUI programmers. • Component-based framework, which leads to high reusability between projects.	• Has an "unlearning" curve for those who are familiar with the Servlet API. • URLs are convoluted by default.

Table 11.1: Frameworks: Their Strengths and Weaknesses

Framework	Strengths	Weaknesses
WebWork	• Simple yet powerful framework. • Interceptors are powerful for managing common aspects. • JSP Tag Library allows you to customize generated HTML. • Good support for Velocity, FreeMarker, and JSP.	• Documentation is poorly organized.[a] • Client-side validation is immature.

a. In the past, WebWork's documentation has been sparse at best. However, WebWork in Action (Manning) solves part of this problem.

FEATURE COMPARISON

A number of small features are nice to have in a web framework when you are developing applications. They are listed in Table , which includes a description of how each framework handles them.

Table 11.2: Feature Comparison

Feature	Framework	Supported?
Sortable/pageable list of data A framework should allow you to easily integrate a component to sort and page through a list of data.	Struts	JSP-based — You can use the Display Tag, the Value List Tag, or the Data Grid Tag.
	JSF	JSP-based — Many tag libraries available. A built-in `dataTable` component does not have sorting out of the box.
	Spring	JSP-based — Many tag libraries available.
	Tapestry	`contrib:Table` component provides this functionality.
	WebWork	JSP-based — Many tag libraries available.

Table 11.2: Feature Comparison

Feature	Framework	Supported?
Bookmarkability Bookmarkability is the ability for users to bookmark pages in your application and get back to them easily. Full controls means that a URL (such as http://company/ 401k.html?id=foo) can be easily sent to co-workers in email messages, and they can click on it to edit a user's record:	Struts	Full control over URLs — You can easily create URLs to edit/ view records.
	JSF	Often, everything is **POST** — sending a post twice results in different behavior each time.
	Spring	Full control over URLs — You can easily create URLs to edit/ view records.
	Tapestry	Can't control URLs — They tend to be quite lengthy and ugly. **Note:** You can use the **URLRewriteFilter** to "pretty up" ugly URLs.
	WebWork	Full control over URLs — You can easily create URLs to edit/ view records.
Easy canceling and multi-button form handling A framework should allow you to easily cancel an operation and return to the previous screen. There should be a way to detect the cancel button has been clicked and cancel validation or any other relevant operations.	Struts	Has an `<html:cancel>` button and means to cancel client-side validation with `onclick` handler (all frameworks allow this).
	JSF	Easy-to-use navigation rules allow you to route cancel actions to other pages.
	Spring	You can override the `processFormSubmission()` method to cancel submit or use `CancellableFormController`.
	Tapestry	You can add a `cancel` listener and easily map a button to it.
	WebWork	You have to handle logic in a method that's called by the form submit.

Table 11.2: Feature Comparison

Feature	Framework	Supported?
Easy testability A framework should give you the ability to test your controllers out of a servlet container quickly and efficiently.	Struts	`StrutsTestCase` and its `MockStrutsTestCase` make this easy.
	JSF	Easiest to test because managed beans are tied to the Servlet API. Mocking dependent objects is easy.
	Spring	Easy because of *spring-mock.jar* for the Servlet API. This library is also useful when testing other frameworks.
	Tapestry	Least amount of support and examples for testing controller (page) classes.
	WebWork	Easiest to test since actions are tied to the Servlet API. Mocking dependent objects is easy.

Table 11.2: Feature Comparison

Feature	Framework	Supported?
Success messages Displaying success messages is an important usability feature in web applications. Users like to know what happened, and a success message is a good way to confirm that an operation succeeded. It's also important to try to eliminate duplicate posts in your application. A duplicate post can happen when a user submits a form and then refreshes the browser on the next page. If you simply forwarded to the next page, and the user was adding a record, the refresh would add an additional record. There are ways to prevent this with tokens and session variables, but the easiest way is to do a redirect after the post. In order for success messages to live through the redirect, you have to somehow pass the messages to the next screen in a URL or in the session.	Struts	Has the best API for setting and retrieving success messages. You can use the **addMessage()** method in any **Action** parent class and the **<html:messages>** to retrieve them. You can stuff them into the session, and the JSP tag will automatically remove them for you.
	JSF	Has a mechanism for setting success messages, but they won't live through a redirect, and it's difficult to get the application's **ResourceBundle** in a managed-bean. Internationalization in JSF could use some improvement — the other frameworks are much better in this regard.
	Spring	Allows you to pass a model object as part of a redirect, so you could put your messages into that.
	Tapestry	Doesn't have anything, though it's pretty easy to implement by adding **set/getMessages** to a common parent page class. Strangely, Tapestry requires you to throw exceptions to redirect.
	WebWork	Has a similar facility to Struts, but messages won't live through a redirect, forcing you to implement your own "stuff in and get from session" logic.

Table 11.2: Feature Comparison

Feature	Framework	Supported?
Validation It's important that users get easy-to-read feedback when they enter an incorrect value. A robust client-side validation implementation will allow low-bandwidth users to use your application more easily.	Struts	Supports Commons Validator, which requires you to define all validation messages. Gives you full control over errors displayed. Client-side validation is one of the best (part of Commons Validator).
	JSF	As of 1.1, default validation messages are very "programmerish." Can be customized, but it doesn't allow you to use labels in messages (will be fixed in 1.2).
	Spring	Supports Commons Validator and creating custom validators. Both require you to define all validation messages. Gives you full control over errors that are displayed. Client-side validation good if using Commons Validator.
	Tapestry	Easily extensible validation framework with defaults for built-in validation rules. Client-side validation is good, but it puts JavaScript functions into page versus an external file).
	WebWork	Supports OGNL expressions in validation rules, which can be very powerful. Client-side validation is new and evolving.

All of the frameworks covered in Table are mature projects that make developing web applications easier. It is hard to say whether one is significantly better than the rest. Your choice may rest on your enthusiasm to develop with a certain framework. You may want to ask yourself, "Which one do I want to learn?"

TIPS AND TRICKS
∎∎∎

There are things you can do to make developing web applications easier. Here are a few of them:

- Use a page decoration tool such as SiteMesh or Tiles. These will allow you to control the layout of your application with a single file. Coupled with CSS, they make life *much* easier. When customers want to change something with the layout (which they often will), it's only a matter of changing a couple of files.

- Use extension-based mapping. Path-based mapping such as */faces/* and */do/* are good, but a lot of stat-tracking engines won't pick those up, so extensions seem to work better.

- Use a generic extension mapping, such as *.html*. There's no reason to advertise the underlying technology that powers your site. It also allows you to easily switch web frameworks and keep your URLs intact. The **UrlRewriteFilter** can help translate old URLs to new ones.

- Use servlet filters. The more logic you can put into filters, the less dependent you'll be on your web framework.

- Learn a new web framework this year. You will be a better developer and gain insight into how things are handled by the other framework. Many features in web frameworks today are borrowed from each other. Learning how your competition operates keeps your web framework competitive.

RECOMMENDED READING
∎∎∎

- *Core JavaServer Faces* by David Geary and Cay Horstmann
- *JavaServer Faces in Action* by Kito Mann
- *Struts Live* by Jonathan Lehr and Rick Hightower
- *Struts in Action* by Ted Husted and team
- *Tapestry in Action* by Howard Lewis Ship
- *WebWork in Action* by Patrick Lightbody and Jason Carreira

SUMMARY
∎∎∎

JSF allows you to inject dependencies with its managed-properties, much like Spring does. This is a technology to watch, especially since so many large companies are jumping on board and providing tools. Struts continues to be one of the most popular web frameworks. It has many tools available, lots of examples, and a plethora of documentation. It's unlikely that Struts will go away anytime soon, particular since WebWork has recently joined the project as Struts 2. Tapestry is a nice component-based framework that contains many of the promises of JSF. Its HTML templates are easy for page designers to use, and it has a vibrant community that is willing to help with any issues. WebWork is a simple framework that allows you to do powerful things. Its interceptors let you to manage and control actions in an AOP-fashion, allowing your actions to be very simple and lightweight. WebWork becoming Struts Action 2 will have a huge impact, not only because of the Struts brand, but also because it has recently added support for JSF.

This chapter showed you how to integrate Spring with the popular Java web frameworks. It also provided the strengths and weaknesses of each framework and compared how they support common web application features. Examples for implementing Spring with each framework are provided in *Appendix A: Examples and References* or previous chapters.

Most important, the overviews and examples in this chapter were designed to show how Spring is all about choice. It doesn't tie you to a specific web framework. Spring tries to be nonintrusive in general, and this is another great example of how it gives the developer more choices.

# Chapter 12

SECURITY

· ·

Securing Spring applications with J2EE and Acegi Security

> *This chapter covers how you can configure authentication and authorization using traditional J2EE (container-managed) security and the Acegi Security framework for Spring. It also shows how you can use Acegi Security to protect and prevent method invocations on Spring-managed beans and configure Access Control Lists (ACLs).*

OVERVIEW
· ·

A web application lives a hazardous existence on the Internet. You must always be sure to protect your resources from the vulnerable, open, and sometimes dangerous superhighway. In such an exposed environment, most web applications have security requirements, such as encrypting passwords or protecting certain pages from unauthorized viewing. You secure your applications by using two very important security measures: *authentication* and *authorization*.

Authentication is the process by which a web application verifies that you are who you say you are (for example, a user who logs in to a web page must enter a user name and password). The web application validates the entered credentials against its user data store, and the login succeeds or fails.

Authorization is the process by which a web application verifies that you are allowed to execute a certain action (for example, to delete a user from the database, you must be an administrator).

In this chapter, you'll use J2EE container-managed authentication to configure authentication and authorization. In the second half of the chapter, you'll use the Acegi Security framework for Spring to mimic all of the security services provided by J2EE.

The exercises in this chapter will show you how to configure authentication that reads user credentials from XML, a database, LDAP, and a Windows domain. To follow along with the exercises, download the **Equinox Chapter 12** project from sourcebeat.com/downloads.

This project is based on Equinox 1.7 with the web and persistence framework installers removed. The download uses Spring MVC and Hibernate (the most popular configuration). For more information about configuring this project, see its README.txt in the root directory.

These exercises have a couple of caveats:

- There's no way to log out. If you redeploy your application with a different authentication mechanism, you aren't prompted to log in again because Tomcat remembers you logged in (often with a cookie) and doesn't prompt you again. To make the browser prompt you to log in again, close all your browser windows (you'll need to quit the application on Mac OS X) and then launch the browser again. You will learn how to add a logout feature as part of this chapter.

- Tomcat will cache the security settings in *web.xml*. Reloading the application will not cause configuration changes in this file to take effect. You'll need to start/stop Tomcat (rather than simply reloading the application) for new security settings to take effect.

J2EE AUTHENTICATION

Container-managed authentication, also known as *declarative security*, involves changing your *web.xml* file to control authentication and authorization, which means you can keep your application's security configuration separate from your code. It also makes your application more portable across application servers and makes it easier for a deployer (versus a developer) to change it.

All configuration settings in your *web.xml* file relate to the root directory of your web application. They do not include your application's context path.

Using container-managed security in a web application is easy; you simply add some XML to your *web.xml* file. To see how simply you can do it, add the lines in Listing 13.1 to the bottom of the *src/main/webapp/web.xml* file (of this chapter's download) to protect the entire application.

Listing 12.1

```
<security-constraint>
    <web-resource-collection>
        <web-resource-name>Secure Area</web-resource-name>
        <url-pattern>/*</url-pattern>
    </web-resource-collection>

    <auth-constraint>
        <role-name>*</role-name>
```

```
        </auth-constraint>
    </security-constraint>

    <login-config>
        <auth-method>BASIC</auth-method>
        <realm-name>Protected Area</realm-name>
    </login-config>
```

This simple example allows all roles in your realm. To add roles by name, add the
<security-role> element in Listing 13.2 after **</login-config>**.

Listing 12.2

```
    <security-role>
        <role-name>ROLE_NAME</role-name>
    </security-role>
```

To add multiple roles (instead of all roles), define multiple **<role-name>** elements
in the **<auth-constraint>** element. See Listing 13.3.

Listing 12.3

```
    <auth-constraint>
        <role-name>administrator</role-name>
        <role-name>user</role-name>
    </auth-constraint>
```

To see how these settings secure the *equinox-security* application, run **ant deploy**,
start Tomcat, and navigate to localhost:8080/equinox-security. A login dialog box
similar to the one in Figure 13.1 should display.

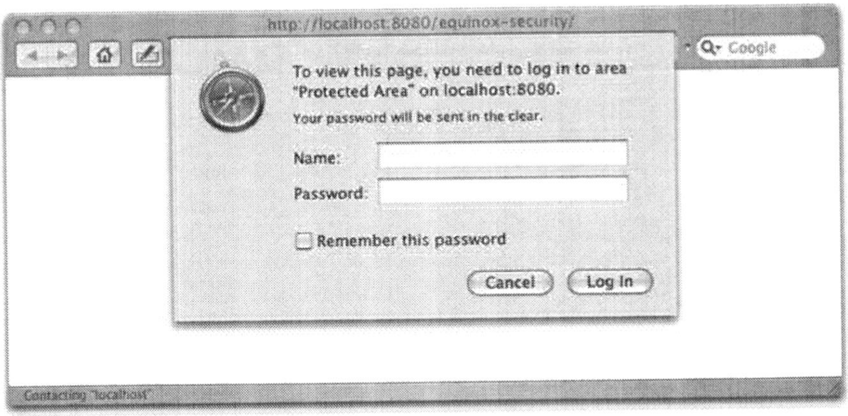

Figure 12.1: Basic login prompt

Because all roles can log in to this application (with `<role-name>*</role-name>`), use one of the default Tomcat users to log in (user name **tomcat** and password **tomcat**). These default users for Tomcat are configured in *$CATALINA_HOME/conf/tomcat-users.xml*.

After configuring container-managed security — if you need to do programmatic security — you can use the helpful security methods in the `HttpServletRequest` interface:

- `getRemoteUser()`: This method returns the authenticated user's login name or null if no authenticated user exists.

- `isUserInRole(String roleName)`: This method determines a role's authorization to certain resources.

- `getUserPrincipal()`: This method returns a `java.security.Principal` object that contains the name of the current authenticated user.

This section covers the following security topics:

- Authentication options
- Configuring Tomcat realms
- Using the Secure Sockets Layer (SSL)
- Java Authentication and Authorization Service (JAAS)
- Security alternatives

For more information about J2EE security, refer to the J2EE 1.4 Tutorial.

AUTHENTICATION OPTIONS

You can configure authentication for a Java web application in a number of ways. These options are configurable with a setting in your *web.xml* file, simplifying switching from one form to another. In the previous example, you used `<auth-method>BASIC</auth-method>` to indicate HTTP Basic authentication. The following list illustrates several other authentication methods.

- HTTP Basic authentication: `<auth-method>BASIC</auth-method>`
- HTTP Digest authentication: `<auth-method>DIGEST</auth-method>`
- HTTPS client authentication: `<auth-method>CLIENT-CERT</auth-method>`
- Form-based authentication: `<auth-method>FORM</auth-method>`

HTTP BASIC AUTHENTICATION

When using HTTP Basic authentication, the server will authenticate a user with a user name and password from the client. Typically, the client is a web browser, which sends the user name and password in the request as an authorization header. This header has an authentication scheme of **Basic** and includes Base-64 encoded **username:password** token. For example, when you authenticated with user name **tomcat** and password **tomcat** in the previous example, your browser sent the following header to the server:

```
Authorization: Basic dG9tY2F0OnRvbWNhdA==
```

TIP: **LiveHTTPHeaders** is a plug-in for Mozilla-based browsers that examines headers as they are sent and received. You can download it at livehttpheaders.moz-dev.org.

Figure 13.2 shows the negotiation process of an HTTP client and server when performing HTTP Basic authentication.

CAUTION: The password in this authentication mechanism is not encrypted. A password sniffer can read it very easily.

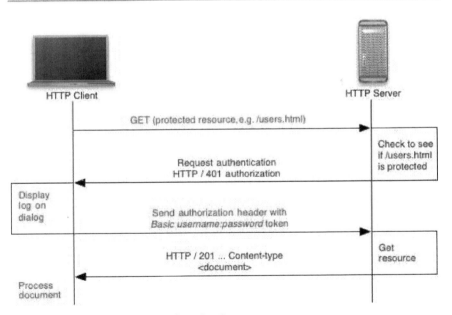

Figure 12.2: HTTP Basic authentication

> **NOTE:** For detailed information about HTTP Basic authentication, see the specification it's based on RFC 1945, Section 11.1.

HTTP Basic authentication does not authenticate the target server; therefore, this is not a secure mechanism. The client has no proof that the server is trustworthy. For a server to prove its identity, it must obtain a Secure Sockets Layer (SSL) certificate from a certificate authority (such as VeriSign). If you need greater security but still wish to use HTTP Basic authentication, you can combine it with SSL or a Virtual Private Network (VPN).

HTTP DIGEST AUTHENTICATION

HTTP Digest authentication also authenticates a user based on a user name and password. However, the client transmits the password in an encrypted form, such as Secure Hash Algorithm (SHA) or Message-Digest algorithm 5 (MD5). In the web arena, HTTP 1.1-enabled browsers will support this. Of the major application servers, Tomcat, JBoss, and Resin support this authentication method. HTTP Digest authentication prompts the user with a user name/password dialog box, which looks similar to the HTTP Basic authentication dialog box. However, the HTTP Digest authentication dialog box indicates that you are accessing a secure site.

To try this in the *equinox-security* application you downloaded, change the **<auth-method>** in *web/web.xml* to **DIGEST**, as in Listing 13.4:

Listing 12.4

```
<login-config>
    <auth-method>DIGEST</auth-method>
    <realm-name>Protected Area</realm-name>
</login-config>
```

Run **ant deploy**, restart Tomcat, and point your browser to localhost:8080/equinox-security. You should see a dialog box similar to the one in Figure 13.3.

> **NOTE:** Most browsers display the same dialog box for basic and digest authentication. However, Internet Explorer for Windows uses a different dialog box that indicates a more secure authentication mechanism is being used.

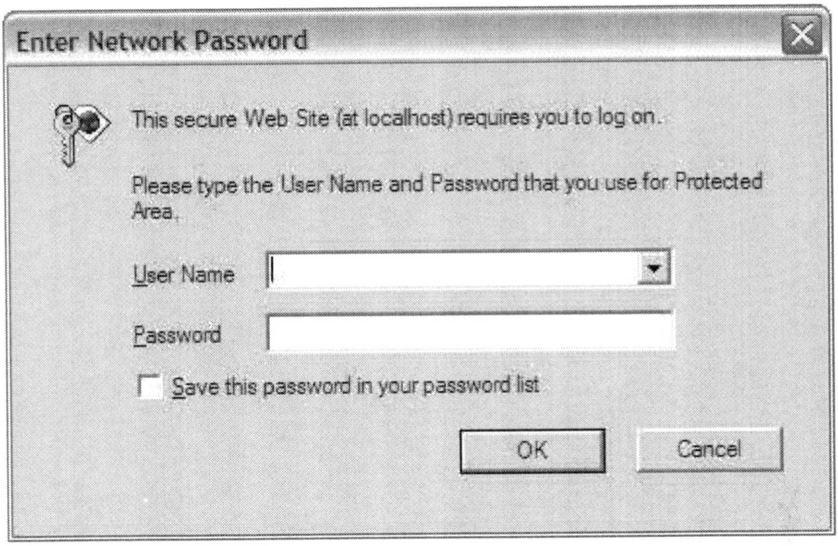

Figure 12.3: Digest login dialog box in Internet Explorer

With HTTP Digest authentication, the authorization header contains more information and the password is encrypted:

```
Authorization: Digest username="tomcat", realm="Protected Area",
    nonce="935d7777d258321c0447286691d44a61",
    uri="/equinox-security/",
    response="88196a77de6948312810f963ff3d3fe8",
    opaque="fcfb979b1cbc533dfacc6d71a843db79",
    qop=auth, nc=00000001, cnonce="01b6730aae57c007"
```

HTTPS CLIENT AUTHENTICATION

HTTPS client authentication requires the user to possess a *public key certificate* (PKC).
It is based on HTTP over SSL — hence, the name HTTPS. To access pages that are
secured with this mechanism, users need to apply for, receive, and install a certificate onto their browsers. This certificate verifies the browser's identity and often
prompts users for a password, even if the certificate is present. PKCs are useful in
applications with strict security requirements and for single sign-on from within the
browser. For servlet containers to be J2EE-compliant, they must support the
HTTPS protocol.

This chapter does not cover the setup and configuration for HTTPS client authentication because it's related to server configuration more so than application configuration and development. The J2EE 1.4 tutorial covers how to configure your server
in the "Understanding Digital Certificates" section.

FORM-BASED AUTHENTICATION

Form-based authentication is the most common choice in web applications because it allows the web designer to customize the look and feel of the login screen. It allows for simple instructions on the login screen and usability features, such as password hints and help links.

IMPLEMENTING FORM-BASED AUTHENTICATION

To understand how form-based authentication works, look at the five main steps in Figure 13.4 that occur during a successful login:

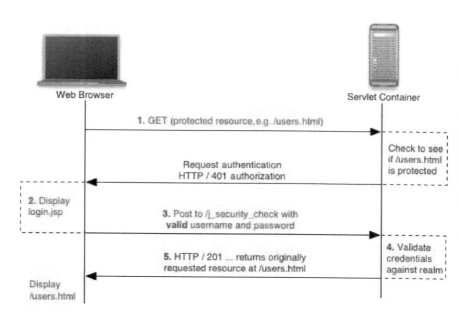

Figure 12.4: Sequence of events with successful form-based authentication

1   A user requests a protected resource (as defined in *web.xml*) by clicking on a link, selecting a bookmark, or typing in a URL.

2   The container sends the login form associated with this protected resource to the client, and the container stores the URL that the user tried to access. That is, the container remembers the fact that the client originally requested the */users.html* URL.

3   The user fills out the form with a user name and password and submits it.

4   The container attempts to authenticate the user with the supplied user name/password combination.

5   If authentication succeeds, the container sends the client to the resource using the stored URL.

This authentication mechanism resembles HTTP Basic authentication, so when authentication fails, it returns an HTTP status code of 401, which means: "This resource requires HTTP authentication." Therefore, your deployment descriptor contains entries for a login form and an error page; the error page displays upon encountering a 401 error. This process, as shown in Figure 13.5, involves the same steps as in Figure 13.4, except step 5 returns a 401 error code and the container returns the configured form-error page.

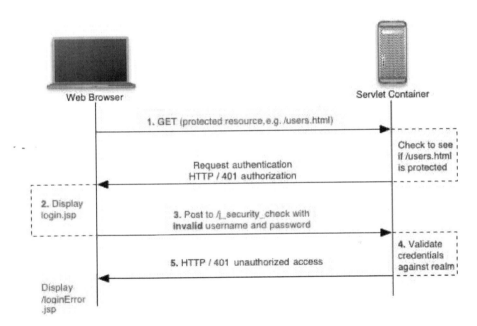

Figure 12.5: Sequence of events with failed form-based authentication

To implement form-based authentication, you need a page with a form. The only specification requirements are that your form's action is **j_security_check** and your user name and password fields are named **j_username** and **j_password**.

1   Create a *login.jsp* page in the *webapp* directory of the *equinox-security* application. Put the code in Listing 13.5 into the page:

Listing 12.5

```
<form id="loginForm" method="post" action="j_security_check">
<p>
    <label for="username">Username</label><br/>
    <input id="username" type="text" name="j_username"/><br/>
```

```
        <label for="password">Password</label><br/>
        <input id="password" type="password" name="j_password"/><br/><br/>

        <button type="submit" class="button">Login</button>
    </p>
</form>
```

2   Create a *loginError.jsp* page in the same directory and put the code in Listing 13.6 into it.

Listing 12.6

```
<p>
    Login failed - please <a href="index.jsp">try again</a>.
</p>
```

3   Change the `<login-config>` element in *webapp/WEB-INF/web.xml* using the format in Listing 13.7.

Listing 12.7

```
<login-config>
    <auth-method>FORM</auth-method>
    <form-login-config>
        <form-login-page>/login.jsp</form-login-page>
        <form-error-page>/loginError.jsp</form-error-page>
    </form-login-config>
</login-config>
```

4   Run **ant deploy**, restart Tomcat, and go to localhost:8080/equinox-security. You should see a window similar to the one in Figure 13.6, prompting you to log in with the form you just created:

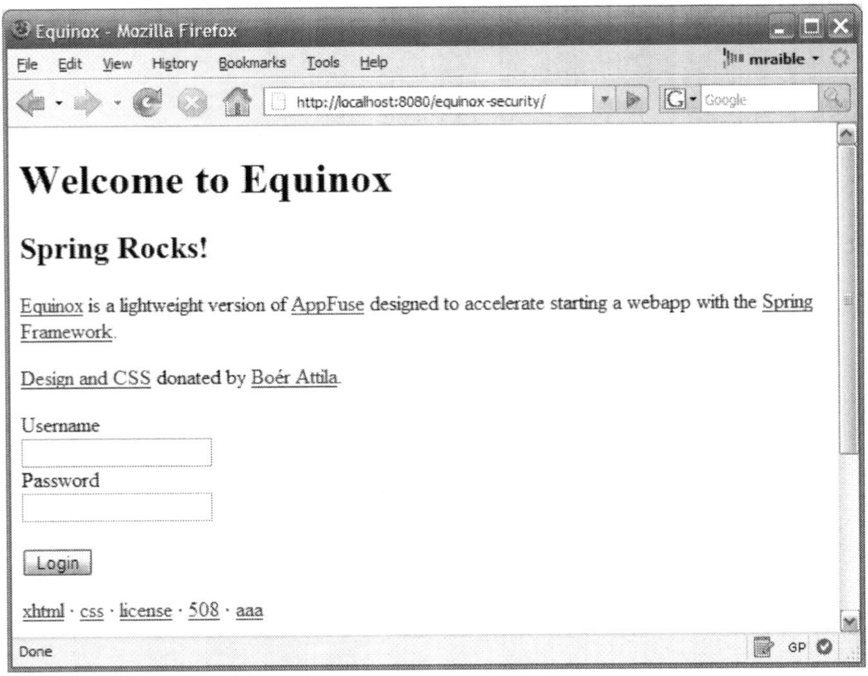

Figure 12.6: Undecorated login form

NOTE: Notice that SiteMesh does not appear to be decorating the page. However, the full HTML is there. The style sheets are protected by `<url-pattern>/*</url-pattern>`, and you need to log in to see them.

Logging in with user name **tomcat** and password **tomcat** gets you one of the CSS or JavaScript files. To fix this issue, change the protected URLs (in *webapp/WEB-INF/web.xml*) to protect only controllers (**.html*) and JSPs (**.jsp*). See Listing 13.8.

Listing 12.8

```
<web-resource-collection>
    <web-resource-name>Secure Area</web-resource-name>
    <url-pattern>*.html</url-pattern>
    <url-pattern>*.jsp</url-pattern>
</web-resource-collection>
```

CAUTION: Although the configuration in Listing 13.8 works on Tomcat, it might not work on all application servers because the `*.jsp <url-pattern>` might prevent users from accessing the *login.jsp* page. You might need to adjust the `<url-pattern>` accordingly.

5   Run **ant deploy** and restart Tomcat. You should see a decorated form similar to the one in Figure 13.7. Logging in will display the welcome page.

NOTE: Behavior can be different on different versions of Tomcat. For example, in 4.1.x and 5.0.x, Tomcat allows you to use `<role-name>*</role-name>` with no `<security-role>` elements defined. However, Tomcat 5.5.x requires you specify a `role-name` as well as a matching `security-role`.

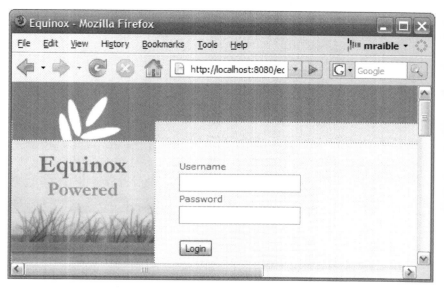

Figure 12.7: Decorated login form

Once you have successfully logged in, the server creates an **HttpSession** for you or matches up with an existing session. This session is active for the duration of the `<session-timeout>` value specified in the *web.xml*. This value determines how long the server retains a user's session between interactions. Thus, if a user clicks a link or somehow sends a request to your application, the server recalculates how long it will wait to expire the session. Once this session expires or is killed by a reboot of the application server, users will be required to log in again. The default is 30 minutes. Some application servers are able to persist sessions to the file system (or a database); therefore, a session can live through a reboot (provided it hasn't timed out).

LOGGING OUT

Currently, it is not possible to configure logout declaratively. Developers usually accomplish logout with one of the following methods:

- Using a JSP or servlet that calls **session.invalidate()** or **session.logout()**
- Placing a link on a page that calls *logout.jsp* or a servlet/controller
- Closing the browser
- Exceeding the minutes of inactivity specified by the session-timeout parameter

---

TIP: It's important that your logout URL is not a protected resource. If it is and a user tries to access it after the session times out, the user needs to log in to log out!

The **HttpSession.logout()** method is new in the Servlet 2.4 specification. This method logs the client out of the web server and invalidates all sessions associated with this client. The scope of the logout is the same as the scope of the authentication. For example, if the servlet container implements single sign-on, the logout logs the client out of all web applications on the servlet container and invalidates all sessions associated with the same client.

To add a logout feature to this chapter's application, perform the following steps:

1   Create a *logout.jsp* page in the *webapp* directory. (Using **session.logout()** in the code results in an error.) See Listing 13.9.

Listing 12.9

```
<% session.invalidate(); %>
<p>
    You have successfully logged out.
    <a href="index.jsp">Login</a> again.
</p>
```

NOTE: This listing violates the "don't protect the logout page" tip; however, I recommend that you protect your controllers and not your JSPs in order to have dynamic resources that any user can access.

---

2   Add a link to the *webapp/decorators/default.jsp* page so authenticated users can click it to log out. Put the HTML in Listing 13.10 directly after the opening **<body>** tag.

Listing 12.10

```
<c:if test="${pageContext.request.remoteUser != null}">
<a href="logout.jsp" style="color: white; position: absolute;
    top: 5px; right: 5px">Logout</a>
</c:if>
```

At this point, you might think that form-based authentication looks good, but it has a few issues you should be aware of.

FORM-BASED AUTHENTICATION TIPS AND TRICKS

Implementing form-based authentication can be a bit tricky. This section covers some useful tips and tricks to make implementation easier.

THE WELCOME FILE

It's important to configure the opening page that users will see. This chapter's application has the **<welcome-file-list>** element in Listing 13.11 in its *web.xml.*

Listing 12.11

```
<welcome-file-list>
    <welcome-file>index.jsp</welcome-file>
</welcome-file-list>
```

In some application servers (such as Tomcat), the default welcome pages are *index.html* and *index.jsp*. However, specifying this element can increase your application's portability. After configuring the welcome file, use JSTL to redirect the user to a protected resource if you want to require everyone to log in. See Listing 13.12.

Listing 12.12

```
<c:redirect url="/users.html"/>
```

CAUTION: It's important to redirect users rather than forwarding them. Using a forward will bypass container-managed security.

In the Servlet 2.4 specification, you can set your welcome file to use a servlet; you were unable to use this technique in earlier versions. The one caveat is that you must map the **<servlet-name>** (specified instead of **<welcome-file>**) as a servlet in *web.xml.* This fact makes it difficult to use this feature in a web framework because web frameworks define only the front controller servlet.

ALLOW LOGIN ON ERROR PAGE

When authentication fails, a browser should prompt you again for valid credentials. The default behavior with form-based authentication is to display an HTTP Status code (401 — Unauthorized) and an error message. To solve this problem, you can use a couple techniques:

- Have the same JSP serve up the login page and the login error page. (This method does not work on all containers.) See Listing 13.13.

Listing 12.13

```
<form-login-config>
    <form-login-page>/login.jsp</form-login-page>
    <form-error-page>/login.jsp?error=true</form-error-page>
</form-login-config>
```

Using this technique enables you to check for the **error** parameter and display a message when authentication fails. See Listing 13.14.

Listing 12.14

```
<c:if test="${param.error != null}">
    <div class="error">
        Invalid username and/or password, please try again.
    </div>
</c:if>
```

•   Have a second JSP page (such as *loginError.jsp*) that simply includes the *login.jsp* page. See Listing 13.15.

Listing 12.15

```
<%@ include file="/taglibs.jsp"%>

<c:import url="login.jsp">
    <c:param name="error" value="true"/>
</c:import>
```

REMEMBER ME

Usually, a server remembers login information by storing some sort of cookie on a user's computer that indicates his or her identity. Because it's dangerous to store user passwords in the cookie, sites usually use a unique token on the server and in the client's browser to identify the user.

NOTE: Some application servers, such as Caucho's Resin, support Remember Me as part of container-managed authentication. However, because this feature is not part of the servlet specification, it is not portable between containers.

After storing this token, you can map a filter to the login page (or to the whole application) that checks for this token and automatically logs in the user upon returning.

A common pattern in web application security is to protect all the controllers for your web framework. This setup is particularly useful when you have more controllers that need to be protected than ones that don't. The easiest way to specify the controllers that don't require authentication is to define a second security constraint that has no `<auth-constraint>` element. Place this before the constraint that has an `<auth-constraint>` defined. See Listing 13.16.

Listing 12.16

```
<!-- Allow anyone to access passwordHint and signup -->
<security-constraint>
    <web-resource-collection>
        <web-resource-name>Unrestricted</web-resource-name>
        <url-pattern>/passwordHint.html</url-pattern>
        <url-pattern>/signup.html</url-pattern>
        <http-method>POST</http-method>
        <http-method>GET</http-method>
    </web-resource-collection>
</security-constraint>
```

CONFIGURING TOMCAT REALMS

In addition to configuring *web.xml*, you must also set up a *realm* for user names and passwords. The Tomcat documentation[1] defines realms:

"A Realm is a 'database' of usernames and passwords that identify valid users of a web application (or set of web applications), plus an enumeration of the list of roles associated with each valid user. You can think of roles as similar to groups in Unix — like operating systems, because access to specific web application resources is granted to all users possessing a particular role (rather than enumerating the list of associated usernames). A particular user can have any number of roles associated with their username."

In all of the examples thus far, you talked to Tomcat's default realm, which is an XML file that contains a list of user names, passwords, and roles. While this works for simple applications, it's a poor way to store your users and their credentials. You'll likely want to store more information about a user, and you'll want to be able to manage users and their information easily.

The good news is that other realm types do exist, from databases to LDAP to JAAS. This section provides a general overview of how to configure these realms in Tomcat for the *equinox-security* application.

---

1. "The Apache Jakarta Tomcat 5 Servlet/JSP Container." Apache Software Foundation. 1999-2003.

   tomcat.apache.org/tomcat-5.5-doc/realm-howto.html#What%20is%20a%20Realm.

> NOTE: At the time of this writing, the latest version of Tomcat is 5.5.20. You can download this version from tomcat.apache.org/download-55.cgi#5.5.20. This version of Tomcat is designed to run on J2SE 5.0 and later and requires configuration to run on J2SE 1.4. Make sure to read the RUNNING.txt file if you are using J2SE 1.4.

To configure a realm for your application on Tomcat 5.5.x, specify a **<Realm>** element in your application's **<Context>** element. This **<Context>** element goes in your application's *META-INF/context.xml* file and will look similar to the one in Listing 13.17. At deploy time, Tomcat will extract this file from your WAR (or expanded WAR) and put it in *$CATALINA_HOME/conf/Catalina/localhost*.

Listing 12.17

```
<Context path="/equinox-security"
    docBase="equinox-security" debug="99"
    reloadable="true" antiJARLocking="true"
        antiResourceLocking="true">

    <Realm className="org.apache.catalina.realm.JDBCRealm" debug="99"
            driverName="com.mysql.jdbc.Driver"
        connectionURL="jdbc:mysql://localhost/equinox "
      connectionName="root" connectionPassword=""
            userTable="users" userNameCol="username"
          userCredCol="password"
          userRoleTable="user_roles" roleNameCol="rolename"/>
</Context>
```

MEMORYREALM

The default realm for Tomcat is a **MemoryRealm** configured in *$CATALINA_HOME/conf/server.xml*. This file specifies the *$CATALINA_HOME/conf/tomcat-users.xml* file for authenticating users. See Listing 13.18.

Listing 12.18

```
<Resource name="UserDatabase" auth="Container"
        type="org.apache.catalina.UserDatabase"
    description="User database that can be updated and saved"
        factory="org.apache.catalina.users.MemoryUserDatabaseFactory"
        pathname="conf/tomcat-users.xml" />
    ...
    <!-- Default realm setting -->
<Realm className="org.apache.catalina.realm.UserDatabaseRealm"
    resourceName="UserDatabase" />
```

The content of *tomcat-users.xml* is self-explanatory; you can easily add new users by inserting an additional **<user>** element. See Listing 13.19.

Listing 12.19

```
<user username="spring" password="rocks" roles="admin,user"/>
```

TIP: If you're using a fresh installation of Tomcat and haven't altered the *server.xml* file, I recommend you replace it with *server-minimal.xml* (in the same directory), which is much more concise. I also recommend deleting all the applications in the *webapps* folder to reduce startup time.

In the previous authentication examples, you used **tomcat/tomcat** to log in to the *equinox-security* application. This combination worked because the **tomcat** user already exists in this file by default. See Listing 13.20.

Listing 12.20

```
<user username="tomcat" password="tomcat" roles="tomcat"/>
```

One of the main problems with using a file-based mechanism is that most servers require a shutdown and restart to pick up any changes. It's great for prototyping, but if you decide to add more user information, you'll probably want to use a database or directory service. Although it is possible to use a file-based realm for user names and passwords and a database to store the rest of the users' information, mainte-nance is easier if you keep everything in the database. For that, Tomcat provides the **JDBCRealm** and **DataSourceRealm**.

ENCRYPTING PASSWORDS

In Tomcat, you can easily store encrypted passwords and configure your realm to encrypt users' passwords before it verifies credentials by adding a **digest** attribute to the **<Realm>** element. The value must be one of the digest algorithms supported by the **java.security.MessageDigest** class (SHA, MD2, or MD5). To expand the previous example, add SHA encrypting to the default **MemoryRealm** in *server.xml*. See Listing 13.21.

Listing 12.21

```
<Realm className="org.apache.catalina.realm.UserDatabaseRealm"
    resourceName="UserDatabase" digest="SHA"/>
```

After making this change, you must encrypt the **tomcat** user's password in *tomcat-users.xml* to its encrypted form. To encrypt the password, execute the command in Listing 13.22.

Listing 12.22

```
java -cp "$CATALINA_HOME/server/lib/catalina.jar;$CATALINA_HOME/bin/
jmx.jar;$CATALINA_HOME/bin/commons-logging-api.jar"
org.apache.catalina.realm.RealmBase -a SHA tomcat
```

CAUTION: On UNIX or Linux, separate the JARs in the classpath with a colon instead of a semicolon.

This command will print out the encrypted password, and you can copy and paste it into the **password** value. See Listing 13.23.

Listing 12.23

```
tomcat:536c0b339345616c1b33caf454454d8b8a190d6c
```

This configuration will work with any realm that can be configured in Tomcat.

JDBCREALM

Tomcat's JDBCRealm allows you to easily configure the database and specify the tables that store your user information. To override the default **MemoryRealm**, create a context file for the *equinox-security* application. In this exercise, you'll set up a MySQL database to store user information, while the application will continue to use the in-memory HSQL database.

Create a *src/main/webapp/META-INF* directory and place a *context.xml* file in it. Next, add a **<Context>** element with a nested **<Realm>** element. See Listing 13.24.

Listing 12.24

```
<Context path="/equinox-security"
    docBase="equinox-security" debug="99"
    reloadable="true" antiJARLocking="true"
        antiResourceLocking="true">

    <Realm className="org.apache.catalina.realm.JDBCRealm" debug="99"
        driverName="com.mysql.jdbc.Driver" digest="SHA"
        connectionURL="jdbc:mysql://localhost/equinox"
    connectionName="root" connectionPassword=""
        userTable="users" userNameCol="username"
        userCredCol="password"
        userRoleTable="user_roles" roleNameCol="rolename"/>
</Context>
```

Tomcat looks for *META-INF/context.xml* in WAR files. If it finds this file, it deploys it to *$CATALINA_HOME/conf/Catalina/localhost/equinox-security.xml* (or your application file name). If you deploy your application as an expanded WAR, Tomcat might not deploy this file to the proper location.

Before you deploy *equinox-security* to Tomcat, create the **equinox** database and add a user to it. The following script will create the appropriate tables and add a **springlive** user. For your convenience, this script is contained in the *metadata/sql/mysql-realm.sql* file of this chapter's download. Run **mysql -u root -p < metadata/sql/mysql-realm.sql** to create and populate the **equinox** database. See Listing 13.25.

Listing 12.25

```
CREATE DATABASE IF NOT EXISTS equinox;
use equinox;

DROP TABLE IF EXISTS users;
CREATE TABLE users (
    username varchar(50) NOT NULL,
    password varchar(50) NOT NULL,
    PRIMARY KEY  (username)
) TYPE=InnoDB;

INSERT INTO users (username, password) VALUES
    ('springlive',' 2a9152cff1d25b5bbaa3e5fbc7acdc6905c9f251');

DROP TABLE IF EXISTS user_roles;
CREATE TABLE user_roles (
    username varchar(50) NOT NULL,
    rolename varchar(20) NOT NULL,
    PRIMARY KEY  (username,rolename)
) TYPE=InnoDB;

INSERT INTO user_roles (username, rolename) VALUES
    ('springlive','tomcat');
```

Because the realm is a Tomcat service rather than an application service, add MySQL's JDBC driver to Tomcat's classpath. First, copy the *~/.m2/repository/mysql/mysql-connector-java/5.0.3/mysql-connector-java-5.0.3.jar* file to your *$CATALINA_HOME/common/lib* directory. Run **ant deploy war** and restart Tomcat; you should be able to log in using **springlive** as the user name and **springlive** as the password.

TIP: If you've configured your application to use a JNDI **DataSource**, you might consider using a **DataSourceRealm** so that your authentication database can use the same connections as your application.

JNDIREALM FOR **LDAP**

The JNDIRealm's configuration is similar to the **JDBCRealm** because it's configured using XML; however, the realms are designed for different data sources. The main purpose of the **JNDIRealm** is to communicate with a Lightweight Directory Access Protocol (LDAP) server. The following steps illustrate setting up an LDAP server on your local machine. These instructions assume a Windows platform.

This example uses OpenLDAP because it is a popular open source LDAP server that ships with Mac OS X server.

1   Download OpenLDAP for UNIX, Linux, or Mac OS X at www.openldap.org/software/download. If you're running Windows, go to lucas.bergmans.us/hacks/openldap for a Windows installer.

2   If you're not using Windows, follow the Quick Start Guide at openldap.org/doc/admin/quickstart.html to install it on your local machine.

3   Edit the *$INSTALL_DIR/slapd.conf* file to include the *cosine.schema* and *inetorgperson.schema* files for recognizing users and groups. See Listing 13.26.

Listing 12.26

```
include     ./schema/core.schema
include     ./schema/cosine.schema
include     ./schema/inetorgperson.schema
```

4   Modify the lines at the bottom of *slapd.conf* to define default settings for this LDAP server. See Listing 13.27.

Listing 12.27

```
database    bdb
suffix      "dc=springlive,dc=com"
rootdn      "cn=Manager,dc=springlive,dc=com"
rootpw      secret
directory   ./data
```

TIP: You can also replace your *slapd.conf* file with the one from *metadata/ldif /slapd.conf*. It already contains these modifications.

5   Restart your server if you have it running as a service.

6   Create an LDAP Data Interchange Format (LDIF) file for your top-level organization entry. This file contains organization units for groups and people. It also contains entries for the **tomcat** user and **developer** role.

The contents in Listing 13.28 are contained in *metadata/ ldif/ entries.ldif* for your convenience.

Listing 12.28

```
# Define top-level entry
dn: dc=springlive,dc=com
objectClass: dcObject
objectClass: organization
o: Spring Live
dc: springlive

# Define Manager Role to authenticate with
dn: cn=Manager,dc=springlive,dc=com
objectclass: organizationalRole
cn: Manager
description: Directory Manager

# Define an entry to contain users
# searches for users are based on this entry
dn: ou=users,dc=springlive,dc=com
objectClass: organizationalUnit
ou: users

# Define a user entry for "springlive" user
dn: uid=springlive,ou=users,dc=springlive,dc=com
objectClass: inetOrgPerson
uid: springlive
sn: Live
cn: Spring Live
userPassword: springlive

# Define an entry to contain LDAP groups (a.k.a. roles)
# searches for roles are based on this entry
dn: ou=groups,dc=springlive,dc=com
objectClass: organizationalUnit
ou: groups

# Define an entry for the "tomcat" role
dn: cn=tomcat,ou=groups,dc=springlive,dc=com
objectClass: groupOfUniqueNames
cn: tomcat
uniqueMember: uid=springlive,ou=users,dc=springlive,dc=com
```

7   Import these entries into OpenLDAP using the **ldapadd** command (all one line, although I needed to insert a return to fit it in the book margins). See Listing 13.29.

Listing 12.29

```
$INSTALL_DIR/ldapadd -x -D "cn=Manager,dc=springlive,dc=com"
  -W -f metadata/ldif/entries.ldif
```

8   Type **secret** when prompted for a password (you configured this password in *slapd.conf*). Running this command results in several "adding new entry" lines displayed in your console. See Figure 13.8.

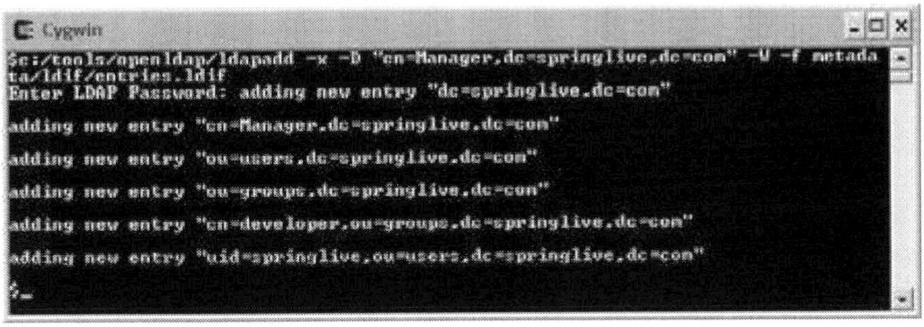

Figure 12.8: Importing LDAP entries

TIP: If errors occur, it's easy to start over by stopping LDAP (using the **kill** command) and removing the contents of the *$INSTALL_DIR/data* directory.

---

9   Replace the contents of *webapp/META-INF/context.xml* with the settings for a **JNDIRealm**. See Listing 13.30.

Listing 12.30

```
<Realm className="org.apache.catalina.realm.JNDIRealm" debug="99"
  connectionName="cn=Manager,dc=springlive,dc=com"
  connectionPassword="secret"
  connectionURL="ldap://localhost:389" userPassword="userPassword"
    userPattern="uid={0},ou=users,dc=springlive,dc=com"
      roleBase="ou=groups,dc=springlive,dc=com"
      roleName="cn" roleSearch="(uniqueMember={0})"/>
```

CAUTION: Adding **digest="SHA"** to this realm and encrypting the **springlive** user's password in *entries.ldif* causes authentication to fail.

---

10   Download LDAP Service Provider 1.2.4 from java.sun.com/products/ jndi/downloads/index.html. Copy its *ldap.jar* into *$CATALINA_ HOME/common/lib*. This file allows Tomcat to talk to LDAP from a **JNDIRealm**.

11 Run **ant -f tomcat.xml remove** while Tomcat is running to undeploy the *equinox-security* application. This step is necessary to remove the *$CATALINA_HOME/conf/Catalina/localhost/equinox-security.xml* file.

NOTE: If you receive a 401 error, you need to add an **admin** user with an **admin** password to *$CATALINA_HOME/conf/tomcat-users.xml.*

---

12 Stop and restart Tomcat so it picks up the new *ldap.jar* in its classpath.

13 Run **ant -f tomcat.xml install** to install the updated WAR with the **JNDIRealm**. You should be able to log in with the **springlive** user name and password.

USING THE SECURE SOCKETS LAYER (SSL)

In this chapter, you've learned how to configure authentication, but authentication does not secure the communication between the browser and the server. If someone were listening with a password sniffer, the security of your application could easily be compromised. Furthermore, these sniffers are easy to come by — try searching Google for "password sniffer."

From the "Guide to Building Secure Web Applications" by the Open Web Application Security Project[2]:

"The most common method of securing the HTTP protocol is to use SSL. The Secure Socket Layer protocol, or SSL, was designed by Netscape and was introduced in the Netscape Communicator browser in 1994. It's most likely the widest spoken security protocol in the world, and is built into all commercial web browsers and web servers."

SSL is a technology that allows web browsers and web servers to communicate over a secure channel. Data is encrypted at the browser (before transmission) and then decrypted at the server before reading the data. This same process, known as the *SSL handshake*, takes place when the server returns data to the client. For more information about the SSL handshake, visit medialab.di.unipi.it/doc/JNetSec/jns_ch11.htm.

The first step to implementing SSL on your web server (in this case, Tomcat) is to generate a certificate. Keep in mind that if you are sending your JSP/Servlet requests through a traditional web server, you will need to set up SSL on those servers.

---

2. Wiesmann, Adrian, et al. "Guide to Building Secure Web Applications." Open Web Application Security Project. 2004. www.owasp.org/documentation/guide/guide_about.html

CONFIGURING SSL ON TOMCAT

Setting up SSL on Tomcat is easy, thanks to excellent documentation and simplistic configuration. Please refer to Tomcat's SSL Configuration How-To for information about setting it up. After you've set up SSL, you should be able to access the *equinox-security* application using https://localhost:8443/equinox-security.

SSL TIPS AND TRICKS

Setting up and using SSL is easy. The hardest part is obtaining and installing a certi-fication from a Certificate Authority (CA). In many cases, however, you won't need to secure your *entire* application, just certain pieces of it, such as when users log in and when they update their passwords.

FORCE SSL IN WEB.XML

The easiest way to secure your application and force SSL for all requests is to modify your *web.xml* file. In the `<security-constraint>` element, add a `<user-data-constraint>` and set its value to `CONFIDENTIAL`. Place this element directly after the `<auth-constraint>` element. See Listing 13.31.

Listing 12.31

```
<user-data-constraint>
    <transport-guarantee>CONFIDENTIAL</transport-guarantee>
</user-data-constraint>
```

The `<transport-guarantee>` element can use one of the following values:

- **NONE**: The application does not requires any no transport guarantee. Using this value is the same as not including the `<user-data-constraint>` element in your *web.xml* file.

- **INTEGRAL**: The application requires that the data be sent between the client and server in such a way that it can't cannot be changed in transit.

- **CONFIDENTIAL**: The application requires that the data be transmitted in a fashion that prevents other entities from observing the contents of the transmission.

Most servlet containers will switch the client to SSL when this value is set to **INTEGRAL** or **CONFIDENTIAL**. Although this feature is great for applications that require it, you need to be careful when implementing it. On most servlet containers, if you set this value to **INTEGRAL** or **CONFIDENTIAL**, your application will be available only on the SSL port. A nice feature is that the server will automatically redirect you to the secure port when users try to access your application on the unsecure port.

This works in Tomcat because its port 8080 connector (in *$CATALINA_HOME /conf/server.xml*) uses **redirectPort="8443"** as an attribute.

SWITCHING SSL PROGRAMMATICALLY

You can switch to and from SSL programmatically by using a JSP tag, such as the **SecureTag** from AppFuse. This tag allows you to use the following code in JSPs to switch to and from SSL. See Listing 13.32.

Listing 12.32

```
<tag:secure/>
<tag:secure mode="unsecured"/>
```

This tag relies on an **SslUtil** class that also allows you to switch to and from SSL in a controller or filter. Listing 13.33 is a usage example in a filter.

Listing 12.33

```
// If using https, switch to http
String redirectString =
    SslUtil.getRedirectString(request, config.getServletContext(),
                        false); // false for http, true for https

if (redirectString != null) {
    // Redirect the page to the desired URL
    response.sendRedirect
        (response.encodeRedirectURL(redirectString));
    return;
}
```

One drawback of using SSL in your web application is that it tends to slow things a bit because of the encryption/decryption process on each end of the connection. If your application has high-performance requirements, you might want to use it only for the parts of your application that really need it, such as when a user logs in or when someone submits a credit card number.

TIP: You can find more information about performance degradation with SSL at www.computerworld.com/securitytopics/security/story/0,10801,58978,00.html. This article also contains links to other articles and options for SSL acceleration.

JAAS

Java Authentication and Authorization Service (JAAS) provides a framework and standard programming interface for authentication and authorization. Together with Java, an application can provide code-centric access control, user-centric access control, or a combination of both. JAAS makes login services independent of authentication technologies and allows Pluggable Authentication Modules (PAM). Most modern application servers actually use JAAS under the covers to configure container-managed security — you're using it without even knowing it!

JAAS can be helpful when you need to use complex authentication schemas or when granting resource specific privileges to the users (for example, inserting a row in the database or assigning write permissions to a file). This security mechanism essentially allows you to specify authentication and authorization via policy files. When you run your application server with a security manager, it checks a policy file, and then the user is allowed to run your application or is prompted for credentials. JAAS allows for complex login schemas, such as a Windows NT domain or Smart Cards (SecurID). More information about the supported login schemas is available at java.sun.com/j2se/1.4/docs/guide/security/jaas/JAASRefGuide.html#AppendixB.

The easiest way to integrate JAAS into your web application is to download and configure Andy Armstrong's JAAS login modules from free.tagish.net/jaas. These modules allow you to configure a JAAS realm in Tomcat that talks to a Windows domain, a database, or a file with user names and passwords in it.

SECURITY ALTERNATIVES

Container-managed security is useful for abstracting security and configuring realm information outside of your application. However, because not all containers support all the different realm types, sometimes it's easier to use an alternative mechanism to handle your security.

SECURITYFILTER

`SecurityFilter` is an open-source project that mimics container-managed security. To the user, it looks exactly like container-managed security, and it supports the programmatic security methods of `HttpServletRequest`. This library has a filter that you specify and map in your *web.xml* file as well as an XML file that contains your security configuration. Like most libraries that mimic container-managed security, it doesn't automatically propagate a user's principal to EJB calls.

JCIFS

JCIFS is an open-source project that implements the CIFS/SMB networking protocol in Java. CIFS is the name of the file-sharing protocol for Microsoft Windows. This library is useful for configuring your web application to authorize users against a Windows domain. It uses a filter that you configure in your *web.xml* file. You configure your Windows domain information as part of the filter. For application users who use Internet Explorer, JCIFS will allow them to log in transparently to your application — without seeing a login dialog. This library is good for integrating your application with a Windows-based intranet. It also supports the programmatic security methods of **HttpServletRequest**.

ACEGI SECURITY

Acegi Security is an open-source project similar to **SecurityFilter** and JCIFS in that it uses filters to control access to web applications. Unlike the other solutions, Acegi Security offers custom realms that you can use to configure your application to use Acegi Security *and* container-managed authentication. This project is closely related to Spring and is actively developed under the same philosophies as Spring. Both projects employ the following philosophies:

- Interface-based architecture
- Interceptors
- Bean contexts

Acegi Security became an official Spring sub-project with its 1.0 release.

ACEGI SECURITY SYSTEM FOR SPRING

Acegi (pronounced a-*cee*-gee) Security is a comprehensive framework for programming and integrating security into your application. Using Acegi Security in your application makes it more portable. While J2EE's security specification standardizes available services, it does not standardize how to configure these services. For this reason, it can be difficult to configure the security settings for your application from one application server to the next.

The goals of Acegi Security are to address the four areas of security that Java applications require:

- Authentication, typically using a user name/password combination
- Securing web requests
- Securing service layer methods so different clients have the same security constraints
- Securing domain objects to limit access

NOTE: In this section, the word "principal" refers to a user, a service, or any system that requires authentication.

This section provides a basic overview of Acegi Security. First, it's important to review the main areas of the Acegi Security framework from its reference documentation.

1. An **Authentication** object holds the principal, the credentials, and the authorities granted to the principal. The object can store additional information associated with an authentication request, such as the source's TCP/IP address.

2. A **SecurityContextHolder** holds the **Authentication** object in a **ThreadLocal**-bound object. This allows authentication information to be retrieved in the middle tier of a Spring application. For example, you can use the code in Listing 13.34 to get an **Authentication** object anywhere in your application.

Listing 12.34

```
Authentication auth =
    SecurityContextHolder.getContext().getAuthentication();
```

3. An **AuthenticationManager** authenticates the **Authentication** object presented via the **SecurityContextHolder**.

4. An **AccessDecisionManager** authorizes a given operation.

5. A **RunAsManager** optionally replaces the **Authentication** object during the execution of a given operation.

6. A *secure object* interceptor coordinates the authentication, authorization, and run-as replacement after handling invocation and execution of a given operation.

7. An **AfterInvocationManager** can modify an **Object** returned from a secure object invocation, such as removing collection elements that a principal does not have authority to access.

8. An Access Control List (ACL) management package obtains the ACLs applicable for domain object instances.

The Acegi Security reference documentation goes into much more depth of how everything works and integrates with each other.

AUTHENTICATION CONFIGURATION AND SETUP

The *equinox-security* project contains a dependency on Acegi Security 1.0 in its *pom.xml* file. Acegi Security transparently depends on Spring, Commons Codec, and Jakarta ORO. The next two sections will show you how to set up and configure basic and form-based authentication using Acegi Security.

BASIC AUTHENTICATION

Perform the following steps to integrate basic authentication into the *equinox-security* application:

1 Remove any **<security-constraint>** and **<login-config>** elements from *src/main/webapp/WEB-INF/web.xml*. You can also delete *src/main/webapp/META-INF/context.xml* because you won't be depending on container configuration anymore.

2 Add the **<filter>** element in Listing 13.35 before any **<filter-mapping>** elements in *src/main/webapp/WEB-INF/web.xml*.

Listing 12.35

```
<filter>
    <filter-name>securityFilter</filter-name>
    <filter-class>
        org.acegisecurity.util.FilterToBeanProxy
    </filter-class>
    <init-param>
        <param-name>targetClass</param-name>
        <param-value>
            org.acegisecurity.util.FilterChainProxy
        </param-value>
    </init-param>
</filter>
```

The **FilterToBeanProxy** delegates filter requests to a Spring-managed bean, while the **FilterChainProxy** allows the filter-chain definition to be stored in a Spring context file. This setup simplifies the security configuration by consolidating it in one location, which is *src/main/webapp/WEB-INF/security.xml* in this example.

3 Add a mapping for this filter to filter all requests for the application. This mapping should come just after the **encodingFilter** filter-mapping in *web.xml*. See Listing 13.36.

Listing 12.36

```
<filter-mapping>
    <filter-name>securityFilter</filter-name>
    <url-pattern>/*</url-pattern>
</filter-mapping>
```

4 Create a *src/main/webapp/WEB-INF/security.xml* file. Because this file has a verbose set of bean definitions, a mostly filled-out version is included in this chapter's download at *src/main/webapp/WEB-INF/security.txt*. Simply rename it with an *.xml* extension.

5 Modify *web.xml* to include *security.xml* as a Spring context file. See
Listing 13.37.

Listing 12.37

```
<context-param>
    <param-name>contextConfigLocation</param-name>
    <param-value>
        /WEB-INF/applicationContext*.xml,
        /WEB-INF/security.xml
    </param-value>
</context-param>
```

The `filterChainProxy` bean contains the filter list that will process the authentication process. These filters each perform specific duties:

- `httpSessionContextIntegrationFilter`: This filter is responsible
  for communicating with the user's session to store the user's
  authentication in the `SecurityContextHolder`.

- `basicProcessingFilter`: This filter processes an HTTP request's
  `BASIC` authorization headers, placing the result into the `ContextHolder`.

- `exceptionTranslationFilter`: This filter handles any
  `AccessDeniedException` and `AuthenticationExceptions` that are
  thrown during filter processing. It provides the bridge between Java
  exceptions and HTTP responses.

- `filterInvocationInterceptor`: This filter is used to define the URLs
  that roles can access. See Listing 13.38.

Listing 12.38

```
<?xml version="1.0" encoding="UTF-8"?>
<beans xmlns="http://www.springframework.org/schema/beans"
       xmlns:xsi="http://www.w3.org/2001/XMLSchema-instance"
       xmlns:aop="http://www.springframework.org/schema/aop"
       xsi:schemaLocation=
           "http://www.springframework.org/schema/beans
           http://www.springframework.org/schema/beans
               /spring-beans-2.0.xsd
           http://www.springframework.org/schema/aop
           http://www.springframework.org/schema/aop
               /spring-aop-2.0.xsd">

    <beans>
        <bean id="filterChainProxy"
            class="org.acegisecurity.util.FilterChainProxy">
            <property name="filterInvocationDefinitionSource">
```

```
                    <value>
                        CONVERT_URL_TO_LOWERCASE_BEFORE_COMPARISON
                        PATTERN_TYPE_APACHE_ANT
                        /images/*=#NONE#
                        /scripts/*=#NONE#
                        /styles/*=#NONE#
                        /**=httpSessionContextIntegrationFilter,
                            basicProcessingFilter,exceptionTranslationFilter,
                            filterInvocationInterceptor
                    </value>
                </property>
            </bean>

            <bean id="httpSessionContextIntegrationFilter"
                class="org.acegisecurity.context
                    .HttpSessionContextIntegrationFilter"/>

            <bean id="basicProcessingFilter"
                class="org.acegisecurity.ui.basicauth.BasicProcessingFilter">
                <property name="authenticationManager"
                    ref="authenticationManager"/>
                <property name="authenticationEntryPoint"
                    ref="basicProcessingFilterEntryPoint"/>
            </bean>

            <bean id="exceptionTranslationFilter"
                class="org.acegisecurity.ui.ExceptionTranslationFilter">
                <property name="authenticationEntryPoint"
                    ref="basicProcessingFilterEntryPoint"/>
            </bean>

            <bean id="filterInvocationInterceptor"
                class="org.acegisecurity.intercept.web
                    .FilterSecurityInterceptor">
                <property name="authenticationManager"
                    ref="authenticationManager"/>
                <property name="accessDecisionManager"
                    ref="accessDecisionManager"/>
                <property name="objectDefinitionSource">
                    <value>
                        PATTERN_TYPE_APACHE_ANT
                        /*.html*=ROLE_USER
                        /*.jsp=ROLE_USER
                    </value>
                </property>
            </bean>

            <bean id="accessDecisionManager"
                class="org.acegisecurity.vote.AffirmativeBased">
                <property name="allowIfAllAbstainDecisions" value="false"/>
```

```
            <property name="decisionVoters">
                <list>
                    <ref local="roleVoter"/>
                </list>
            </property>
        </bean>

        <bean id="roleVoter" class="org.acegisecurity.vote.RoleVoter"/>

        <bean id="authenticationManager"
            class="org.acegisecurity.providers.ProviderManager">
            <property name="providers">
                <list>
                    <ref local="daoAuthenticationProvider"/>
                </list>
            </property>
        </bean>

        <bean id="daoAuthenticationProvider"
            class="org.acegisecurity.providers.dao
                .DaoAuthenticationProvider">
            <property name="userDetailsService" ref="inMemoryDaoImpl"/>
            <property name="userCache" ref="userCache"/>
        </bean>

        <bean id="inMemoryDaoImpl"
            class="org.acegisecurity.userdetails.memory.InMemoryDaoImpl">
            <property name="userMap">
                <value>
                    tomcat=tomcat,ROLE_USER
                </value>
            </property>
        </bean>

        <bean id="basicProcessingFilterEntryPoint"
            class="org.acegisecurity.ui.basicauth
                .BasicProcessingFilterEntryPoint">
            <property name="realmName" value="Protected Area"/>
        </bean>

        <bean id="userCache"
            class="org.acegisecurity.providers.dao.cache
                .EhCacheBasedUserCache">
            <property name="cache">
                <bean class="org.springframework.cache.ehcache
                    .EhCacheFactoryBean">
                    <property name="cacheManager">
                        <bean class="org.springframework.cache.ehcache
                            .EhCacheManagerFactoryBean"/>
                    </property>
```

```
                <property name="cacheName" value="userCache"/>
            </bean>
        </property>
    </bean>
</beans>
```

6   Run **ant -f tomcat.xml remove** while Tomcat is running.

7   Stop Tomcat and then run **ant clean deploy**.

8   Start Tomcat and navigate to localhost:8080/equinox-security. If you'd like to install Maven 2, you can also run **mvn jetty:run** to use the **maven-jetty-plugin**.

CAUTION: One issue I found with the Jetty plug-in is that it doesn't seem to protect the welcome file as served up by Jetty. For this reason, you might need to click the **View Demonstration** button to be prompted to log in.

---

9   In the *security.xml* file is an **inMemoryDaoImpl** bean that contains the **tomcat** user with a **tomcat** password and a **ROLE_USER** role. This role has access to the application in the **filterInvocationInterceptor** bean. See Listing 13.39.

Listing 12.39

```
/*.html*=ROLE_USER
/*.jsp=ROLE_USER
```

By restricting the **filterInvocationInterceptor** to URLs ending with *.html* and *.jsp*, you limit security interception to these extensions and do not block access to style sheets, images, or JavaScript files. Using **tomcat** for the user name and password should result in a successful login.

TIP: You can use **#NONE#** in the **filterChainProxy** bean's **filterInvocaion-DefinitionSource** to exclude certain paths from being processed. For example, putting Listing 13.40 after **PATTER_APACHE_ANT** will prevent images, style sheets and scripts from being processed.

Listing 12.40

```
/images/*=#NONE#
/scripts/*=#NONE#
/styles/*=#NONE#
```

NOTE: The ability to use regular expressions or Ant path matching with Acegi Security gives it a huge advantage over the Servlet APIs security mechanism. With the Servlet API, you can do only path matching (/path/*) or extension matching (*.extension).

To better help you understand how Acegi Security works and why you need all the bean definitions in *security.xml*, see the following list for each bean definition and its responsibility.

- **httpSessionContextIntegrationFilter**: This class populates the **SecurityContextHolder** with information obtained from the **HttpSession**. It queries the **HttpSession** to retrieve the **Context** to store against the **ContextHolder** for the duration of the web request. At the end of the web request, this filter persists any updates made to the **ContextHolder** back to the **HttpSession**.

- **basicProcessingFilter**: This Servlet filter talks to the **authenticationManager** bean to perform authentication. It uses the **basicProcessingFilterEntryPoint** property to determine custom settings for this authentication method.

- **exceptionTranslationFilter**: Responsible for delegating authentication failures to the **authenticationProcessingFilterEntryPoint** bean and returning "Access Denied" when principals don't have permission to access URLs or methods.

- **filterInvocationInterceptor**: This implementation of **AbstractSecurityInterceptor** performs security handling of HTTP requests. This bean's **objectDefinitionSource** property contains the rules for who can see what.

- **accessDecisionManager**: This **AccessDecisionManager** grants access if any of its listed **decisionVoters** return an affirmative response.

- **authenticationManager**: This **ProviderManager** takes a list of **AuthenticationProvider** implementations and calls their **authenticate()** methods. If the first provider in the list fails, it will continue until it gets to the end of the list or finds a successful provider.

- **daoAuthenticationProvider**: This **AuthenticationProvider** implementation retrieves principal details from a **UserDetailsService**. The **UserDetailsService** interface has one method, **loadByUsername(String username)**, which makes it easy to use a custom security implementation. This bean also allows you to configure a **userCache** for more efficient user retrieval.

- **inMemoryDaoImpl**: This **UserDetailsService** implementation looks up users' credentials from an in-memory database that's created based on the values in this bean's **userMap** property.

- **basicProcessingFilterEntryPoint**: This implementation of **AuthenticationEntryPoint** contains the realm name to be displayed in the login dialog. Other implementations include **Authentication-ProcessingFilterEntryPoint** for form-based authentication and **CasProcessingFilterEntryPoint** for single sign-on with Yale Central Authentication Service (CAS).

NOTE: When configuring roles in the **objectSourceDefinition** property of the **filterInvocationInterceptor** bean, you must specify a role in your rules. You can separate multiple roles with a comma. You cannot currently use a wildcard (*) like you can with container-managed authentication. See Listing 13.41.

Listing 12.41

```
<property name="objectDefinitionSource">
    <value>
        CONVERT_URL_TO_LOWERCASE_BEFORE_COMPARISON
        PATTERN_TYPE_APACHE_ANT
        /admin/*=ROLE_ADMIN,ROLE_DBA
    </value>
</property>
```

FORM-BASED AUTHENTICATION

With the building blocks in place for Acegi Security, it's easy to switch from basic authentication to form-based authentication.

1   In *src/main/webapp/WEB-INF/security.xml*, add a new bean definition for form-based authentication processing. This bean uses the **org.acegi-security.ui.webapp.AuthenticationProcessingFilter** class to handle authentication. It doesn't matter where you define this bean, but it makes sense to put it with the other filters, just after the **httpSession-ContextIntegrationFilter**. See Listing 13.42.

Listing 12.42

```
<bean id="authenticationProcessingFilter"
    class="org.acegisecurity.ui.webapp
        .AuthenticationProcessingFilter">
    <property name="authenticationManager"
        ref="authenticationManager"/>
    <property name="authenticationFailureUrl"
        value="/loginError.htm"/>
    <property name="defaultTargetUrl" value="/"/>
    <property name="filterProcessesUrl" value="/j_security_check"/>
</bean>
```

In addition to the properties listed here, you can define two others.

- **alwaysUseDefaultTargetUrl**: Setting this to **"true"** will cause successful authentication to always redirect to the **defaultTargetUrl**.

- **exceptionMappings**: a **java.util.Properties** object that maps a fully-qualified exception class name to a redirection url. See Listing 13.43.

Listing 12.43

```
<property name="exceptionMappings">
    <value>
        org.acegisecurity.AccountExpiredException=/accountExpired.jsp
        org.acegisecurity.LockedException=/accountLocked.jsp
    </value>
</property>
```

Any **AuthenticationException** thrown that cannot be matched in the **exceptionMappings** will be redirected to the **authenticationFailureUrl**.

2   In this same file, add an **authenticationProcessingFilterEntryPoint** bean that contains the login page and indicates whether to force HTTPS. See Listing 13.44.

Listing 12.44

```
<bean id="authenticationProcessingFilterEntryPoint"
    class="org.acegisecurity.ui.webapp
    .AuthenticationProcessingFilterEntryPoint">
    <property name="loginFormUrl" value="/login.htm"/>
    <property name="forceHttps" value="false"/>
</bean>
```

3   Change the filter chain in the `filterChainProxy` bean to use the `authenticationProcessingFilter` bean instead of the `basicProcessingFilter` bean. See Listing 13.45.

Listing 12.45

```
/**=httpSessionContextIntegrationFilter,
    authenticationProcessingFilter,
    exceptionTranslationFilter,filterInvocationInterceptor
```

4   Change the `authenticationEntryPoint` in the `exceptionTranslationFilter` bean to point to the `authenticationProcessingFilterEntryPoint`. See Listing 13.46.

Listing 12.46

```
<bean id="exceptionTranslationFilter"
    class="org.acegisecurity.ui.ExceptionTranslationFilter">
    <property name="authenticationEntryPoint"
        ref="authenticationProcessingFilterEntryPoint"/>
</bean>
```

5   Rename *src/main/webapp/login.jsp* to *src/main/webapp/login.htm* and *src/main/webapp/loginError.jsp* to *src/main/webapp/loginError.htm*. This renaming is necessary because **.jsp* is protected in the `filterInvocationInterceptor` bean. The user will receive a URL redirect error from the browser if your login page is protected by your security rules.

NOTE: The extension should be .htm, not *.html*. The *.html* extension is used by Spring MVC to map controllers, hence the reason for using .htm. In a real-world environment, it's better to not protect **.jsp* or add anonymous mappings so anonymous users can get to them. AppFuse uses anonymous mappings if you're interested in this feature.

6   Run `ant -f tomcat.xml deploy reload`. Log in to localhost:8080/equinox-security with the `tomcat` user.

7   The logout link you created in the J2EE authentication section no longer displays because the `request.getRemoteUser()` doesn't work by default with Acegi Security. To fix this link, add a bean definition with a `class` attribute of `org.acegisecurity.wrapper.SecurityContextHolderAwareRequestFilter`. See Listing 13.47.

Listing 12.47

```
<bean id="securityContextHolderAwareFilter"
    class="org.acegisecurity.wrapper
    .SecurityContextHolderAwareRequestFilter"/>
```

8   After defining this bean, add it to the list of filters in the **filter-ChainProxy** bean. The order in the **filterChainProxy** is critical, so place it after the **authenticationProcessingFilter** and before the **exceptionTranslationFilter**. See Listing 13.48.

Listing 12.48

```
... authenticationProcessingFilter,securityContextHolderAwareFilter,
    exceptionTranslationFilter ...
```

9   Run **ant -f tomcat.xml deploy reload**; you should see the logout link after you log in.

10   Acegi Security 1.0 added the ability to use a **LogoutFilter** instead of a JSP to log out. To configure it, simply add the contents of Listing 13.49 to *security.xml*.

Listing 12.49

```
<bean id="logoutFilter" class="org.acegisecurity.ui.logout
    .LogoutFilter">
    <constructor-arg value="/"/>
    <constructor-arg>
        <list>
            <bean
             class="org.acegisecurity.ui.logout
                .SecurityContextLogoutHandler"/>
        </list>
    </constructor-arg>
    <property name="filterProcessesUrl" value="/logout.jsp"/>
</bean>
```

The first constructor argument is the URL to redirect to after logout. The second is a list of **LogoutHandler** references. If you're using Acegi's Remember Me feature, you'll need to add the **rememberMeServices** bean to the list of **LogoutHandlers**. See Listing 13.50.

Listing 12.50

```
<list>
    <ref bean="rememberMeServices"/>
    <bean
        class="org.acegisecurity.ui.logout
            .SecurityContextLogoutHandler"/>
</list>
```

After you've added this listing to *security.xml*, you'll need to add it to the **filter-ChainProxy** bean. See Listing 13.51.

Listing 12.51

```
/**=httpSessionContextIntegrationFilter,logoutFilter,
    authenticationProcessingFilter ...
```

CONFIGURING REALMS

Acegi Security supports different realms called *authentication providers*, which implement the **AuthenticationProvider** interface. All of the implementations mentioned in this section are configured as the **userDetailsService** property of a **DaoAuthenticationProvider**. See Listing 13.52.

Listing 12.52

```
<bean id="daoAuthenticationProvider"
  class="org.acegisecurity.providers.dao.DaoAuthenticationProvider">
    <property name="userDetailsService" ref="inMemoryDaoImpl"/>
</bean>
```

If you have multiple providers, define them as beans with different IDs. After defining the provider bean, reference it in the **providers** property of the **authenticationManager** bean. See Listing 13.53.

Listing 12.53

```
<bean id="authenticationManager"
    class="org.acegisecurity.providers.ProviderManager">
    <property name="providers">
        <list>
            <ref local="daoAuthenticationProvider"/>
        </list>
    </property>
</bean>
```

In this example, the **authenticationManager** is responsible for looking up user's information and ensuring that the credentials are correct.

Acegi Security supports many different types of authentication providers that allow you to talk to different data stores for user and role information. The list of supported authentication providers includes the following:

- In Memory
- JDBC
- JAAS

Additionally, Acegi Security supports password encryption for all of these authentication providers.

IN MEMORY

The **InMemoryDaoImpl** is the easiest provider to configure. To use it, define it as a bean in your *security.xml* file. Reference this bean in the **userDetailsService** property of the **daoAuthenticationProvider** bean (as in the previous section). See Listing 13.54.

Listing 12.54

```
<bean id="inMemoryDaoImpl"
    class="org.acegisecurity.userdetails.memory.InMemoryDaoImpl">
    <property name="userMap">
        <value>
            tomcat=tomcat,ROLE_USER
            springlive=springlive,ROLE_USER
        </value>
    </property>
</bean>
```

Users are defined as **username=password,rolename1,rolename2**, etc. You can define multiple users by specifying multiple lines. If you add the **springlive** user to your *src/main/webapp/WEB-INF/security.xml* file and run **ant -f tomcat .xml deploy reload**, you can log in as the **springlive** user.

PASSWORD ENCRYPTION

To enable password encryption with Acegi Security, add a **passwordEncoder** property to the **daoAuthenticationProvider** bean. The possible **Password-Encoder** implementations are available in the **org.acegisecurity.providers .encoding** package.

1   To change the list of current users to use password encryption, first encrypt their passwords. The SHA encrypted forms of **tomcat** and **springlive** are shown in Listing 13.55.

Listing 12.55

```
tomcat:536c0b339345616c1b33caf454454d8b8a190d6c
springlive:2a9152cff1d25b5bbaa3e5fbc7acdc6905c9f251
```

2   Change the plain-text passwords in the **inMemoryDaoImpl** bean to use their encrypted versions. See Listing 13.56.

Listing 12.56

```
<bean id="inMemoryDaoImpl"
    class="org.acegisecurity.userdetails.memory.InMemoryDaoImpl">
    <property name="userMap">
        <value>
            tomcat=536c0b339345616c1b33caf454454d8b8a190d6c,ROLE_USER
            springlive=2a9152cff1d25b5bbaa3e5fbc7acdc6905c9f251,
                ROLE_USER
        </value>
    </property>
</bean>
```

3   Add the **passwordEncoder** bean and reference it as a property in the **daoAuthenticationProvider** bean. See Listing 13.57.

Listing 12.57

```
<bean id="daoAuthenticationProvider"
    class="org.acegisecurity.providers.dao
        .DaoAuthenticationProvider">
    <property name="userDetailsService" ref="inMemoryDaoImpl"/>
    <property name="passwordEncoder" ref="passwordEncoder"/>
</bean>

<bean id="passwordEncoder"
    class="org.acegisecurity.providers.encoding.ShaPasswordEncoder"/>
```

JDBC

If you're porting an existing application that uses a **JDBCRealm** to use Acegi Security, use the **JdbcDaoImpl** provider. The basic configuration for this provider is in Listing 13.58.

Listing 12.58

```
<bean id="jdbcDaoImpl"
    class="org.acegisecurity.userdetails.jdbc.JdbcDaoImpl">
    <property name="dataSource" ref="dataSource"/>
</bean>
```

By default, the **JdbcDaoImpl** class uses one query for fetching a user's information and a second query for grabbing the user's roles, or authorities. These queries are as follows in Listing 13.59

Listing 12.59

```
"SELECT username,password,enabled FROM users WHERE username = ?";
"SELECT username,authority FROM authorities WHERE username = ?";
```

You can implement this provider in the *equinox-security* application by performing the following steps:

1   Log in to MySQL using **mysql -u root -p** and press Enter when prompted for a password. Drop the **equinox** database using **drop database equinox**.

2   Re-create the database using the following script or by loading the *metadata/sql/mysql-acegi.sql* file. The main changes between this file and *metadata/sql/mysql-realm.sql* are that it has an additional **enabled** column in the **users** table and it uses **authorities/authority** instead of **user_roles/rolename**. See Listing 13.60.

Listing 12.60

```
CREATE DATABASE IF NOT EXISTS equinox;
use equinox;

DROP TABLE IF EXISTS users;
CREATE TABLE users (
    username varchar(50) NOT NULL,
    password varchar(50) NOT NULL,
    enabled bit default 1,
    PRIMARY KEY  (username)
) TYPE=InnoDB;

INSERT INTO users (username, password)
VALUES ('springlive',' 8e86cbb973c3813c1d33b7525c0f00916595907a');

DROP TABLE IF EXISTS authorities;
CREATE TABLE authorities (
    username varchar(50) NOT NULL,
```

```
        authority varchar(20) NOT NULL,
        PRIMARY KEY   (username,authority)
) TYPE=InnoDB;

INSERT INTO authorities (username, authority)
        VALUES ('springlive','ROLE_USER');
```

The **dataSource** bean (in *src/main/webapp/WEB-INF/applicationContext-hibernate.xml*) already points to this database, so you can reuse that bean definition in the **jdbcDaoImpl** bean — defined in step 3.

> 3   Add a **jdbcDaoImpl** bean. See Listing 13.61.

Listing 12.61

```
<bean id="jdbcDaoImpl"
     class="org.acegisecurity.userdetails.jdbc.JdbcDaoImpl">
     <property name="dataSource" ref="dataSource"/>
</bean>
```

> 4   Change the **daoAuthenticationProvider** to use the **jdbcDaoImpl** for its **userDetailService** property. See Listing 13.62.

Listing 12.62

```
<bean id="daoAuthenticationProvider"
     class="org.acegisecurity.providers.dao
        .DaoAuthenticationProvider">
     <property name="userDetailsService" ref="jdbcDaoImpl"/>
     <property name="passwordEncoder" ref="passwordEncoder"/>
</bean>
```

> 5   Run **ant -f tomcat.xml deploy reload** and log in with the **springlive** user name and **sourcebeat** password.

The **JdbcDaoImpl** is a flexible class that you can easily modify to fit with your database schema, thanks to Spring's IoC container. To modify the queries, set the new query strings as properties on this bean. Modifying these queries will allow you to easily port from a **JDBCRealm** with Acegi Security. The customization in Listing 13.63 makes the **jdbcDaoImpl** bean talk to the original **equinox** database in MySQL.

Listing 12.63

```
<bean id="jdbcDaoImpl"
     class="org.acegisecurity.userdetails.jdbc.JdbcDaoImpl">
     <property name="dataSource" ref="dataSource"/>
     <property name="usersByUsernameQuery">
```

```
        <value>SELECT username,password,enabled as 'true' FROM users
            WHERE username = ?</value>
    </property>
    <property name="authoritiesByUsernameQuery">
        <value>SELECT username,rolename FROM user_roles
            WHERE username = ?</value>
    </property>
</bean>
```

CAUTION: Be sure that your SQL matches your table and column names. If your SQL is wrong, it will result in failed authentication with no errors about the invalid SQL.

---

6   Change the **RoleVoter** bean to set the **rolePrefix** property to an empty string. See Listing 13.64.

Listing 12.64

```
<bean id="accessDecisionManager"
    class="org.acegisecurity.vote.AffirmativeBased">
    <property name="allowIfAllAbstainDecisions" value="false"/>
    <property name="decisionVoters">
        <list>
            <bean class="org.acegisecurity.vote.RoleVoter">
                <property name="rolePrefix" value=""/>
            </bean>
        </list>
    </property>
</bean>
```

The **usersByUsernameQuery** must contain three columns, just like the original query. If you don't want to fake the **enabled** column as shown here, you can add the **enabled** column to the **users** table.

JAAS

In addition to supporting users configured in files and databases, Acegi Security supports delegating requests to JAAS. To make JAAS work, you need a login configuration file and a **LoginModule** implementation. From there, you create a bean definition for **JaasAuthenticationProvider** and configure its properties appropriately.

To test JAAS with the *equinox-security* application, use the Tagish JAAS Login Modules created by Andy Armstrong. For your convenience, the *tagishauth.jar* (version 1.0.3) is included in this project's *pom.xml*. Complete the following steps to configure Acegi Security to work with the **FileLogin** module:

1   Create a *src/main/webapp/WEB-INF/users.txt* file with a single user. The password must be MD5 encrypted. Colons must separate the roles after the password. The **jaasuser** in Listing 13.65 has a password of **test1**.

Listing 12.65

```
# Passwords for com.tagish.auth.FileLogin
jaasuser:5a105e8b9d40e1329780d62ea2265d8a:ROLE_USER
```

2   Create a *src/main/webapp/WEB-INF/login.conf* file that tells the **LoginModule** class where the password file is. See Listing 13.66.

Listing 12.66

```
FileLogin
{
  com.tagish.auth.FileLogin required debug=true
    pwdFile="${catalina.home}/webapps/equinox-security/WEB-INF
      /users.txt";
};
```

JAAS works quite differently from most authentication systems. Everything is a principal, even roles. Acegi Security uses an **Authentication** object. This object has a single principal and an array of **GrantedAuthority** objects. To bridge the gap between JAAS and Acegi Security, you must implement an **Authority-Granter** interface.

3   Create a **JaasAuthorityGranter.java** file in *src/main/java/org/appfuse/web* to grant authorities for this JAAS implementation. See Listing 13.67.

Listing 12.67

```
package org.appfuse.web;

// organize imports using your IDE

public class JaasAuthorityGranter implements AuthorityGranter {

    public Set grant(Principal principal) {
        Set grantedRoles = new HashSet();
        String role = null;

        // check for "GROUP" in principal.toString();
        if (principal.toString().indexOf("GROUP") > -1) {
            role = principal.getName();
            grantedRoles.add(role);
        }
```

```
            return grantedRoles;
        }
    }
```

4   Add a **jaasAuthenticationProvider** bean definition to *src/main/ webapp/WEB-INF/security.xml* that brings everything together. See Listing 13.68.

Listing 12.68

```
. . <bean id="jaasAuthenticationProvider"
    class="org.acegisecurity.providers.jaas.JaasAuthenticationProvider">
    <property name="loginConfig" value="/WEB-INF/login.conf"/>
    <property name="loginContextName" value="FileLogin"/>
    <property name="callbackHandlers">
        <list>
            <bean class="org.acegisecurity.providers.jaas
                .JaasNameCallbackHandler"/>
            <bean class="org.acegisecurity.providers.jaas
                .JaasPasswordCallbackHandler"/>
        </list>
    </property>
    <property name="authorityGranters">
        <list>
            <bean class="org.appfuse.web.JaasAuthorityGranter"/>
        </list>
    </property>
</bean>
```

5   In the **authenticationManager** bean, comment out the reference to the **daoAuthenticationProvider** bean and add the **jaasAuthenticationProvider** bean. See Listing 13.69.

Listing 12.69

```
<bean id="authenticationManager"
    class="org.acegisecurity.providers.ProviderManager">
    <property name="providers">
        <list>
            <!--ref local="daoAuthenticationProvider"/-->
            <ref local="jaasAuthenticationProvider"/>
        </list>
    </property>
</bean>
```

6   Run **ant -f tomcat.xml deploy reload** and log in to localhost:8080/ equinox-security with the user name **jaasuser** and password **test1**.

> **NOTE:** The main advantage of using a JAAS `FileLogin` module over Acegi Security's `InMemoryDaoImpl` is you can add and remove users from the JAAS file and they'll be picked up immediately without requiring that you restart your application. With the `InMemoryDaoImpl`, you must alter the file and reload your web application.

SECURING METHOD INVOCATIONS

Acegi Security is an effective tool for securing methods on your Spring-managed beans. To do this, define a bean that uses the `MethodSecurityInterceptor`.

1   Add a user with a **ROLE_ADMIN** role. If you're still using the JAAS `FileLogin` module, add the line in Listing 13.70 to *src/main/webapp/WEB-INF/users.txt*.

Listing 12.70

```
admin:5a105e8b9d40e1329780d62ea2265d8a:ROLE_ADMIN:ROLE_USER
```

The password for this user is **test1**. Acegi Security also has a **ROLE_USER** role so you don't need to change the existing URL-to-role configuration.

2   Create a `securityInterceptor` bean in *src/main/webapp/WEB-INF/security.xml*. This bean determines the methods that each role can access. See Listing 13.71.

Listing 12.71

```
<bean id="securityInterceptor"
    class="org.acegisecurity.intercept.method.aopalliance
        .MethodSecurityInterceptor">
    <property name="authenticationManager"
        ref="authenticationManager"/>
    <property name="accessDecisionManager"
        ref="accessDecisionManager"/>
    <property name="objectDefinitionSource">
        <value>
            org.appfuse.service.UserManager.getUser=ROLE_ADMIN
            org.appfuse.service.UserManager.getUsers=ROLE_USER
            org.appfuse.service.UserManager.removeUser=ROLE_ADMIN
            org.appfuse.service.UserManager.saveUser=ROLE_ADMIN
        </value>
    </property>
</bean>
```

The `securityInterceptor` bean depends on the `authenticationManager` bean to verify authenticated users. The `accessDecisionManager` bean currently has only one voter, the **RoleVoter**, which determines permissions. It's recommended that you use Acegi Security's default **ROLE_** prefix to simplify distinguishing user names from role names.

The **objectDefinitionSource** property shows the methods and who can access them. Based on these rules, users with the **ROLE_USER** role can call **getUsers()**, but they cannot call **getUser()**, **removeUser()**, or **saveUser()**.

3   In the *src/main/webapp/WEB-INF/security.xml* file, add an **<aop:config>** element with a nested **<aop:advisor>** element that configures this interceptor to intercept the **userManager** bean's methods. This interceptor checks permissions before invoking a method and throws an exception if the user isn't authenticated or doesn't contain the proper role. See Listing 13.72.

Listing 12.72

```
<aop:config>
    <aop:advisor id="userManagerMethods"
        advice-ref="securityInterceptor"
        pointcut=
            "execution(* org.appfuse.service.UserManager.*(..))"/>
</aop:config>
```

NOTE: This syntax is part of Spring 2.0's improved AOP syntax. For more information, see *Chapter 6: Aspect Oriented Programming with Spring* in Spring's Reference Documentation.

4   Run **ant -f tomcat.xml deploy reload populate** and log in to localhost:8080/equinox-security with the user name **admin** and password **test1**. Click the **View Demonstration** button to view users; when you try to click a user, you should see the error in Figure 13.9.

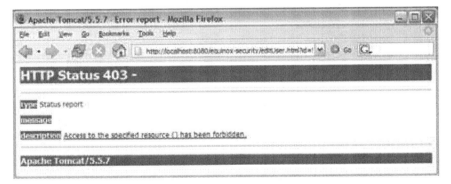

Figure 12.9: "Access Denied" error

To override the default "Access Denied" error page in the *equinox-security* application, use the following steps to create a JSP and map an error page for it in *web.xml*.

1 Create an *accessDenied.jsp* file in the *src/main/webapp* directory with a simple "Access Denied" message. See Listing 13.73.

Listing 12.73

```
<h1>Access Denied</h1>
<p>You don't have permission to perform this operation.</p>
```

2 Add an **<error-page>** in *src/main/webapp/WEB-INF/web.xml* that maps the 403 error code to this page. See Listing 13.74.

Listing 12.74

```
<error-page>
    <error-code>403</error-code>
    <location>/accessDenied.jsp</location>
</error-page>
```

3 Run the command **ant -f tomcat.xml deploy reload** and try to edit a user again. You should see a page similar to the one in Figure 13.10.

Figure 12.10: Customized "Access Denied" error

NOTE: SiteMesh does not process this page because it doesn't properly decorate error pages in Tomcat. To work around this issue, put some basic CSS and HTML structure in the *accessDenied.jsp* page or use the **<page:applyDecorator>** tag to wrap the page.

SECURING DOMAIN OBJECTS WITH ACLS

Restricting method calls to particular user roles is an excellent way to add security to your service layer. You can go a step further and lock down your domain objects so only certain users or roles can view them. Using AOP, you can modify the object returned from a secure method invocation. Acegi Security has this feature built in to its ACL capabilities.

The **AfterInvocationManager** handles the decision making for returning objects to users. This **AfterInvocationProvider** is the single concrete implementation of this interface. There are two types of providers:

- **BasicAclEntryAfterInvocationCollectionFilteringProvider** filters collections and removes objects where the user does not have the appropriate ACL.

- **BasicAclAfterInvocationProvider** ensures the principal has the appropriate permission to the returned object.

Figure 13.11 shows the relationship that exists between these interfaces and implementations.

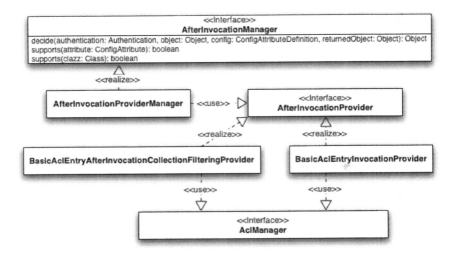

Figure 12.11: AfterInvocationManager

To make ACL-based object security easier to implement, Acegi Security ships with anAclManager implementation: **BasicAclProvider**. This class has a **BasicAclDao** dependency provided by the **JdbcExtendedDaoImpl** class. Using **JdbcExtendedDaoImpl** allows you to use custom database structures by setting the default query strings to use. Using the default data structures, this class talks to two database tables:

- **acl_object_identity** stores information about a domain object.

- **acl_permission** stores access information, specifying the principals and their permissions to objects in the **acl_object_identity** table. The permissions in this table are stored as integers (or masks) and indicate what a user can do with a particular object. Here are the available permission masks:

- **Mask integer 0** = no permissions
- **Mask integer 1** = administer
- **Mask integer 2** = read
- **Mask integer 4** = write
- **Mask integer 6** = read and write permissions
- **Mask integer 8** = create
- **Mask integer 14** = read and write and create permissions

---

NOTE: These masks are consistent with Acegi Security documentation and the sample application. However, you could change these masks to be more like a binary bit mask; for example, 0001 = administrator, 0010 = read, 0100 = write, 1000 = create. This would allow you to use 0110 to signify read and write permissions.

In the following exercise, you will modify the default[3] domain objects in the *equinox-security* application. You'll configure ACL settings for the "Julie Raible" user, which has a primary key of 5. You will configure the principals and their permissions as follows:

- **superuser**: Can read, write, and delete (administrative role)
- **readwrite**: Can read and write but not delete
- **nocando**: No permissions; cannot read or write

To implement these business rules, follow the steps below:

1   In *src/main/webapp/WEB-INF/security.xml*, change the **authentica-tionManager** bean so the **daoAuthenticationProvider** is the first (or only) one in the list of providers. See Listing 13.75.

Listing 12.75

```
<bean id="authenticationManager"
    class="org.acegisecurity.providers.ProviderManager">
    <property name="providers">
        <list>
            <ref local="daoAuthenticationProvider"/>
```

---

3. These objects are the ones that are in the database after you run **ant populate**.

```
            <ref local="jaasAuthenticationProvider"/>
         </list>
      </property>
   </bean>
```

2   Add the **admin**, **tomcat**, and **manager** principals to the MySQL **equinox** database. The encrypted passwords are the same as the user names for each user. See Listing 13.76.

Listing 12.76

```
INSERT INTO users (username, password) VALUES
    ('superuser','8e67bb26b358e2ed20fe552ed6fb832f397a507d');
INSERT INTO users (username, password) VALUES
    ('readwrite','accf881e821ed62ca842d34164426a7d9215a948');
INSERT INTO users (username, password) VALUES
    ('nocando','3131a0e3591641dcd157f027b92d09f99af39312');

INSERT INTO authorities (username, authority) VALUES
    ('superuser','ROLE_USER');
INSERT INTO authorities (username, authority) VALUES
    ('readwrite','ROLE_USER');
INSERT INTO authorities (username, authority) VALUES
    ('nocando','ROLE_USER');
```

In this example, all the users have the **ROLE_USER** role so they can log in according to the allowed roles specified in the **filterInvocationInterceptor** bean.

3   Add a number of new bean definitions to your *src/main/webapp/WEB-INF/security.xml* file. You can use any of the following bean definitions.

- **SimpleAclEntry.ADMINISTRATION**: This bean indicates the administer permission. The initialized value is from the **SimpleAclEntry** class and its **ADMINISTRATION** static variable.

- **SimpleAclEntry.READ_WRITE**: This bean indicates read/write permission.

- **SimpleAclEntry.READ**: This bean indicates read permission.

- **aclUserAdminVoter**: This implementation of **AccessDecision-Voter** determines whether a principal has administer permissions for the **org.appfuse.model.User** object. It's similar to **RoleVoter**, which determines access based on role.

- **aclUserUpdateVoter**: This implementation of **AccessDecision-Voter** determines whether a principal has read/write permissions for the **org.appfuse.model.User** object.

- **aclUserReadVoter**: This implementation of **AccessDecision-Voter** determines whether a principal has read permissions for the **org.appfuse.model.User** object.

- **aclAccessDecisionManager**: This is an implementation of **AccessDecisionManager**. This bean uses an instance of **AffirmativeBased**, which returns **"true"** if any voter returns an affirmative response. It contains a list of **decisionVoters**, which includes **roleVoter** and the ACL voters mentioned earlier.

- **aclManager**: This implementation of **AclManager** gets **AclEntry** instances for a particular domain object. It has a list of providers that looks up ACL information from a data store.

- **basicAclProvider**: This **AclProvider** gets ACL entries for objects from a DAO.

- **basicAclExtendedDao**: This extension of **JdbcDaoImpl** retrieves ACLs. Set it as the **BasicAclDao** on the **basicAclProvider** bean.

- **afterInvocationManager**: This implementation of **AfterInvocationManager** specifies a list of providers. These providers determine whether a principal has appropriate access to an object; if not, it throws an **AccessDeniedException**.

- **afterAclCollectionRead**: This implementation of **AfterInvocationProvider** removes objects from a collection if the principal doesn't have appropriate permissions as defined by the **aclManager** property. Set it as a provider on the **afterInvocationManager** bean.

- **afterAclRead**: This implementation of **AfterInvocation-Provider** determines whether a principal has appropriate permissions to access an object. Set it as a provider on the **afterInvocationManager** bean.

See Listing 13.77.

TIP: If you don't want to type the (lengthy) XML in Listing 13.77, you can download the completed application for this chapter and copy the XML from its *src/main/webapp/WEB-INF/security.xml* file.

CAUTION: The **staticField** properties in the first three beans must not contain white space or line breaks between the **<value>** tags and the class name. If one exists, you'll receive a **java.lang.ClassNotFoundException** error.

Listing 12.77

```
<!-- ===================== ACL-BASED SECURITY ===================== -->

<!-- ACL permission masks used by this application -->
<bean id="SimpleAclEntry.ADMINISTRATION"
    class="org.springframework.beans.factory.config
        .FieldRetrievingFactoryBean">
<property name="staticField"
value="org.acegisecurity.acl.basic.SimpleAclEntry.ADMINISTRATION"/>
</bean>

<bean id="SimpleAclEntry.READ_WRITE"
    class="org.springframework.beans.factory.config
        .FieldRetrievingFactoryBean">
<property name="staticField"
value="org.acegisecurity.acl.basic.SimpleAclEntry.READ_WRITE"/>
</bean>

<bean id="SimpleAclEntry.READ"
    class="org.springframework.beans.factory.config
        .FieldRetrievingFactoryBean">
<property name="staticField"
value="org.acegisecurity.acl.basic.SimpleAclEntry.READ"/>
</bean>

<!-- An access decision voter that reads ACL_USER_ADMIN settings -->
<bean id="aclUserAdminVoter"
class="org.acegisecurity.vote.BasicAclEntryVoter">
<property name="aclManager" ref="aclManager"/>
<property name="processConfigAttribute" value="ACL_USER_ADMIN"/>
<property name="processDomainObjectClass"
    value="org.appfuse.model.User"/>
<property name="requirePermission">
    <list>
        <ref local="SimpleAclEntry.ADMINISTRATION"/>
    </list>
 </property>
</bean>

<!-- An access decision voter that reads ACL_USER_UPDATE settings -->
<bean id="aclUserUpdateVoter"
class="org.acegisecurity.vote.BasicAclEntryVoter">
<property name="aclManager" ref="aclManager"/>
<property name="processConfigAttribute" value="ACL_USER_UPDATE"/>
<property name="processDomainObjectClass"
    value="org.appfuse.model.User"/>
<property name="requirePermission">
    <list>
        <ref local="SimpleAclEntry.ADMINISTRATION"/>
```

```
            <ref local="SimpleAclEntry.READ_WRITE"/>
        </list>
    </property>
</bean>


<!-- An access decision voter that reads ACL_USER_READ settings -->
<bean id="aclUserReadVoter"
class="org.acegisecurity.vote.BasicAclEntryVoter">
<property name="aclManager" ref="aclManager"/>
<property name="processConfigAttribute" value="ACL_USER_READ"/>
<property name="processDomainObjectClass"
    value="org.appfuse.model.User"/>
<property name="requirePermission">
    <list>
        <ref local="SimpleAclEntry.ADMINISTRATION"/>
        <ref local="SimpleAclEntry.READ_WRITE"/>
        <ref local="SimpleAclEntry.READ"/>
    </list>
</property>
</bean>


<!-- An access decision manager used by the business objects -->
<bean id="aclAccessDecisionManager"
class="org.acegisecurity.vote.AffirmativeBased">
<property name="allowIfAllAbstainDecisions" value="true"/>
<property name="decisionVoters">
    <list>
        <ref local="roleVoter"/>
        <ref local="aclUserAdminVoter"/>
        <ref local="aclUserUpdateVoter"/>
        <ref local="aclUserReadVoter"/>
    </list>
</property>
</bean>


<!-- ========= ACCESS CONTROL LIST MANAGER DEFINITIONS ========= -->

<bean id="aclManager"
class="org.acegisecurity.acl.AclProviderManager">
<property name="providers">
    <list>
        <ref local="basicAclProvider"/>
    </list>
</property>
</bean>


<bean id="basicAclProvider"
class="org.acegisecurity.acl.basic.BasicAclProvider">
<property name="basicAclDao" ref="basicAclExtendedDao"/>
</bean>
```

```
<bean id="basicAclExtendedDao"
class="org.acegisecurity.acl.basic.jdbc.JdbcExtendedDaoImpl">
<property name="dataSource" ref="dataSource"/>
</bean>

<!-- ============== "AFTER INTERCEPTION" AUTHORIZATION =========== -->

<bean id="afterInvocationManager"
    class="org.acegisecurity.afterinvocation
        .AfterInvocationProviderManager">
<property name="providers">
    <list>
        <ref local="afterAclRead"/>
        <ref local="afterAclCollectionRead"/>
    </list>
</property>
</bean>

<!-- Processes AFTER_ACL_COLLECTION_READ configuration settings -->
<bean id="afterAclCollectionRead"
    class="org.acegisecurity.afterinvocation
        .BasicAclEntryAfterInvocationCollectionFilteringProvider">
<property name="aclManager" ref="aclManager"/>
<property name="requirePermission">
    <list>
        <ref local="SimpleAclEntry.ADMINISTRATION"/>
        <ref local="SimpleAclEntry.READ_WRITE"/>
        <ref local="SimpleAclEntry.READ"/>
    </list>
</property>
</bean>

<!-- Processes AFTER_ACL_READ configuration settings -->
<bean id="afterAclRead" class="org.acegisecurity.afterinvocation
    .BasicAclEntryAfterInvocationProvider">
<property name="aclManager" ref="aclManager"/>
<property name="requirePermission">
    <list>
        <ref local="SimpleAclEntry.ADMINISTRATION"/>
        <ref local="SimpleAclEntry.READ_WRITE"/>
        <ref local="SimpleAclEntry.READ"/>
    </list>
</property>
</bean>
```

4 Create database tables to store ACL information for each object. The
script in Listing 13.78 will create the tables and insert permissions for the
User object with an **id** equal to **5**.

Listing 12.78

```
use equinox;

DROP TABLE IF EXISTS acl_object_identity;
CREATE TABLE acl_object_identity (
    id int(11) NOT NULL auto_increment,
    object_identity varchar(255) NOT NULL,
    parent_object int(11) default NULL,
    acl_class varchar(255) NOT NULL,
    PRIMARY KEY (id),
    UNIQUE KEY object_identity (object_identity)
) TYPE=InnoDB;

DROP TABLE IF EXISTS acl_permission;
CREATE TABLE acl_permission (
    id int(11) NOT NULL auto_increment,
    acl_object_identity int(11) NOT NULL,
    recipient varchar(100) NOT NULL,
    mask int(11) NOT NULL,
    PRIMARY KEY (id),
    UNIQUE (acl_object_identity, recipient)
) TYPE=InnoDB;

INSERT INTO acl_object_identity VALUES
    (1, 'org.appfuse.model.User:5', null,
    'org.acegisecurity.acl.basic.SimpleAclEntry');
INSERT INTO acl_object_identity VALUES
    (2, 'org.appfuse.model.User:6', null,
    'org.acegisecurity.acl.basic.SimpleAclEntry');

INSERT INTO acl_permission VALUES (null, 1, 'superuser', 1);
INSERT INTO acl_permission VALUES (null, 1, 'readwrite', 6);
INSERT INTO acl_permission VALUES (null, 1, 'nocando', 0);

--- Mask integer 0  = no permissions
--- Mask integer 1  = administer
--- Mask integer 2  = read
--- Mask integer 6  = read and write permissions
--- Mask integer 14 = read and write and create permissions
```

TIP: You can specify the role name in addition to (or as an alternative to) the principal's name in the `acl_permission` table.

---

5   Change the **securityInterceptor** bean to specify an **afterInvocationManager** property. Then change the **objectDefinitionSource** to check the **getUser()** and **getUsers()** roles for domain object permissions. You don't need to specify ACL rules on **saveUser()**

and **removeUser**() because the rules are only applied *after* method invocation. You can only specify ACL rules on secure methods with roles defined. See Listing 13.79.

Listing 12.79

```
<bean id="securityInterceptor"
    class="org.acegisecurity.intercept.method.aopalliance
    .MethodSecurityInterceptor">
    <property name="authenticationManager"
        ref="authenticationManager"/>
    <property name="accessDecisionManager"
        ref="accessDecisionManager"/>
    <property name="afterInvocationManager"
        ref="afterInvocationManager"/>
    <property name="objectDefinitionSource">
        <value>
            org.appfuse.service.UserManager.getUser=
                ROLE_ADMIN,AFTER_ACL_READ
            org.appfuse.service.UserManager.getUsers=ROLE_USER,
                                                AFTER_ACL_
                                                COLLECTION_READ
            org.appfuse.service.UserManager.removeUser=ROLE_ADMIN
            org.appfuse.service.UserManager.saveUser=
                ROLE_ADMIN,ROLE_READWRITE
        </value>
    </property>
</bean>
```

6 Run **ant -f tomcat.xml deploy reload** to deploy and refresh the application.

7 Log in to localhost:8080/equinox-security/users.html with the *superuser/ superuser* user. You should be able to see "Julie Raible" as a user in the list. See Figure 13.12.

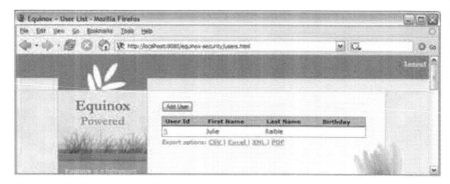

Figure 12.12: User list for `superuser` principal

This record displays because the **acl_permission** table has the record in Listing 13.80. You entered this record in step 4).

Listing 12.80

```
mysql> select * from acl_permission where recipient = 'superuser';
+----+----------------------+-----------+------+
| id | acl_object_identity  | recipient | mask |
+----+----------------------+-----------+------+
| 1  |                    1 | superuser |    1 |
+----+----------------------+-----------+------+
```

This record says that the **superuser** principal has administer permissions (**mask = 1**) for the object with **id = 1** in the **acl_object_identity**. The record with **id = 1** has **org.appfuse.model.User:5** for its **object_identity** value. By default, this value is the class name plus colon (:) plus the value that the **getId()** method returns.

   8   Log out and log back in with the **nocando/nocando** user. Now you won't see any records. See Figure 13.13.

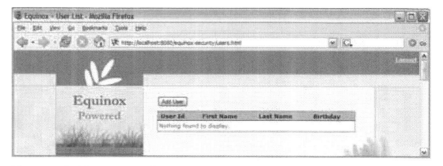

Figure 12.13: User list for `nocando` principal

You might have noticed how you need to specify ACLs for *all* objects. To solve this problem, create a parent object that has default permissions and have entries for child objects for which you want to change permission. If you implement ACL-based security in your application, you should create a user interface to edit ACLs for the secured objects. In addition to this example, you might find AppFuse's Acegi ACL tutorial helpful.

ADDITIONAL ACEGI SECURITY FEATURES

In addition to the features mentioned here, Acegi Security includes features such as Remember Me, SSL switching, anonymous users, user switching, and authentication with LDAP. Examples of Remember Me, SSL switching, and anonymous users can be found in AppFuse's *security.xml*. The latter two have examples in Acegi's sample applications.

ACEGI SECURITY VERSUS J2EE SECURITY

It can be difficult to choose between container-managed security and Acegi Security. To help you decide, refer to Table , which illustrates the pros and cons of each approach.

Table 12.1: Acegi Security and J2EE: Their Pros and Cons

Security Framework	Pros	Cons
Acegi Security	• Security configuration is self-contained in the application — you don't need to worry about application server portability. • It solves many of the shortcomings of J2EE security and allows all the same things with the option to customize. • It supports single sign-on with CAS. • It's evolving and improving rapidly. • It allows you to secure methods of any Spring-managed bean and filtering objects based on their ACLs.	• It requires a lot of XML to configure. • The learning curve can be a little steep and seem overwhelming at first. • Realm information is packaged with the application, making it tough for a deployer to change.
J2EE security	• It is easy to set up from an application perspective. • User realm configuration is in the hands of the deployer. • Because it's a standard, many sources of documentation are available.	• It can be difficult to port from one application server to the other. Even though the application-developer configuration is standardized, the realm configuration for servers is not. • Service layer methods can be secured only if you are using EJBs.

In general, I'd recommend you use container-managed security for small, prototype applications. Container-managed authentication is also a good choice if you're using EJBs and want to secure method invocations without wiring them up as Spring beans. However, if you want the power and flexibility of security method invocations and filtering objects based on ACLs, Acegi Security is the framework for you. The code samples in this chapter provided you with the foundation and reference you'll need to implement Acegi Security into your project.

AUTHORIZATION

After users log in to the application, you might have requirements for what they can do or see. Setting these permissions is much simpler with container-managed security and Acegi Security because the user's role is available to you. Using your own authentication architecture, you could probably achieve a similar result, but you might not be able to take advantage of the wealth of available plug-ins. By plug-ins, I mean tag libraries and other Java-related packages that allow for role-based configuration. For example, the Request Tag Library allows you to show and hide parts of your user interface based on a user's role. The Tiles templating framework also allows you to configure showing and hiding sections of your template based on roles.

In the last section on Acegi Security, you learned how to protect certain users and roles from invoking methods on your service layer. It's equally important to hide links in the view so users never see an "Access Denied" error. If a user sees this type of error after clicking a visible link, it's probably an oversight in your application code. But if a user is altering the parameters or path of a URL, an "Access Denied" error is entirely appropriate.

PROTECTING PAGES AND URLs

You need consider what choices a user should have after logging in. Usually, choices are presented as links, but they can also be menu-type systems, such as pick-lists or DHTML drop-down menus. One simple way to control what links a user might see is to use something similar to the `<request:isUserInRole>` tag to show or hide links on the basis of a user's role. If you're using Acegi Security, you can use its `AuthorizeTag` to hide links based on roles or its `AclTag` to hide links based on specific permissions for an object.

One practice recommended by web application developers is to place your JSP files and fragments under the *WEB-INF* directory when deploying your application. If you use this method, you will prevent browsers from directly accessing JSP pages using a URL, and it forces you (as a developer) to follow the MVC pattern. Your JSP pages will be protected because all resources under *WEB-INF* are secluded and not accessible from a URL. The Servlet specification mandates that security be provided inside *WEB-INF*, and it ensures good separation of controller and view by forcing each request to go through a servlet controller. However, some containers don't support this method— they allow access to *WEB-INF* through the browser or they don't allow you to render JSP pages that live under *WEB-INF*. If your servlet container is J2EE compliant, however, it should allow you to do protect your pages this way.

NOTE: Equinox 1.2+ does not place the JSPs in the WEB-INF directory, mainly because having them under the *web* directory is easier to understand. *Chapter 6: View Options* shows you how to move your JSPs under *src/main/webapp/WEB-INF/jsp* and how to configure Spring appropriately.

After securing the locations of your pages, you need to secure access to them so that unauthorized users cannot execute the logic to get to them. You can do secure access in a couple of different ways. The built-in method with servlets is to use a different security constraint for each servlet (or group of servlets) that you want to protect, which means you need to create servlet mappings for each servlet or group. (Your *web.xml* can become quite large if you have many servlets.) An easier way is to proxy all requests through an initial servlet that checks permissions and forwards appropriately. Other alternatives include using a filter or putting a tag library at the top of every JSP file. This tag library verifies whether the user has access to that page.

The problem with programmatically checking for user roles and dispatching accordingly or displaying an error message (as in the case of the JSP) is that it can become a maintenance nightmare. Container-managed authentication or framework-based solutions such as Acegi Security are much easier to work with.

TOOLS FOR AUTHORIZATION

Several helpful tools are available to help you protect principals from unauthorized access.

USERROLEAUTHORIZATIONINTERCEPTOR

The `UserRoleAuthorizationInterceptor` is an *interceptor* included in Spring's MVC module. It allows you to specify which roles can access certain URLs. It uses the `HttpServletRequest` API and its `isUserInRole()` method. For more information about configuring this interceptor, please see the *Intercepting the request* section in *Chapter 5: Advanced Spring MVC*.

STRUTS MENU

Struts Menu is an open-source project that allows you to configure menu items and links in an XML file. It started as a plug-in for Struts, but you can now use it in any web framework that supports JSPs. Struts Menu allows you to choose different menu styles (for example, drop-down menus, DHTML, or tabs) and has a **Permissions Adapter** for setting permissions programmatically from your application. It also allows you to define roles in its XML configuration file. You can use the built-in **RolesPermissionAdapter** to check security access for the roles you define in the *menu-config.xml* file. To configure this access, add **permissions="rolesAdapter"** to the **<menu:useMenuDisplayer>** tag. See Listing 13.81.

Listing 12.81

```
<menu:useMenuDisplayer name="Velocity" permissions="rolesAdapter">
```

TILES

You can use the Tiles templating framework as a plug-in with Struts and as a view option with Spring MVC. You can use it to create templates of your JSP pages so you need to change only a page or two (depending on how many layout templates you have) to alter the entire look and feel of your site. The Tiles tag libraries and definitions XML file allow you to define role attributes.

ACEGI SECURITY TAG LIBRARIES

Acegi Security ships with a JSP tag library designed to simplify writing JSPs. To use this tag library in the *equinox-security* application, simply add the line in Listing 13.82 to *web/taglibs.jsp*:

Listing 12.82

```
<%@ taglib uri="http://acegisecurity.org/authz" prefix="authz" %>
```

You could use a prefix such as "**a**" or "**auth**," but "**authz**" is the prefix recommended by the Acegi Security team. By using this prefix, you'll enable other developers to easily understand how your application works.

AUTHORIZETAG

The **AuthorizeTag** is similar to the Request tag library in that it can show and hide information based on a principal's roles. In Acegi Security's terminology, a principal's roles are *granted authorities*. Listing 13.83 is an example of how to use this tag to hide the **Add User** button in the *web/userList.jsp* page:

Listing 12.83

```
<authz:authorize ifAnyGranted="ROLE_READWRITE,ROLE_ADMIN">
    <button onclick="location.href='editUser.html'">Add User</button>
</authz:authorize>
```

Adding the elements in Listing 13.83 to the existing *web/userList.jsp* will hide it from all principals because neither **ROLE_READWRITE** nor **ROLE_ADMIN** is assigned to users in the **authorities** table. Next, add records to the **authorities** table. See Listing 13.84.

Listing 12.84

```
INSERT INTO authorities (username, authority)
    VALUES ('superuser','ROLE_ADMIN');
INSERT INTO authorities (username, authority)
    VALUES ('readwrite','ROLE_READWRITE');
```

Deploy and log in with the **nocando** user name and password; the **Add User** button should be hidden. See Figure 13.14.

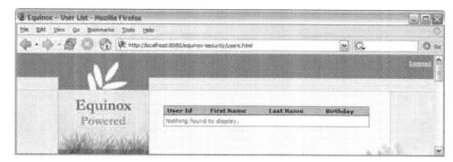

Figure 12.14: Hidden **Add User** button for ROLE_USER

Log out and log back in as **readwrite**. You should see the **Add User** button, as in Figure 13.15.

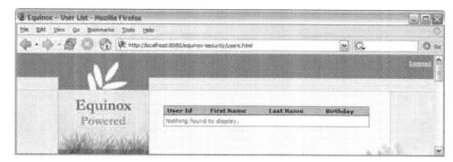

Figure 12.15: Add User button for ROLE_READWRITE

In addition to the `ifAnyGranted` attribute, the `ifAllGranted` and `ifNot-Granted` attributes exist for more fine-tuned control of who can see what. The `AuthorizeTag` verifies the authorizations in the following order:

1   `ifNotGranted`: None of the listed roles must be granted for the tag to output its body.

2   `ifAllGranted`: All the listed roles must be granted for the tag to output its body.

3   `ifAnyGranted`: Any of the listed roles must be granted for the tag to output its body.

AUTHENTICATIONTAG

You can use the `AuthenticationTag` to print out the principal's user name. Use the code in Listing 13.85 to print out **readwrite** if you're logged in as that user.

Listing 12.85

```
<authz:authentication operation="principal"/>
```

TIP: You could also use JSP's Extension Language to produce the same output as long as you're using Acegi Security's `SecurityContextHolderAwareRequest-Filter`. See Listing 13.86.

Listing 12.86

```
${pageContext.request.remoteUser}
```

ACLTAG

The `AclTag` controls access to an object based on the object's ACL. If you followed the Acegi Security tutorial, your *equinox-security* application should have a **read-write** user that's not allowed to invoke the **UserManager.removeUser()** method. Using this tag, you can easily hide the **Delete** button for this principal when viewing a user's details. In *web/userForm.jsp*, change the **Delete** button's code so only principals with the **administer** permission will see it. See Listing 13.87.

Listing 12.87

```
<c:if test="${not empty param.id}">
    <authz:acl domainObject="${user}" hasPermission="1">
        <input type="submit" class="button"
            name="delete" value="Delete"/>
    </authz:acl>
</c:if>
```

AUDITING AND MONITORING SECURITY

Projects often have requirements to audit the security of the web application by capturing security events — authentication and authorization failures in addition to successful logins. Spring's `org.springframework.context.ApplicationListener` interface simplifies auditing based on the Observer design pattern. Acegi Security has a couple of classes that implement this interface: `org.acegisecurity.event.authentication.LoggerListener` and `org.acegisecurity.event.authorization.LoggerListener`. Each listens for events related to their respective area: authentication or authorization. The following bulleted items are sample event types:

- `AuthenticationCredentialsNotFoundEvent`

- `AuthenticationFailureBadCredentialsEvent`

- `AuthorizationFailureEvent`

- `AuthorizedEvent`

- `PublicInvocationEvent`

To configure the `LoggingListener` for authentication in the *equinox-security* project, perform the following steps:

1   Define a bean in *src/main/webapp/WEB-INF/security.xml* that uses `LoggerListener` in its `class` attribute. It will be instantiated and managed according to the standard bean lifecycle. See Listing 13.88.

Listing 12.88

```
<bean id="loggerListener"
    class="org.acegisecurity.event.authentication.LoggerListener"/>
```

2   Add a new `<logger>` to *src/main/webapp/WEB-INF/classes/log4j.xml* so the events will show up in your application logs. See Listing 13.89.

Listing 12.89

```
<logger name="org.acegisecurity.event.authentication
    .LoggerListener">
    <level value="WARN"/>
</logger>
```

3　Run **ant -f tomcat.xml deploy reload** and try to log in with an invalid user name. Figure 13.16 shows logging in with an invalid user name followed by a valid user name with an incorrect password.

Figure 12.16: Security events logged using **LoggerListener**

Publishing these security-related events in your application's event log is an excellent example of separation of concerns. The security management is not directly coupled with the actions that must occur as a result of one or more security events. Event examples include authentication and displaying "Access Denied" exceptions to the user.

SUMMARY

This chapter has provided you with the security information you need to integrate security into your Spring-based application. For container-managed security, you learned how to add **<security-constraint>** elements to your *web.xml*. From there, you saw how to configure Tomcat with various user realms (XML file, database, LDAP) to check credentials. Finally, you learned how to configure Tomcat for SSL and how to force your web application to switch between HTTP and HTTPS.

In the second half of the chapter, you explored the configuration and setup of the Acegi Security framework for Spring. This powerful library can do basic and form-based authentication and perform secure method invocations and protect objects based on their ACLs. Finally, you learned how to use JSP tags to show and hide information based on a user's role and an object's ACL.

ADVANCED FORM PROCESSING

Handling forms, wizards, and flows with Spring MVC

Spring MVC is a full-fledged web application framework. It can easily handle complex data types, nested forms, indexed properties, and wizards. It even has a "page flow" component that allows you to configure navigation rules external to your controllers.

*Chapter 4: Spring's MVC Framework gave you the basics of Spring MVC. This chapter will provide even more about how to use forms and how to handle common issues in web development. These issues typically revolve around handling non-string types such as **Integer**, **Date**, and **Boolean**; displaying drop-down lists and using check boxes; and editing nested objects. Unlike many web frameworks, Spring MVC also has built-in support for multi-page forms, called wizards, using its **AbstractWizardFormController** or Spring Web Flow.*

To follow along with the exercises, download the MyUsers Chapter 13 project from source-beat.com/downloads. This project is based on Equinox 1.7 with the web and persistence framework installers removed. The download uses Spring MVC and Hibernate (the most popular configuration). For more information about configuring this project, see its README.txt in the root directory. If you have MySQL installed, it should create the database for you automatically.

NON-STRING FIELDS

An HTTP request sends input fields in a form as string parameters. If your command object has string properties, Spring's data binding can populate these properties without any additional configuration. However, if you have non-string fields (such as **Integer**, **Double**, or **Date**), you must register custom **Property-Editor** classes in your **SimpleFormController**.

In this section, you'll add three non-string properties to the **User** object: an **Integer**, a **Double**, and a **Date**.

1   Add the properties and accessor methods in Listing 14.1 to the **src/main/java/org/appfuse/model/User.java** class.

Listing 13.1

```
private Date birthDate;
private Integer siblings;
private Double temperature;

public Date getBirthDate() {
    return birthDate;
}

public void setBirthDate(Date birthDate) {
    this.birthDate = birthDate;
}

public Integer getSiblings() {
    return siblings;
}

public void setSiblings(Integer siblings) {
    this.siblings = siblings;
}

public Double getTemperature() {
    return temperature;
}

public void setTemperature(Double temperature) {
    this.temperature = temperature;
}
```

2   Modify the *src/main/java/org/appfuse/model/User.hbm.xml* mapping file to add the properties in Listing 14.2.

Listing 13.2

```
<property name="birthDate" column="birth_date"/>
<property name="siblings" column="no_siblings"/>
<property name="temperature" column="temperature"/>
```

3   Add each property as a new row of data in *src/main/webapp/userForm.jsp*[1]. See Listing 14.3.

---

1. The **<form>** tag in this example is from Spring 2.0's Form Tag Library.

Listing 13.3

```
<tr>
    <th><fmt:message key="user.birthDate"/>:</th>
    <td>
        <form:input path="birthDate" id="birthDate" size="11"/>
        <form:errors path="birthDate" cssClass="fieldError"/>
    </td>
</tr>
<tr>
    <th><fmt:message key="user.siblings"/>:</th>
    <td>
        <form:input path="siblings" id="siblings" size="5"/>
        <form:errors path="siblings" cssClass="fieldError"/>
    </td>
</tr>
<tr>
    <th><fmt:message key="user.temperature"/>:</th>
    <td>
        <form:input path="temperature" id="temperature"
            size="4"/> &deg;F
        <form:errors path="temperature" cssClass="fieldError"/>
    </td>
</tr>
```

4 Add i18n keys and values for each of the new properties in *src/main/resources/messages.properties*. See Listing 14.4.

Listing 13.4

```
user.birthDate=Birth Date
user.siblings=No. of Siblings
user.temperature=Body Temperature
```

5 Run **ant deploy** (or **mvn jetty:run** if you'd prefer to use Maven 2) and try to add a new user in your browser. You should receive an error that the string-to-date conversion failed. See Figure 14.1.

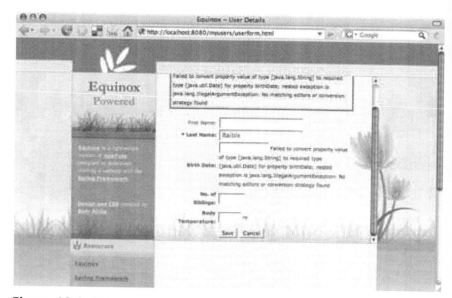

Figure 13.1: Property conversion errors

To show more user-friendly error messages, add **typeMismatch.*** keys to your application's i18n bundle. Add the key-value pairs in Listing 14.5 to *src/main/resources/messages.properties*:

Listing 13.5

```
# -- conversion errors --
typeMismatch.java.lang.Integer={0} must be an integer.
typeMismatch.java.lang.Double={0} must be a double.
typeMismatch.java.util.Date={0} must be a date.
```

Run **ant -f tomcat.xml deploy reload** and try the previous operation again. This time, the conversion error message is more user-friendly. See Figure 14.2.

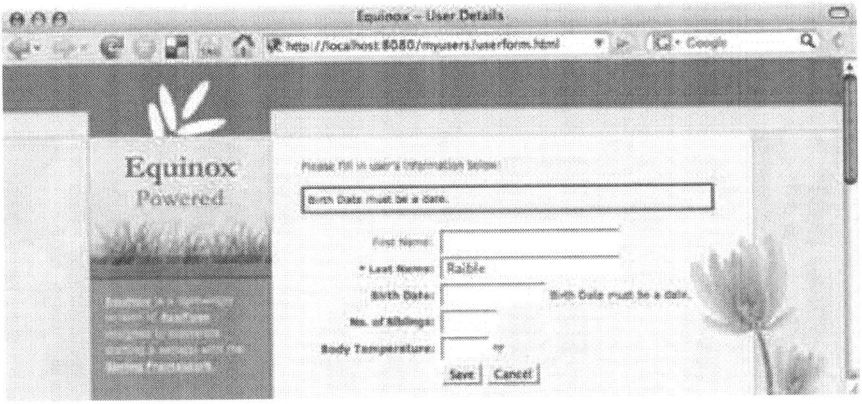

Figure 13.2: User-friendly conversion error

You can use messages to handle conversion errors. This way, you don't need to specify validation rules for each property type; rather, you can just display errors when conversion fails. In addition to specifying **typeMismatch.*className***, you can specify **typeMismatch.*fieldName***.

The class that makes this all possible is the **DefaultMessageCodesResolver**, which is part of the **org.springframework.validation** package. Spring MVC handles validation of property types for you. You simply need to override the default error messages to make them more user-friendly.

6   To convert strings into the specified object types, register a **PropertyEditor** for each type in the **initBinder()** method of **UserFormController**. See Listing 14.6.

Listing 13.6

```
protected void initBinder(HttpServletRequest request,
                          ServletRequestDataBinder binder) {
    // convert java.util.Date
    SimpleDateFormat dateFormat = new SimpleDateFormat("MM/dd/yyyy");
    dateFormat.setLenient(false);
    binder.registerCustomEditor(Date.class, null,
            new CustomDateEditor(dateFormat, true));

}
```

NOTE: In Spring 2.0, converters are automatically registered for **Integer** and **Double** types. In versions prior to 2.0, this was not the case, and you had to register them in your **initBinder()** method in the **FormController** using the code in Listing 14.7.

Listing 13.7

```
// convert java.lang.Integer
binder.registerCustomEditor(Integer.class, null,
    new CustomNumberEditor(Integer.class, true));

// convert java.lang.Double
binder.registerCustomEditor(Double.class, null,
    new CustomNumberEditor(Double.class, true));
```

7 Run **ant -f tomcat deploy reload** and add a new user by filling in the new fields. Figure 14.3 shows an example with values for each new field.

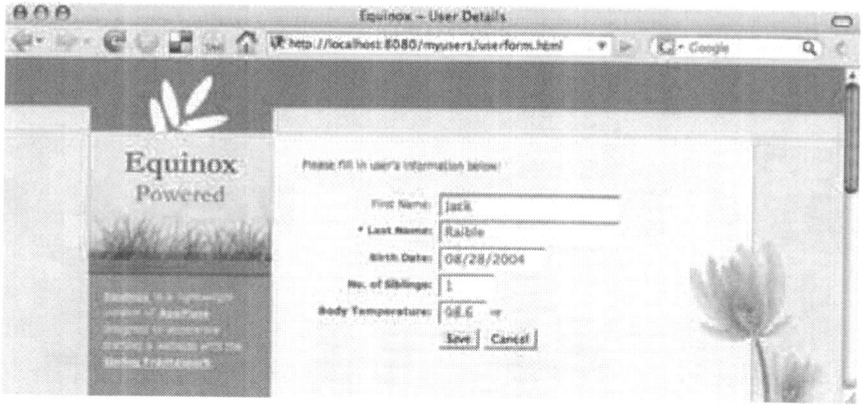

Figure 13.3: Form with non-string fields

ADDING A DATE SELECTOR

The one thing missing from this example is a pop-up calendar to select the date. To add one, complete the following steps.

1 Download the **DHTML / JavaScript Calendar** from www.dynarch.com/projects/calendar.

2 Extract the *jscalendar-1.0.zip* file to your hard drive and copy the following files to the *myusers* project folder:

 • Copy calendar.js into src/main/webapp/scripts.

 • Copy calendar-setup.js into src/main/webapp/scripts.

 • Copy lang/* into src/main/webapp/scripts/lang.

 • Copy calendar-green.css into src/main/webapp/styles.

3   In *src/main/webapp/userForm.jsp*, replace the `<title>` element with the code in Listing 14.8 to include the JavaScript and CSS files:

Listing 13.8

```
<head>
    <title><fmt:message key="userForm.title"/></title>
    <link href="${ctx}/styles/calendar-green.css" type="text/css"
        rel="stylesheet"/>
    <script type="text/javascript"
        src="${ctx}/scripts/calendar.js"></script>
    <script type="text/javascript"
        src="${ctx}/scripts/calendar-setup.js"></script>
    <script type="text/javascript"
        src="${ctx}/scripts/lang/calendar-en.js"></script>
</head>
```

4   Add a button after the `birthDate` field (see Listing 14.9) to invoke the calendar.

Listing 13.9

```
<form:input path="birthDate" id="birthDate" size="11"/>
<button id="birthDateCal" type="button" class="button">...</button>
```

5   Add JavaScript to the bottom of the page to initialize the calendar for the `birthDateCal` button. See Listing 14.10.

Listing 13.10

```
<script type="text/javascript">
    Form.focusFirstElement($('userForm'));
    Calendar.setup({
        inputField  : "birthDate",     // id of the input field
        ifFormat    : "%m/%d/%Y",      // the date format
        button      : "birthDateCal"   // id of the button
    });
</script>
```

6   Run **ant deploy** and open MyUsers in your browser. Click the button next to the **Birth Date** field to display a pop-up calendar. See Figure 14.4.

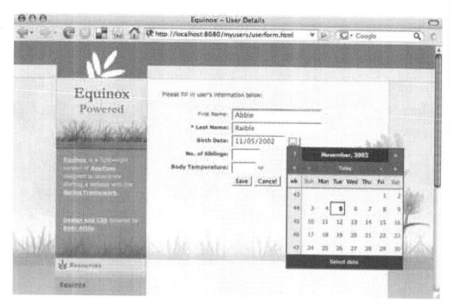

Figure 13.4: Date selector

In this section, you have seen how Spring makes it easy to convert strings from request parameters into real object types. For the most part, it's a matter of registering editors in the **initBinder()** method. Also, adding **typeMismatch.*** messages to your i18n **ResourceBundle** makes it easy to present user-friendly conversion-error messages.

DROP-DOWN LISTS AND CHECK BOXES

The **referenceData()** method in the **SimpleFormController** is designed specifically for pulling and displaying information in drop-down lists (or **<select>** elements) on a form. In this exercise, you'll add a drop-down list of countries to the form.

1 Add a **country** property and accessor methods to the **src/main/java/ org/appfuse/model/User.java** object. See Listing 14.11.

Listing 13.11

```
private String country;
public String getCountry() {
    return country;
}
```

```
public void setCountry(String country) {
    this.country = country;
}
```

2   Map this property to a column in *src/main/java/org/appfuse/model/ User.hbm.xml*. See Listing 14.12.

Listing 13.12

```
<property name="country" column="country"/>
```

3   Override the **referenceData()** method in *src/main/java/org/appfuse/web/ UserFormController.java*. This method returns a **java.util.Map** of bean name and bean instance pairs as expected by the **ModelAndView**. The **NameValue** object referenced in this method should already exist in the *src/main/java/org/appfuse/web* directory. See Listing 14.13.

Listing 13.13

```
protected Map referenceData(HttpServletRequest request) {
    final Locale[] available = Locale.getAvailableLocales();

    List countries = new ArrayList();

    for (int i = 0; i < available.length; i++) {
        final String value = available[i].getCountry();
        final String name =
            available[i].getDisplayCountry(request.getLocale());

        if (!"".equals(value) && !"".equals(name)) {
            NameValue country = new NameValue(name, value);

            if (!countries.contains(country)) {
                countries.add(new NameValue(name, value));
            }
        }
    }

    Collections.sort(countries, NameValue.CASE_INSENSITIVE_ORDER);
    Map countryMap = new HashMap();
    countryMap.put("countries", countries);

    return countryMap;
}
```

4   Add a **country** drop-down list to *src/main/webapp/userForm.jsp*. See Listing 14.14.

Listing 13.14

```
<tr>
    <th><fmt:message key="user.country"/>:</th>
    <td>
        <form:select path="country">
            <form:option value="" label=""/>
            <form:options items="${countries}"
                itemValue="value" itemLabel="name"/>
        </form:select>
        <form:errors path="country" cssClass="fieldError"/>
    </td>
</tr>
```

5   Add a **user.country** key and value to *src/main/resources/messages.properties*. See Listing 14.15.

Listing 13.15

```
user.country=Country
```

6   Run **ant -f tomcat.xml deploy reload** and add a new user. You should see a **Country** drop-down list as shown in Figure 14.5.

Figure 13.5: Country drop-down list

Check boxes present an interesting challenge for framework developers. Unlike the other input fields, check boxes will not send a request parameter when they're unchecked. Therefore, there has to be a mechanism to indicate the field was *unchecked*. Spring MVC accomplishes this by adding a hidden field that has the same name as the check box field, except it has an underscore (_) as a prefix. See an example in Listing 14.16.

Listing 13.16

```
<input type="hidden" name="_${status.expression}"/>
<input type="checkbox" name="${status.expression}" value="true"/>
```

The good news is the code in Listing 14.16 was required for Spring versions prior to 2.0, but in 2.0, there's a **<form:checkbox>** tag that does this for you.

To add a check box to the user form, perform the following steps:

1   Add an **enabled** property to the **User** object. See Listing 14.17.

Listing 13.17

```
private Boolean enabled;

public Boolean getEnabled() {
    return enabled;
}

public void setEnabled(Boolean enabled) {
    this.enabled = enabled;
}
```

2   Map this property to a column in *src/main/java/org/appfuse/model/ User.hbm.xml*. See Listing 14.18.

Listing 13.18

```
<property name="enabled" column="enabled"/>
```

3   Add an **enabled** check box to *src/main/webapp/userForm.jsp*. See Listing 14.19.

Listing 13.19

```
<tr>
    <th><label><fmt:message key="user.enabled"/>?</label></th>
    <td>
```

```
            <form:checkbox path="enabled"/>
            <form:errors path="enabled" cssClass="fieldError"/>
        </td>
    </tr>
```

4   Add a **user.enabled** key and value to *src/main/resources/messages.properties*.
    See Listing 14.20.

Listing 13.20

```
user.enabled=Enabled
```

5   Run **ant -f tomcat.xml deploy reload** and go to the **Add User**
    screen. You should be able to toggle this new field on and off and have
    your selection persisted to the database.

NESTED OBJECTS AND INDEXED PROPERTIES

A common use-case in web applications is to have an object composed from two
separate database tables. For example, one table stores user account information,
and another table stores address. To display and edit nested objects, you'll create an
Address object and make it a property on the **User** object.

1   Create an **Address.java** class in the *src/main/java/org/appfuse/model*
    directory. See Listing 14.21.

Listing 13.21

```
package org.appfuse.model;

public class Address extends BaseObject {
    private Long id;
    private String city;
    private String state;
    private String zip;

    // generate getters and setters with your IDE
}
```

2   Create an *Address.hbm.xml* mapping file in the same directory as your
    Address object. See Listing 14.22.

Listing 13.22

```xml
<?xml version="1.0" encoding="UTF-8"?>
<!DOCTYPE hibernate-mapping PUBLIC
    "-//Hibernate/Hibernate Mapping DTD 3.0//EN"
    "http://hibernate.sourceforge.net/hibernate-mapping-3.0.dtd">

<hibernate-mapping>
    <class name="org.appfuse.model.Address" table="address">
        <id name="id" column="id">
            <generator class="increment"/>
        </id>
        <property name="city"/>
        <property name="state"/>
        <property name="zip"/>
    </class>
</hibernate-mapping>
```

3   Open *src/main/webapp/WEB-INF/applicationContext-hibernate.xml* and add the *Address.hbm.xml* mapping file to the list of mappings. See Listing 14.23.

Listing 13.23

```xml
<property name="mappingResources">
    <list>
        <value>org/appfuse/model/Address.hbm.xml</value>
        <value>org/appfuse/model/User.hbm.xml</value>
    </list>
</property>
```

4   Modify the *src/main/java/org/appfuse/model/User.java* class to have an **address** property. See Listing 14.24.

Listing 13.24

```java
private Address address;

public Address getAddress() {
    return address;
}

public void setAddress(Address address) {
    this.address = address;
}
```

5   Modify the *src/main/java/org/appfuse/model/User.hbm.xml* mapping file to have a **many-to-one** mapping for its **address** property. See Listing 14.25.

Listing 13.25

```
<many-to-one name="address" class="org.appfuse.model.Address"
    column="address_id" cascade="all"/>
```

6   Modify the **formBackingObject()** method in **UserFormController** to set an empty **Address** object on a **User** object if none exists. This is to prevent the **<form:*>** tags from throwing exceptions when the **address** property is null. See Listing 14.26.

Listing 13.26

```
protected Object formBackingObject(HttpServletRequest request)
        throws ServletException {
    String userId = request.getParameter("id");

    User user = null;
    if ((userId != null) && !userId.equals("")) {
        user = mgr.getUser(userId);
    } else {
        user = new User();
    }

    if (user.getAddress() == null) {
        user.setAddress(new Address());
    }

    return user;
}
```

7   Add fields to the *src/main/webapp/userForm.jsp* file to allow editing of a user's address. See Listing 14.27.

Listing 13.27

```
<tr>
    <td colspan="2">
        <fieldset>
            <legend>Address</legend>
            <table>
                <tr>
                    <th style="text-align: left">City</th>
                    <th style="text-align: left">State</th>
                    <th style="text-align: left">Zip</th>
```

```
                    </tr>
                    <tr>
                        <form:hidden path="address.id"/>
                        <td>
                            <form:input path="address.city"/>
                            <form:errors path="address.city"
                                cssClass="fieldError"/>
                        </td>
                        <td>
                            <form:input path="address.state" size="2"/>
                            <form:errors path="address.state"
                                cssClass="fieldError"/>
                        </td>
                        <td>
                            <form:input path="address.zip" size="10"/>
                            <form:errors path="address.zip"
                                cssClass="fieldError"/>
                        </td>
                    </tr>
                </table>
            </fieldset>
        </td>
    </tr>
```

8   Run **ant -f tomcat.xml deploy reload** and go to the **Add User** screen. Your browser should look similar to Figure 14.6.

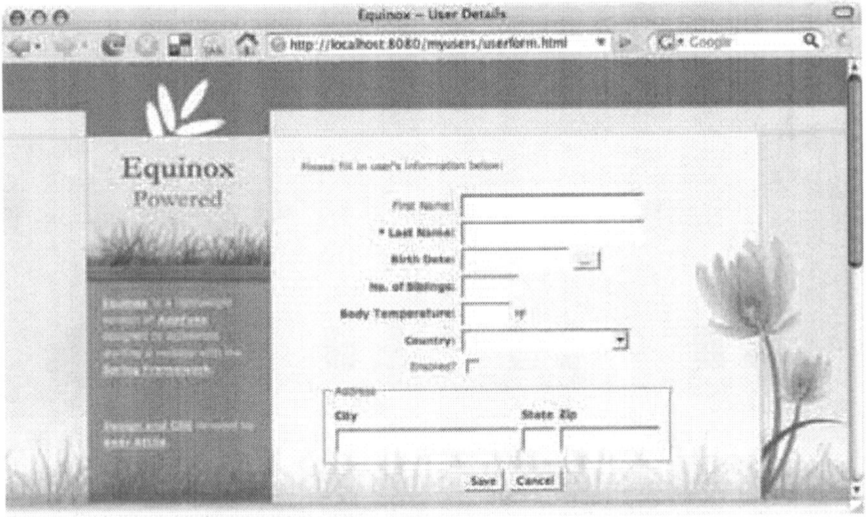

Figure 13.6: Nested address object

9   To make the **City** field required, simply add the validation rule in Listing 14.28 to *src/main/webapp/WEB-INF/validation.xml*.

Listing 13.28

```
<field property="address.city" depends="required">
    <arg key="City" resource="false"/>
</field>
```

Now if you redeploy and reload, both **Last Name** and **City** will be required.

CUSTOM PROPERTYEDITORS

A custom **PropertyEditor** can transform a string in a form into a real object. In this exercise, you'll create an **AddressEditor** class that handles converting a one-line address into an **Address** object with all its different properties set. This single-input field will expect users to enter addresses in the *city-state-ZIP* format with the following rules:

- The last comma will separate the city from the remainder of the text.

- The remainder of the text will use the two blanks separating the state and the ZIP to determine the final two fields.

- All fields will remove additional spaces.

Spring makes it easy to register custom editors. You can register them in the **init-Binder()** method of a **FormController**, or you can simply name them the same as your POJO + "Editor" (for example, **PersonEditor** for **Person**) and put it in the same package as your POJO. To make things simple, this example will modify the *web/userForm.jsp* page to which you just added an address.

When creating a custom **PropertyEditor**, you must extend **PropertyEditor-Support** and override two methods: **getAsText()** and **setAsText()**. The **getAsText()** method returns a string suitable for presentation to be edited, whereas the **setAsText(String text)** method sets the **Address** object properties value by parsing the input string. In the event of an illegal format, the **setAs-Text()** method will throw an **IllegalArgumentException**.

The following steps describe how to create an **AddressEditor** and modify the previously developed form to use it:

1   Create an **AddressEditor.java** class and put it in the *src/main/java/org/appfuse/web* directory. See Listing 14.29.

Listing 13.29

```java
package org.appfuse.web;

import java.beans.PropertyEditorSupport;
import org.appfuse.model.Address;
import org.springframework.util.StringUtils;

public class AddressEditor extends PropertyEditorSupport {
    /**
     * Parse the Address from the given text.
     * Assumes a format where the last comma separates the city and
     * state and the last space separates the state and zip
     */
    public void setAsText(String text)
        throws IllegalArgumentException
    {
        if (!StringUtils.hasText(text)) {
            // treat empty String as null value
            setValue(null);
        } else {
            String trim = text.trim();
            int lastComma = trim.lastIndexOf(",");
            int lastSpace = trim.lastIndexOf(" ");

            if ((lastComma >= 0) && (lastSpace >= 0) &&
                    (lastSpace > lastComma)) {
                Address address = new Address();
                address.setCity(trim.substring(0, lastComma));
                address.setState(trim.substring(
                    lastComma + 1, lastSpace).trim());
                address.setZip(trim.substring(lastSpace + 1));
                setValue(address);
            } else {
                throw new IllegalArgumentException(
                    "Could not parse address: " + text);
            }
        }
    }

    /**
     * Format the Address as a one-line String
     */
    public String getAsText() {
        Object value = getValue();

        if ((value != null) && (value instanceof Address)) {
            Address address = (Address) value;

            if (StringUtils.hasText(address.getCity())) {
```

```
                    return address.getCity() + ",  " + address.getState()
                    + " " + address.getZip();
                }
            }

        return "";
        }
    }
```

2   Register this property editor in the `initBinder()` method of
    `UserFormController`. See Listing 14.30.

Listing 13.30

```
    protected void initBinder(HttpServletRequest request,
                              ServletRequestDataBinder binder) {
        ...

        // convert org.appfuse.model.Address
        binder.registerCustomEditor
            (Address.class, new AddressEditor());
    }
```

3   Revise the *src/main/webapp/userForm.jsp* file to use a single-text input for
    the address field. See Listing 14.31.

Listing 13.31

```
<tr>
    <th>Address:</th>
    <td>
        <form:input path="address" id="address" size="30"/>
        <form:errors path="address" cssClass="fieldError"/>
    </td>
</tr>
```

4   Run **ant -f tomcat.xml deploy reload** and navigate to add a new user.
    Your revised form should look like the one in Figure 14.7.

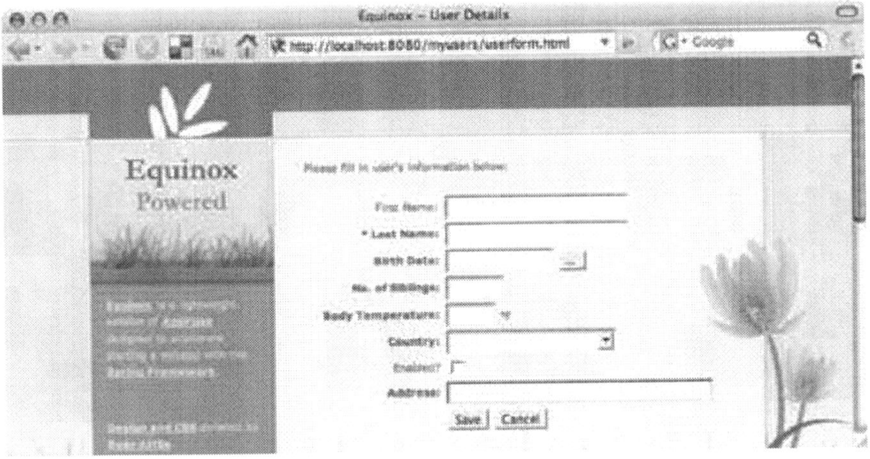

Figure 13.7: One-line **Address** field

Notice that there is only one text box in which to enter the city, state, and ZIP. Also, using a custom **PropertyEditor** allows you to use a regular **<spring:bind>** tag instead of requiring **<spring:nestedPath>**.

You should now be able to add a new user with an address in the form of *city, state ZIP*. Using a custom **PropertyEditor** can be a great help in simplifying forms, as well as converting strings into real object types.

INDEXED PROPERTIES

Similar to a single-nested object, *indexed properties* represent a collection of child objects. These objects are usually represented in the form of a **java.util.List** or **java.util.Set** in a command object.

In this section, you'll add a set of **Phone** objects to the **User** object and configure the MyUsers application to allow viewing, editing, adding, and deleting. In this example, the **Phone** objects are *indexed properties*. They get this name because they are displayed in the UI by their index, which is the order in which they appear in the collection.

    1   Create a **Phone.java** class in the *src/main/java/org/appfuse/model* directory. See Listing 14.32.

Listing 13.32

```
package org.appfuse.model;

public class Phone extends BaseObject {
    private Long id;
    private String type;
```

```
    private String number;

    public Phone() {}

    public Phone(String type, String number) {
        this.type = type;
        this.number = number;
    }

    // generate getters and setters with your IDE
}
```

2   Create a *Phone.hbm.xml* mapping file in the same directory. See
     Listing 14.33.

Listing 13.33

```xml
<?xml version="1.0" encoding="UTF-8"?>
<!DOCTYPE hibernate-mapping PUBLIC
    "-//Hibernate/Hibernate Mapping DTD 3.0//EN"
    "http://hibernate.sourceforge.net/hibernate-mapping-3.0.dtd">

<hibernate-mapping>
    <class name="org.appfuse.model.Phone" table="phone">
        <id name="id" column="id">
            <generator class="increment"/>
        </id>
        <property name="type"/>
        <property name="number"/>
    </class>
</hibernate-mapping>
```

3   Modify the **src/main/java/org/appfuse/model/User.java** class to
     have a **phones** property. See Listing 14.34.

Listing 13.34

```java
private Set phones;

public Set getPhones() {
    return phones;
}

public void setPhones(Set phones) {
    this.phones = phones;
}
```

4   Modify *User.hbm.xml* to contain a **`<set>`** of **`Phone`** objects. See Listing 14.35.

Listing 13.35

```
<set name="phones" cascade="all">
    <key column="user_id"/>
    <one-to-many class="org.appfuse.model.Phone"/>
</set>
```

5   Add the mapping file to the list of **`mappingsResources`** for the **`sessionFactory`** bean, located in *src/main/webapp/WEB-INF/applicationContext-hibernate.xml*. See Listing 14.36.

Listing 13.36

```
<property name="mappingResources">
    <list>
        <value>org/appfuse/model/Address.hbm.xml</value>
        <value>org/appfuse/model/Phone.hbm.xml</value>
        <value>org/appfuse/model/User.hbm.xml</value>
    </list>
</property>
```

6   To simplify viewing the UI, open *src/main/webapp/userForm.jsp* and comment out from the **`<tr>`** before **`siblings`** to the **`</tr>`** after **`enabled`**. See Listing 14.37.

Listing 13.37

```
<%--tr>
    <th><fmt:message key="user.siblings"/>:</th>
....
<tr>
    <th><fmt:message key="user.enabled"/>?</th>
    <td>
        <form:checkbox path="enabled"/>
        <form:errors path="enabled" cssClass="fieldError"/>
    </td>
</tr--%>
```

7   Comment out the **`<tr>`** around the **`Address`** row. See Listing 14.38.

Listing 13.38

```
<%--tr>
    <th>Address:</th>
    <td>
        . . .
    </td>
</tr--%>
```

8   Remove (or comment out) the validation rule to make **City** a required field in *src/main/webapp/WEB-INF/validation.xml*. See Listing 14.39.

Listing 13.39

```
<!--field property="address.city" depends="required">
    <arg key="City" resource="false"/>
</field-->
```

9   Add code to show the phone numbers assigned to the user. See Listing 14.40.

Listing 13.40

```
<tr>
    <td colspan="2">
        <fieldset>
            <legend>Phone Numbers</legend>
            <table>
                <tr>
                    <th style="text-align: right">Type</th>
                    <th style="text-align: left">Number</th>
                </tr>
                <c:forEach var="no" items="${user.phones}"
                    varStatus="s">
                <form:hidden path="phones[${s.index}].id"/>
                <tr>
                    <td style="text-align: right">
                        <form:input path="phones[${s.index}].type"
                            size="5"/>
                        <form:errors path="phones[${s.index}].type"
                            cssClass="fieldError"/>
                    </td>
                    <td>
                        <form:input path="phones[${s.index}].number"
                            size="15"/>
                        <form:errors path="phones[${s.index}].number"
                            cssClass="fieldError"/>
                    </td>
```

```
        </tr>
      </c:forEach>
    </table>
  </fieldset>
</td>
</tr>
```

Most of code in this snippet should be familiar to you. The main thing to take notice of is the **varStatus** attribute on **<c:forEach>**. This variable ("**s**," in this example) specifies the index in the bind path for the indexed properties. See Listing 14.41 for an example.

Listing 13.41

```
<form:hidden path="phones[${s.index}].id"/>
```

10 Modify the SQL in the **populate** target (in *build.xml*) to add some phone numbers for the first user. See Listing 14.42.

Listing 13.42

```
<sql driver="${jdbc.driverClassName}" url="${jdbc.url}"
    userid="${jdbc.username}" password="${jdbc.password}">
  <classpath refid="compile.classpath"/>
  <![CDATA[
    INSERT INTO app_user (id, first_name, last_name)
      values (5, 'Julie', 'Raible');
    INSERT INTO app_user (id, first_name, last_name)
      values (6, 'Abbie', 'Raible');

    INSERT INTO phone (id, type, number, user_id)
      values (1, 'home', '303-555-1212', 5);
    INSERT INTO phone (id, type, number, user_id)
      values (2, 'work', '720-555-1212', 5);
  ]]>
</sql>
```

11 Run **ant -f tomcat.xml deploy reload populate** and go to localhost:8080/myusers/userform.html?id=5 in your browser. The results should be similar to those shown in Figure 14.8.

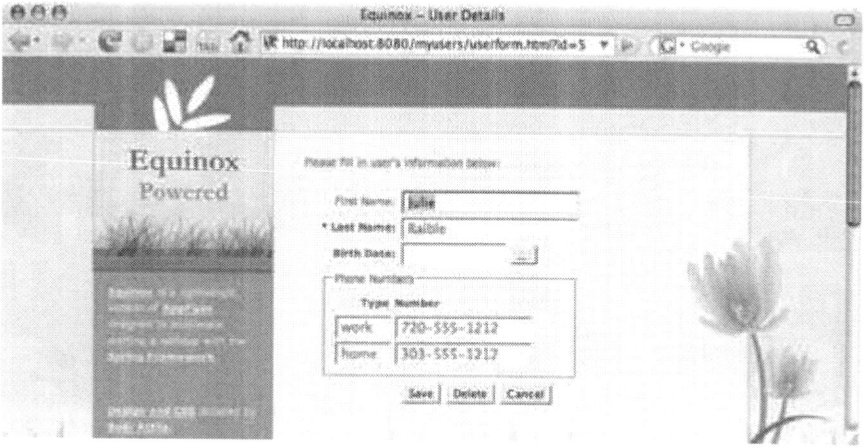

Figure 13.8: Viewing phone indexed properties

You should be able to update the **Type** and **Number** fields, save your changes, and see the persisted values when you edit the user again. While this is useful, the UI is useless until you can add and delete phone numbers as well.

ADDING INDEXED PROPERTIES

Since the number of indexed properties is static, you have to write some custom logic to allow users to add a phone number. You'll need to provide input fields on the form itself, as well as modify **UserFormController** to detect when a new record has been added.

1   Edit *src/main/webapp/userForm.jsp* and add the following HTML just after the closing **</c:forEach>**. See Listing 14.43.

Listing 13.43

```
<tr>
    <td style="text-align: right">
        Add New &raquo;
        <input type="text" name="new.phone.type" value=""
            size="5"/>
    </td>
    <td>
        <input type="text" name="new.phone.number"
            value="" size="15"/>
    </td>
</tr>
```

2   In **UserFormController**, override the **onBind()** method. In it, check to see if anything's been entered into the **new.phone.type** field. If something has been entered, this will serve as the indicator to add a new record. See Listing 14.44.

Listing 13.44

```
protected void onBind(HttpServletRequest request, Object o)
throws Exception {
    User command = (User) o;

    // check if user entered a "type" on the "Add New" row
    String type = request.getParameter("new.phone.type");
    if (!"".equals(type)) {
        if (command.getPhones() == null) {
            command.setPhones(new HashSet());
        }

        String number = request.getParameter("new.phone.number");
        command.getPhones().add(new Phone(type, number));
    }

    super.onBind(request, command);
}
```

3   Run **ant -f tomcat.xml deploy reload**. You should be able to view and add additional phone numbers, as shown in Figure 14.9.

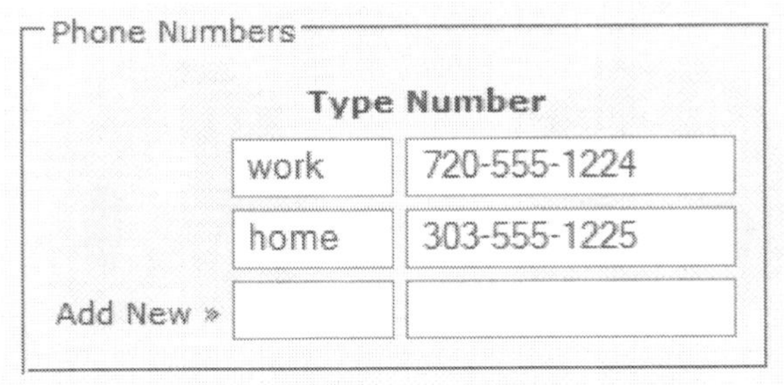

Figure 13.9: Adding phone indexed properties

DELETING INDEXED PROPERTIES

To allow deleting of indexed properties, add a **Delete** check box next to each phone number. If a user checks a box and clicks **Save**, the phone number will be removed from the user's set of phones.

1   Add a **Delete** column and an associated check box. As part of adding this
new column, move the **Add New »** text into its own **<td>**. Listing 14.45
contains the restructured code with changes in bold.

Listing 13.45

```
<table>
    <tr>
        <th style="text-align: left">Delete?</th>
        <th style="text-align: right">Type</th>
        <th style="text-align: left">Number</th>
    </tr>
    <c:forEach var="no" items="${user.phones}" varStatus="s">
    <spring:bind path="user.phones[${s.index}].id">
        <input type="hidden" name="${status.expression}"
            value="${status.value}"/>
    </spring:bind>
    <tr>
        <td>
            <spring:bind path="user.phones[${s.index}].id">
            <input type="checkbox" name="deletePhone"
                value="${status.value}"/>
            </spring:bind>
        </td>
        <td style="text-align: right">
            <spring:bind path="user.phones[${s.index}].type">
            <input type="text" name="${status.expression}"
                value="${status.value}" size="5"/>
            <span class="fieldError">${status.errorMessage}</span>
            </spring:bind>
        </td>
        <td>
            <spring:bind path="user.phones[${s.index}].number">
            <input type="text" name="${status.expression}"
                value="${status.value}" size="15"/>
            <span class="fieldError">${status.errorMessage}</span>
            </spring:bind>
        </td>
    </tr>
    </c:forEach>
    <tr>
        <td>Add New &raquo; </td>
        <td>
            <input type="text" name="new.phone.type" value=""
                size="5"/>
        </td>
        <td>
            <input type="text" name="new.phone.number" value=""
```

```
                    size="15"/>
             </td>
        </tr>
</table>
```

2 Add logic to the **onBind()** method of **UserFormController** to remove phones that are checked in the UI. Place this code just after the **Add New** logic you added in the previous section. See Listing 14.46.

Listing 13.46

```
// check for deleted phone numbers
if (command.getPhones() != null) {
    String[] deletePhones = request.getParameterValues
        ("deletePhone");
    Set phones = new HashSet(command.getPhones());
    for (int i = 0; deletePhones != null
        && i < deletePhones.length; i++) {
        String phoneId = deletePhones[i];
        for (Iterator it = phones.iterator(); it.hasNext();) {
            Phone p = (Phone) it.next();
            if (p.getId().toString().equals(phoneId)) {
                command.getPhones().remove(p);
            }
        }
    }
}

super.onBind(request, command);
```

3 Run **ant -f tomcat.xml deploy reload**. The check boxes display and give you the ability to remove phone numbers from a user's information, as shown in Figure 14.10.

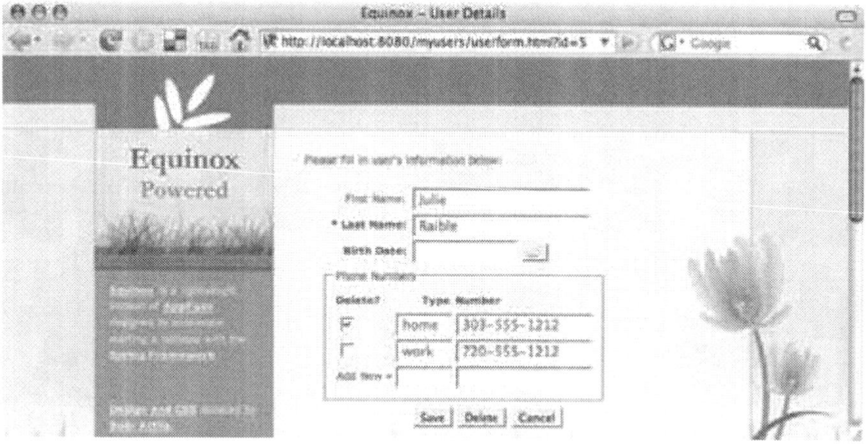

Figure 13.10: Deleting phone indexed properties

This section demonstrated how Spring MVC makes it easy to display and edit indexed properties of a command object. The next section will show you how to break up a form into multiple pages so it behaves like a *wizard*.

ABSTRACTWIZARDFORMCONTROLLER

The previous examples have provided you with the knowledge to use the different form elements with Spring, as well as how to work with its nested properties. However, if you have a form with a large number of properties, it can become unwieldy and intimidating to users. When you have a form that captures a lot of data, it often makes more sense to use a *wizard* that spans multiple pages. Spring MVC makes it easy to compose and process multi-page forms using its `AbstractWizardFormController`.

HOW ABSTRACTWIZARDFORMCONTROLLER WORKS

When extending `AbstractWizardFormController`, the only method you *must* implement is `processFinish()`. This method gathers the results of the wizard's pages and persists them as needed. To help the controller navigate between pages, you can define the pages in a wizard form in the class's constructor or as a `<list>` of values in *action-servlet.xml*. The code in Listing 14.47 is an example of a `pages` property.

Listing 13.47

```
<property name="pages">
    <list>
        <value>wizard/name</value>
        <value>wizard/address</value>
        <value>wizard/phone</value>
    </list>
</property>
```

Similarly, you can specify these pages in a constructor if you prefer not to configure them in XML. See Listing 14.48.

Listing 13.48

```
public WizardFormController() {
    setPages(new String[] {"wizard/name", "wizard/address",
                           "wizard/phone"});
}
```

To determine which page to call in its workflow, **AbstractWizardFormController** talks to its **getTargetPage()** method. This method uses a number of request parameters to determine its page flow. **AbstractWizardFormController** uses the following request parameters:

- **target#**: The number (#) is the page's index in the list of pages. It specifies which page the controller should show when the user submits the current page.

- **finish**: If this parameter is present in the request, the page calls the **processFinish()** method and removes the command object from the session.

- **cancel**: If this parameter is present in the request, the page calls the **processCancel()** method. The default implementation removes the command object from the session and throws a **ServletException** stating that **processCancel()** is not implemented.

- **page**: This parameter indicates the index of the current page. It's recommended that you specify this parameter in a hidden field.

The following steps illustrate capturing and validating a wizard form for adding a new user.

1   Create a **UserWizardController.java** class in *src/main/java/org/appfuse/web*. This class should use the same **User** command class and

depend on the **UserManager** service. The only method you need to implement at this point is **processFinish()**. See Listing 14.49.

Listing 13.49

```
package org.appfuse.web;

// organize imports using your IDE

public class UserWizardController
    extends AbstractWizardFormController {
    private static Log log =
        LogFactory.getLog(UserWizardController.class);
    private UserManager userManager;

    public UserWizardController() {
        setCommandClass(User.class);
    }

    public void setUserManager(UserManager userManager) {
        this.userManager = userManager;
    }

    protected ModelAndView processFinish(HttpServletRequest request,
                                         HttpServletResponse response,
                                         Object command,
                                         BindException errors)
    throws Exception {
        log.debug("executing 'processFinish'...");

        User user = (User) command;
        userManager.saveUser(user);
        request.getSession()
                .setAttribute("message", "User added successfully.");

        return new ModelAndView(new RedirectView("users.html"));
    }
}
```

2   Add a **userWizardController** bean definition to *src/main/webapp/WEB-INF/action-servlet.xml*. See Listing 14.50.

Listing 13.50

```
<bean id="userWizardController"
    class="org.appfuse.web.UserWizardController">
    <property name="commandName" value="user"/>
    <property name="userManager" ref="userManager"/>
    <property name="pages">
```

```
          <list>
               <value>wizard/name</value>
               <value>wizard/address</value>
               <value>wizard/other</value>
          </list>
     </property>
  </bean>
```

3   Create a wizard directory in *src/main/webapp* and create a *name.jsp* file in it. Populate this file with the code in Listing 14.51. The important parameters to note are **_target** and **_page**.

Listing 13.51

```
<%@ include file="/taglibs.jsp"%>

<form:form commandName="user" method="post" action="userwizard.html">
<form:errors path="*" cssClass="error"/>
<input type="hidden" name="_page" value="0"/>
<table>
<tr>
<th><label for="firstName">
    <fmt:message key="user.firstName"/>:</label></th>
    <td>
        <form:input path="firstName" id="firstName"/>
        <form:errors path="firstName" cssClass="fieldError"/>
    </td>
</tr>
<tr>
<th><label for="lastName" class="required">*
    <fmt:message key="user.lastName"/>:</label></th>
    <td>
        <form:input path="lastName" id="firstName"/>
        <form:errors path="lastName" cssClass="fieldError"/>
    </td>
</tr>
<tr>
    <td></td>
    <td>
        <input type="submit" class="button" name="_target1"
            value="Next &raquo;"/>
        <input type="submit" class="button" name="_cancel"
            value="Cancel"/>
    </td>
</tr>
</table>
</form:form>
```

4   Run **ant -f tomcat.xml deploy reload** and navigate to localhost:8080/myusers/userwizard.html[2] in your browser. You should see something similar to Figure 14.11.

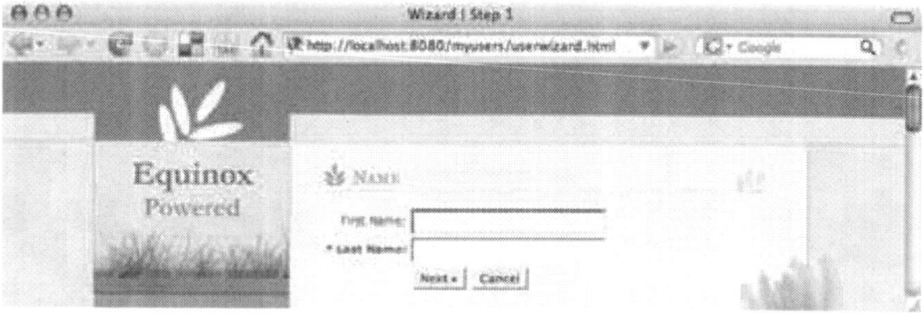

Figure 13.11: Wizard: Page 1

5   If you click the **Cancel** button, an error message will tell you that the cancel operation is not supported. To fix this issue, override **processCancel()** with the code in Listing 14.52.

Listing 13.52

```
protected ModelAndView processCancel(HttpServletRequest request,
                                     HttpServletResponse response,
                                     Object command,
                                     BindException errors)
throws Exception {
    return new ModelAndView(new RedirectView("users.html"));
}
```

6   Once you've proven cancel works, add an *address.jsp* page to the *src/main/webapp/wizard* directory with the following contents. See Listing 14.53.

Listing 13.53

```
<%@ include file="/taglibs.jsp"%>

<title>Wizard | Step 2</title>

<h3>Address Information</h3>
```

---

2. The controller is available at this location because of the **ControllerClassName-HandlerMapping** that's registered in *action-servlet.xml*. This **HandlerMapping** implementation automatically registers controllers by their names in all lowercase without the word "controller."

```
<form:form commandName="user" method="post" action="userwizard.html">
<input type="hidden" name="_page" value="1"/>
<table>
    <tr>
        <th>City:</th>
        <td>
            <form:input path="address.city" size="15"/>
            <form:errors path="address.city" cssClass="fieldError"/>
        </td>
    </tr>
    <tr>
        <th>State:</th>
        <td>
            <form:input path="address.state" size="2"/>
            <form:errors path="address.state" cssClass="fieldError"/>
        </td>
    </tr>
    <tr>
        <th>Zip:</th>
        <td>
            <form:input path="address.zip" size="10"/>
            <form:errors path="address.zip" cssClass="fieldError"/>
        </td>
    </tr>
    <tr>
        <td></td>
        <td>
            <input type="submit" class="button" name="_target0"
                value="&laquo; Prev"/>
            <input type="submit" class="button" name="_target2"
                value="Next &raquo;"/>
            <input type="submit" class="button" name="_cancel"
                value="Cancel"/>
        </td>
    </tr>
</table>
</form:form>
```

Notice how the **Next** and **Previous** buttons at the bottom of the page use the `_target` attribute to determine which page to go to next. When you first attempt to access the address page, you'll get a `NullValueInNestedPathException` because `user.getAddress()` returns null. To solve this issue, you can override the **form-BackingObject()** method in **UserWizardController**. See Listing 14.54.

Listing 13.54

```
protected Object formBackingObject(HttpServletRequest request)
throws Exception {
    User command = new User();
    command.setAddress(new Address());

    return command;
}
```

7   Run **ant -f tomcat.xml deploy reload** and attempt to navigate to the
     address page again. This time you should see fields for entering data, as
     shown in Figure 14.12. You should also be able to enter address
     information and click **Previous** and **Next** without losing any data.

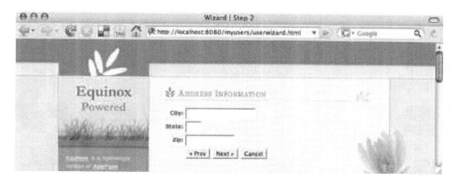

Figure 13.12: Wizard: Page 2

8   To add the third and final page, create a *src/main/webapp/wizard/other.jsp*
     page. This page will have a **Finish** button that triggers the end of the
     wizard. See Listing 14.55.

Listing 13.55

```
<%@ include file="/taglibs.jsp"%>

<title>Wizard | Step 3</title>

<h3>Other Information</h3>

<form:form commandName="user" method="post" action="userwizard.html">
<input type="hidden" name="_page" value="2"/>
<table>
<tr>
    <th><fmt:message key="user.birthDate"/>:</th>
    <td>
```

```
        <form:input path="birthDate" id="birthDate" size="11"/>
        <form:errors path="birthDate" cssClass="fieldError"/>
    </td>
</tr>
<tr>
    <td></td>
    <td>
        <input type="submit" class="button" name="_target1"
            value="&laquo; Prev"/>
        <input type="submit" class="button" name="_finish"
            value="Finish"/>
        <input type="submit" class="button" name="_cancel"
            value="Cancel"/>
    </td>
</tr>
</table>
</form:form>
```

After deploying, if you try to enter a date on this page, you will get an error like the one in Figure 14.13 stating you have entered an invalid date.

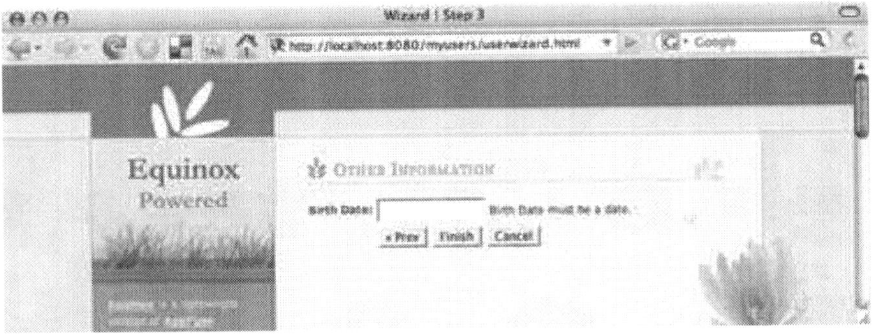

Figure 13.13: Page 3 with binding error

This is because you haven't registered any property editors for **java.util.Date**. To submit a date successfully, override the **initBinder()** method in **UserWizardController**. See Listing 14.56.

Listing 13.56

```
protected void initBinder(HttpServletRequest request,
                          ServletRequestDataBinder binder) {
    // convert java.util.Date
    SimpleDateFormat dateFormat =
        new SimpleDateFormat("MM/dd/yyyy");
```

```
        dateFormat.setLenient(false);
        binder.registerCustomEditor(Date.class,
            new CustomDateEditor(dateFormat, true));
}
```

9 Run **ant -f tomcat.xml deploy reload**. You should be able to
   navigate back and forth in this wizard and add a new user successfully. The
   result will look similar to Figure 14.14.

Figure 13.14: User added successfully

VALIDATING WIZARDS

1 Validating a command object's properties in a wizard is easy with
   Commons Validator. Specify a **page** property on the **<field>** in *src/main/*
   webapp/WEB-INF/validation.xml. See Listing 14.57.

Listing 13.57

```
<field property="lastName" depends="required" page="0">
```

2 Also, add a hidden **page** field with the current page's number. See
   Listing 14.58.

Listing 13.58

```
<input type="hidden" name="page" value="0"/>
```

You will need to configure a **ConfigurablePageBeanValidator** with the page
number in order to do partial bean validation with Commons Validator. You can
read more on how to configure this in the Spring Modules' Reference Documentation.

If you'd prefer to use Spring's Validator interface (and your own implementations)
for validating command object properties, the **AbstractWizardFormController**

has **validatePage()** methods you can use. Just remember to validate the entire object in the **processFinish()** method.

SPRING WEB FLOW

Spring Web Flow is a Spring sub-project that allows you to define *page flows* in your web application. By defining a page flow, you can control how a user *flows* from one page to the next. A web flow is defined in XML (or programmatically in Java) and allows you to specify complex navigation rules. By abstracting this information from controllers, you can reuse them and simplify your code.

If you create your own **AbstractWizardFormController**, you can only use the logic in your class in the context of that wizard. With web flows, your controller is completely unaware of which pages are being displayed and instead just reports success or failure for method outcomes.

To use a web flow in your project, you will need to use Web Flow *Actions* rather than Spring's command controllers. The main difference between the two is Web Flow Actions take a single method parameter: **RequestContext**. The following list contains the main actions you can implement to create your web flow.

- **AbstractAction**: This is the base **Action** implementation that provides convenience methods for subclasses. It's analogous to implementing a controller interface with Spring MVC. This action must implement **Event doExecute (RequestContext)**

- **MultiAction**: This is an action implementation that bundles many action execution methods into one class. Spring determines which method to call using a **method** attribute on an **<action>** element. If no **method** attribute is defined, the **<action-state>** element's **id** attribute is used.

- **FormAction**: This is a subclass of **MultiAction** that contains logic for dealing with input forms, including setup, bind, and validate. This subclass includes the following methods:

  - **setupForm (RequestContext)**: Creates a form.

  - **bindAndValidate (RequestContext)**: Binds values and validates if any validators are present.

  - **bind (RequestContext)**: Binds all incoming event parameters to the form object.

  - **validate (RequestContext)**: Validates the form object using a registered validator.

- `resetForm(RequestContext)`: Resets the form by reloading the backing form object and reinstalling any custom property.

Spring Web Flow 1.0 was released in early October 2006. While it has a Java API for defining flows, this section will only show you how to define flows in XML. The examples in this section were written using Spring Web Flow (SWF) 1.0.

CREATE A WEB FLOW

Two entities make up a flow definition: actions and views. The flow in Listing 14.59 defines viewing a list, editing a form, and saving that form. Notice how the actions are defined using `<action-state>` and `<action bean="..."/>`, while the views are defined by the `<view-state>` tag.

Listing 13.59

```
<action-state id="search">
    <action bean="userListAction"/>
    <transition on="success" to="userList"/>
</action-state>

<view-state id="userList" view="pages/userList">
    <transition on="*" to="userForm">
        <action bean="userFormAction"/>
    </transition>
</view-state>

<view-state id="userForm" view="pages/userForm">
    <transition on="submit" to="saveUser.action">
        <action bean="userFormAction"/>
    </transition>
    <transition on="cancel" to="showList.action"/>
</view-state>
```

The `<action>` tag can have an optional **method** attribute. If you don't specify it, then the **id** of the `<action-state>` is the method name. The `<view-state>` tag's **view** attribute defines a logical view name that's resolved by a defined `ViewRe-solver`.

Events that trigger transitions are signaled by the **_eventId** request parameter. The value of this parameter must match the value of the **on** attribute in a `<transi-tion>`. The **on** attribute of a `<transition>` can be a static string, an OGNL expression, or a block of Java code. The **_eventId** must be stored in a hidden field or as a hyperlink parameter.

In addition to an **_eventId** request parameter, you also need a **_flowExecution-Key** field to track the flow. If you're creating hyperlinks to invoke state transitions, you'll need to code both of these parameters into your URLs. If you're using forms, you can specify these as hidden fields. See Listing 14.60.

Listing 13.60

```
<input type="hidden" name="_flowExecutionKey"
    value="${flowExecutionKey}"/>
<input type="hidden" name="_eventId" value="submit"/>
```

> NOTE: You can also use _eventId_eventName on submit buttons to easily signify events when clicking buttons.

To see how you might use Spring Web Flow, follow these steps to implement the "add user" wizard you just created.

1 Create a **UserFormAction.java** class in *src/main/org/appfuse/web/flow* (you'll need to create the flow directory). See Listing 14.61.

Listing 13.61

```
package org.appfuse.web.flow;

// organize imports with your IDE

public class UserFormAction extends FormAction {
    private UserManager userManager;

    public void setUserManager(UserManager mgr) {
        this.userManager = mgr;
    }

    public UserFormAction() {
        setFormObjectName("user");
        setFormObjectClass(User.class);
        setFormObjectScope(ScopeType.FLOW);
    }

    public Object createFormObject(RequestContext context)
    throws Exception {
        User user = (User) super.createFormObject(context);
        user.setAddress(new Address());
        return user;
    }
}
```

This class has a dependency on **UserManager** to save the user when the flow is complete. Its constructor initializes a number of default values, and it overrides the **createFormObject()** method to provide an empty **Address** object.

> **NOTE:** In many cases, you can use SWF's `FormAction` class without subclassing it. SWF allows you to call middle-tier beans and pass your form object to them.

2   Create a *flow-user.xml* file in *src/main/webapp/WEB-INF* and add the code in Listing 14.62 to it.

Listing 13.62

```xml
<?xml version="1.0" encoding="UTF-8"?>
<flow xmlns="http://www.springframework.org/schema/webflow"
        xmlns:xsi="http://www.w3.org/2001/XMLSchema-instance"
        xsi:schemaLocation="http://www.springframework.org/
            schema/webflow
            http://www.springframework.org/schema/webflow
                /spring-webflow-1.0.xsd">

    <start-state idref="setupForm"/>

    <action-state id="setupForm">
        <action bean="userFormAction"/>
        <transition on="success" to="nameForm"/>
    </action-state>

    <view-state id="nameForm" view="flow/name">
        <transition on="submit" to="addressForm">
            <action bean="userFormAction" method="bindAndValidate"/>
        </transition>
        <transition on="cancel" to="finish"/>
    </view-state>

    <view-state id="addressForm" view="flow/address">
        <transition on="previous" to="nameForm">
            <action bean="userFormAction" method="bindAndValidate"/>
        </transition>
        <transition on="submit" to="otherForm">
            <action bean="userFormAction" method="bindAndValidate"/>
        </transition>
        <transition on="cancel" to="finish"/>
    </view-state>

    <view-state id="otherForm" view="flow/other">
        <transition on="previous" to="addressForm"/>
        <transition on="submit" to="save">
            <action bean="userFormAction" method="bindAndValidate"/>
        </transition>
        <transition on="cancel" to="finish"/>
    </view-state>

    <action-state id="save">
```

```
        <action bean="userFormAction"/>
        <transition on="success" to="finish"/>
    </action-state>

    <end-state id="finish" view="externalRedirect:/users.html"/>
</flow>
```

This flow has a number of **bindAndValidate** actions states for transitioning from one form to another. One difference between Spring Web Flow and **AbstractWizardFormController** is you can easily control whether a form's values are bound. With **AbstractWizardFormController**, you have no choice — values are always bound. In this example, the **previous** event from **otherForm** will simply redisplay the **addressForm <view-state>**. However, the **previous** event from **addressForm** calls **bindAndValidate()** as part of its transition.

The **<end-state>** specifies an ending view and handles the process of cleaning up any session variables associated with the flow.

3   Configure the flow and its URL in *src/main/webapp/WEB-INF/action-servlet.xml*.

   a   Add the XSD for SWF to the top of the file. See Listing 14.63.

Listing 13.63

```
<beans xmlns="http://www.springframework.org/schema/beans"
    xmlns:xsi="http://www.w3.org/2001/XMLSchema-instance"
        xmlns:flow="http://www.springframework.org/schema
            /webflow-config"
        xsi:schemaLocation="http://www.springframework.org
            /schema/beans
            http://www.springframework.org/schema/beans
                /spring-beans-2.0.xsd
            http://www.springframework.org/schema/webflow-config
            http://www.springframework.org/schema/webflow-config
                /spring-webflow-config-1.0.xsd">
```

   b   Create a **flowRegistry** bean that loads the flow definition created in step 2. See Listing 14.64.

Listing 13.64

```
<flow:registry id="flowRegistry">
    <flow:location path="/WEB-INF/flow-*.xml"/>
</flow:registry>
```

   c   Create a **flowExecutor** bean that is responsible for executing the flow. When no **repository-type** attribute is defined on the

`<flow:executor>` tag, the default type of **continuation** is used. There are three types of storage (or execution) repositories available in SWF. They are **simple**, **client**, and **continuation**. These storage mechanisms will be covered later in this chapter. See Listing 14.65.

Listing 13.65

```
<flow:executor id="flowExecutor" registry-ref="flowRegistry"/>
```

d   Create a **flowController** bean that serves as a front controller for web flows in your project. You can define a **defaultFlowId** property on this bean if you want it to only serve up a single page flow. See Listing 14.66.

Listing 13.66

```
<bean id="flowController"
    class="org.springframework.webflow.executor.mvc
        .FlowController">
    <property name="flowExecutor" ref="flowExecutor"/>
</bean>
```

e   Create a bean definition for the **userFormAction** bean that *flow-user.xml* refers to the code in Listing 14.67.

Listing 13.67

```
<bean id="userFormAction"
    class="org.appfuse.web.flow.UserFormAction"
        autowire="byName"/>
```

4   When creating the wizard, you created three JSPs to capture users' input. You'll need to do the same thing for this example. For the most part, the flow-friendly JSPs are the same as the wizard JSPs, except they require different hidden fields. Create a *src/main/webapp/flow* directory, and put the three files in Listing 14.68 into it. The web-flow-specific code is underlined.

Listing 13.68

```
src/main/webapp/flow/name.jsp
<%@ include file="/taglibs.jsp"%>

<title>Flow | Step 1</title>

<h3>Name</h3>
```

```
<form:form commandName="user" method="post" action="flow.html">
<input type="hidden" name=" flowExecutionKey"
    value="${flowExecutionKey}"/>
<table>
<tr>
<th><label for="firstName">
    <fmt:message key="user.firstName"/>:</label></th>
    <td>
        <form:input path="firstName" id="firstName"/>
        <form:errors path="firstName" cssClass="fieldError"/>
    </td>
</tr>
<tr>
<th><label for="lastName" class="required">*
    <fmt:message key="user.lastName"/>:</label></th>
    <td>
        <form:input path="lastName" id="firstName"/>
        <form:errors path="lastName" cssClass="fieldError"/>
    </td>
</tr>
<tr>
    <td></td>
    <td>
        <input type="submit" class="button" name=" eventId submit"
            value="Next &raquo;"/>
        <input type="submit" class="button" name=" eventId cancel"
            value="Cancel"/>
    </td>
</tr>
</table>
</form:form>

<script type="text/javascript">
    Form.focusFirstElement($('user'));
</script>
```

In Page 1, the two possible transitions are "submit" and "cancel". See Listing 14.69 and Listing 14.70.

Listing 13.69

```
src/main/webapp/flow/address.jsp
<%@ include file="/taglibs.jsp"%>

<title>Flow | Step 2</title>

<h3>Address Information</h3>

<form:form commandName="user" method="post" action="flow.html">
```

```
<input type="hidden" name=" flowExecutionKey"
    value="${flowExecutionKey}"/>
<table>
    <tr>
        <th>City:</th>
        <td>
            <form:input path="address.city" size="15"/>
            <form:errors path="address.city" cssClass="fieldError"/>
        </td>
    </tr>
    <tr>
        <th>State:</th>
        <td>
            <form:input path="address.state" size="2"/>
            <form:errors path="address.state" cssClass="fieldError"/>
        </td>
    </tr>
    <tr>
        <th>Zip:</th>
        <td>
            <form:input path="address.zip" size="10"/>
            <form:errors path="address.zip" cssClass="fieldError"/>
        </td>
    </tr>
    <tr>
        <td></td>
        <td>
            <input type="submit" class="button"
                name=" eventId previous"
                value="&laquo; Prev"/>
            <input type="submit" class="button" name=" eventId submit"
                value="Next &raquo;"/>
            <input type="submit" class="button" name=" eventId cancel"
                value="Cancel"/>
        </td>
    </tr>
</table>
</form:form>
```
src/main/webapp/flow/other.jsp

Listing 13.70

```
<%@ include file="/taglibs.jsp"%>

<title>Flow | Step 3</title>

<h3>Other Information</h3>

<form:form commandName="user" method="post" action="flow.html">
```

```
<input type="hidden" name=" flowExecutionKey"
    value="${flowExecutionKey}"/>
<table>
<tr>
    <th><fmt:message key="user.birthDate"/>:</th>
    <td>
        <form:input path="birthDate" id="birthDate" size="11"/>
        <form:errors path="birthDate" cssClass="fieldError"/>
    </td>
</tr>
<tr>
    <td></td>
    <td>
        <input type="submit" class="button" name=" eventId previous"
            value="&laquo; Prev"/>
        <input type="submit" class="button" name=" eventId submit"
            value="Finish"/>
        <input type="submit" class="button" name=" eventId cancel"
            value="Cancel"/>
    </td>
</tr>
</table>
</form:form>
```

5   Run **ant -f tomcat.xml deploy reload** and navigate to
    localhost:8080/myusers/flow.html?_flowId=flow-user. The result should
    look something like Figure 14.15.

NOTE: Passing in a `_flowId` parameter is required because you didn't define a
`defaultFlowId` property on the `flowController` bean. This allows you to have
a single controller that executes all flows rather than requiring you to define one for
each flow.

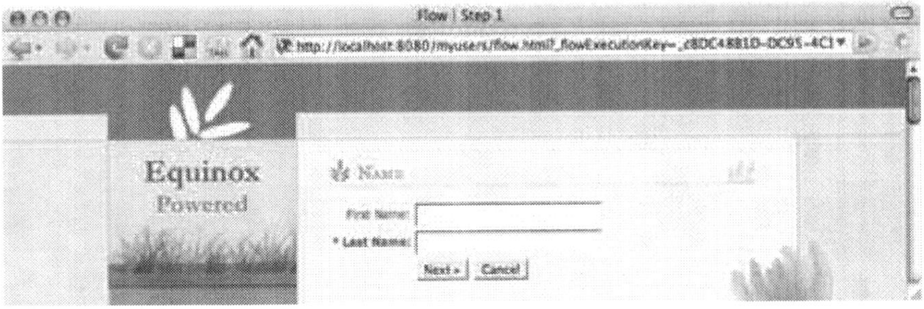

Figure 13.15: Flow: Page 1

You should be able to enter values on this form, navigate to the address form, and
navigate to the other/birth date form. Clicking the **Back** button or pressing the

Refresh button during execution of the wizard should not cause any adverse effects. This is a feature of web flow — it handles these browser-related issues for you.

WARNING: Pressing your keyboard's Enter key will invoke the first **Submit** button that appears in your form. You may need to add custom HTML or Java-Script to handle this behavior if you want a specific event to fire when pressing Enter.

When you click **Finish** on the birth date form, you should get an error about an invalid date, as shown in Figure 14.16.

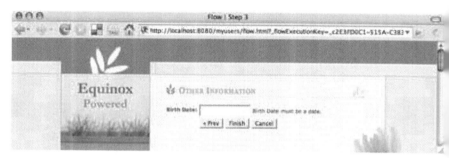

Figure 13.16: Flow: date binding error

To fix this mismatch, **override initBinder()** from the **FormAction** class. Open *src/main/java/org/appfuse/web/flow/UserFormAction.java* and add the method in Listing 14.71.

Listing 13.71

```
protected void initBinder(RequestContext context,
                    DataBinder binder) {
    // convert java.util.Date
    SimpleDateFormat dateFormat =
        new SimpleDateFormat("MM/dd/yyyy");
    dateFormat.setLenient(false);
    binder.registerCustomEditor(Date.class,
            new CustomDateEditor(dateFormat, true));
}
```

To save the new user created in the flow, add a **save** method to this class. See Listing 14.72.

Listing 13.72

```
public Event save(RequestContext context) throws Exception {
    User user = (User) context.getModel().get("user");
    userManager.saveUser(user);
    return success();
}
```

The wizard will then call this method (as indicated by **id="save"**) when the following state is called. Remember to run **ant -f tomcat.xml deploy reload** for these changes to take effect. See Listing 14.73.

Listing 13.73

```
<action-state id="save">
    <action bean="userFormAction"/>
    <transition on="success" to="finish"/>
</action-state>
```

FLOW STORAGE STRATEGIES

In this exercise, you defined a **flowExecutor** that handled the flow execution strategy and flow storage (also called a *registry*). By default, this is not required. At a minimum, you can configure your *action-servlet.xml* to define only a **flowController** and any flows you have. For example, Listing 14.74 is the Spring 1.2 syntax:

Listing 13.74

```
<bean id="flowController"
    class="org.springframework.webflow.executor.mvc.FlowController">
    <property name="flowLocator" ref="flowRegistry"/>
</bean>


<bean name="flowRegistry"
    class="org.springframework.webflow.config.registry
    .XmlFlowRegistryFactoryBean">
    <property name="flowLocations" value="/WEB-INF/flows/*-flow.xml"/>
</bean>
```

It is also possible to customize **argumentExtractor** property with a **FlowExecutorArgumentExtractor** that allows a different type of controller parameterization. For example, you could use a **REST**-style request mapper (see **RequestPathFlowExecutorArgumentHandler**).

If you use these definitions, the wizard will use a default storage strategy. Table 14.1 lists the possible storage strategies and their advantages and disadvantages.

Table 13.1: Storage Strategies

Class Name	Advantages	Disadvantages
ContinuationFlow-ExecutionRepository (default)	Handles **Back** and **Refresh** buttons on the browser.	Can result in many copies of the flow execution being stored in the session.
ClientContinuationFlow-ExecutionRepository	Handles **Back** and **Refresh** buttons on the browser. Reduces memory used on server.	Can be a security concern because state is stored on client (in a hidden field).
SimpleFlowExecution-Repository	Minimal overhead	Does not allow for duplicate submissions — best used when you can hide the **Back** button.

For information about Spring Web Flow's flow execution repositories, please see its reference documentation.

Spring Web Flow is a relatively new part of the Spring code base, but it's a very full-featured system. You can integrate it with Struts and JSF as well as Spring MVC and Spring MVC's portlet support. In the future, there will be more out-of-the-box support for other Java web frameworks. The main advantage of using a page-flow system like Spring Web Flow is your actions are unaware of navigation concerns. Instead, they just have methods that report error or success status.

SUMMARY

This chapter covered the more advanced features of Spring MVC. It showed you how to bind to non-string fields, populate drop-down lists, and handle check boxes. In addition, you learned how to display and edit nested objects and lists of objects. You used the **AbstractWizardFormController** to create a wizard, and a brief introduction to Spring Web Flow was provided.

The knowledge you gained from this chapter should provide you with all of the knowledge you need to develop a web application with Spring MVC. Not only is it a robust framework that makes for easy POJO manipulation, but it also drastically simplifies wizard creation. You can also use the Spring Web Flow project to abstract your page navigation concerns to an XML-based or Java-based configuration mechanism.

Examples and References

This appendix contains examples and references.

JSF AND SPRING CRUD EXAMPLE

This section shows you how to create a JSF, Spring, and Hibernate application using test-first development. You will use two techniques for testing the web layer of this application (both described in *Chapter 9: Testing Spring Applications*):

• **BasePageTestCase** class to look up managed beans from the *faces-config.xml* file

• Canoo's WebTest with JavaScript enabled

After writing the tests, managed beans, and JSPs, you will configure validation.

DEPENDENCIES AND CONFIGURATION

To follow along with the examples in this section, download the **Chapter 11** bundle from sourcebeat.com/downloads. This zip file contains the three starter projects you'll need to complete the exercises in this appendix. Each project is a stripped-down version of Equinox 1.6. These projects use Maven 2's Ant Tasks to download their dependencies. They will be downloaded on the fly when you first run **ant** (or **mvn**) from the command line. Be prepared — this process may take awhile.

Instead of using Ant, you can try Maven 2 to build Equinox. However, describing how to use Maven 2 is outside the scope of these examples. Maven 2 will become the default build system in Equinox 2.0 and AppFuse 2.0. A free book on Maven 2 is available at www.mergere.com/m2book_download.jsp.

For the JSF example, you'll use the *equinox-jsf* project, which already contains Eclipse and IDEA project files. For instructions on configuring this project with a Postgre-SQL database and your IDE, please see the README.txt in the project's root directory. Besides configuring the MyFaces dependencies in *pom.xml*, nothing JSF-related is setup. This example uses the MyFaces JSF implementation (version 1.1.2).

CONFIGURING JSF IN WEB.XML

To configure MyFaces as your web framework, you need to add a number of elements to the *src/main/webapp/WEB-INF/web.xml* file:

1   Configure a `<listener>` to load the *faces-config.xml* file and initialize MyFaces. Place this element directly after the existing `<listener>` for Spring's `ContextLoaderListener`. See Listing A.1.

Listing A.1

```
<listener>
    <listener-class>
        org.apache.myfaces.webapp.StartupServletContextListener
    </listener-class>
</listener>
```

2   Add an entry for the `FacesServlet`, which is much like Spring's `DispatcherServlet`. Place this element directly after the `<listener>` element. See Listing A.2.

Listing A.2

```
<servlet>
    <servlet-name>faces</servlet-name>
    <servlet-class>javax.faces.webapp.FacesServlet</servlet-class>
    <load-on-startup>1</load-on-startup>
</servlet>
```

3   Add a `<servlet-mapping>` to send all URLs ending in **.html* to the `FacesServlet`. Place this element directly after the `<servlet>` element. See Listing A.3.

Listing A.3

```
<servlet-mapping>
    <servlet-name>faces</servlet-name>
    <url-pattern>*.html</url-pattern>
</servlet-mapping>
```

4   This file already contains a `<context-param>` for setting the default `ResourceBundle` for JSTL. The setting in Listing A.4 tells the `<fmt:message>` tag to use the *messages.properties* `ResourceBundle` from *WEB-INF/classes* (the root of the classpath).

Listing A.4

```
<context-param>
    <param-name>
        javax.servlet.jsp.jstl.fmt.localizationContext
    </param-name>
    <param-value>messages</param-value>
</context-param>
```

More information about using JSTL and JSP in a JSF application is available in the article "Getting around JSF: The role of JSP" by Kito Mann.

JSF TAG LIBRARIES

JSF has a number of tag libraries for JSPs. The download for this tutorial does not have any tag libraries defined, however. To define them, create a *src/main/webapp/ taglibs.jsp* file and populate it with the code in Listing A.5. This file is included at the top of most JSP pages.

Listing A.5

```
<%@ page language="java" errorPage="/error.jsp" %>
<%@ taglib uri="http://java.sun.com/jsp/jstl/core" prefix="c" %>
<%@ taglib uri="http://java.sun.com/jsp/jstl/fmt" prefix="fmt" %>
<%@ taglib uri="http://java.sun.com/jsf/html" prefix="h" %>
<%@ taglib uri="http://java.sun.com/jsf/core" prefix="f" %>
<%@ taglib uri="http://displaytag.sf.net" prefix="display" %>
<%@ taglib uri="http://www.opensymphony.com/sitemesh/decorator"
    prefix="decorator" %>
<%@ taglib uri="http://myfaces.apache.org/tomahawk" prefix="t"%>

<c:set var="datePattern"><fmt:message key="date.format"/></c:set>
<c:set var="ctx" value="${pageContext.request.contextPath}"/>
```

The first two **taglib** lines in this file are for JSTL. The next two, with the "h" and "f" prefixes, are common to all JSF applications that use JSP. The **display** tag is covered in *Chapter 6: View Options*, and the SiteMesh **decorator** tag is covered in *Chapter 5: Advanced Spring MVC*. The last tag is for MyFaces' Tomahawk components. In this example, it is used for a pop-up calendar. The **<c:set>** tag sets a **datePattern** to format dates in JSPs. This value is currently in the *src/main/ resources/messages.properties* file, allowing you to change the formatting based on your locale.

date.format=MM/dd/yyyy

NOTE: You may be familiar with declaring your tag libraries in *web.xml*, but this is not necessary with a Servlet 2.3+ container. If the *.tld* file is stored in the tag library's

JAR file (in the *META-INF* directory) and has a `<uri>` element defined, you can use that `<uri>` in your `taglib` declaration without touching *web.xml*.

After modifying *src/main/webapp/WEB-INF/web.xml* and creating *src/main/webapp/taglibs.jsp*, build and deploy the Equinox-JSF application using **ant deploy**. After executing this command, start Tomcat and navigate to localhost:8080/equinox-jsf. The default Equinox welcome page (see Figure A.1) should render without issues.

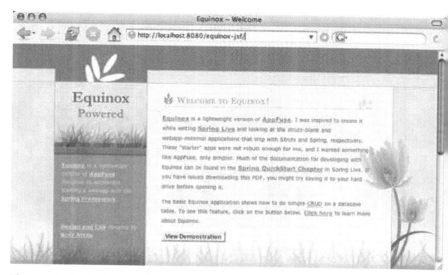

Figure A.1: Equinox welcome page

NOTE: If SiteMesh doesn't decorate your page, make sure *src/main/webapp/taglibs.jsp* has all the `taglib` declarations specified.

NOTE: If your JSP tags don't seem to execute when you're developing web applications, do a **View Source** on the page. If no `taglib` declaration exists for the tag, the tag will not be evaluated, and you will see it exactly as you typed it in the JSP.

To prove that JSF is configured and working properly, add the code in Listing A.6 to the top of the *src/main/webapp/index.jsp* file, directly after the `<title>` tag. You must place all JSF tags inside an `<f:view>` tag.

Listing A.6

```
<f:view>
    <h1><h:outputText value="Hello JSF!"/></h1>
</f:view>
```

Run **ant deploy** and refresh your browser; you will receive an error, as shown in Figure A.2.

An Error has occurred in this application. Please check your log files for further information.

Figure A.2: Error received when using JSF tags without FacesServlet

This error occurs because the welcome file is *index.jsp*. The FacesServlet only processes URLs that end with **.html*. In order for JSF's JSP tags to work, they must be processed by this servlet. By default, JSF's **ViewResolver** dispatches from the URL ending with **.html* (or whatever you have configured in *web.xml*) to a JSP file with the same name. If you try to access localhost:8080/equinox-jsf/index.html, you should see something similar to Figure A.3:

Figure A.3: Hello World with JSF

If you see "Hello JSF!" at the top of your page, you've set up everything correctly. Now remove this tag from *index.jsp* so you don't receive an error every time you try to access localhost:8080/equinox-jsf.

NOTE: You could also use the **UrlRewriteFilter** to redirect requests from *index.jsp* to *index.html* to ensure that JSF processes the *index.jsp* request. This is covered in *Chapter 6: View Options*.

CREATE THE MASTER SCREEN

Testing is an important part of any application, and testing a JSF application is no different. Unlike the other frameworks, not much information is available for testing managed beans, so this section draws from the MyFaces test suite, as well as my own experience.

1   Create a **BasePageTestCase.java** class in *src/test/java/org/appfuse/web*.
     This initializes JSF and Spring. It also allows you to grab managed beans by
     calling **getManagerBean("userList")**, where **userList** is the name of
     the managed bean in *faces-config.xml*. The mock classes in the following code
     are from *spring-mock.jar*, which is already in your classpath. See Listing A.7.

Listing A.7

```java
package org.appfuse.web;

// organize imports with your IDE

public class BasePageTestCase extends TestCase {
    protected final Log log = LogFactory.getLog(getClass());
    protected static FacesContext facesContext;
    protected static MockServletConfig config;
    protected static MockServletContext servletContext;
    protected static WebApplicationContext ctx;

    // This static block ensures that Spring's BeanFactory and JSF's
    // FacesContext is only loaded once for all tests.
    static {
        servletContext = new MockServletContext("");
        // This static block ensures that Spring's BeanFactory
            and JSF's
        // FacesContext is only loaded once for all tests.
        servletContext.addInitParameter(ContextLoader.
            CONFIG_LOCATION_PARAM,
                                    "/WEB-INF/applicationContext*
                                        .xml");

        ServletContextListener contextListener =
            new ContextLoaderListener();
        ServletContextEvent event =
            new ServletContextEvent(servletContext);
        contextListener.contextInitialized(event);

        config = new MockServletConfig(servletContext);
        facesContext = performFacesContextConfig();
        ctx = FacesContextUtils.getRequiredWebApplicationContext
            (facesContext);
    }

    protected static FacesContext performFacesContextConfig() {
        StartupServletContextListener facesListener =
            new StartupServletContextListener();
        ServletContextEvent event =
            new ServletContextEvent(servletContext);
        facesListener.contextInitialized(event);
```

```java
        LifecycleFactory lifecycleFactory = (LifecycleFactory)
            FactoryFinder.getFactory(FactoryFinder.LIFECYCLE_FACTORY);

        Lifecycle lifecycle =
            lifecycleFactory.getLifecycle(getLifecycleId());

        FacesContextFactory facesCtxFactory = (FacesContextFactory)
            FactoryFinder.getFactory(FactoryFinder.
                FACES_CONTEXT_FACTORY);

        FacesContext ctx =
            facesCtxFactory.getFacesContext(servletContext,
                                    new MockHttpServletRequest(),
                                    new MockHttpServletResponse(),
                                        lifecycle);

        return ctx;
    }

    protected static String getLifecycleId() {
        String lifecycleId =
            servletContext.getInitParameter(FacesServlet.
                LIFECYCLE_ID_ATTR);

        return (lifecycleId != null) ? lifecycleId
                                     : LifecycleFactory
                                        .DEFAULT_LIFECYCLE;
    }

    /**
     * Get managed bean based on the bean name.
     *
     * @param beanName the bean name
     * @return the managed bean associated with the bean name
     */
    protected Object getManagedBean(String beanName) {
        return getValueBinding(getJsfEl(beanName))
            .getValue(facesContext);
    }

    private Application getApplication() {
        ApplicationFactory appFactory = (ApplicationFactory)
            FactoryFinder.getFactory(FactoryFinder.
                APPLICATION_FACTORY);
        return appFactory.getApplication();
    }

    private ValueBinding getValueBinding(String el) {
        return getApplication().createValueBinding(el);
```

```
        }

        private String getJsfEl(String value) {
            return "#{" + value + "}";
        }
    }
```

Once you create this class, writing a test for a managed bean is easy.

    2   Create a **UserListTest.java** class in *src/test/java/org/appfuse/web*. See Listing A.8.

Listing A.8

```
package org.appfuse.web;

// organize imports with your IDE

public class UserListTest extends BasePageTestCase {
    private UserList bean;

    protected void setUp() throws Exception {
        super.setUp();
        bean = (UserList) getManagedBean("userList");

        // create a new user
        User user = new User();
        user.setFirstName("Matt");
        user.setLastName("Raible");
        user.setBirthday(new Date());

        // persist to database
        UserManager userManager =
            (UserManager) ctx.getBean("userManager");
        userManager.saveUser(user);
    }

    public void testSearch() throws Exception {
        assertTrue(bean.getUsers().size() >= 1);
    }
}
```

This class won't compile yet; you must first create the **UserList** class.

    3   Create a **UserList.java** class in *src/main/java/org/appfuse/web*. See Listing A.9.

Listing A.9

```
package org.appfuse.web;

// organize imports with your IDE

public class UserList {
    private UserManager userManager;

    public void setUserManager(UserManager userManager) {
        this.userManager = userManager;
    }

    public List getUsers() {
        return userManager.getUsers();
    }
}
```

The majority of this code is the setter for dependency injection. You're testing the `getUsers()` method.

4   Modify *src/main/webapp/WEB-INF/faces-config.xml* to include a managed bean definition for **userList**. See Listing A.10.

Listing A.10

```
<managed-bean>
    <managed-bean-name>userList</managed-bean-name>
    <managed-bean-class>org.appfuse.web.UserList</managed-bean-class>
    <managed-bean-scope>request</managed-bean-scope>
    <managed-property>
        <property-name>userManager</property-name>
        <value>#{userManager}</value>
    </managed-property>
</managed-bean>
```

5   Run the **UserListTest** using the command **ant test -Dtest-case=UserList**. The result should look similar to Figure A.4.

```
○ ○ ○                    Spring Live – Chapter 11                    ⬭
New  Bookmarks  Configure   Customize  Close
alotta:~/dev/equinox-jsf mraible$ ant test -Dtestcase=UserList
Buildfile: build.xml

compile:

test:
    [junit] Testsuite: org.appfuse.web.UserListTest
    [junit] Tests run: 1, Failures: 0, Errors: 0, Time elapsed: 0.496 sec

    [junit] -------------- Standard Output ------------------
    [junit] DEBUG - UserDAOHibernate.saveUser(35) | userId set to: 1
    [junit] ------------------------------- -----------------

BUILD SUCCESSFUL
Total time: 6 seconds
alotta:~/dev/equinox-jsf mraible$ ▊
```

Figure A.4: Running the `UserListTest`

6   Create a *src/main/webapp/userList.jsp* page to display the list of users, as you did with JSTL and the display tag. See Listing A.11.

Listing A.11

```jsp
<%@ include file="/taglibs.jsp"%>

<f:view>
<f:loadBundle var="messages" basename="messages"/>

<title><fmt:message key="userList.title"/></title>

<h:form id="editUser">
<h:commandButton value="Add User" action="add" immediate="true"
    styleClass="button"/>

<h:dataTable value="#{userList.users}" var="user" styleClass="list"
    rowClasses="odd,even" id="userList">
    <h:column>
        <f:facet name="header">
            <h:outputText value="#{messages['user.id']}"/>
        </f:facet>
        <h:commandLink action="#{userForm.edit}" value="#{user.id}">
            <f:param name="id" value="#{user.id}"/>
        </h:commandLink>
    </h:column>
    <h:column>
        <f:facet name="header">
            <h:outputText value="#{messages['user.firstName']}"/>
```

```
            </f:facet>
            <h:outputText value="#{user.firstName}"/>
        </h:column>
        <h:column>
            <f:facet name="header">
                <h:outputText value="#{messages['user.lastName']}"/>
            </f:facet>
            <h:outputText value="#{user.lastName}"/>
        </h:column>
        <h:column>
            <f:facet name="header">
                <h:outputText value="#{messages['user.birthday']}"/>
            </f:facet>
            <h:outputText value="#{user.birthday}">
                <f:convertDateTime pattern="#{messages['date.format']}"/>
            </h:outputText>
        </h:column>
    </h:dataTable>

    </h:form>
    </f:view>
```

This page is wrapped in an **<f:view>** tag, and it loads the default **Resource-Bundle** named **messages**. To use i18n messages with JSF tags, you *must* use the **<f:loadBundle>** tag. JSF 1.1 provides no way to set the default **ResourceBundle** or **messages** variable. In most JSF pages, you also need an **<h:form>** tag to allow processing of the HTTP POST that occurs when users click links or buttons.

The **commandButton** following the **<h:form>** tag has an **action** attribute that indicates where to go next. The mapping of **action="add"** to a particular page is done in *faces-config.xml* with a navigation rule (covered in Step 6).

Following the **commandButton** is an **<h:dataTable>**, which you can use for editing or displaying data. It has column tags that allow you to internationalize headers, format values, and link to other pages. The **<h:dataTable>** does not support sorting and paging out-of-the-box, but you can get paging functionality using MyFaces's **DataScroller** component. For sorting, you must implement custom comparator logic. An example of this is in the sample application that ships with MyFaces.

After editing *userList.jsp*, run **ant populate deploy** and open localhost:8080/equinox-jsf/userList.html in your browser. Your results should resemble those in Figure A.5.

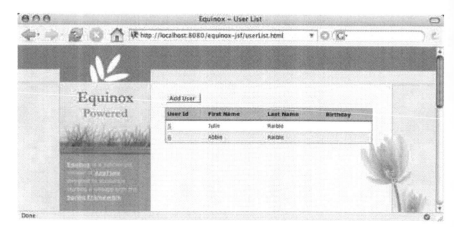

Figure A.5: View the user list using the `<h:dataTable>`

7   To map the **add** action from the **Add User** button, create a navigation rule in *src/main/webapp/WEB-INF/faces-config.xml*. Place this directly after the `</application>` element. See Listing A.12.

Listing A.12

```
<navigation-rule>
    <from-view-id>/userList.jsp</from-view-id>
    <navigation-case>
        <from-outcome>add</from-outcome>
        <to-view-id>/userForm.jsp</to-view-id>
    </navigation-case>
</navigation-rule>
```

8   The *userList.jsp* file contains another kind of action; rather than having a simple string literal such as **add**, it references a method in another managed bean. The **commandLink** in Listing A.13 references the **userForm**-managed bean and its **edit()** method.

Listing A.13

```
<h:commandLink action="#{userForm.edit}" value="#{user.id}">
    <f:param name="id" value="#{user.id}"/>
</h:commandLink>
```

Clicking this link results in an error because the **userForm** bean isn't defined in *faces-config.xml*. Before you create and define the **UserForm** class, take a brief look at using the display tag to display a list of data.

USING THE DISPLAY TAG WITH JSF

While the `<h:dataTable>` tag doesn't support sorting out-of-the-box, you can use JSP tags, such as `displaytag`, `ValueList`, or Jakarta's Data Grid Tag Library, to get easy sorting and paging. The display tag also supports exporting to CSV, Excel, XML, and PDF. The code in Listing A.14 illustrates how to refactor the *userList.jsp* page to use this tag. You can use this technique with any of the other tag libraries. To use the display tag, open *web/userList.jsp* and replace the `<h:dataTable>` with the following code:

Listing A.14

```
<%-- Step 1: Use a hidden dataTable to pull userList into request --%>
<h:dataTable var="user" value="#{userList.users}"
    style="display:none"/>

<display:table name="userList.users" class="list"
    requestURI="/userList.html"
    id="userList" export="true" pagesize="10">
    <display:column sortable="true" titleKey="user.id" media="html">
        <a href="javascript:viewUser('${userList.id}')">
            ${userList.id}</a>
    </display:column>
    <display:column property="id" media="csv excel xml pdf"
        titleKey="user.id"/>
    <display:column property="firstName" sortable="true"
        titleKey="user.firstName"/>
    <display:column property="lastName" sortable="true"
        titleKey="user.lastName"/>
    <display:column sortable="true" titleKey="user.birthday"
        sortProperty="birthday">
        <fmt:formatDate value="${userList.birthday}"
            pattern="${datePattern}"/>
    </display:column>
</display:table>

<%-- JSF Hack for the Display Tag, from James Violette ~
        http://www.emeraldjb.com/roller/page/jviolett --%>
<%-- Step 2. Create a dummy actionLink, w/ no value --%>
<h:commandLink action="#{userForm.edit}" id="editUserLink">
    <f:param name="id" value=""/>
</h:commandLink>
<%-- Step 3. Write a JavaScript function that's easy to call --%>
<script type="text/javascript">
function viewUser(id) {
    var f = document.forms['editUser'];
    f.elements['editUser:_link_hidden_']
        .value='editUser:editUserLink';
    f.elements['id'].value=id;
```

```
      f.submit();
  }
  highlightTableRows("userList");
</script>
```

You must complete the following three steps to make the display tag work with JSF:

1 Expose the **userList**-managed bean to the page. Since the bean isn't exposed until the first tag calls it, you can use a hidden **<h:dataTable>** tag. Several other ways are available to expose beans to a page when it first loads, but this is the simplest.

2 Create an **actionLink** with no value. This will create hidden fields you can use to call the action specified. Use the **<f:param>** tag to specify parameters to pass to this action.

3 Write a JavaScript function that specifies the link clicked and its parameter values and then submits the form.

Run **ant deploy populate**; you'll have a sortable and pageable list of users, complete with exporting capabilities! Two principles in this example are specific to the display tag:

a If you leave out the **property** attribute from a **<display:column>** tag, the body of the tag will be rendered. This content will be rendered in the output, so the **id** and **birthday** columns have logic to control content, based on the view type being used (HTML, XML, Excel, or PDF).

b To format the date, use the **<fmt:formatDate>** tag. If you don't specify the **property** attribute of a column, the content of the column is assumed to be a string and is sorted as such. By formatting the date in a comment in **yyyyMMdd** format, sorting will work.

CREATE THE DETAIL SCREEN

The **UserForm**-managed bean in this example edits, saves, and deletes a user.

1 Create a **UserFormTest** class in *src/test/java/org/appfuse/web* and populate it with the code in Listing A.15:

Listing A.15

```
package org.appfuse.web;

// organize imports using your IDE

public class UserFormTest extends BasePageTestCase {
    private UserForm bean;
```

```
private String userId;

protected void setUp() throws Exception {
    super.setUp();
    bean = (UserForm) getManagedBean("userForm");
    // verify that "userForm" has been defined as a managed-bean
    assertNotNull("you need to define 'userForm'
        in faces-config.xml",
        bean);

    // create a new user
    User user = new User();
    user.setFirstName("Matt");
    user.setLastName("Raible");

    // persist to database
    UserManager userManager =
        (UserManager) ctx.getBean("userManager");
    userManager.saveUser(user);
    userId = user.getId().toString();
}

protected void tearDown() throws Exception {
    super.tearDown();
    bean = null;
}

public void testEdit() throws Exception {
    bean.setId(userId);
    assertEquals(bean.edit(), "success");
    assertNotNull(bean.getUser().getFirstName());
}

public void testSave() throws Exception {
    bean.setId(userId);
    bean.edit();
    assertNotNull(bean.getUser());
    bean.getUser().setFirstName("Jack");

    assertEquals(bean.save(), "success");
    assertNotNull(bean.getUser());
}

public void testRemove() throws Exception {
    User user = new User();
    user.setId(new Long(userId));
    bean.setUser(user);
    assertEquals(bean.delete(), "success");
}
}
```

2   Modify *src/main/webapp/WEB-INF/faces-config.xml* to include a managed bean definition for **userForm**. Place this directly after the **userList**-managed bean. See Listing A.16.

Listing A.16

```
<managed-bean>
    <managed-bean-name>userForm</managed-bean-name>
    <managed-bean-class>
        org.appfuse.web.UserForm
    </managed-bean-class>
    <managed-bean-scope>request</managed-bean-scope>
    <managed-property>
        <property-name>id</property-name>
        <value>#{param.id}</value>
    </managed-property>
    <managed-property>
        <property-name>userManager</property-name>
        <value>#{userManager}</value>
    </managed-property>
</managed-bean>
```

3   Create the **UserForm** class in *src/main/java/org/appfuse/web* with the contents in Listing A.17.

Listing A.17

```
package org.appfuse.web;

// user your IDE to organize imports

public class UserForm {
    private String id;
    public User user = new User();
    public UserManager mgr;

    public String getId() {
        return id;
    }

    public void setId(String id) {
        this.id = id;
    }

    public User getUser() {
        return user;
    }

    public void setUser(User user) {
```

```
        this.user = user;
    }

    public void setUserManager(UserManager userManager) {
        this.mgr = userManager;
    }

    public String edit() {

        if (id != null) {
            // assuming edit
            setUser(mgr.getUser(id));
        }

        return "success";
    }

    public String save() {
        mgr.saveUser(getUser());
        addMessage("user.saved", getUser().getFullName());

        return "success";
    }

    public String delete() {
        mgr.removeUser(getUser().getId().toString());
        addMessage("user.deleted", getUser().getFullName());

        return "success";
    }

    // Convenience methods
    public static String getRequestParameter(String name) {
        return (String) FacesContext.getCurrentInstance()
            .getExternalContext().getRequestParameterMap().get(name);
    }

    public void addMessage(String key, String arg) {
        // sure is a lot of work to get the named ResourceBundle in
JSF, eh?
        ApplicationFactory factory = (ApplicationFactory)
            FactoryFinder.getFactory(FactoryFinder.
                APPLICATION_FACTORY);
        String bundleName =
            factory.getApplication().getMessageBundle();
        ResourceBundle messages =
            ResourceBundle.getBundle(bundleName);

        // it's even more work to format a message with args
```

```
MessageFormat form =
    new MessageFormat(messages.getString(key));

String msg = form.format(new Object[] { arg });

// add message to session so it can live past redirects
// the MessageFilter class will take care of removing it
HttpSession session = (HttpSession)
    FacesContext.getCurrentInstance().getExternalContext()
                                    .getSession(true);
    session.setAttribute("message", msg);
    }
}
```

4   Run the **UserFormTest** using **ant test -Dtestcase=UserForm**. The
results are shown in Figure A.6.

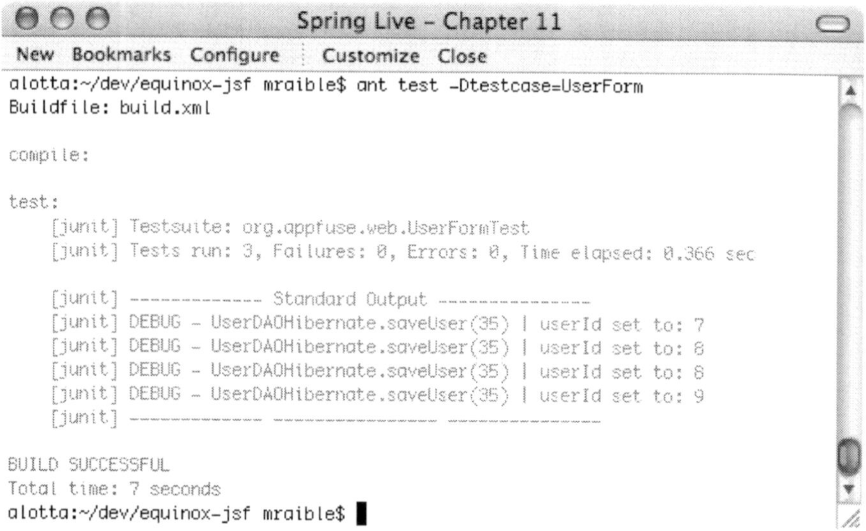

Figure A.6: Running the **UserFormTest**

5   Create a *src/main/webapp/userForm.jsp* page to interact with the **UserForm**-
managed bean. See Listing A.18.

Listing A.18

```
<%@ include file="/taglibs.jsp"%>

<f:view>
<f:loadBundle var="messages" basename="messages"/>
```

```
<head>
   <title><fmt:message key="userForm.title"/></title>
   <!-- JSCalendar -->
   <script type="text/javascript"
       src="${ctx}/scripts/popcalendar.js"></script>
   <link rel="stylesheet"
       href="${ctx}/scripts/jscalendar-WH/theme.css"
       type="text/css"/>
</head>

<h:messages errorClass="error" layout="table" style="width: 100%"/>

<p>Please fill in user's information below:</p>

<h:form id="userForm">
<h:inputHidden value="#{userForm.user.id}">
   <f:convertNumber/>
</h:inputHidden>
<h:panelGrid columns="3" styleClass="detail" columnClasses="label">

   <h:outputLabel for="firstName"
       value="#{messages['user.firstName']}"/>
   <h:inputText value="#{userForm.user.firstName}" id="firstName"/>
   <h:message for="firstName" styleClass="errorMessage"/>

   <h:outputLabel for="lastName"
       value="#{messages['user.lastName']}"/>

   <h:inputText value="#{userForm.user.lastName}" id="lastName"/>
   <h:message for="lastName" styleClass="errorMessage"/>

   <h:outputLabel for="birthday"
       value="#{messages['user.birthday']}"/>
   <t:inputCalendar monthYearRowClass="yearMonthHeader"
           weekRowClass="weekHeader" id="birthday"
           currentDayCellClass="currentDayCell"
           value="#{userForm.user.birthday}"
           renderAsPopup="true" addResources="false"/>
   <h:message for="birthday" styleClass="errorMessage"/>

   <%-- Put in empty <td></td> --%>
   <h:inputHidden value=""/>

   <h:panelGroup>
       <h:commandButton
           value="Save" action="#{userForm.save}" id="save"
           styleClass="button"/>
   <c:if test="${not empty userForm.id}">
       <h:commandButton value="Delete" action="#{userForm.delete}"
           id="delete"
```

```
            styleClass="button"/>
    </c:if>
        <h:commandButton value="Cancel" action="cancel"
            immediate="true"
            id="cancel" styleClass="button"
            onclick="bCancel=true"/>
    </h:panelGroup>
    <h:inputHidden value=""/>
</h:panelGrid>
</h:form>

<script type="text/javascript">
    Form.focusFirstElement(document.forms['userForm']);
</script>

</f:view>
```

This page uses the **<f:formatNumber>** tag to auto-convert the **user.id** hidden field. It also contains code for the MyFaces custom **InputCalendar** component. To use this component, include the JavaScript and CSS lines in your **<head>**, and use the **<t:inputCalendar>** tag in your JSP. The JavaScript and CSS files are included in the JSF version of Equinox and this tutorial's download. These files are not required by default, but I found issues with the default versions.

To automatically place asterisks (and add colons) next to required fields, use a custom **javax.faces.Label** renderer. AppFuse has an example of this in its **LabelRenderer.java** class. After creating this class, configure it (see render-kit settings in AppFuse's *faces-config.xml*).

6   Modify *src/main/webapp/WEB-INF/faces-config.xml* to route edit requests from */userList.jsp* to */userForm.jsp*. Replace all the existing **<navigation-rule>** elements with the code in Listing A.19:

Listing A.19

```
<navigation-rule>
    <from-view-id>/userList.jsp</from-view-id>
    <navigation-case>
        <from-outcome>add</from-outcome>
        <to-view-id>/userForm.jsp</to-view-id>
    </navigation-case>
    <navigation-case>
        <from-outcome>success</from-outcome>
        <to-view-id>/userForm.jsp</to-view-id>
    </navigation-case>
</navigation-rule>
<navigation-rule>
    <from-view-id>/userForm.jsp</from-view-id>
    <navigation-case>
```

```
        <from-outcome>cancel</from-outcome>
        <to-view-id>/userList.jsp</to-view-id>
    </navigation-case>
    <navigation-case>
        <from-outcome>success</from-outcome>
        <to-view-id>/userList.jsp</to-view-id>
    </navigation-case>
  </navigation-rule>
```

7   Save all your files and run **ant deploy**. Then open your browser to localhost:8080/equinox-jsf/userList.html. You should see a window similar to Figure A.7.

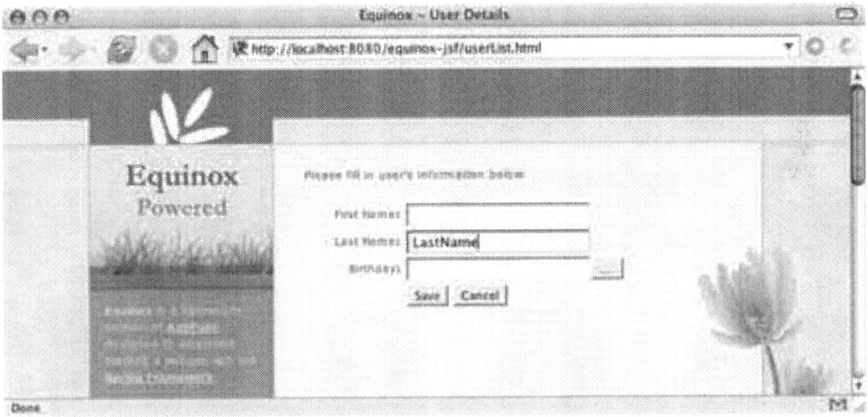

Figure A.7: Entering a new user

a   Click the **Add User** button to add a new user.

b   Populate the **Last Name** field and click **Save**.

c   Verify the list screen displays with a success message above the table, as shown in Figure A.8.

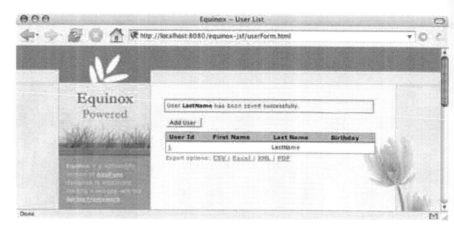

Figure A.8: Displaying success message

The *src/main/webapp/messages.jsp* file renders the success message in this screen. This file is included in *src/main/webapp/decorators/default.jsp*. Its contents are as follows in Listing A.20.

Listing A.20

```
<%-- Success Messages --%>
<c:if test="${not empty message}">
    <div class="message">${message}</div>
</c:if>
```

CONFIGURE VALIDATION

Most web applications require some sort of validation to ensure the entered data meets specific requirements. The following steps show how you can make **Last Name** a required field.

1   Add a **required** attribute to the **<h:inputText>** for the **Last Name** field and set it to **"true"**. See Listing A.21.

Listing A.21

```
<h:inputText value="#{userForm.user.lastName}"
    id="lastName" required="true"/>
```

2   Run **ant deploy** and try to add a user without a last name. You will receive a validation error like the one shown in Figure A.9.

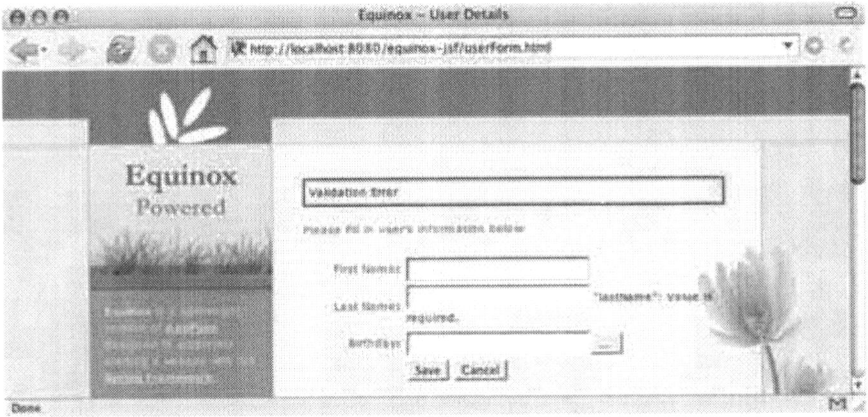

Figure A.9: Server-side validation error

The error messages on this page are rendered by the `<h:messages>` tag above the form and the `<h:message>` tag following the `<h:inputText>`.

NOTE: You can change the default "required" validation message by adding the following line to *src/main/resources/messages.properties*:

```
javax.faces.component.UIInput.REQUIRED=This is a required field.
```

CLIENT-SIDE VALIDATION

The JSF Specification does not include anything for client-side validation. At the time of this writing, neither Sun's Reference nor MyFaces include a client-side validation feature. If you'd like to use Commons Validator for client-side validation, you have a couple of options:

1   David Geary's Core JSF contains a tutorial and JAR files for integrating Commons Validator. This was included in Equinox versions prior to 1.5. I removed it because of conflicts between this JAR and Spring. Previous versions (December 2005) of Spring Live include instructions for integrating this validator. It also continues to be included and used in AppFuse.

2   The JSF-Comp project on SourceForge has a set of client-side validators. Something similar will likely be included in MyFaces' Tomahawk components in the near future.

3   Shale supports Commons Validator for client-side validation. The default server-side validation errors are a bit ugly, but you can prevent users from seeing them by adding client-side validation.

4   Cagatay Civici has written a good article on JSF and client-side validation on his blog at jroller.com/page/cagataycivici?entry= diaries_of_a_jsf_client.

Congratulations! You have implemented a working JSF application that hooks into Spring for its middle tier and back end. Now you must create tests that navigate the UI and verify functionality.

TESTING THE USER INTERFACE

User interface tests are an invaluable asset to a project. They verify that your view renders the proper information and doesn't produce errors. *Chapter 6: View Options* introduced you to JWebUnit, which is a testing framework on top of HttpUnit. *Chapter 9: Testing Spring Applications* introduced you to Canoo WebTest for testing UIs with Ant.

The capabilities of both libraries are similar. JWebUnit is based on HttpUnit, and Canoo WebTest used it at one time as well. They both rely on its JavaScript interpreter, Rhino. Unfortunately, HttpUnit often reports errors where none exist. Normally, this isn't an issue because you can disable JavaScript by not including the Rhino JAR. However, JSF uses Java-Script for its **commandLinks** and buttons, so it's helpful to have JavaScript enabled to test a JSF UI.

In the fall of 2004, Canoo switched from using HttpUnit to using HtmlUnit. While HtmlUnit also uses Rhino, its JavaScript support is *much* better. Because of this, these examples use Canoo WebTest rather than JWebUnit for testing this application's UI.

The Ant tasks and targets are already configured to run the Canoo tests, but you must first write them.

1   Create a *config.xml* file in the *test* directory and add the XML in Listing A.22 to it:

Listing A.22

```
<config host="${host}" port="${port}"
    protocol="http" basepath="${webapp.name}"
    resultpath="${test.dir}/data" resultfile="web-tests-result.xml"
    summary="true" saveresponse="true"/>
```

2   Create a *web-tests.xml* file in the same directory and add test targets to it. See Listing A.23.

Listing A.23

```xml
<!DOCTYPE project [
    <!ENTITY config SYSTEM "config.xml">
]>
<project basedir="." default="run-all-tests">
    <!-- Include messages.properties so we can test against
         keys, rather than values -->
    <property file="${resources.dir}/messages.properties"/>
    <property name="host" value="localhost"/>
    <property name="port" value="8080"/>

    <!-- runs all targets -->
    <target name="run-all-tests" depends="UserTests"
        description="Call and executes all test cases (targets)">
        <echo>All UserTests passed!</echo>
    </target>

    <!-- Verify adding a user, viewing and deleting a user works -->
    <target name="UserTests" description="Tests User CRUD">
        <webtest name="userTests">
            &config;
            <steps>
                <!-- View add screen -->
                <invoke url="/userList.html"/>
                <clickbutton label="Add User"/>

                <verifytitle text="${userForm.title}"/>

                <!-- Enter data and save -->
                <setinputfield name="userForm:firstName"
                    value="Test"/>
                <setinputfield name="userForm:lastName" value="Name"/>
                <clickbutton label="Save"/>

                <!-- View user list -->
                <verifytitle text="${userList.title}"/>

                <!-- Delete first user in table -->
                <invoke url="/userList.html"/>

                <clicklink href="viewUser"/>
                <verifytitle description="view user form"
                    text="${userForm.title}"/>
                <clickbutton label="Delete"/>
                <verifytitle description="view user list"
                    text="${userList.title}"/>
```

```
        </steps>
      </webtest>
    </target>
</project>
```

3   Run the tests in Tomcat by running **ant test-web** (if Tomcat is already running) or **ant test-tomcat** if you want Cargo to start it for you. The result should be similar to Figure A.10.

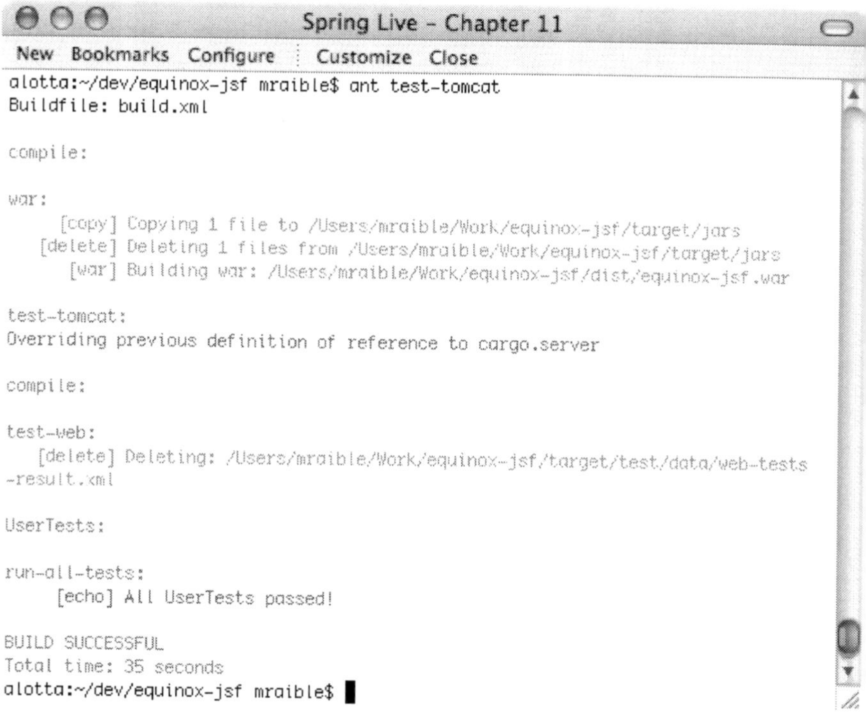

```
● ● ●                    Spring Live - Chapter 11                        ⬭
  New  Bookmarks  Configure  ┆  Customize  Close
alotta:~/dev/equinox-jsf mraible$ ant test-tomcat
Buildfile: build.xml

compile:

war:
    [copy] Copying 1 file to /Users/mraible/Work/equinox-jsf/target/jars
  [delete] Deleting 1 files from /Users/mraible/Work/equinox-jsf/target/jars
     [war] Building war: /Users/mraible/Work/equinox-jsf/dist/equinox-jsf.war

test-tomcat:
Overriding previous definition of reference to cargo.server

compile:

test-web:
    [delete] Deleting: /Users/mraible/Work/equinox-jsf/target/test/data/web-tests
-result.xml

UserTests:

run-all-tests:
    [echo] All UserTests passed!

BUILD SUCCESSFUL
Total time: 35 seconds
alotta:~/dev/equinox-jsf mraible$ ▮
```

Figure A.10: Testing the user interface

This section has shown you how to integrate a JSF web layer with a Spring middle tier and back end. All the code shown in this section is in the JSF version of Equinox 1.6.

TAPESTRY AND SPRING CRUD EXAMPLE
••

This section shows you how to create a Tapestry application using test-first development. You will use JUnit and a **BasePageTestCase** that instantiates page classes for you. This is necessary because Tapestry pages and components are often abstract. At runtime, Tapestry uses information from the class and its matching page or component specification to enhance the class. Enhancement is the process of creating a subclass on-the-fly that has implementations of abstract methods. More information about the class enhancement process is available on Tapestry's wiki.

DEPENDENCIES AND CONFIGURATION

For the Tapestry example, you'll use the *equinox-tapestry* project, which already contains Eclipse and IDEA project files. For instructions on configuring this project with a PostgreSQL database, and your IDE, please see the *README.txt* in the project's root directory. Besides configuring the Tapestry dependencies in *pom.xml*, nothing Tapestry-related is setup. This example uses Tapestry version 4.0.2.

For testing the UI, you will be using JWebUnit. After writing tests, page classes, templates, and specifications, you'll configure validation for the application.

CONFIGURING TAPESTRY IN WEB.XML

To configure Tapestry as your web framework, add a few elements to the *src/main/webapp/WEB-INF/web.xml* file:

1   Add a **<filter>** entry for Tapestry's **RedirectFilter**. This filter redirects requests from the root of the web application directly to Tapestry's **ApplicationServlet**, where the Home page for your application is served up. See Listing A.24

Listing A.24

```
<filter>
    <filter-name>redirect</filter-name>
    <filter-class>org.apache.tapestry.RedirectFilter
        </filter-class>
</filter>
```

2   Add a **<filter-mapping>** for this filter. See Listing A.25.

Listing A.25

```
<filter-mapping>
    <filter-name>redirect</filter-name>
    <url-pattern>/</url-pattern>
</filter-mapping>
```

3   Add a **<servlet>** entry for the **ApplicationServlet**. This is a **Front Controller** servlet, like Spring's **DispatcherServlet**. See Listing A.26.

Listing A.26

```
<servlet>
    <servlet-name>tapestry</servlet-name>
    <servlet-class>
        org.apache.tapestry.ApplicationServlet
    </servlet-class>
    <load-on-startup>1</load-on-startup>
</servlet>
```

4   Add a **<servlet-mapping>** to send all URLs ending with "*.html*" to the **ApplicationServlet**. Place this directly after the **<servlet>** element. In addition, add a number of mappings to support Tapestry 4's Friendly URLs feature. See Listing A.27.

Listing A.27

```
<servlet-mapping>
    <servlet-name>tapestry</servlet-name>
    <url-pattern>/app</url-pattern>
</servlet-mapping>

<servlet-mapping>
    <servlet-name>tapestry</servlet-name>
    <url-pattern>*.html</url-pattern>
</servlet-mapping>

<servlet-mapping>
    <servlet-name>tapestry</servlet-name>
    <url-pattern>*.direct</url-pattern>
</servlet-mapping>

<servlet-mapping>
    <servlet-name>tapestry</servlet-name>
    <url-pattern>*.sdirect</url-pattern>
</servlet-mapping>

<servlet-mapping>
    <servlet-name>tapestry</servlet-name>
    <url-pattern>/assets/*</url-pattern>
</servlet-mapping>

<servlet-mapping>
    <servlet-name>tapestry</servlet-name>
    <url-pattern>*.svc</url-pattern>
</servlet-mapping>
```

5 Create a *tapestry.application* file in the *src/main/webapp/WEB-INF* directory. This file configures services, third-party components, and pages. Its name must match the name that you assigned to the `ApplicationServlet`, which is "tapestry" in this example. See Listing A.28.

Listing A.28

```
<?xml version="1.0" encoding="UTF-8"?>
<!DOCTYPE application PUBLIC
    "-//Apache Software Foundation//Tapestry Specification 4.0//EN"
    "http://jakarta.apache.org/tapestry/dtd/Tapestry_4_0.dtd">

<application name="tapestry">
    <page name="error" specification-path="/pages/error.page"/>
    <page name="Home" specification-path="/pages/home.page"/>

    <library id="contrib" specification-
        path="/org/apache/tapestry/contrib/Contrib.library"/>
</application>
```

The Home page in this file already exists in the *src/main/webapp/pages* directory.

6 Create a *hivemodule.xml* file in *src/main/webapp/WEB-INF*. This file is used to override framework defaults, as well as configure friendly URLs. See Listing A.29.

Listing A.29

```
<?xml version="1.0" encoding="UTF-8"?>
<module id="org.appfuse.tapestry" version="1.0.0">
    <contribution configuration-id="tapestry.url.ServiceEncoders">
        <page-service-encoder id="page" extension="html"
            service="page"/>
        <direct-service-encoder id="direct" stateless-
            extension="direct" stateful-extension="sdirect"/>
        <asset-encoder id="asset" path="/assets"/>
        <extension-encoder id="extension" extension="svc" after="*"/>
    </contribution>

    <contribution configuration-id=
        "tapestry.InfrastructureOverrides">
        <property name="exceptionPageName" value="error"/>
    </contribution>
</module>
```

7 Run **ant deploy**, start Tomcat (if it's not running), and open localhost:8080/equinox-tapestry in your browser. Your browser will redirect you to localhost:8080/equinox-tapestry/app, and you will see the welcome page for Equinox, as shown in Figure A.11.

Figure A.11: Equinox welcome page

The Equinox-Tapestry example still uses SiteMesh for page decoration, so you will use some JSPs and JSTL code. For JSTL i18n, the *web.xml* file already contains a **<context-param>** for setting the default **ResourceBundle**. The setting below tells the **<fmt:message>** tag to use the **messages.properties Resource-Bundle** from *WEB-INF/classes* (the root of the classpath). See Listing A.30.

Listing A.30

```
<context-param>
    <param-name>
        javax.servlet.jsp.jstl.fmt.localizationContext
    </param-name>
    <param-value>messages</param-value>
</context-param>
```

TIP: Tapestry has a **RenderBody** component that offers similar functionality of SiteMesh. However, this tutorial uses SiteMesh because it works for all the frameworks used in Equinox. In the future, this may change since a patch was submitted to SiteMesh's JIRA that allows you to use a Tapestry page for your decorator.

CREATE THE MASTER SCREEN

The first class of this example displays the list of current users in the database. First, create a unit test.

1. Create a `BasePageTestCase.java` class in *src/test/java/org/appfuse/web*. This class extends Spring's `AbstractDependencyInjectionSpring-ContextTests` and has convenience methods for instantiating page classes. The mock classes in Listing A.31 are from *spring-mock.jar*, which already exists in your classpath.

Listing A.31

```
package org.appfuse.web;

// organize imports using your IDE

public class BasePageTestCase
    extends AbstractDependencyInjectionSpringContextTests {
    protected final Log log = LogFactory.getLog(getClass());
    protected final static String EXTENSION = ".html";

    protected String[] getConfigLocations() {
        return new String[] {"/WEB-INF/applicationContext*.xml"};
    }

    protected IPage getPage(Class clazz) {
        return getPage(clazz, null);
    }

    protected IPage getPage(Class clazz, Map properties) {
        Creator creator = new Creator();
        if (properties == null) {
            properties = new HashMap();
        }

        Messages messages = new MessageFormatter(log, "messages");
        properties.put("messages", messages);

        return (IPage) creator.newInstance(clazz, properties);
    }
}
```

Once you create this class, writing a test for a page class is easy.

2. Create a `UserListTest.java` class in *src/test/java/org/appfuse/web*. See Listing A.32.

Listing A.32

```
package org.appfuse.web;

// organize imports using your IDE

public class UserListTest extends BasePageTestCase {
    private UserList page;
    private UserManager userManager;

    public void setUserManager(UserManager userManager) {
        this.userManager = userManager;
    }

    protected void onSetUp() throws Exception {
        Map map = new HashMap();
        map.put("userManager", userManager);
        page = (UserList) getPage(UserList.class, map);

        // create a new user
        User user = new User();
        user.setFirstName("Abbie");
        user.setLastName("Raible");
        user.setBirthday(new Date());

        // persist to database
        userManager.saveUser(user);
    }

    protected void onTearDown() throws Exception {
        page = null;
    }

    public void testSearch() throws Exception {
        assertTrue(page.getUserManager().getUsers().size() >= 1);
    }
}
```

This class won't compile until you create the **UserList** class.

3   Create a **UserList.java** class in *src/main/java/org/appfuse/web*. See Listing A.33.

Listing A.33

```
package org.appfuse.web;

// organize imports using your IDE
```

```
public abstract class UserList extends BasePage {
    public abstract UserManager getUserManager();
    public abstract String getMessage();
    public abstract void setMessage(String message);

    private DateFormat dateFormatter =
        new SimpleDateFormat("MM/dd/yyyy");

    public String getFormattedDate(java.util.Date date) {
        if (date == null) {
            return "";
        }

        return dateFormatter.format(date);
    }
}
```

This class is fairly simple. In fact, most of the code is for the **message** variable and its accessors, which display success messages.

NOTE: You could put these methods in the **BasePage** class, but exposing them here demonstrates how to set success messages.

The **getUserManager()** method is an abstract method that Tapestry will implement when it enhances this class. You must specify this property's value in this page's specification file.

4   Run the **UserListTest** using the command **ant test -Dtest-case=UserListTest**. The result should look similar to Figure A.12.

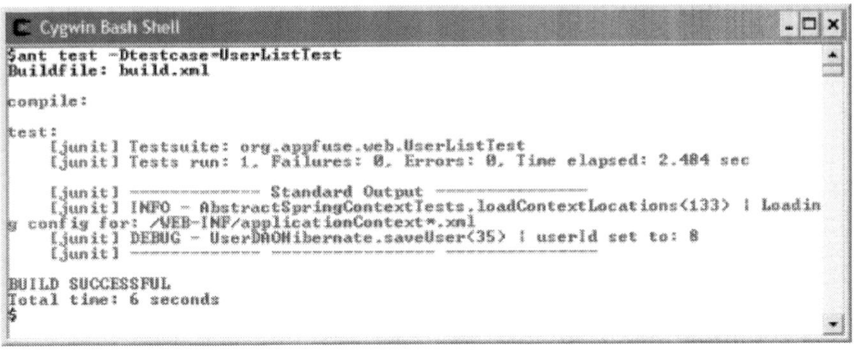

Figure A.12: Running the **UserListTest**

5   Create an *src/main/webapp/pages/users.html* page to display the list of users, as you did with JSTL and the display tag. The **contrib:Table**

component allows you to easily create a list of pageable and sortable data. See Listing A.34.

Listing A.34

```
<title><span key="userList.title"/></title>

<span jwcid="@If" condition="ognl:message != null">
    <div class="message">
        <span jwcid="@Insert" value="ognl:message" raw="true"/>
    </div>
</span>

<a jwcid="@PageLink" page="userForm" id="formLink"
    style="display:none"/>
<button class="button"
    onclick="location.href=document.getElementById('formLink')
        .href">Add User</button>

<table jwcid="table@contrib:Table" class="list" id="userList"
    rowsClass="ognl:beans.evenOdd.next"
    row="ognl:row" source="ognl:userManager.users"
    columns="id, firstName, lastName, birthday"
    arrowUpAsset="ognl:assets.upArrow"
    arrowDownAsset="ognl:assets.downArrow">
    <tr jwcid="birthdayColumnValue@Block">
        <span jwcid="@Insert"
            value="ognl:getFormattedDate(row.birthday)"/>
    </tr>
</table>

<script type="text/javascript">highlightTableRows("userList");
    </script>
```

The **If** component near the top of this template displays messages from the page if there are any. The **Add User** button does nothing at this point, but you'll set it to go to the userForm page after creating it.

6 Tapestry makes it very easy to internationalize your web application. The title for this page is **<span key="userList.title"/>**. This value will be replaced with the **userList.title** key in this page's **ResourceBundle**. Each page has its own **ResourceBundle**, which is named the same as the page. Create a *users.properties* file in the *webapp/pages* directory with the keys in Listing A.35.

NOTE: Unlike Struts, Spring, and JSF, the Tapestry architecture promotes only one **ResourceBundle** per page. Tapestry 4 added the ability to have a global

`ResourceBundle`, but the implementation does not allow you to configure the location of that bundle. See TAPESTRY-881 for more information.

Listing A.35

```
#-- messages for users.html page --
userList.title=Equinox ~ User List

id=Id
firstName=First Name
lastName=Last Name
birthday=Birthday
date.format=MM/dd/yyyy
```

The `contrib:Table` component will automatically look up the keys for column headings based on the column names.

7   Create a page specification for this page at *src/main/webapp/pages/users.page*. See Listing A.36.

Listing A.36

```
<?xml version="1.0" encoding="UTF-8"?>
<!DOCTYPE page-specification PUBLIC
    "-//Apache Software Foundation//Tapestry Specification 4.0//EN"
    "http://jakarta.apache.org/tapestry/dtd/Tapestry_4_0.dtd">

<page-specification class="org.appfuse.web.UserList">
    <inject property="userManager" type="spring"
object="userManager"/>

    <property name="message" persist="flash"/>
    <property name="row"/>

    <bean name="evenOdd" class="org.apache.tapestry.bean.EvenOdd"/>
    <asset name="upArrow" path="/images/arrow_up.png"/>
    <asset name="downArrow" path="/images/arrow_down.png"/>
</page-specification>
```

8   Add this page to the list of pages for this application in *src/main/webapp/ WEB-INF/tapestry.application*. See Listing A.37.

Listing A.37

```
<page name="Home" specification-path="/pages/home.page"/>
<page name="users" specification-path="/pages/users.page"/>

<library id="contrib" specification-path="/org/apache/tapestry/
    contrib/Contrib.library"/>
```

9   Run **ant deploy populate**, navigate to localhost:8080/equinox-tapestry and click the **View Demonstration** button. You should see something similar to Figure A.13.

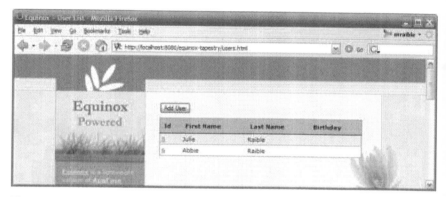

Figure A.13: View the user list using the `contrib:Table`

NOTE: Tapestry caches page templates by default. While this is great for production, it can be frustrating for development. To disable caching, create a `CATALINA_OPTS` environment variable with the following value:

`-Dorg.apache.tapestry.disable-caching=true`

CREATE THE DETAIL SCREEN

The `UserForm` page in this example edits, saves, and deletes a user.

1   Create a `UserFormTest` class in *src/test/java/org/appfuse/web*, and populate it with the code in Listing A.38.

Listing A.38

```
package org.appfuse.web;

// organize imports with your IDE
```

```java
public class UserFormTest extends BasePageTestCase {
    private UserForm page;
    private Long userId;
    private UserManager userManager;

    public void setUserManager(UserManager userManager) {
        this.userManager = userManager;
    }

    protected void onSetUp() throws Exception {
        Map map = new HashMap();
        map.put("userManager", userManager);
        map.put("engineService", new MockPageService());
        page = (UserForm) getPage(UserForm.class, map);

        // create a new user
        User user = new User();
        user.setFirstName("Jack");
        user.setLastName("Raible");

        // persist to database
        userManager.saveUser(user);
        userId = user.getId();
    }

    protected void onTearDown() throws Exception {
        page = null;
    }

    public void testEdit() throws Exception {
        RequestCycle cycle = new MockRequestCycle();
        cycle.setServiceParameters(new Object[] {userId});

        page.edit(cycle);
        assertNotNull(page.getUser());
    }

    public void testSave() throws Exception {
        RequestCycle cycle = new MockRequestCycle();
        cycle.setServiceParameters(new Object[] {userId});

        page.edit(cycle);
        assertNotNull(page.getUser());
        ILink link = page.save(cycle);
        assertEquals("users" + EXTENSION, link.getURL());
    }

    public void testRemove() throws Exception {
        User user = new User();
        user.setId(userId);
```

```
                page.setUser(user);

                ILink link = page.delete(new MockRequestCycle());
                assertEquals("users" + EXTENSION, link.getURL());
        }
}
```

2   Create the **UserForm** class in *src/main/java/org/appfuse/web*. See
    Listing A.39.

Listing A.39

```
package org.appfuse.web;

// organize imports using your IDE

public abstract class UserForm extends BasePage implements
    PageBeginRenderListener {
    private final Log log = LogFactory.getLog(UserForm.class);
    public abstract IEngineService getEngineService();
    public abstract UserManager getUserManager();
    public abstract void setUser(User user);
    public abstract User getUser();

    public void pageBeginRender(PageEvent event) {
        if ((getUser() == null) &&
            !event.getRequestCycle().isRewinding()) {
            setUser(new User());
        } else if (event.getRequestCycle().isRewinding()) {
            setUser(new User());
        }
    }

    public void cancel(IRequestCycle cycle) {
        log.debug("entered 'cancel' method");

        cycle.activate("users");
    }

    public void edit(IRequestCycle cycle) {
        Object[] parameters = cycle.getListenerParameters();
        Long id = (Long) parameters[0];

        log.debug("fetching user with id: " + id);

        setUser(getUserManager().getUser(id.toString()));
        cycle.activate(this);
    }

    public ILink save(IRequestCycle cycle) {
```

```
        log.debug("entered 'save' method");

        getUserManager().saveUser(getUser());

        UserList nextPage = (UserList) cycle.getPage("users");
        nextPage.setMessage(getMessages().format("user.saved",
            getUser().getFullName()));
        // redirect to next page
        return getEngineService().getLink(false,
            nextPage.getPageName());
    }

    public ILink delete(IRequestCycle cycle) {
        log.debug("entered 'delete' method");

        getUserManager().removeUser(getUser().getId().toString());

        UserList nextPage = (UserList) cycle.getPage("users");
        nextPage.setMessage(getMessages().format("user.deleted",
            getUser().getFullName()));
        // redirect to next page
        return getEngineService().getLink(false,
            nextPage.getPageName());
    }
}
```

3   Run the **UserFormTest** using the command **ant test –Dtestcase= UserForm**. The result should be similar to what's shown in Figure A.14.

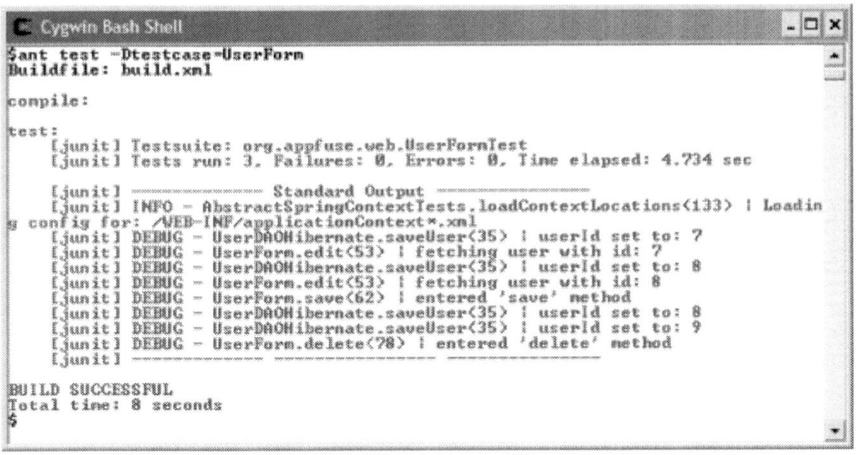

Figure A.14: Running the **UserFormTest**

4   Create a *src/main/webapp/pages/userForm.html* template to display the form.
See Listing A.40.

Listing A.40

```html
<head>
    <title><span key="userForm.title"/></title>
    <link href="styles/calendar.css" type="text/css"
        rel="stylesheet"/>
</head>

<body jwcid="@Body">

<p>Please fill in user's information below:</p>

<form jwcid="form" id="userForm">
<input type="hidden" jwcid="@Hidden" value="ognl:user.id"/>
<table class="detail">
<tr>
    <th>
        <label for="firstName">
            <span key="firstName">First Name</span></label>:
    </th>
    <td>
        <input jwcid="@TextField" type="text"
            value="ognl:user.firstName" id="firstName"
            displayName="message:firstName"/>
    </td>
</tr>
<tr>
    <th>
        <label jwcid="@FieldLabel"
            field="ognl:components.lastNameField">Last Name</label>:
    </th>
    <td><input jwcid="lastNameField" type="text" id="lastName"/></td>
</tr>
<tr>
    <th>
        <label for="birthday">
            <span key="birthday">Birthday</span></label>:
    </th>
    <td>
        <input jwcid="@DatePicker" type="text" size="11"
            value="ognl:user.birthday" id="birthday"
            translator="translator:date,pattern=MM/dd/yyyy"/>
    </td>
</tr>
<tr>
    <td></td>
    <td>
```

```
            <input type="submit" class="button" jwcid="@Submit"
                value="Save" id="save" listener="ognl:listeners.save"/>
        <span jwcid="@If" condition="ognl:user.id != null">
            <input type="submit" class="button" jwcid="@Submit"
                value="Delete" id="delete"
                listener="ognl:listeners.delete"/>
        </span>
            <input type="submit" class="button" jwcid="@Submit"
                value="Cancel" id="cancel"
                    listener="ognl:listeners.cancel"
                onclick="form.onsubmit = null"/>
        </td>
    </table>
    </form>

    </body>
```

This page uses a number of components. At the top is a *calendar.css* file, which over-rides the default colors and positioning of the pop-up calendar provided by the **DatePicker** component. In Tapestry, this component is entirely self-contained. The JavaScript for the calendar that's rendered is contained within the JAR file for the component.

You don't always need the **Body** component, but it's in this template because it's necessary for client-side validation. Within the **Form** component is a **Hidden** component for the user's id, which contains two **TextField** components for the user's first and last names. At the bottom of the screen are **Submit** components, which call the different listener methods in the **UserForm** class.

5 Create a *userForm.properties* file in the *src/main/webapp/pages* directory. See Listing A.41.

Listing A.41

```
# Messages used for labels, errors and success messages
userForm.title=Equinox ~ User Details

user.saved=User <strong>{0}</strong> has been saved successfully.
user.missing=No user found with this id.
user.deleted=User <strong>{0}</strong> successfully deleted.

firstName=First Name
lastName=Last Name
birthday=Birthday
date.format=MM/dd/yyyy
```

6 Create the page specification at *web/pages/userForm.page*. See Listing A.42.

Listing A.42

```xml
<?xml version="1.0" encoding="UTF-8"?>
<!DOCTYPE page-specification PUBLIC
    "-//Apache Software Foundation//Tapestry Specification 4.0//EN"
    "http://jakarta.apache.org/tapestry/dtd/Tapestry_4_0.dtd">

<page-specification class="org.appfuse.web.UserForm">
    <inject property="engineService" object="engine-service:page"/>

    <component id="form" type="Form"/>

    <property name="user"/>
    <inject property="userManager" type="spring"
        object="userManager"/>

    <component id="lastNameField" type="TextField">
        <binding name="value" value="user.lastName"/>
        <binding name="displayName" value="message:lastName"/>
    </component>

</page-specification>
```

7 Add this page to the list of pages for this application in *src/main/webapp/WEB-INF/tapestry.application*. See Listing A.43.

Listing A.43

```xml
<page name="userForm" specification-path="/pages/userForm.page"/>
```

Now you must add a link to the *users.html* template so you can view the details page.

8 Change the **Form** and **Submit** components to use a **PageLink** and an **onclick** handler in the button. See Listing A.44.

Listing A.44

```html
<a jwcid="@PageLink" page="userForm" id="formLink"
    style="display:none"/>
<button class="button"
    onclick="location.href=document.getElementById('formLink').href">
    Add User</button>
```

You must do it this way because there is no core component that allows clicking a **<button>** to go to another page. Other options are to use a **PageLink** with an **<a href="...">** or to add some logic to the **UserForm.edit()** listener and allow that to be called without any service parameters.

9 Add a row to the table that allows you to click on the user's id to view the details page. `Block` and `DirectLink` components override the default column value for `id` and put a link around it. Place the HTML in Listing A.45 inside the `<table>` element:

Listing A.45

```
<tr jwcid="idColumnValue@Block">
    <a jwcid="@DirectLink" parameters="ognl:row.id"
        listener="ognl:requestCycle.getPage('userForm')
            .listeners.edit">
        <span jwcid="@Insert" value="ognl:row.id"/>
    </a>
</tr>
```

10 Run **ant deploy**, open your browser to localhost:8080/equinox-tapestry and click the **View Demonstration** button (see Figure A.15). Click the **Add User** button to add a new user. 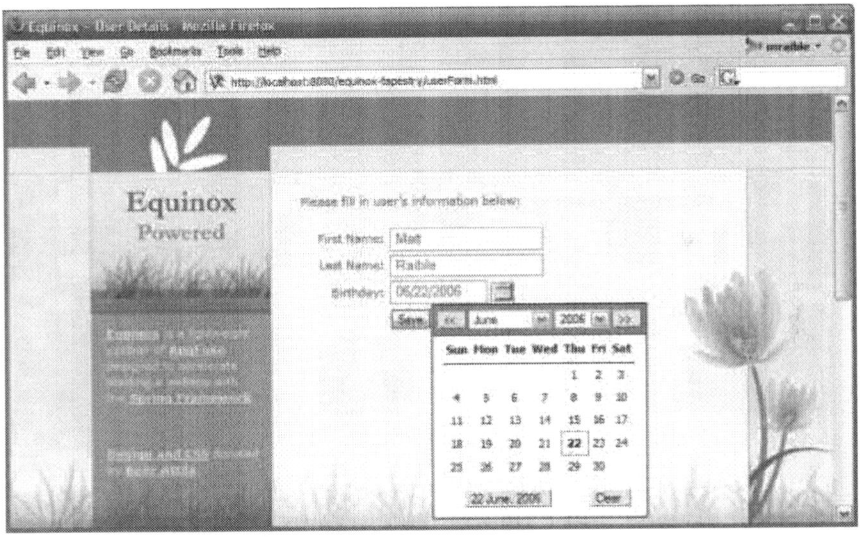

Figure A.15: Adding a new user

11 Click the **Save** button. This will route you to the list screen, where a success message displays and the user is listed, as shown in Figure A.16.

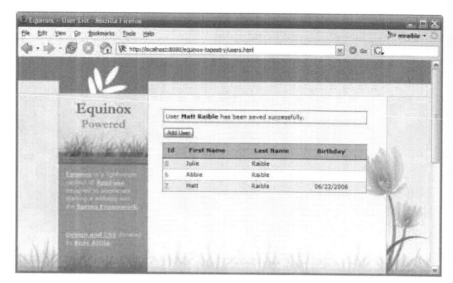

Figure A.16: Displaying success message

CONFIGURE VALIDATION

Most web applications require some sort of validation to ensure the entered data meets specific requirements. The following steps show how you can make **Last Name** a required field:

1   Add a **ValidationDelegate** to the *userForm.page* page specification. This class is a helper bean to handle validation for the **Form** component. See Listing A.46.

Listing A.46

```
<bean name="delegate"
    class="org.apache.tapestry.valid.ValidationDelegate"/>
```

2   Add a **getValidationDelegate()** method to **UserForm** to get the **delegate** bean. See Listing A.47.

Listing A.47

```
protected IValidationDelegate getValidationDelegate() {
    // be nice to unit tests
    if (getSpecification() != null) {
        return (IValidationDelegate)
            getBeans().getBean("delegate");
```

```
        } else {
            return new ValidationDelegate();
        }
    }
```

3   Modify the **Form** component in the page specification to make the form validation-aware. See Listing A.48.

Listing A.48

```
<component id="form" type="Form">
    <binding name="delegate" value="ognl:beans.delegate"/>
</component>
```

4   Modify the **lastNameField** component to add a **validators** binding. See Listing A.49.

Listing A.49

```
<component id="lastNameField" type="TextField">
    <binding name="value" value="user.lastName"/>
    <binding name="validators" value="validators:required"/>
    <binding name="displayName" value="message:lastName"/>
</component>
```

5   Add a **Conditional** component to the top of the *userForm.html* page, directly after the **<body>** tag. See Listing A.50.

Listing A.50

```
<span jwcid="@If" condition="ognl:beans.delegate.hasErrors">
    <div class="error">
        <span jwcid="@Delegator"
            delegate="ognl:beans.delegate.firstError">
            Error Message
        </span>
    </div>
</span>
```

6   Unlike most other web frameworks, Tapestry doesn't automatically return you to the input page when validation fails. You must add your own logic in the method that you want to enforce validation. Refactor the **UserForm.save()** method to route the user back to the input page when validation errors occur. See Listing A.51.

Listing A.51

```
public ILink save(IRequestCycle cycle) {
    log.debug("entered 'save' method");

    if (getValidationDelegate().getHasErrors()) {
        return null;
    }

    getUserManager().saveUser(getUser());

    ...
}
```

7 Run **ant deploy**, and try to add a user without a last name. You should
get a validation error like the one shown in Figure A.17.

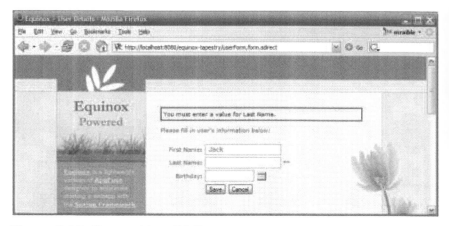

Figure A.17: Server-side validation error

CLIENT-SIDE VALIDATION

Configuring client-side validation with Tapestry is easy.

1 Set the **clientValidationEnabled** binding to **"true"** on the **Form**
component (in *src/main/webapp/pages/userForm.page*). See Listing A.52.

Listing A.52

```
<component id="form" type="Form">
    <binding name="delegate" value="ognl:beans.delegate"/>
    <binding name="clientValidationEnabled" value="true"/>
</component>
```

2   Run **ant deploy** and try to add a user without a last name. You should see
     a JavaScript alert telling you the field is required (see Figure A.18).

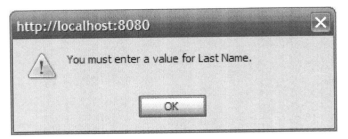

Figure A.18: Client-side validation error

Congratulations! You have implemented a working Tapestry application that hooks
into Spring for its middle tier and back end. Now you must create tests that navigate
the UI and verify functionality.

TESTING THE USER INTERFACE

The download for this section is already configured for JWebUnit, both for creating
tests and running them. To test that everything works as expected through the UI,
complete the following steps:

1   Create a **UserWebTest.java** class in *src/test/java/org/appfuse/web* and
     populate it with the code in Listing A.53.

Listing A.53

```
package org.appfuse.web;

// organize imports using your IDE

public class UserWebTest extends WebTestCase {

    public UserWebTest(String name) {
        super(name);
        getTestContext().setBaseUrl
            ("http://localhost:8080/equinox-tapestry");
        getTestContext().setResourceBundleName("messages");
    }

    public void testWelcomePage() {
        beginAt("/");
        assertTitleEqualsKey("index.title");
    }

    public void testAddUser() {
```

```
        beginAt("/userForm.html");
        assertTitleEqualsKey("userForm.title");
        setFormElement("TextField", "Spring");
        setFormElement("lastNameField", "User");
        submit("Submit");
        assertTextPresent("saved successfully");
    }

    public void testListUsers() {
        beginAt("/users.html");

        // check that table is present
        assertTablePresent("userList");

        // check that a set of strings are present somewhere in table
        assertTextInTable("userList",
                    new String[] {"Spring", "User"});
    }

    public void testEditUser() {
        beginAt("/users,$DirectLink.sdirect?sp=1" +
getInsertedUserId());
        assertFormElementEquals("TextField", "Spring");
        submit("Submit");
        assertTitleEqualsKey("userList.title");
    }

    /**
     * Convenience method to get the id of the inserted user
     * Assumes last inserted user is "Spring User"
     */
    public String getInsertedUserId() {
        beginAt("/users.html");
        assertTablePresent("userList");
        assertTextInTable("userList", "Spring");
        String[][] sparseTableCells =
                getDialog().getSparseTableBySummaryOrId("userList");
        return sparseTableCells[sparseTableCells.length-1][0];
    }
}
```

2   Run the tests in Tomcat by running **ant test-web** (if Tomcat is already
    running) or **ant test-tomcat** if you want Cargo to start it for you. The
    result should look something like Figure A.19.

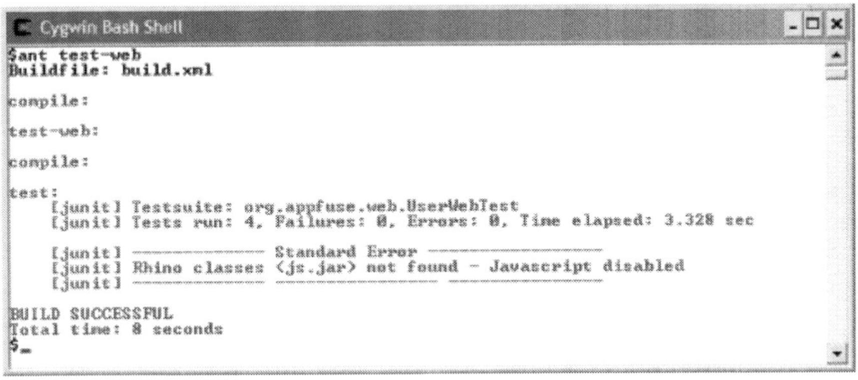

Figure A.19: Testing the user interface

This section has shown you how to integrate a Tapestry web layer with a Spring middle tier and back end. All the code shown in this section is in the Tapestry version of Equinox 1.6.

WebWork and Spring CRUD example

This section shows you how to create a WebWork, Spring, and Hibernate application using test-first development. You will use two techniques for testing the web layer of this application:

- JUnit to test WebWork Actions
- JWebUnit to test the user interfaces

After writing the tests, Actions, and JSPs, you will configure validation.

Dependencies and configuration

For the WebWork example, you'll use the *equinox-webwork* project, which already contains Eclipse and IDEA project files. For instructions on configuring this project with a PostgreSQL database, and your IDE, please see the *README.txt* in the project's root directory. Besides configuring the WebWork dependencies in *pom.xml*, nothing WebWork-related is set up. This example uses WebWork version 2.2.2.

Configuring WebWork in *web.xml*

To configure WebWork as your web framework, add a few elements to the *src/ main/webapp/WEB-INF/web.xml* file.

1   Add an entry for the **FilterDispatcher**, which is similar to Spring's **DispatcherServlet**. Unlike most Java web frameworks, WebWork uses a filter instead of a servlet for its front controller. It also supports using a servlet, but using a filter allows dynamic elements to be added anywhere in the HTML page (for example, JavaScript in the **<head>**). See Listing A.54.

Listing A.54

```
<filter>
    <filter-name>webwork</filter-name>
    <filter-class>
        com.opensymphony.webwork.dispatcher.FilterDispatcher
    </filter-class>
</filter>
```

2   Add a **<filter-mapping>** for the **FilterDispatcher**. Place this before the **<listener>** element. See Listing A.55.

Listing A.55

```
<filter-mapping>
    <filter-name>webwork</filter-name>
    <url-pattern>/*</url-pattern>
</filter-mapping>
```

This file already contains a **<context-param>** for setting the default **Resource-Bundle** for JSTL. The setting below tells the **<fmt:message>** tag to use the *messages.properties* **ResourceBundle** from *WEB-INF/classes* (the root of the classpath). See Listing A.56.

Listing A.56

```
<context-param>
    <param-name>
        javax.servlet.jsp.jstl.fmt.localizationContext
    </param-name>
    <param-value>messages</param-value>
</context-param>
```

WebWork only recently added support for a global **ResourceBundle**. In prior versions, it worked much like Tapestry, where you would create properties files to match an Action or a package. This tutorial uses the global approach.

3   Create a *webwork.properties* file in *src/main/resources* with the contents in Listing A.57:

Listing A.57

```
webwork.objectFactory=spring
webwork.action.extension=html
webwork.custom.i18n.resources=messages
```

WEBWORK TAG LIBRARIES

1   WebWork has a tag library that is quite useful when developing with JSPs. It gives you access to the `OgnlValueStack` and makes development much easier. The download for this tutorial does not have any tag libraries defined. To define them, create a *src/main/webapp/taglibs.jsp* file and populate it with the code in Listing A.58. This file is included at the top of most JSP pages.

Listing A.58

```
<%@ page language="java" errorPage="/error.jsp" %>
<%@ taglib uri="http://java.sun.com/jsp/jstl/core" prefix="c" %>
<%@ taglib uri="http://java.sun.com/jsp/jstl/fmt" prefix="fmt" %>
<%@ taglib uri="http://displaytag.sf.net" prefix="display" %>
<%@ taglib uri="http://www.opensymphony.com/sitemesh/decorator"
    prefix="decorator" %>
<%@ taglib uri="/webwork" prefix="ww" %>

<c:set var="datePattern"><fmt:message key="date.format"/></c:set>
<c:set var="ctx" value="${pageContext.request.contextPath}"/>
```

The first two lines in this file are for JSTL. The display tag is described in *Chapter 6: View Options*, and the SiteMesh **decorator** tag is described in *Chapter 5: Advanced Spring MVC*. The **webwork** tag is WebWork's JSP Tag Library, which renders forms and validation errors. You can also use it to render internationalized text, or you can use JSTL's **<fmt:message>** tag. The **<c:set>** tag sets a **datePattern** for formatting dates in JSPs. This value is currently in the *src/main/resources/messages.properties* file so you can change the formatting based on a user's locale.

> **date.format=MM/dd/yyyy**

After modifying *src/main/webapp/WEB-INF/web.xml* and creating *src/main/webapp/taglibs.jsp*, build and deploy the *equinox-webwork* application using **ant deploy**. After executing this command, start Tomcat and navigate to localhost:8080/equinox-webwork. The default Equinox welcome page should render without any issues (see Figure A.20).

Figure A.20: Equinox welcome page

CREATE THE MASTER SCREEN

Testing is an important part of any application, and testing a WebWork application is easier than most. The generic command pattern provided by XWork doesn't depend on the Servlet API at all. This makes it easy to use JUnit to test your Actions.

1   Create a **UserActionTest.java** class in *src/test/java/org/appfuse/web*. This initializes Spring's context and tests the **UserAction** class. See Listing A.59.

Listing A.59

```
package org.appfuse.web;

// use your IDE to organize imports

public class UserActionTest extends
    AbstractDependencyInjectionSpringContextTests {
    private UserAction action;
    private String userId;

    public void setUserAction(UserAction action) {
        this.action = action;
    }

    protected String[] getConfigLocations() {
        return new String[] {"/WEB-INF/applicationContext*.xml",
```

```
                            "/WEB-INF/action-servlet.xml"};
    }

    protected void onSetUp() throws Exception {
        UserManager mgr = (UserManager)
            applicationContext.getBean("userManager");

        // add a test user to the database
        User user = new User();
        user.setFirstName("Jack");
        user.setLastName("Raible");
        mgr.saveUser(user);
        userId = user.getId().toString();

        ActionContext.getContext().setSession(new HashMap());
        LocalizedTextUtil.addDefaultResourceBundle("messages");
    }

    protected void onTearDown() throws Exception {
        ActionContext.getContext().setSession(null);
    }

    public void testSearch() throws Exception {
        assertEquals(action.list(), ActionSupport.SUCCESS);
        assertTrue(action.getUsers().size() >= 1);
    }
}
}
```

This class won't compile yet; you must first create the **UserAction** class.

   2   Create a **UserAction.java** class (that extends XWork's
          ActionSupport) in *src/main/java/org/appfuse/web*. See Listing A.60.

Listing A.60

```
package org.appfuse.web;

// use your IDE to organize imports

public class UserAction extends ActionSupport {
    private final Log log = LogFactory.getLog(UserAction.class);
    private UserManager mgr;
    private List users;

    public void setUserManager(UserManager userManager) {
        this.mgr = userManager;
    }

    public List getUsers() {
        return users;
```

```
    }

    public String list() {
        users = mgr.getUsers();
        return SUCCESS;
    }
}
```

WebWork actions are typically both the controller and the model. In this example, the **list()** method acts as the controller, and the **getUsers()** method retrieves data from the model. This simplification of the MVC paradigm makes it easy to program with WebWork.

  3   Create an *action-servlet.xml* file in the *src/main/webapp/WEB-INF* directory. Set its dependencies as you normally would with Spring. See Listing A.61.

Listing A.61

```
<?xml version="1.0" encoding="UTF-8"?>
<!DOCTYPE beans PUBLIC "-//SPRING//DTD BEAN//EN"
    "http://www.springframework.org/dtd/spring-beans.dtd">

<beans>
    <bean id="userAction" class="org.appfuse.web.UserAction"
    singleton="false">
        <property name="userManager" ref="userManager"/>
    </bean>
</beans>
```

  4   Add *action-servlet.xml* to the list of context files loaded by the **ContextLoaderListener**. To do this, open *src/main/webapp/WEB-INF/web.xml* and change the **contextConfigLocation** context parameter. See Listing A.62.

Listing A.62

```
<context-param>
    <param-name>contextConfigLocation</param-name>
    <param-value>
        /WEB-INF/applicationContext*.xml
        /WEB-INF/action-servlet.xml
    </param-value>
</context-param>
```

  5   Run the **UserActionTest** using **ant test -Dtestcase=UserAction**. The result should look something like Figure A.21.

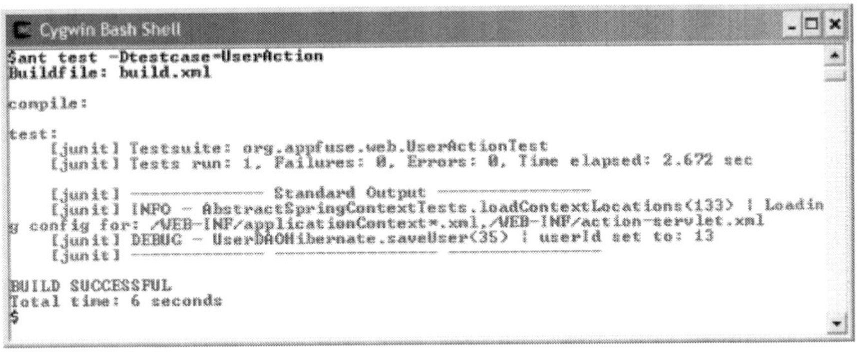

Figure A.21: Running the `UserActionTest`

6   Create a *src/main/webapp/userList.jsp* page to display the list of users. See Listing A.63.

Listing A.63

```
<%@ include file="/taglibs.jsp"%>

<title><fmt:message key="userList.title"/></title>

<ww:set name="users" value="users" scope="request"/>
<button onclick="location.href='editUser.html'">Add User</button>

<display:table name="users" class="list" requestURI="" id="userList"
    export="true" pagesize="10">
    <display:column property="id" sortable="true"
        href="editUser.html"
        paramId="id" paramProperty="id" titleKey="user.id"/>
    <display:column property="firstName" sortable="true"
        titleKey="user.firstName"/>
    <display:column property="lastName" sortable="true"
        titleKey="user.lastName"/>
    <display:column sortable="true" titleKey="user.birthday"
        sortProperty="birthday">
        <fmt:formatDate value="${userList.birthday}"
            pattern="${datePattern}"/>
    </display:column>
</display:table>

<script type="text/javascript">highlightTableRows("userList");
    </script>
```

The most important line in Listing A.63 is the one near the top that contains the `<ww:set>` tag. This tag calls `getUsers()` on the `UserAction` and sets the resulting `List` into the request scope, where the `<display:table>` tag can grab it.

The Spring 1.x Primer

This is necessary because the display tag doesn't have any knowledge of the **ValueStack** used by WebWork.

7   Create an *xwork.xml* file in the *src/main/resources* directory. Define an **<action>** and set its **class** attribute to match the id of the bean you created in Step 3. See Listing A.64.

Listing A.64

```
<!DOCTYPE xwork PUBLIC "-//OpenSymphony Group//XWork 1.1.1//EN"
    "http://www.opensymphony.com/xwork/xwork-1.1.1.dtd">

<xwork>
    <!-- Include webwork defaults (from WebWork JAR) -->
    <include file="webwork-default.xml"/>

    <package name="default" extends="webwork-default">

      <action name="users" class="userAction" method="list">
        <result name="success"
            type="dispatcher">userList.jsp</result>
      </action>
    </package>
</xwork>
```

The **dispatcher** result type simply forwards you to the *userList.jsp* file. Other result types include **redirect** and **chain**. Redirect performs a client-side redirect and chain forwards you to another action. For a full list of result types, see WebWork's Result Types documentation.

The **method** attribute of this action has a **list** attribute, which calls the **list()** method when the *users.html* URL is invoked. If you exclude the **method** attribute, it calls the **execute()** method. **ActionSupport** implements this method by default.

8   Run **ant deploy populate** and open localhost:8080/equinox-webwork/ users.html in your browser. You should get a result similar to that in Figure A.22.

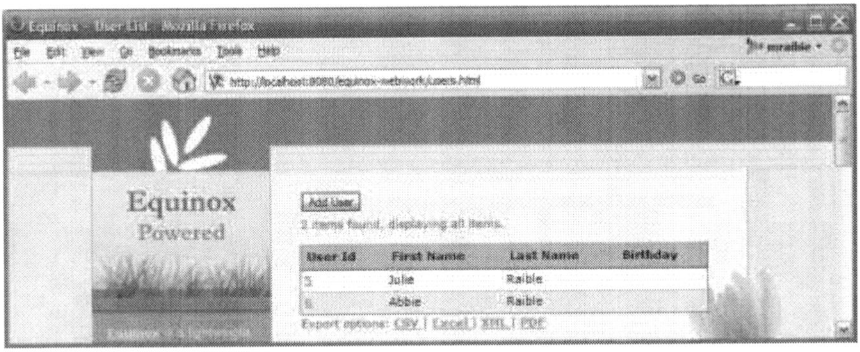

Figure A.22: Viewing the user list

CREATE THE DETAIL SCREEN

To create the detail screen for this application, add **edit()**, **save()**, and **delete()**
methods to the **UserAction** class. Before doing this, create tests for these methods.

1   Open *src/test/java/org/appfuse/web/UserActionTest.java* and add test methods
     for edit, save, and delete operations. See Listing A.65.

Listing A.65

```java
public void testEdit() throws Exception {
    action.setId(userId);
    assertEquals(action.edit(), "success");
    assertNotNull(action.getUser().getFirstName());
}

public void testSave() throws Exception {
    action.setId(userId);
    action.edit();
    assertNotNull(action.getUser());
    action.getUser().setFirstName("Jack");

    assertEquals(action.save(), "success");
    assertNotNull(action.getUser());
}

public void testRemove() throws Exception {
    User user = new User();
    user.setId(new Long(userId));
    action.setUser(user);
    assertEquals(action.delete(), "delete");
}
```

2   Update the *src/main/java/org/appfuse/web/UserAction.java* class. The cancel
    and delete properties capture the click of the **Cancel** and **Delete** buttons.
    The **execute()** method routes the different actions on the form to the
    appropriate method. See Listing A.66.

Listing A.66

```java
public class UserAction extends ActionSupport {
    private final Log log = LogFactory.getLog(UserAction.class);
    private UserManager mgr;
    private List users;
    private User user;
    private String id;
    private String cancel;
    private String delete;

    public void setCancel(String cancel) {
        this.cancel = cancel;
    }

    public void setDelete(String delete) {
        this.delete = delete;
    }

    public void setUserManager(UserManager userManager) {
        this.mgr = userManager;
    }

    public List getUsers() {
        return users;
    }

    public void setId(String id) {
        this.id = id;
    }

    public User getUser() {
        return user;
    }

    public void setUser(User user) {
        this.user = user;
    }

    public String delete() {

        mgr.removeUser(user.getId().toString());

        List args = new ArrayList();
```

```
        args.add(user.getFullName());
        ActionContext.getContext().getSession().put("message",
                getText("user.deleted", args));

        return "delete";
    }

    public String edit() {
        // check for an add
        if (id != null) {
            user = mgr.getUser(id);
        } else {
            user = new User();
        }
        return SUCCESS;
    }

    public String execute() {
        if (cancel != null) {
            return "cancel";
        }

        if (delete != null) {
            return delete();
        }

        return save();
    }

    public String save() {
        log.debug("entering 'save' method");

        mgr.saveUser(user);

        List args = new ArrayList();
        args.add(user.getFullName());

        ActionContext.getContext().getSession().put("message",
                getText("user.saved", args));

        return SUCCESS;
    }

    public String list() {
        users = mgr.getUsers();
        return SUCCESS;
    }
}
```

3 Run the tests in `UserActionTest` using the command **ant test -Dtestcase=UserAction**. Your results should resemble Figure A.23.

```
C Cygwin Bash Shell                                                    _ □ x
$ant test -Dtestcase=UserAction
Buildfile: build.xml

compile:

test:
    [junit] Testsuite: org.appfuse.web.UserActionTest
    [junit] Tests run: 4, Failures: 0, Errors: 0, Time elapsed: 2.968 sec

    [junit] --------------- Standard Output ---------------
    [junit] INFO - AbstractSpringContextTests.loadContextLocations(133) | Loadin
g config for: /WEB-INF/applicationContext*.xml,/WEB-INF/action-servlet.xml
    [junit] DEBUG - UserDAOHibernate.saveUser(35) | userId set to: 13
    [junit] DEBUG - UserDAOHibernate.saveUser(35) | userId set to: 14
    [junit] DEBUG - UserDAOHibernate.saveUser(35) | userId set to: 15
    [junit] DEBUG - UserAction.save(86) | entering 'save' method
    [junit] DEBUG - UserDAOHibernate.saveUser(35) | userId set to: 15
    [junit] DEBUG - UserDAOHibernate.saveUser(35) | userId set to: 16
    [junit] ---------------

BUILD SUCCESSFUL
Total time: 7 seconds
$_
```

Figure A.23: Running the `UserActionTest`

4 Create a *src/main/webapp/userForm.jsp* page to display the form. See Listing A.67.

Listing A.67

```
<%@ include file="/taglibs.jsp"%>

<head>
    <title><fmt:message key="userForm.title"/></title>
    <link href=
        "<ww:url value="/webwork/jscalendar/calendar-green.css"/>"
            rel="stylesheet" type="text/css" media="all"/>
</head>

<p>Please fill in user's information below:</p>

<ww:form name="userForm" action="saveUser" method="post">
    <ww:hidden name="user.id" value="%{user.id}"/>
<ww:textfield label="%{getText('user.firstName')}"
    name="user.firstName"
        value="%{user.firstName}" id="user.firstName"/>
<ww:textfield label="%{getText('user.lastName')}"
    name="user.lastName"
        value="%{user.lastName}" required="true"/>
<ww:datepicker label="%{getText('user.birthday')}"
    name="user.birthday"
        size="11" format="%{getText('cal.date.format')}"/>
<tr>
```

```
        <td></td>
        <td>
            <input type="submit" class="button" name="save" value="Save"
                onclick="this.blur()"/>
        <c:if test="${not empty param.id}">
            <input type="submit" class="button" name="delete"
                value="Delete" onclick="form.onsubmit=null"/>
        </c:if>
            <input type="submit" class="button" name="cancel"
                value="Cancel"/>
        </td>
    </ww:form>

<script type="text/javascript">
    Form.focusFirstElement(document.forms["userForm"]);
</script>
```

WebWork reduces the amount of HTML you need to write for a form. The `<ww:form>` tag writes the `<form>` and `<table>` tags for you. The `<ww:text-field>` tag writes the whole row, including the `<tr>` and `<td>` tags to hold the input field's label. Finally, the `<ww:datepicker>` tag is used to render a pop-up calendar component, much like the one in MyFaces and Tapestry.

5   Update the *src/main/resources/xwork.xml* file to include the **editUser** and **saveUser** actions, in addition to the **users** action. Add the **default-interceptor-ref** element to the top of this file to set properties from request parameters on the action. See Listing A.68.

Listing A.68

```
<default-interceptor-ref name="defaultStack"/>

<!-- List of Users -->
<action name="users" class="userAction" method="list">
    <result name="success" type="dispatcher">userList.jsp</result>
</action>

<!-- Edit User -->
<action name="editUser" class="userAction" method="edit">
    <result name="success" type="dispatcher">userForm.jsp</result>
    <result name="error" type="dispatcher">userList.jsp</result>
</action>

<!-- Save User -->
<action name="saveUser" class="userAction">
    <result name="cancel" type="redirect">users.html</result>
    <result name="delete" type="redirect">users.html</result>
    <result name="success" type="redirect">users.html</result>
</action>
```

6 Run **ant deploy reload -f tomcat.xml**, open your browser to localhost:8080/equinox-webwork/users.html, and click the **Add User** button (see Figure A.24).

Figure A.24: Adding a new user

7 Click the **Save** button. This action routes you to the list screen, where a success message displays and the new user displays in the list, as shown in Figure A.25.

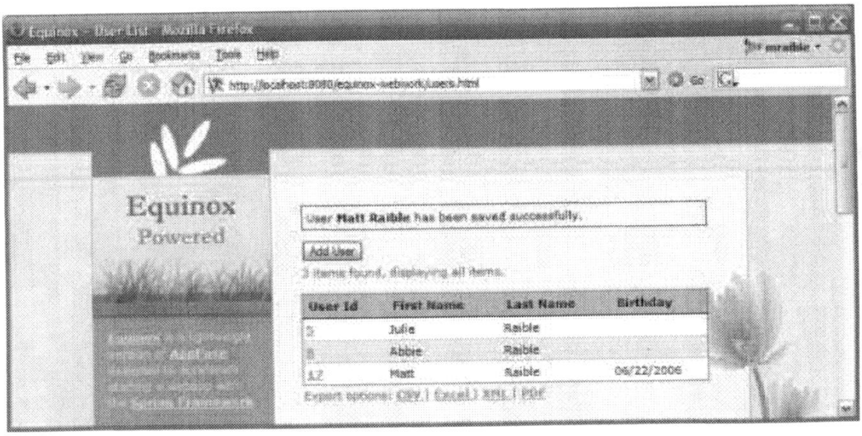

Figure A.25: Displaying success message

The *src/main/webapp/messages.jsp* file renders the success message in this screen. This file is included in the *decorators/default.jsp*. It also handles displaying validation errors. See Listing A.69.

Listing A.69

```
<%-- Error Messages --%>
<ww:if test="hasFieldErrors()">
    <div class="error">
      <ww:iterator value="fieldErrors">
          <ww:iterator value="value">
             <ww:property/><br/>
          </ww:iterator>
      </ww:iterator>
    </div>
</ww:if>

<%-- Success Messages --%>
<c:if test="${not empty message}">
    <div class="message">${message}</div>
</c:if>
```

CONFIGURE VALIDATION

Most web applications require some sort of validation to ensure the data entered meets specific requirements. The following steps demonstrate how to make the **Last Name** a required field:

1   Create a *validators.xml* file in *src/main/resources*. In it, define which **requiredstring** validator to use. The one shown here is the default XWork validator. See Listing A.70.

Listing A.70

```
<validators>
    <validator name="requiredstring"
        class="com.opensymphony.xwork.validator.validators
            .RequiredStringValidator"/>
</validators>
```

NOTE: The full list of validators is available in WebWork's documentation.

---

2   Create validation rules for the **UserAction** by creating a *UserAction-validation.xml* file in the *src/main/java/org/appfuse/web* directory. See Listing A.71.

Listing A.71

```
<?xml version="1.0" encoding="UTF-8"?>
<validators>
    <field name="user.lastName">
        <field-validator type="requiredstring">
            <param name="trim">true</param>
            <message key="errors.required">
                Last Name is required.
            </message>
        </field-validator>
    </field>
</validators>
```

3   Create a new **saveUserWithValidation** **<action>** in *src/main/resources/xwork.xml*. See Listing A.72.

Listing A.72

```
<!-- Save User (Validation Enabled) -->
<action name="saveUserWithValidation" class="userAction"
    method="save">
    <result name="input" type="dispatcher">userForm.jsp</result>
    <result name="success" type="redirect">users.html</result>
    <result name="error" type="dispatcher">userForm.jsp</result>
</action>
```

4   In order to invoke validation when the **save ()** method is called, remove the **<default-interceptor-ref .../>** tag from *xwork.xml* and replace it with the code in Listing A.73.

Listing A.73

```xml
<interceptors>
    <interceptor-stack name="defaultStack">
        <interceptor-ref name="exception" />
        <interceptor-ref name="alias" />
        <interceptor-ref name="servlet-config" />
        <interceptor-ref name="prepare" />
        <interceptor-ref name="i18n" />
        <interceptor-ref name="chain" />
        <interceptor-ref name="model-driven" />
        <interceptor-ref name="fileUpload" />
        <interceptor-ref name="static-params" />
        <interceptor-ref name="params" />
        <interceptor-ref name="conversionError" />
        <interceptor-ref name="validation">
            <param name="excludeMethods">cancel,execute,delete,edit,
                list</param>
        </interceptor-ref>
        <interceptor-ref name="workflow">
            <param name="excludeMethods">input,back,cancel</param>
        </interceptor-ref>
    </interceptor-stack>
</interceptors>
```

By default, the `ValidationInterceptor` excludes `input()`, `back()`, and `cancel()` methods. The previous configuration overrides these defaults to include all CRUD methods but `save()`.

5   Change the `execute()` method in `UserAction.java` to return `success` instead of `save()`. See Listing A.74.

Listing A.74

```java
public String execute() {
    if (cancel != null) {
        return "cancel";
    }

    if (delete != null) {
        return delete();
    }

    return SUCCESS;
}
```

6   In *xwork.xml*, change the **success** result on the **saveUser** action to call the **saveUserWithValidation** action. This new result should use **type="chain"** to forward to another action. See Listing A.75.

Listing A.75

```
<action name="saveUser" class="userAction">
    <result name="cancel" type="redirect">users.html</result>
    <result name="deleteSuccess" type="redirect">users.html</result>
    <result name="success" type="chain">saveUserWithValidation
        </result>
</action>
```

7   Run **ant deploy reload -f tomcat.xml**, and try to add a new user without a last name. You should receive a validation error stating that last name is a required field. See Figure A.26.

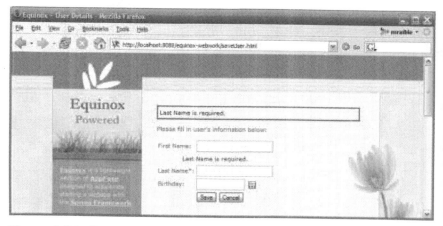

Figure A.26: Server-side validation error

NOTE: The asterisk next to the **Last Name** field is not tied to the validation rules for this action. It appeared there when you specified **required="true"** in the **<ww:textfield>** tag.

CLIENT-SIDE VALIDATION

To enable client-side validation with WebWork, complete these two simple steps:

1   Add **validate="true"** to the **<ww:form>** tag in *src/main/webapp/ userForm.jsp*, as in Listing A.76.

Listing A.76

```
<ww:form name="userForm" action="saveUser" method="post"
    validate="true">
```

2 Add an **onclick** handler to the **Cancel** button in this page so validation will be disabled when users click **Cancel**. See Listing A.77.

Listing A.77

```
<input type="submit" class="button" name="cancel"
    value="Cancel" onclick="form.onsubmit=null"/>
```

3 Run **ant deploy** and try to add a user without a last name. You will receive an error similar to the one in Figure A.27 (inserted with JavaScript) to alert you that "Last Name is required."

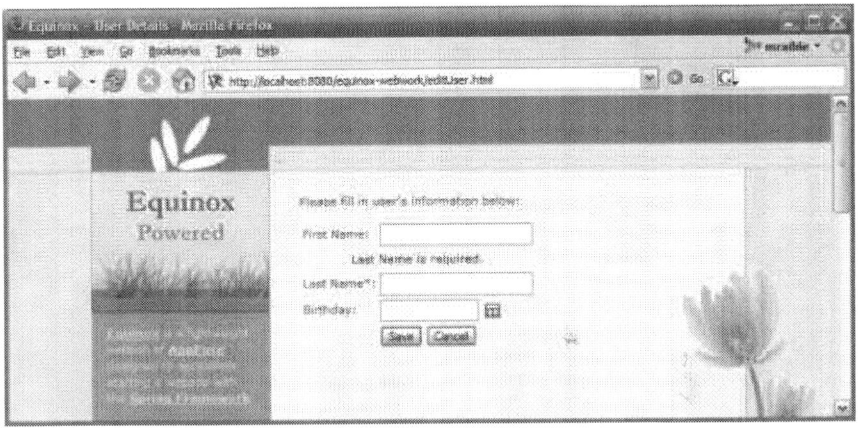

Figure A.27: Client-side validation error

For more information on WebWork's validation framework, see its reference documentation.

TESTING THE USER INTERFACE

The download for this section is already configured for JWebUnit, both for creating tests and running them. To test that everything works as expected through the UI, complete the following steps:

1 Create a **UserWebTest.java** class in *src/test/java/org/appfuse/web* and populate it with the code in Listing A.78.

Listing A.78

```
package org.appfuse.web;

// organize imports using your IDE

public class UserWebTest extends WebTestCase {

    public UserWebTest(String name) {
        super(name);
        getTestContext().setBaseUrl
            ("http://localhost:8080/equinox-webwork");
        getTestContext().setResourceBundleName("messages");
    }

    public void testWelcomePage() {
        beginAt("/");
        assertTitleEqualsKey("index.title");
    }

    public void testAddUser() {
        beginAt("/editUser.html");
        assertTitleEqualsKey("userForm.title");
        setFormElement("user.firstName", "Spring");
        setFormElement("user.lastName", "User");
        submit("save");
        assertTitleEqualsKey("userList.title");
    }

    public void testListUsers() {
        beginAt("/users.html");

        // check that table is present
        assertTablePresent("userList");

        //check that a set of strings are present somewhere in table
        assertTextInTable("userList",
                new String[]{"Spring", "User"});
    }

    public void testEditUser() {
        beginAt("/editUser.html?id=" + getInsertedUserId());
        assertFormElementEquals("user.firstName", "Spring");
        submit("save");
        assertTitleEqualsKey("userList.title");
    }

    public void testDeleteUser() {
        beginAt("/editUser.html?id=" + getInsertedUserId());
        assertTitleEqualsKey("userForm.title");
```

```
            submit("delete");
            assertTitleEqualsKey("userList.title");
    }

    /**
     * Convenience method to get the id of the inserted user
     * Assumes last inserted user is "Spring User"
     */
    public String getInsertedUserId() {
            beginAt("/users.html");
            assertTablePresent("userList");
            assertTextInTable("userList", "Spring");
            String[][]sparseTableCells =
                    getDialog().getSparseTableBySummaryOrId("userList");
            return sparseTableCells[sparseTableCells.length-1][0];
    }
}
```

2   Run the tests in Tomcat by running **ant test-web** (if Tomcat is already
    running) or **ant test-tomcat** if you want Cargo to start it for you. The
    result should look similar to Figure A.28.

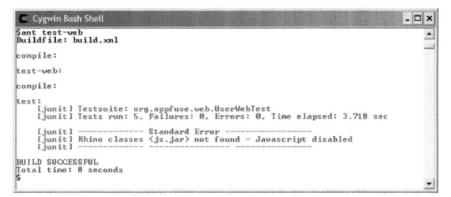

Figure A.28: Testing the user interface

This section has shown you how to integrate a WebWork front end with a Spring
middle tier and back end. All the code in this section is in the WebWork version of
Equinox 1.6.

INDEX

testing with a different locale 330
language bug 330
patch 328
reference materials
    QuickStart Guide 328
testing web layers 307

K

KeyHolder 255
King, Gavin 222
Kodo JDO 272

L

Laddad, Ramnivas 338
LazyInitializationException 290
LDAP
    importing entries 441
    LDAP Service Provider 1.2.4 441
    server setup 439–442
LDAP Data Interchange Format (LDIF) *See*
    LDIF
LDIF 439
    creating a file 439–440
Lehr, Jonathan 417
lifecycle
    beans 52–66
Lightbody, Patrick 417
Lightweight Directory Access Protocol *See*
    LDAP
ListableBeanFactory 51
ListUsers action 54
    IoC-ready 54
LiveHTTPHeaders 423
LocaleEditor property editor 102
LocalOjbConfigurer 274
LocalPersistenceManagerFactoryBean 265
LocalSessionFactoryBean 26
log4j.xml file 63, 333
    adding a logger 339
logger variable 229
logging
    changing the log4j.xml file settings 23
    code example 63
    modifying the log4j.xml file 34
loggingInterceptor bean 339
    replacing 352
LoggingListener 486
LoginModule 463

logout.jsp page
    creating 431
LogoutHandler 457

M

mailSender bean 151, 322
    injecting 152
MailSender interface 150
mailSession bean 153
Manager application
    $CATALINA_HOME/conf/tomcat-us-
        ers.xml file 17
    allowing administrative access 17
Mann, Kito 417
mapping
    <filter mapping> 130
    alternatives 227
    data 240
    data mapping 240
    DelegatingActionProxy class 41
    mapping the User object to the app_user table
        263
    servlet-mapping 78
MappingSqlQuery class 251, 252
mappiong
    metatdata 240
MemoryRealm 435–436
Message-Digest algorithm 5 (MD5) 424
messages.jsp file 86, 99, 100
messages.properties file 88, 108, 316
    adding keys 45
    configuring messages 41–42
    creating 326
    loading from the classpath 70
messageSource bean 87
    example 70
MessageSource interface 69, 70
Metadata Mapper, *See also* object-relational map-
        per (ORM) 240
method injection, *See* getter-based injection 54
methodNameResolver property 212
methods
    defined 396
MethodSecurityInterceptor 466
Miller, Charles 220
MimeMessagePreparator class 151
mock object
    defined 281

OJB.properties file 275
ojbConfigurer bean
    adding 274–275
onSubmit() method 91, 99, 113
    exception handling 140
    sending email 152
OpenLDAP 439, 440
OpenSessionInViewFilter 148, 236
OpenSessionInViewInterceptor 148, 237
    adding as an interceptor 237
    correcting the lazy-loading error 237–238
    lazy-loading error 237
org.appfuse.service.impl package
    creating 31–32
org.jpox.identifier.case property 265
org.springframework.orm.jdo 260
org.springframework.orm.jdo.support 260
org.springframework.test package
    classes 287–288
ORM
    metadata mapping 240
    tools 7, 240

P

package.jdo file 264
page flows 525
page-parsers 120
    FastPageParser 121
    HTMLPageParser 121
PAM 445
parameters
    _flowId 533
password
    encrypting 436–437
passwordEncoder bean 460
passwordEncoder property 459
PDF 195–196
    creating a UserPDFView class 195
    creating the View class 195
    iText document 195
    testing 196
Perl5RegexpMethodPointcut class 342
persistence
    defined 219
    preparing for exercises 221–222
    Spring strategies 220–221
    strategies
        overview 219–222

persistence layer
    unit test 18
persistence strategies 219–278
persistence strategies See also Hibernate, iBATIS,
        JDBC, JDO, OJB
PersistenceBroker 274
PersistenceBrokerDaoSupport 275
PersistenceBrokerTemplate 274
PersistenceBrokerTransactionManager 274
PersistenceBrokerTransactionManager class 385
persistenceManagerFactory bean 264
PGInstaller 368
Plain Old Java Objects See POJOs
PlatformTransactionManager 244, 376
    as a variable 375
PlatformTransaction-Manager class 373
PlatformTransactionManager class 375–376
PlatformTransactionManager interface 365
Pluggable Authentication Modules (PAM) 445
POJOs 109
    and Spring JDBC 251
    testing 290
    userManager bean 369
populate target 295–296
POST request 74
PostgreSQLDialect 368
preInterceptors
    adding the notificationAdvisor bean 356
preInterceptors property 339
primary keys
    retrieving 247–249
    using Spring to generate 248
PROPAGATION_MANDATORY 362
PROPAGATION_NESTED 362
PROPAGATION_NEVER 362
PROPAGATION_NOT_SUPPORTED 362
PROPAGATION_REQUIRED 362
PROPAGATION_REQUIRES_NEW 362
PROPAGATION_SUPPORTS 362
PropertiesBeanDefinitionReader 52
PropertiesEditor property editor 102
PropertiesMethodNameResolver 212
property conversion errors 492
property editors
    ByteArrayPropertyEditor 101
    ClassEditor 101
    CustomBooleanEditor 101
    CustomCollectionEditor 101

9744710R0

Made in the USA
Lexington, KY
24 May 2011